D1161518

WATCH TOWER PUBLICATIONS INDEX

of Subjects Discussed and Scriptures Explained 1971—1975

"If you keep seeking for it as for silver, and as for hid treasures you keep searching for it, in that case you will understand the fear of Jehovah, and you will find the very knowledge of God."—Prov. 2:4, 5.

PUBLISHERS
WATCHTOWER BIBLE AND TRACT SOCIETY
OF NEW YORK, INC.
INTERNATIONAL BIBLE STUDENTS ASSOCIATION
Brooklyn, New York, U.S.A.

Made in the United States of America

USE OF THIS INDEX

For the convenience of readers of the Watch Tower publications, the Watch Tower Society is pleased to provide this five-year index, which includes the annual indexes for 1971 through 1974 as well as listings for publications issued in 1975. Regular use of this index will help you tremendously in finding the information you seek, whether it be for reports, compositions, talks, field-service presentations or in answer to a question.

The **Watch Tower Publications Index 1971-1975** is in two parts. The first is the Subject Index, listing sources of information on hundreds of topics. This index classifies information according to the specific subject under consideration, not necessarily the title of the article. Subjects appear in alphabetical order.

So, to locate information in the Subject Index, determine in your own mind what the subject is, select a noun that expresses it and look under that word to find references. If information has not been catalogued under the word or expression that you select, you will often find that there is a cross reference there that tells you where the information is listed. Sources of information are clearly shown by symbols and page numbers. Throughout this index, on even-numbered pages, footnotes show the principal publications specified by the various symbols. A complete list of all symbols and the corresponding titles, along with the years of publication, appears on page six.

The second portion of the **Watch Tower Publications Index 1971-1975** is the Scripture Index. It contains thousands of scriptures used in the Watch Tower publications during the past five years. Listings cover Genesis through Revelation and are in order according to Bible book, chapter and verse. Symbols and page numbers direct you to the publications where these scriptures are commented upon. Thousands more scriptures than are listed in this index have been quoted and cited in the Society's publications to show what the Bible teaches on various matters and in refutation of false doctrines; but these have not been indexed. Only those Scripture verses on which specific explanation has been provided are listed in the Scripture Index. It is good to keep in mind that a Scripture citation or quotation may appear on one page and the explanation or clarification of the Bible verse on the following page. For that reason, if you do not immediately find the comments on the text you are looking up, be sure to read the surrounding material.

We hope that this index will aid all sincere students of the Bible, whether they be young or old, to reap rich rewards by finding "the very knowledge of God" in answer to their own questions and those of others.

ABBREVIATIONS OF PUBLICATION TITLES

Symbol	Title	Year of Publication
bi8	New World Translation of the Holy Scriptures (Large-print edition)	1971
dn	Divine Rulership—The Only Hope of All Mankind	1972
dy	Divine Victory—Its Meaning for Distressed Humanity	1973
fu	A Secure Future—How You Can Find It	1975
g	Awake!	
gc	Is There a God Who Cares?	1975
hu	Human Plans Failing as God's Purpose Succeeds	1974
ka	God's Kingdom of a Thousand Years Has Approached	1973
kj	"The Nations Shall Know that I Am Jehovah"—How?	1971
km	Kingdom Ministry	
ml	There Is Much More to Life!	1975
nc	When All Nations Collide, Head On, with God	1971
og	One World, One Government, Under God's Sovereignty	1975
or	Organization for Kingdom-preaching and Disciple-making	1972
pm	Paradise Restored to Mankind —By Theocracy!	1972
po	God's "Eternal Purpose" Now Triumphing for Man's Good	1974
sg	Theocratic Ministry School Guidebook	1971
sl	Man's Salvation out of World Distress at Hand!	1975
te	Listening to the Great Teacher	1971
tp	True Peace and Security —From What Source?	1973
ts	Is This Life All There Is?	1974
w	The Watchtower	
yb	Yearbook of Jehovah's Witnesses	

SUBJECT INDEX

AARON
high priest: ka 103-5; pm 175-6
house of Aaron: po 114-15, 118
prophetic significance: ka 103-5; pm 176
(SEE ALSO HIGH PRIEST, LEVITES, PRIESTHOOD, PRIESTS)

ABACUS
discussion: g71 11/22 17-20

ABBA
w74 448

ABEL
death: w73 300; w71 74; te 80
faith: w73 435-6
wife: w75 75

ABHORRENT THING
pm 345-6

ABILITY(IES)
proper view of: w74 530-1
use of: w71 444

ABIMELECH (Gideon's Son)
po 122

ABORIGINES
discussion: g72 2/22 21-6
preaching to: w72 536

ABORTION
Bible view: w75 191-2; g75 8/22 5-6; w74 509; w73 420; tp 156-7; g73 3/22 11; g73 12/22 27-8
clergy view: w73 419-20; g73 4/22 29; g72 7/22 30; w71 484; g71 4/8 30; g71 10/22 30
comments on: w75 248; g75 6/8 30; g73 2/8 12-13; g72 3/22 30; g72 6/8 30
dangers: g73 3/22 9-11; g73 5/8 29
definition: g74 2/8 13
DES: g74 1/22 16
discussion: g75 8/22 3-6; w73 419-20; g73 3/22 8-11
doctors' view: w74 509; g72 11/22 30; g71 2/22 29; g71 7/8 30; g71 7/22 19
effects: g75 8/22 4-5; g74 6/22 7-8; g73 3/22 10-11; g73 5/8 29; g71 12/8 31
experiences:
women refuse: w75 192, 266; g74 8/22 23
fetus a person: g75 6/8 30; g73 4/8 29-30; g73 12/22 27-8; g71 2/22 29
India: g75 8/22 4
Japan: g74 6/22 7-8; g73 12/22 31
legalized in U.S.: w73 419-20; g73 3/22 29
methods: g74 1/22 15-16; g73 3/22 9-10
minipill: g74 1/22 15; g73 4/8 29
nurses quit: g75 8/22 5; g74 8/8 30
prevalence: g73 2/8 12-13; g73 3/22 8; g73 5/8 4; g72 1/22 4; g72 5/8 31; g72 5/22 8; g72 11/22 30; w71 484; g71 6/22 29-30; g71 9/8 29; g71 9/22 30; g71 12/8 31
rackets: g74 8/22 29
research on fetus: g73 6/22 30; g73 12/22 27-8
statistics: g73 3/22 8; g73 12/22 31; g72 3/22 30-1
chart: g75 8/22 5
when life begins: g75 8/22 5-6; w74 509; g74 2/8 13; tp 156
Witness refuses: g71 1/8 25-6
women's liberation: g74 2/8 30
(SEE ALSO ILLEGITIMATE BIRTHS, MORAL BREAKDOWN, PREGNANCY)

ABRAHAM (Abram)
Abrahamic covenant: po 85-7, 104
acknowledged God as Sovereign: w75 660
attempt to sacrifice Isaac: po 91-2; w72 503; w71 120-1
basis for God's dealings: w71 272
burial place: w75 735-6
entered Canaan: po 86
faith: w75 281-2; w74 22-3, 309; po 86, 90-2
uncircumcised yet blessed: po 90, 163-4
friend of God: w74 309-10
"kings" from: po 87, 100
prophet: po 98
prophetic significance: po 162, 180; w71 121
seed: w74 330, 696-7; po 85, 87, 161-8, 180-1
Terah's age at birth of: w75 64
wife: w75 75-6

ABU DHABI
automobiles: g75 12/8 31
Jehovah's witnesses: yb76 26-7; yb75 26-7; yb74 26-7; yb73 26-7; yb72 36-7
population: g75 12/8 31; yb73 26; yb72 36

ABYSS
Satan and demons: w74 239-40; po 186; w73 344-5; ka 28-9, 42-4, 149, 156; kj 370-1, 395
(SEE ALSO TARTARUS)

ACCIDENTS
after working hours: g75 11/8 31
airplanes: g75 1/22 31; w74 394; ts 10; g73 2/22 31; g73 4/8 25-6; g72 2/22 29; g72 7/22 29; g72 12/8 30
laws of chance: g75 3/22 21-2
automobiles: g75 2/22 31; w74 452-3; g74 3/22 8-11; g74 7/22 29; g74 11/8 30; g73 7/8 31; g73 8/8 31; g73 10/22 31; g73 12/22 30; g72 2/22 29; g72 6/8 3-4; g72 9/8 31; g72 9/22 30; g72 10/8 31; g72 11/8 30; g71 4/8 31; g71 6/22 3-4; g71 8/22 22; g71 10/22 30; g71 11/8 3-4
infant safety: g74 1/8 31
seat belts: g75 6/8 31
victim awakes from eight-year coma: g75 9/8 30-1
bicycles: g74 7/22 29-30; g73 6/22 27; g73 11/22 31
boats: g73 12/8 31
causes: ts 10-12; w73 669; g72 11/22 12, 30
choking: g73 12/8 30
drowning: g73 6/22 17-19; g71 8/8 16
fate: ts 10-12
fires: g71 12/8 12-17
first aid: g74 9/22 8
influence of smoking: g73 8/22 19
kite gliding: g75 5/22 30-1
motorcycles: g75 5/8 30; g74 9/22 30-1; g72 11/22 30-1; g71 12/22 31
pedestrian: g71 8/22 31
prevention: g71 6/8 30
shoe styles: g72 10/22 30
skis: g74 3/8 30-1; g73 4/8 31
space travel: g71 11/22 6
sports: g73 1/8 31; g72 12/8 30; g71 11/22 29
statistics: g74 3/22 8-9; g73 8/8 30-1; g71 10/22 10
stepping on objects: g75 9/8 31
trucks: g71 7/22 30
weapons: g75 11/22 12, 29; g72 2/22 29
(SEE ALSO DISASTERS, SAFETY)

ACCOUNTS
congregation: km 2/74 8; or 151-3

ACNE
discussion: g71 1/8 17-19

ACTIVE FORCE
(SEE HOLY SPIRIT)

ACTS (Book)
authenticity: g71 4/8 27-8

ACUPUNCTURE
healing method: g72 7/22 30; g72 9/8 12-16; g71 7/8 31

ADAM
commission: w72 487
communication with Eve: w74 308-9
communication with Jehovah: po 44-5
creation: po 37-40, 42
purpose in: po 33-4, 40-1, 45, 48-9, 54-5
"day you eat" (Ge 2:17): po 43-4, 62-3
death: po 62-3
disobedience: fu 14-16; ml 15-16; po 58-9; w73 433-5; tp 48, 52; w72 426, 649-50; g72 5/22 13
language: g71 2/22 8
"last Adam": w71 275
name: po 40; pm 10
perfection: w71 499-500
poetry: w74 308
punishment: w73 133; g73 6/8 8; g73 7/8 27-8
result of sin to offspring: fu 15; po 62-3; w72 487-8; w71 486-7; te 89-90; g71 9/8 3-4; g71 10/8 19-20; g71 12/8 27-8
rib: po 46-7
soul: po 38-40
speech: sg 5
time between creation of, and Eve's creation: w75 285, 579
(SEE ALSO PARADISE, SIN)

ADAM AND EVE
account confirmed: ts 30; g74 6/22 27; pm 8-12; w71 48
blessings: w73 77-8
children: g74 6/22 27-8
clothing: w72 222
communication: w74 308-9

conscience: w75 209; w72 556-8
disobedience: w75 617-18; fu 14-16; ml 15-16; og 16-18; w74 595-6; po 56-9; w73 433-5; tp 51-2; w72 262-3, 426-7; pm 15-17; g72 5/22 13; g72 6/8 7; te 39-41
food eaten: po 49-50
free moral agents: gc 12; g74 10/8 12; w71 499
  relative freedom: g72 8/22 4
knowledge of good and bad: po 58
losses due to sin: w74 190; w72 427; pm 148; w71 486-7; g71 12/8 27-8
marriage: po 45-7; pm 9-10
nakedness realized: po 58-9
not fear dying: ts 17
one flesh: po 47
opportunity for everlasting life: po 54-5
perfection: gc 11-12; w71 499-500, 539
procreation mandate: po 45-6; w71 742
punishment: g73 7/8 27-8
purpose in living: w74 660, 669; g74 8/22 6; g74 10/8 10
rebellion: pm 15-16; g72 10/22 10-11; w71 616; nc 11-12
sin identified: g72 4/8 27-8
sin of, unforgivable: w75 459
test of obedience: fu 14-15; w74 529-30; po 43-4, 56-9; ts 30-4; g74 10/8 11-12

ADMINISTRATION
Jehovah's: w75 286; sl 330-3, 365; w74 601, 616-19, 621-3, 636; hu 12-14, 17-18, 23-9; po 156-7; ts 131; w72 170-1; w71 568-71; g71 6/8 12-13

ADOBE
houses: g71 1/8 23-4

ADONAY (Adon, Adonai)
substituted for divine name: bi8 1352
use in Hebrew Scriptures: w73 702; bi8 1352

ADONIS
kj 150-1

ADOPTION
children: g74 8/8 28

ADULTERY
artificial insemination: g74 8/8 27-8
avoiding: w73 538-40
Bible view: w73 539-40; tp 146-7, 150; w71 452
clergy view: w74 100, 562; g72 4/22 18, 30; w71 451; kj 158
confessing to mate: g74 11/8 27; w73 351-2
definition: w72 767
divorce: w74 511-12; tp 150-1; w72 766-8
  guilty mate: w74 671-2
experience: g72 9/22 26
forgiving: w74 511-12
innocent mate: w73 351-2
in one's heart: w71 142, 287
spiritual: kj 242-64
statistics: g74 4/22 4
wife swapping: g71 7/22 30
worldly view: g74 12/22 29
  (SEE ALSO FORNICATION, MARRIAGE, MORAL BREAKDOWN)

ADVANCEMENT
importance: w72 306-8
making manifest: w74 114-19; sg 188-92; km 7/71 3
proper view of: w75 87-92; g74 10/22 19-20

ADVENTISTS
beginning of: ka 185
experiences:
  Adventists accept truth: yb73 44; yb72 173, 183
Second Adventists: yb75 34, 36
  (SEE ALSO SEVENTH-DAY ADVENTISTS)

ADVERSITY
people unite during: w71 298

ADVERTISING
deception: g74 3/8 9-12, 26; g73 7/22 13-14
guns: g73 2/22 30
packaging: g73 9/8 22-3
prize tickets: w73 127
psychology: g74 3/8 9-12; w73 158
smoking: w75 12; g75 5/22 29; g73 10/22 30
statistics: g75 4/22 29; g73 3/8 30
television: g73 12/22 30
tickets for prizes in "drawings": g75 7/8 28

AFARS AND ISSAS TERRITORY
Jehovah's witnesses: yb76 24-5; yb75 24-5

AFFECTION(S)
heart: w71 134

AFFLICTION
four hundred years (Ge 15:13): po 105-6

AFGHANISTAN
famine: g73 6/22 4
Jehovah's witnesses: yb76 28-9; yb75 28-9; yb74 28-9; yb73 28-9; yb72 38-9, 209-13
population: yb73 28; yb72 38
religion: yb72 209

AFRICA
animals: g71 12/22 25-6
animism: yb73 141-2
catching wild animals: g75 8/22 7-9
Cherubim and Seraphim sect: g71 9/8 16-18
chiefs: yb73 163-5
children: g72 7/8 24-6; g71 10/22 8
cholera: w74 132
Christendom's religions: g75 3/8 15; w74 677-9; g74 11/22 5; w73 151-3; g72 3/8 8-10
  "converted" people by force: w75 254
colonialism: w74 677; g74 6/22 25-6
Conference of Churches: w74 677-9
diamonds: g74 7/22 25
drought: g74 7/22 4, 6; g74 10/8 3, 5-6
drums: g71 7/8 23
economics: g74 6/22 24-5
  poverty: w75 68
elephants: g75 11/8 30
failure to unite: g74 6/22 23-4, 26
false "Watchtower movements": yb76 73-4, 81, 94-7
famine: g75 2/22 9-11; w74 196; g74 3/8 5-8; g74 7/22 6; g74 9/8 30
festival singer: g74 2/8 24-6
fishing: g72 6/8 25-6
food: g74 6/22 29
history: g74 12/22 18
internal strife: g74 6/22 23-4
ivory: g75 11/8 30
Jehovah's witnesses: yb76 67-242; yb75 5-11; w75 351; g75 3/8 15; w73 153-5; g73 1/22 15-16; g73 10/8 30; w72 70-1, 144; w71 11-14, 118, 122-7, 155-8, 533-4
lake dwellers: g71 1/22 24-6
languages: g75 2/22 26; g73 1/22 25-6; g73 8/22 22-3
marriage: w73 151-5; w71 124-5, 158; g71 10/22 7-8
mathematics: g75 5/22 17-19
music: g71 3/22 11
names: g72 5/8 31; g72 7/8 24-6
Organization of African Unity (OAU): g74 6/22 23-6
polygamy: w75 200; g75 12/8 13-17
refugees: g74 6/22 24
Sahara Desert: g75 7/22 29
superstitions: g74 1/22 26; g72 6/8 26; g71 9/8 18
travel in: g72 1/8 21-4
witchcraft: g72 3/8 8-11; g71 7/8 16-20
women: g75 12/8 13-14; g71 10/22 6-8
  (SEE ALSO INDIVIDUAL COUNTRIES BY NAME)

AGENT
Chief, of life: w73 104; w72 680-701

AGNOSTICISM
experience: g71 6/22 21-2

AGRICULTURE
Africa: g74 6/22 25
desert cultivation: w74 624; g71 9/22 30
earth's, expanded: g71 11/22 20
earth's potential: ts 135-6; g74 11/8 29-30
fertilizer: g75 3/8 31; g74 5/22 10-11; g73 11/22 20; g72 5/8 30; g72 7/22 7; g71 4/22 12; g71 10/22 29-30; g71 11/22 29-30
giant vegetables: g75 12/22 30
gleaning: g75 12/8 30
grain production: g74 7/22 3-4, 30; g74 11/22 29
"green revolution": g74 6/22 6-7; tp 13-14; g73 2/22 29; g73 5/8 29; g73 6/22 3-4, 6-7; g72 7/22 3-13, 29
high-yield grain: g71 3/22 29
India: g72 7/22 4, 8-11
irrigation: g75 3/8 29; g72 7/22 8; g71 1/22 29
Japan: g75 8/22 18

g, Awake!; **ka**, God's Kingdom of a Thousand Years; **kj**, "The Nations Shall Know that I Am Jehovah"; **km**, Kingdom Ministry; **or**, Organization; **pm**, Paradise Restored—By Theocracy!; **po**, God's "Eternal Purpose"; **sg**, Theocratic School Guidebook; **sl**, Man's Salvation out of World Distress!; **te**, Listening to the Great Teacher; **tp**, True Peace and Security; **ts**, Is This Life All There Is?; **w**, Watchtower; **yb**, Yearbook. **Complete list on page 6.**

land used for: g74 6/22 10; g74 7/22 7
mixed culture: g71 5/22 17-20
percent of population engaged in: g74 7/8 29-30
pesticides: g72 5/8 30; g72 8/8 31; g71 4/22 11-12; g71 9/22 29
rice: g72 7/22 3-4, 7-8
soil: g74 5/22 10; g71 5/22 17-18
Soviet Union: g74 6/22 30; g74 7/22 3, 6
surplus destroyed: g71 12/22 30
United States: w74 197; g71 5/22 29
vegetable garden: g74 5/22 9-12
waste in mechanized farming: g75 12/8 30
world food potential: g75 7/22 30

AHAB (King of Israel)
warfare with Ben-hadad: kj 28-30

AHASUERUS
(ALSO CALLED XERXES)
prophetic significance: w71 172-3

AHAZIAH
w74 459

AID TO BIBLE UNDERSTANDING (Book)
experiences with: km 9/75 1
preparation of: yb75 199
release: yb72 42; w71 598, 600

AIR
air-cushion vehicles: g73 11/22 21-3
composition: g71 1/8 6; g71 4/22 6
forest oxygen production: g75 3/8 8
number of atoms in a breath of: g75 11/8 7
oxygen deficient: g71 10/22 29
pollution: g75 12/22 8-9; g73 2/22 30; w72 614; g72 1/22 29; g72 3/8 29; g72 6/8 3; g72 7/22 29; g72 8/8 15-16, 18-19; g72 9/8 29-30; g72 10/8 10-11; g71 1/8 6-7; g71 4/22 6-8; g71 6/8 9-11; g71 10/8 6; g71 10/22 10; g71 12/8 29
purification: g72 2/22 12
(SEE ALSO ATMOSPHERE)

AIR-CONDITIONING
g75 1/8 7-8; g73 7/22 30

AKELDAMA
w75 367

ALADURA
experiences: g71 9/8 16-18

ALASKA
birds: g72 3/8 26
disaster: w71 298
discussion: g75 9/22 5-9
Jehovah's witnesses: yb76 24-5; yb75 24-5; g75 2/8 24-6; g75 9/22 8-9; w74 141-2; yb74 24-5; yb73 6, 24-5; yb72 34-5; g72 3/22 16
oil: g75 9/22 5-6
Alaska pipeline: g75 6/22 29; g75 9/22 5-7
population: yb73 24; yb72 34
proportion of unmarried men to women: g75 4/22 31

ALBINOS
w75 73-4
(SEE ALSO GENETICS)

ALCOHOL
in outer space: g75 1/22 30

ALCOHOLIC BEVERAGES
additives: g72 2/8 29
automobile accidents: g75 8/8 30; w74 452-3; w73 669; g71 4/8 31; g71 6/22 3-4; g71 11/8 3-4
beer: g75 5/8 31; w74 452-4; g72 2/8 21-3
breweries closing: g75 6/8 31
churches: g75 8/8 30
Bible view: w75 218; w73 71-2, 667-70; tp 158; w72 596; g72 1/8 20; g71 6/22 6-7
consumption statistics: g73 12/8 30; g71 6/22 3
death: g74 7/22 31
discussion: w73 666-70; g72 2/8 21-3
effect on body: g75 2/8 17; g75 10/22 30; w74 451-2; g74 2/8 19; w73 667-8; g72 2/8 22-3; g72 12/8 31; g71 1/22 14; g71 6/22 4-5; g71 9/8 4
"empty" calories: w74 452
lands with most excessive drinkers: g75 8/8 30
liquor: w74 452, 454; g72 2/8 21-3
mescal: g73 5/22 26
moderation: w73 670; g71 8/22 26
moonshine whiskey: g75 11/8 31
pulque: g73 5/22 25-6
tequila: g73 5/22 26
use of grain: g74 6/8 31
whiskey: g71 9/8 4
wine: w74 452-4; g73 1/8 31; g72 2/8 21-2; g71 7/8 29; g71 7/22 30; g71 8/22 24-6
youth: w73 666-70
(SEE ALSO DRUNKENNESS)

ALCOHOLISM
Bible view: w74 455; w73 667-70; tp 158-9; g71 6/22 6-7
cancer: w74 452
causes: g75 2/8 18; w74 453-4; ts 13; g71 6/22 5-6
child: g75 2/8 16-17; w74 451, 453; w73 668; g73 9/8 30
clergy: g74 7/22 29; g73 5/22 29; g72 7/22 30
cost: g75 2/8 18; w74 453; g71 6/22 3-4
discussion: w74 451-5; g71 6/22 3-8
doctors: g74 4/22 29
effects: g75 9/8 30; w74 451-3; w73 71, 669; g73 8/8 25; g72 11/22 30; g71 6/22 3-5
Jews: w75 560
not "disease": w74 456
pregnant women: g75 9/8 30; g74 1/8 31
babies born drunk: g75 7/22 29-30
prevalence: w75 560; w74 451; g74 4/8 29; tp 158-9; g73 11/8 30; g72 5/22 31; g72 9/22 30; g71 6/22 3; g71 8/22 26
solution: w74 454-5
treatment: g71 6/22 7-8
truth overcomes: g74 8/8 4-5; w73 670; yb73 15-17; w72 125, 454-5; g71 6/22 8
women: w74 451, 453-4
youth: g75 2/8 16-18; g75 9/8 30; g74 4/8 29; g74 12/8 30

ALEXANDER THE GREAT
death: w71 715
discussion: g72 1/22 13-17
empire divided: w71 715-16
established world power: po 132
role in Bible prophecy: w71 714-15
siege of Tyre: pm 263, 265
visit to Jerusalem: g74 4/8 24
(SEE ALSO GREECE)

ALGERIA
Jehovah's witnesses: yb76 24-5; yb75 24-5; yb74 24-5; yb73 24-5; yb72 34-5
population: yb73 24; yb72 34

ALIEN RESIDENTS
(SEE TEMPORARY RESIDENTS)

ALLEGIANCE
(SEE FLAG SALUTE)

ALLIANCES
political, Bible times: kj 249

"ALL SCRIPTURE IS INSPIRED OF GOD AND BENEFICIAL" (Book)
yb75 199

ALPHABET
Hebrew: g71 9/8 20
Roman: g73 5/8 14

ALPHAEUS
w75 222

ALTAR(S)
copper: w74 221; w73 31; w72 606, 714-15
Ezekiel's vision: kj 387-8
symbolic: w73 31; ka 97-8, 109; w72 714-16, 718, 721
(SEE ALSO SACRIFICES, TABERNACLE, TEMPLE)

ALUMINUM
w74 102; g74 11/22 18-19; g74 12/22 30

AMALEKITES
kj 24-5

AMAZON RIVER
g75 3/8 8

AMBASSADORS
Bible times: w74 650
Christian: w74 650-2; w73 686; ka 76-81
Jehovah's witnesses: pm 72-7

AMEN
Jesus Christ: w73 262
prayer: w72 334

AMERICA
discovery: g71 11/22 20
(SEE ALSO UNITED STATES OF AMERICA)

AMERICAN LEGION
persecution of Witnesses: yb75 182-3; w71 520-1

AMERICAN SAMOA
Jehovah's witnesses: yb76 24-5; yb75 24-5; yb74 24-5

AMMONITES
destruction: w75 421-3
fall to Babylon: w73 61-2; kj 235-6

AMNON
Tamar violated by: w72 220

AMOEBAS
g74 1/22 11; g73 10/22 10

AMON
king of Judah: kj 102
AMORITES
po 104; g74 4/8 16
ANABAPTISTS
g72 3/8 19
ANANIAS
lie to Peter: te 72-3
ANATOMY
(SEE HUMAN BODY)
ANCESTOR WORSHIP
Christendom: g71 9/22 30-1
discussion: ts 60-4; g72 3/22 17-19
examples: w75 54-5
experiences: yb75 13; yb73 240-1
Lesotho (Basutoland): yb76 193
(SEE ALSO WORSHIP)
ANCIENT WORTHIES
misconception regarding resurrection: yb75 146
ANDORRA
Jehovah's witnesses: yb76 30-1; yb75 30-1; yb74 30-1; yb73 30-1; yb72 40-1; w71 680
population: yb73 30; yb72 40
ANGELS
description: w72 152
duties: w74 760-2
executioners: w72 44-5
Gabriel: g73 5/22 14
gathering "chosen ones": ka 328-9
humility: w72 201
Jehovah's "wife": po 61, 79
joy over repentance: w72 431
kindness of: w75 675-6
language: g71 2/22 8
loyalty: po 79
materialization: g73 7/22 4-5; g72 9/22 7
meaning of term: po 30
Michael: po 137-8
misconceptions: w72 151
number: po 32, 79
organization: w72 153-4
personality: w74 436
preaching work: w73 405; g72 6/8 28; te 101
protection: yb75 187-90; w74 760-2; yb74 127-8, 140-1; te 99-102
seven angels sound trumpets (Re 8-11): yb75 135-9
sons of God: po 30-1; w72 651-3
spirits: po 32-3; g72 6/8 28
subjection to God: w72 153-4; kj 49-51
symbolic representation: w72 633
(SEE ALSO CHERUBS, SERAPHS)
ANGELS THAT SINNED
access to heaven: w74 640
debased: w74 640
demons: po 78
identified: w74 21-2; g73 5/22 14-15; w71 509; g71 5/22 3-4, 28
judgment: po 77-8
marriage: po 71-3; g71 5/22 3, 28
materialization: ts 83-5
offspring: po 73-6; w71 509
spirits in prison: ts 85; w72 427-8; w71 607-8
"stars": ts 83
Tartarus: po 78; ts 84-5; w72 427; bi8 1366
(SEE ALSO DEMONS, SPIRITISM)
ANGER
causes: w71 359
discussion: w75 647-8
effects: w75 647-8; g74 5/22 28; w72 196; g72 10/8 31; w71 163-4
examples: w75 647-8; g73 9/8 30
God's anger: ts 187-8; w71 357-60
self-control: w74 314-15; g74 5/22 28; w72 68-9; w71 164
ANGLICAN CHURCH
(SEE CHURCH OF ENGLAND)
ANGLO-AMERICAN WORLD POWER
"false prophet": kj 363
final world power: g75 10/8 14
seventh world power: w71 717-18, 720-4, 728; kj 350-1
two-horned beast: kj 363
United Nations: kj 351
(SEE ALSO GREAT BRITAIN, UNITED STATES OF AMERICA)
ANGOLA
Jehovah's witnesses: yb76 28-9, 198-208; yb75 28-9; yb74 28-9; yb73 28-9; yb72 38-9
persecution: yb76 204-8
population: yb73 28; yb72 38
ANGUILLA
Jehovah's witnesses: yb76 28-9; yb75 28-9; yb74 26-7; yb73 26-7; yb72 36-7; w71 679
population: yb73 26; yb72 36
ANIMALS
adaptability: g74 1/8 20-3; g74 8/22 24
Africa:
catching wild animals: g75 8/22 7-9
ancient Israel: g72 7/8 7-8
antibiotics in feed: g72 4/8 30-1
behavior no guide: g71 1/22 3-4
benefits to man: g72 7/8 3
bestiality: w72 32; g72 1/22 5
breeding: g74 8/8 27; g74 11/8 14; g73 10/22 16-17
Colombia: g75 3/22 13-15
communication: g71 7/22 20
"dats" fraud: g71 9/22 31
death: ts 18-21
discipline young: g73 1/22 21-2
disease: g72 1/8 30; g72 7/8 31; g71 5/8 30; g71 11/8 21-3
domesticating wild: g74 8/22 25-6
enmity: g72 5/22 29
extinction: g74 5/8 30; g74 8/22 25; g73 5/8 16-18, 30; g73 12/22 14, 16; g72 6/8 31; g71 4/22 13
species in danger: g75 8/8 29; g75 11/8 30; g75 12/22 30
food before the Flood: w75 606
hearing: g75 6/8 19-20
heartbeats: g73 11/22 19
hibernation: g74 1/8 20-1; g72 1/8 20
instinct: ts 18-20
jumping: g74 10/22 21-3
killing characteristics: ts 20-1
killing (reasons): w73 159; g73 10/22 25-6
largest: g73 12/22 14
man-killing: w75 639
man's behavior compared: g73 5/8 16-18; w72 515; g72 7/8 6
man's dominion: w73 159; ka 144-5; g72 7/8 5-6
materialists: w72 516
memory: ts 19-20
mental illness: g73 6/8 31
microscopic: g74 1/22 10-12
no concept of past, future: ts 18-21
peace with man: w75 606-8; ts 142; ka 144-5
pets: g74 8/22 31; g72 5/8 31; g72 7/8 3-8; g71 8/22 29-30
play: g75 10/22 24-6
poisonous: g72 10/22 30
souls: ts 38-40
speed: g74 2/22 12-15
spirit: ts 49-50
sterilization: w73 159
stress affects: g71 10/8 30
symbolic: w72 538
training: g73 1/22 20-2; g72 7/8 5-6
trapping: g73 5/8 18; g72 12/22 21-3
variety: ts 145-6
wildlife preservation: g74 8/8 23; g73 5/8 16-18, 30
winter: g74 1/8 20-3
wisdom in creation: g72 7/8 3; g72 10/22 8

List by Name

amoeba: g74 1/22 11
antelope: ts 19; g74 10/22 22; g71 1/8 15
ape: g72 1/22 10
bat: g75 6/8 20
bear: g74 1/8 21-2; g74 3/22 14; g73 1/22 20; g73 2/8 26; g73 5/8 16-18; g72 1/8 18-20; g72 3/22 29
buffalo: g71 12/22 25-6
bull: w75 639
camel: g71 1/8 22
cat: g75 10/22 24; g73 1/22 21; g72 1/8 30; g71 3/22 23
cheetah: g74 2/22 12; g71 6/8 23
chimpanzee: g73 1/22 21
cottontail rabbit: g74 1/8 20
cougar: g74 10/22 22
cow: g73 2/22 19
coyote: g75 9/22 31
deer: g75 3/22 14; g74 1/8 22; g74 10/22 22; g73 1/22 21; g72 6/22 22-3; g71 3/8 20; g71 10/8 30
dog: g75 7/8 31; ts 19-20; g74 7/22 17-19; g74 9/8 31; g73 6/22 19; g72 2/8 31; g72 6/8 29; g72 8/22 30; g71 3/8 29; g71 6/8 23; g71 7/8 15; g71 11/8 21-3; g71 12/8 30
dolphin: g74 2/22 13; g73 12/22 15
earthworm: g75 3/22 13, 15; g72 10/22 7
elephant: g75 10/22 30; g75 11/8 30; g74 5/8 30; g73 2/22 19; g71 5/22 10; g71 12/22 26
fighting cock: g74 1/22 31

g, Awake!; **ka**, God's Kingdom of a Thousand Years; **kj**, "The Nations Shall Know that I Am Jehovah"; **km**, Kingdom Ministry; **or**, Organization; **pm**, Paradise Restored—By Theocracy!; **po**, God's "Eternal Purpose"; **sg**, Theocratic School Guidebook; **sl**, Man's Salvation out of World Distress!; **te**, Listening to the Great Teacher; **tp**, True Peace and Security; **ts**, Is This Life All There Is?; **w**, Watchtower; **yb**, Yearbook. **Complete list on page 6.**

fox: g75 10/22 26
frog: g75 3/22 14; g74 1/8 20
gazelle: g74 2/22 12; g71 12/22 25
giraffe: g71 12/8 10-11
goat: g73 1/22 21
gorilla: g74 8/8 20-3
greyhound: g75 10/22 31
grizzly bear: g73 5/8 16-18
ground squirrel: g74 1/8 21
guinea pig: g73 2/22 19
hippopotamus: g73 11/22 30-1
hog: g73 2/22 19
horse: g73 2/22 19; g71 9/22 31
impala: g74 10/22 22
jack rabbit: g74 10/22 21
jumping mouse: g74 10/22 21
kangaroo: g74 10/22 21
klipspringer: g74 10/22 22
koala: g71 10/22 20
leopard: g74 10/22 22
lion: g75 10/22 25; g75 12/22 30; ts 20-1; g74 10/22 22; g72 9/22 30-1; g71 12/22 26
mammoth: g74 4/22 31; g73 8/22 31
margay: g75 3/22 14-15
monkey: g71 3/8 12; g71 8/22 30
moose: g71 3/8 20
mouse: g73 2/22 19
musk ox: g74 8/22 24-6
otter: g75 10/22 26
panda: g73 11/22 16-19
pig: g75 3/22 29; g75 10/22 24-5
porcupine: g74 12/22 31
porpoise: g73 12/22 15
pronghorn: g74 2/22 12
rabbit: g75 10/22 31; g74 1/8 22-3; g74 2/22 12; g74 10/22 31; g73 2/22 19; g71 5/8 29
rabbit deer: g75 3/22 14
raccoon: g73 1/22 20
rat: g75 3/8 30; g75 6/8 29; g75 9/22 30; g73 1/22 21; g72 10/22 31; g71 5/22 31; g71 12/22 31
red squirrel: g74 1/8 22
rhinoceros: g75 4/22 30; g75 8/8 29; g72 6/8 9-11
sea snake: g75 3/22 31
sheep: w75 432; g74 11/8 14-16; g73 2/22 19
sloth: g71 3/22 15
snake: g75 6/8 19; g74 1/8 20-1; g71 3/8 19-20; g71 5/8 31
snowshoe rabbit: g74 1/8 22-3
springbuck: g74 10/22 22
squirrel: g73 1/22 21
tiger: g74 10/22 22; g73 5/8 30
viper: g75 5/22 30; g72 10/22 30
walrus: g74 9/8 30
water flea: g74 1/22 11-12
whale: g75 7/22 30; g74 3/8 23; g73 12/22 13-16
white fox: g74 1/8 20
white-tailed deer: g74 10/22 22
wildebeest: g71 12/22 25
wolf: g73 1/22 21
woodchuck: g74 1/8 21; g72 1/8 20
(SEE ALSO BIRDS, FISH, FISHING, INSECTS, MARINE LIFE)

ANIMAL WORSHIP
po 42, 44-5; g72 7/8 6, 8
(SEE ALSO IDOLATRY, WORSHIP)

ANIMISM
yb73 141-2

ANNA
prophetess: kj 345

ANNIVERSARY
wedding: w71 735-6

ANOINTED
Abraham, Isaac and Jacob: po 98
(SEE ALSO CONGREGATION OF GOD, JESUS CHRIST)

ANOINTING
evidence of, to heavenly hope: w75 105-6
holy spirit: w75 105-8; po 158-9
Jesus Christ: w74 251; po 144-5; ka 64-6; w71 242, 713
meaning of term: w74 361
wrong assumptions regarding: w75 105-8

ANT
g75 9/22 29; g72 6/22 30; g72 10/22 8; g72 11/22 21

ANTARCTICA
iceberg: g72 8/22 16

ANTIBIOTICS
bacteria resist: g71 3/22 29
colds: g73 12/22 9
dangers: g72 4/8 30-1; g71 11/22 30; g71 12/8 31

ANTIBODIES
g72 12/22 17-18

ANTICHRIST
misconceptions: w73 648

ANTICLERICALISM
yb72 50; w71 740; g71 8/22 14

ANTONIA, CASTLE OF
w75 366-7; sl 17

ANXIETY
causes: g74 8/22 17-18
overcoming: g74 2/22 11; g74 8/8 3-7; g74 8/22 18-19

APARTMENTS
storage: g74 9/8 14
window gates: g75 7/22 29

APATHY
children: g74 2/8 3-4
dangers: w74 50-1
overcoming: w74 445-6
religious: w74 444-6

APOCRYPHA
discussion: w75 414-15; w73 601-2
Jerome's comments on: w75 414
Josephus' comments on: w75 414
Second Maccabees: g75 1/22 28

APOLLO
god: w72 586; kj 157

APOSTASY
Christendom: w75 166-8, 253-4, 729-30; sl 208-14; w74 592; po 170; w71 628-9; kj 78-9
Constantine: w74 592
definition: w75 167; ka 369-70
discussion: w75 201-4, 252-4; ka 369-78
false teachers: w72 191-2
first and second centuries (C.E.): w75 201-2, 252-3; w74 740; ka 371-3, 377-8; w72 191; w71 79-80
first-century restraint: ka 384-8
foretold: w75 167-8, 201, 252-3; po 169-70; ka 369-73, 386-7; w71 80, 501-2, 628

APOSTLES
attitude toward Kingdom: w74 50
correspondency with sons of Jacob: w71 747
faith: w72 99
faithfulness: w74 532
first chosen: w71 747
foundation stones: po 158
gifts in men: w71 750-3
governing body: w71 748, 759
humility: w71 606-7; te 27-9
integrity tested: w72 136, 142-3; w71 486, 488, 493-4, 541; te 173-4; g71 10/22 27-8
meaning of term: w75 726; po 158; w71 319
miraculous gifts: w75 95; g74 12/22 27-8
older men: w71 688
Paul: w75 727
persecution: w74 214-16
preaching: w73 717-18
replacement for Judas: w71 319-20, 688-90
restraining force against apostasy: ka 384-8
temporary: w75 727
theatrical spectacle: w74 215-16, 318
wrong views held: w74 296
(SEE ALSO INDIVIDUAL APOSTLES BY NAME)

APOSTLES' CREED
w73 238-9

APPENDIX
g74 2/8 16; g72 12/8 30

APPLE
g75 2/22 31; g74 9/22 7; g73 5/22 15; g73 9/22 21-4; g71 5/22 19

APPOINTED TIMES OF THE NATIONS (Gentile Times)
beginning: sl 41; po 174, 176-7; ts 156-9; w73 645; w72 188, 351, 748; kj 57, 231-2, 352
discussion: w74 163-5; po 174-7; ts 155-60; ka 259-61
end: w75 621, 661; sl 8, 41, 243, 316; og 25; w74 236-7; po 176-7; ts 159-60; w73 645, 722-3; ka 228-30, 259-61; g73 10/8 17-18; w72 187-8, 324, 351, 748; pm 72, 74, 331, 368; w71 619-21, 717-18; kj 57-8, 65, 73, 105, 176, 233-5, 306, 345-6, 352-3, 356; nc 18-22
end announced before 1914: w75 686; yb75 37; w74 506-7; ka 186; yb73 96; g73 10/8 17-18; pm 332
length: sl 198; w74 163-5, 557; ts 155-6; w73 645; tp 74-6; w72 188; pm 129; kj 57, 231-5, 352
Maccabean kingdom not interrupt: po 175
Nebuchadnezzar's dream of tree: w74 164; po 176; ts 152-60; ka 260-1; tp 74-6
physical evidences of end: ts 160-3
(SEE ALSO CHRONOLOGY, 1914, SIGN)

APPOINTMENT(S)
keeping: w72 28-9
(SEE ALSO MINISTERIAL SERVANTS, OLDER MEN)

APPRECIATION
cultivating: w75 14, 20, 29
discussion: w75 13-22, 29
for Bible knowledge: g74 6/22 16
for Christian meetings: w71 678-80
for deliverance: yb74 208-9; w72 302-8

for family relationships: w75 13-16
for Jehovah: w75 18; w73 67-8; ka 400-1, 410-11; w71 265-76
for Jehovah's provisions: w75 19-22, 29; w74 189-91; g74 6/8 5-6
for Jehovah's sovereignty: w74 538-9
for one's blessings: w75 556-9
how to express: te 43-6
Jehovah's: w75 17-18, 713-14
meaning: w75 13; g74 7/22 16

APPROACHABILITY
w74 367-8, 544

APPROVAL
Jehovah's: w72 99-100

AQUARIUM
discussion: g72 9/22 13-16

AQUEDUCTS
discussion: g73 1/8 13-15

ARABIC
interest in: g74 12/8 30

ARABS
cooperation with Jews in crime: g75 4/22 29
oil: g74 2/22 17-22; g74 8/8 8, 10
opposition to modern Israel: g74 2/22 18-20
United States: g74 2/22 18-20
war with modern Israel: g74 11/8 5

ARCHAEOLOGY
ancient writing: w71 410; g71 11/22 24-6
Assyria: g72 6/22 27
Bible confirmed: w74 77, 79; g72 1/8 28; g72 9/8 31
Caesarea: g72 1/8 28
Capernaum: w75 671
China: g75 9/22 29
copper in Palestine: w75 112
dating: g73 5/8 19-20; g71 4/8 31; g71 5/8 31
Egypt: g75 5/8 29
Hadrian's statue: g75 9/22 30-1
Hittites: w71 348-9
impalement: g71 2/22 30
Lachish Letters: w74 79
limitations: g75 5/8 29
Nabunaid Chronicle: w71 315-16
Pompeii: g71 2/8 20
Pontius Pilate: w74 79; g72 1/8 28; w71 340
Queen Helena's palace: g75 11/8 30
Rosetta stone: g71 11/22 24-6
sites looted: g72 1/22 30
"Stone Age": g73 5/8 19-20
"tomb of Peter": w72 671
(SEE ALSO BIBLE AUTHENTICITY, FOSSILS, SCIENCE)

ARCHIPPUS
w75 733

ARCHITECTURE
Babylonian: w74 490
discussion: w74 490-1
religious: g75 1/8 21-2
  Christendom's: w74 490-1
skyscrapers: g74 2/8 20-3
tallest buildings: g74 2/8 21; g74 4/22 30-1; g73 7/8 30
World Trade Center: g74 2/8 20-3

ARCTIC
icebergs: g72 2/8 11
polar bear: g73 2/8 26
temperature: g72 2/8 10

AREOPAGUS (Mars Hill)
Paul's sermon: w72 119; g72 11/22 17-18; w71 323-4

ARGENTINA
armaments: g74 11/8 6
Catholic church: w72 391; yb72 50; w71 740; g71 2/22 3-6
description: yb72 46-7, 51
disasters: g74 5/22 7-8; yb72 66; g72 4/8 29
food shortage: g72 10/8 30
Jehovah's witnesses: yb76 24-5; w75 246-7, 488-9; yb75 22, 24-5; yb74 24-5; g74 5/22 8; yb73 6-7, 24-5; yb72 34-5, 46-125; w71 23, 216-18
  conventions: yb72 73-6, 81-3, 87-93, 105-6, 116-21
  persecution: yb72 61-2, 82-8, 105-6, 109-11
kidnapping: g75 5/22 6, 8
map: yb72 49
meat: g71 5/22 29
population: yb73 24; yb72 34, 47
tunnel: g71 8/22 23

ARGUMENTATION
g75 1/8 9-12; g74 7/8 3-4; g74 12/22 14-15

ARIUS
Trinity doctrine: g73 1/8 16-19

ARK (Noah's)
capacity: g75 6/8 5
claims of discovery: g75 9/8 17-21
construction: w75 10; ka 333; w72 488
description: w74 23, 380; w71 168; te 128
living conditions in: w75 752
symbolic: km 11/75 1; w74 634-5, 667-8
(SEE ALSO FLOOD [NOACHIAN])

ARK OF THE COVENANT
brought to Jerusalem: po 125
disappearance: w72 745
Jehovah's heavenly temple: w72 606
location: kj 165
symbolic: w72 710

ARMAGEDDON
attack of Gog: w75 88, 637-8; w73 344-5
battle: w73 755-7; ka 19-28; w71 623-4; kj 372-3; nc 26-8; g71 4/22 25
  length: w73 677-8
children: w72 51-2, 633-4; w71 63-4
death of some faithful ones: sl 268-9
description: w75 637-8, 758; w73 293, 296-7; pm 389-94; kj 366-8, 376-7
discussion: w75 515-16; w74 227-39; w73 619-22, 745-6, 749, 753-60; ka 19-28; dy 18-25
disposal of dead: w73 345-6
events preceding: w75 681-2
fear of nations: w73 753-4
fighters: sl 256-7, 264-7; w73 620-2, 677-8; dy 20, 22-4
gathering of nations: g74 11/8 7-8; w73 619-20; dy 18-20; kj 363-4
hardships: w74 61; w73 746, 749, 757-60
Har-Magedon: w74 77, 229-32, 318; w73 296-7; kj 298, 363-4, 366-7, 372-3
issue: w74 233-5, 238; w73 620-1; dy 21, 23
Jehovah: w73 753-5, 757
meaning of term: w75 515; w74 229-30, 232; g74 11/8 8
Megiddo: w75 387-8, 515; w74 229-32
misconceptions: w73 745
part of great tribulation: w73 293; ka 317; kj 298
protection during: w75 637-8; w74 171-2, 318, 667-8, 765-6; ka 399-401, 408-9
purpose: w72 4; w71 625-6
quotations using term: w75 515; g75 2/22 29; g75 3/22 29; g75 10/22 31; g74 12/22 29; w73 745; g73 12/22 30; g71 10/8 28
requirements for survival: w74 668; w72 51-3, 326-7, 372-4; w71 64, 624; nc 27-8; g71 4/22 29
role of Christ: ka 163-4
role of Witnesses: w73 623, 678; dy 27
  preaching good news: w74 333-40
some anointed survive on earth: w74 765-6
time for exultation: w75 88
time of: w74 635; w73 620-1; ka 336-7; dy 21-2
warning: w72 56-7
who are destroyed: sl 273-82; w74 123, 238-9; w73 296-7, 677-8, 756-7; ka 21-2; tp 38-43; g73 10/8 22-5; w72 587
who survive: w73 623, 678, 756-7; ka 27-30; dy 26-7
winepress: w75 620; sl 264-5, 348; og 23
(SEE ALSO LAST DAYS, TRIBULATION)

ARMAMENTS
arms race: g74 11/8 3-7; g74 12/8 30; w72 613; g72 10/8 3, 5, 10, 29; g71 7/8 6-8
cost: w75 487, 634; g75 4/8 29; g75 8/22 18; gc 9; g74 11/8 6-7; g74 12/8 8; tp 14; g73 10/8 28-9; g72 9/8 29; g72 10/8 3-4
  per person: g75 10/22 30
destructive power: g72 10/8 4, 9-10
limitation talks: g74 11/8 3
statistics: g72 10/8 3-4, 9-10
stockpile: w75 487; g74 11/8 3-6; g72 10/8 4, 9-10; g71 7/8 6-8
(SEE ALSO WAR, WEAPONS)

ARMOR
Christian: w73 159-60

ARMY
crime statistics: g75 3/22 30
food supplies: g75 6/8 31
Germany: g75 2/22 19-23
United States: g71 6/22 29
use of horses: g72 10/22 25

g, Awake!; **ka**, God's Kingdom of a Thousand Years; **kj**, "The Nations Shall Know that I Am Jehovah"; **km**, Kingdom Ministry; **or**, Organization; **pm**, Paradise Restored—By Theocracy!; **po**, God's "Eternal Purpose"; **sg**, Theocratic School Guidebook; **sl**, Man's Salvation out of World Distress!; **te**, Listening to the Great Teacher; **tp**, True Peace and Security; **ts**, Is This Life All There Is?; **w**, Watchtower; **yb**, Yearbook. **Complete list on page 6.**

ARRIAN
g74 4/8 24

ARSON
g75 6/8 30

ART
Chinese: g73 8/8 12-15
decline: g72 7/22 31
erotic: g73 11/22 30
life story of a famous artist: g75 7/8 12-16
oil painting: g74 5/8 21-3
religious: g73 11/22 30
scroll paintings: g73 8/8 14-15
smuggled: g73 4/22 29
stained glass: g75 8/8 29-30
thefts: g71 6/22 31; g71 7/8 29

ARTAXERXES I
(ALSO CALLED ARTAXERXES LONGIMANUS)
Nehemiah to Jerusalem: g71 12/8 8

ARTEMIS
w72 586; kj 157

ARTIFICIAL INSEMINATION
g74 8/8 27-8

ARTIFICIAL RESPIRATION
g73 7/22 8-12

ARUBA
Jehovah's witnesses: yb76 28-9; yb75 28-9; yb74 28-9; yb73 28-9; yb72 38-9
population: yb73 28; yb72 38

ASAPH
attitude toward prosperity of wicked: w75 50-1
meditation on Jehovah's activity: w72 523-4

ASBESTOS
g74 9/8 20; g71 6/22 30

ASCENSION
Jesus Christ: g72 9/22 5-8

ASCENSION ISLAND
Jehovah's witnesses: yb76 230-1; yb73 30-1; yb72 40-1
population: yb73 30; yb72 40

ASCETICISM
Bible view: w74 575; w71 538

ASHDOD
pm 267

ASHTORETH (Astarte)
w74 457-8

ASIA
Jehovah's witnesses: w71 14-16, 533
religions: w71 14
(SEE ALSO INDIVIDUAL COUNTRIES BY NAME)

ASPIRIN
colds: g73 12/22 9
danger: g73 6/22 29; g72 2/22 29; g72 10/22 30; g71 1/22 30; g71 5/22 30
(SEE ALSO DRUGS, MEDICINE)

ASSASSINATION
King Faisal: g75 8/8 30
meaning of term: w71 248
Trujillo: yb72 164

ASSEMBLIES
circuit: g74 6/8 16, 20
early Christians: w71 396-400
Israel: w71 392-6
prison: g75 4/22 21-2
(SEE ALSO CONVENTIONS)

ASSEMBLY HALLS
g75 3/8 27; km 4/75 4; km 10/75 8; g74 6/8 16-20; km 5/74 1

ASSOCIATIONS
Bible view: w74 153, 271-2, 564-5, 607; w73 144, 421-4; g71 5/8 27-8
children: km 4/75 3
disfellowshiped persons: w74 153, 464-5, 468, 544
Greek term: w74 271-2
results of bad: w73 588-9; g71 5/8 27-8
selectivity: w74 93, 112, 564-5; g74 2/8 10; g74 5/8 6-7; w73 72-3, 318-20, 422-4; w72 304-5; w71 6-7, 562-3, 606
value of good: w74 212-13

ASSYRIA
archaeological finds: g72 6/22 27
captivity of Jews: kj 203
destruction: g72 6/22 28; kj 245
discussion: g72 6/22 27-8
Esar-haddon: w75 242
historical records: w72 314-16; w71 410
invasion of Israel: w71 672; kj 238-9, 243
invasion of Judah: sl 172
Jehovah's judgment: po 18-19
Nineveh: g72 6/22 28; kj 245
religion: g72 4/22 12; g72 6/22 28

ASTHMA
g72 3/8 30

ASTROLOGERS
visit young Jesus: po 142-3

ASTROLOGY
Babylon: g73 11/22 3, 5
Bible view: g74 2/22 5-6 g73 11/22 6-7
discussion: g73 11/22 3-7
Israel: g73 11/22 6
magi: g73 12/22 5
modern-day: g73 11/22 3-7; kj 224; g71 10/8 10, 21
origin: g73 11/22 3-5
scientific basis lacking: w75 715; g75 8/8 4
Tarot cards: g75 8/8 4
use in psychiatry: g72 11/8 29
zodiac: g75 11/8 30; g73 11/22 4-5
(SEE ALSO SPIRITISM)

ASTRONOMY
asteroids: g74 1/8 12
Babylon: g74 4/8 23
Bible: g74 1/8 14-15
"black holes": g74 1/8 14
comet: g73 8/8 30
constellations: g75 6/22 18
eclipses: g73 8/8 30
Eros: g75 8/22 14-15
evolutionists' problems: g75 6/22 18
galaxies: g75 6/22 17-19; g75 8/22 31; g71 2/22 31
Jupiter: g75 8/22 13-14
Kohoutek: w74 40
largest known object: g75 4/8 30
largest telescopes: g74 12/22 30
Mars: g75 8/22 14
Mercury: g75 8/22 13
meteors: g74 5/22 31
Milky Way: g75 6/22 17-18
moon: w74 295; w72 293; g72 1/22 30
quasimoon: g71 11/22 30
origin-of-universe theories: w75 200; g75 6/22 19; g75 12/22 29
proof of God's existence: g75 6/22 18
pulsars: g74 1/8 14; g72 9/22 31
quasars: g74 1/8 13-14; g71 5/8 29; g71 6/8 29
radio astronomy: g71 11/22 30
Saturn: g75 8/22 15-16
solar system: g75 6/22 17-18
stars: g75 6/22 17-18; g75 8/22 31; g71 1/8 8
telescopes: g72 12/22 24-6; g71 8/8 30
universe: g75 6/22 16-19
Venus: g75 8/22 12-13; g75 12/22 29; g71 3/8 30-1
(SEE ALSO HEAVENS, SOLAR SYSTEM, STARS)

ATHANASIAN CREED
w73 131-2

ATHANASIUS
Trinity doctrine: g73 1/8 16-19

ATHEISM
Communism: w75 233-4; g73 4/8 5-6, 9-11
England: g74 12/8 30
existentialism: w73 451-2
experience: g71 4/8 3-7
results: w73 38

ATMOSPHERE
biosphere: g71 4/22 5
composition: g73 7/8 6; g71 4/22 5-6
function: g73 7/8 5-6
nitrogen: g71 4/22 6-7
ozone: g71 7/22 29
SST endangers: g71 7/22 29
(SEE ALSO AIR)

ATOMIC ENERGY
hydrogen atoms: g71 8/8 30
oil production: g75 7/22 30
power plant wastes: g71 4/22 30
problems: g74 1/8 4; g74 8/22 22
reactors: g74 11/8 29; g73 2/22 20-3, 30; g72 2/22 31; g72 9/22 9-12

ATOMIC RADIATION
fallout decreases: g72 1/8 30
harmful effects: g74 8/22 22; g72 9/22 9-12

ATOMIC WEAPONS
arms race: g74 11/8 3-4; g72 10/8 3, 5, 10, 29; g71 7/8 6-7
destructive power: g75 8/22 30; g72 10/8 4, 9-10
fallout: g72 1/8 30
Hiroshima: yb73 221, 242-3; g72 9/22 9
number of nations having: w74 550
potential number: g74 11/8 29
plutonium: g75 8/22 30
size of stockpiles: w75 487; g74 11/8 4; g72 10/8 4, 9-10; g71 7/8 6-7
terrorists could make: g74 6/22 30; g74 11/8 5-6
testing: g74 11/8 4-5; g71 2/8 29; g71 4/22 16, 30; g71 9/8 30; g71 12/22 29
threat to human existence: g73 1/8 30; g72 10/8 4, 10; g71 5/22 31

ATOMS
number in a breath of air: g75 11/8 7
size: g74 1/22 13
smasher: g72 5/8 29
structure: g73 11/22 23; g72 3/8 12-15; g71 6/8 29; g71 7/22 11; g71 8/8 3-4

ATONEMENT DAY
description: w74 175-6; ka 94
discussion: po 115-17, 155
incense: w72 711
prophetic significance: w74 221-3; po 117, 155; ka 94-7, 103; w72 716-17
prophetic significance of sacrifices: w71 536-7
purpose: w74 176
sacrifices not remove sin: po 115-17

ATTENTION
importance of paying: w72 410-11; sg 24-9

ATTITUDE
negative: w74 589, 591

AUCTIONEERS
g75 5/8 31

AUGUSTINE
g74 12/22 28; g72 12/8 6

AUSTRALIA
aborigines: ts 26-7; g72 2/22 21-6
air pollution: g73 8/8 31
alcoholic beverages: g74 12/22 31
Cyclone Tracy: g75 3/22 24-6; km 3/75 4
description: g72 5/22 25-6; g71 3/22 22
divorce: g74 4/22 4
draft: g73 5/8 31
drugs: g73 12/8 5
earthquakes: g72 3/8 29
economy: g71 3/22 23
employment: g71 3/22 22-3
gambling: w74 579
Great Barrier Reef: g72 10/22 27
immigration: g71 3/22 21-3
Jehovah's witnesses: yb76 5-6, 24-5; w75 217-18; yb75 24-5; g75 3/22 26; km 4/75 1; yb74 24-5; w73 53; yb73 7-8, 24-5; g73 9/22 13-14; w72 533-6; yb72 34-5
preaching in the outback: w75 677-80
printery (Watch Tower): g73 9/22 13-14
moral breakdown: g74 4/22 4-5; g74 6/22 30-1; g73 4/22 6; g71 5/22 30; g71 8/22 29; g71 10/8 30
population: yb73 24; yb72 34
protests Malawi persecution: g73 8/22 30
radio: g71 7/8 25-6
rating of its products: g75 10/22 30
religion: w75 172; g74 9/8 29-30; g71 3/22 21-2; g71 5/8 3
rights of unborn: g72 2/22 30
size: w75 677
suicides: g71 5/22 30
surgery: g71 8/22 30
television's effect on students: g75 5/22 31
tires: g72 5/8 30
unemployment: g75 3/22 7-8
witchcraft: w74 323

AUSTRIA
Jehovah's witnesses: yb76 6, 24-5; yb75 24-5; yb74 24-5; yb73 8-9, 24-5; yb72 34-5, 41-2, 44; g72 5/22 24; g72 9/22 17-21; g72 10/22 17; km 11/72 6
population: yb73 24; yb72 34

AUTHORITY
discussion: tp 132-44; w72 261-73
disrespect of: g74 2/8 4-5; w72 261-4, 268-9
Jehovah: w72 266, 272-3
meaning of term: w72 262
superior authorities: tp 135-9; w72 266-7
within congregation: tp 142-4
within home: tp 139-42

AUTOMOBILES
abandoned: g75 12/8 31; g74 3/22 30
Abu Dhabi: g75 12/8 31
accidents: g72 12/22 31
causes: w74 452-3; g74 3/22 8-11; g73 7/8 31; g72 9/22 30; g72 10/8 31; g72 11/22 30; g71 4/8 31; g71 6/22 3-4; g71 8/22 22; g71 11/8 3-4
children: g74 1/8 31; g72 2/22 29; g71 8/22 31
deaths: g75 2/22 31; g74 2/22 28; g74 5/22 16; g74 11/8 30; g73 10/22 31
decrease: g74 7/22 29
new tool: g72 9/8 31
prevention: g71 6/8 30
statistics: g74 3/22 8-9; g72 6/8 3-4; g72 9/22 30; g71 10/22 30
victim awakes from eight-year coma: g75 9/8 30-1
young drivers: g74 3/22 8-11
air pollution: g72 6/8 3; g71 4/22 8, 20-1, 28
control devices: g73 2/22 30
armored: g75 3/22 29
automated: g72 4/8 29
automatic transmissions: g74 1/22 29
care: g75 7/22 9
company bankrupt: g71 3/22 30; g71 4/8 30
cost to operate: g74 8/22 30
displaying Tetragrammaton on: km 9/74 8
driving: w74 676; g74 3/22 10-11; g74 5/22 16; g74 12/8 29-30; g73 1/8 29-30; g73 1/22 29; g72 12/8 31
in dangerous areas: g75 11/22 13
smoking: g73 1/22 29
use of drugs: g72 10/8 31
drunken drivers: g72 11/22 30
failures: g75 8/22 19
gasoline: g74 3/22 30
hitchhiking: g73 2/8 30-1
Hitler's swindle: w75 241
hot rods: g74 6/22 12
imports: g71 6/22 29
insurance: g74 3/22 9
left- or right-hand driving: g72 11/8 21-3
number: g74 2/22 29; g74 11/8 31; g73 6/8 4; g71 12/22 31
production: g71 10/22 9
protecting from theft: g73 4/22 17
purchasing: g75 7/22 9
racing: g74 6/22 12
reducing driving expenses: g75 7/22 9-10
repairs: g71 6/22 29
sales: g75 2/8 30
sales fraud: g74 12/8 29
seat belts: g75 6/8 31; g73 2/8 30; g72 3/22 30
speed: g74 6/22 12; g74 11/8 30
taxicabs: g75 7/22 31; g72 7/8 16-19
thefts: g74 9/22 31; g71 9/8 29; g71 11/8 29
tires: g72 5/8 30; g72 6/22 30; g72 9/8 22-3
traffic congestion: g74 11/8 31
U.S. president: g72 10/8 30
Witkars: g75 2/22 24-5
(SEE ALSO TRANSPORTATION)

AUTOPSY
g71 6/22 22

AVENGER OF BLOOD
w73 302-4, 308

AVIATION
accidents: g75 1/22 31; w74 394; ts 10; g73 2/22 31; g73 4/8 25-6; g72 3/22 29; g72 7/22 29; g72 12/8 30
laws of chance: g75 3/22 21-2
airport: g73 1/22 22-4
airport duty-free shops: g75 2/8 30-1
fuel economy: g75 4/22 30
fuel shortage: g74 4/8 30; g73 12/22 31
hijacking of plane: g74 5/22 13-16; g71 6/8 18
New Guinea: g73 4/8 24-6
Orville Wright's comment on the airplane: g75 8/22 19
passengers screened: g71 12/22 30
pollution dangers: g71 7/22 29
private aircraft sales: g74 10/8 31
safety: g71 8/8 30
supersonic planes: g71 7/22 29
white-outs: g75 2/8 25
witnessing during air travel: g75 2/8 25-6
(SEE ALSO TRANSPORTATION)

AWAKE! (Magazine)
appreciation for: g73 10/22 5, 28; g72 11/8 18; km 1/72 3; w71 94
circulation: g75 3/8 30
distribution:
1942-74: yb75 241
experiences with: g74 8/22 23; w72 318
"extra" copies for congregation: km 8/75 8
first issue: yb75 241
German edition: yb74 243-4
name changes: yb75 123, 211
printeries: g73 9/22 10-16
production: yb75 32, 245; w74 30; yb72 256; w71 29
release: yb75 123, 211
statement of ownership: g75 11/8 23; g74 11/8 8; g73 11/8 11; g72 11/8 31; g71 11/8 31

subscription: km 2/72 8
subscription rate: km 7/71 1
(SEE ALSO GOLDEN AGE)

AWAKENESS
importance: g71 11/22 3-4

AZAZEL
sl 64-6

AZORES
Jehovah's witnesses: yb76 28-9; yb75 28-9; yb74 28-9; yb73 28-9; yb72 38-9
population: yb73 28; yb72 38

AZTECS
g72 4/22 11

BAAL
name: w74 457
orgies: w74 457-8; w73 586-8
worship: w74 457-8; w73 586-8; w72 684-5

BAAL OF PEOR
w74 457; w72 502-3, 684

BAAL-ZEPHON
kj 19

BABEL
w74 41-2, 490
(SEE ALSO BABYLON)

BABIES
badness: w71 606
baptism: g74 3/22 27-8; w72 511-12
birth: g72 10/22 8
birth at home: g74 6/8 21-4
blind baby "sees" with bat's sonar method: g75 8/22 29
book *Birth Without Violence:* g75 10/8 30-1
contact with mother after delivery: g75 11/8 31
crying: g75 5/22 30
death: g74 6/8 21, 23; g74 12/8 9; g73 7/8 14-15; g72 3/22 30; g72 6/8 5; g71 12/8 27-8
decision whether to have: g74 11/8 9-11
deformed: g71 2/8 31
development in womb: g74 2/8 12-16; g74 3/22 29; w73 420; g73 12/22 27-8
effects of—
  alcoholism of mother: g75 7/22 29-30; g75 9/8 30
  drugs used by mother: g74 2/8 14; g72 5/8 30
  incestuous marriage: w75 72-4
  mercury in food: g71 4/8 29
  noises before birth: g75 8/22 30
  pesticides: g72 5/8 30; g72 7/8 30
  smoking by mother: g74 5/22 31
fatness: g71 6/22 30
feeding: g75 11/22 30; g74 7/8 13-16; g73 2/22 17; g73 7/8 12-15; g71 6/22 30
genetic disorders: w75 191
growth: w72 112-13
handicapped: g73 6/22 28-9
helplessness: g71 5/22 16
human milk: g75 10/8 30; g75 11/22 30; g74 7/8 13, 15-16; g73 7/8 13-15
jaundiced: g72 6/22 29; g71 12/22 30
love needed: g72 1/8 30; g72 5/22 10-11; g72 9/8 30
mongoloid: g75 6/22 20-3
nursing: g75 10/8 30; g74 7/8 13-16
premature: g72 9/8 30
swimming: g72 1/22 30
weaning: g72 11/22 14
(SEE ALSO CHILDBEARING, CHILDBIRTH)

BABYLON (Babel)
astrology: g73 11/22 3, 5
astronomy: g74 4/8 23
captivity of Jews: w72 587, 723-4, 745, 763-5; kj 137-8, 168, 203-6, 271, 339-40
conquest of city: w72 745; w71 315-16
date of overthrow: w71 316, 649
decline: pm 227
desolation foretold by Bible: w75 136-7
desolation of Jerusalem: g72 5/8 27-8
divination: w73 60
fall: sl 113; po 20-1; w71 315-16; kj 340
founding: po 84; w72 572
Judaism: w72 669-70
language: w75 464
leaving Babylon 537 B.C.E.: sl 113, 119-21; ts 158; w72 300-1, 305-7; pm 28-32; g72 3/8 28
Nebuchadnezzar: kj 224-7
origin of religious myths: ts 27-9
priestly celibacy: g75 5/8 28
religion: ts 44; w73 605; w72 745; pm 165, 220; w71 509-10
  influence on ancient world: ts 28-9, 44-5
ruins: w75 136-7; w72 745-6
  restoration efforts: w75 294
rulers: pm 227
sorcery: g74 9/8 28
Tower of Babel: w74 490; w72 428
visited by Peter: w72 669
ziggurats: w74 490
(SEE ALSO NIMROD)

BABYLON THE GREAT
bloodguilt: w73 306-8; tp 26-7; w71 629
Christendom: sl 236; kj 255, 289-90, 343
destruction: w75 270-1, 682, 743-4; sl 247, 334-5, 339-43; w74 53-4, 170-1, 318, 552, 719; w73 676; ka 312-13, 316-17, 394-5; tp 34-5; g72 10/8 22; kj 190-1, 206-7, 209, 253-7, 289-90, 292, 302, 359-60
exiled people: w72 255; kj 80
experience:
  changing employment: w71 533-4
fall: kj 300
fornication: w75 691-2; g74 10/22 9
God's people in captivity: sl 114; yb75 109-11
identified: w75 682; sl 234, 335; g75 11/22 23; w74 718; ka 312; w72 587, 589, 630, 636, 724, 749; dn 28; g72 10/8 18, 22; kj 179-80, 190-1
leaving: w75 692; sl 161; w74 564-5; yb74 86; ka 315; w72 185; pm 221-2; g72 10/8 22; w71 561-2
liberation of captives: sl 107, 127, 134, 139, 158, 165, 190; w72 725; pm 161-2, 172; kj 300-1, 343, 354, 380-1
mourning over her: w74 171
persecution of God's people: w72 749; kj 207, 379
relationship to ancient Babylon: pm 220
rides scarlet-colored wild beast: w75 743; w71 629

"BABYLON THE GREAT HAS FALLEN!" GOD'S KINGDOM RULES! (Book)
yb75 231

BACCHUS
kj 150

BACKACHES
discussion: g73 8/8 23-5
exercise: g75 6/8 31
sleeping positions: g75 6/8 31
surgery: g75 1/8 30

BACTERIA
g74 7/22 13; g73 2/22 19; g73 3/8 9-11; g73 7/8 7; g71 3/22 29; g71 8/22 11-12

BAD(NESS)
"babes as to": w74 112; w71 606

BAHAI
g74 1/22 17-18

BAHAMAS
government: g73 5/8 8-10
history: g73 5/8 8-9
independence: g73 5/8 8-10
Jehovah's witnesses: yb76 24-5; yb75 24-5; yb74 24-5; yb73 24-5; yb72 34-5
population: yb73 24; yb72 34

BAHREIN ISLANDS
Jehovah's witnesses: yb74 26-7; yb73 26-7; yb72 36-7
population: yb73 26; yb72 36

BALAAM
prophet: w73 586-9

BALAK
w73 586

BALANCE
mental health: g75 4/22 3-4
physical, affected by cold: g73 1/8 31
spiritual—
  elders: w75 368-74
  field service: w74 563-9, 575-6
  maintaining: w74 564; w72 599

BAMBOO
g73 1/8 22-4; g71 5/8 11

BANGLADESH
cholera: g75 3/22 29-30
crisis: g74 6/22 5, 7, 10; g74 11/22 29
famines: g75 2/22 9
Jehovah's witnesses: yb76 26-7; yb75 26-7
population density: g74 3/22 31; g74 6/22 10

BANKRUPTCY
auctions: g75 5/8 31
automobile company: g71 3/22 30; g71 4/8 30
cause: g72 3/8 3
churches: g75 3/8 30
large companies: g75 12/8 30
statistics: g74 11/8 30; g72 3/8 3; g71 2/8 29
suicide: g71 3/22 30

BANKS
cost of borrowing money: g75 5/8 30
discussion: g75 6/8 9-13
embezzlements: g75 11/8 29; g74 7/8 31
experience: w71 533
failures: g75 6/8 9; g71 5/22 29
inflation: g74 11/22 30
robbery: g74 7/8 31; g73 4/22 8; g73 11/8 30; g71 1/22 23
(SEE ALSO ECONOMICS, MONEY)

BANS
getting literature: yb74 141-3, 193-4, 198-201, 229
meeting under: yb74 134-6, 139, 143-5, 152, 161-2, 181-2, 194, 200; w72 136-7; or 186; yb72 86-93
number: w72 340
preaching under: yb76 59-64, 194-5; yb75 258; yb74 20, 132-3, 139, 141-3, 155-6, 159; w72 70-1, 137-8; yb72 85-8
printing under: yb74 139-41, 157-60, 201
Witnesses during World War II: w71 721

Countries

Argentina: yb72 84-8, 116; w71 23
Australia: w73 53; w72 535
Botswana (Bechuanaland): yb76 146, 180, 189, 196, 209, 213, 216; yb74 17
Brazil: yb73 51-2, 64-7
Cameroon: yb75 5-6; yb74 11; yb73 19-20
Canada: yb75 95-6; w74 284-5; w72 148, 150; w71 22
Central African Republic: yb74 36, 39
Czechoslovakia: yb72 139-41
Dominican Republic: yb72 153-63; w71 18-19, 343
East Germany: yb74 225-6, 229-31
France: yb76 15; w71 17
Gabon: yb76 10-11; w71 251-4
Germany: yb74 103-4, 108-10, 112-13, 115-16; w71 16
Ghana: yb73 154-6, 166, 168-70, 175, 177-8
Great Britain: yb73 123-9; w71 667
India: w73 763-4
Kenya: yb75 7; yb74 12
Lesotho (Basutoland): yb76 146, 159, 189, 209
Malagasy Republic: w71 90
Malawi (Nyasaland): yb76 120, 152, 170-1; g75 12/8 5
Morocco: yb75 8
Newfoundland: yb76 59-64
Nicaragua: yb72 186-90
Pakistan: yb72 199
Rhodesia (Southern Rhodesia): yb76 154, 167
Russia: w74 218
Singapore: yb74 20; w72 341-9
South Africa: yb76 138-9, 141-6; w74 475
Spain: w75 456
Sri Lanka (Ceylon): yb76 246
Swaziland: yb76 146, 179, 189, 194-5, 209
Taiwan: yb72 218-26, 228
Tanzania: yb74 13-14
Turkey: w74 218
Uganda: yb74 13
Zaïre (Belgian Congo): yb76 177
Zambia (Northern Rhodesia): yb76 130-3, 156-7, 173-5; yb74 14; yb72 238-40, 252-3
(SEE ALSO PERSECUTION)

BAPTISM
Greek word: w73 273-4

Holy Spirit

Jesus Christ: po 144

Water

after 36 C.E.: or 17
attire for women: w73 254-5
clarification of belief: kj 177-8
command: w74 344
Cornelius: w72 691-2
delaying: w74 342-4
discourse and questions: w73 280; w72 492-3
discussion: w73 269, 273-80
"Divine Purpose" Assemblies (1974): w75 470
Ethiopian eunuch: w72 691
experiences: yb73 226; w71 343
 obstacles overcome: w74 342-3
 pond dug: yb76 182
 prison inmates baptized: yb76 155; g75 4/22 21-3, 25-6, 28; w74 639
immersion: g74 3/22 27-8; w73 273-4; g72 3/8 18
 by brother: w73 479-80
importance: w74 343-4; w72 379; w71 64
infant: g74 3/22 27-8; w73 276; w72 511-12
Jesus Christ: w74 603; w73 5, 274; w72 175-6, 379, 601, 606, 623, 715-16; dn 16; te 184
Jesus' disciples: w73 7
Jews: w72 688-91
John's baptism: w73 273-5
Lutheran church: g72 3/8 18
meetings with candidates before: yb75 254; or 18-19
misconceptions: yb76 72-3; g74 3/22 28
picture of, in *National Geographic:* g75 11/8 29
publications studied prior to: km 3/74 4
public declaration: tp 184-6; w72 601
questions for candidates: or 19-52
rebaptism: w73 341
reports: yb76 3, 23, 31; w75 18-19, 23, 27, 86; sl 202; yb75 5, 31, 253-4, 257; km 5/75 1-2; km 11/75 1; w74 15, 26; yb74 254; g74 3/8 20; km 11/74 1; km 12/74 1; w73 23, 28; yb73 23, 32, 255; w72 50, 307, 458, 492; pm 258; yb72 42-3; w71 24, 562; kj 179
 number since release of *Truth* book: km 12/75 1
request good conscience: w74 58-9, 603; tp 185-6
requirements: w74 340, 343; km 3/74 4; w73 154, 276-80, 336-41, 543, 636; tp 184-5
responsibilities: w72 379-80
Samaritans: w72 690-1
significance: w74 603; w73 273-80, 309-10; or 17-18; te 183-6
when prevented: w73 479-80
(SEE ALSO DEDICATION)

BAPTIST, JOHN THE
(SEE JOHN THE BAPTIST)

BAPTISTS
abortion: g74 4/22 30; w73 419
attitude toward Witnesses: g71 1/8 29
beliefs: g73 2/22 6-7
Bible discredited: tp 34; g73 2/22 6-7
church program: w71 643
clergy: g74 1/8 30; g74 1/22 31; w71 740; g71 7/8 30
 comments on church failure: g75 2/8 31; w71 548
 quitting: g75 3/22 31
decline: g74 5/8 29; g73 2/22 3; g72 2/8 29; g72 6/22 29; g71 5/8 31
discussion: w71 547-52
disunity: w71 547-8
experiences:
 become Witnesses: g73 2/22 9-10; yb73 40, 46-7; w71 368-9, 551-2
fight in church: g75 6/8 29
homosexuality: w73 356
money raising: w71 505
pornography: g74 12/22 31
Soviet Union: g75 4/8 31; w73 708; g73 4/8 15
woman president: w71 644; g71 7/8 30

BARAK
w74 231-2

BARBADOS
coral island: g72 10/22 28
home construction: g72 10/22 28
Jehovah's witnesses: yb76 6, 24-5; yb75 24-5; yb74 24-5; yb73 24-5; yb72 34-5
population: yb73 24; yb72 34
tourism: g72 5/8 14

BARBER, C. W.
yb75 148, 195-7

BARBERS
ancient: g72 11/8 13
experiences: yb73 10, 56-7
home barbering: g72 11/8 12-14

BARBOUR, N. H.
yb75 36-8; w73 395

BARLEY
harvest:
 sheaf of firstfruits: w75 603

BARNABAS
dispute with Paul: w75 344-6

BARNACLE
ts 146-7

BAROMETER
patterned after the jellyfish: w75 560

BARRENNESS
physical: g74 8/8 28

BARUCH
Jeremiah's secretary: w75 563; w72 634

BARUCH, BERNARD
comment on Bible: g75 10/8 15

BASKETBALL
g75 2/8 29; g75 6/8 29
BAT
blind baby "sees" with bat's sonar method: g75 8/22 29
echolocation: g75 6/8 20
BATH
'brought to life by' (Titus 3:5): w72 607-8
BATH-SHEBA
w73 479
BATTERY
solar: g72 10/8 27
BATTLE OF ARMAGEDDON, THE (Book)
w74 723
BEACH(ES)
formation: g71 8/22 20-2
BEAR
grizzly: g73 5/8 16-18
Kodiak: g72 1/8 18-20
polar: g72 3/22 29
BEARD
discussion: w73 139-40
when inadvisable: w75 501
BEASTS
symbolic: ts 154
Of Revelation
beast out of the sea (wild beast): w75 228-9, 743; sl 250; w73 676-8; ka 22-6; pm 46-7; kj 363
beginning: ka 22-3
destruction: w73 677-8
froglike expressions: kj 363
mark of, on hand or forehead: w73 741; ka 33, 80
seven heads: w74 381; ka 23
victory over: w73 660-1
scarlet-colored wild beast: kj 256
abyss: w74 718
desolates harlot: w75 743-4; w74 552, 719; ka 311-13, 316; g72 10/8 22
destruction: ka 317-18; w71 622; nc 23-4
identified: w75 743; yb75 203; g75 2/8 8; w74 552, 718; ka 309-10, 314, 394; w71 621, 718; nc 22-3
image of the beast: sl 250-1; w73 676; w71 723; kj 363-4
kings have one thought: w74 552
"peace and security": g75 2/8 9
rulers give authority: g75 2/8 8-9
seven heads and ten horns: g75 2/8 8-9; w74 552
two-horned beast: kj 363
false prophet: w73 677; ka 24
"wild beasts of earth" (Re 6:8): w74 359
BEAUTY
Bible view: w73 523
cleanliness: g71 7/22 24
BEDS
water: g72 3/22 29-30
BEEF
shortage: g72 10/8 30
BEER
alcohol content: w74 452-4
breweries closing: g75 6/8 31
churches: g75 8/8 30
consumption statistics: g75 5/8 31
discussion: g72 2/8 21-3
BEES
African: g75 1/22 29; g72 3/22 31
communication: g71 3/8 11
hive in carcass: g74 4/8 21
honeybee: g75 1/22 29; g75 5/22 23
honeycombs:
honeycomb-type grain elevators: w75 560
insecticides: g75 1/22 29
pollination: g72 10/22 7
queen: g73 4/8 19
sting: g75 1/22 29; g73 9/22 30
BEGGING
ts 101; g73 11/22 26; g72 11/22 30
BELGIUM
Catholic church: g72 7/22 17-26
Jehovah's witnesses: yb76 6-7, 24-5; yb75 24-5; yb74 24-5; w73 571-3; yb73 24-5; yb72 34-5; g72 7/22 23-6; w71 680
population: yb73 24; yb72 34
BELIEFS
surveys: g72 9/8 30; w71 675-6; g71 3/22 3, 22
BELIZE (British Honduras)
Jehovah's witnesses: yb76 24-5; yb75 24-5; yb74 24-5; yb73 24-5; yb72 34-5
BELLS
horses (Zec 14:20): pm 402-3
BEN-HADAD
kj 28-30
BEQUIA
Jehovah's witnesses: yb76 24-5; yb75 24-5; yb74 24-5; yb73 24-5; yb72 34-5
population: yb73 24; yb72 34
BERLIN
description: g71 5/22 21-4
Jehovah's witnesses: yb76 26-7; yb75 16, 26-7; yb74 24-5, 222-4; w73 29; yb73 14, 24-5; yb72 34-5; w71 17, 531-2
population: yb73 24; yb72 34
wall: yb74 228-9
(SEE ALSO GERMANY)
BERMUDA
home construction: g72 10/22 28
Jehovah's witnesses: yb76 24-5; yb75 24-5; yb74 24-5; yb73 24-5; yb72 34-5
population: yb73 24; yb72 34
BESTIALITY
w72 32; g72 1/22 5
BETEL NUT
addiction: tp 162-3; w72 594
cancer: w74 742
BETHEL FAMILY(IES)
allowance: g73 9/22 11
appreciation for privileges: km 5/74 5-6; w73 284, 403; yb72 106-7; km 11/72 4
background of members: g75 1/8 14-17
contributes relief to Honduras: g74 12/22 26
discussion: g75 1/8 13-17; or 145-7; km 11/72 3-4
elders: km 9/75 1
experiences: g75 1/8 14-17
field service: km 5/74 6
food: w73 313-14; g73 6/22 21
governing body: w75 60; w71 669-70
growth: yb75 243-4
history:
the "Vow": yb75 51-2
number in families: yb76 259; yb75 258; g75 1/8 13; km 5/75 1; yb74 255; km 5/74 4; yb73 256; g73 6/22 21; w71 335
older members: g75 11/8 16
privileges: km 5/74 4-6; w71 458-9
purpose: g73 9/22 11
requirements: km 5/75 1; km 5/74 5; or 146; km 10/72 1; km 4/71 4
schedule: w72 408; or 146; km 11/72 3-4
South Africa: yb76 186-7, 193, 234, 242
training: w73 110
BETHEL HOME
closed in 1918: yb75 110
court cases: g74 9/8 15-16; g71 6/8 26
Germany: yb74 242-4, 246-7
investigation by authorities: yb75 95-7
original purchase: yb75 51
picture: w73 313
reopened in 1919: yb75 120-2
South Africa: yb76 186-7, 193, 233-6, 241
taxation: g74 9/8 15-16
tours: g75 1/8 17
Towers Hotel: km 3/75 1
comments on Witness purchase and use: w75 631
U.S. expansion: yb75 52, 145, 243-4; w73 397; g73 6/22 20-4
visitors: g73 8/22 16; km 8/73 1
wireless misreport: yb75 96-7; yb73 107-8
BETHLEHEM
name: w72 78
restored 537 B.C.E.: po 134
BETH-SARIM
yb75 193-4
BETHZATHA
pool: w75 367
BEVERAGES
coffee: g73 1/8 31; w72 596; g71 1/22 19; g71 9/8 30
fruit "drinks": g75 4/8 23
green-pea: g74 7/22 20
Guyana: g74 7/22 20
hot: g74 2/8 19
orange juice: g72 3/22 29
papaw: g74 7/22 20
pineapple peel: g74 7/22 20
potato: g74 7/22 20
soft drinks: g73 1/8 31; g73 8/22 3
tastes in U.S.: g73 1/8 31
tea: g71 1/22 19
thirst-quenching effect: g74 8/22 29
tropical fruit: g73 1/22 13-14
BIBLE
accurate history: g74 4/8 25-6; g74 10/8 9-10
age: w74 483
aids to keeping events in proper order: w75 446-7
aids to understanding: w73 207-18

- application of counsel: w73 37-8; w72 35-6
- Author: g75 10/8 8-9; w71 228; sg 15
- banned: w74 743
- basis for beliefs: w75 82-6; w73 644-6
- candor of writers: g74 4/8 25; g74 6/22 11; g73 2/8 4; w72 320; w71 95
- Catholic church:
  - attitude toward Bible study: w73 547-8; g72 10/22 29
  - discredit Bible: w75 710; g75 3/22 30-1; g73 3/22 16-19; g72 4/8 23-4; w71 676; g71 8/8 26; g71 12/22 5
  - shortage: g71 9/22 29
- chapter and verse division: w71 228; sg 15
- charts:
  - Bible books (writers, time covered, time and place written): bi8 1367
- clergy discredit: yb76 47; w75 710; g75 3/22 30-1; g75 9/8 30; g74 7/8 22-3; g74 8/22 9-12; g74 9/8 30; g74 9/22 30; g73 2/22 6-7; g73 4/8 30; w72 169; g72 1/22 5, 29; g72 4/8 23-4; g72 8/22 18; w71 48-51, 464-5, 548, 561, 628, 675-6; g71 1/22 29; g71 9/22 15; g71 12/22 5
- clergy oppose use of: w74 743-4
- codex: w74 553-4
- comments on sex: g74 6/22 11
- context: w73 207-18
- criticism: w75 148; g75 10/8 9; w74 72; g73 3/22 16-19; g72 1/22 27-8; g72 2/22 27-8; g72 6/22 6-7; w71 324
- discussion: w75 131-50; g75 10/8 8-29
- divine name: fu 8-10; pm 388; w71 229, 387, 389-91, 453-5; sg 17
- epitome of Bible events: w75 446-7, 579-88
- experiences:
  - found in garbage: yb73 20
  - reading arouses interest: g72 3/8 23
- finding scriptures: km 2/75 4; sg 97
- footnotes: w73 702
- games: g72 6/22 14-16
- Genesis' compilation: w71 409-10
- geographical and geological accuracy: w74 77-80; g72 9/8 31
- God's Word: w75 141-50, 286
- Greek Scriptures: w71 453-5
- guide for human conduct: w75 151-8; g75 1/22 6; g75 10/8 8-29
- harmony with true science: w75 133-5
- ignorance: g75 6/8 29; g72 2/8 24; g71 4/8 30
- inspiration: w75 133-50; fu 5; g75 10/8 8-9; w73 645-6; g72 2/8 27-8; w71 228-9; sg 15-17; g71 11/8 27-8
- interpretation: w74 629; g74 8/22 9-11; w73 548
- knowledge "complete" (1 Co 13:10): w75 95-6
- learning order of books: yb73 57
- memorizing Bible facts: g75 9/22 25-6
- miracles: g75 3/22 30-1; g74 4/8 25-6; w71 291-4
- moral standards: g75 10/8 15-18; w74 483-6; w72 35-6
- myths wrongly attributed to: g75 10/8 10-11
- names: w71 58-9
- no pious frauds: w71 324
- number of languages in which circulated: w75 131; w74 394, 700; tp 6; w72 388; g72 12/8 29; g72 12/22 5; w71 227; sg 14; te 13
- number of words, verses, chapters: w71 228; sg 15
- original languages: w71 227; sg 14; te 13
- original manuscripts: w75 149-50
- "pattern of healthful words": w73 528
- Pentateuch: g72 2/22 27-8
  - published in Russia: w75 487
- percentage without Bible in their language: w74 394
- poetry: g73 2/8 27-8
- powerful: w74 445; tp 143-4
- practicality: w72 259-60
- preservation: w75 149-50; g75 10/8 9
- printing: yb75 213, 218-21; g73 9/22 8
- proper view: g75 10/8 8-18; w74 179-82, 265; tp 111-12, 143-4
- public reading: w71 59; sg 32-3, 122-9, 146
- punctuation: g73 6/8 7; w71 227-8, 255; sg 14-15
- quoting: w73 209-10
- reading: w74 179-80; w73 201-7; w71 62, 105, 263; sg 21, 23
  - statistics: w75 200
- reasons for disbelief: w75 148; ts 177; g73 10/22 3, 21-2; g71 4/8 30
- reasons for examining: w74 148
- rejection of: w71 324; kj 157; g71 4/8 30
- Soviet Union:
  - attitude toward Bible: w75 487
- spurious texts: g73 8/8 6-7; w71 537-8
- standard: w74 529
- study: g75 1/22 23; g75 10/22 14-15; w74 114-15, 179-82, 211; g74 8/8 4-5; w73 122, 201-18; km 12/73 3; w71 60-2
- superscriptions: w72 61-2
- supposed discrepancies: w75 149
- symbolism: w74 629
- theme: po 65; w71 230; sg 18
- time used in writing: w71 227; sg 14
- use in field service: km 2/75 4; km 9/75 8; km 12/75 7; w73 209-10; or 114, 116; yb72 85-6; sg 97
- view of Isaac Newton: w75 651
- why beneficial: w75 131-2; g75 10/8 12-29; w74 148; ts 88, 189-90; g74 1/22 17-18; g74 8/8 4-5; g74 9/22 11; g74 10/8 25; g74 12/8 25; w73 38, 164-5, 252-3, 326-7, 505; tp 111-13; g73 1/22 4; w72 35-6, 67-9, 195-6, 259-60, 543; g72 9/22 27-8; w71 31, 229-30; sg 17-19; te 11-14; g71 1/22 4; g71 10/8 29
- why humans used to write: w75 147
- why only certain histories: po 65
- why symbolism used: ts 151-2
- Witnesses' view and use: w74 629, 631-2, 637, 768; w71 465, 676-7
- words stolen: pm 212-14
- writers: w75 141-9; g72 1/22 27-8; g72 2/8 27-8; g72 2/22 27-8; w71 228-9, 409-10; sg 15-17; te 12; g71 3/8 25; g71 11/8 27-8
- writing style: w74 15; g73 9/8 20

Quotations

- all races find answers to world problems: g74 12/8 25
- best reference: g72 9/8 31
- makes best people in the world: g72 10/22 10
- no Bible study ever really done: g72 2/8 24
- no other book so revolutionary influence: g74 12/8 25
- no other work of antiquity as accurate: w75 150
- read Bible and you will live a better man: w72 388
- Ten Commandments and Sermon on the Mount are best guides: g75 10/8 15

(SEE ALSO BIBLE MANUSCRIPTS, BIBLE TRANSLATIONS)

BIBLE AUTHENTICITY

- Acts (book): g71 4/8 27-8
- Ammonites: w75 421-3
- Arch of Titus: w75 139-40
- Babylon: w75 136-7
- candor of writers: g74 4/8 25; g73 2/8 4; w72 320
- Christian Greek Scriptures: w75 150; g72 6/22 5-8
- chronology: g72 4/8 16-20; g72 5/8 27-8
- circumcision: w75 135-6
- copper in Palestine: w75 112
- discussion: w75 133-50
- earth: w75 133
- Flood: g75 6/8 5-8; g75 11/22 29; g73 1/22 24
- geographical accuracy: w74 77-80; g72 1/8 27-8; g72 9/8 31
- Gospel accounts: w75 149
- harmony of scriptures explained:
  - Numbers 3:22, 28, 34—Numbers 3:39: g72 3/8 28
  - Numbers 4:3, 30, 47—Numbers 8:24: g72 3/8 27
  - Deuteronomy 8:18—Luke 18:24: g71 11/22 27-8
  - 2 Kings 25:8—Jeremiah 52:12: g72 3/8 27
  - Proverbs 26:4—Proverbs 26:5: w72 127-8
  - Matthew 10:5, 6—Acts 1:8: w71 159-60
  - Luke 24:50, 51—Acts 1:9-11: g72 9/22 6
  - Acts 7:16—Genesis 25:15-19: w75 735-6
  - Acts 9:7—Acts 22:9: w72 159-60
- Hittites: w71 348-9
- internal harmony: w75 148-9; g71 12/22 6, 8
- Isaiah (book): g73 3/22 18-19
- Jerusalem: w75 138-40
- Jesus Christ: w75 237, 249-51; g72 2/8 8

g, Awake!; **ka**, God's Kingdom of a Thousand Years; **kj**, "The Nations Shall Know that I Am Jehovah"; **km**, Kingdom Ministry; **or**, Organization; **pm**, Paradise Restored—By Theocracy!; **po**, God's "Eternal Purpose"; **sg**, Theocratic School Guidebook; **sl**, Man's Salvation out of World Distress!; **te**, Listening to the Great Teacher; **tp**, True Peace and Security; **ts**, Is This Life All There Is?; **w**, Watchtower; **yb**, Yearbook. **Complete list on page 6.**

resurrection: g75 5/8 30
Jonah (book): w75 709-10; g73 3/22 17-18
Joseph: w71 381
Luke (Gospel): g71 12/22 6-8
Matthew (Gospel): g71 12/22 6-8
medical science: w75 133-6; g75 12/8 25
miracles: g74 4/8 25-6; w71 291-4
Moabites: w75 421-3
Nabunaid Chronicle: w71 315-16
Nineveh: w75 137; g72 6/22 28
numerical differences: g72 3/8 27-8
Paul's Rome voyage: g71 4/8 27-8
Pentateuch: g73 3/22 16-17; g72 2/22 27-8
Peter (second book): g71 2/8 27-8
Philistines: w75 421-3
Pontius Pilate: g72 1/8 28; w71 340
prophecy: w75 136-40; g75 10/8 13-14; w73 37; g73 1/22 7-9
reliability of Bible text: w75 150
sanitary provisions of Law: w75 133-5
sun and moon stood still: g74 1/8 14-15
textual criticism: g72 2/22 27-8
Zechariah (book): pm 94

Quotations

authenticity and integrity of New Testament finally established: w75 150; g71 12/22 8
authentic source of information: g72 9/8 31
confirm essential soundness of existing texts: w75 150; g72 6/22 7
interval between composition and evidence negligible: g71 12/22 8
through a thousand years so little alteration: g72 6/22 8
(SEE ALSO ARCHAEOLOGY, FLOOD [NOACHIAN])

BIBLE CANON

Apocrypha: w75 414-15; w73 601-2
evidence of authenticity: w71 227-9; sg 14-17
Jerome's comments on: w75 414
Josephus' comments on: w75 414
(SEE ALSO BIBLE TRANSLATIONS, SPURIOUS TEXTS)

BIBLE HOUSE

yb75 42

BIBLE IN LIVING ENGLISH, THE (Byington)

release: g72 10/22 20-1
use of God's name: w72 605-6

BIBLE MANUSCRIPTS

Alexandrine: g72 6/22 7
Chester Beatty: w75 150; g72 6/22 6-8
Christian Greek Scriptures (copies extant): g72 6/22 5; g71 12/22 8
copying: w75 150; g72 3/8 27; g72 6/22 7-8
Dead Sea Scrolls: g72 4/8 5; g72 6/22 6, 8
divine name: g72 6/22 8
Fouad Papyri: w71 389-90; bi8 1354-5
Septuagint: w73 702; w71 389-90, 454
Sinaitic: g72 6/22 7
vellum: g71 12/22 8
ways numbers written: ka 208-9
(SEE ALSO BIBLE TRANSLATIONS)

BIBLE STUDENTS MONTHLY (Tract)

distribution: yb75 85
Fall of Babylon: yb75 94-5; yb73 107-8

BIBLE STUDIES

answers to questions: sg 35-6, 94
attitude of Witness: km 1/74 4
befriending students: km 8/71 3
benefits: g75 10/22 14-15
children: km 7/74 4; w73 559-64; w72 114-17; te 5-6
coming to know Jehovah: w74 339
conducting anytime: km 1/74 4; km 11/73 6
directing interest to organization: w74 338; w73 406; or 124
discontinuing: w71 85
discussion: or 121-5; km 11/72 5-6
experiences:
  arranging study with meeting attender: km 10/71 7
  brings happiness: g73 7/22 19
  children: yb75 13-14; km 11/73 5; g71 4/8 23
  clergymen: w75 650; w72 381
  conduct of student changes: g73 4/22 26-8; w71 209
  illiterate conductor: km 11/73 6
  including other family members: km 11/73 5
  interested ones seek: w71 383
  marriage saved: w74 317
  older persons: km 11/73 5
  prisons: g75 4/22 25-8
  rapid advancement: w75 181; g73 2/22 24; w71 221-2; g71 5/8 7
  starting on first call: km 6/73 2
  studying with one's relatives: g73 2/22 24
  use of Bible alone: km 11/73 4
  young Witness conducts: km 8/73 4
family: w74 86-7; km 2/73 7-8; km 1/72 7-8; w71 104-7, 532, 556, 585-6; sg 37-8; km 5/71 3-4
Harp of God studies: yb75 128
hearts reached: w74 338-9; sg 75-8
indecisive ones: km 7/72 4
"*Lamp*" book: km 11/71 8
locations for: w75 181
method used: or 122-5
need: w75 180-1
number: w75 23, 27; yb75 31-2, 257; w74 26; yb74 30; km 11/74 1, 4; w73 23, 462, 639; yb73 23; w72 27; yb72 33; w71 24
pastoral work: yb75 85-6
prayer: sg 77-8
preparation: sg 39, 50-1
preparing for opposition: w74 339-40
reporting: km 7/74 4; or 127
six-month program: yb75 239-40; g75 10/22 14
starting: km 1/75 4; km 11/73 3-6; or 122; km 1/72 8; km 2/72 8; km 11/72 6; km 2/71 8; km 5/71 4; km 7/71 3; km 10/71 7
starting new ones in service: w74 340; km 7/72 4
teaching: w74 338-40; g74 7/8 4; or 122-5; km 5/72 3; sg 49-54, 75-8
use of booklets: km 10/75 1, 8
(SEE ALSO FIELD SERVICE)

BIBLE STUDY OVERSEER

duties: w72 460; or 76-7

BIBLE TEXTS

discussion: g72 6/22 5-8
(SEE ALSO BIBLE MANUSCRIPTS)

BIBLE TRANSLATIONS

African languages: yb73 142-3; g73 1/22 26
American Standard Version: yb75 219; w71 391
archaic language addressing God: w74 15
Authorized Version: kj 304-5
  Society edition: yb75 218-19
Bible in Living English, The (Byington): yb75 221
Children's Living Bible, The: w74 362
Chinese:
  first: w74 744-5
discussion: w74 361-4; g71 3/8 23-6
divine name: yb73 142-3; g73 1/22 26; w71 389-91, 453-5
English: g71 12/22 22
  first: w74 743-4
footnotes: g71 3/8 26
Hexapla: w71 454
Kingdom Interlinear Translation of the Greek Scriptures, The: yb75 221
Morrison: w74 744-5
New English Bible, The: w74 361, 363-4
New World Translation of the Christian Greek Scriptures:
  anarthrous nouns: w75 702-4
  divine name: yb75 219-20
  effect on Witnesses' speech: yb75 220
  foreign editions: yb75 220-1
  release: yb75 213, 219
  translation committee: w74 767-8
New World Translation of the Holy Scriptures (1961 edition):
  release: yb75 220
New World Translation of the Holy Scriptures (1963 large-print edition): yb75 220
New World Translation of the Holy Scriptures (1970 revision):
  German edition: yb73 9, 13; g72 6/8 29
New World Translation of the Holy Scriptures (1971 revision):
  accuracy: w74 361-2, 364
  divine name: bi8 1352-5, 1358-60
  footnotes: w73 702
  release: yb75 220-1
  translation committee: w74 767-8
number of languages: w74 361; g72 12/8 29
reasons for new ones: g72 6/22 5-6; g71 3/8 23
requirements for good translation: w74 361-4
Revised Standard Version Common Bible, The: w73 601-3
Septuagint: po 132-3; w71 389-91, 454
translation problems: w74 15, 361-4; g72 5/22 27-8; w71 59; g71 3/8 23-6
Tyndale: w74 743-5; g71 12/22 22
value of: g74 12/8 25

Vulgate: w71 455
Wycliffe: w74 743
(SEE ALSO BIBLE, BIBLE MANUSCRIPTS)

BICYCLES
accidents: g74 7/22 29-30; g73 11/22 31
champion cyclist learns truth: g75 8/8 7-8
discussion: g73 6/22 25-7
sales: g74 4/8 30
speed record: g73 11/22 31

BILL OF RIGHTS
g72 7/8 10-12

BILLS
Christians pay: w71 127-8

BINGO
Bible view: g74 6/22 13; g74 10/22 27-8
church money raising: g74 4/8 29; g74 10/22 27-8
synagogue money raising: w74 524

BIONICS
discussion: w75 560

BIRDS
courting: g74 5/22 23-6
disease: g74 12/8 30
diving: g71 9/22 13-15
eggs: g72 2/22 16
extinction: g74 5/8 30; g73 3/8 30; g72 6/8 31; g71 1/8 31; g71 4/22 13; g71 5/22 31
eyes: g71 7/22 19
flying ability: g74 2/22 14-15
food: g72 2/8 23
habit of tilting neck: g74 8/22 26
Japan: g72 3/8 30
light's effects: g71 7/8 15
mating time: g74 5/22 23-6
migration: g74 1/8 22; w73 579-80; g72 3/8 30; g71 7/8 12
navigation: w75 71; g75 2/8 29; g71 6/8 29
nests: g71 6/22 12; g71 7/22 13-15
pesticides: g73 1/22 30; g71 1/8 31; g71 4/22 11
pouches: g71 12/22 29
poultry feed: g71 3/22 29
singing: g74 5/22 25
speed: g74 2/22 14-15
training: g73 1/22 21
tropics: g72 3/8 26
varieties: ts 145-6
waterproofing: g71 5/8 10
wisdom in creation: g74 2/22 15

List by Name
Arctic tern: g71 7/8 12
bird-of-paradise: g74 5/22 24
blackbird: w75 248
black-poll warbler: w73 579-80
black skimmer: g71 7/22 13-14
bobwhite: g74 5/22 25
bowerbird: g74 5/22 26
cardinal: g74 5/22 24
chickadee: g72 2/8 23
chicken: g73 2/22 19; g71 1/8 16; g71 8/8 30
condor: g75 3/22 15
cormorant: g71 9/22 14-15
dipper: g71 7/22 14-15
duck: g73 2/22 19; g71 5/8 10
eagle: g75 3/22 15; g75 7/22 31; g74 2/22 14; g71 1/8 31
emu: g74 2/22 14
ferret: g71 7/8 15
finfoot: g71 12/22 29
flicker: g72 2/8 23
frigate: g74 2/22 15; g74 5/22 23
gannet: g71 9/22 13
golden plover: g74 1/8 22
goldfinch: g71 6/22 12
grebe: g74 5/22 26; g71 9/22 15
harpy eagle: g75 3/22 15
heron: g74 8/22 26
homing pigeon: w75 71; g75 2/8 29
hummingbird: g75 3/22 15; g74 2/22 14; g74 5/22 25
indigo: g74 5/22 25
killdeer: g71 7/22 13
kingfisher: g71 9/22 14
loon: g71 9/22 15
lyrebird: g74 5/22 23-4
murre: g71 7/22 13
nighthawk: g71 7/22 13
night heron: g74 5/22 24-5
oriole: g71 7/22 15
osprey: g74 5/8 30; g71 9/22 14
ostrich: g74 2/22 14; g72 2/22 16
ovenbird: g71 7/22 15
owl: g74 2/22 15; g72 2/8 23
oxpecker: g72 6/8 11
peacock: g74 5/22 23
pelican: g71 1/8 31; g71 9/22 13-14
penguin: g75 12/22 20-2; g74 5/22 24
peregrine falcon: g74 2/22 14-15; g73 3/8 30
pigeon: g74 12/8 30; g71 6/8 29
red-winged blackbird: g74 5/22 23
roadrunner: g74 2/22 14
robin: g72 2/8 23; g71 7/22 14-15
ruffed grouse: g74 5/22 25
sage grouse: g74 5/22 23
sandpiper: g71 7/22 13
skimmer: g71 9/22 14
starling: g71 2/22 19; g71 7/8 15
stork: g74 5/22 24; pm 219; g71 1/8 31
swan: ts 24
swift: g74 2/22 15; g71 7/22 15
tern: g74 5/22 24; g71 9/22 14
tomtit: g72 3/22 20-2
waxwing: g74 5/22 24
white stork: g74 1/8 22
woodcock: g74 5/22 25-6
woodpecker: g74 5/22 25; g71 5/22 31
wren: g71 7/22 14
(SEE ALSO ANIMALS, INSECTS, MARINE LIFE)

BIRTH
at home: g74 6/8 21-4
book *Birth Without Violence:* g75 10/8 30-1
discussion: g74 2/8 14-15; g73 2/22 16-17; g73 7/8 7-8; g72 11/22 13-16
handicapped from: g73 6/22 28-9
hormone injections: g74 1/22 13, 15
infant mortality: g74 6/8 21, 23
multiple: g74 1/22 13; g73 3/8 31; g73 3/22 30
parthenogenesis: g71 12/22 8
potential health dangers: w75 191-2
practices: g72 5/22 29
statistics: g74 7/8 13; g72 4/22 30
stool: g72 11/22 14
vertical: g71 6/8 31
(SEE ALSO BABIES, CHILDBIRTH, PREGNANCY)

BIRTH CONTROL
ban on: g75 9/8 30; g72 6/22 10; w71 407-8; g71 1/8 30
Catholics defy church: g74 10/22 29
Catholic view: g74 11/22 29-30; g73 3/8 29; g73 6/22 9; g73 9/22 31; g71 5/8 29; g71 8/22 14
Christian view: w75 159-60; w73 256
contraceptives: g74 1/22 15-16; w73 255-6; g73 1/22 30; g73 4/8 29; g73 9/8 31; g73 11/22 31
  youths: g75 7/8 30
governmental efforts: g74 6/22 7-8
Islam: g74 11/22 29
pills: g75 12/22 29; g74 1/22 15-16
sterilization: w75 158-60; g73 1/8 29-30
  increase: g75 9/22 30

BIRTHDAYS
discussion: te 123-6
faithful servants', not recorded in Bible: po 139
Witnesses adjust view of: yb75 147
(SEE ALSO CHRISTMAS)

BISHOP
meaning of term: w75 730
Roman Catholic Church: g75 1/22 30; g75 2/22 21; w74 592, 742; g74 12/22 29; w72 626-7; dn 20-2; yb72 142-3; g72 1/22 29-30; g72 4/22 6-7, 9, 16-17; g72 8/8 30; w71 407; g71 9/8 31; g71 9/22 9; g71 11/22 12
  admissions about church: g75 3/22 16-18
  suppress book on church role in World War II: w75 715
  Synod: g72 1/8 30-1; g72 1/22 31; g72 3/22 9-11; g72 5/8 9-12

BLESSINGS
appreciation for: w75 556-9
Christian: w75 60
Jehovah's: w74 191; w71 92-4
parental: w73 447-8

BLIND(NESS)
accomplishments: w72 547
baby "sees" with bat's sonar method: g75 8/22 29
causes: w74 319-20; g74 1/22 30; g73 6/22 28
cure: g74 4/22 30
experiences:
  minister becomes Witness: w74 411
  Witnesses who are physically blind: yb73 165-6; w72 407; g72 1/22 23; g72 2/22 20; g72 5/8 17-20; g71 12/22 4
India: g72 6/22 16
Jehovah "appoints": w74 319-20
Keller, Helen: g75 10/22 4

rehabilitation: g74 4/22 30
spiritual: w74 319-20
witnessing to physically blind persons: g73 3/8 11
(SEE ALSO HANDICAPPED)

BLOOD
anemia: w74 524
antibody produced after transfusion: g75 4/8 30-1
aspirin's effect upon: g72 10/22 30
bleeding: g72 12/22 23
blood banks: g75 3/22 29; g73 2/22 29
blood donors: w75 445; g75 1/22 30; g74 10/22 30-1; g73 11/22 30; g72 3/8 30; g72 5/8 23; g72 8/8 12; g71 3/8 29; g71 4/22 30; g71 11/8 8
building up: g74 6/22 21-2
cells: g74 7/22 12-14; g72 12/22 17-18; g71 3/8 16-18
chart: g74 7/22 13
circulation: g74 7/22 12-15; w72 387
composition: g74 5/22 19
covenant validation: po 112-13
crime detection: g73 4/22 30-1
discussion: g73 5/8 27-8
early Christians: g73 5/8 28; w71 118
experiences:
girl refuses unbled meat: yb76 8
respect for: g71 9/22 8
fractions: w74 351-2
function in body: g73 4/8 22
hemophilia treatment: g75 2/22 30
Jesus Christ: w72 607-8; pm 276-7
platelets: g74 7/22 13-14
prohibition on use: g74 5/22 20; w73 224, 301-2; tp 164-5; g73 5/8 27-8; w72 190-1, 544; g72 7/8 27; w71 118; g71 9/22 27-8
reinjection for sports stamina: g74 8/8 30
sacred: w73 300-2; g73 5/8 27
schizophrenics: g75 4/22 4, 8
sensitivity: g74 5/22 18-19
serums: w74 351-2
spleen: g71 3/8 16-18
storage: g72 4/8 29-30; g71 4/8 29-30
surgery without: g75 11/22 29; g74 6/22 17-22; g74 1/22 29; g74 5/22 18-19, 21-2; g73 2/8 19, 29; g73 6/8 15; g72 6/8 30; g72 6/22 29; g72 7/8 30-1; g72 8/22 29; g71 3/22 14; g71 6/8 31; g71 11/8 6-7
synthetic: g73 7/8 31; g72 6/22 29-30
use in foods: w73 224; g73 5/8 28; g71 10/22 31
vitamins: w72 63-4
wasted: g72 7/8 27-8
worship of: g72 7/22 23
(SEE ALSO BLOOD TRANSFUSION, PLASMA VOLUME EXPANDERS)

BLOODGUILT
Babylon the Great: w73 306-8
Christendom: sl 216-17; w73 93, 126-7, 149-50, 306-8; w72 312, 324, 391, 574-5; w71 629; kj 103-5; g71 9/8 31
cities of refuge: w73 303-12
discussion: w73 300-12
for failure to preach: w74 123-4
Israel: w73 148, 302-6; kj 101-3, 115
Jerusalem: w73 123-6; kj 139-40, 268-70
nations: sl 217
when given transfusion: w73 543-4

BLOOD, MEDICINE AND THE LAW OF GOD (Booklet)
yb75 225

BLOOD SUBSTITUTES
(SEE PLASMA VOLUME EXPANDERS)

BLOOD TRANSFUSION
alternatives: w74 524; g74 6/22 17-22; g73 6/8 15
Bible view: yb75 222-3; g75 6/8 27-8; w74 351-2; g74 5/22 20; tp 164-5; g72 7/8 27; w71 118-19; g71 9/22 27-8
blood donors: g75 1/22 30; g74 10/22 30-1; g72 3/8 30; g72 8/8 12; g71 3/8 29; g71 4/22 30; g71 11/8 8
child-custody cases: yb75 223-4
clarification of belief: yb75 222-3
cost: g73 10/22 30-1
court cases: w74 166; g74 1/22 29; g74 5/22 19-22; g73 2/22 29; g72 9/22 17-21; g71 3/22 13-14; g71 11/8 6-8
court orders: w75 759; g74 5/22 21-2; w73 543-4
dangers: g75 3/22 29; g75 4/8 30-1; g75 11/22 29; g74 4/22 30; g74 6/22 17, 19, 21, 29-30; g73 2/8 13; g73 6/8 15; g73 10/22 30-1; g72 7/8 28; g72 9/22 19-20; g72 10/22 30; g71 4/8 29-30; g71 2/22 29; g71 8/22 31; g71 11/8 6
carbon monoxide: g75 1/22 30
diseases: w75 445; g75 6/8 27, 29; g75 7/8 30; w74 592; g74 2/22 30; g74 5/22 18, 20, 30; g74 10/22 30-1; g73 5/22 31; g73 6/8 15; g73 7/8 31; g73 11/22 30; g73 12/8 30; g72 3/8 30; g72 5/8 21, 23; g71 2/8 30-1; g71 3/22 13; g71 4/22 30; g71 5/22 30; g71 6/22 8, 30; g71 7/22 30-1
wrong blood type: g71 12/22 30
death rate: w75 445; g74 5/22 18; g73 5/22 31; g72 3/8 30; g72 7/8 27; g71 3/22 13; g71 6/22 8; g71 11/8 6
dialysis machines: g74 9/22 29
discussion: g75 6/8 27-8; g74 5/22 17-22
doctors' disregard of patients' rights: w75 759; g74 3/22 20-1; g72 12/22 29; g71 11/8 7-8
doctors recommend alternatives: g74 4/22 30; g74 6/22 19, 21; g74 9/22 29; g73 6/8 15
doctors testify to dangers: w75 445; g75 11/22 29; g74 3/22 21; g74 5/22 19; g71 3/22 14
doctors urged to respect patients' views: g75 6/8 28; g71 4/8 30
doctors' views on Witnesses' cases: g74 3/22 21; g74 5/22 19-20; g74 6/22 19-21
fluorocarbons as substitute: g74 6/22 22
freezing serum no protection: w75 445
heart surgery without: g75 11/22 29
history: yb75 222-3; g74 3/22 19
hospital form: g74 5/22 20-2; g71 7/22 31
hospital pioneers bloodless surgery: g74 12/22 30
integrity maintained to death: yb75 223-4; g72 9/22 17-18; w71 531-2
issue clarified: w72 501-2
"No Blood Transfusion" card: km 6/75 3
precautions to avoid transfusions: g74 6/8 23-4; w73 543-4
profits: g74 2/22 30
recoveries without blood: yb76 231-2; yb75 224-5; w74 166, 524; g74 1/22 29; g74 3/22 21; g74 6/22 18-21; g73 2/8 19, 29; w72 531; g72 6/8 30; g72 6/22 29; g72 8/22 29; g72 10/8 29; g71 11/8 6-7
serums: w74 351-2
stored blood: g72 4/8 29-30
surgical procedures that lessen need for: g74 6/22 18-19, 21-2; g73 6/8 15
testing for compatibility: g74 5/22 19
transfusion no guarantee: g74 5/22 20
unnecessary: g74 5/22 19; g74 6/22 19-21; g71 2/22 29
Witness stand upheld: g72 10/8 29

Quotations
liquid Russian roulette: w75 445
resistance to, not motivated by desire for self sacrifice: w75 475
(SEE ALSO BLOOD, PLASMA VOLUME EXPANDERS)

BLUSHING
g74 3/22 12-14

BOASTFULNESS
w74 247, 532; te 147-50

BOATS
accidents: g73 12/8 31
canoes: g73 12/8 21
disaster: g72 2/8 12-16
fishing trawlers: g74 2/22 23
Germany: g72 5/22 18-19
number in U.S.: g73 12/8 31
thefts: g71 10/8 31
witnessing from: g74 6/22 15-16

BOAZ
prophetic drama: w72 76-90

BODY ODOR
g74 3/8 24-6

BODY OF A TALK
sg 47-8

BODY OF CHRIST
(SEE CONGREGATION OF GOD)

BOLEKAJA
Nigerian truck: g72 3/8 24-6

BOLIVIA
description: g71 6/8 21-3
Jehovah's witnesses: yb76 7-8, 24-5; yb75 24-5; yb74 24-5; yb73 24-5; g72 5/22 24; yb72 34-5, 124; g72 6/8 24; w71 211; g71 6/8 23; g71 9/22 8
population: yb73 24; yb72 34
religion: w71 740; g71 8/22 15-16; g71 9/22 29

BONAIRE
Jehovah's witnesses: yb76 28-9; yb75 28-9; yb74 28-9; yb73 28-9; yb72 38-9
population: yb73 28; yb72 38

BONES
burial after great tribulation: kj 373-5, 377
valley of dry bones: kj 336-43

BONSAI
dwarf trees: g71 6/8 15-16

BOOKKEEPING
home: g71 6/22 13-15

BOOK OF LIFE
discussion: ka 159

BOOKS
about diet and reducing: g74 4/22 21
about occultism: w74 323; g74 2/22 5-6
best sellers: g73 9/22 8; g71 4/8 19-20
codex: w74 553-4
evaluating what one reads: g73 1/8 5
freezing: g72 9/8 29
libraries: or 81; km 5/72 4; g71 1/22 31
mildew: g74 9/8 13-14
parochial-school textbooks: g75 2/22 30
production costs: g75 5/8 30
religious: w75 48; g72 1/8 31
scrolls: w74 553
suppression of book on Catholic church role in World War II: w75 715

List by Name
Birth Without Violence: g75 10/8 31
Boy and Girl, Man and Woman: g72 1/22 4-5
The Great War and Modern Memory: w75 684
The Money Motive: g75 10/22 31
(SEE ALSO LITERATURE, READING)

BOOMERANG
g72 2/22 24

BOREDOM
discussion: g74 2/22 10-11; w72 156-8
work: g72 5/22 31

BORIC ACID
insecticide: g72 11/22 31

BORN AGAIN
discussion: g74 8/22 27-8
other sheep: g74 8/22 28

BORROWING
Bible view: w75 4-5; w71 526-7, 766
discussion: g73 3/22 7; w71 766-7; g71 12/8 23-4

BOSOM POSITION
ts 101, 107

BOTSWANA
Jehovah's witnesses: yb76 30-1, 180-1, 213-16; yb75 30-1; yb74 17, 30-1; yb73 30-1; yb72 40-1
persecution: yb76 195-6
population: yb73 30; yb72 40

BOUGAINVILLE ISLAND
Jehovah's witnesses: yb76 28-9; yb75 28-9; yb74 28-9; yb73 28-9; yb72 38-9
population: yb73 28; yb72 38

BOUNDARIES
theocratic: w73 431-7

BOXING
g71 5/8 30

BOYS TOWN
w75 172

BRAILLE
Watch Tower publications: km 4/75 3; km 10/75 7; yb74 77

BRAIN
alcohol's effect: w74 452; g72 12/8 31
capacity: w75 263; g74 12/8 18-21
cell renewal: g72 8/8 30-1
damage: g74 12/8 20
designed to serve forever: w75 684
effect of cold-water submergence: g75 8/22 31
epilepsy: g71 8/8 21-2
evidence of Creator: w75 263
function: g73 4/8 22
language: g75 8/22 30; g74 12/8 21
marijuana: g72 2/8 30
memory: g74 12/8 16-21
neurons: w75 684
psychosurgery: g75 4/22 12
superiority of human: ts 17-18; tp 105
(SEE ALSO HUMAN BODY)

BRANCH OFFICES (Watch Tower)
branch overseers: or 89-90
special program of instruction: yb73 65, 77-8
number: yb76 259; w75 27; yb75 30, 257; yb74 32, 255; w73 23; yb73 23, 256; w72 27, 461; yb72 33; w71 722
purpose: w74 282
rotation of elders: yb73 257
training: w73 110

List by Location or Country
Alaska: yb73 6-7
Argentina: yb72 106-8, 114-15, 117, 121-3
Australia: yb73 7-8
Austria: yb73 8-9
Brazil: yb73 37-8, 52-3, 70-2, 77-9, 84-6
Chile: g71 2/8 24-6
Czechoslovakia: yb72 132-7, 139
Dominican Republic: yb72 166-70
Ghana: yb73 187-8
Great Britain: yb73 92-3, 95-6, 101-6, 125, 135-6, 139-41
Guatemala: yb73 197, 199, 202
Italy: yb73 17
Japan: yb73 233-4, 251-4
Luxembourg: yb76 45
Mauritius: yb76 197-8
Newfoundland: yb76 64
Nicaragua: yb72 174-5, 191-2; w71 731
Philippine Republic: yb73 20-1
Rhodesia (Southern Rhodesia): yb76 168
South Africa: yb76 76, 84, 89, 135, 186-7, 208-9, 222, 232-6, 240-2; yb73 21-2
Spain: g72 9/8 24
Sri Lanka (Ceylon): yb76 249-50
Tahiti: km 4/75 1
Taiwan: yb72 227-8, 232-3
Watchtower Farms: km 5/75 4
Zambia (Northern Rhodesia): yb76 175; yb72 243, 246-7

BRAZIL
Amazon River: g73 1/8 31
armaments: g74 11/8 6
carnival: g73 3/8 6
Catholic church: w75 172; g74 1/8 30; g74 11/22 4; g73 12/8 17; w72 391; g72 2/22 30; w71 740; g71 2/8 30
cemetery: g72 3/8 31
coffee: g75 10/22 30
description: yb73 33-4
disasters: g71 5/8 29
entertainment: g75 3/22 29
floods: g74 5/22 29; g74 7/8 24-6
Indians: g72 6/8 21-3
institution for aged: g73 1/22 12
internal problems: g71 6/8 18
Jehovah's witnesses: yb76 24-5; yb75 22, 24-5; w74 207-8; yb74 24-5; g74 5/8 25; g74 7/8 26; km 3/74 1; yb73 24-5, 33-88; g73 9/22 12-13; w72 59-60; yb72 34-5, 44; g72 6/8 23; w71 23; g71 4/8 20-3
printery (Watch Tower): g73 9/22 12-13; km 5/73 1
kidnapping: g75 5/22 7
music: g71 5/22 11-12
population: yb73 24, 33; yb72 34
spiritism: g74 1/8 30; g74 2/22 3-5
voodoo: w75 172

BREAD
leaven: w75 591-2, 597, 601-4
Memorial: w72 166; g72 3/22 27-8
modern Oriental: g73 2/22 25-6
(SEE ALSO MEMORIAL)

BREAST-FEEDING
g75 9/22 30; g75 10/8 30; g75 11/22 30; w74 684; g74 7/8 13-16; g73 2/22 17; g73 7/8 12-15

BREATH
bad breath: w72 414; g71 9/8 24-6
Greek words: ts 48
Hebrew words: ts 48-9
of life: po 40

BREATHING
process: g72 1/22 11; g71 9/22 16-19

BRIBES
different from fines: w75 223
moral breakdown: g72 3/22 3
resisting: w71 533

BRIDE OF CHRIST
(SEE CONGREGATION OF GOD)

BRIDE PRICE
marriage custom: g71 4/8 24-6

BRIDGE(S)
Bosporus: g74 4/22 25-6
Brooklyn: g73 7/22 30

BRITAIN
(SEE GREAT BRITAIN)

BRITISH HONDURAS
(SEE BELIZE)

BRITISH ISLES
(SEE GREAT BRITAIN)

BROOKLYN TABERNACLE
description: yb75 52

g, Awake!; **ka**, God's Kingdom of a Thousand Years; **kj**, "The Nations Shall Know that I Am Jehovah"; **km**, Kingdom Ministry; **or**, Organization; **pm**, Paradise Restored—By Theocracy!; **po**, God's "Eternal Purpose"; **sg**, Theocratic School Guidebook; **sl**, Man's Salvation out of World Distress!; **te**, Listening to the Great Teacher; **tp**, True Peace and Security; **ts**, Is This Life All There Is?; **w**, Watchtower; **yb**, Yearbook. **Complete list on page 6.**

purchase: yb75 51
sold: yb75 110

BROTHERHOOD
Christian brotherhood: w74 635

BROTHER-IN-LAW MARRIAGE
discussion: w73 255-6
examples: w73 383-4
Ruth: w72 82-3, 86-8

BROTHERS
use of term:
experience: g71 1/22 26

BROWN, CLAUDE
service in Ghana: yb73 145-7, 149-50

BROWN, W. R.
service in Africa: yb73 145, 147, 149-50, 154-7, 166-7, 185

BRUNEI
Jehovah's witnesses: yb76 28-9; yb75 28-9; yb74 28-9; yb73 28-9
population: yb73 28

BUDDHISM
beliefs: ts 53, 56; g74 1/8 16-18; yb73 246; g72 2/22 17-20; g71 2/22 24
hell: ts 89-90; g73 7/22 27
nirvana: g74 1/8 17-18; g72 2/22 18
transmigration of souls: g74 1/8 16
trinity: w74 75-6; g73 2/22 27-8
Borobudur: g72 2/22 17-20
celibacy: g75 5/8 28
China: g73 8/8 15
earthquake damage to statue: g75 9/22 31
experiences:
Buddhists accept Bible truth: w75 43; yb74 53-4; g71 2/22 23-6
fear of demons: g71 2/22 25-6
funerals: ts 61-3
India: g74 11/22 8-9
Japan: yb73 210-11
meditation: g74 1/8 16-17, 19
membership: w71 14
monks: g71 2/22 23-4
origin: g74 1/8 16, 18-19
rosary: w74 259
Soviet Union: g73 4/8 15
Tibetan: g74 11/22 9

BUDGET
"bargains": g73 7/22 13-15
fighting inflation: w75 4-6
money: g74 8/22 7; g71 3/8 8-10; g71 6/22 13-15

BULL(S)
bullfighting: g75 9/8 9-12
Christian view: g75 9/8 12
life story of a matador: g75 9/8 13-16
religion: g75 9/8 12, 16
man-killing: w75 639
symbolic: w72 295; kj 39-40

BULLETIN, THE
yb75 86, 133; w72 759

BULRUSHES
g75 4/22 29-30

BULWARK
symbolic: w74 753-4

BURDEN
lightening others': w71 259-60

BURIAL
Gog's crowd: kj 369-70, 373-5, 377
permit denied: w75 71
sea: g72 3/8 29
(SEE ALSO CEMETERIES, DEAD, FUNERALS)

BURMA
earthquake: g75 9/22 31
Jehovah's witnesses: yb76 8, 24-5; yb75 24-5; km 4/75 1; yb74 24-5; w73 762-3; yb73 24-5; yb72 34-5; w71 368-9
population: yb73 24; yb72 34

BURNS
eye: g74 9/22 8
treatment: g75 8/8 19; g74 9/22 8; g73 7/22 12; g73 11/22 22; g72 11/8 18

BURUNDI
internal warfare: g72 10/8 14
Jehovah's witnesses: yb76 26-7; yb75 26-7; yb74 26-7; yb73 26-7; yb72 36-7
population: yb73 26; yb72 36

BUS
steam: g72 3/8 30

BUSH MEDICINE
w73 697-701

BUSINESS
ancient Israel: w71 765-6
avoiding being cheated: g74 12/8 7
"bargain" sales: g73 7/22 13-15
between Christians: w73 287-8, 703-4
Bible principles: w75 291-3; w71 764-7
big corporations: g75 3/8 29; g71 2/8 3-6
bankruptcy: g75 12/8 30
business meetings with religious services: g75 9/8 29
churches: w74 166; g71 2/8 17
corporation name changes: g75 6/8 30
corruption: g75 7/8 29; g71 2/8 4-5
crime: g73 4/22 4, 7-8, 10
decline of confidence in: g75 12/8 30
dishonesty: g75 2/8 30; g74 9/8 4; g73 7/22 13-14; g73 9/8 31; w72 598; g71 2/8 4-5; g71 7/8 29; g71 8/22 30
employees: w75 291; g72 8/22 29
experiences:
honesty: w75 293
office buildings: w74 364-6
stores with no tobacco: w75 292
failures: g71 4/8 30-1
importance of listening: g74 11/22 22-3
industrial spying: g73 7/8 9-11
inflation: g75 1/8 29
letters: sg 85-7
luxuries: w75 172
mini-business: g73 8/8 8-11
planned obsolescence: g71 2/8 5
prize tickets: w73 127
profit motive: g74 8/8 8-9
self-employment: g73 8/8 8-11
selling by smell: g75 7/8 6-8
smoking in places of: w74 223-4
value of written contract: w73 287-8; g73 7/22 14
witnessing to businessmen: km 3/71 3-4

BUTTERFLIES
g72 11/22 21

BUYING
avoiding being cheated: g74 12/8 7
bargaining: g75 8/8 16-17; g74 12/8 6
"bargains": g73 7/22 13-15
clothing: g72 1/8 25-6
credit cards: g71 2/8 29
discussion: g73 7/22 13-15
effect of inflation: g74 9/8 31
food: g74 5/8 14-15; g73 8/22 3-5, 30; g73 9/8 21-3
installment buying: g75 10/22 29
luxuries: w75 172
mobile homes: g71 11/22 13-16
saving money: g75 4/8 22-3; g75 8/8 16-18; g74 3/8 12; g71 3/8 8-10

CAESAR
Caesars of Rome: g74 4/8 22
Christians in Caesar's household: w72 592
Christian's obligation: w74 62-3; g74 2/22 27-8; w73 142; tp 135-9; w72 640; te 135-8
Julius: g72 4/8 4
Tiberius: g75 12/22 27
(SEE ALSO GOVERNMENTS)

CAESAREA
discussion: g72 1/8 27-8

CAIN
attitude: w73 300-1; w72 650
killed Abel: w73 300-1, 435-6, 441; w72 438; w71 74-5; te 80
name: w71 58
punishment: w75 665; w73 300-1
wife: w75 75; g74 6/22 27-8; g71 11/22 26

CALF
worship: w72 295; kj 25, 28, 98-9, 240

CALLING
Christian: w74 657-9

CAMBODIA
Jehovah's witnesses: yb74 30-1; yb73 30-1; yb72 40-1
population: yb73 30; yb72 40

CAMEL
heat endurance: g71 1/8 22

CAMERA
ultrasonic motion-picture: g75 8/8 30

CAMEROON
Jehovah's witnesses: yb76 24-5; yb75 5-6, 24-5; yb74 11, 28-9; w73 529-30; yb73 19-20, 28-9; yb72 38-9; w71 157
population: yb73 28; yb72 38

CANAAN (Ham's Son)
curse: po 83

CANAAN (Land)
Israelite occupation: po 104

CANAANITES
Amorites: g74 4/8 16
Baal worship: w74 457-8; w72 568
'error completed': po 104

extermination: w73 582
occultism: w74 715
religion: w74 144, 457-8

CANADA
alcoholism: g74 4/8 29
Bay of Fundy: g73 11/8 8-11
Bill of Rights: g72 7/8 10
CN Tower: g75 6/8 21-4
crime: g75 3/22 29; g75 7/8 30
disaster: g71 7/22 21-2
drugs: g73 12/8 5
economy: w72 616
farming: g73 9/22 21-4
government records: g73 6/8 16-26
history: g71 5/22 13-15
homosexual "marriage" illegal: g75 2/22 30
illegitimacy: g74 4/22 4-5
Jehovah's witnesses: yb76 24-5; w75 41-4; yb75 20-1, 24-5; g75 2/8 25-6; yb74 24-5; g73 1/8 11-12; g73 2/22 24; yb73 9-10, 24-5; w72 146-51, 318, 510; yb72 34-5; g72 6/8 24
 assembly halls: g74 6/8 16, 19
 conventions: g75 3/8 16; g75 10/22 16
 court cases: g75 3/8 16, 19, 21-3
 persecution: w74 284-5; g73 6/8 16-26; w72 144, 148-51; g72 7/8 9-10; w71 22
 Quebec: g75 3/8 16, 18-23, 25-8; g73 6/8 21, 23-5
 service experiences: w74 141-3
King, William Mackenzie: g75 7/8 31
mental illness: g71 7/8 30-1
moral breakdown: g73 10/8 10; g72 2/8 31; g72 3/8 30-1; g72 4/22 31; g72 7/22 29; g71 4/22 31; g71 11/8 29; g71 12/8 30
oil: g74 1/8 7
parochial schools: g75 2/22 30
police strike: w72 261; g71 2/22 18
population: yb73 24; yb72 34
Quebec: g75 3/8 16-28
religion: w75 323; g75 1/22 7; g75 3/8 17-19, 23-7; g75 5/22 30; g75 11/8 29; w74 555; g74 2/8 29; g73 6/8 16-26; g73 7/22 30; g72 2/22 30; w71 484; g71 1/22 30; g71 2/8 30
smoking: g72 7/8 30
terrorism: g71 6/8 17-19
time spent watching television: g75 11/8 30
unemployment: g71 3/22 30
wheat: g74 7/22 30

CANALS
Suez: g75 6/22 29; g74 10/22 16-18

CANARY ISLANDS
Jehovah's witnesses: yb76 30-1; yb75 30-1; yb74 30-1; yb73 30-1; yb72 40-1
population: yb73 30; yb72 40

CANCER
alcoholism: w74 452
breast: g75 9/22 30; g74 12/22 29
causes: g75 2/8 19; g75 10/22 30; w74 742; g74 1/22 15-16; g74 9/8 19-21; g73 7/8 15; g73 11/22 29; g73 12/8 7; g72 2/8 29; g71 3/8 30; g71 8/22 31; g71 9/8 30; g71 10/8 11
cervix: w75 191
death statistics: w75 634; g74 1/8 30; g74 5/22 30; g74 9/8 17-18; g74 12/22 29
diet: g75 2/8 19; g74 9/8 22-3; g71 7/8 30
discussion: g74 9/8 17-23
fish: g72 8/22 31
increase: g74 1/8 30; g74 1/22 30; g74 9/8 17-18; tp 20
Laetrile: g74 9/8 22
number of cases in U.S.: g75 5/22 30
pollution: g74 9/8 20
prevention: g74 9/8 22-3
research: g74 9/8 17
smoking: w75 12; g75 10/22 30-1; g74 5/22 30; g74 9/8 18, 20, 23; w72 595
Soviet Union: g74 5/22 30
symptoms: g74 9/8 19
treatment: g74 9/8 21-2
 cost: g75 5/22 30
types: g74 9/8 18-19

CANNIBALISM
w74 394, 684; g73 2/8 29-30; g73 12/8 21

CANTOR
experience: g71 11/8 12-15

CAPERNAUM
home of Jesus: w75 669
Jesus' miracles: w75 669-70
ruins: w75 671; w74 78

CAPE VERDE ISLANDS
Jehovah's witnesses: yb76 28-9; yb75 28-9; yb74 28-9; yb73 28-9; yb72 38-9
population: yb73 28; yb72 38

CAPITAL ORGANIZATION
(SEE JEHOVAH'S ORGANIZATION)

CAPITAL PUNISHMENT
Bible view: g75 11/22 10, 26-8; g74 7/22 27-8; w73 302; w72 480
Canada: g72 4/22 31
Great Britain: g72 9/8 30
Israel: g72 1/8 15-16
modern views: g71 3/8 31
origin of: g75 11/22 27
Saudi Arabia: g75 8/8 30
United States: g72 1/8 6; g72 8/22 29

CAPTIVITY
Israel, by Assyria: kj 30, 168, 203, 340
Israel in Egypt: w72 38-40; w71 381-2
 exodus: w72 40; pm 59-60
Jews in Babylon: w72 723-4; kj 31-2, 129-30, 137-8, 168, 203-6, 336, 339-40
Jews return from Babylon: w72 172-3, 300-1, 305-7, 500, 724; pm 28-32; g72 3/8 28; kj 206, 329
spiritual Israel: kj 207-8, 315
spiritual Israel released: w72 173; kj 208, 317, 325-32

CARBON DIOXIDE
g72 10/22 7

CARBON 14
radioactive clock: g72 4/8 5-20

CARBON MONOXIDE
blood donors: g75 1/22 30
effect on blood: g74 7/22 13
poisoning: g73 2/22 23
soil microorganisms: g72 2/22 12

CARDINALS
Roman Catholic Church: g71 11/22 10-12
statements on conscience: g75 2/22 18

CARDS
(SEE PLAYING CARDS)

CAREER
experiences:
 giving up worldly: w74 605, 653-5

CARIBBEAN
travel: g72 5/8 13-16

CARMEL (Mount)
w74 79

CARNEGIE, ANDREW
w72 491

CARNIVAL
discussion: g73 3/8 5-8
effects: g74 5/22 31

CARPETS
g74 2/22 25-6

CARRIACOU
Jehovah's witnesses: yb76 24-5; yb75 24-5; yb74 24-5; yb73 24-5; yb72 34-5
population: yb73 24; yb72 34

CARROT
g73 3/22 23

CARS
(SEE AUTOMOBILES)

CASTE SYSTEM
yb76 251-2

CATECHISM
Catholic church: w71 297-8
Common Catechism: g75 5/22 29

CATHOLIC
(SEE GREEK ORTHODOX CHURCH, ROMAN CATHOLIC CHURCH)

CATHOLIC ACTION
persecution of Witnesses: yb75 180-2, 191

CATTLE
disease: g72 11/8 30
dung: g75 11/22 30
farming: g73 6/22 23-4
grain needed: w74 196-7
(SEE ALSO MEAT)

CAVES
Gibraltar: g71 10/22 26
Jeita: g71 11/8 10-11

CAYMAN ISLANDS
Jehovah's witnesses: yb76 26-7; yb75 26-7; yb74 26-7; yb73 26-7; yb72 36-7; w71 522
population: yb73 26; yb72 36

CEDAR POINT, OHIO, CONVENTIONS
1919
attendance: yb75 122

Golden Age released: yb75 122-3; w73 398; ka 192-3, 233
report: w72 85; pm 50-1, 202, 298
significance: yb75 124; w74 507-8; kj 330
talks given: yb75 122-3; w72 198; kj 64, 301

1922

discussion: yb75 130-3, 135-6
report: w72 85
resolution: yb75 135-6
Service Day: yb75 132-3
talks given: yb75 131; w73 398; ka 234-5; pm 111-12
(SEE ALSO CONVENTIONS)

CEDARS OF LEBANON
w75 541

CELIBACY
admitted to be unscriptural: g75 1/22 9; g71 11/22 12
Catholic teaching: w73 549; g72 1/22 31; g71 12/22 30
discussion: g75 5/8 27-8; g72 5/8 9-12
origin of priestly: g75 5/8 28
priests dissatisfied with: w74 102; g71 8/8 24-5
vows: w73 608
(SEE ALSO ROMAN CATHOLIC CHURCH)

CELLS
aging process: g71 2/22 13-15
complexity: g73 10/22 9-11
description: g71 2/22 12-13; g71 9/8 5-7
growth: g72 10/22 7-8
human: g74 10/8 7; g72 10/22 7-8; g71 3/8 16-18, 26; g71 8/8 5-6
scientists' claim: g71 1/8 29
(SEE ALSO HUMAN BODY)

CEMETERIES
Brazil: g72 3/8 31
pet: g71 8/22 29-30

CENSORSHIP
Watch Tower publications: yb73 123-4, 127-8

CENSUS
Nigeria: g74 6/8 11-12

CENTRAL AFRICAN REPUBLIC
Jehovah's witnesses: yb76 9, 24-5; yb75 24-5; yb74 24-5, 34-41; yb73 24-5; yb72 34-5
population: yb73 24; yb72 34
religion: yb74 34-5

CENTRAL AMERICA
travel in: g72 9/8 25-6

CEPHAS
(SEE PETER)

CESIUM 137
g75 5/22 31

CEYLON
(SEE SRI LANKA)

CHAD
famine: g74 3/8 6
Jehovah's witnesses: yb76 24-5; yb75 24-5

CHAIR
rocking chair: g74 11/8 22-3

CHAIRMAN(SHIP)
congregations' older men: w75 729-30; w72 20; yb72 28-9; w71 691, 693, 695-701
governing body: w71 759, 761-2
public meeting: km 12/73 4
(SEE ALSO GOVERNING BODY, OLDER MEN, OVERSEERS)

CHALLENGES
environment: g71 10/22 3-4
moral principles: w72 515-16, 548

CHANCE
chance and creation: g72 10/22 5-8
discussion: g75 3/22 20-3
gambling: w72 593-4

CHAPLAINS
g75 2/22 19, 21
(SEE ALSO CLERGY)

CHARCOAL
g71 5/8 30

CHARIOT
symbolic: w72 103-4, 152-5, 659; pm 222-8, 233; kj 35-7, 41-51, 144, 164, 182, 184-94, 209-10, 212

CHARITY
assistance for fellow Witnesses: w74 476, 569-70; yb74 99; g74 5/22 8; g74 7/8 26; g74 12/22 26; g73 6/22 15; yb72 99-100, 137, 179, 225-6, 252-3; w71 424-5; g71 3/22 25
Bible view: g74 10/22 28; w73 305; g73 4/8 27-8; g73 11/22 24, 26
discussion: g73 11/22 24-6
fraudulent organizations: w75 519
motive: g73 11/22 24
preaching work: w74 282
statistics: g74 8/22 30
use of funds: w75 519; g74 9/22 31; g73 11/22 24-6; g71 1/22 30
(SEE ALSO CONTRIBUTIONS, LOVE)

CHARLEMAGNE
discussion: g73 5/8 12-15

CHARM(S)
occult: w74 715-16

CHARTS
abortions in Japan and the United States: g75 8/22 5
alcoholism: g71 6/22 5
animals' ability to jump: g74 10/22 23
Baptist problems: w71 549
best sellers: g71 4/8 19
Bible books (writers, time covered, time and place written): bi8 1367
Chart of the Ages: po 10
Chinese characters and translation: g75 5/22 10
Christendom's failure: g71 4/8 5
church attendance in the United States: w75 324
comparison of employee theft with shoplifting: w75 291
costs of industrial materials: g74 11/22 18
creative days: w73 83
crisis dates of problems: g71 10/8 17
decline in number of nuns: g75 1/22 8
endocrine functions: g72 6/22 19
genetic dangers in incestuous marriages: w75 74
gold and dollars: g71 8/22 5
inflation in United States: g75 1/22 20
Jehovah's witnesses:
conventions in Brazil: yb73 77
conventions in Great Britain: yb73 140
full-time preachers: yb73 252; km 2/71 3
increase: w73 41; yb73 71, 75; w71 14, 16, 18, 20-3, 25
literature placements: yb73 251
missionary homes: yb73 255
1972 conventions: g72 10/22 23
printing in Brazil: yb73 72
service reports: yb76 24-31; w75 24-7; yb75 24-31; w74 27-30; yb74 24-31; w73 24-7; yb73 24-31; w72 22-5; yb72 34-41; w71 26-9
teachings and practices: w71 677
temporary pioneers: km 2/71 4
theocratic organization of Jehovah's witnesses: w71 749
languages: g72 12/22 13
life cycle in lake: g71 4/22 9
marriages prohibited under Mosaic law: w75 73
monetary inflation: g73 11/22 10
monsoon rains move farther south: g75 3/8 5
Mosaic law (crime and compensation): g72 1/8 16
nitrogen cycle: g71 4/22 7
oxygen cycle: g71 4/22 7
planting vegetables: g74 5/22 12
price increases: w75 5
relatives of Jesus: w75 221
removal of common stains: g75 8/8 11
seven times: w74 163
sign of last days: w71 69
6,000 years of human history: g71 10/8 27
2,300 days, beginning and end: w71 726
unemployment in the United States: g75 7/8 3
weapon stockpiles: g74 11/8 4
work changes that some have made: g75 7/8 5
world population: g75 2/8 3; g71 4/22 16
zone of life: g71 4/22 5

CHART TALKS
yb75 44, 50

CHEATING
avoiding being cheated: g74 3/8 10-12; g74 12/8 7
gambling: w74 580, 585
schools: w74 245-6; g73 4/8 31; g71 6/22 30
sports: g73 1/8 29
supermarkets: g74 11/8 30-1
(SEE ALSO DISHONESTY, MORAL BREAKDOWN, STEALING)

CHEESE
g72 11/8 19-20

CHEJU ISLAND
g74 11/22 24-6

CHEMICALS
DDT: ts 147-8
fertilizers: g71 4/22 12
food additives: g72 2/8 29; g72 4/8 31; g71 3/8 29
hexachlorophene: g72 1/22 30-1
pollution: g75 10/22 30

toiletries: g72 4/8 31

CHEMISTRY
catalyst: w74 302
discussion: g71 7/22 11-12
organic molecules produced in laboratory: g75 12/8 21

CHERUBS
discussion: po 29-30, 32; kj 38-41
Jehovah 'sitting upon': po 29
living creatures: w72 102; kj 38, 45-6
subjection to God: w72 153; kj 49-51
(SEE ALSO ANGELS, SERAPHS)

CHESS
g73 1/22 6; g73 3/22 12-14

CHICKENS
g71 1/8 16; g71 8/8 30

CHIEFTAIN
Ezekiel's vision: w73 426-8; kj 401-5

CHILDBEARING
artificial insemination: g73 4/22 31
attitudes toward: g74 6/22 7, 11; g74 8/8 28; g74 11/8 9-10
book *Birth Without Violence:* g75 10/8 30-1
Christian view: w75 158-60; g74 6/22 11; g74 11/8 11
discussion: g73 2/22 16-19
incestuous marriages: w75 72-4
long pregnancy: g71 7/22 30
(SEE ALSO BABIES, PREGNANCY)

CHILDBIRTH
abortion rejected: w75 192; g74 8/22 23; g71 1/8 25-6
alcoholism: g75 9/8 30
at home: g74 6/8 21-4; g72 11/22 29-30
baby's early contact with mother: g75 11/8 31
cesarean section: w75 159
childbed fever: w75 134-5
description: g74 2/8 14-15
drug addiction: g71 1/8 30-1
drugs taken during: g74 7/8 14
handicapped: g73 6/22 28-9
history: g72 11/22 13-16
induced labor: g74 1/22 16
measles (rubella): w75 191-2
miracle of: g73 7/8 7-8
music during: g75 7/8 30
practices: g72 5/22 29
premature: g72 9/8 30
Rh factor: w74 351
safety: g74 6/8 21-3
statistics: g74 7/8 13; g74 11/8 9
stillborn: g72 5/8 30
vertical: g71 6/8 31
(SEE ALSO ABORTION, BIRTH, BIRTH CONTROL)

CHILDREN
ability to learn: g74 10/22 30; w72 112; w71 104-5
abnormalities due to incestuous marriages: w75 72-4
accident statistics: g72 2/22 29
accidental poisonings: g71 5/8 29; g71 12/8 31
adoption: g74 8/8 28; w72 363-4
Africa: g71 10/22 8
alcoholism: g75 2/8 16-18; w74 451, 453; g73 9/8 30
appreciation for parents: g74 12/22 6; w71 107
Armageddon: w72 51-2, 633-4; w71 63-4
associations: w74 93, 271-2
baby-sitters: g71 3/22 30
baptism: g74 3/22 27-8; w72 511-12
belief in God: w73 553-6, 559-62
Bible studies: w75 436-7; g74 2/8 9-10; w73 559-64; km 1/72 7-8; w71 104-7; sg 37-8; km 5/71 3-4
Caesar's laws: te 135-8
changing: g73 3/8 30
child survives forty-minute submergence: g75 8/22 31
clothing: g72 1/8 26
confidence in parents: w72 31, 259-60; g72 4/8 4; w71 587-92
confirmation: w71 170-1
congregation's interest in: km 4/75 3
consideration for: g73 11/22 14
cost to raise: g74 10/8 30
creativity study: w75 217-18
daydreaming: g75 4/22 7
death: w74 132; g74 12/8 9; g72 6/8 5-6; g71 12/8 27-8
delinquency: w75 37, 439; g75 11/22 5; g74 2/8 4-6; w73 552-3, 558-9; g73 11/22 30; g72 5/22 30; g72 7/8 31; g71 1/22 23; g71 9/8 29; g71 12/8 30
father not necessarily at fault: km 7/75 3
desire for independence: w75 61
discussion: w75 439-44
disease: g74 6/8 30-1; g71 2/8 30; g71 4/8 29
disfellowshiping: w74 470-1; or 173, 175-6
divided households: w75 437-8; tp 177; w71 212-13
drugs: g74 2/8 5-6; g74 4/22 15; g74 5/8 3-8; w73 182, 185; g72 8/22 30; g72 9/8 29; w71 249-50; g71 9/8 29; g71 12/8 30
education: w75 542-4; g75 5/8 21; g74 4/8 29
evolution theory: w71 40-2
experiences:
aid to parents: g74 12/22 22
conducting Bible studies: yb75 13-14; g71 4/8 23
effective Witnesses: g72 6/8 24; km 10/72 7; w71 368-9
essay contest won: w72 444
flag salute: yb74 117
girl refuses meat of unbled animal: yb76 8
help family members to Bible truth: w71 369
impression made by Bible truth: w75 763; g74 7/22 21, 23; w73 29; g72 6/8 24; w71 106-7; g71 9/22 8
impression made by honest adult: g74 1/8 26
insisted on quitting church: yb74 248
integrity: g75 2/22 4; yb74 117-19, 121-5; g72 6/8 24
letter of appreciation to parents: w72 403; w71 368
refused to buy cigarettes: yb75 16
respect for blood: g71 9/22 8
search for truth: w73 318
witnessing in school: g74 5/22 26; w72 402; g72 8/8 19; km 8/72 3
Witness youth persuades gunmen to surrender: g75 1/22 30
fallacy of parental permissiveness: w75 71
father's influence: g72 8/22 29-30
gifts: w74 741; g73 12/22 7; w71 345-6; te 143-6
goal for future: g75 9/22 22-5
Greek words: w72 112, 114
growth: w73 520; w72 112-13, 425
handicapped: g73 6/22 28-9
happiness: g74 7/22 21-3
health: g74 4/8 29
homeless: g72 4/22 30
honor due parents: g75 10/22 27-8
hyperactivity: g75 4/22 6; g72 8/8 31
illegitimate: w74 224
love for brothers and sisters: w71 74-5; te 79-82
mathematics: g75 7/22 30; g71 2/8 9-12
meeting attendance: w75 61-2, 319-20; w73 671-2; or 92-3; w71 555; sg 27; te 157-8
memories: g74 7/22 21-3
mental retardation: g75 6/22 20-3
mistreatment: w75 327; g73 1/22 30; g73 9/8 29-30
murder: g72 12/8 30
names: g72 7/8 24-6
need for association: km 4/75 3
need of love: w72 457; g72 1/8 30; g72 5/22 10-11; g72 7/22 29; g72 9/8 30; g72 10/22 30
obedience: g75 10/22 27; w74 119; w73 670-2; w72 362-4; w71 213, 259-60; te 31-4, 135-8; g71 3/22 8
obligations to parents: w74 119; w73 671-2; tp 140-2; w71 259-60; g71 3/22 8
opposed parents: w73 671-2
orphans: g71 6/8 30-1
parental authority: w73 318; w72 163-4
parental companionship: w75 156-7; w74 741; g74 2/8 10; g74 7/22 22-3; w73 559-60, 562; sg 80
parental responsibility: w75 314, 433-7, 451-3; g74 2/8 7-11; g74 8/22 4-6; w72 51-2, 109-11, 360, 364, 425, 543; g72 8/8 4; g72 11/8 30; w71 170-1, 581-92; kj 166-7; g71 3/22 7-8
parental training: w75 14-15, 155-7; g75 5/8 21; w74 81-94, 267-72; g74 7/22 23; w73 552-64; g73 2/22 17-19; g73 8/8 31; w72 109-17, 259-60, 360-3; g72 5/8 5-8; g72 11/22 27-8; w71 170-1, 369-72, 555-6; g71 9/8 8-11
failure of worldly guidance: g75 10/8 6-7
unselfishness: g75 6/8 14-16
parental unity: g72 9/22 27-8

parents learn by listening to: g75 7/8 30
personality development: w72 113
persuading: g75 1/8 9, 12
praise Jehovah: te 107-10
prayer: g74 12/22 22; g72 11/22 27-8; te 47-50
privileges in congregation: km 4/75 3
public schools:
problems: g74 2/8 3-7; w71 584-5
reading: g75 12/22 30; g74 2/8 4, 9-10; sg 23; g71 10/22 30
value of reading aloud to: w75 519
Witness children commended: g75 12/8 22
respect for others: w74 90-1, 265-6; g74 2/8 4-5
results of parental neglect: g75 3/8 29; g75 4/22 9
resurrection: ts 180-1; w72 448
rock concerts: g75 6/8 30
runaways: g71 3/22 5-9
screaming at: w71 163-4
serving others: te 27-30
sex education: g75 1/8 30; g74 2/8 6, 9; g72 1/22 3-9; g72 7/22 29-30; w71 589; g71 1/22 29-30
shaking: g73 1/22 30
shyness: w75 197-9
sinfulness: w72 359-60
smoking: g73 11/22 30; g71 1/22 31
spiritual advancement: w74 119
spray cans: g71 1/22 29
suicide: g75 8/22 30
teaching about God: w74 84-5; g74 2/8 9-10; w73 553-5; w72 114-17; g72 11/22 27-8; km 1/72 7-8; w71 599; te 5-6
television's effect: g75 5/22 31; g75 12/22 30; w74 262, 272; g74 9/8 8-11; g73 1/22 31; g73 3/8 30; g73 3/22 3; g71 1/8 11; g71 3/22 30; g71 12/8 30
toys: g74 7/22 22; g71 1/8 9-12; g71 9/8 30; g71 12/8 30
vandalism: g74 8/22 3-6
venereal disease: g72 2/8 17, 19; g71 11/8 31
view of churches: g75 3/22 30; g75 8/22 29-30
weapon accidents: g72 2/22 29
Witnesses: km 10/72 7-8
witnessing in school: w75 440-3
work: g72 5/8 5-8; w71 231-2; te 95-8
(SEE ALSO FAMILY, PARENTS, YOUTH)

CHILDREN (Book)
yb75 193

CHILD TRAINING
ancient Israel: w75 759
anticipating problems: w74 89-90
appreciation for: w71 107
avoiding unfavorable comparisons: w74 269-70
belief in God: w73 553-6, 559-62
communication: w74 268-9; g74 11/22 21-2
congregation meetings: w75 61-2, 319-20; sg 27
counsel: w74 89-90, 92-3
daily routine: w74 84-5
discipline: w75 14-15, 156-7; w74 82, 92-3, 267-8; g74 2/8 8; g74 4/22 14-15; w73 556-8; w72 740; w71 555-6, 588-9, 592
divided household: w75 437-8
drugs: g74 5/8 3-8; w73 182-7; w71 249-50
early: w75 435; w74 267-8; g74 2/8 7-8; g73 2/22 17-19; w72 111-17; g72 5/8 5-6; w71 104-5
effect of proper training: g75 1/22 30; g74 7/22 23; w72 403; w71 106-7, 191, 368; g71 2/22 11; g71 9/22 8; g71 10/22 16
experiences involving Witness children: w75 763; g75 2/22 4; w74 272; g74 2/8 10; w71 368
failure of worldly guidance: g75 10/8 6-7
fallacies to avoid: w75 71; w74 263, 267-72; w73 553-4, 556-8, 560; g73 10/22 24; w72 111, 113-14, 270; g71 5/22 30
father's role: w75 14-15, 156-7, 433-4; w73 561-2
goal: w74 82
good habits: w72 452; g71 7/22 26
holidays: g73 12/22 7
home Bible instruction: w75 436-7; w74 84-7; g74 2/8 8-10; km 7/74 4; w73 532-3, 553-6, 559-64; w72 114-17; km 1/72 7-8; w71 104-7, 170-1; sg 37-8; te 5-6; km 5/71 3-4
household chores: g74 2/8 9; g72 5/8 5-8; w71 312; g71 9/8 8-11
imparting moral values: g74 4/22 13-14; w73 561-2
Israel: w71 361-2
love: g74 4/22 15-16; w72 740
"mental-regulating": w75 157; g74 2/8 8-9
mother's role: w75 434, 436; w74 85; w71 104
parental companionship: w75 156-7; w74 270-1; g74 2/8 10; g74 4/22 15-16; g74 7/22 22-3; w73 559-60, 562
parental example: w74 263; g74 4/22 15; w73 451; g73 12/8 7; w71 370-2, 583, 589
parental role in education: g75 5/8 21
parental unity: w72 270-1
parents' responsibility: w75 155-7, 314, 433-7, 451-3; w74 81-94; g74 2/8 7-11; g74 8/22 4-6; w73 553-64; w72 51-2, 109-11, 163-4, 360-3; w71 361-2, 367-72
persuasion: g75 1/8 9, 12
reading: g75 12/22 30; g74 7/22 21; sg 23
respect for parents and others: w74 90-1; g74 2/8 4-5; w72 163-4
results of parental neglect: g75 3/8 29; g75 4/22 9; w74 267, 270-1; g74 8/22 4-5; w72 259-60
sex education: g75 1/8 30; g74 2/8 6, 9; g74 4/22 13-14; g72 1/22 8-9; g72 7/22 29-30; w71 589
toys: g71 1/8 9-12
unselfishness: g75 6/8 14-16
(SEE ALSO FAMILY, PARENTS)

CHILE
cannibalism: w74 394
description: g72 12/22 24-6
food: g72 3/22 25-6; g72 10/8 30
glacier: g73 8/22 26-7
government: g71 1/8 29
hiking: g73 8/22 24-7
Jehovah's witnesses: yb76 24-5; yb75 22-5; yb74 24-5; w73 628; yb73 24-5; w72 155; yb72 34-5, 123; g72 6/22 11-13; g71 2/8 24-6; g71 6/22 8
population: yb73 24; yb72 34
religion: w75 684; w74 101, 217; g72 6/22 9-13; w71 408; g71 1/8 29
sheep: g74 11/8 14-16
telescope: g72 12/22 24-6

CHILION
name: w72 78

CHINA (People's Republic [Communist])
acupuncture: g72 9/8 12-16; g71 7/8 31
ancient zodiac signs found: g75 11/8 30
archaeology: g75 9/22 29
birth control: g73 11/22 31
Christendom's missionaries: g75 9/22 21; w74 656
Communism: yb74 47, 52-6; g74 7/8 5-9
crime: g74 2/22 29-30; g74 7/8 7-8
description: g71 12/8 29
discussion: g74 7/8 5-9
doctors: g74 5/22 30; g73 1/22 31
earthquake: g75 4/22 29
education: g74 7/8 6-7
fear: g74 8/8 30
health: g74 7/8 7
history: g74 7/8 5-6
hospital costs: g75 12/8 31
Jehovah's witnesses: yb75 208; yb74 41-4, 46-9, 51-6, 59-60, 63; g74 7/8 9; w72 521, 524-5, 532
oil production: g75 9/8 31
Peking: g73 4/8 30
population: g75 2/22 30; g74 7/8 5
relations with Japan: g72 11/22 29
religion: g75 1/8 30-1; w74 198
science: g71 12/8 29
secret societies: g75 5/8 12
Shanghai: g73 4/8 30
tunnels: g74 8/8 30
United Nations: g72 3/8 7; g72 10/8 4, 12; g71 1/8 29; g71 6/22 29; g71 12/8 29
United States: g74 1/22 30; g73 11/8 30; g71 9/8 29
wars: g75 5/8 9-12; w72 444
weapons detection in ancient: g75 6/8 24

CHINA (Republic of [Taiwan])
abacus: g71 11/22 17-20
description: yb72 213-14
discussion: g73 7/22 20-3
Jehovah's witnesses: yb76 30-1; yb75 30-1; yb74 30-1; yb73 30-1; g73 7/22 22-3; yb72 40-1, 214-34
National Palace Museum: g73 8/8 12-15
population: yb73 30; yb72 40
religion: g72 3/22 18; w71 422

CHINESE (Language)
chart of Chinese characters and translation: g75 5/22 10
discussion: g75 5/22 9-13
first Bible: w74 744-5
number speaking: g75 11/8 29
spoken language: g75 5/22 11-12
writing: g75 5/22 10

CHOICE
big or little things: w71 572-4
freedom of choice: w71 37

CHOLERA
g75 3/22 29-30; g73 10/22 30; g71 11/22 30

CHRIST
kings of Judah: kj 220
(SEE ALSO JESUS CHRIST, MESSIAH)

CHRISTENDOM
abortion: w73 419-20
apostasy: w75 166-8, 201-4, 253-4, 729-30; sl 208-14; w74 592; po 170; ka 374-85, 388-94; w71 628-9; kj 78-9
atrocities against Jews: g75 2/22 17-19; g71 12/8 3-4
attitude toward Bible: g74 8/8 30; g74 8/22 9-11; tp 33-4; g73 4/8 30; g73 5/22 23-4; w72 169; g72 1/22 5, 29; g72 4/8 23-4; w71 548, 561, 628, 675-6; kj 157; g71 4/8 30; g71 8/8 26
attitude toward Jehovah's witnesses: yb74 36-8, 40, 56, 100, 103-5, 108-28; w73 748-9; yb73 117-19, 151-9, 191; g73 6/8 16-26; w72 147-50, 574-5, 749; yb72 127, 131, 133, 138, 140, 150-1, 153-4, 160-1, 178, 185-7, 225, 235, 237, 241-2; w71 508; kj 315
attitude toward Jesus Christ: g75 3/8 29; g74 3/8 29; pm 325-6; w71 8; g71 1/8 29
attitude toward Kingdom: w74 101, 614; hu 8-9; w73 616; dy 12-13
Babylon the Great: ka 312-13, 316, 394; w72 587; kj 80, 180, 190-1, 206-7, 255, 289-90, 343
beginning: w75 597, 691; sl 208-9, 226, 235; po 170; ka 182-3; w72 625-6; dn 19-21; g72 6/8 12-16; w71 628-9
beliefs: w74 620; ts 37, 46, 64-8; hu 21; w73 232-3, 238-9; g73 1/8 16-19; g73 2/22 27-8; g73 3/22 16-19; g73 7/22 27; w72 100, 508; g72 3/22 5-8; w71 355-6, 627-8, 646-7; kj 159-61; g71 6/22 23-4
Bible knowledge lacking: g75 6/8 29; g73 2/22 6-8; g72 2/8 24; g72 12/22 29; g71 4/8 30
bloodguilt: sl 216-17; w74 145; w73 93, 126-7, 306-8; w72 312, 324, 391, 574-5; w71 629; kj 103-5; g71 9/8 31
children's view of churches: g75 8/22 29-30
church attendance: w75 200, 323-4; g75 4/8 24; g75 12/22 30; g74 9/8 29-30; g73 3/22 29; g72 4/8 21; g71 5/8 3
church buildings: w75 263; g75 4/8 24-5, 31; w74 490-1; g73 3/22 29; g72 8/8 30; g71 2/22 30
churches not preaching gospel: w73 743-4; g73 9/22 4-6
church gambling: w74 524; g74 11/8 12-13; g71 11/8 30
church membership: w75 323; sl 206; g75 6/8 30; g74 7/8 29; g74 8/8 30; w73 612, 688-9; dy 6; g73 9/22 3; pm 257; g72 10/22 29; g71 11/8 30
tax: w75 364
church mergers: g72 3/8 16; g72 7/22 30
church programs: w73 742-4; g73 9/8 29; w72 509; g72 4/8 22; w71 643-4; g71 3/8 29
striptease dancer: g75 6/22 30-1
class distinctions: ka 375-8; g73 5/8 29; g71 7/22 9
clergy: w75 201-4; yb74 35-8, 40; ka 374-84; g73 2/22 29; g73 9/22 3-4; w72 6-7, 214, 380, 453, 760; yb72 5-6; g72 1/8 30-1; g72 4/8 21-4, 30; g72 5/8 9-12; g72 8/8 30; g72 11/8 29; g72 12/8 29; w71 330, 484, 675-6, 739-40; g71 4/8 29-30; g71 7/22 4-9; g71 8/8 24-6; g71 8/22 13-14; g71 11/22 9-12; g71 12/8 3-4; g71 12/22 30
Communism: w73 707-8; g73 1/8 30; g73 4/8 3-19; g73 5/8 31; g72 4/22 3-5; w71 408; g71 1/8 29
"converted" people by force: w75 254
Crusades: g72 4/22 12-13; g72 10/22 29; kj 104
daughter organization of Babylon the Great: sl 235-6
decline: w75 41, 631; g75 1/8 30; g75 4/8 24-6; g75 9/8 24-5; w74 556; w73 688-9; tp 85-6; g73 1/8 29-30; g73 1/22 30; g73 2/22 3; g73 4/8 3-16; g73 6/8 30; g73 9/8 4; w72 323, 340; g72 1/8 31; g72 2/8 29; g72 2/22 30; g72 3/22 29; g72 4/8 21-4, 30; g72 4/22 30; g72 5/22 30; g72 6/22 9-11, 29; g72 7/22 31; g72 8/8 30; g72 8/22 17-18; w71 329-30, 407-8, 472, 484, 739-40; kj 317-18; g71 1/8 29; g71 1/22 29; g71 2/8 30; g71 3/22 3-4, 31; g71 4/8 29-30; g71 5/8 3, 5, 31; g71 8/8 29; g71 9/22 9-12; g71 10/8 31; g71 11/8 30; g71 12/22 30-1
destruction: sl 231, 236, 240-1, 338; w74 53-4, 318, 697-8, 719, 749; g74 4/8 19-20; w73 93, 126-7, 136; ka 202-4, 312-13, 316, 394-6; g73 12/8 19-20; w72 45, 51-3, 326, 357-8, 392-4, 420-2, 472-3, 764-6; w71 471-2; kj 30, 88, 93, 112-13, 119-27, 129-36, 140-1, 159, 180, 189-91, 200-2, 209-10, 212, 216-20, 274-5, 277-8, 289-90, 292, 298-9, 302, 309, 359-60
dishonesty: ts 109
disunity: g74 8/22 8-12; g74 9/8 29; g74 12/8 14-15; w73 613; dy 6-7; g73 1/8 16-19; g72 1/22 30; g72 3/22 10-11; g72 4/8 21-2, 24, 30; g72 4/22 8, 13-17; g72 6/8 29; g72 6/22 9-10; g72 7/8 31; g72 7/22 30; g72 8/8 30; w71 297-8, 355-6, 407-8, 547-8, 644; g71 5/8 12-16; g71 6/22 16-19; g71 7/22 6-9, 29; g71 8/22 13-14; g71 9/8 27; g71 10/8 29; g71 10/22 30; g71 11/8 30; g71 11/22 10-12
Edom's counterpart: sl 218, 223, 226-8
efforts to unite: g71 7/22 29
evangelism: g74 12/8 12-15; w73 742-4
evolution theory: g74 7/8 21-3; w72 586; w71 41, 46-51, 56
exposed by Witnesses: yb75 228-9, 235
failure: w75 355-8, 754; g75 1/8 4; g75 3/8 15; g75 6/22 31; w74 620-1, 656; hu 21-2; g74 2/8 29-30; g74 8/22 30; g74 9/8 29-30; w73 151-3, 483-4, 743-4; g73 2/22 29; g73 4/8 3-16; g73 8/22 6-8; g73 9/8 3-7; w72 423, 639; g72 1/8 30-1; g72 3/8 29, 31; g72 3/22 11; g72 9/8 30; w71 254, 419-22, 483, 548; g71 2/8 16-19, 30; g71 4/8 5; g71 5/8 3-6; g71 6/8 30; g71 8/22 30; g71 9/8 31; g71 10/22 29; g71 11/8 29-30
financial problems: g71 1/22 30; g71 2/8 30; g71 3/8 29; g71 3/22 31
"holy place":
desolated: w75 741-4
identified: w75 742, 744
hypocrisy: w74 263; g73 2/22 7-8; w71 549; kj 199-200
idolatry: w74 459; g73 1/8 27-8; yb72 112-13; g72 7/22 23; kj 103, 119, 134, 146, 156-61
influence waning: g74 12/22 8-9; g73 6/8 30; g72 4/8 21; g72 9/22 29; g71 1/22 30; g71 2/22 5-6; g71 4/8 30-1; g71 10/22 29
laity: w75 202; g74 12/8 14-15
League of Nations: w72 189, 197; w71 560; kj 60-1, 73
meaning of term: w71 629
membership: w74 614; hu 8; g71 5/8 3
militant preachers denied war was evil: w74 217
missionaries: g75 9/22 21; w74 677
money raising: w75 263; g75 9/8 25-6; tp 31-2; w72 419-20; w71 505-7, 709; g71 8/22 13-14
morals: w74 14, 100-1, 562-3, 592; po 170-1; w73 355-6; tp 28-32; g73 9/8 5, 7; w72 100; g72 3/8 29; g72 3/22 4; g72 4/8 22-3; g72 4/22 18-20, 30; g72 9/22 29; w71 451-2, 628; g71 5/8 29; g71 5/22 7; g71 7/22 4-5, 9-10; g71 10/22 30; g71 11/8 30
paganism approved: yb73 142-3, 206, 214; g72 2/22 30; g72 6/8 23; g71 7/22 29; g71 8/22 15-16; g71 9/22 30-1; g71 12/8 25-6
pagan origin of doctrines and practices: w75 55-6; w74 490-1, 740; ts 43-5, 96; g74 2/8 28; g74 12/22 4; g73 3/8 5-8; w72 63
pictured by:
Israel: w73 149-50, 166; w72 199; kj 67-72, 85, 90-2, 122, 130, 199-202, 216-17
Jerusalem: w74 717-18, 749; po 173; ka 305, 315, 395; w72 45, 324, 472-3, 675-9, 764; kj 99, 111-13, 146, 161-2, 173, 175-6, 189-90, 210, 216, 238, 268-71, 277-8, 286, 343, 359
man without marriage garment: w74 696-9
Oholah and Oholibah: w73 92-3; kj 245
political activity: w75 203-4, 357-8; w74 614-15, 677-9; hu 8-9; w73

165-6, 675-6; ka 250, 381-2, 384; g73 1/22 29; g73 5/22 24; g73 6/8 16-19, 23-5; g73 9/8 3-6; g73 11/8 29; g73 12/8 16-19, 29; w72 340, 366-7, 573-4; yb72 142-3; g72 2/22 30; g72 3/8 19; g72 4/22 3-11, 14-17, 30; g72 6/22 9-10, 24-6; g72 7/8 31; w71 420, 644, 740; kj 152-3, 296-8; g71 1/8 29; g71 3/8 30; g71 5/8 3-4; g71 7/22 6-8; g71 8/22 29; g71 12/8 3-4
population: ka 392; w71 8; kj 317
prayers: g74 1/8 10
Reformation: w72 199; yb72 126; kj 69
reincarnation: g75 4/8 27
Russia: g73 5/22 24
sermons: g73 1/22 30; w72 366; g72 5/8 29; w71 408, 643
spiritism: yb72 113-14; g71 7/8 17
spiritual condition: sl 12; w74 756-8, 760; w73 136, 146, 748; w72 6-7, 357; yb72 5-7; w71 548-9, 553
Sunday schools: w74 555; w72 340; w71 484
surveys: w71 675-6
symbolic representation: w75 589-605
violence: w75 294; w72 391, 394; g72 4/22 17; w71 420, 740; g71 2/22 3-6, 30; g71 7/8 30
war: g75 2/22 18-23; g75 5/8 9-12; g75 7/8 30; w74 217, 678-9; tp 24-7; g73 5/8 23; g73 8/8 20; g73 10/8 23-4; w72 625-7, 748-9; pm 215-16, 307-8; dn 19-20; g72 2/22 30; g72 4/22 5-17; g72 6/8 26; g72 10/8 7, 14; g72 10/22 29; g72 12/8 29; w71 215, 463, 644, 647; kj 59-61, 78, 104-5, 152-3, 158, 258-9; g71 3/8 30; g71 6/22 16-19; g71 8/22 30; g71 9/8 31; g71 11/8 30
warned: yb75 135-6, 138
wealth: ts 67-8; tp 31-2; g73 3/22 29; w72 419-20; g72 2/22 30; g72 6/8 29; w71 419-20; kj 131-6; g71 1/22 30; g71 2/8 17; g71 6/8 30; g71 9/22 29
world conversion: w74 615; hu 9
World Council of Churches: w73 675; g73 12/8 18; g71 3/8 31
worldliness: w74 217, 631; g74 12/8 13-15; w73 613-15; dy 8-10; w72 625-7, 639; dn 19-22; g72 10/8 18

Quotations

acquiescence of the churches sustained Third Reich: g75 7/8 30
apostasy of churches like rejection of Christ by Jews: g71 1/8 29
average member knows little about his faith: w73 744
cast Bible aside to follow modern fashion: g72 3/8 29
church currently in state of decline: w72 323
churches are in the eye of a storm: w75 684
churches have glorified war: g72 4/22 10
churches neglect the home visit: w75 759
churches not demand integrity and morality: g75 1/8 4; g74 9/8 5
churches war recruiting agencies: g73 6/8 18
church failed to provide spiritual leadership: g74 8/22 30
church follows flag: tp 25; g72 4/22 10
church is dying: g75 4/8 26
church is most anemic and sickliest: g71 5/8 31
church more a field for evangelism than force for it: w72 423
clergy admits responsible for selfishness: g73 8/22 6
clergy have sold us out: g71 6/8 30
constant compromise with evil: tp 25
death of churches soon: g74 5/8 31
denied calling and failed by conforming to world: g74 12/8 13
doing everything except preaching Gospel: g73 9/22 5
hungry sheep not being fed: g74 7/22 30
if all the churches disappeared, would anybody care?: w75 631
indistinguishable from a business: w74 556; g73 6/8 30
Jesus would not be tolerated if he returned in flesh: g75 3/22 30
Jesus would see Christians are not Christians any more: g75 8/22 29-30
Kingdom insignificant to churches: w74 101
kingdom of Christ converted into a kingdom of this world: w75 253
major cause of church's decline—clergy: g73 2/22 29
many who profess Christianity hardly practice it: g71 11/8 29
ministers' Bible knowledge leaves much to be desired: g72 2/8 24
ministers spiritual cheerleaders: g73 7/22 30
mounting ignorance of contents of Bible: g71 4/8 30
murder of six million Jews by baptized Christians: w75 294
no Christian army advancing: g72 9/8 30
not much impact on human relations in Africa: g75 3/8 15
not take stand unless we know direction wind is blowing: g72 4/22 9
our customary Christianity is Satan's pet child: g71 3/22 4
pampers to rich and powerful even when corrupt: g71 10/22 29
preach Christianity without Christ: g72 3/8 29
religion—a nonreligious role: g73 7/22 30
responsible for Communism: g73 4/8 7
Russian church seriously ill: g73 4/8 14
sick church in a sick community: g71 9/8 31
theology has no integrity or standards of its own: g75 6/22 31
theology is nine parts Greek thought to one part Christian: w75 55-6; ts 43
very foundations are crumbling: g72 9/22 29
waning power of religion reason life so stressful: w74 524
we may all be more pagan than we like to think: g71 5/22 7
when war pulpit is recruiting platform: g73 5/8 23
(SEE ALSO CHURCH[ES], CLERGY, ROMAN CATHOLIC CHURCH, WORSHIP)

CHRISTENDOM OR CHRISTIANITY—WHICH ONE IS "THE LIGHT OF THE WORLD"? (Booklet)
yb75 228

CHRISTIAN GREEK SCRIPTURES
authenticity: g71 12/22 8
directed to anointed: w74 376
divine name: yb73 142-3; w71 453-5
number of manuscripts extant: g72 6/22 5
(SEE ALSO BIBLE, BIBLE TRANSLATIONS)

CHRISTIANITY
Christian service: w75 716-22
identified: w75 536-8; w74 557-9
imitation: sl 207-8
superiority over Judaism: w73 213-18
way of life: w75 698-9

Quotation

rapid spread: g72 11/22 8

CHRISTIANS
conduct: w74 314-17, 340, 379-80; w73 590-6; g73 4/22 22-5
goals: w74 219; g74 8/22 7-8
hated: w73 656-9
holiness: w73 591-6
identification: w74 540, 543
light of world: w74 477-8
meaning of term: g74 11/8 19; w72 422
personal advancement: w74 114-19
preaching: w74 37
victory over world: yb74 252-3; w73 656-61
view of world: tp 120-31
(SEE ALSO JEHOVAH'S WITNESSES)

CHRISTIANS (Early)
apostasy: w75 729-30; w74 592, 740
attitude toward worship: w74 378
blood: g73 5/8 28; w71 118
codex: w74 554
congregation difficulties: w75 343-4
congregations: w72 729-31
direction by body of elders: w75 729-30
contributions: g74 1/8 28; g74 10/22 28
discussion: w73 213-18
exposed religious error: g74 11/22 28
flight from Jerusalem: w75 340-1; ml 22; w74 426; ka 301-2; tp 92; w72 108-9; g71 12/8 5-6
growth: ka 222-7; w71 399-400
holidays: g73 12/22 4, 7
identification: w75 536-8
images: w74 48
Jewish arguments against: w73 214-15
life sacred: w71 344
love: w75 340-1; w74 47-8
military service: w74 47; tp 126-7; g73 5/8 23; g72 4/22 21-2
misrepresentation: w74 47-8
morals: g72 4/22 22
neutrality: w75 497; w74 47-8

no clergy-laity distinction: w73 51; w71 330
persecution: w74 48, 215-16, 650; w73 42-3, 46, 214; w72 415-16; g72 6/8 13-15; g72 12/8 20; w71 213, 447, 485-6, 488-9, 716
personality change: w73 116; g73 8/22 6
prayer: g74 6/8 7
preaching: w74 61, 183, 185, 556-7; w73 51, 681-3, 687-8, 717-18; ka 222-7, 297-8; g72 11/8 8; g72 11/22 8; w71 330
progressive truths: w72 501-2
refusal to compromise: g75 12/8 4; w71 489; g71 9/8 14
relief measures: w71 414-15
respect for rulers: w71 488
resurrection: w72 242
separate from world: w75 358; w74 48; tp 126-7
testimony from outsiders: w74 48; w71 330
unity: w74 540, 542-3; w71 549-50
zeal: w72 210
(SEE ALSO APOSTLES)

CHRISTIAN SCIENCE
beliefs: g72 12/22 30
war: g72 4/22 7

CHRIST JESUS
(SEE JESUS CHRIST)

CHRISTMAS
celebrated by non-Christians: yb73 212
Christmas vacation: g72 10/22 29
clergy comments: g71 8/22 16
date: w75 739-40; g75 12/22 27-8; w74 739-40; po 139-40; g73 12/22 4-5; te 126; g71 8/22 16
discussion: w74 739-41; g73 12/22 3-7
effect on children: g73 12/22 3, 7
effect on emotions: g74 12/22 3-4
explaining Christian view: w74 741
gifts: w75 739-40; g74 12/22 3-4; g73 12/22 3-4, 7
groups forbidding: g74 12/22 29
holly: g73 12/22 5-6
Mexico: g71 6/22 23-4
mistletoe: g73 12/22 5-6
not a festival of early church: g73 12/22 4
origin: w75 739-40; w74 740; g74 12/22 4; g73 1/8 28; g73 12/22 4-6
piñata: g71 6/22 23-4
star: po 140, 142-3; g73 12/22 5
tree: g73 12/22 5-6
wise men: g74 12/22 4; g73 12/22 5
Witness children: w74 741
Witnesses adjust view of: yb75 147
(SEE ALSO HOLIDAYS)

CHRISTS (False)
w75 273, 275

CHRIST'S PRESENCE
as days of Noah: w75 10-11
attitude of clergy: g74 3/8 30
attitude of mankind: ka 334-5
coming: w75 9-11; w74 751; ka 327-8, 336-7
discussion: w74 397-400; ka 167-9, 187-8, 205-11, 259-61; g73 7/22 3-6
Greek word: w74 399-400; ka 167-9
Manifesto: w71 621; nc 20-1
manner: w74 255, 399-400, 748, 750
misconceptions: yb75 36-7; w74 397, 506-7; ka 184-7, 206-11, 228; g73 7/22 3-5
not 70 C.E.: w74 400
purpose: w74 398
revealing: g73 7/22 6
sign: w75 632-5; w74 40, 72-4, 99-101, 131-3, 195-6, 750-1; po 172-4; g74 5/8 17-19; ka 165-9, 212, 256, 307-8, 320-8; tp 78-88; g73 7/22 5-6; g73 10/8 20-2
time: w74 165, 398, 557; po 174-7
(SEE ALSO LAST DAYS, SIGN[S])

CHROMOSOMES
number: w75 72; w73 731-2; g73 10/22 11-12

CHRONICLES (First Book)
discussion: w71 571-2

CHRONICLES (Second Book)
discussion: w71 571-2

CHRONOLOGY
appointed times of the nations: w74 163-5; po 174-7; ts 155-60; w73 645; ka 186-7, 259-61; w72 187-8, 324, 351; pm 72, 74, 129, 332, 368; w71 619-21; nc 18-22
confirmation of Bible's: g72 4/8 16-20
connected historical events from 4026 B.C.E. to 98 C.E.: w75 446-7
connected historical events from 4026 B.C.E. to 1975 C.E.: w75 579-88
date of Adam's creation: w75 63; w74 507
miscalculations: ka 206-11
date of Jerusalem's destruction: ts 158-9; g72 5/8 27-8
480th year (1 Ki 6:1): po 120
450-year period (Ac 13:20): po 121-2
400 years of affliction: po 104-6
God's rest on seventh day:
beginning of: w75 285
Israel in Egypt: po 108
Jewish: w75 63-4
miscalculation regarding 1 Ki 6:1: w74 507; ka 206-11
radiocarbon dating: g72 4/8 5-15, 17-19
secular, often unreliable: w75 63; g72 5/8 28
seventy weeks: po 131-2, 144-5; g71 12/8 6-9
seventy-year desolation: ts 158-9
6,000 years of human history: yb75 256; w74 507; g71 10/8 26-7
proper view of: w74 378-9, 635
time between Adam's creation and Eve's: w75 285
2,300 "evenings and mornings": yb75 247
(SEE ALSO DATES)

CHURCH(ES)
abortion: w73 419-20
American Indians: g75 1/22 31
art thefts: g71 7/8 29
attacks on: g71 8/22 14
attendance: w75 200, 323-4; g75 4/8 24; g75 12/22 30; w74 15; g74 1/8 29-30; g74 9/8 29-30; g73 3/22 29; g73 9/8 4; g72 4/8 21; g72 11/8 29; g72 12/22 30; g71 5/8 3
attending wedding in: w74 766-7
attitude toward money: g74 8/8 31
buildings: w75 263; w74 490-1; g72 8/8 30; g71 2/22 30
largest: g75 1/8 22
business enterprises: g71 2/8 17
children's view of: g75 3/22 30; g75 8/22 29-30
choirs: w75 112
class distinctions: w74 491; g71 7/22 9
closed: w75 631; g73 3/22 29; g73 9/22 4
collections: g73 11/22 24-5; w71 505-6
credit card: w75 651
Communism: w73 707-8
criticism proper: g74 11/22 27-8
decline: w75 41, 172, 200, 323-4, 631, 684; g75 2/8 31; g75 3/8 30; g75 4/8 24-6, 31; g75 9/8 30; w74 15, 556; g74 1/8 29-30; g74 5/8 31; g74 7/8 29; tp 85-6; g73 1/8 29-30; g73 1/22 30; g73 2/22 3; g73 5/8 30; g73 6/8 30; g73 9/22 3-4; g73 10/22 31; w72 323, 340; g72 2/22 30; g72 3/22 29; g72 4/8 21-4, 30; g72 4/22 30; g72 5/22 30; g72 6/22 9-11, 29; g72 7/22 31; g72 8/8 30; g72 8/22 17-18; g72 10/8 12; w71 329-30, 407-8, 472, 484, 739-40; g71 1/8 29; g71 1/22 29; g71 2/8 30; g71 3/22 3-4, 31; g71 4/8 29-30; g71 5/8 3, 5, 31; g71 8/8 29; g71 9/22 9-12; g71 10/8 31; g71 11/8 30; g71 12/22 30-1
destruction: w74 53-4, 318; g74 4/8 19-20; g73 12/8 19-20; w71 471-2
disunity: w74 678-9; g74 9/8 29; g74 12/8 14-15
end predicted: g72 6/22 29
evangelism: w74 492; g74 12/8 12-15; w73 742-4
experiences:
couple quit because of immorality in: g74 10/8 28
members quit to become Witnesses: g74 3/8 22; w72 327
failure: w75 355-8, 759; g75 1/8 4; g75 3/8 29; g75 4/8 17, 25; g75 6/22 31; g75 9/8 25-6; w74 100-1, 263, 324, 492; g74 2/8 29-30; g74 7/22 30; g74 8/22 30; g74 9/8 29-30; w73 483; g73 2/22 29; g73 5/8 29; g73 8/22 6-8; g73 9/22 3-5; g73 11/8 30; w72 423, 639; g72 3/8 29, 31; g72 3/22 11; g72 9/8 30; w71 254, 419-22, 483, 548; g71 5/8 3-6, 31; g71 6/8 30; g71 8/22 30; g71 9/8 31; g71 10/22 29; g71 11/8 29-30
fight in: g75 6/8 29
financial problems: g71 1/22 30; g71 2/8 30; g71 3/8 29; g71 3/22 31
financial support: g75 3/8 30;

g75 5/8 29; g75 9/8 24-6; g74 8/22 30; g73 9/8 4
fund-raising schemes: w75 263, 651; g75 9/8 25-6; w74 524; g74 11/8 12-13; tp 31; g73 12/8 29; w72 419-20; w71 505-7, 709; g71 6/8 30; g71 7/22 29-30; g71 8/22 13-14
gambling: g75 1/8 31; g74 10/22 27; g74 11/8 12-13; g73 11/22 30; g71 11/8 30
homosexual: g74 2/8 30; g73 5/22 29
influence waning: w75 364, 684; g75 4/8 26; w74 360; g74 1/22 30; g73 6/8 30; g73 10/22 31; g72 4/8 21; g72 9/22 29; g71 1/22 30; g71 2/22 5-6; g71 4/8 30-1; g71 10/22 29
laity: g74 12/8 14-15
magazines: w75 327; g75 3/8 30
meaning of term in Bible: w74 491
members' comments: g72 8/8 30
membership: w75 323; g75 5/8 29; g75 6/8 30; g74 7/8 29; g73 9/8 4; pm 257; g72 10/22 29; g71 5/8 3; g71 11/8 30
name removed from rolls: yb74 86, 248
tax: w75 364
mergers: g75 11/22 21-4; g72 3/8 16; g72 7/22 30
moral condition: g75 4/8 25; w74 14, 100-1; g74 9/8 5; w73 355-6; tp 28-32; g73 9/8 5, 7, 29; w72 100; g72 3/8 29; g72 4/8 23-4; g72 4/22 18-20, 30; w71 451-2, 628; g71 5/8 29; g71 5/22 7; g71 10/22 30; g71 11/8 30
music: w71 643-4; g71 3/8 29
not preaching gospel: w74 100-1; w73 743-4; g73 9/22 4-6
not teaching children: g75 6/8 29
nudism: g75 5/22 30
political activities: w75 357-8; w74 217, 677-9; g74 1/22 29; g74 5/22 29; g74 8/8 31; g74 9/8 29; g74 11/22 3-6; g74 12/8 14; w73 675-6; g73 1/22 29; g73 6/8 16-19, 23-5; g73 8/8 20; g73 9/8 3-6; g73 9/22 4; g73 11/8 29; g73 12/8 16-19, 29; g73 12/22 29; w72 340, 366-7, 639; yb72 142-3; g72 2/22 30; g72 3/8 19; g72 4/22 3-11, 14-17, 30; g72 6/22 9-10, 24-6; g72 7/8 31; w71 420, 740; g71 1/8 29; g71 3/8 30; g71 5/8 3-4; g71 7/22 6-8; g71 8/22 29; g71 12/8 3-4
prayers: g74 1/8 10
programs: w73 742-4; w72 509; g72 4/8 22; w71 643-4; g71 3/8 29
striptease dancer: g75 6/22 30-1
pubs in churches: w74 492
revolutions: w74 678-9
seminaries: g75 3/8 27
social activities: w72 639
Sunday schools: w74 555
survival strategies: w75 631
taxation: w71 407; g71 3/22 3-4
vandalism: g75 2/8 31
victims of crime: g75 12/22 30
violence: g74 11/22 4-5; g72 4/22 17; w71 420, 740; g71 2/22 3-6, 30; g71 7/8 30
war: g75 2/22 18-23
worldliness: w75 631; g75 6/22 31; w74 100-1, 217; g74 9/8 29; g74 10/8 17; g74 11/8 12-13; g74 12/8 13-15; g73 12/8 16-19, 29; g73 12/22 29; w72 639
(SEE ALSO CHRISTENDOM, CLERGY, INDIVIDUAL CHURCHES BY NAME)

CHURCH AND STATE
alliance ended: sl 245
Catholic church: g73 12/8 16-19; g71 7/22 6-8
effect of alliance: g73 12/8 16-20
England: g75 4/8 25-6; g74 8/8 30
Romania: w73 708
Russian Orthodox: w73 708; g73 5/22 24

CHURCH OF ENGLAND
Archbishop of Canterbury: g74 8/8 30; g74 9/8 30
attendance: w75 172; g75 4/8 24
cathedrals: w75 263
clergy: g75 4/8 25; g74 8/22 30; yb73 148-9; g73 7/8 31; g72 1/8 31; g72 11/22 30; g72 4/22 30; w71 451; g71 3/8 29
decline: w75 172; g75 4/8 24-6, 31; g74 5/8 31; g73 5/8 30; g72 4/22 30
experiences:
members accept truth: g72 7/8 20
opposition to Witnesses: w71 508
failure: g75 4/8 25; g72 3/8 31
money: w75 263; w74 524
origin: kj 69
political activities: g74 5/22 29
polygamy: w72 366
Queen Elizabeth's visit to Pope Paul VI: g75 5/22 15
(SEE ALSO EPISCOPAL CHURCH)

CHURCH OF SCOTLAND
g72 7/22 31

CIGARETTES
(SEE SMOKING)

CIRCUIT ASSEMBLY
yb76 165-6, 250, 257; yb75 23, 204-5; km 10/75 8; g74 6/8 16-20; yb73 18, 235; km 3/73 4; or 87, 89, 105-6, 153-4; yb72 81, 176-7, 250-1
(SEE ALSO CONVENTIONS)

CIRCUIT OVERSEERS
adjustment: km 2/72 1
Bible studies: km 5/71 4
big-city territory: w75 206
duties: or 82-7; yb72 109; km 6/71 2
experiences:
accommodations: w75 205
Australian outback: w75 677-80
difficulties endured: yb73 67-8, 207-8; yb72 93-6, 149-50, 163, 175-6, 251
distances traveled: w73 54-5; yb73 233-5
humility: w74 412
informal witnessing: g73 2/22 24
Philippine Republic: w71 475-6
public talks: yb76 165
travels: yb76 214
travels on horseback: yb76 194
under ban: yb72 85-6, 93
financial support: w75 207
history: w73 663
meeting for field service: km 12/75 8
meeting time during visit of: km 12/75 8
meeting with elders: km 12/75 3-4; km 8/74 7
number: yb75 258; yb74 255; w71 335
pilgrims: yb75 48-51, 85; yb74 85-6, 95-6; yb73 91-2, 106
report to Society: km 12/75 4
responsibility: km 8/75 6
rotation: w71 700
"servants to the brethren": yb76 149-50; yb75 204
slide programs: yb75 232-3
visit: km 5/75 3-4; km 1/73 3
working with: km 1/73 3; or 85-6
zone servant: yb75 167-8, 204

CIRCUMCISION
Abraham and household: w71 441-2, 446
discussion: w71 441-7
hearts: sl 34; w71 442-4
meaning of term: w71 441
Moses' son: w75 415-16
why eighth day: w75 135-6

CIRCUMSTANCES
proper view: g71 12/22 3-4

CITIES OF REFUGE
avenger: g75 11/22 26-7; w73 302-4, 308
discussion: w73 302-312
manslayer: w73 303-5
map: w73 303
number: w73 303
other sheep: w73 311-12
purpose: w73 303-5
remnant: w73 311
symbolic: w74 667-8; w73 306-12, 543

CITY (Cities)
complexity: g74 11/22 14
decay: g71 9/8 29; g71 10/8 19, 28, 30
effects of breakdown in services: g74 11/22 14-15
fear: g75 10/22 29
financial problems: g75 12/8 30
overseer: or 82
population: g71 12/22 16
growth compared to rurals: g75 9/8 30
reasons for growth: g74 11/22 13-14
symbolic: pm 140-1
visitors' costs: g72 3/22 30

List by Name
Capernaum: w74 78
Jehovah-shammah: kj 401-6
Jerusalem: w74 78-9
Megiddo: w74 77
Shanghai: g72 5/8 29
Tokyo: g75 4/22 31; g71 10/22 29; g71 11/22 30

CIVILIZATION
disintegration: g71 1/22 19
industrial: g75 8/22 17-20
quote on average age of great civilizations: g75 6/22 30

CLAMS
g71 4/22 30

CLEANING
agents dangerous: g72 1/22 30-1
detergents: g72 9/8 30
methods: g74 5/8 14-15
mixing cleaners: g75 12/22 30
planning: g74 5/8 14
value of organization: g74 5/8 13

CLEANLINESS
bathing: g74 3/8 25

home: km 1/75 3
Israelite laws: w72 448
Kingdom Hall: km 1/75 3
moral: or 154-82
physical: km 1/75 3; g74 3/8 25; w72 413-14; g71 7/22 24-6
spiritual: w74 340; w72 414; g71 7/22 24-5

CLEMENT OF ROME
w72 670

CLERGY
alcoholism: g74 7/22 29; g72 7/22 30
anticlericalism: yb72 50; w71 740; g71 8/22 14
attitude toward abortion: w73 419-20; g73 4/22 29
attitude toward adultery: w74 562
attitude toward Bible: yb76 47; sl 289; g75 9/8 30; w74 36-7, 52, 743-4; g74 1/8 30; g74 3/8 30; g74 4/8 29-30; g74 8/22 9-12; g74 9/8 30; g74 9/22 30; w73 602-3; g73 2/22 6-7; g73 6/22 30; g72 1/22 5, 29; g72 4/8 23-4; g72 10/22 29; w71 464-5, 628, 675-6; g71 1/22 29; g71 4/8 30; g71 5/8 5; g71 8/8 26; g71 9/22 15
attitude toward fornication: g75 11/22 30
attitude toward homosexuality: w74 483, 493, 562; g74 5/22 29; g73 10/8 15, 31; g73 11/8 29
attitude toward Kingdom: w74 52, 101; w73 616; dy 13, 21; g73 12/8 18-19
attitude toward sex: g74 4/22 13, 30; g73 10/8 15
attitude toward Witnesses: yb75 154-5, 180-1, 184, 188; w74 763; yb74 95-6, 100, 103-4, 108, 112-13, 222, 237; g73 6/8 16-19, 23-5; w72 147-50; yb72 48, 153-4, 160, 235, 237, 241-2; w71 287, 508; g71 11/8 13-15
beginning: w75 201-2, 253-4; po 170
beliefs: g74 8/22 9-12; g74 12/8 14-15; w73 132, 232-3; g73 3/22 16-19; w72 508; g72 9/8 30; w71 408, 646-7, 675-6; g71 7/22 29
Bible ignorance: w75 650; g73 2/22 9; g72 2/8 24; g72 12/22 29; g71 4/8 30
black robes: g75 5/22 29
chaplains: g75 2/22 19, 21; g73 5/8 30; w72 760; g72 12/8 29; w71 644
church programs: w73 742-4; w71 643
clergy-laity distinctions: w75 202; g75 3/22 17; w73 51; ka 375-8; w71 330-1
comments on Witnesses' zeal: g73 2/22 8; w72 423-4; g71 1/8 29
Communism: g73 1/8 30; g73 4/8 4-16; g73 12/8 17; g71 1/8 29
confusion: g74 5/22 30-1
definition: ka 375
discredit Bible: w75 710; g75 3/22 30-1; w74 14; g74 1/8 30; g74 7/8 22-3, 30; g73 3/22 16-19; g73 5/22 23-4; g72 1/22 29; g72 8/22 18; w71 48-51, 675-6; g71 8/8 26; g71 12/22 5
dishonesty: ts 98-9, 109
disunity: g74 8/22 8-12; g72 6/8 29; g72 7/8 31; w71 407; g71 5/8 12-16; g71 7/22 6-8; g71 11/22 10-12
drugs: g74 7/22 29
evolution theory: g74 7/8 21-3; g73 10/22 22; w71 46-51, 56
experiences:
admiration for Witnesses: g74 3/8 30; g72 6/8 16; g71 1/8 24; g71 9/22 12
become Witnesses: w75 478; w74 411; yb74 37; w72 284, 327, 381, 679; g71 7/22 20
clergymen lack interest in parishioners: g74 3/8 22; yb73 18; g71 5/8 6
family members become Witnesses: yb72 183, 207-8; g72 2/8 24
inability to use Bible: yb74 35-6; yb73 148-9
opposition to Witnesses: yb76 18-19, 51, 53, 55, 57-8, 83, 98-100, 102, 113, 116-17, 120, 138-9, 141-3, 151-2, 168-70, 183, 188, 206, 220, 244; yb75 95-7, 101-2, 109; w74 80, 143; yb74 36-8, 40, 95-6, 100, 103-4, 108, 112-13; g74 5/8 20; w73 119-20; yb73 39-41, 58-9, 61, 63, 117-18, 151-9, 191, 201; w72 60, 147-50, 283-5; yb72 48, 105-6, 127, 131, 133, 138, 140, 150-1, 153-4, 160-1, 178, 185-7, 225, 235-7, 241-2; w71 18, 252, 508; g71 11/8 13-15
priest recommends studying with Witnesses: w74 143; yb72 194
failure: w75 631, 651, 759; g75 12/8 30-1; w74 100-1, 556; g74 5/22 30-1; g74 6/8 31; g74 8/22 30; w73 743-4; g73 2/22 29; g73 4/8 7-8, 14; g73 4/22 29-30; g73 8/8 20; g73 8/22 6-8; g73 9/8 3-7; w72 366-7; g72 3/8 31; g72 8/22 18; g71 5/8 5; g71 6/8 30; g71 11/22 10
false shepherds: w73 165-6; pm 307-9
false teachers: ts 97-9, 109
fight: g74 1/22 29; g73 12/22 30
hypnotism: g74 9/8 27-8
hypocrisy: w74 36-7
in United States Congress: g73 4/8 29
Jehovah's judgment of: ts 116
Jehovah's name: w72 31, 55; w71 646-7, 649
loss of prestige: g74 1/22 30; g74 3/22 6; g71 2/22 5-6
Manifesto: w71 621; nc 20-1
man of lawlessness: w75 167-8, 201-4, 252-4; ka 374-5, 378, 380
marriage: g72 5/8 9-12; g71 6/8 30; g71 8/8 24-5
missionaries: g73 8/8 29
money: g75 3/22 30; w74 624; g74 3/8 29-30; g74 5/8 31
moral decay: g75 12/8 30-1; w74 14, 100-1, 562; g74 10/22 30; g74 11/22 30; g74 12/22 29-30; w73 355-6; g73 2/22 7; g73 4/8 7; g73 5/22 24, 29; g73 7/8 31; g73 9/8 5, 7, 29; w72 6-7, 281, 366, 453; yb72 5-6, 198-9; g72 1/22 29; g72 4/8 22-3; g72 5/8 9-10; g72 6/8 29; g72 6/22 12, 30; g72 8/8 30; g72 9/22 29; g72 11/22 30; g72 12/8 29; w71 451, 557, 628, 709-10; g71 5/8 5-6, 30-1; g71 5/22 30; g71 6/8 30; g71 7/8 30; g71 7/22 4-5, 9-10; g71 10/8 31; g71 11/8 30
motion pictures: g71 3/8 31
pagan practices: g74 10/8 30
political activities: w75 203-4, 560; w74 101, 166, 217, 244; g74 5/22 29; g74 6/8 30; g74 11/22 3-6; w73 675-6; ka 381-2, 384; g73 1/22 29; g73 6/8 16-19, 23-5; g73 8/8 18; g73 11/8 7; g73 12/8 16-19, 29; w72 340, 366-7; yb72 142-3; g72 7/8 31; g72 12/22 29; w71 644, 740; kj 296-8; g71 1/8 29; g71 2/22 3-6; g71 5/8 3-4; g71 7/22 6-8; g71 12/8 3-4
polygamy: w75 200
prayers: g75 3/22 30
predict church's end: g73 2/22 3; g72 6/22 29; g72 8/22 17; g71 5/8 31
prostitution: g74 9/22 30
psychiatrists replacing: g75 8/22 25-6
qualifications: w72 380
quitting: g75 3/8 23-4; g75 3/22 16-18; g74 3/8 30; g73 9/22 3-4; w72 214; g72 4/8 21, 30; g72 6/22 10-11; g72 8/22 30; w71 330, 407-8, 484, 740; g71 1/22 31; g71 5/8 29-30; g71 8/8 24-5; g71 8/22 13; g71 11/8 30
salaries: g74 3/8 29-30; g73 7/22 29-30; g73 11/22 29; g72 10/8 30
sermons: g73 1/22 30; g73 9/8 3-4; w72 366; w71 643
shortage: w72 214, 367; g72 4/8 21, 30; g72 4/22 30; g72 5/22 30; g72 6/22 10; g72 8/8 30; g72 8/22 17, 30; g72 11/22 30; w71 329-30, 408, 484, 739-40; g71 2/8 16-17, 30; g71 2/22 30; g71 4/8 29-30; g71 8/22 13, 30; g71 11/8 30; g71 12/22 30
smuggling: g74 10/22 30
symbolic representation: w71 177
titles: w75 203; kj 303-4
unions for: g74 8/22 30
violence: w74 244; w72 391; g71 2/22 3-6, 30
war: g75 2/22 18-23; g75 7/8 30; w74 217, 244; ts 46; yb74 94; g74 10/22 13-14; g74 11/22 4-5; w73 549; g73 4/22 29-30; g73 5/8 23; g73 6/8 17-18; g73 7/22 30; g73 8/8 20; g73 10/8 15, 24; w72 626-7, 748-9, 760; pm 215-16, 307-8; g72 4/22 5-17; g72 6/8 26; g72 10/8 7; g72 10/22 29; g72 12/8 29; w71 215, 644; g71 7/22 7
witchcraft: yb76 193
Witnesses expose: yb75 55, 94-5, 97-8, 126, 135-7, 155, 181, 235
women: g73 6/22 30
worldliness: g74 6/8 31
(SEE ALSO CHRISTENDOM, CHURCH[ES], PRIESTS)

CLEVELAND, OHIO, CONVENTION (1946)
yb75 206-7, 210-11

CLIMATE
change affects health: g72 3/8 30
changes in earth's: g75 10/8 30
effect of human activities: g75 3/8 5
Palestine: g75 3/8 6

CLOCKS
creation: w72 291-3; g71 7/8 13-15
humans' inner: g71 2/22 30
leap second: g72 8/8 29
radioactive: g72 4/8 5-20; g71 4/8 31; g71 5/8 31

CLOPAS
w75 222

CLOTHING
Adam and Eve: w72 222
appropriate: km 8/74 8; w73 31, 138, 140; w72 222-4, 665-8, 757
asbestos: g71 6/22 30
avoid rape: g73 4/22 15-16; g71 2/22 30
Bible term "naked": w74 20
Bolivia: g71 6/8 21
care of: g75 8/8 9-12; g74 9/8 13-14; g72 1/8 26
chart on removal of common stains: g75 8/8 11
cleaning: g75 8/8 9-11
current styles: km 6/75 4; w73 138, 140, 144; w72 222-4, 665-8
customs vary: g71 10/22 6
cutting costs: g71 3/8 9; g71 5/8 8-10
Ghana: g71 10/22 6
making own: g73 8/22 9-12; g71 5/8 8-10; g71 5/22 29
men: g72 5/8 16; g71 3/22 29
mildew: g74 9/8 13-14
modesty: w74 118-19; g74 3/8 15-16
moths: g74 9/8 14
Panama Indians: g71 9/22 20-2
purchasing: g73 7/22 14-15; g72 1/8 25-6
reasons for wearing: g71 1/22 12
repair and remodeling: g75 8/8 11-12
shoes: g71 8/22 17-19
storage: g74 9/8 12-14
Surinam: g71 7/8 24
winter: g71 1/22 12-14
women: w73 254-5; w72 671-2; g71 7/8 24
pantsuits: w75 500
wool: g74 11/8 15-16; g73 2/8 24-6

CLOUD(S)
discussion: g73 7/8 6-7
symbolic: w74 256, 298, 751; kj 48

COAL(S)
fuel: g74 1/8 4
mining: g73 12/22 29
oil from: g74 4/22 29
symbolic: kj 184, 187, 189-90, 196

COBRA
symbolic: w74 762-3

COCA
addictive: w72 594

COCAINE
g75 6/8 29; g73 4/8 30

COCKROACH
g72 11/22 31

COCONUTS
monkeys: g71 8/22 30
uses: g71 6/22 25-6

CODEX
early Christians: w74 553-4

COFFEE
g75 4/22 9; g75 10/22 30; g75 12/8 31; g73 9/22 29-30; w72 596; g71 9/8 30

COINS
disease-causing germs on: g75 7/22 31

COLD(S)
balance affected by: g73 1/8 31
cause: g73 12/22 8-9
discussion: g73 12/22 8-10
treatment: g73 12/22 9-10; g72 9/8 30; g71 1/8 29-30; g71 3/8 30
(SEE ALSO DISEASE, HEALTH)

COLLECTIONS
Christian view: pm 83; w71 506-7
churches: w71 505-6; g71 3/22 31
(SEE ALSO CONTRIBUTIONS)

COLLEGE
closings: g71 6/22 30
crime: g73 2/22 29
dangers to Christian youths: w75 543
degrees: g71 6/22 30
discussion: g71 6/8 3-8
drugs: g72 4/22 31; g71 4/8 16-17; g71 6/8 6
effect: w73 117-18; g73 4/22 31
experience:
Witness gives talk: yb73 239-40
failure: g75 5/8 21
graduates: w72 207; g71 12/22 29
graduates without jobs: g74 2/8 30-1
medical: g74 8/22 31
morals: g74 11/8 31; g73 11/22 30; g72 8/8 30; g71 6/8 5-6
rape: g74 1/8 30
religion: g74 9/22 12
shortage of funds: g73 6/8 29; g71 6/8 4; g71 6/22 30; g71 12/8 30
sports: g72 5/22 31
student despair: km 5/73 4
student riots: g71 6/8 4-5; g71 8/8 10-12
students' ability to use English language: g75 12/22 30
suicides: g72 6/8 30
value: g75 6/8 29-30; g74 11/8 31
(SEE ALSO SCHOOLS)

COLLISION
nations with God: w71 611-31; nc 3-29

COLOMBIA
airplane skyjacked: g74 5/22 13-16
animals: g75 3/22 13-15
earthquakes:
corpses thrown out of tombs: w75 640
employment: g73 8/8 8-11
food shortage: g72 10/8 30
internal problems: w72 579
Jehovah's witnesses: yb76 24-5; w75 413; yb75 24-5; w74 39; yb74 24-5; yb73 24-5; w72 281-6; yb72 34-5
population: yb73 24; yb72 34
students riot: g71 8/8 10-12

COLOR
discussion: g71 6/22 9-12
emotional effect: g74 3/22 15
paint: g74 3/22 15
rainbow: g75 1/22 14-16
sky: g71 6/22 11
source: g71 6/22 10

COLOSSIANS (Book)
counsel to ancient congregation: w73 682-6
time and place written: w73 682

COLPORTEURS
beginning: yb75 39-40, 61
discussion: yb76 91-2, 245-6; yb75 61-4
expansion: yb75 86
(SEE ALSO PIONEERS)

COLUMBUS, CHRISTOPHER
earth's food potential: g71 11/22 20

COLUMBUS, OHIO, CONVENTIONS

1924
resolution: yb73 150; w72 148; kj 83-5

1931
name "Jehovah's witnesses" adopted: yb75 149-51; w73 398; ka 238-40; yb73 112, 218; w72 47; w71 183, 651; kj 172
public talk: yb75 151-2
releases: ka 266; w72 47

1937
doorstep phonograph work: yb75 158
(SEE ALSO CONVENTIONS)

COMETS
w74 40; g73 8/8 30

COMFORT
drawing, from Scriptures: w71 263
loneliness: w71 262-3
mourners: w73 29; g71 12/8 28

COMMANDMENTS
"new commandment": w71 191
Ten Commandments: g72 11/22 6-8; g71 1/8 3-4
(SEE ALSO COVENANTS, LAW)

COMMENDATION
right view: g72 2/22 3-4

COMMERCE
big business: g71 2/8 3-6
problems: g71 4/8 31
Satan controls: g74 10/22 8

COMMERCIALISM
w75 248

COMMISSION
Christians': w71 423-6
Ezekiel's: w72 187, 253

COMMITTEE
(SEE JUDICIAL COMMITTEE, OVERSEERS)

COMMON MARKET
g73 2/8 31

COMMUNICATION
animals: g71 7/22 20
approachability: w74 367-8
Bible times: w74 307-10
CN Tower: g75 6/8 21-4
definition: w74 305
drums: g71 7/8 23

in congregation: w74 306, 313, 367-8
listening: g74 11/22 21-3
marriage mates: w74 305-11; g74 4/22 8-12; g72 8/8 3-4
parents with children: w75 156; w74 261-5, 267-72; g74 4/22 14-16; g72 8/8 3-4
radio: g71 7/8 25-6
satellites: g72 2/8 29; g71 12/8 19
telephone: g74 9/22 16
television: g74 9/8 8; g71 12/8 19

COMMUNISM
atheism: w75 233-4
Baptists: g73 5/8 31
Catholic church: w74 71, 341; g74 3/22 29; g74 4/22 29; g74 11/22 4-5, 30; g73 6/8 29; g73 12/8 17; g73 12/22 29; g72 10/8 7-9; w71 408; g71 1/8 29; g71 7/22 6-7
China: yb74 47, 52-6; g74 7/8 5-9
Christendom responsible: g73 4/8 6-7; g72 4/22 3-5
clergy compromise: g73 1/8 30; g73 4/8 7-11, 14-16; g71 1/8 29
conditions under rule: w72 580
Cuba: w74 707, 710
evolution theory: ml 13-14
experiences:
  Communists become Witnesses: w75 247; yb75 19-20; g73 2/22 24; w72 71, 281-2
  Communist-trained revolutionary becomes Witness: w74 710-14
fight against religion: g73 4/8 4-19
goal: g71 7/8 5
growth: g75 7/22 5-8; g71 7/8 5-9
Italy: g75 8/8 29
Jehovah's witnesses: w74 250; yb74 52-6, 59-60, 223-32; g74 7/8 9; g73 4/8 17-19
  Communist leaders petitioned by: yb75 234-5
  tactics against Witnesses: yb74 53-6, 59-60, 223-6, 229-32; w72 144
king of the north: g71 7/8 9
Lenin: g73 4/8 5
Marx, Karl: g71 7/8 5
religion: w74 198; g74 2/8 31; w73 707-8; g73 12/8 17
resemblance to religion: w73 604
Russian Orthodox Church: g74 2/8 31; g73 4/8 4-14
Stalin: g73 4/8 9
youth: g73 4/8 6, 10, 13
(SEE ALSO CHINA, SOVIET UNION)

COMMUNIST LANDS
Jehovah's witnesses: yb75 18-20; w74 31; yb72 45
  persecution: w74 373; yb74 223-32; g73 4/8 17-19; w72 71, 144
religion: w73 707-8; g71 9/8 27

COMMUNITY RESPONSIBILITY
w71 235-6, 629-31

COMORO ISLANDS
Jehovah's witnesses: yb76 24-5; yb74 24-5

COMPASSION
Jehovah: w75 517-18; w74 281-2; ts 123-4
Jehovah's witnesses: w74 281-2
mercy: w71 411-15; g71 8/8 27-8

COMPENSATION
crime: g72 5/22 30

COMPETITION
g74 4/22 31; w73 506; g73 1/8 29; g73 3/22 13-14; g73 10/22 30

COMPLACENCY
examples: w72 675-9; yb72 50

COMPLAINING
against God's organization: w74 413
examples: w71 147

COMPOSITION
drawing for painting: g74 5/8 23
suit audience: g73 9/8 18-19
word choice: g73 9/8 17-20

COMPREHENSIVE CONCORDANCE OF THE NEW WORLD TRANSLATION OF THE HOLY SCRIPTURES
yb75 221, 251

COMPROMISE
avoiding: w74 202-3; w72 122-3
Christendom: w74 273
examples: yb74 107, 109, 111, 129-30, 148-50, 170-1, 175-8

COMPUTERS
Bible: g72 1/22 27-8
capabilities: w74 555; g72 6/22 3-4
comparison with human abilities: w75 263
miniaturization: g73 3/22 26

CONCENTRATION CAMPS
Auschwitz: yb76 40; yb74 173
Buchenwald: yb76 39-40
compromisers: w74 202, 218
Dachau: yb74 169-71, 206
death marches: w74 676; yb74 205-9
evacuation: yb74 205-8
Jehovah's witnesses: yb76 39-41; w74 676; yb74 163-78, 191-204, 211-12; w72 396-9; w71 489-90
  integrity: w75 85; yb74 118-19, 163-9, 172-4, 183, 194, 196-7, 202-4, 208-12; w72 397-8; g72 4/22 22-3; w71 425, 494; g71 10/22 4
  meetings: yb74 194
  spiritual food: yb76 40; yb74 191-4, 198-204
  treatment: yb74 139, 161, 164-70, 173-4, 183, 196-8, 202-4
Mauthausen: yb74 171-2, 206
Ravensbrück: yb76 41; yb74 173-4, 199-200, 204
Sachsenhausen: yb74 165-9, 183, 193-4, 201-3, 206-7
women: yb74 172-4
(SEE ALSO PERSECUTION, PRISONS)

CONCEPTION
biological description: g74 2/8 12-13
DNA: g73 12/22 27-8
genetic dangers: w75 72-4
hormones: g74 1/22 13, 15-16
miraculous: po 136-8; ts 128-9
preventing: w75 158-60; g74 1/22 15-16
sex of offspring: w73 731-2
(SEE ALSO BIRTH CONTROL)

CONCERN
showing: w74 675-6

CONCLUSION
public speaking: g74 12/22 15; sg 48-9, 175-7

CONCORDANCES
producing: g72 1/22 27

CONCORDATS
Vatican and—
  Hitler: w75 398; g72 4/22 16
  Mussolini: w75 364
  Trujillo: yb72 158

CONCUBINES
forsaking concubinage: w72 598

CONDUCT
aids to proper: g75 1/22 6; w73 591, 595-6
Christian: w75 752-8; w74 187, 379-80, 562, 564-6, 570-1; or 184-5; g71 10/22 3-4
  between sexes: w74 10-13; w73 31-2, 592-6
  divided household: w74 314-17
  field service: km 8/74 8
  honesty: g72 10/22 22
conventions: w75 761
experiences:
  aids others to accept Bible truth: w73 187-8; w72 381-2, 510; w71 209; g71 6/22 8
  blessings for good: g72 3/8 11
  favorable comments about Witnesses: w75 628-9; g75 10/22 16-18; g74 11/8 17-21; w72 125, 403, 555; yb72 241-2, 246; g72 10/22 17-19, 21-3
  fellow worker aided to accept truth: yb76 6-7
guests: w73 599-600
loose: w73 574-6
secular employment: w72 269-70
standard for proper: tp 111-12
(SEE ALSO MORAL BREAKDOWN)

CONFERENCES
1972, Stockholm, Sweden: g72 9/22 29
1975, Helsinki, Finland: g75 9/22 29; g75 11/8 3-7

CONFESSION
Bible view: g74 11/8 27-8; w72 694-8
Catholic church: w74 198; g74 11/8 27-8; g73 6/8 29; g71 5/22 29; g71 7/22 4
decline in number going to: g75 7/22 31
judicial committee: or 165

CONFIDENCE
Christian faith: w75 374-80; ts 176-7
decline of: g75 12/8 30
in elders: w75 764-6
lack of, in world: w75 764
parents and children: w72 163-4; g72 4/8 4; w71 587-92
private information: w71 222-4
public speaking: sg 181-4

CONFIRMATION
discussion: w71 170-1
godparents: w72 511

CONFORMITY
Christian position: w72 543
youth: w72 473-6

CONFUCIANISM
Communist China: w74 198
membership: w71 14

CONGO (Kinshasa)
(SEE ZAIRE REPUBLIC)

CONGO REPUBLIC
Jehovah's witnesses: yb76 9-10, 24-5; yb75 24-5; yb74 24-5; yb73 24-5; yb72 34-5; w71 679
population: yb73 24; yb72 34

CONGO RIVER (Zaïre)
g72 11/8 24-6

CONGREGATION(S)
all contribute to growth: w74 533, 573; w73 372-3
all contribute to spirituality: w74 212-13, 531, 533, 575
appointment of elders: w75 86; km 8/75 3; w73 469-74; w72 458; or 61-3, 69; yb72 26-9; w71 688-90, 699-701
appreciating: w73 400-7, 461
attitude toward elders: w73 141-6, 335; tp 142-3; w72 271-2, 464-5
attitude toward sexual immorality: w75 755-6
Bible study overseer: w72 460; or 76-7
children: km 4/75 3
circuit overseer: km 5/75 3-4; km 8/75 6; km 1/73 3-4
city overseer: or 82
conduct within: w74 300, 313, 316, 367-8; w73 331-43; w72 223-4; sg 72-3
confidential matters: km 7/75 3
congregation book study conductor: km 1/75 4; w72 461; or 81-2
conversation: sg 82-4
cooperation in: w73 140-6; w72 464-5, 467-8
difficulties: w73 703-4; w72 15-17, 465-7; or 58, 155-9; yb72 20-3; w71 438
disassociated persons: w72 124; or 171
discipline: km 5/73 8
disfellowshiped persons: km 11/74 4; w71 383-4
elders: w72 9-21, 25-7, 126, 201-4, 458-62; or 11, 53-70, 150; yb72 10-33, 42; km 11/72 7; w71 603-4, 663, 690-701; km 9/71 3-4
  benefit to: w75 86
  meetings: or 63-70
  moving to another congregation: km 8/75 5-6; km 2/73 7; km 6/73 3
  recommendation: w72 591, 599
  shepherds: w73 39
"extra" magazines for: km 8/75 8
false teachers: w72 191-2
field overseer: w72 460-1; or 73-6
field service: w71 459, 753-4
files: km 2/74 8
finances: km 3/73 4; km 10/73 8; w72 461; or 149-53
foreign-speaking, in the United States: km 7/75 4
forming new: km 7/75 4; or 101-3
helping inactive ones: yb74 254-5; km 1/74 3
helping new ones: km 5/74 7
incorporated: km 5/75 3
Jehovah's blessing: w74 52-3
judicial committee: w72 604
Kingdom Ministry: or 97
loving interest in all associates: km 12/75 4-5; w74 569-71; w73 371-6, 627-9; w72 17-19, 456-62, 467-8; yb72 23-6; w71 375-6, 414; sg 190; g71 8/8 28; km 6/71 3-4
male authority: w72 271
"marked" person: w73 318-20
meetings: km 4/75 4; km 7/75 1, 3; km 12/75 5; w74 566-8; km 8/74 7-8; km 12/74 3-4; w73 253-4, 533-5; w72 133-4, 447; or 71-2, 91-105; km 3/72 4; km 4/72 4; km 7/72 4; km 9/72 7-8
  when attendance exceeds seating capacity: km 7/75 4
ministerial servants: km 1/75 4; km 2/75 4; w72 20-1, 25-7, 126, 287; or 60-1; yb72 29-33; km 11/72 7
  qualifications: km 8/75 3
modern-day:
  history of: yb76 56, 65-6, 86-7, 104; yb75 39, 124, 133
moral cleanness: km 12/75 5-6; w73 144-5, 336-43; w72 191-2, 604; or 86-7, 154-82
naming: or 102
needy ones: w74 569-70
New York city: km 9/75 1
number: yb76 3, 23, 31; w75 27, 605; sl 203, 329; yb75 3, 5, 30-2, 258; w74 30; yb74 32; ka 283; yb73 256; w72 333, 457; pm 254; yb72 43; w71 24, 332, 560
  United States: km 11/75 4
older persons: w74 265-6, 533, 537-8, 570; km 11/74 3; w73 400-1; km 3/72 3
opportunities to serve: w72 203-4; km 2/72 7-8; sg 190-1
overall spirit of: km 12/75 4
personalities vary: w73 109
prayer: w72 334-5; or 92; km 1/72 8; km 9/72 8
preaching: w71 701-3
presiding overseer: w72 458-9; or 70-3
report: km 1/73 4; km 8/73 4
singing: w75 29-31
small: or 102-3
social gatherings: km 7/74 3
spiritual qualities: w71 664-5
tact: sg 72-3
theocratic organization: yb75 165-6
theocratic rule: w73 142, 146, 458-9; yb73 116; w72 458, 729-31; w71 681-701; kj 330
Theocratic School overseer: w72 460-1; or 79-81
tobacco users: km 7/73 4; km 11/73 7
unbaptized wrongdoers: km 10/75 8
United States:
  number of new congregations: km 8/75 8
unity: w74 313; km 3/74 3; w73 732-3
view of worldly courts: w73 703-4
Watchtower study conductor: w72 460; or 78-9
women's privileges: w73 255
youth: w75 443-4; w73 146
(SEE ALSO KINGDOM HALLS, MEETINGS)

CONGREGATIONAL CHURCH
clergy: g71 4/8 29

CONGREGATION BOOK STUDY
conductor: km 12/74 3; w72 461; or 81-2; km 12/72 8
  capable ministerial servant: km 1/75 4
discussion: km 5/75 2; km 9/74 7-8; or 100-1
field service: or 101
readers: or 101; sg 146
teaching at: km 5/72 3
time held: km 8/74 8

CONGREGATION COMMITTEE
(SEE JUDICIAL COMMITTEE, OVERSEERS)

CONGREGATION OF GOD
(ALSO CALLED ANOINTED, BODY OF CHRIST, BRIDE OF CHRIST, CHOSEN ONES, HOLY NATION, ISRAEL OF GOD, KINGDOM CLASS, LITTLE FLOCK, NEW CREATION, 144,000, ROYAL HOUSE, ROYAL PRIESTHOOD, SPIRIT BEGOTTEN, SPIRITUAL ISRAEL, SPIRITUAL SONS)
ambassadors: w74 107-8, 650-2; ka 76-81
anointing: w74 251-2; po 158-9; ka 106-8
  wrong assumptions regarding: w75 105-8
appreciation for: w73 400-7
begetting: g74 8/22 27; w73 730, 732; w72 608
beginning: w74 621-2; po 158-9; hu 24; w72 717; w71 397-9, 655, 746, 755-6
born again: g74 8/22 27
bride of Christ: sl 358-60; w74 431-2, 686-7, 690, 700; ts 105-6; w73 199-200; w71 275
brothers of Christ: w74 287-8; ka 276-7
calling: w73 731-3; w71 568-71, 703-4
'chosen before founding of world': w74 287; g74 7/8 28
chosen ones: w74 749-50
commission: w71 423-6
death of members: w73 740-1; w72 518-20
"executed with ax": w73 740-1; ka 32-4
faithful and discreet slave: ka 337-57; w72 755; or 8-12; w71 81, 462-3, 750, 754
firstfruits: ka 106
foreordained: po 157, 164; g74 7/8 28; ka 73-5
foundation: w72 719; w71 319, 397, 747
Gentiles: w74 126-8, 619, 695-6, 699; po 164-8; hu 18-19; w71 655
hated by nations: w74 650-1
heavenly language: w74 42
holiness: w73 741
identification: w72 457; or 12; w71 423-6
immortality: ts 183
inheritance: w74 287-8; w73 494-5
Israel of God: w74 126-8; po 159-

61; w72 173; pm 101, 144-6, 251-8; w71 430, 747; kj 68, 302, 352
Jehovah is ruler: w71 746-7
Jesus is head: w73 458-9; w72 729-31, 755-7; w71 747
Jews given first opportunity: w74 687-95
joint heirs: w74 690
judges: ka 31, 117-19, 124-5, 131, 136-7, 139-42
justification: w74 252, 607; ka 110-11; w72 518-19, 608
kings: w74 106-8; po 161; ka 30-1, 48-9, 72-5
language in heaven: ka 49
members: w74 619; hu 18-20; tp 68-9
misconceptions: w74 636-7; w71 421-2
neutrality: w74 107-8; w73 741, 749; ka 288
"never see death": w74 376-7
new covenant: po 157, 159-61; w73 198-200, 415-16
New Jerusalem: w74 599; w72 720; pm 149-53
number: w74 619; hu 19-20; g73 5/8 6-7; w72 518; w71 430, 714
pictured by—
Esther: w71 176
Jacob's sons: w71 747
Mordecai: w71 175
24 older persons: w73 62
wise virgins: w74 506-9; ka 169-83, 189-204
priests: w74 157, 251-4, 690; po 183; ts 130-1; ka 107-12, 116; w72 717-18; pm 88, 103-5; w71 570, 714
qualifications: w74 106-8, 254; ts 141; w73 740-1
racial equality: ka 50-2
restoration: w73 221-3, 251-2, 394-400; w72 750-1
resurrection: w74 253-6, 558-9; ts 170; w73 243, 727-9; ka 31-2, 36-42, 242-4
sealing: w74 61, 252; w73 730; w72 636
seed of Abraham: w74 696-7
seed of God's woman: w74 106
selecting members: w74 478, 699-700; po 171; tp 67-9
some on earth after great tribulation: ka 401, 406, 411
some on earth through past ages: w74 561
spiritual temple: w73 440; w72 607, 719; kj 274-5
sympathetic to mankind: ts 141
temple-building: w72 750-1
unity: w74 620-1; hu 20-3
virgins: w74 108, 431-2; ka 173
(SEE ALSO CONGREGATION, REMNANT)

CONGREGATION PUBLISHERS
aiding new ones: km 9/75 7-8; km 9/74 1
aiding weaker ones: w73 42-3
experiences:
bus group: yb72 63-4
field service: w71 459
inactivity: km 12/75 7-8; w73 41-2; km 12/71 4
new ones: or 128-30
introducing themselves to elders: km 9/75 8
number: w75 23, 27; yb75 5, 30, 32; km 12/74 1
record card: km 2/74 8; or 127
requirements: km 3/71 4
spiritual assistance: km 6/71 3-4
(SEE ALSO FIELD SERVICE)

CONSCIENCE
Adam and Eve: w75 209; w72 556-8
body of elders': w75 219
clergy comments: g75 2/22 18-19, 21
consideration for others': w75 218-19; g74 3/22 22-3; w73 30, 139-41, 145-6; w72 563-7, 591, 599, 757
Darwin, Charles, view of: w75 208
David: w75 210-11
discussion: w75 208-20; w73 164-5, 357-9; w72 556-67, 588-600
employment: w75 215-16; w73 409-11; w72 591-600
experiences: w75 215-16; w73 357-9, 409-11
faculty of, universal: w75 210-11
Freud, Sigmund, view of: w75 208
guide: g75 4/8 9; w73 140-1; w72 589-99
Hitler's view of: w75 209
honesty: g74 12/8 5-6
Joseph (son of Jacob): w75 209-11
keeping good: w74 58-9, 205
law: w75 114; w73 30, 36-7; w72 556-63
meaning of term: w73 357; w72 556
not imposing your conscience upon others: w75 707; km 6/75 4; w72 599
pagan writers: w75 211
patriotic exercises: w75 217
paying fines: w75 223-4
proof of God's existence: w75 114
request to God (1 Pe 3:21): w74 602-3; w73 31, 309-10; tp 185-6; w72 120-1, 698-701
seared: w75 212; w72 565
subjection: tp 138
superior to rules: w75 217-18
taxes: w75 214-15
training: w75 211-13, 218-19; w73 164-5
variation in decisions based on: w75 217

CONSCIENTIOUS OBJECTION
Brazil: yb73 79-81
civilian work as substitute for military: g74 12/8 23
Ghana: yb73 162-3
Great Britain: yb73 98-100, 120-2, 124
Netherlands: g74 12/8 22-5
Spain: yb73 22
United States: yb75 101, 103
(SEE ALSO MILITARY SERVICE)

CONSENSUAL MARRIAGE
(SEE MARRIAGE)

CONSERVATION
wildlife: g73 5/8 16-18, 30;

CONSIDERATION
showing: w74 45-6, 675-6; g73 11/22 13-15

CONSOLATION (Magazine)
yb76 140-1; yb75 123, 162; yb73 123, 160-1
(SEE ALSO AWAKE!)

CONSTANTINE
baptism: w72 625; dn 19
Christendom founded by: w75 597
Church and State: w74 592
cross: w72 573; g72 11/8 27-8
fusion religion: ka 382; w72 625-6; dn 19-20; g72 6/8 15
murderer: w72 311-12; g72 6/8 14; kj 103; g71 9/8 18
Nicene council: w75 356; sl 209; g73 1/8 16-17; kj 103
Pontifex Maximus: sl 208-9, 235; ka 382; w72 625-6; dn 19-20
set up clergy class: po 170
Trinity doctrine: w75 356; sl 209; w72 625; dn 19
(SEE ALSO APOSTASY)

CONSTELLATIONS
g75 6/22 18

CONSTITUTION OF THE UNITED STATES
Fourth Amendment: g71 11/8 5
Thirteenth Amendment: g71 11/8 5

CONSTRUCTION
adobe house: g71 1/8 23-4
assembly halls: g74 6/8 16-20; km 5/74 1
earthquake-prone areas: g71 4/8 10
highways: g72 6/8 4
houses: g74 8/8 30-1; g72 10/22 28
insects' ability: g71 10/22 18-20
Kingdom Halls: g72 8/22 19-23
tall buildings: g74 2/8 21; g74 4/22 30-1; g72 12/8 30
tallest towers: g74 8/8 31
vandalism: g74 6/8 14-15
World Trade Center: g74 2/8 21-3

CONTENTMENT
w75 123-4; g75 6/22 3-5; g74 8/8 5-6; g72 5/8 3-4

CONTEXT
Bible: w73 207-18

CONTRACEPTIVES
w75 159-60; g75 7/8 30; g75 12/22 29; w73 255-6; g73 1/22 30; g73 4/8 29; g73 9/8 31; g71 8/22 14
(SEE ALSO BIRTH CONTROL)

CONTRACT
between Christians: w73 287-8

CONTRIBUTIONS
assemblies: or 153-4
assembly halls: g74 6/8 18-19
"charitable" organizations: g74 9/22 31; g73 11/22 24-6; g71 1/22 30
collections: w73 507-8; w71 505-6; g71 3/22 31
congregation "garage sale": km 10/73 8
contribution boxes: w73 298
decline: g71 5/22 29
discussion: w74 282; w73 297-9; tp 31-3; or 148-54; w71 283-5, 506-7

early Christians: g74 1/8 28; g74 10/22 28
elders: g74 1/8 28
experiences:
 brothers give so publishing continues: yb74 105
 child contributes for preaching work: w72 444
 Witnesses support branch office expansion: yb76 234-5
literature: w74 3
motive: g73 4/8 27-8; g73 11/22 24; w71 284
three basins: yb73 95
tithing: g74 1/8 27-8
use of money: w73 298-9; g73 11/22 24-6; w72 313-14
Witnesses in stricken areas: yb75 209-10; w74 476; yb74 216-17; g74 5/22 8; g74 7/8 26; g74 12/22 26; km 11/74 1; w73 95-6, 134-5, 267-8; yb73 95; g73 3/8 13-14, 16, 19; g73 6/22 15; yb72 137, 179, 225-6, 252-3; g72 8/8 26; g72 8/22 16; g71 3/22 25
 how funds gathered: km 3/73 4
Witnesses' view: g74 1/8 28; w73 297-9; w72 461; pm 83

CONVENTIONS

cafeteria: g75 10/22 17-18; g72 10/22 21-2; g71 10/22 14
children: w75 629
conduct at: km 5/73 7-8; km 6/72 3
conduct of Witnesses (quotes): w75 628-9, 761; g75 10/22 16-17; w74 44, 149, 516, 632, 635, 637-9; yb74 239, 251; g74 3/8 29; g74 9/8 6; g74 11/8 17-21; g74 12/8 4-5; w73 453, 456, 486; g73 7/22 23; g73 11/8 14-17, 20; yb72 41-2, 246; g72 10/22 17-19, 21-3; w71 91, 595-9, 601; g71 3/22 26; g71 10/22 13-15
convention trains: yb75 57-8
dramas: yb75 233-4
effort to attend: yb76 210, 254; w75 680; yb75 23; g75 10/22 23; w73 348; yb73 165-6; g73 11/8 18-19; g71 4/8 21; g71 6/8 24-5; g71 10/22 12
experiences:
 attendance despite tragedy: w74 518
 attendance during political uprising: w75 351
 difficulties overcome: g75 10/22 23; yb74 218-19, 236-9; g73 11/8 19
 literature shipment: yb73 176
 love among Witnesses impresses others: g75 10/22 17, 19-20
 money lost: w74 638; g74 1/8 26; w73 633; g73 11/8 19
 nuns discourage giving Witnesses rooms: yb75 191
 overcome clergy opposition: g74 5/8 20
 prison inmates baptized: w74 639
 television interview: w74 207
 visitors' interest aroused: w74 632; g74 11/8 17; g73 11/8 18
 Witnesses pay parking fees: g72 10/22 22
 Witness returns lost money: g74 11/8 20
first international in one city: yb75 210
handbill distribution: km 5/75 3
lost and found department: w73 633; w71 191; g71 10/22 15-16
opposition: w75 548-51; yb74 237; yb73 62, 126-7, 130; yb72 82-3, 105-6, 109-10; w71 520-1
organized groups: km 9/71 4
rooming accommodations: g73 8/22 16; g72 10/22 21; g71 10/22 14; km 5/71 4
seat saving: km 5/75 3; km 5/73 7; km 6/72 3
trailer cities: yb75 191, 210-12, 214-15
travel suggestions: km 6/72 2-3
volunteer service: w75 630; g75 10/22 18-19; g74 11/8 19-20; g73 11/8 19-20; g72 10/22 21-2
when banned: yb75 11

List by Year

1892, Allegheny, Pa.: yb75 44
1914, South Africa (Durban): yb76 80
1916, Niagara Falls, N.Y.: w72 147
1917, Boston, Mass.: yb75 92
1919, Cedar Point, Ohio: sl 100-1, 146-8, 165-6; yb75 122-4; w74 507-8; w73 398; ka 192-3, 233; w72 85, 198; pm 50-1, 298; kj 64, 301, 330
1922, Cedar Point, Ohio: yb76 91; yb75 130-3, 135-6; w73 398; ka 234-5; w72 85; pm 111-12
 Germany (Leipzig): yb74 91-2
1923, Los Angeles, Calif.: sl 161; yb75 136; ka 264-5
1924, Columbus, Ohio: yb75 136; w72 148; kj 83-5
1925, Indianapolis, Ind.: yb75 137; w74 756
1926, England (London): yb75 137; yb73 110-11; w71 718
1927, Canada (Toronto): yb75 137-8
 Scotland (Glasgow): yb73 111
1928, Detroit, Mich.: yb76 102; yb75 139; w74 764; pm 300
1931, Columbus, Ohio: yb76 108; sl 109-10; yb75 149-52; w73 398; ka 238-40, 266; yb73 112, 218; w72 47; w71 183, 651, 719; kj 172
 Czechoslovakia: yb72 131
 India (Madras): yb76 246
1932, Czechoslovakia: yb72 131
1935, Washington, D.C.: sl 201; yb75 156; ka 267-9; yb73 113; w72 638; pm 78; kj 178
 Zambia: yb72 236-7
1936, Switzerland (Lucerne): yb74 151, 154; yb72 133
1937, Columbus, Ohio: yb75 158
 Czechoslovakia: yb72 133
 France (Paris): yb74 161
1938, England (London): yb75 160-1; yb73 115
1939, New York, N.Y.: yb75 180-1; yb73 118; w71 520
1940, Great Britain: yb73 123
1941, St. Louis, Mo.: yb76 148; yb75 190-3; w74 725; w72 57-8; w71 473-4
1942, New World Theocratic Assemblies, Cleveland, Ohio: yb75 202-3, 218; yb73 61; w71 724, 730
 Klamath Falls, Oreg.: w71 521
 South Africa (Johannesburg): yb76 148
1943, "Call to Action" Assembly: yb75 197
 "Free Nation" Theocratic Assembly: yb73 128
 Brazil: yb73 61
1944, "United Announcers" Theocratic Assembly: yb75 246-7; yb73 129-30; w71 725
 Brazil: yb73 61-2
 Ghana: yb73 165-6
 Great Britain: yb73 128
1945, Argentina: yb72 73-6
 Great Britain: yb73 130-1
1946, Glad Nations Theocratic Assembly, Cleveland, Ohio: yb75 206-7, 210-11; yb72 174
 Brazil: yb73 69
 Czechoslovakia: yb72 138
 Germany (Nuremberg): yb74 215-16
 South Africa (Johannesburg): yb76 164
1947, Czechoslovakia: yb72 138-9
 Ghana: yb73 169
1948, Czechoslovakia: yb72 139
 Germany (Berlin): yb74 222-3
 Germany (Cassel): yb74 218-20
 South Africa (Johannesburg): yb76 166
1949, Argentina: yb72 82-3
 Brazil: yb73 69-70
 Germany (Berlin): yb74 223-4
 Ghana: yb73 174
1950, Theocracy's Increase Assembly, New York, N.Y.: yb75 212-14, 234; w72 478
 Japan: yb73 226, 229-30
1951, "Clean Worship" Assembly, Germany: yb76 43; yb74 236-7
 Japan: yb73 232-3, 254
1952, "Press On to Maturity" District Assembly: yb73 171, 174-8
 South Africa (Johannesburg): yb76 189-90
1953, New World Society Assembly, New York, N.Y.: yb75 214-16, 227
 Argentina: yb72 88-93
 Germany: yb74 237
1954, Japan: yb73 245
1955, "Triumphant Kingdom" Assemblies: yb73 135, 179
 Germany: yb74 237-8
 South Africa (Johannesburg): yb76 191-2
 Zambia: yb72 244
1956, Argentina: yb72 105-6
 Japan: yb73 239-40
 Taiwan: yb72 227
1957, "Life-giving Wisdom" District Assemblies: yb75 227
 Japan: yb73 245-6
 Taiwan: yb72 227-8
1958, Divine Will International Assembly, New York, N.Y.: yb76 45, 192, 197, 252; yb75 216-18, 235, 253; w73 400; yb73 76, 203-4
 Sri Lanka (Ceylon): yb76 252

1959, Awake Ministers District Assemblies: yb73 204
Ghana: yb73 183-4
South Africa (Johannesburg): yb76 193
Zambia: yb72 246
1961, United Worshipers District Assemblies: yb75 220
Germany (Hamburg): yb74 238-9
Zambia: yb72 247
1962, "Courageous Ministers" District Assemblies: yb75 237-8
1963, "Everlasting Good News" Assemblies: yb75 220, 230-1, 235-6; yb73 139, 246; w71 476
Germany: yb74 239
India (New Delhi): yb76 254
Pakistan: yb72 212
Taiwan: yb72 231-2
Zambia: yb72 247-8
1965, "Word of Truth" Assembly: yb73 139
1966, "God's Sons of Liberty" District Assemblies: yb75 233
Nicaragua: yb72 192-3
Zambia: yb72 250
1967, Argentina: yb72 116-21
Brazil: yb73 76-7
Zambia: yb72 251
1968, "Good News for All Nations" District Assemblies: yb75 239-40; yb73 139
Zambia: yb72 252
1969, "Peace on Earth" International Assemblies: yb75 236; yb73 140, 250, 252
England (London): yb76 229
Germany: yb74 249
1970, "Men of Goodwill" District Assemblies: yb75 245-6; yb73 73, 185-7; kj 333
Africa: w71 122-7, 155-8; g71 3/22 24-6; g71 7/8 23
Brazil: g71 4/8 20-3
1971, "Divine Name" District Assemblies: yb75 246-8; yb73 250; w72 54-7, 492-3; yb72 41-2; w71 63, 317-18, 483, 595-605; g71 6/8 32; g71 6/22 32; g71 8/8 29; g71 8/22 29; g71 10/22 12-17
Philippine Republic: g71 6/8 24-6
1972, "Divine Rulership" District Assemblies: yb75 249; yb73 9, 16, 19, 141, 250, 253; g73 2/8 14-15; w72 95, 316-18, 600-7; g72 9/8 29; g72 9/22 29; g72 10/22 17-23
Greenland (Godthåb): yb73 11-12
1973, "Divine Victory" International Assemblies: yb75 236-7, 250-2; w74 206-8, 342, 349; yb74 3; g74 3/8 29; w73 94-5, 348-50, 456, 629-39, 722-5; g73 8/8 29; g73 8/22 13-16; g73 11/8 13-20; km 4/73 3-4; km 9/73 1; km 10/73 1
Brazil: yb75 22
Germany: yb74 249-52
Guatemala: km 1/74 1
Mexico: km 1/74 1
Nigeria: km 3/74 1
South Africa (Johannesburg): yb76 238-9; km 3/74 1
South America: km 3/74 1
1974, "Divine Purpose" District Assemblies: w75 44, 470; yb75 254-5; g75 3/8 16; g75 4/22 26; w74 349-51, 632-9; g74 8/8 29; g74 9/8 29; g74 11/8 17-21
1975, "Divine Sovereignty" District Assemblies: w75 94-5, 349-51, 624-30; g75 10/22 16-23; km 5/75 3
Greece: w75 547-52; g75 9/8 29
(SEE ALSO MEETINGS)

CONVERSATION
clear expression: g74 12/22 13
discussion: g75 3/22 10-12; sg 78-84
everyday speech: w73 535-6; sg 58
listening: g75 3/22 12; sg 79
mealtime: sg 79-80
parents with children: w73 532-3, 535-6; sg 80
persuasion: g75 1/8 9-12
public speaking: sg 144-6
telephone: g75 2/22 30
upbuilding: g75 3/22 11-12; w74 439-40; km 10/74 7; g73 11/22 15; sg 82-4, 189
use of experiences: g75 3/22 11
use of questions: g75 3/22 11

CONVERSION
turning back from sin: w74 602; tp 182-3
world: w74 615; hu 9

COOKING
beef:
ways to serve: g74 10/22 24-6
breakfast: g74 2/8 17-18
camping: g73 8/22 25
can openers: g72 2/8 30
Greek: g75 3/8 9-11
hints: g72 11/8 19-20
hot meals: g74 2/8 17-19
Japanese: g74 8/8 13-16
money-saving meals: g73 8/22 4-5
preserving nutrition: g74 9/22 5-6
rice dishes: g74 8/8 13-14; g73 12/8 24-6
salad: g73 11/8 21-3
soups: g74 2/8 18-19; g74 8/8 13-15
(SEE ALSO FOOD)

COOK ISLANDS
Jehovah's witnesses: yb76 28-9; yb75 28-9; yb74 28-9; yb73 28-9; yb72 38-9
population: yb73 28; yb72 38

COOPERATION
congregation: w72 464-5, 467-8
family: w72 156, 484
God's new order: w72 463

COPPER
African tribes: g73 7/8 25-6
Bible times: g73 7/8 25
coins: g74 3/22 30
demand for: g74 11/22 18-19
discussion: g73 7/8 25-6
mining: g75 1/8 18-20
mountains: pm 222-5
Palestine: w75 112

COPYISTS
Bible copyists: g72 6/22 7

CORAL
g72 10/22 27-8

CORINTH
congregation: w74 210, 466-7; w72 191, 297-8, 434, 439, 563-4; w71 300-1, 351; g71 5/22 9-10
licentiousness: w72 297

CORK
discussion: g71 9/22 24

CORN
blight: g72 10/8 30
use of corncobs: g71 12/22 29
waste in mechanized farming: g75 12/8 30
where grown: g71 11/22 20

CORNELIUS
conversion: po 165-6; w72 692
generosity: w75 318

CORNERSTONE
discussion: pm 187-90
identified: pm 188
(SEE ALSO JESUS CHRIST, TEMPLE)

CORRECTION
overseers: w72 15-18; yb72 20-5

CORRUPTION
consequences: gc 16-17
labor unions: g74 6/8 13-14
police: g75 11/22 6, 8; g72 3/22 3
political: g73 1/8 30; g73 11/8 3-5; w71 299-300

COSMETICS
dangers: g75 9/8 29
use by Christian women: w72 667-8

COSMIC RAYS
g72 4/8 8; g71 5/8 30; g71 11/22 6

COSTA RICA
Jehovah's witnesses: yb76 24-5; yb75 24-5; w74 208; g74 10/8 26; yb74 24-5; w73 134-5; yb73 24-5; g73 3/8 14; yb72 34-5; w71 730-2
population: yb73 24; yb72 34
religion: g71 8/22 13-14

COST OF LIVING
increase: w72 579; g72 10/8 30; g71 10/8 4; g71 11/8 30

COTTAGE MEETINGS
yb75 43-4

COUNCILS
Boston commends Witnesses: w72 542

Council of Elvira
celibacy: g75 5/8 28

Council of Laodicea
saints: g75 1/22 27

Council of Nicaea (Nicene)
Constantine: w75 356; kj 103
spiritism possibility: g71 2/22 26
Trinity: w75 356, 703

Council of Trent
celibacy: g75 5/8 28
confession to priest: g74 11/8 27-8
saints: g75 1/22 27

COUNSEL
application of Bible's: w72 35-6
bartenders: g74 12/8 31
discussion: w75 267-9; w73 503-5
how to give: w75 267-8; w74 92-3, 435-6; w73 145, 503-5
how to receive: w75 268-9; w74 266, 410; km 3/74 3; w73 143, 145, 492; w72 604, 740
Jehovah's counsel: w74 614; hu 7
listening before giving: g74 11/22 21-3
need: w75 267; tp 112-13; or 159-61
overseers: w75 371-2; w74 435-6; km 3/74 3; w73 145, 503-5
servants: w72 15-17; w71 347
Theocratic School: km 5/74 8; sg 98-108
ways to obtain: km 10/74 8

COURAGE
basis: w74 522-3; w73 659
benefits: w74 202
demonstrating: w74 522
examples: w74 743-5
 modern-day Witnesses: yb75 19-20, 181, 183-4, 188-90; yb74 52-6, 113-21, 123-6, 128, 135-6, 142, 155-6, 158-9, 166-8, 174, 181, 186, 188-9; g74 3/8 13-15, 20; w72 70-1

COURSE IN THEOCRATIC MINISTRY (Booklet)
yb75 197

COURTS
Argentina: yb72 109-10
Bethel home case: g71 6/8 26
blood-transfusion cases: w74 166; g74 1/22 29; g74 5/22 21-2; g73 2/22 29; g72 9/22 17-21; g71 3/22 13-14; g71 11/8 6-8
blood transfusions ordered: w75 759; w73 543-4; g71 11/8 7-8
British tax case: yb73 131-3
Christian view of worldly: w73 703-4
conduct in: sg 94-5
divorce because of religion: g73 12/22 30
experiences: w72 534-5
 Witness lawyer: yb75 178; w73 117, 120-2
failure: g74 9/8 30
father's right: g71 9/22 30
flag-salute cases: yb75 169, 172
jury: g75 4/8 30; w73 190-2
lie detector: g72 12/8 30
paying fines: w75 223-4
"plea bargaining": g75 11/22 9-10
security in courtrooms: g75 4/8 29
selective service case: yb73 133-5
suing a fellow Christian: w73 703-4
taxation cases: g74 9/8 15-16
Turkey: g74 2/8 29
unattractive defendants: g75 5/22 29-30
U.S. Supreme Court: yb75 169, 172, 208; g74 9/22 30; g72 7/8 11-12; w71 722; g71 9/8 14-15; g71 9/22 29
(SEE ALSO JUDGE, LAW)

COURTSHIP
w74 8-13, 607; w73 592-4

COURTYARD(S)
court of Gentiles: w72 606-7
Jehovah's spiritual temple: w72 753
symbolic: ka 98, 101, 110-11; w72 721
tabernacle: w72 606-7, 714
temple built by Solomon: w72 606-7
temple built by Zerubbabel: w72 606-7

COVENANTS
Greek word: bi8 1365-6
Hebrew word: bi8 1365-6
seriousness: w72 357-8; kj 121

Abrahamic Covenant
not canceled by Law covenant: po 105
purpose: w74 330
when made: po 104

Christ's Covenant with Followers for a Kingdom
congregation of God: po 161

Kingdom Covenant Made with David
discussion: sl 102-7; po 125-9, 136, 142; ka 54-8, 62
Jesus Christ: w74 68-9; po 126-7, 129, 136, 142; ka 58-63
not fail in 607 B.C.E.: po 128-9, 136, 142

Law Covenant
abolished: po 159; g74 1/8 28; g72 11/22 5-8; w71 745
 allowed Jews to join Christ's "bride": ts 104-6
animals that kill a man: w75 639
basis for release: ts 105
bilateral: po 113-14
"ceremonial law": g75 2/8 27
Christians: g75 2/8 27-8
circumcision: w75 135-6
compensating victims of crime: w75 390
discussion: tp 102-3; w72 681-5
'elementary things': w71 416
fat: w72 190-1
Gentiles: w74 463-4
God's justice: w75 116-17
God's mercy: w75 115-16
illegitimate child: w74 224
inauguration: po 109-10; w72 681-4
incest: w75 73-6
keeping perfectly: po 117-18
meaning of term: po 112
mediator: w72 682-3
national covenant: po 103-10; kj 198-9
not forced on Israel: po 110, 113
not nation of priests: po 114
not prior to Moses: g74 5/8 20
priesthood: po 114-16, 118
purpose: po 105, 109-10; w73 464; w72 127, 489, 559, 681-2
ransom provisions: w75 429-30
replaced: w73 217; w72 685-8
sanitary provisions: w75 133-5
shadow of greater reality: g74 10/8 21-2
stealing: w75 115-16; w74 204-5
Ten Commandments: po 110; g71 1/8 3-4
treatment of offenders: w72 471-2; g72 1/8 14-16
"tutor": w73 581
unsolved murders: g75 11/22 27
validation: po 112-13; w72 681-4
where and when made: po 109-10; w72 489, 681-4; kj 118, 241

New Covenant
"blood of the covenant": w72 685-8; pm 276-7; g72 3/22 28
conscience: w72 559-60
discussion: w73 198-200, 217
inauguration: w72 606; g72 3/22 28; w71 745
mediator: sl 97; po 159-61; w72 166, 685-8; w71 746-7
participants: po 160-1
replaced Law covenant: po 157, 159; ts 106-7; w73 217; w72 559-60, 685-8
superior to Law covenant: w73 287, 415-16
validating: sl 98; po 159-61; w72 685-8
written in heart: w73 415-16

COVETOUSNESS
idolatry: g73 11/22 28
meaning of term: g73 11/22 28

COWARDICE
w74 522-3

CRAFTSMEN
handicrafts: g75 1/8 31
shortage of: g74 2/8 30-1

CREATION
before it existed: po 26
building blocks: g72 3/8 12-15
"chance" favors: g75 3/22 23
clergy viewpoint: g73 10/22 22
dinosaurs: w73 447
earth: g71 1/8 5
evidence of Creator: ml 6-7; g75 4/8 8-9; w74 643, 720; g74 1/22 9-11, 13; g74 2/8 15-16; g74 2/22 15; g74 3/8 23; g74 3/22 14, 26; g74 5/22 22; g74 9/22 29; g74 10/8 8; g74 10/22 30; w73 35-7, 163-4; g73 5/22 6-8, 13; g73 10/22 8-12, 15-21, 24-5; w72 168, 388; pm 147; g72 10/22 4-8; w71 43-6, 152, 325-7, 613; nc 4-5; g71 4/8 6-7; g71 7/22 17-18; g71 8/8 3-7; g71 8/22 11-12; g71 9/8 7
first: po 26-9
learning from: ts 146-7
light's effects: g71 7/8 13-15
man: w74 594; po 33-42; ts 30; w73 77-8; g71 4/8 7
man copies from animal: w75 560
microscopic: g74 1/22 9-13
orderliness: g74 1/22 9-13; w73 35-6; w72 265; g72 10/22 5; g71 8/8 3-7
scientists' attempts to create life: g75 12/8 21
set free from enslavement: w71 431-3
teaching of in schools: g72 10/22 29
variety: ts 145-6
vegetation: w71 152
why scientists do not acknowledge: g75 3/8 31
wisdom shown: g74 1/22 9-13; g74 2/22 15; w73 163-4; g73 4/8 20-3; g73 5/22 5-8, 13; g73 7/8 5-8; w72 388; g72 10/22 4-8; w71 325-7; g71 8/22 10-12
woman: po 46-7

Quotations
back of all this order must be Supreme Being: g71 8/8 5
convinced of God by order: g73 3/8 29

God used very advanced mathematics in constructing universe: g72 10/22 5; g71 8/8 5
natural law reveals superior Intelligence: g71 8/8 4-5
order and design in nature demands a Designer: w71 152
viewing reaches of space confirms belief in Creator: g72 10/22 5
(SEE ALSO EARTH, MAN, UNIVERSE)

CREATION DRAMA
yb74 96-7
(SEE ALSO PHOTO-DRAMA OF CREATION)

CREATIVE DAYS
day three: w73 82-3
day six: po 36, 50-1; w73 82-3
day seven: po 51-3
"morning" begins: po 131-2
sacred sabbath: po 189-90
discussion: po 35-6, 50-3

CREATOR
(SEE JEHOVAH)

CREATURE WORSHIP
Bible view: po 42, 44-5; w72 539-40
dangers: w72 539
examples: yb75 88; ts 60-2; yb74 98, 106-7, 174-5
(SEE ALSO IDOLATRY, WORSHIP)

CREDIT
buying on: g75 4/8 23
Soviet Union: g75 10/22 29
credit cards: g75 5/8 29-30; g71 2/8 29
churches: w75 651
losses: g73 4/8 29

CREEDS
Athanasian: w75 355

CRIME
apathy to crime: g73 3/22 3-4
automobile thefts: g74 9/22 31; g71 9/8 29; g71 11/8 29
bank robbery: g74 7/8 31
burglary: w74 515; g73 4/22 14-15; g72 4/8 3; g72 5/8 30; g72 5/22 30; g72 8/22 29; g72 9/22 30; g72 12/8 31; g71 6/22 30-1
Canada: g75 3/22 29
capital punishment: g75 11/22 10; g74 7/22 27-8; g71 3/8 31
cargo thefts: g75 5/8 30; g71 6/22 31
causes: w75 36-7; g75 1/8 3-5; g75 1/8 29; g75 3/22 29; g75 11/22 6-10; w74 100-1, 262; ts 13-14; g74 3/22 4; g73 4/22 9-14, 30; w72 263-4; g72 1/8 10, 12; g72 12/8 30; g71 5/8 30; g71 10/22 11
children: w75 37; g75 5/22 29; g75 11/22 5; g74 8/22 3-6; g72 6/8 29-30; g71 9/8 29; g71 12/8 30
China: g74 7/8 7-8
churches victims of: g75 2/8 31; g75 12/22 30
church members: g71 6/8 30
college: g73 2/22 29
compensating victims of: w75 390
contributing factors: g74 4/22 30; g73 12/8 3-4, 6, 11-12; g72 7/22 29
cost: w75 35, 163; g75 1/22 31; g73 3/22 5-6; g73 4/22 4; g73 10/8 21; w72 614; g72 1/8 12; g71 5/22 31; g71 10/8 8
discussion: w75 35-8; g75 11/22 3-16; g73 4/22 3-28; g73 10/8 10-11, 21
elimination of: w75 36-8; g75 11/22 15-16; g73 4/22 18-21; g72 1/8 16-17
churches fail: w74 100-1; g74 2/8 29; g73 11/8 30
embezzlement: g75 11/8 29; g74 7/8 31
employee theft: g75 11/8 29-30; g75 11/22 5; tp 18; w72 614; g72 5/22 30; g72 6/22 31; w71 306; g71 7/8 29; g71 10/8 13
experiences:
account of a New York City police officer: g75 11/22 5-10
former criminals become Witnesses: g75 4/22 21-8; yb73 16-17; g73 4/22 24-8; w72 454
Witness youth persuades gunmen to give up: g75 1/22 30
fear of: g75 11/22 3; g74 9/8 4
females: w75 464; g73 9/8 30; g71 8/8 30
fingerprinting: g71 1/22 31
gambling: w72 593; g71 11/8 29-30
government: g73 11/8 3-4; g72 3/8 30-1
Great Britain: w72 614
hitchhiking: g73 2/8 30-1
increase: w75 35; sl 12; g75 1/8 30; g75 3/8 29; g75 3/22 29; g75 5/22 30; g75 6/8 30; g75 10/22 29; g75 11/22 3-5; w74 99, 102, 341, 515; g74 2/22 29-30; g74 5/22 29; g74 8/8 29; g74 11/8 29; g74 11/22 29; tp 17-18; g73 1/8 30-1; g73 3/8 29; g73 3/22 5-7; g73 4/22 3-9, 30; g73 10/8 10-11, 21; g73 11/8 30; g73 12/8 30; w72 263-4, 614; g72 2/8 31; g72 6/22 31; g72 10/22 4; g72 11/8 29-30; g71 2/8 29-30; g71 5/22 30-1; g71 8/8 30; g71 10/8 5, 30; g71 10/22 30; g71 11/8 29
Israel (Republic): w75 263
Japan: g75 4/22 31
Jews and Arabs cooperating in: g75 4/22 29
kidnapping: g75 5/22 6-9; w74 244
labor unions: g74 6/8 13-15
looting: g73 3/8 15
military personnel: g75 3/22 30
murder: w75 36, 263; g75 11/22 3-10; w74 99; g74 6/22 31; g74 9/8 4, 10, 30; g73 3/8 30; g73 4/22 5; w72 480; g72 1/8 15; g72 9/22 4; g72 10/8 30; g72 12/8 30; g71 5/8 31; g71 8/22 29
narcotics: g73 4/22 9, 26-8; g73 12/8 3-4, 6, 11-12; g72 9/8 29; g71 5/8 30
organized: g75 1/22 31; g75 3/8 30; g75 11/22 5
pornography: g75 12/22 29
permissiveness: g75 1/8 3-5
pickpockets: g73 4/22 17; g71 11/8 3
policemen: g75 11/22 5-10; g73 4/22 4, 8, 12
assaults on: g71 2/22 16-18
protection against: g75 11/22 11-16; g74 7/22 17-19; g73 4/22 14-17; g72 1/8 12; g72 5/8 30; g72 9/22 30
punishment: g75 11/22 9-11; g73 4/22 10-12; w72 480; g72 1/8 5-16; g72 4/22 31; g72 5/22 31; g72 8/22 29; g72 9/8 30
rape: g75 2/22 30; g74 3/8 13-16
robbery: g75 11/22 4-5; g73 3/8 29; g73 4/22 8, 15-17; g72 7/8 18; g71 1/22 23; g71 10/8 31; g71 11/8 3
rurals: g75 5/8 30-1
schools: g75 9/8 30; g72 1/22 31
self-defense: g75 9/8 27-8
sex: g73 4/22 15-17; g72 12/8 29; g71 1/22 18; g71 2/22 30; g71 6/8 29; g71 10/22 30
shoplifting: g75 3/22 7; g75 6/22 30; g73 4/22 4, 7-8; g73 12/8 3, 30; g72 3/22 30; g72 11/8 30; g72 12/8 30; g71 9/22 30
number per year: g75 9/8 31
small town: w74 515; g74 7/8 30
statistics: g75 1/8 30; g75 5/22 30; g75 11/22 3-7, 29; w74 99, 102; g74 3/8 30; g74 5/22 29; g74 8/8 29; g73 3/22 5-6; g73 4/22 4-6; g73 9/22 31; g73 11/8 30; w72 614; g72 11/8 29-30; g71 6/8 29; g71 8/8 30; g71 10/8 5; g71 10/22 30
unreported crimes: w74 341; g74 4/22 29-30; g74 6/22 30-1; g73 4/22 6
television: g74 9/8 10-11; g73 3/22 3-4; g71 12/8 30
truck hijackings: g71 6/22 31
vandalism: g75 2/8 29-30; g75 5/22 29; g74 6/8 14-15; g74 8/22 3-6; g73 3/22 5-6
"victimless crime": g75 1/8 3-5
victims: g72 4/22 31; g72 5/22 30
vigilantes: g72 4/22 31
(SEE ALSO JUVENILE DELINQUENCY, MORAL BREAKDOWN)

CRISES
discussion: g75 2/8 3-9
food: g75 2/8 7, 30
what concerns Americans most: g75 7/22 30

CRITICISM
Biblical criticism: g72 2/22 27-8; g72 6/22 6-7; w71 324
of brothers: w74 437-8, 441
of family members: w74 45-6
of organization: w74 437-8
religious: g74 11/22 27-8

CROSS
Constantine's vision: g72 11/8 27-8
crux simplex: bi8 1360-1
discussion: g72 11/8 27-8; bi8 1360-1
early Christians: g72 11/8 27-8
Greek words: g72 11/8 27-8; bi8 1360-1
Jesus' impalement: g74 9/22 27-8; g72 11/8 27-8
origin: g74 9/22 27; g74 10/8 30
Witnesses adjust view of: yb75 148-9
worship: g74 9/22 28; w72 572-3; kj 151-2
(SEE ALSO TORTURE STAKE)

CROWD
dangers of following: g75 2/22 5-7
CROWN
kj 228-9
CRUCIFIXION
(SEE IMPALEMENT)
CRUSADES
results: g72 4/22 12-13
CRUX
crux simplex (illustration): bi8 1361
meaning of word: bi8 1360
CRYSTALS
g71 8/8 30
CUBA
armaments: g74 11/8 6
Communism: w74 707, 710
experience of revolutionary: w74 707, 710-11
Jehovah's witnesses: w71 19, 342-3, 678; g71 10/22 28
Witnesses hijacked to: g74 5/22 13-16
CUNEIFORM
Assyria: w72 314-16
CURIOSITY
g73 8/8 3-4
CURSE
on Cain: w75 665
on ground: w75 664-6; g75 12/22 7; po 63, 71, 82; pm 17-18
CURTAIN
separating Holy from Most Holy: w72 606
CUSTOMS
Christian attitude toward: yb76 219; w74 8-9
dishonesty: g71 7/22 30
Ghana: g71 10/22 5-8
God-displeasing: g74 2/8 27-8
handshaking: g73 1/8 25-6
Japan: g73 2/8 20-3
Moslem women: g75 2/22 29
parental blessing: w73 447-8
respecting others': g71 10/22 5-8
wedding: g72 8/8 20-3; g71 4/8 24-6; g71 10/22 8
(SEE ALSO HOLIDAYS)
CYCLONES
Australia: g75 3/22 24-6; km 3/75 4
East Pakistan: g71 1/8 29
CYPRIAN
ka 378
CYPRUS
early Christians: w71 19
Jehovah's witnesses: yb76 11, 24-5; yb75 24-5; w74 80; yb74 24-5; g74 10/22 13-15; km 10/74 1; yb73 24-5; yb72 34-5; w71 19-20; g71 3/8 14-15
population: yb73 24; yb72 34
story of a guerrilla fighter: g71 3/8 13-15
war: g74 10/22 12-15
CYRUS THE GREAT
Babylon conquered by: w72 745-6; w71 315-16; kj 340, 350
ensign of: po 21-2
foreordained: g74 7/8 28
joint rule with Darius: w72 349-51
prophecy fulfilled by: sl 96; po 21-2, 130; kj 31, 300
prophetic significance: sl 96, 115, 134; kj 300
release of Jews: po 130-1; ts 158-9; w72 746; pm 28-32; w71 649; kj 340-1, 345
CZECHOSLOVAKIA
Catholic church: g73 6/8 31
description: yb72 125-6, 129
doctors:
women: g75 11/22 31
Jehovah's witnesses: yb72 126-41
map: yb72 129
religion: yb72 126
DAHOMEY
description: g71 1/22 24-6
Jehovah's witnesses: yb76 11-12, 24-5; yb75 24-5; yb74 24-5; w73 111-12; yb73 24-5; yb72 34-5; w71 85, 155, 388; g71 1/22 24, 26
polygamy: g74 1/22 21
population: yb73 24; yb72 34
DAILY TEXT
discussion: sg 37
explanation: yb76 261; yb75 261; yb74 261; yb73 261; yb72 261
(SEE ALSO YEARBOOK)
DAMS
problems caused by: g74 7/8 30
DANCING
ballroom: w72 569-70
church programs: g75 6/22 30-1
discussion: w72 567-71
experience:
career given up for Bible truth: g71 12/8 25-6
Israel: w72 567
propriety: w75 504
reflects despair: w75 57
religious: w72 567-8
rock 'n' roll: w72 567-9
DANIEL (Book)
king of the north: g74 2/22 22
king of the south: g74 2/22 22
'reports out of north': w74 334
DANIEL (Prophet)
faith: km 6/75 2; w72 141
service in Babylon: w71 712
son of man: kj 55
vision of God's kingdom established: kj 233-4
DANTE
w73 232-3
DARIUS I
(ALSO CALLED DARIUS II AND HYSTASPIS)
pm 25-6, 30, 227
DARIUS THE MEDE
(ALSO CALLED DARIUS I)
identification: w72 349-51
reign: ts 158
DARKNESS
spiritual: w74 560-5, 571-2
symbolic: w74 755
DARWIN, CHARLES
w75 208; ml 7, 9, 13; g73 10/22 4-6, 15, 17, 23; w71 40, 48, 52-3; g71 7/22 18
DATES
Jewish traditional: w75 63-4
radiocarbon: g72 4/8 5-20
secular, often unreliable: g72 5/8 28

B.C.E.

4026, Adam's creation: w75 63
2370, Floodwaters fall: sl 290-1; pm 284
1943, beginning of 430-year period until Israelites leave Egypt: po 86
1918, Isaac born; beginning 450-year period: po 121-2
1913, beginning of 400-year affliction: po 106
1513, end of 400-year affliction and 430 years after Abraham crossed Euphrates: po 86, 106, 108-9
exodus from Egypt: sl 366; po 108-9; pm 59
1512, tabernacle built: pm 60
1034, Solomon begins temple: kj 27
1027, Solomon completes temple: kj 27
997, Israel divided into two kingdoms: w72 309; pm 291; kj 28, 97-9, 101, 240-1
740, ten-tribe kingdom of Israel destroyed: w72 309; pm 291; kj 30, 203, 243, 245, 251, 261, 322
632, Nineveh's destruction: pm 291
617, first Jewish captives taken to Babylon: w72 723, 763
Zedekiah made king of Judah: w72 102
613, Ezekiel's vision of Jehovah's war chariot: w72 102
612, Ezekiel's vision of unclean worship in Jerusalem's temple: w72 42
607, fall of Jerusalem: ts 158-9; pm 136, 162; g72 5/8 27-8; kj 32, 57, 99, 101, 112-13, 115, 124, 134, 169, 188, 190, 198, 201, 205, 218, 231, 235, 253-4, 261-3, 273, 286, 289, 312, 322, 351-2, 383
539, Babylon overthrown: sl 113; w71 315-16; kj 340, 350
537, Cyrus' decree for release of Jews: ts 158; pm 28; kj 32, 34, 206, 299-300, 340, 345
536, foundation laid for rebuilt temple: pm 33, 55, 92
522, temple building stopped: pm 192
520, temple building resumed: pm 42, 196
515, temple built by Zerubbabel completed: sl 321; pm 60-1
455, Jerusalem's walls rebuilt: sl 321
2, birth of Jesus: ka 63

C.E.

14, Tiberius Caesar began rule: w73 767
29, Jesus became Christ (Messiah) and began ministry: w73 767
33, Jesus' death: w73 767-8
Pentecost, congregation of God begins to be formed: po 158-9, 162; pm 347; kj 52
66, siege of Jerusalem: w74 425-6
70, Jerusalem destroyed by Romans: w74 427-9; pm 330; kj 135, 146, 210, 233, 273, 316
325, Nicene council: sl 209

1054, final break between Greek and Latin churches: kj 69
1529, Martin Luther establishes Protestant movement: kj 69
1534, king of England becomes head of church: kj 69
1877, end of appointed times of nations in 1914 announced: w71 468
1879, first *Watchtower* published: yb75 38; w73 395; w71 756
1881, colporteur work began: yb75 61
Zion's Watch Tower Tract Society organized: w71 757
1884, Zion's Watch Tower Tract Society incorporated: yb75 40; w73 395; w71 757
1886, *Divine Plan of the Ages* published: yb75 40
1896, Society's name changed to Watch Tower Bible and Tract Society: w71 757
1908, Bethel purchased: yb75 51
1912, Photo-Drama of Creation: yb75 59
1914, International Bible Students Association incorporated: w71 757
1916, death of Charles T. Russell: yb75 78-9
1917, *The Finished Mystery* released: yb75 91
1918, Watch Tower Society's officers arrested: yb75 104; pm 370-1
1919, *Golden Age* released: sl 101-2; yb75 123; w74 507; w73 398; kj 64
remnant of spiritual Israel liberated from Babylon the Great: sl 127, 134, 164, 190
service directors appointed: yb73 116
Watch Tower Society's officers released from prison: yb75 116-17; w72 198; kj 63, 329
1920, began printing on Society presses: yb75 128-9
organized field service began: yb75 124
1924, WBBR began to broadcast: yb75 141
1927, first Kingdom Hall built: yb75 167
Society factory at 117 Adams St. began to operate: yb75 145
1931, name "Jehovah's witnesses" adopted: yb75 149-50; w73 398; w72 47, 637, 751; pm 105, 364; kj 66, 320
1932, elimination of elective elders: yb75 165; w71 693
1936, return-visit work begun: w72 50
1937, "other sheep" used as servants: yb75 166
use of phonograph at door began: yb75 158-9
1938, congregation organization made more theocratic: yb75 166; w71 693, 719, 724-5
1939, first *Watchtower* subscription campaign: yb75 162
1940, street distribution of magazines began: yb75 163
1943, Gilead School opened: yb75 200-1; w73 399
Theocratic School began in congregations: yb75 197-8; w73 399
1944, end of 2,300 days: w71 725-8
Society's charter changed: yb75 246-7
1959, Kingdom Ministry School began: yb75 202; w73 399-400
1974, quotations concerning significance of: g75 2/22 29
1975, six thousand years of man's existence: w75 285; yb75 256

Clarification of Beliefs

1921, image of wild beast: w71 723
1925, name of Jehovah: w71 651
Satan hurled down to earth: w71 469
1926, eighth world power: w71 718
1928, pagan origin of Christmas: yb75 147
1929, Ezekiel's chariot vision: w72 154-5; kj 53
1931, man with writer's inkhorn: w72 47; kj 171-2
1935, flag salute: yb75 168-9
great crowd: yb75 156; w72 50, 721, 753; pm 78-9; kj 178, 307
1936, Jesus did not die on cross: yb75 148-9
1938, congregation organization conforms to theocratic rule: yb73 116; w71 693, 719, 724-5; kj 330
1939, neutrality: w71 720
1944, governing body: w71 755
1945, sanctity of blood: yb75 222-3
1950, princes in New Order: yb75 213-14
1951, use of term "religion": yb75 225
1952, need of disfellowshiping: yb75 225-6
1962, "superior authorities": yb75 238
1971, appointed elder arrangement: yb75 247-9
end of 2,300 days: w71 724-8
(SEE ALSO CHRONOLOGY)

DATES OF PROPHETIC SIGNIFICANCE

B.C.E.

997 B.C.E.: kj 97-101
607 B.C.E.: w73 645; pm 162; kj 57, 99, 101, 103, 111-13, 134, 169, 231, 235, 253-4, 261-3, 352
537 B.C.E.: kj 206, 299-300, 316, 322-3, 329
455 B.C.E.: pm 155, 158

C.E.

33 C.E.: pm 347
70 C.E.: kj 135, 146, 210, 233, 273, 351
1914 C.E.: w75 621; sl 41-2, 103-4, 190, 316; og 25; w73 645; ka 186, 259-61; tp 74-6; g73 10/8 17-18; w72 324, 351; pm 331, 368-9; w71 467-8; kj 34, 73, 88, 105, 129, 176, 233-5, 306, 346, 352-4, 356-7
1919 C.E.: sl 127, 134, 164, 190; kj 53, 207-8, 300-1, 311, 317-18, 320, 323, 325, 342, 346-7, 354, 380-1
1938 C.E.: yb75 247
1944 C.E.: yb75 247; w71 724-8
(SEE ALSO CHRONOLOGY)

DATING
w74 10-13, 607; w73 74, 319, 592-4; w72 31; w71 593-5

DAVID
anointed as king: po 124-5
ark of the covenant: po 125
birth: po 123
character: w73 323-4
conscience: w75 210-11
covenant: w74 68; po 125-9, 136, 142; ka 54-8, 62; w71 302; kj 219-20
integrity: w71 524, 527-30
Jerusalem taken: kj 240
prophetic significance: po 125
sat on Jehovah's throne: po 127-8
transgressions: w75 40, 147-8; w74 495; g73 2/8 4; w72 551, 554, 556
why forgiven: w75 40

DAVID, CITY OF
po 123

DAWN CIRCLES
yb75 44

DAY(S)
creative days: po 35-6, 50-3, 131-2, 189-90; g71 8/8 9
day of Jehovah's anger: ts 187-8
"day you eat" (Ge 2:17): po 43-4, 62-3
good day: g71 8/8 8-10
Jews: w73 767; g72 11/22 6-7
Lord's: w74 356-7
prophetic: ts 156
"that day" (Zec 14:6): pm 380-3
"two evenings": w73 175
use of term: sl 293, 299-300; w74 356, 629; po 52-3
(SEE ALSO CREATIVE DAYS)

DAY OF ATONEMENT
(SEE ATONEMENT DAY)

DAY OF JEHOVAH
discussion: sl 318; w74 49-56
preparing for: w75 752-8
proper view: sl 302-9; w74 54-5; w73 543; ka 365-8, 397; g72 10/8 14-15, 17, 21

DAYSTAR
w74 298

DDT
ts 147-8

DEACON(S)
yb75 164; g71 8/22 30

DEAD
acquitted from sin: w74 607
body parts from: w74 684
burial customs: ts 22, 61-2; g72 3/8 29
"come to life" (Re 20:5): w74 95-6
communicating with: ts 74-8; g73 6/8 7, 27-8
condition: g75 10/22 5; ts 60, 90-3, 98, 120-1; g74 6/8 28; w73

230-41, 639-40; g73 6/8 6; g72 3/22 18-19; g72 6/8 6; g72 8/8 27-8; w71 707-8; te 67-70; g71 3/8 27-8; g71 5/22 27
discussion: g75 10/22 3-13; g72 6/8 5-8; w71 707-10; g71 3/8 27-8
fear of: ts 69-73; g74 12/8 26; w73 603-6; te 70
forgotten: ts 23
freezing: ts 22; g71 8/22 30
in God's sight: w74 95-6
misconceptions: g75 10/22 5-7; ts 26-9, 69-72, 74, 88-92, 96; g74 6/8 27-8; w73 208-9, 229-33; g73 6/8 5-8; g72 3/22 18; g72 4/22 8; w71 709-10; g71 3/8 28
mourning for: ts 61-2; g74 12/8 26-8
prayers for: ts 61, 64-9
proper view: w73 604, 606
resurrection hope: g75 10/22 8-13; ts 166-75; g74 6/8 28; g74 12/8 28; g73 6/8 6, 8; g72 6/8 7-8; w71 295-6, 708-10; te 83-6; g71 12/8 28
rites for: ts 61-9; g74 12/8 26-7; w73 603-6
skyscraper tomb: g72 3/8 31
spirit returns to God: ts 47-8, 50-3
spiritually: w74 757-60; w73 208-9
works: g72 7/22 27-8
worship: ts 60-9; w73 603-6; g72 3/22 17-18
(SEE ALSO IMMORTALITY OF THE SOUL, SPIRITISM)

DEAD SEA (Salt Sea)
description: pm 384
Ezekiel's vision: kj 392-6
symbolic: pm 384-6

DEAD SEA SCROLLS
discovery: g72 6/22 6
"Fragment of Mark": g72 12/22 27-8
Isaiah: g72 4/8 5; g72 6/22 6, 8

DEAF (Deaf-Mutes)
Jehovah "appoints": w74 319-20
Keller, Helen: g75 10/22 4
spiritually: w74 319-20
(SEE ALSO HANDICAPPED)

DEATH
abolition: w73 232-49, 606, 624-6; ka 159-60; dy 29-30; g72 6/8 8; w71 276, 708
babies: g74 6/8 21, 23; g72 3/22 30; g72 6/8 5-6; g71 12/8 27-8
belongs to Christians: w71 352
cause: g75 1/8 27; po 55-60, 62-3; ts 34-5, 126; tp 48, 50-2; g72 6/8 7; w71 707; g71 2/22 15; g71 12/8 27
ceremonies at death: ts 22; g74 12/8 26-7
clergy comments on: g71 3/8 28
comfort to survivors: g75 5/8 22-3; g75 10/22 3, 12; g74 12/8 27-8; w73 29; g72 6/8 7-8; w71 708-9; g71 12/8 28
condition: g75 10/22 5-8; ts 60, 90-3, 98, 120-1; g74 6/8 28; w73 133, 230-41, 639-40; g72 3/22 18-19; g72 6/8 6; g72 8/8 27-8; w71 707-8; te 67-70; g71 3/8 27-8; g71 5/22 27
customs at death: ts 69-70
'day of death better': ts 15-16
differing views on: ts 7-16
discussion: g75 10/22 3-13; w73 230, 234-6, 239-43, 246-7, 639-40; g72 6/8 5-8; w71 707-10; g71 3/8 27-8
drug-related: g75 2/22 30
enemy: w73 604-6; w71 707
experiences:
mourners comforted: g74 12/8 28
priest seeks truth about: w75 650
Witnesses' attitude arouses interest: g71 3/8 7
fate: ts 9-12
fear of: w75 53-4, 57; g75 10/22 4, 12; ts 13, 17, 174-5, 190; yb74 182-3; w73 603-6
'hurled into lake of fire': ts 118-19
key of death: w73 239-40, 243
knowledge wasted: ts 25
medical redefining: w74 684
"mercy killing": g74 5/8 27-8
misconceptions: g75 10/22 5-7; ts 9-10, 26-9, 88-92, 96; g74 6/8 27-8; w73 229-33, 603-5; g73 6/8 5-8; g72 3/22 18; g72 4/22 8; w71 709-10; g71 3/8 28
molds life pattern: ts 5-6, 9, 13-16
'never see at all': yb75 2/28; w74 376-7
not physical necessity: w74 375
prolonging: g74 5/8 28
proper view: w73 604, 606
second death: sl 268-9; g75 10/22 13; w74 238-9, 382-3; ts 119-21, 183, 185-6; ka 26, 157-8
slaves to: w74 370
some never die: ts 164-6
spirit returns to God: ts 47-8, 50-3; g72 8/8 27-8
spiritual: w75 286; w74 757-60
statistics: g74 5/22 16; g74 9/8 17-18
suicide: g75 8/8 24-5; g75 9/22 29-30; g75 10/22 31; g72 2/8 23; g72 3/8 30; g72 6/8 30; g72 8/22 30; g72 9/8 31; g72 12/8 29; g71 4/8 30; g71 5/22 30; g71 6/22 5; g71 11/8 30-1
symbolic representation: w74 358-9
symbolic use of word: ts 104
unnatural for man: ts 21-2
"wages" of sin: w74 607
will: g71 12/22 13-16

DEATH VALLEY
description: g71 2/8 7-8

DEBATES
clergy-Blackwell: w73 119-20

DEBORAH
association with Barak: w74 231-2

DEBT, DEBTOR
avoiding: w75 4-5
Christians pay: w71 127-8
effect on banks: g75 6/8 12
New York city: g75 7/8 31
United States: g75 1/22 20; g75 5/22 4; g75 6/8 11; g75 9/22 30
world: g75 6/8 11

DE CECCA, GIOVANNI
yb75 104, 108, 116

DECEPTION
beginning on earth: ts 79-80
religious: ts 63-4, 68, 70, 72-3

DECISION(S)
appealing judicial committee's: or 178-9
making: w74 701; w72 35-6, 589-91
elders: w75 372-4
serving God: w72 754
(SEE ALSO SUPREME COURT DECISIONS)

DECLARATION(S)
against Hitler regime: yb74 133, 136-9, 155
"Divine Name" District Assembly: w72 54-7
"Divine Victory" International Assemblies: yb75 236-7; w73 722-5
"Peace on Earth" International Assemblies: yb75 236
(SEE ALSO RESOLUTIONS)

DECLARING RIGHTEOUS
(SEE JUSTIFICATION)

DEDICATION
after great tribulation: w74 603
baptism: w74 603; g74 3/22 27-8; w73 479-80; w72 601; or 17-18
conscience: w73 31
discussion of Bible usage: w72 683-701
Hebrew word: w72 684
how made: w74 602
Israelites: w72 752
Jesus Christ: w73 274
living up to one's: w72 121-4
meaning of term: w73 636
proper view: w71 554-6
requirements: w74 343
when baptism prevented: w73 479-80
(SEE ALSO BAPTISM)

DEED
document: w73 287-8
Israelite contracts: w73 288

DEER
rabbit (*Pudu*): g75 3/22 14

DELIVERANCE
authority of darkness: w71 428-34
discussion: w72 227-55, 297-308
Jews from Babylon: w72 300-1, 500

DELUGE
(SEE FLOOD [NOACHIAN])

DEMOCRACY
crime threatens: g72 3/8 30-1
decline of: g75 9/8 29
Greece: g75 6/8 25-6
quotation by historian Alexander Tyler: g75 6/22 29-30

DEMONISM
avoiding demonic harassment: w74 715-16
Bible view: w74 715-16; ts 76-8, 87
books on occult: w74 323; g74 2/22 5-6
breaking free: yb76 150; ts 86-8
bush medicine: w73 697-701
discussion: w74 323-8; g74 2/22 3-6; w73 176-81, 186
divination: g75 8/8 3, 5-6; g72 3/8 8-9
drugs: g74 5/8 4-5
evidences of: ts 78, 86, 88
examples:
Bible accounts: g71 5/22 28
Bible truth overcomes demons: w74 328, 396; g74 2/22 3-6; g74 7/22 9; g72 6/8 28; w71 710
fetishism: g75 7/22 24-6; w73 486; g71 7/8 19
modern-day: g75 5/22 30; w74 166, 715-16; g74 2/22 3-6;

g74 11/22 7-10; g72 3/8 8-9; g72 6/8 27-8; w71 710; g71 2/22 25-6; g71 5/8 30; g71 5/22 3-4, 27-8; g71 6/22 30; g71 7/8 16-18; g71 7/22 29; g71 9/8 16-18; g71 9/22 8
extrasensory perception (ESP): w74 323, 326; g74 4/22 27-8
faith a protection against: w75 51-3
hypnotism: g74 9/8 27-8
idols: w74 396; g74 2/22 4-5
Italy: g71 7/8 29-30
magic: g75 7/22 26
meditation: w75 43; g75 11/8 10-11, 29; g74 1/8 19
possession: g75 2/8 11
practices connected with: ts 76, 86
spirit mediums: g75 3/22 27-8; ts 74-8, 86-7
suicide: g75 10/22 31
(SEE ALSO DIVINATION, SPIRITISM)

DEMONS
abyssing: w75 622; sl 319; og 27; w74 6; ka 28-9, 42-4; kj 395
access to heaven: w74 640
activities: w74 21-2; po 78-9; ts 78, 85-8; w73 176-7, 180-1, 186, 699-700; g71 5/22 3-4, 27-8
approach to: w73 176-81, 185-6; g73 6/8 7, 27-8
belief in existence: g74 6/22 30
"believe and shudder": w74 21-2
debased: w74 640
discussion: g72 6/8 27-8
exorcising: w74 323, 326-7, 447; g74 10/22 10
influence on men: g75 4/8 6-7; w74 326-7, 755-7; ts 85-8; g74 2/22 3-6; w73 176-81, 185-6, 484-6, 699-700; g72 6/8 27-8; g71 5/22 3-10; g71 10/8 20-2
judgment: po 77-8
materialization: ts 83-5
not harmed by literal fire: w74 381
not live in fear of: w74 716
origin: w74 21-2; po 71-3, 77-8; ts 83-5; w73 180-1, 484-5; g73 6/8 7-8, 28; w72 427-8, 651-3; g72 6/8 27; g71 5/22 3-4, 28
possession: g75 2/8 11
reality of existence: g74 2/22 4
release from the abyss: ka 149-50, 153
resisting: w74 447; ts 87; g74 10/22 9-10; w73 485-6
Tartarus: po 78; ts 84-5
teachings: w74 755-7
(SEE ALSO ANGELS THAT SINNED, SATAN THE DEVIL, SPIRITISM)

DENMARK
calling at homes: g71 12/22 10-12
greatest "empire": g75 10/8 30
Jehovah's witnesses: yb76 24-5; yb75 15, 24-5; yb74 24-5; yb73 10-12, 24-5; yb72 34-5; g72 3/22 16; g71 3/22 29
moral breakdown: yb73 10-11; g73 4/22 6
population: yb73 24; yb72 34
religion: g75 11/22 30
sex education: g72 1/22 3-9
taxes: g74 2/8 30
tolerance: g71 3/22 29

DEODORANTS
g74 3/8 24-6; g72 2/8 30

DEPENDABILITY
how demonstrated: w74 152-3
value: w72 28-30

DEPRESSION
emotional: g75 4/22 5-6; g74 12/22 3-4; g73 10/8 12; g72 11/22 3-4
financial: g75 3/22 8; g75 7/8 29
overcoming: g74 2/22 11; w72 521-2; yb72 57; w71 261-4
experience: w75 245

DESERTS
ants locate water in: g75 4/8 30
Death Valley: g71 2/8 7-8
farming: ts 135-6; g71 9/22 30
preaching in the Australian outback: w75 677-80
reclaiming: w74 624
reefs below: g74 12/8 31
Sahara: g75 3/8 5; g75 7/22 29
sheep farm: g75 11/22 29
trees used to halt: g75 7/22 29

DESIRABLE THINGS OF THE NATIONS
discussion: pm 75-82, 89-91
identified: w75 394-6; pm 76-9, 174

DESIRE
heart: w71 134
wrong: g71 5/22 10

DESOLATION
Jerusalem (607-537 B.C.E.): ts 158-9; w72 744-6; pm 131-6, 237; g72 5/8 27-8
Jerusalem (70 C.E.): w72 748

DESPAIR
finding freedom from: w75 56-8

DESTRUCTION
everlasting: ts 181-3, 185
symbolic representation: w74 652, 666; ts 111, 115-16
world: w74 664-6, 668; g74 4/8 7-8; tp 37-45
(SEE ALSO ARMAGEDDON, FLOOD [NOACHIAN])

DETERGENTS
g75 8/8 30; g72 9/8 30

DETERIORATION
entropy: g71 7/8 3-4

DETERMINATION
Jehovah's witnesses: w75 85
value: w72 274-6

DETROIT, MICH., CONVENTION (1928)
pm 300

DEVIL
(SEE SATAN THE DEVIL)

DEVIL WORSHIP
g71 5/22 3-10; g71 8/22 15-16, 30

DEVOTION
godly: w75 119-25
"sacred secret" of: w75 286
to Jehovah: w75 380-2

DIAMONDS
discovery: g72 5/8 31
discussion: g74 7/22 24-6
improvement: g72 7/8 29
mining: g74 7/22 25-6

DIANA
goddess: w72 586

DICTATORS
support by Catholic Hierarchy: yb72 134-5, 143, 158; g72 4/22 16-17; g71 12/8 3-4

DID MAN GET HERE BY EVOLUTION OR BY CREATION? (Book)
experiences with: g74 10/22 11; w72 402; km 11/72 6
may be most widespread antievolutionary document (quote): g74 8/8 30
release: yb75 239
use in field service: km 8/75 2

DIET
balanced: g74 2/8 17; g73 8/22 4
effects: w74 167-8; g73 12/22 9; w72 413; g72 1/8 30; g72 6/8 18; g72 7/8 30; g72 12/22 8-11, 19-20; g71 2/22 31; g71 4/8 29; g71 7/8 30; g71 7/22 31; g71 9/22 30; g71 11/22 30-1
food additives: g71 3/8 29
food shortages: g74 9/22 3-7
hot meals: g74 2/8 17-19
old age: g72 1/22 20-2
poor: g73 1/22 4
pregnancy: g72 8/8 23
protein: g74 2/8 17; g74 9/22 4-5; g74 10/22 26; g73 8/22 4
reducing diets: g74 4/22 21-4; g71 9/22 30
unprocessed foods: g74 10/22 30
vegetable: g75 2/8 30
youth: g72 6/8 31
(SEE ALSO FOOD, HEALTH)

DIFFERENCES, SETTLING PERSONAL
(SEE SETTLING PERSONAL DIFFERENCES)

DIFFICULTIES
Christian method of settling: w72 465-7; or 155-9; w71 438
dealing with congregational: or 159-82; yb72 20-3

DIGESTIVE SYSTEM
g71 3/22 16-20

DINOSAURS
g75 6/8 7; w73 447

DISASSOCIATION
(SEE DISFELLOWSHIPING)

DISASTERS
causes: w74 735
cloudburst: g72 7/22 29
crater: g71 7/22 21-2
cyclones: g75 3/22 24-6; g71 1/8 29
droughts: w74 196; g74 3/8 5-7; g74 10/8 3; g71 5/22 31; g71 7/8 29
earthquakes: g75 2/22 29; g75 11/8 30; w74 72-4, 243, 318; g74 5/8 16-19; w73 95-6, 134-5; tp 83; g73 2/8 29; g73 2/22 30; g73 3/8 12-16; g73 6/22 30; g73 10/22 30; yb72 66; g72 6/8 29; w71 298;

g71 3/22 29; g71 4/8 8-11; g71 7/22 21-2
experiences:
aid from Witnesses:
g75 3/22 26; yb75 209-10; g74 6/8 10; g74 7/22 30; g74 12/22 24-6; km 11/74 1; w73 95-6, 134-5; g73 3/8 13-16; g73 6/22 15; yb72 99-100, 179, 225-6, 253; g72 8/8 26; g72 8/22 15-16
fires: g74 4/8 31; g73 1/22 30; g72 2/8 12-16; g72 4/8 29; g71 11/22 3; g71 12/8 14, 16
floods: g74 5/22 7-8, 29; g74 7/8 24-6; g74 12/22 21-6; g73 6/22 14-17; g73 10/22 30; yb73 21; yb72 99-100, 178-9; g72 4/8 29; g72 6/22 30-1; g72 8/8 24-6, 29; w71 298; g71 5/8 29
fumes from mixed cleaners: g75 12/22 30
hurricanes: g74 12/22 21-6; yb72 143; g72 8/22 13-16; w71 611
landslide: g72 8/8 29
looting of victims: g74 6/8 10
not fate: ts 10-12
not retribution for sins: g74 5/22 8
people unite during: w71 298
sea: g72 2/8 12-16; g72 8/8 29
tidal waves: g71 1/8 29
tornadoes: g74 1/8 31; g74 4/22 31; g74 6/8 8-10; g74 7/22 30; yb72 100
typhoon: g71 10/22 29
volcanic eruptions: g75 12/22 4-5; g73 3/22 31; g73 5/22 19-20; yb72 177-8; g71 2/8 20

DISCERNMENT
importance: g73 11/22 14-15

DISCIPLE(S)
discussion: w73 269-73, 277-80
Jesus Christ: w73 6-8, 14, 16, 269-73; w71 438; te 55-8
steps necessary to becoming: w74 601-3
making disciples: w75 177-83; w73 269-73
meaning of term: w74 600; w73 269
proof of being: w72 107
requirements: g75 1/22 23; w73 277-80

DISCIPLINE
animals: g73 1/22 21-2
children: w75 14-15, 156-7; w74 82; g74 4/22 14-15; w73 556-8; w72 740; g72 1/8 29; w71 555-6, 588-9, 592
congregational: w73 145-6; km 5/73 8
how to receive: w74 410; w73 492; w72 740; w71 660-1
meaning of term: w75 14-15; w71 659
need: tp 112-13; g72 1/8 29; w71 659
persecution: sl 144-5
(SEE ALSO CHILD TRAINING)

DISCOURAGEMENT
overcoming: w75 505-8; g75 2/22 3-5; w72 521-2; km 4/72 3; w71 261-4

DISCRIMINATION
employment: w74 388

DISEASE (Also Symptoms and Disorders)
animals: g72 1/8 30; g72 7/8 31; g72 8/22 31; g71 5/8 30; g71 11/8 21-3
body's resistance: g74 10/8 7
causes: w74 167-8; g74 9/8 19-21; g74 11/8 30; g74 11/22 30; g73 12/22 8-9; g72 5/8 29; g71 3/8 6; g71 6/8 9; g71 7/8 31; g71 8/8 29; g71 11/8 21-3; g71 12/8 30
diagnosis errors: g71 6/22 22
discussion: w74 131-4
dogs: g71 11/8 21-3
enduring: w73 476
epidemics: g71 3/8 3-6
extent in world: g74 6/8 30-1
fever: g75 12/8 25-7
germs on money: g75 7/22 31
increase: tp 19-20; g71 3/8 4; g71 10/8 6
nutrition: g74 9/8 22-3
plants: g72 7/22 6-7
prevention: g74 8/22 19; g74 9/8 22-3; g74 12/22 12; g73 1/8 21-2; g72 1/8 30; g72 6/8 17-20; g71 7/22 25; g71 9/22 18-19
prevention of, by Mosaic law: w75 133-5
serums: w74 351-2
sin: w74 134
vaccinations: w74 351
viruses: g73 12/22 8-9; g71 8/8 29
vitamins: g72 8/8 31
why Jehovah permits: ts 59
Witness view of treatment of: w75 415

List by Name
acne: g71 1/8 17-19
asthma: g72 3/8 30
atherosclerosis: g75 7/22 18-19, 21-2
athlete's foot: g75 9/8 7-8; g72 3/22 24
backaches: g75 1/8 30; g73 8/8 23-5
bilharziasis: g73 1/8 20-2
bronchitis: g73 12/22 10
bunions: g72 3/22 24
calluses: g72 3/22 24
cancer: w75 12, 191, 634; g75 5/22 30; g75 9/22 30; g75 10/22 30-1; w74 452; g74 1/8 30; g74 1/22 30; g74 9/8 17-23; g74 12/22 29; tp 20; g73 7/8 15; g73 11/22 29; g73 12/8 7; g72 2/8 29; g71 3/8 30; g71 7/8 30; g71 8/22 31; g71 9/8 30; g71 10/8 11
lung cancer: w75 12; w74 131; g74 5/22 30; g74 9/8 17-18, 20, 23
Chagas' disease: w74 592
cholera: g75 3/22 29-30; w74 131-2; g74 12/22 30; g73 10/22 30; g71 7/22 30; g71 11/22 30
cirrhosis: w74 452; g73 8/8 25; g71 6/22 5
colds: g73 12/22 8-10; g72 9/8 30; g71 1/8 29-30; g71 3/8 30
corns: g72 3/22 23
diabetes: g74 1/22 15-16; g71 11/22 30-1
diarrhea: g73 11/8 12
dysentery: g73 11/8 12
epilepsy: g71 8/8 20-3
esophageal varices: g73 8/8 25
fallen arches: g72 3/22 24
fatigue: g74 2/22 8-11
fungus infections: g75 9/8 7-8
gallstones: g72 2/22 29; g71 5/22 25-6
gingivitis: g72 7/8 21
gonorrhea: g75 5/8 5-8; g74 8/8 30; g72 2/8 17-18; g72 7/22 30; g72 12/8 29; g71 5/8 30; g71 7/8 31; g71 8/22 29
hay fever: g74 1/22 16
headaches: g72 8/8 8-12
heart disease: w75 634; g75 2/22 31; g75 7/22 16-22; g75 10/22 29; g75 12/22 29; w74 131; g74 1/8 31; g74 2/8 29; tp 20; g73 2/22 30; g73 7/8 3; g72 1/8 30; g72 3/22 19; g72 6/8 17; g71 2/22 29; g71 3/8 10; g71 4/22 31; g71 10/8 11
hemophilia: g75 2/22 30
hemorrhoids: g75 1/8 25-6
hepatitis (jaundice): g75 6/8 29; g74 1/8 31; g74 5/22 18-20, 30; g74 6/8 30; g74 6/22 17, 19, 21; g74 10/22 30-1; g72 3/8 30; g72 5/8 21-3; g72 6/22 29; g71 2/8 30-1; g71 4/22 30; g71 5/22 30; g71 6/22 8; g71 7/22 31; g71 12/22 30
herpes-virus: g75 5/8 5, 7-8; w74 424
hoof-and-mouth: g73 7/8 29
hydatidosis: g71 11/8 22
hyperactivity: g72 8/8 31
influenza: w75 634; g73 12/22 10; g72 1/8 30; w71 406; g71 3/8 3-6; g71 10/8 16
ingrown toenails: g72 3/22 23-4
kidney disease: g74 7/8 30
kidney stones: g75 1/22 25-6
leptospirosis: g71 11/8 22
leukemia: g72 9/22 18-20
loose bowels: g73 11/8 12
malaria: g75 8/22 31; w74 132; g74 12/22 30; g73 11/8 30; g71 5/22 30
measles (rubella): w75 191-2
multiple sclerosis: g75 8/8 26; g72 2/22 9-12; g71 4/8 29
nervous breakdown: g74 8/22 16-19
neuroses: g75 4/22 5
paralysis: g75 2/22 12-16
periodontal disease: g72 2/8 30
piles: g75 1/8 25-6
pneumonia: g74 12/22 11-12
polio: w74 133; g71 1/22 15
progeria: g71 2/8 30
pyorrhea: g72 7/8 21-3
rabies: g72 7/8 31
Rh factor: w74 351
river blindness: g74 1/22 30
salmonellosis: g71 12/8 30
schistosomiasis: g74 7/8 30; g73 1/8 20-2; g73 8/8 29
schizophrenia: g72 3/8 29
scurvy: g74 12/22 20
sickle-cell anemia: g72 1/8 30
smallpox: g74 1/22 30; g73 11/8 30; g72 8/22 31; g71 12/22 31
snail fever: g74 7/8 30; g73 1/8 20-2; g73 8/8 29
stroke: g73 11/8 31; g72 3/22 31
syphilis: g75 5/8 6-8; g74 2/8 14; g74 2/22 30; g74 5/22 18; g72 2/8 17-18, 20; g71 5/8 30
toxocariasis: g71 11/8 23
toxoplasmosis: g72 1/8 30
tuberculosis: w74 133
tumors: g74 9/8 18-19

typhoid: w74 132; g72 8/8 29
ulcers: g74 4/22 30; g74 6/8 29
varicose veins: g74 7/22 15
venereal disease: w75 364; g75 5/22 31; g75 7/22 29; w74 131, 319, 424; g74 2/8 14; g74 3/22 31; g74 4/22 30; g74 9/22 30; g74 10/8 29-30; g73 3/8 29; g73 4/22 31; g73 5/8 4; g73 5/22 30; g73 6/8 30; g73 9/22 30-1; w72 219, 339; g72 1/8 29; g72 2/8 17-20; g72 8/22 29; g71 1/8 30; g71 1/22 29; g71 3/22 30; g71 5/8 30; g71 7/8 31; g71 9/8 29; g71 11/8 31; g71 11/22 29; g71 12/8 30
(SEE ALSO HEALTH, MEDICINE)

DISFELLOWSHIPING
aiding disfellowshiped who stop wrong course: w74 467-73
association with disfellowshiped:
showing common courtesy: w74 464-5, 468, 544
balanced view of disfellowshiped: w74 466-73
children: w74 470-1; or 173, 175-6
committee: or 159
confession: w72 437-8; or 165
congregation file: km 2/74 8
disassociation: w72 124; or 171
discussion: w74 460, 463-73; or 170-4
effect on family relationships: w74 470-2
elders' view of disfellowshiped: w74 467-70, 472
extending mercy: or 166-7
greeting disfellowshiped persons: w74 465; km 11/74 4
grounds: w75 287; km 2/74 4, 6; w73 594; km 9/73 8; w72 543
meaning of 'spiritual fellowship': w74 468, 471
prayer for disfellowshiped persons: w71 383-4
proper view of: w74 153
reinstatement: w74 466, 468-9, 472-3; or 176-8
free to preach: km 12/74 4
relatives: or 172-3
reporting wrongdoing to committee: w72 465, 467; or 181
restrictions: or 62, 171-4, 176-7
Scriptural basis: w71 452-3
statistics: w74 466; w73 42; yb72 170-1
status while disfellowshiped: or 174
meetings in private home: km 11/74 4
those continuing in wrongdoing: w74 465-6, 472
those no longer associating: km 2/74 6
unbaptized persons: km 10/75 8; or 174-5
visiting relatives: w74 471-2
when made congregational requirement: yb75 225-6
why God commands: w74 460
worldly courts: w73 703-4
(SEE ALSO JUDICIAL COMMITTEE)

DISGUSTING THING
first century C.E.: w75 274, 741-2; w74 683; ka 298-304; w71 31
twentieth century C.E.: w75 274, 743-4; ka 308-16; w71 31

DISHONESTY
avoiding being cheated: g74 12/8 7
business: w75 291; g75 2/8 30; g74 3/8 27-8; g74 12/8 29; w73 597-8; w72 598; g71 2/8 4-5; g71 6/22 29; g71 7/8 29; g71 8/22 30
Christendom: g72 7/22 20; g72 9/22 29
cost: g75 9/8 31
effects: g74 12/8 3, 5; g73 1/22 28
employee: w75 291, 293; g75 9/8 31; g75 11/8 29-30; g75 11/22 5; w74 341; g74 3/8 28; g72 5/22 30; g72 6/22 31; g72 8/22 29; w71 524-5; g71 4/8 13, 29; g71 10/8 13
examples: w74 582, 585; g74 12/8 5
examples in Bible: w71 426-7; te 151-3
Greek word: w73 470-1
inflation accompanies: g75 2/22 31
prevalence: w75 163; w74 341; g74 10/22 30; g73 1/22 27-8; g71 6/22 30; g71 7/22 30
religion: w75 390
taxicabs: g72 7/8 18-19
youths: w74 245-7
(SEE ALSO MORAL BREAKDOWN)

DISLOYALTY
Bible examples:
"evil slave": w75 110-11
Judas Iscariot: w75 109
discussion: w75 109-11

DISOBEDIENCE
Bible examples:
Adam and Eve: fu 14-16; gc 14-18; ml 15-16; w74 595-6; po 56-9; ts 30-4; tp 48-52; w72 262-3, 426-7; te 39-41
Israelites: w73 586-9; w71 618; nc 14-16
prevalence: w72 261-2

DISPERSION (Diaspora)
w73 582

DISTRESS
cause of: ml 18-20; w73 617-19; dy 16-18; g71 10/8 18-22

DISTRICT ASSEMBLIES
discussion: or 106-7
(SEE ALSO CONVENTIONS)

DISTRICT OVERSEER
beginning of work: yb75 204
duties: or 87-9
experiences: w71 476
number: yb75 258; yb74 255; w71 335
rotation: w71 700

DIVIDED HOUSEHOLD
(SEE FAMILY)

DIVINATION
astrology: g73 11/22 5-7; g71 10/8 10, 21
Babylon: w73 60; kj 224-6
Bible view: w75 52; ts 76-8, 87; g74 2/22 5-6
Buddhists: g74 1/8 18
dreams: g75 1/22 5-6
extrasensory perception (ESP): g74 4/22 27-8
fortune-telling: g75 8/8 3-6
omens: g75 1/22 6
palmistry: g75 2/8 29
practices: ts 76, 87
(SEE ALSO DEMONISM, SPIRITISM)

"DIVINE NAME" DISTRICT ASSEMBLIES (1971)
list of cities: w71 63, 317-18; g71 6/8 32; g71 6/22 32
report: w72 492-3; yb72 41-2; w71 483, 595-605; g71 8/8 29; g71 8/22 29; g71 10/22 12-17
Resolution: w72 54-7; g71 10/22 15
(SEE ALSO CONVENTIONS)

DIVINE PLAN OF THE AGES, THE (Book)
yb75 40; po 9-10; yb74 83-4; w72 146

"DIVINE PURPOSE" DISTRICT ASSEMBLIES (1974)
Canada: w75 44
discussion: yb75 254-5; w74 632-9; g74 11/8 17-21
list of cities: w74 349-51
statistics: w74 633, 639; g74 8/8 29; g74 9/8 29; g74 11/8 17-20
baptism: w75 470
(SEE ALSO CONVENTIONS)

DIVINE RIGHT OF KINGS
kj 304-5

"DIVINE RULERSHIP" DISTRICT ASSEMBLIES (1972)
Austria: g72 10/22 17
experiences: g73 2/8 14-15
Germany: g72 10/22 18
list of cities: w72 95, 316-18
program: w72 600-7
releases: w72 605-6; g72 10/22 20-1
report: yb73 9, 16, 19, 141; w72 600-7; g72 9/8 29; g72 9/22 29; g72 10/22 17-23
Spain: g72 10/22 17-18

"DIVINE SOVEREIGNTY" DISTRICT ASSEMBLIES (1975)
discussion: w75 624-30; g75 10/22 16-23
experiences: g75 10/22 19-23
Greece: w75 547-52
handbill distribution prior to: km 5/75 3
list of cities: w75 95, 349-51
seating: km 5/75 3
statistics: g75 8/22 29; g75 9/8 29; g75 10/22 16-17, 20

"DIVINE VICTORY" INTERNATIONAL ASSEMBLY (1973)
Detroit: w73 456
discussion: yb75 236-7, 250-2; w74 206-8; w73 629-39; g73 11/8 13-20; g73 8/22 13-16
Germany: yb74 249-52
list of cities: w73 94-5; km 4/73 3
releases: yb74 252; w73 638
Resolution: w73 637-8, 722-5
statistics: yb75 22; w74 206,

342, 349; yb74 3; g74 3/8 29; km 1/74 1; km 3/74 1; w73 639, 725; g73 8/8 29; g73 11/8 13, 20; km 9/73 1; km 10/73 1
(SEE ALSO CONVENTIONS)

DIVINE WILL INTERNATIONAL ASSEMBLY (1958)
yb75 216-18, 235, 253

DIVISIONAL CAMPAIGNS
yb75 153-4

DIVORCE
adulterous mate may obtain: w74 671-2
annulment: g74 9/22 13-14
avoiding: w73 695; g73 9/22 26-8
Caesar's laws: w74 671-2
Catholic church: g74 5/8 30; g74 9/22 13-15; w72 597
causes: g75 3/22 9; w74 9, 11; g74 4/22 6-10
clergymen: g75 12/8 30-1
discussion: g73 9/22 26-8; w71 309-10
effects: g75 3/22 30; g74 4/22 4
grounds:
court rules religion not: g73 12/22 30
Scriptural: w74 160, 511-12, 671-2, 703-4; w73 154-5; tp 150; g73 9/22 27; w72 31-2, 766-8
Italy: g74 5/8 30; g74 9/22 13-15
legal fees: g75 3/22 30
minister performs: g74 12/22 30
"no fault": g73 7/22 31
sea gypsies: g75 9/22 15
separation: w75 286-8, 575-6; w74 511
Soviet Union: g73 10/8 11
statistics: w75 483; g74 1/22 31; g74 4/22 3-4; g74 5/22 3; g74 9/8 4; g73 10/8 11; g72 4/8 29; g72 12/8 29; w71 309; g71 4/8 30; g71 4/22 31; g71 11/22 31
when government forbids: tp 151
when husband beats wife: w75 286-8
(SEE ALSO ADULTERY, MARRIAGE)

DNA
"chance" could not form: w74 720
description: g71 2/22 12-13; g71 8/8 6; g71 9/8 5-7

DOCTORS
abortion: w75 248; g71 7/8 30; g71 7/22 19; g71 9/22 30
acupuncture: g72 9/8 12-16
advice on population problems: g75 6/8 30
Africa: g72 3/8 8-11
alcoholism: g74 4/22 29; g74 7/8 31
cardiologists: g74 4/8 31
China: g74 5/22 30
cost of visit: g72 12/8 31
dentists: g74 4/8 31
disregard of patients' rights: w75 759; g74 5/22 17, 21-2; g71 11/8 7-9
experiences:
abortion rejected: g71 1/8 25-6
surgeon accepts truth: w75 265-6
Witness surgeon: g74 3/22 17-23
hypnotism: g74 9/8 27-8
inabilities: w73 185
intolerance: g74 3/22 20-1
irregular practices: g71 2/8 30; g71 3/8 29; g71 8/22 30
lawsuits: g75 5/8 31; g71 3/22 13-14
lengthen dying process: g74 5/8 28
medical literature: g72 1/8 26
mistakes: g74 5/8 28; g73 8/8 31; g71 6/22 22
morals: g74 11/22 30
negligence: g73 2/8 11-12
operating without blood: w75 445; g74 3/22 21; g74 5/22 17-19, 21-2; g74 6/22 17-22; g73 2/8 19, 29; g72 6/8 30; g72 7/8 30-1; g71 3/22 14; g71 6/8 31; g71 11/8 6-7
operation statistics: g71 1/8 31
precautions to avoid transfusions: g74 6/8 23-4; g74 6/22 18-22
prescriptions: g73 12/8 7, 30
recommend blood substitutes: g74 6/22 19, 21
research on human fetus: g73 12/22 27-8
respect for patients' rights: g74 5/22 17, 20-2; g74 6/22 20-1
respect patients' religious convictions: g75 6/8 28-9; g74 3/22 20-1; g71 4/8 30
responsibility: g74 7/8 7
rights of patients: g74 2/8 31; g73 7/8 31
sex with patients: g73 12/8 31
shortage: g73 1/22 31
smoking: g71 2/22 29
suicides: g74 2/8 31
sympathy needed by: g74 3/22 22-3; w73 291; g73 5/8 29
unlicensed: g73 3/22 30
unnecessary surgery: g72 4/8 30; g72 9/8 30-1; g72 10/8 31
warn of transfusion dangers: w75 445; g74 3/22 21; g74 5/22 19; g74 6/22 19, 21
wine recommended: g71 7/22 30
Witness view of: w75 415
wives: g74 7/8 31
women: g75 4/8 31; g75 11/22 31; g74 7/8 31
world's view of: g73 1/22 30-1
(SEE ALSO HOSPITALS, MEDICINE, SURGERY)

DOG
attack dog: g74 7/22 17, 19
biting people: g74 9/8 31
bloodhound: g71 12/8 30
cost: g74 7/22 19; g71 7/8 15
discussion: g71 11/8 21-3
drug detection: g72 2/8 31
greyhound: g75 10/22 31
guard dog: g75 5/22 8; g74 7/22 18-19
help schizophrenics: g74 7/22 31
large dogs: g75 7/8 31
memory: ts 19-20
number in United States: g74 7/22 18; g72 6/8 29
popular dogs: g71 12/8 30
population growth: g71 3/8 29
protection: g74 7/22 17-19
silencer: g72 8/22 30

DOME OF THE ROCK
location: sl 17, 18

DOMESTICS
identified: w75 45-7, 77; ka 341-3

DOMINICA
Jehovah's witnesses: yb76 28-9; yb75 28-9; yb74 26-7; yb73 26-7; yb72 36-7
population: yb73 26; yb72 36

DOMINICAN REPUBLIC
description: yb72 142
Jehovah's witnesses: yb76 24-5; yb75 24-5; yb74 24-5; yb73 24-5; yb72 34-5, 143-71; w71 18-19, 343
persecution: yb72 151-63
population: yb73 24; yb72 34
religion: yb72 142-3
rocking chair: g74 11/8 22
water: g72 1/22 18

DOOR
repairing: g74 7/8 20

DOUBT
dangers: w74 113, 436-8
discussion: w72 387-8
overcoming: w74 113; w72 543

DRAFT
(SEE SELECTIVE SERVICE)

DRAGNET (Illustration)
w75 593, 596, 599-601

DRAGON
fiery-colored (Re 12:3): w75 228-9
meaning of term: w73 447

DRAGONFLY
g71 9/8 21-3

DRAMAS
conventions: yb76 233; yb75 233-4; w73 634, 636-7; g73 11/8 17-18; w72 602; g72 10/22 19-20; w71 600-1; g71 3/22 25
(SEE ALSO PHOTO-DRAMA OF CREATION, PROPHETIC DRAMAS)

DREAMS
Daniel interprets: pm 376; w71 619-20; nc 18-20
discussion: g75 1/22 3-6
divination: g75 1/22 5-6
Freud, Sigmund, view of: g75 1/22 4-5
Nebuchadnezzar: w74 164; po 176; ts 152-3, 156-9; pm 375; w71 619-20; nc 18-19
need for: g75 1/22 3-4
old men (Joe 2:28): w71 32
unpleasant: g75 1/22 4

DRESS
(SEE CLOTHING)

DRINKING
avoiding stumbling others: w75 300-1
Bible view on alcoholic beverages: w73 71-2, 667-70
Christian view: w75 300-2
youths: g75 2/8 16-18

DRIVING
(SEE ACCIDENTS, AUTOMOBILES)

DROUGHT
Africa: g74 3/8 5-7; g74 7/22 4, 6; g74 10/8 3, 5-6; g73 10/8 6
Kenya: g71 5/22 31
Mexico: g71 7/8 29
prediction: g74 12/22 29
United States: g74 7/22 7

DROWNING
discussion: g73 6/22 17-19
mouth-to-mouth resuscitation: g73 7/22 8-12
pools: g73 8/8 31

DRUGS
addiction: ts 13-14; g74 6/22 13; g74 7/22 29; g73 2/8 30; g73 7/8 30; g73 12/8 3-15; w72 339-40, 594-6, 614-15; g72 4/22 31; g72 5/8 30; g72 6/22 31; g72 7/8 30; g72 7/22 30-1; g72 8/22 3-4, 30; g72 9/8 29; g72 9/22 29; g72 11/8 31; w71 247-51; g71 1/8 30-1; g71 1/22 30; g71 2/8 20; g71 3/8 30; g71 3/22 6, 30-1; g71 4/8 16-18; g71 5/8 27-8, 30; g71 5/22 30; g71 6/8 31; g71 6/22 29-30; g71 7/8 30; g71 9/8 29; g71 10/8 7-8, 28, 31; g71 11/22 29; g71 12/8 30; g71 12/22 30
  causes: w72 740
  effect on community: g73 12/8 3-6
Alaska: g73 4/8 30
amphetamines: g74 2/22 8, 10; w73 184-5; g73 12/8 6-7
antibiotics: g72 4/8 30-1; g71 3/22 29; g71 8/22 12; g71 11/22 30; g71 12/8 31
aspirin: g72 2/22 29; g72 10/22 30; g71 1/22 30; g71 5/22 30
barbiturates: g73 12/8 5-7
betel nut: w72 594-6
Bible view: g74 5/8 4-8; w73 176-87, 287, 336-8, 340-3; tp 160-2
cancer: g74 9/8 21-2; g71 3/8 30
children: g75 4/22 30; g75 6/8 30; g74 2/8 5-6; g74 5/8 3-8; g74 12/8 29
cocaine: g75 6/8 29; g73 4/8 30; w72 594-6
coca plant leaves: w72 594-6
cost: g73 9/22 29; g73 12/8 3, 6
dangers: g75 1/22 31; w74 394; g74 5/8 4-6; g74 6/22 13; g74 7/8 30; w73 176-87; tp 160-2; g73 1/22 30; g73 2/22 10; g73 7/22 19; g73 12/8 6-7, 9, 11-13, 15; g72 1/22 29; g72 2/8 23; g72 3/22 31; g72 5/8 30-1; g72 7/22 31; g72 8/22 3-4; g71 2/8 31; g71 3/8 30; g71 4/8 16-18; g71 4/22 30; g71 8/8 31
deaths: g75 2/22 30
dogs: g72 2/8 31
experiences:
  addiction overcome: w75 246; g73 12/8 9, 13-15; g72 3/22 16
  drugs fail to enlighten: g74 3/22 7; g74 11/22 7-8
  peddlers accept Bible truth: g74 4/8 27-8; g73 12/22 26
  users accept Bible truth: g74 5/8 8; g74 10/22 11; g74 11/22 10-12; g73 2/8 15; g73 4/22 26-8; g73 7/22 7; g73 12/8 13-15; g72 3/8 23; g72 3/22 16; g72 9/22 26
family influence: g74 4/22 15; g72 9/22 29
fertility: g73 3/22 30
heroin: g75 2/22 30; g73 12/8 6, 11; w72 596
ineffective: g72 9/8 30; g71 2/8 30-1
LSD: g74 5/8 5, 7-8; g74 11/22 7-8, 10; g73 12/8 6, 11-13; g72 1/22 29; g72 2/22 30; g72 10/22 30; w71 247; g71 4/8 18
marijuana: g75 1/22 31; g75 6/8 30; w74 394; g74 3/8 31; g74 3/22 30; g74 5/8 5-6; g74 10/8 30; g74 12/8 29-30; w73 177-9, 182-3, 186-7; tp 160-1; g73 5/22 30; g73 7/8 30; g73 12/8 6-7; g72 10/8 31
methadone: g74 5/8 30; w73 336-8, 340; g73 9/8 30-1; g72 5/8 30
methaqualone: g73 8/8 30
morphine: w72 596
opium: w72 596
pain-killing: g73 2/22 10
penicillin: g74 12/22 12; w72 387
placebo: g71 11/22 30
poisons: g73 12/8 7
proper use: w73 336-7
public preaching: km 7/73 4
reducing: g74 4/22 22; w73 184; g71 9/22 30
sleep-inducing: g75 3/8 13; g72 2/8 23; g72 10/22 30
spiritism: g74 5/8 4-5; tp 161
thalidomide: g73 6/22 28; g73 12/22 25; g71 2/8 31
tobacco: g74 7/22 30
traffic in: g73 3/22 30; g72 4/22 31; g72 9/8 29
tranquilizers: w75 246; g75 11/8 30; g72 5/8 30-1
use during pregnancy: g74 2/8 14
use for mental illness: g75 4/22 11-12
  (SEE ALSO MEDICINE)

DRUMS
communication: g71 7/8 23

DRUNKENNESS
automobile accidents: g71 4/8 31
babies: g75 7/22 29-30
Bible view: w74 455; w73 71-2, 667-70; tp 158-9; g71 6/22 6-7
death: g74 7/22 31
discussion: g71 6/22 3-8
effects: w74 451-2; w73 667-9; g71 6/22 3-5
elephants: g75 10/22 30
enduring husband's: g72 3/22 15; g71 6/22 8
statistics: g71 6/22 3
youths: g75 2/8 18; g75 9/8 30
  (SEE ALSO ALCOHOLIC BEVERAGES, ALCOHOLISM)

DUBAI
Jehovah's witnesses: yb76 26-7; yb75 26-7; yb74 26-7

DUMAH
meaning of term (Isa 21): w75 31

DUNG
fuel: g75 11/22 30

DUPLESSIS, MAURICE
g75 3/8 18-22, 26

DUST
clouds: g74 3/8 8

DUTIES
Christians: w73 136-46

DYSENTERY
discussion: g73 11/8 12

EAGLE(S)
attacks on lambs: g75 7/22 31
harpy: g75 3/22 15
symbolic: w74 750, 752; ka 336; kj 39-40

EARLY CHRISTIANS
  (SEE CHRISTIANS [EARLY])

EARRINGS
piercing ears for: w74 318-19; g74 6/8 30

EARS
animals: g75 6/8 19-20; g71 5/8 29
creased earlobes: g75 2/22 31
diagram of human ear: g75 6/8 18
figurative: sl 149-50
grasshopper: w75 560
human: g75 6/8 17-20; g73 4/8 21; g71 8/22 10
pierced: w74 318-19; g74 6/8 30; g71 9/22 30
  (SEE ALSO HEARING)

EARTH
ability to recover from abuse: g75 12/22 4-8
acres per person: ts 134-5
area required for world population at one location: g75 4/22 30
Armageddon's effect: g75 8/22 27-8
astronauts' comments on: ml 8; g75 3/8 30; g74 8/22 29; g73 4/22 30; g73 5/22 13
atmosphere: g75 4/8 8; g73 7/8 5-6; g71 4/22 5-6
belts: g72 7/8 29
'burned up': w74 666; ka 27-8
climate: g75 10/8 30
continual phenomenon: g71 2/22 18
creation: w71 43; g71 1/8 5
crust: g74 5/8 16-17
curse on ground: w75 664-6; g75 12/22 7; po 63, 71, 82; pm 17-18
designed for human life: g75 12/22 10; po 35; w73 163-4; g73 7/8 5-7; w72 291-4
distance to moon: g72 10/22 4
effect of Flood: po 76
endures forever: g75 8/22 27-8; w74 4; tp 38-9; w72 658-9
energy from sun: g75 8/22 16
evidence of Creator: g75 4/8 8-9; w71 613; nc 4-5
filling the earth: ts 134-5; g74 6/22 10-11; tp 108-9
food potential: g75 7/22 30; ts 135; g74 10/8 5; tp 109; g72 10/22 5-6; g72 12/22 8-11; g71 11/22 20
God's purpose for: w74 291, 377-8, 660-2, 669; po 35, 40-1, 45, 48-9, 54-5, 61-2, 64, 188, 190; g73 5/22 15; w72 4; pm 9-10, 14-15, 18; g72 9/8 3-4; w71 36-7, 615-17; nc 9-10, 13; g71 8/22 11-12
'hangs upon nothing': w75 133
knowledge of, incomplete: g74 1/22 13
land sinking: g75 10/22 30
man's abuse of: g74 10/8 6, 15-16
'meek inherit': w74 377-8, 662; g71 7/8 27-8
mineral resources: g74 11/22 16
moon affects: g75 3/8 30
motions: g72 10/22 4-5
ownership of: w74 594-9
paradise: g75 12/22 3-12; po 48-9,

g, Awake!; **ka,** God's Kingdom of a Thousand Years; **kj,** "The Nations Shall Know that I Am Jehovah"; **km,** Kingdom Ministry; **or,** Organization; **pm,** Paradise Restored—By Theocracy!; **po,** God's "Eternal Purpose"; **sg,** Theocratic School Guidebook; **sl,** Man's Salvation out of World Distress!; **te,** Listening to the Great Teacher; **tp,** True Peace and Security; **ts,** Is This Life All There Is?; **w,** Watchtower; **yb,** Yearbook. **Complete list on page 6.**

54-5, 61, 64; w71 615-17; te 179-82; nc 9-14; g71 4/22 22-7
perishable: w71 480
population capacity: g75 4/22 30; tp 108
quasimoon: g71 11/22 30
rotation: g71 2/22 18
"ruining" (Re 11:18): g75 12/22 8-11; w72 355; g72 7/8 29; w71 561, 626; g71 4/22 24-5; g71 7/22 29
seismic waves: g74 5/8 16-17
sun's distance: g72 2/8 9
symbolic: sl 297, 305-6; w72 238-40; pm 71-4; w71 479, 512
water: g75 6/8 8; g73 7/8 6-7; w71 350; g71 4/22 8
weight: w71 43, 613; nc 4-5
zone of life: g71 4/22 5
(SEE ALSO CREATION, SOLAR SYSTEM)

EARTHQUAKES
Argentina: yb72 66
atomic tests: g71 9/8 30
Australia: g72 3/8 29
Burma: g75 9/22 31
Canada: g71 7/22 21-2
causes: g74 5/8 16
China: g75 4/22 29
dead bodies thrown out: w75 639-40
deaths since 1914: w74 73, 318; g74 5/8 18-19
deaths since 1968: w75 635; w74 243
discussion: w74 72-4; g74 5/8 16-19
first century (C.E.): w74 73
frequency of: g75 10/22 29
geysers' warning: g71 12/22 29
God's role: g74 5/8 19
"great quaking": g74 5/8 19
Hawaii: g73 6/22 30
Iran: g72 6/8 29; g71 4/8 11
Japan: g75 4/22 29
Mexico: g73 10/22 30; g73 11/22 30
Nicaragua: w75 341-2; w73 95-6, 134-5; g73 2/8 29; g73 3/8 12-16
Pakistan: g75 2/22 29
Peru: w75 634; g75 3/22 26; g71 4/8 11
power exerted: g71 4/8 10
predicting: g75 4/22 29; g75 10/22 29; g74 5/8 17-18; g73 2/22 30; g72 3/8 29; g71 9/22 31
Richter scale: g74 5/8 16-17; g72 12/22 26
sign of last days: g74 5/8 17-18; w72 339
statistics: w75 634-5; w74 73, 243; g74 5/8 18-19; tp 83
survival suggestions: g71 4/8 11
symbolic: g74 5/8 19
Turkey: g75 11/8 30
United States: w71 298; g71 3/22 29; g71 4/8 8-11
various places: w74 74; g74 5/8 18; tp 83
warning: g71 2/22 30-1; g71 12/22 29
(SEE ALSO DISASTERS, LAST DAYS)

EARTHWORM
role in fertilizing soil: g72 10/22 7

EASTER
Ashtoreth (Astarte): g75 4/22 29
eggs: g75 4/22 29
origin: g75 4/22 29; g73 1/8 28

EAST GERMANY
(SEE GERMANY [EAST])

EATING
avoiding stumbling others: w75 300-2
Christian view: w75 300-2
frozen foods: g75 5/8 31
importance: w71 477; te 187-8
overeating: g74 4/22 21-2; g71 2/22 6
self-control: g74 4/22 23
(SEE ALSO DIET, FOOD, HEALTH)

EBED-MELECH
w75 563; w72 140, 634

ECCLESIASTES (Book)
discussion: w73 639-40

ECCLESIASTICS INDICTED (Tract)
yb75 136

ECLIPSE
Moslem belief: g73 8/22 31
solar: g73 8/8 30

ECOLOGY
crisis: g75 12/22 8-9; g73 4/22 29
discussion: g71 1/8 5-8
evidence of Creator: w71 326-7
wetlands: g75 2/8 12-15
(SEE ALSO ENVIRONMENT, POLLUTION)

ECONOMICS
Africa: g74 3/8 8
debt in the United States: g75 6/8 11; g75 6/22 30
debt in world: g75 6/8 11
economists bewildered: g75 1/22 20-1
food: g75 4/8 20-3; w74 341; g74 1/22 6-7; g73 8/22 3-5, 30; g73 11/22 9-11
Great Britain: g74 5/8 9-12
great tribulation: g74 1/22 8
Japan: g74 6/8 25-6
military spending: g75 4/8 29; g75 7/8 30
problems: w75 3-6, 12; g75 1/22 16-21; g75 2/8 6; g75 2/22 29; g75 5/22 3-5; g75 6/8 9-11; g75 6/22 30; g75 7/8 29; w74 102, 248-9, 295, 341, 492, 550-1; g74 1/22 3-8; g74 3/22 4, 29-30; g74 4/8 3-4, 19, 29; g74 6/22 4-7, 29-30; g74 7/22 29; g74 8/8 8-11, 29; g74 8/22 29-30; g74 9/8 29-30; g74 10/8 29-30; g74 11/22 16-20, 30; g74 12/8 10-11; g73 4/22 4, 30; g73 5/8 21-3; g73 10/8 7-10; g73 11/8 29; g73 11/22 8-12; g71 4/8 31; g71 8/22 3-10; g71 10/8 30; g71 10/22 21-4
sale of luxuries: w75 172
stock market: w74 71; g74 2/8 30; g74 8/22 30; g74 11/8 29
theory of supply and demand: g75 1/22 16-19
world trade: g75 11/8 30

Quotations
500-year span of economic history closes: g75 2/22 29
money lust a cause of economic woes: g75 10/22 31
(SEE ALSO INFLATION, MONEY)

ECSTASY
religious: w75 325; g75 5/22 27-8

ECUADOR
army ants: g75 9/22 29
food: g73 1/22 13-14
Jehovah's witnesses: yb76 24-5; yb75 23-5; yb74 24-5; yb73 24-5; yb72 34-5
Mt. Chimborazo: g75 10/8 31
music: g71 9/8 19-20
population: yb73 24; yb72 34
Vilcabamba: g75 3/8 7-8

ECUMENISM
Bible view: g75 11/22 22-4; g74 11/22 27-8
Christendom: g75 11/22 21-2
rewriting history: g74 12/22 17

EDEN
place: w71 539-40

EDOM(ITES)
counterpart: sl 218, 223, 226-8
destruction: sl 223, 225-6, 230-1; kj 314-16
location: w73 751-2
meaning of term: w73 751
opposed God's people: sl 219-25
prophecy against: w75 31-2

EDUCATION
benefits: w72 156-7; g72 9/8 5-6; w71 733-5
Bible times: w75 759
Catholic church: g71 5/22 29; g71 9/22 9-12
college: g75 6/8 29-30; g71 6/8 3-8; g71 6/22 30
"developing nations": g74 4/8 29
discipline: g72 1/8 29
discussion: g74 2/8 3-10
evolution theory: w71 40-2
failure of secular: w75 759; g75 5/8 16-21; g74 2/8 3-7, 30-1; g74 3/22 30; g74 9/22 12; g71 6/8 3-8
God's new order: sl 364-5
importance of home: g73 8/8 31
Japan:
teacher regrets militaristic education: w75 715
Kingdom Ministry School: yb73 75-6, 136-8, 207; yb72 115-16, 190-1, 229-30, 232, 247; g72 1/8 21, 24
mathematics: g71 2/8 9-12
morals: g75 5/8 17, 20
parental guidance: g75 5/8 21; g72 1/22 8-9
principles of teaching: g74 1/8 23-6
science:
knowledge decline: g75 7/22 30
sex, for children: g75 1/8 30; g74 2/8 6, 9; g72 1/22 3-9; g71 1/22 29-30
television: g74 9/8 8, 10
Theocratic School: w74 411; w73 111-12; or 98-100; yb72 256
Watch Tower reading schools: w74 410-11; w73 111-12; yb73 73-4, 159-60, 181-2; yb72 240; w71 12, 157; g71 4/8 22-3
Watch Tower Society's view on schooling: w75 542-4, 759; w71 733-5
(SEE ALSO COLLEGE, SCHOOLS, SEMINARY, STUDY, TEACHING)

EFFICIENCY
thinking ability: g73 1/8 3-8
work methods: w72 483-4

EGGS
food: g73 4/8 23; g72 10/22 31
formation of: g71 1/8 16
ostrich: g72 2/22 16

EGYPT
archaeological finds: g71 11/22 24-6
inscriptions of pharaohs: g75 5/8 29
Aswan Dam: g74 7/8 30
captivity of Israel: po 106-9; w72 38-40; w71 381-2
exodus: w72 40; pm 59-60
childbirth: g72 11/22 14-15
divorce: g74 4/22 4
famine in Joseph's day: w71 381
Hyksos: w71 381-2
medicine: w75 134
Necho: g74 10/22 17
plagues: w74 333; w72 39-40; kj 16-19
religion: g72 4/22 12
standards: g71 9/8 13
Suez Canal: g75 6/22 29; g74 10/22 16-18
world power: w72 38
(SEE ALSO UNITED ARAB REPUBLIC)

EINSTEIN, ALBERT
w75 114; g71 8/8 4-5; g71 10/8 12

EISENHOWER, MRS. IDA
g75 4/22 30

ELAM
place: g73 6/8 31

ELDERS
(SEE OLDER MEN)

ELECTIONS
political: g73 1/8 30

ELECTIVE ELDERS
yb75 164-6; yb73 100, 110, 116

ELECTRICITY
appliances: g74 11/8 30
atomic production: g73 2/22 20-3, 30; g72 9/22 9-12
consumption: g72 8/8 14-15
economical use of: g75 1/8 7-8
fuel cells: g72 8/8 29
fish: g72 8/22 31
home repairs: g74 7/8 18-20
light bulbs: g75 1/8 8; g73 7/22 15
power failure: g74 3/8 17-19; g72 8/8 13
power lines: g72 7/8 29
production: g74 1/8 3-5; g74 4/22 29; g72 1/22 18-19; g72 8/8 15; g72 10/8 26-8; g71 5/8 17-19
public utilities: g72 10/8 26-8
safety hints: g72 11/22 12
sources of: g74 8/22 20-3
windmills: g75 9/22 30

ELECTRONICS
computers: g72 1/22 27-8; g72 6/22 3-4; g71 10/22 30
electron microscope: g72 9/8 29
music: g72 5/22 22
radio: g71 7/8 25-6
transistors: g71 12/8 18-20

ELECTRONS
g73 11/22 23; g72 3/8 12-15

ELEMENTS
carbon: g72 3/8 13
discussion: g72 3/8 12-15
hydrogen: g71 12/22 23
number in creation: g71 7/22 11-12
oxygen: g71 12/22 23

ELEPHANT
g75 10/22 30; g75 11/8 30; g71 5/22 10

ELIHU
speech to Job: w71 363

ELIJAH
ascension to heavens: w74 298
pictures John the Baptist: g75 4/8 28; ts 57-8; w71 239
transfiguration: w74 297-8

ELIJAH WORK
beginning: w71 239

ELIMELECH
name: w72 77
prophetic significance: w72 77, 79-80

ELISHA
healed Naaman's leprosy: w74 402-3
prophetic drama: w74 406-7
qualities: w74 403, 405

ELIZABETH
related to Jesus' mother: w75 222

ELOHIM
discussion: bi8 1352
false gods: bi8 1356-7
Hebrew word: po 36
New World Translation footnote: w73 702
(SEE ALSO JEHOVAH)

EL SALVADOR
illegitimacy: w71 452
Jehovah's witnesses: yb76 12-14, 24-5; yb75 24-5; w74 206; yb74 24-5; w73 134-5; yb73 24-5; g73 3/8 14; yb72 34-5; g72 10/8 24; km 11/72 6
population: yb73 24; yb72 34
war: g72 4/22 14

EMBLEMS
Memorial: w72 166; g72 3/22 27-8

EMBRYO
development: g74 2/8 13-16
living creature: g73 12/22 27-8

EMIGRATION
discussion: g71 12/8 21-3

EMOTIONS
anger: g74 5/22 28; w71 163-4
blushing: g74 3/22 13-14
color: g74 3/22 15
depression: g75 4/22 5-6
effect of organ transplants on: w75 519
effect on physical health: g74 2/22 10-11; g74 5/22 27-8; g74 8/22 17-19; w73 291-2; w72 195-6; g72 8/8 11
emotional ills: g73 9/22 19-20; g71 9/22 23
heart: w71 134
humor: g72 1/8 3-4
kidneys: w75 479-80
moods: w73 522-3
music: w74 301-2; g74 6/22 14
overcoming emotional barriers: g75 1/8 9-12
self-control: w74 12-13
sports: g74 6/22 13
(SEE ALSO MENTAL ILLNESS)

EMPATHY
benefits of exercising: w71 580
demonstrating: g74 11/22 21-3
need of: w74 46; w73 324; g73 1/22 3-4

EMPLOYMENT
absenteeism: w74 453; g74 4/8 30; g74 7/22 29; g73 9/8 8, 31
armed: w73 127-8
attitude toward: w74 151; g74 7/22 29; g74 9/8 4; w73 137, 260-1; g73 7/22 24-6; g73 8/8 30; g73 9/8 8-11; w72 205-9, 269-70, 299; g72 3/22 30; g72 5/8 5; g72 9/22 16; w71 231-2; te 95-8; g71 4/8 12-15; g71 12/8 29
automobile industry: g75 2/8 30
boredom: g72 5/22 31
choosing: g74 2/8 30-1; g73 8/8 8-9; g73 9/8 10-11
Christian conduct: w71 223
college graduates: g71 6/8 7-8
confidential matters: km 7/75 3
conscience: w75 215-16; w73 358-9, 409-11; w72 591-600
dissatisfaction: g73 9/8 8-11
doctors of philosophy (Ph.D): g75 4/8 29-30
employee dishonesty: w75 291, 293; g75 11/8 29-30; g75 11/22 5; g74 9/8 4; g74 11/8 30-1; g73 3/22 31; g73 5/22 29; g73 7/8 9-11; g73 9/8 31; w72 614; g72 5/22 30; g72 6/22 31; g72 8/22 29; w71 306, 524-5; g71 4/8 13, 29; g71 7/8 29; g71 10/8 13
experiences:
changing: w73 358, 409-11
conduct of Witnesses: w75 293; w74 411-12; g74 3/8 28; w73 358-9; w72 381, 510; yb72 241-2; g72 3/8 11
gives up judgeship: w74 655
paralyzed Witness shows trust in Jehovah: w74 702
putting Kingdom interests first: w74 412, 653-5; g73 11/8 19; yb72 79; km 12/72 3-5; w71 680
refusal to paint military or church buildings: yb76 231
refusing military or religious work: w71 533-4; g71 12/22 24
turning down advancement: w74 654-5
Witnesses stop tobacco farming: w74 456
witnessing to workmates: w71 221-2
four-day week: g75 7/22 29
gambling establishments: w72 593-4
Germany: g73 3/22 20-1
giant corporations: g71 2/8 3-6
giving employer full measure: w71 260; g71 4/8 15
growing tobacco: km 2/74 3-6; w73 409-10; w72 595-6
"guest workers": g73 3/22 20-2
holiday activities: w74 741

honesty: w75 293, 698; g74 3/8 27-8
house of prostitution: w72 591-2
"humble" jobs: w75 297-9
income statistics: g74 8/22 30; g72 10/8 30
informal witnessing: w72 400-1
mini-business: g73 8/8 8-11
need for faith: w72 598-9
obtaining: g75 5/8 14-15; g75 7/8 3-6
older persons: g75 4/22 30; g72 11/8 30
part-time: g75 9/22 9-12
sales: g73 8/8 9
self-employment suggestions: g75 8/22 9-11; g75 9/22 11-12; g75 11/8 13
selling tobacco: km 2/74 3-4, 6
stress: g71 11/8 30-1
three-day workweek: g74 11/8 30
unemployment: g75 2/22 4; g75 3/22 7-9; g75 7/8 3-6; g75 11/8 30; g75 12/22 29
  preferred: g75 11/22 30
wages: g74 8/22 30
women: g74 10/8 31; g72 5/22 7; g71 3/22 30
  (SEE ALSO LABOR UNIONS, WORK)

ENAMEL
g72 1/22 12

ENCOURAGEMENT
examples of giving: w73 45-9; w71 374
need of: w71 375
responsibility to give: w71 374-6

ENCYCLICALS
Paul VI, *Sacerdotalis Caelibatus* (Priestly Celibacy): g75 5/8 27

END OF THE WORLD
misconceptions: g72 5/22 30
  (SEE ALSO ARMAGEDDON, TIME OF THE END)

ENDURANCE
aids: w75 542; w74 64, 202-3, 219-20, 249-50, 373, 380, 479; yb74 227-8; w73 40-51; tp 186-90; g73 3/8 25-6; w72 133-9, 145-6, 494-7, 521-32; or 185
examples:
  Bible accounts: w72 140-3, 523-4; g72 12/8 24-5; w71 110-12, 120, 487-8; g71 1/22 27-8
  Jehovah: w73 100-1
  modern-day Witnesses: yb76 207-8; yb75 183-4, 186-90, 208-9; g75 12/22 16-19; w74 56; yb74 54-6, 59-60, 63, 115-26, 163-4, 166-9, 172-4, 180-90, 194, 196-7, 202-4, 208-12, 224, 226-31; w73 761-2, 765; w72 70-1, 143-4, 521, 524-5, 532; yb72 47, 51-4, 58-60, 93-9, 151, 153, 160-2; g72 12/8 10-13, 15-17; w71 114, 117-18, 489-90, 494-5; g71 9/22 27-8
hardships: w75 331-3
hindrances: w73 41-5; w72 144-5
need: km 4/75 1; w74 155; w73 40-5, 80-1, 657; or 182-7; w71 496-7, 584; g71 1/22 27-8; km 11/71 7
preaching: w71 119-20
"to the end" (Mt 24:13): w74 55-6
  (SEE ALSO FAITHFULNESS)

EN-EGLAIM
kj 393-4

ENEMY(IES)
loving: g73 2/22 15
prayer for: g71 1/22 6-7

ENERGY
consumption:
  United States: g75 4/8 30; g75 10/8 7
crisis: g74 1/8 3-8, 29; g74 5/8 9-10; g74 8/22 22-3; g73 10/8 9-10
  oil: g74 8/8 8-11
electricity: g75 1/8 7-8; g73 2/22 20-3; g73 7/22 30; g72 7/8 29; g72 8/8 13-19; g72 10/8 26-8; g71 5/8 17-19
  when fails: g74 3/8 17-19
firewood: g75 11/22 30
food industry: g74 6/8 29
light: g72 10/8 25-8
nuclear: g74 8/22 22
ocean waves: g74 8/8 11
oil: g75 1/22 30
peat: g75 2/8 30
recycling: g75 6/22 29
solar: g74 8/22 20-1
sources: g74 1/8 4-5; g74 8/22 20-3
stars: g75 8/22 31
tidal power: g74 8/22 21; g73 11/8 10-11
trash: g74 4/22 29
water: g74 1/8 4-5; g74 8/22 21
windmills: g75 9/22 30

ENGAGEMENT
avoiding haste: w75 383
breaking: w75 382-4
conduct during: w73 592-4
confessing past immorality: g74 11/8 27
  (SEE ALSO COURTSHIP)

EN-GEDI
kj 393-4

ENGINEERING
aqueducts: g73 1/8 13-15
tunnel: g71 8/22 23

ENGINES
g72 8/8 29-30

ENGLAND
(SEE GREAT BRITAIN)

ENGLISH
development: g71 12/22 20-3
first Bibles: w74 743-4
number speaking: g75 11/8 29
spoken by British: g73 2/8 30
students' ability to use: g75 12/22 30
use of word "billion": g75 1/8 29
words: g75 1/8 29; g71 7/22 10; g71 12/22 20-3

ENOCH (Son of Jared)
prophet: po 68
transferred: po 68-70; w72 650-1; w71 616-17; nc 12
walked with God: po 69

ENOSH
calling on name of Jehovah: po 67-8; w71 648
meaning of name: po 66-7

ENTERTAINMENT
beneficial: w72 403-4; g72 6/22 13-16
Bible games: g72 6/22 14-16
bullfighting: g75 9/8 9-12
Christian view: w75 502-4; w71 280, 311-15
cost: g75 1/8 30
dancing: w75 503-4; w72 567-71; g71 12/8 25-6
experiences:
  actors: w71 532-3
  checker player: w71 280
  Oriental dancer: g71 12/8 25-6
growth industry: g75 3/22 29
hobby: g71 7/8 20-3
'idols': w74 145-6
Japan: g73 2/8 23
motion pictures: g75 1/8 30; g72 1/8 30; w71 606; g71 11/8 29
music: w75 504
oil painting: g74 5/8 21-3
overindulgence: w71 280
playing cards: g75 6/22 27-8
selectivity: w71 314-15
sports: w75 502-3; w74 145-6; g73 2/22 13-15; g71 7/8 10-12; g71 8/8 16-19; g71 9/22 6-8; g71 11/22 29
television: w75 503; g75 6/22 26; g74 9/8 8-11; g73 1/22 31; g72 1/22 29; g72 5/8 29; g71 11/22 21-3; g71 12/8 30
wrong associations: w74 563, 565
  (SEE ALSO SOCIAL GATHERINGS)

ENTHUSIASM
public speaking: g72 9/8 17-20; sg 163-5
teaching: g74 1/8 24

ENTROPY
discussion: g71 7/8 3-4

ENVIRONMENT
chemicals in: g75 10/22 30
cost to clean: g72 10/8 30
crisis: g75 12/22 8-9; w73 583; g73 4/22 29
DDT contamination: ts 148
earth: g72 9/22 29
effects of deforestation: g74 7/8 25-6
Jehovah's witnesses: g74 6/22 11
  (SEE ALSO EARTH, POLLUTION)

ENVY
guarding against: w73 477, 505-7

EPAPHRAS
w73 682, 684

EPHAH
measure of capacity: pm 217
woman inside (Zec 5:7): pm 218-22

EPHRAIM (Tribe)
union with Judah: kj 343-5

EPHRATHAH
name: w72 78

EPICUREANS
w73 70-2, 75, 430; g72 11/22 17-18

EPIDEMICS
cholera: g71 7/22 30
influenza: g71 3/8 3-6
typhoid: g72 8/8 29

EPILEPSY
g71 8/8 20-3

EPISCOPAL CHURCH
church service: w72 509
evolution theory: g74 7/8 22
failure: w73 387
homosexuality: w73 356
ministers: w71 675

problems: g71 3/22 31
pub in church: w74 492
women leaders: g73 6/22 30
(SEE ALSO CHURCH OF ENGLAND)

EQUATORIAL GUINEA
Jehovah's witnesses: yb76 24-5; yb75 24-5; yb74 28-9; yb73 28-9; yb72 38-9
population: yb73 28; yb72 38

"EQUIPPED FOR EVERY GOOD WORK" (Book)
yb75 198

EROS
planet: g75 8/22 14-15

EROSION
beaches: g71 8/22 22

ESAR-HADDON
w75 242; w71 672

ESAU
attitude: sl 219, 224-5; po 94-5; w73 496-8; w72 707
birthright: w73 497-8; w72 438
discussion: w73 496-8
foreknown: po 94; ts 58-9
name: w71 58
not 'forced' to be bad: po 94
prophetic significance: sl 224

ESKIMOS
adaptability: g73 2/8 6-7
experiences: w75 43; g75 2/8 26; w74 142
musk ox: g74 8/22 25-6

ESP
(SEE EXTRASENSORY PERCEPTION)

ESTHER (Queen)
name: w71 175
prophetic drama: w71 172-85

ETERNAL TORMENT
belief admitted to be unbiblical: w75 56
belief in: ts 88-9, 96, 110-11; w73 232-3; w71 646
Bible view: w75 56; g75 10/22 7; w74 382-4; ts 91-4, 98, 114-16, 120-1, 123-4; w73 231-41; g72 3/8 17; w71 627-8
Buddhist view: ts 89-90
Catholic view: w75 56; ts 89, 91
does not reflect God's personality: ts 123-4
not good motivation to serve God: w75 58
results of belief: ts 89-90; yb72 54-5
scriptures misapplied to support:
Luke 16:22, 23: ts 98-102
Revelation 14:10: ts 121-3
Revelation 20:10: ts 117-21
(SEE ALSO HELL, IMMORTALITY OF THE SOUL)

ETHIOPIA
advertising: g75 4/22 29
Falasha sect: g75 7/8 30
famine: g74 3/8 6; g74 7/22 6
church demands money: g74 7/22 30; g74 10/8 17
Jehovah's witnesses: yb76 26-7; yb75 7-8, 26-7; yb74 12-13, 26-7; yb73 26-7; yb72 36-7; w71 680
champion cyclist learns truth: g75 8/8 7-8
population: yb73 26; yb72 36
religion: g71 4/8 30-1

EUNUCH(S)
Ethiopian: w72 691

EUODIA
w75 343-4

EUPHRATES RIVER
garden of Eden: w71 540
symbolic: w74 230-1

EUREKA DRAMA
yb75 60

EUROPE
Common Market: g73 2/8 31
Conference on Security and Cooperation in Europe: g75 9/22 29; g75 11/8 3-7
crime: g75 1/8 30
economy: g74 1/22 4-5; g73 5/8 21-2
Jehovah's witnesses: yb75 14-20; w71 16-18
music: g71 3/22 10
oil: g74 1/8 4-6
railroads: g72 3/8 30
Thirty Years' War: g71 6/22 16-19
(SEE ALSO WORLD WAR I, WORLD WAR II, INDIVIDUAL COUNTRIES BY NAME)

EUSEBIUS PAMPHILUS (of Caesarea)
comment on Christians' flight to Pella: w75 340

EUTHANASIA
(SEE MERCY KILLING)

EVANGELICAL CHURCH
experience:
witnessing to members of: w72 284

EVANGELIST(S)
discussion: w74 335-40
first century: w74 336-7
instilling evangelizing spirit: w74 338-40
worldly: g72 10/8 30

EVANGELIZING
churches: w74 492; g74 11/22 30; g74 12/8 12-15
Lausanne Congress: g74 12/8 12-15
meaning of term: w74 492
true Christians: km 5/75 1; w74 335-40
use of literature: g74 9/22 30
(SEE ALSO MISSIONARIES, PREACHING)

EVE
creation: po 46-7
deceived: po 57-8; w72 178, 426-7; g72 4/8 28
disobedience: fu 14-16; po 56-9; w73 433-5; tp 51-2; w72 649-50; g72 5/22 13; w71 31
not "woman" of Genesis 3:15: ts 126-7
punishment: g73 7/8 27-8
temptation: w73 595
time between Adam's creation and creation of: w75 285, 579

EVERLASTING LIFE
(SEE LIFE EVERLASTING)

EVIL
babes as to: w71 606
demon influence: g75 4/8 6-7
discussion: gc 3-31
effects on people: g73 5/8 3-4; w71 579-80
"evil day": po 18-19
hating bad: w74 153
Jehovah permits: gc 3-21; w74 643-4; g74 4/8 16-17; g74 10/8 14-17; g74 10/22 7-8
"principle of evil": g73 12/8 27-8
returning, to no one: g74 3/8 3-4; g74 5/22 27-8; g72 3/8 11
(SEE ALSO WICKEDNESS)

EVILDOER(S)
paradise: w74 6, 362-3; pm 12-13, 395; w71 255-6

EVIL SLAVE
description: w75 110-11; w74 589-91; ka 357-62
identified: pm 363-4
judgment: pm 364

EVOLUTION
accepted as fact: g74 9/22 17-19, 26
acquired characteristics: g74 9/22 19
"ape-men": g73 10/22 18-21
appreciation for *Awake!*: g73 10/22 5, 28
astronomy: g75 6/22 18
Australia: g72 2/22 24-5
Australopithecus: g73 10/22 19-20; g72 4/22 30; g71 8/8 30
Bible view: g73 10/22 21-3; w72 538; w71 43-6; kj 148-9
Buddhism: g72 2/22 17-18
cells: g73 10/22 9-12; g71 9/8 7
chance: g75 3/22 22-3
chemical evolution: w74 720
child training: g73 10/22 24; w72 111
chimpanzees: g75 6/8 30
chromosomes: g73 10/22 11-13
clergy support: g74 7/8 21-3
Communism: ml 13-14
confusion: g74 4/8 29; g74 12/22 30
criticism of: ml 9-11; w74 720; g74 10/8 30
Darwin: ml 7, 9, 13; g74 9/22 19-20; g73 10/22 4-6, 15, 17, 23; w71 40, 48, 52-3; g71 7/22 18
dating methods: g73 5/8 19
discussion: g74 9/22 17-26; g73 10/22 3-25, 28, 30; w71 40-57
dishonesty: g74 9/22 19-20, 25-6; g73 10/22 6-7
DNA: w74 720
doubts concerning: g75 6/22 18, 30; g74 4/8 29; g73 10/22 3-7, 30
experiences:
evolutionist becomes Witness: g71 4/8 3-7
Witnesses defend Bible truth in school: w75 440, 443-4; g74 5/22 26
eyes: g73 10/22 13-14; w72 388; g71 7/22 18
fish: w75 715; g72 6/8 29
fossils: g75 6/22 30; g75 12/8 30;

g74 4/8 29; g74 9/22 19-22; g74 11/22 30; g73 10/22 17-21; g72 4/22 30
frog: g75 6/8 30
Genesis "kinds": g73 10/22 8-9, 11, 15-18, 21
gorilla: g74 8/8 23
horses: g74 9/22 19-20
human voice disproves: g72 1/22 10
immunity disproves: g71 8/22 11-12
inconsistencies: g74 11/22 30
insects: g74 9/22 20-1
Jehovah's witnesses: g73 10/22 28
language: g72 2/22 25; g71 2/22 7-8; g71 3/8 11-12
Leakey's claims: g73 1/8 30
life in outer space: g75 2/8 29; g73 5/22 3, 6, 11-13
man unique: g71 3/8 11-12
meaning of term: w71 40
missing links: ml 11; g73 10/22 17-21; g71 8/8 30
mutations: g75 3/22 23; g75 6/8 30; g74 9/22 22-4; g73 2/8 6; g73 10/22 12-15; w71 42
natural selection: g75 3/22 23; g74 9/22 23
origin of life: ml 9-10; g74 9/22 20; g73 10/22 9-12; w71 44
plants: g74 9/22 20
prediction: w71 56-7
religious acceptance: g74 7/8 21-3; g73 10/22 22; w71 46-51, 56; kj 148-9, 156
reptiles: g74 9/22 21
resemblance not proof: g74 9/22 25
results: ml 12-14; g73 10/22 3, 23-5; w72 617-18; dn 3-5; w71 54-7, 286
secular education in schools: g74 9/22 17, 26; w73 117-18; g73 10/22 6-7; g72 10/22 29; w71 40-2
space programs: g75 2/8 29; g73 10/22 23-4
spider: g75 5/22 23
spiritism: w71 56
spontaneous generation: g74 9/22 20
"Stone Age": g73 5/8 19-20
time estimates: g73 10/22 8-9
Toynbee's comment on: ml 7
transitional forms: g73 10/22 15-21
trees: w75 715
vertebrates: g74 9/22 21-2
vestigial organs: g74 2/8 16
why believed: g75 1/8 12; g74 9/22 18-19, 26; g73 12/22 30
scientists: g75 3/8 31

Quotations

breeding procedures refute evolution: g73 10/22 16
chemical evolution not true science: w74 720
everything in evolution is very speculative: g71 3/8 11
evolutionists suppress criticism: g73 10/22 6
families appear suddenly: g73 10/22 17-18
high-ranking scientists reject: g73 10/22 5
hypothesis collapses on origin of life: g73 10/22 10
lacks actual mechanism and sheer plausibility: g75 6/22 30
life only from similar life: g73 10/22 17
man's evolution remains mystery: g74 9/22 22
man unique, abyss separates from animals: g73 12/22 30
more illogical than biological: g72 2/8 30
more philosophy than evidence: g74 12/22 30
most mutations harmful: g73 10/22 13
one with three million noughts is odds against chance producing a horse: g75 3/22 23
science failed to prove theory: g72 10/22 29
scientists in direct opposition to theory: g73 10/22 4
theory rejected by many because it conflicts with Bible: w71 45
weakened faith in natural selection: w72 388
wild guesses: g71 12/22 29
(SEE ALSO CREATION)

EXCITEMENT

craving for: g74 6/22 12-14

EXCLUSIVE DEVOTION

Christians tested: w71 116-18
discussion: w75 380-2
required by God: w72 250-1

EXECUTION

escaping divine: w72 51-3; w71 631-3
Saudi Arabia: g75 8/8 30

EXERCISE

body-building: g73 5/22 21-4
massage: g73 9/8 26
physical: g75 2/22 30-1; g75 6/8 31; g75 10/22 30; g74 2/22 11, 31; g74 4/22 23; g74 8/22 7; g74 9/8 23; g73 5/22 31; g73 6/22 27; g73 8/8 23-5; g72 6/8 19-20; g72 8/22 12

EXILE

Assyrian: kj 30, 168, 203
Babylonian: kj 31-2, 94-5, 109-10, 129-30, 137-8, 168, 203-6, 271

EXODUS (from Egypt)

crossing Red Sea: w72 40
date: pm 59

EXORCISM

w74 323, 326-7; g74 10/22 10

EXPERIENCES

(SEE FIELD SERVICE)

EXPERIMENTS

bacteria immunity: g71 8/22 12

EXTEMPORANEOUS SPEAKING

discussion: sg 58-63, 120-1, 145, 162-3

EXTORTION

purgatory: w71 709-10

EXTRASENSORY PERCEPTION (ESP)

g75 2/22 27-8; w74 323, 326; g74 4/22 27-8; g74 7/22 30

EYES

birds: g71 7/22 19
blindness: g74 4/22 30
care: g71 7/22 19
construction: g71 7/22 16-18
contact lenses: g71 11/22 30
discussion: g71 7/22 16-19
eyeglasses: g75 5/22 29; g71 7/22 18-19
farsightedness: g71 7/22 19
first aid for burns: g74 9/22 8
insects: g71 7/22 19; g71 9/8 23
Jehovah: pm 166, 199, 203
nearsightedness: g71 7/22 18-19
optic nerve: g73 4/22 30
plastic cornea: g73 8/8 30
"simple eye": w73 407-8
spiritual blindness: sl 149
symbolic: w73 407-8
transplanting: g73 8/8 30
wisdom shown: w72 388

EZEKIEL (Book)

commentary:
chapter 1: kj 35-54
chapter 2: kj 55-72
chapter 3: kj 73-92
chapter 4: kj 93-109
chapter 5: kj 109-13
chapter 6: kj 115-22
chapter 7: kj 123-41
chapter 8: kj 143-61
chapter 9: kj 162-81
chapter 10: kj 183-93
chapter 11: kj 194-212
chapter 21: kj 214-36
chapter 23: kj 238-64
chapter 24: kj 265-78
chapter 33: kj 279-92
chapter 34: kj 294-311
chapter 36: kj 313-34
chapter 37: kj 336-48
chapter 38: kj 350-68
chapter 39: kj 369-82
chapter 40: kj 383-6
chapter 47: kj 387-98
chapter 48: kj 400-7
Jehovah's name: w72 75, 155
not record of "space visit": w74 273
time and place written: kj 34

EZEKIEL (Prophet)

Bible writer: kj 34
captive in Babylon: kj 36, 95, 142-3, 214
commission from Jehovah: w72 187, 199, 253, 279-80; kj 56-7, 67, 74, 76-7, 88-9, 115-16
muteness: kj 276-7, 287
name: w72 199; kj 70
prophetic scenes enacted: w72 310, 543; kj 95-7, 100, 105-10, 142, 343-4
prophetic significance: w72 155, 188-90, 252-5, 324; kj 53
roll of book eaten: w72 200, 253, 278; kj 71-2, 74-7, 81
son of man: w72 186-7; kj 55
temple vision: w72 585-7; kj 383-92
valley of dry bones: kj 336-43
vision of land division: kj 399-401
visions of God: w72 42-54, 101-4, 152-3, 186, 253, 508-9; kj 37-49, 54, 74, 93, 143-4, 183-6, 210-12
watchman: w73 147; w72 277-9; kj 85-8, 279-81, 285-6
wife: w73 125; kj 272-3

EZRA (Copyist)

writer: w71 571-2

FABRICS

wool: g73 2/8 24-6

FACE

acne: g71 1/8 17-19
artificial parts: g72 6/8 30
peeling: g71 10/22 31

FACTORY (Factories)
Watch Tower
Brooklyn:
 Bible-printing: yb75 218, 220-1
 Concord Street: yb75 129-30
 construction of Adams Street factory: yb75 144-5
 equipment: g75 1/8 14; km 5/75 1
 expansion: yb75 242-3; km 10/74 1; g73 9/22 10
 first printing on own presses: yb75 129
 first rotary press: yb75 128-9
 former Squibb complex: yb75 243
 Myrtle Avenue: yb75 128-9
 new Wood-Hoe press: km 8/74 1
 paper: g73 9/22 10
 press erection: yb75 130
 self-contained: g73 9/22 11
 77 Sands Street: yb75 242
 tours: g75 1/8 17
countries that print: yb75 244-5; w73 538; g73 9/22 11-16
expansion world wide: g73 9/22 10-16
Germany: yb74 97-8, 220-1, 242-6; km 10/74 1
Ghana: yb75 6
number of rotary presses world wide: yb75 245
production in U.S.:
 1975: km 5/75 1
 1974: yb75 245; km 5/75 1; km 1/74 1; km 4/74 1; km 11/74 3
 1973: km 5/75 1; km 5/73 1
 1972: km 5/72 1
 1970: w71 562
 1927: yb75 130
production world wide:
 1975: yb76 23
 1974: yb75 32, 241, 259; g75 1/8 13; km 12/74 1
 1973: w74 30; yb74 255
 1972: yb73 256
 1971: yb72 43-4
 1970: w71 29
South Africa: yb76 186-7, 193, 233-6, 241
Watchtower Farms: yb75 244; km 5/74 1, 4; km 10/74 1; w73 313-14; g73 6/22 21-2; g73 9/22 10
 tours: g75 1/8 17
 (SEE ALSO BETHEL HOME)

FADS
avoiding: w75 499-504; w73 138, 144; w72 475-6
results: g73 11/22 29

FAITH
avoiding shipwreck of one's: w75 505-11
basis: w75 82-6; w74 17-19, 397; w73 438, 685, 691-2; tp 98-9; w71 304; g71 6/8 13-14
benefits: w75 50-4, 302-4; ts 190; g74 9/8 30
Christendom: g74 12/8 14-15
dead: w74 20-2
definition: w74 16
demonstrating: w74 18-26, 31, 378-80, 755, 759, 763; yb74 254-5; w72 121-4, 305-6, 598-9; yb72 218; w71 478; te 190
developing: w74 645-6
discussion: w75 49-53; w74 16-26; tp 180-1; w72 387-8
examining own: w72 302
examples:
 Abraham: w75 281-2; w74 22-3; w71 120-1
 Daniel: g75 6/75 2; w72 141; w71 365
 early Christians: w73 116; tp 92; w72 142-3; g72 12/8 20; w71 488-90
 Elihu: w71 363
 Jeremiah: w72 140; w71 364-5
 Jesus: g72 12/8 24; w71 109-10, 366, 488
 Job: g72 12/8 24-5; w71 112, 487
 Josiah: w71 363-4
 maidservant to Naaman's wife: w74 405
 modern-day Witnesses: w74 572-3; g73 11/8 17; w72 70-1, 381, 397-8, 520-1, 524-5, 531-2; yb72 47, 51-4, 97, 108, 119, 150-3, 156-8, 160-2; g72 6/8 24; g72 12/8 10-17; w71 114, 117-18, 489-90, 494-5, 531-4; g71 8/8 13-15
 Noah: w75 748-9; w74 23-4; tp 93-4
 psalmist (Ps 116): w75 303-4
 Rahab: w74 24-5
 Ruth: w71 92-3
 Sarah: w75 281-2
 Shadrach, Meshach and Abednego: w72 123, 140-1; g72 9/8 7; te 139-42
fight for: yb74 4-5
fruit of the spirit: w71 504
gift of spirit: w71 502
heart: w72 695-6
importance: ka 402-3
in God's existence: w73 35-8
in Jesus' name: w73 102-4, 659-60
lack: w74 344; yb74 254-5
rewarded: w75 302-4; w74 574
strengthening: w74 344; w73 40-51; w72 30, 494-5; or 185; yb72 218; w71 286, 527-30
tested: w71 120-1
weakening influences: w73 41-2, 44-5, 69-75; w72 144-5, 494; g71 9/8 30
why Jehovah requires exercise of: ts 177
"word of faith" (Ro 10:8): w74 17-19

FAITHFUL AND DISCREET SLAVE
channel for spiritual food: w75 45-7, 78-9; ka 342-5; w71 750, 754
discussion: w75 77-9; ka 338-57; or 8-12
"domestics": w75 45-7, 77-9; ka 341-4
"evil slave" (Mt 24:48): w75 110-11; ka 357-62
Gog cannot disincorporate: sl 260-1
governing body: w72 458, 755; or 10-11; w71 81, 758
identified: yb75 88; ka 338-42, 345-7; w72 636; w71 81, 462-3, 750, 758
inspection by Master: ka 349-55
misconception: yb75 88
proper view of: w75 508-9; w74 50
'the master's belongings': ka 353-7; w71 750, 754
when began: w75 46
 (SEE ALSO GOVERNING BODY, REMNANT)

FAITHFULNESS
aids to keeping: w75 90-2; w74 249-50, 373, 479, 523, 532, 534, 538-9; w73 40-51; w72 30, 121-4, 133-9, 145-6, 494-7; or 185; yb72 218; w71 92-4, 112-14, 286
discussion: w75 77-9; w74 528-39
examples:
 Bible accounts: w74 532, 535-7; w72 123, 140-3, 523-4; g72 9/8 7; g72 12/8 24-5; w71 92-4, 110-12, 120, 362-6, 487-8; te 139-42
 modern-day Witnesses: yb76 39-41; yb75 183-4, 186-90, 208-9, 223-4; g75 12/22 16-19; w74 56, 373, 533, 537-8; yb74 52, 54-6, 59-60, 63, 115-26, 149, 163-4, 166-9, 172-4, 180-90, 194, 196-7, 202-4, 208-12, 224, 226-31; yb73 126-30, 217-21; w72 70-1, 143-4, 381, 397-8, 520-1, 524-5, 531-2, 631; yb72 97, 108, 119, 150-3, 156-8, 160-2; g72 6/8 24; g72 12/8 10-13, 15-17; w71 114, 117-18, 489-90, 494-5, 531-4; g71 1/8 25-6; g71 8/8 13-15
how demonstrated: w74 152-3, 529-30, 534, 537-9; w72 305-6; w71 478; te 190
importance: w74 533, 539
in small matters: w74 529-30
Jehovah: w74 528-9, 534-7
modesty: w74 532
motive: w71 92-4
righteousness: w74 534
role ability plays: w74 530-1
 (SEE ALSO ENDURANCE)

FAITH HEALING
 (SEE HEALING)

FALCON
g73 3/8 30

FALKLAND ISLANDS
Jehovah's witnesses: yb72 40-1
population: yb72 40

FALLOUT
 (SEE ATOMIC RADIATION)

FALSE PROPHET
Anglo-American World Power: ka 24; kj 363
destruction: sl 272-3
identified: sl 271

FAMILY
attitude within: w73 478
basis for unity: w74 88-9; w72 131-2, 259-60, 270-1, 287; g72 2/22 5-8; g72 9/22 27-8; km 7/72 3; w71 223, 581
Bible reading: w73 532
 reading aloud: w73 205-7
Bible study: w75 436-7; w74 86-7; g74 2/8 9-10; w73 205-7, 532-3, 559-64; km 2/73 7-8; w72 114-17; km 1/72 7-8; w71 104-7, 532, 556, 585-6; sg 37-8; km 5/71 3-4
breakdown: w74 261-7, 270, 391, 675; g74 4/22 3-5; g74 9/8 4;

g, Awake!; **ka**, God's Kingdom of a Thousand Years; **kj**, "The Nations Shall Know that I Am Jehovah"; **km**, Kingdom Ministry; **or**, Organization; **pm**, Paradise Restored—By Theocracy!; **po**, God's "Eternal Purpose"; **sg**, Theocratic School Guidebook; **sl**, Man's Salvation out of World Distress!; **te**, Listening to the Great Teacher; **tp**, True Peace and Security; **ts**, Is This Life All There Is?; **w**, Watchtower; **yb**, Yearbook. **Complete list on page 6.**

w71 581-2; g71 2/22 30; g71 10/22 10
children: w75 155-7, 434-7; w74 119; g74 4/22 13-16; w73 552-64; w72 259-60, 270-1, 359-65
Christian view of having: g74 6/22 11
communication: w74 89-90, 92-3
companionship of parents with children: w75 156-7; w74 270-1; g74 2/8 10; g74 4/22 15-16; g74 7/22 22-3; w73 523, 559-60, 562; km 7/73 3; sg 80
conduct: w74 45-6
confidential matters: km 7/75 3
congregation spirituality: km 7/72 3
consideration for members: g75 5/22 24-6; w74 45-6, 313-17
cooperation: w74 117-19, 313-17; g74 5/8 13-14; w72 156, 484
cutting expenses: g71 3/8 8-10
discussion: w75 151-8, 433-8; w71 581-6
disfellowshiped members: or 172-3
divided household: w75 437-8; km 8/75 7; w74 314-17; g74 4/22 9; w73 475; tp 176-7; km 2/73 8; or 185-6; km 5/72 4; w71 201-13
drugs: g72 9/22 29
effect of television: g74 9/8 9-10
experiences:
aiding unbelieving mate: w71 211
opposition by relatives: g73 1/22 15-16; w71 533-4, 574-5
overcoming opposition: g73 1/22 15-16; g72 5/22 24; w71 679-80
parents talk to school class: w74 272
training of children: g71 2/22 11
united by truth: w74 317; g74 2/8 11; g74 4/22 16; g74 9/8 7; yb73 228-9, 240-1; w72 455; yb72 246-7; g72 4/8 25; g72 10/8 23-4; km 5/72 4; w71 202, 204-6, 209, 211-12, 376; g71 4/22 23
failure of worldly guidance: g75 10/8 6-7
family merit and family responsibility: w72 543
father's headship: w75 153-4, 433-4; w72 270-1, 445-7; g72 2/22 7-8; g72 9/22 27-8; w71 582-3; g71 9/22 30
father's influence: g72 8/22 29-30
generosity within: g74 12/22 6
Ghana: g71 10/22 7
husband's responsibilities: w75 153-4, 314, 434; w74 117-18; w73 471; tp 175-6; g72 2/22 7-8; g72 5/22 13-14; w71 104
Jehovah's: w74 313
letter writing: sg 88-90
love for other members: w74 439; g73 1/22 3-4; w72 131-2; g72 2/8 3; g72 4/8 4; w71 516, 583-4
mealtime conversation: g74 9/8 10; sg 79-80
meetings: w72 409
need for a sound guide: g75 10/8 3-7
parents' responsibility toward children: w75 155-7, 314, 433-7; w74 81-94; g74 2/8 7-11; g74 4/22 13-16; w73 532-3, 535-6, 553-64; tp 175-7; km 2/73 7-8; w72 109-11; g72 9/22 27-8; w71 170-1, 361-2, 369-72; g71 3/22 7-8
preservation of marriage: w72 131-2
privacy: w74 314
rebellion in, not necessarily father's fault: km 7/75 3
recreation: w74 273; km 7/73 3; w71 314
respect within: w74 90-1
settling difficulties: g74 4/22 5-16; w73 324; km 9/73 8; w71 582-4
tact: sg 73
trust: g72 4/8 4
unity: w74 313-17
violence: g74 11/8 30
wife's responsibilities: w75 154-5, 314, 434, 436; w74 118-19; g74 5/8 14; tp 176; g72 2/22 8; g72 5/22 6-7, 10-11
witnessing to relatives: w74 185-6
(SEE ALSO CHILDREN, MARRIAGE, PARENTS)

FAMINE(S)

physical:
Afghanistan: g73 2/8 29
Africa: g75 2/22 10; g74 3/8 5-8; g74 7/22 4, 6; g74 9/8 30; g73 10/8 6-7
Bangladesh: g75 2/22 9
causes: w75 195-6; g75 1/22 29; w74 196-7; g74 3/8 6-7; g74 7/22 3-7; g74 9/8 30; g74 11/8 29-30; tp 13-15; g73 6/22 6-12; g73 8/22 30
Christian view: w75 196, 634; g75 2/22 8, 11; w74 40, 248-9
coping with: g74 9/22 6-7
discussion: w75 195-6; g75 2/22 7-11; g73 6/22 3-13, 16; g73 10/8 5-7, 21
effects of: g75 2/22 10-11
Ethiopia: g74 7/22 6
India: g75 2/22 9-11; g74 7/22 7; g73 5/8 29; g73 6/22 3-4, 7-9; g72 7/22 3
Iraq: g75 2/22 9
Ireland: g72 7/22 6
Nigeria: g75 2/22 9
predictions for future: g75 3/22 29; w74 195-6, 243; g74 2/8 29; g74 3/22 3; g74 5/8 29; g74 6/22 5-6, 29; g74 7/22 3-7; g74 10/8 29; g74 11/8 10; g74 11/22 29; tp 13-14, 82; g73 6/22 5-6, 16-17; g73 7/8 29; g73 9/22 29; g73 10/8 5-7; g73 11/8 29; g72 7/22 3, 10-12; g71 10/8 7, 28, 30
religion: g74 7/22 29; g73 6/22 8-9
statistics: w74 295; g74 7/22 3-6; g72 7/22 11; g71 10/8 7, 17
symbolic representation: w74 358
technology fails to solve: w74 40, 197; g73 6/22 7, 10

Quotations

by 1985 worldwide famines: tp 14
500 million starving in less developed lands: g74 7/22 5
hungry multiplying twice as fast as well fed: tp 13
in 1973 close to having 50-60 million die: g74 7/22 5
millions on brink of starvation: g74 9/22 3
things much worse than when we wrote *Famine—1975!*: g75 2/22 29
(SEE ALSO FOOD SHORTAGES, LAST DAYS)

FARMING

accidents: g73 8/8 30
beef: w74 196-7; g73 6/22 23-4
commodity market: g75 6/22 12-13
cultivating deserts: w74 624; ts 135-6; g71 9/22 30
discussion: g75 6/22 9-13
earth's potential: ts 135-6; g74 11/8 29-30
fertilizers: g75 3/8 31; g74 5/22 10-11; g74 10/8 31; g72 5/8 30; g72 7/22 7; g71 4/22 12; g71 10/22 29-30; g71 11/22 29-30
giant vegetables: g75 12/22 30
grain production: g75 6/22 9; g74 7/22 3-4, 30
green revolution: g74 6/22 6-7; tp 13-14; g73 2/22 29; g73 5/8 29; g73 5/22 30; g72 7/22 3-13, 29
high-yield grain: g71 3/22 29
income: g74 9/8 29; g73 3/8 30; g73 5/8 30
irrigation: g75 3/8 29; g72 7/22 8; g71 1/22 29
land cost: g75 6/22 10-11; g74 3/8 29
land used for: g74 6/22 10; g74 7/22 7
mixed culture: g71 5/22 17-20
modern: g73 6/22 23-4
number of farms declines: g74 10/8 30
paid not to: g73 5/22 30
percent of population engaged in: g75 6/22 9; w74 197; g74 7/8 29-30; g72 7/22 9
pesticides: g72 5/8 30; g72 8/8 31; g71 4/22 11-12; g71 9/22 29
petroleum shortage: w74 197; g74 1/8 29
problems: g75 6/22 10-11; g74 3/8 7, 29; g73 12/8 29-30
profit incentive: g75 6/22 11-13
rice: g72 7/22 3-4, 7-8
rooftop: g73 11/22 30
seas: g72 5/22 26; g71 11/8 16-19
soil: g71 5/22 17-18
surplus destroyed: g71 12/22 30
United States: g75 6/22 9-13; g74 6/22 29; g73 6/22 16-17; g71 5/22 29
vegetable garden: g74 5/22 9-12
waste in mechanized: g75 12/8 30

FARMS

Watchtower Society's: yb75 244; km 5/75 4; w73 313-15; g73 6/22 20-4
windmills: g75 9/22 30

FAROE ISLANDS

Jehovah's witnesses: yb76 24-5; yb75 24-5; yb74 24-5; yb73 24-5; yb72 34-5
population: yb73 24; yb72 34

FASHIONS

(SEE CLOTHING)

FASTING

discussion: w71 536-8
health benefits: g74 4/22 23
Israel: pm 234-9; w71 536-7

FAT

Law covenant: w72 190-1

FATALISM
dangers of belief: ts 12
discussion: ts 9-12; g74 7/8 27-8
Hindus: ts 9

FATHER
experiences:
pioneering: km 12/72 5-6; w71 339
training of children: g71 2/22 11
failure: g71 1/8 30
importance: g72 8/22 29-30
Jehovah: w74 313, 447-8; w71 583, 633
Jesus Christ: ts 167
responsibility to family: w75 14-15, 433-4; w74 83, 86, 90, 117-18, 122; g74 7/22 22-3; tp 175-6; g72 1/8 4; g72 9/22 27-8; w71 104, 582-3
right of: g71 9/22 30
teaching children about God: g74 2/8 8-10
(SEE ALSO FAMILY, HEADSHIP, HUSBAND)

FATHERLESS BOY
discussion: w74 82-3

FATIGUE
g74 2/22 8-11; g74 3/22 11; g74 8/22 17

FAULT(S)
view of others': w73 323-4

FAULTFINDING
by elders: w74 434-5
end results: w74 591

FAVORITISM
avoiding: w71 448

FEAR
among nations: g74 4/8 6-7
animals: w75 606
causes: g74 3/22 4; g73 4/22 3-4, 6-7
cowardice: w74 522-3
dominates our lives (quote): w75 635
effects: yb74 130; g72 4/8 3
freedom from: w74 754-5
increase: g75 10/22 29; w74 102; g72 9/8 30; g72 10/22 4; g71 2/22 31; g71 10/8 5
love throws, outside: w73 210-11
of crime: g75 11/22 3
of death: ts 13, 17, 174-5, 190
of persecution: w74 219
of the dead: ts 69-73
of torment in hell: w75 58; ts 89-90, 98
overcoming: w74 202-3, 219-20; ts 190

Of God
demonstrating: g72 9/8 28
effects: w74 408
importance: w73 750-1; kj 63-4; g71 9/8 4
Jehovah's anger: w71 357-60
meaning of term: w74 179; w73 491; g72 9/8 28

Of Man
conquering: g71 1/8 27-8
of neighbors: w74 201-3
(SEE ALSO INTEGRITY, OBEDIENCE)

FEARLESSNESS
Jehovah's witnesses: w74 755, 762-3

FEDERAL COMMUNICATIONS COMMISSION
debate between Rutherford and Catholic church: yb75 155

FEDERAL COUNCIL OF CHURCHES
(SEE NATIONAL COUNCIL OF CHURCHES)

FEET
care: g72 3/22 22-4
injuries from stepping on objects: g75 9/8 31
washing: te 27-9

FELLOWSHIP
spiritual: w74 468, 471

FERMENTATION
w75 591-2

FERTILIZERS
chemicals: g75 8/8 14-15; g71 4/22 12
cost: g74 10/8 31
debate over best type: g75 8/8 15; g74 12/22 31
"drip" irrigation: g75 3/8 29
earthworms: g75 8/8 14
need: g72 7/22 7
organic: g73 11/22 20; g71 10/22 29-30
sewage: g75 3/8 31; g72 5/8 30; g71 11/22 29-30
shortage: g74 6/8 29; g74 6/22 29
indifference to problem: g74 10/22 29; g74 12/8 8-9
(SEE ALSO AGRICULTURE)

FESTIVALS
African singer: g74 2/8 24-6
Ching Ming: g72 3/22 17-18
fertility festivals: g75 7/22 11-12
Israel's: po 115, 117
Purim: w71 185
Saturnalia: g73 3/8 7-8

Festival of Booths (Ingathering)
Haggai: pm 53-4
sacrifices: pm 399-400
symbolic: w72 721-2; pm 400-1
time of observance: pm 399

Festival of Unfermented Cakes
firstfruits of barley harvest: w75 603

Festival of Weeks
two wave loaves: w75 601-2

FETISHISM
Bible truth frees from: g75 7/22 26; g74 3/8 21; g71 7/8 19
definition: w74 395
discussion: g75 7/22 24-6
practices: g74 1/22 26

FETUS
research on aborted: g73 6/22 30
unborn child: w73 420; g73 4/8 29-30; g73 12/22 27-8; g71 7/22 19

FEVER
discussion: g75 12/8 25-7

FIELD OVERSEER
congregation report: km 8/73 4
duties: w72 460-1; or 73-6
(SEE ALSO OVERSEERS)

FIELD SERVICE
adaptability: km 12/75 8; w73 270-3; or 115-16; sg 150, 172-5
appearance: km 8/74 8; sg 184-7; g71 7/22 26
appreciating: w73 405-6
attitude of publisher: km 3/75 4; km 7/75 4; w74 60, 124-5, 183-4, 568-9; km 1/74 4; w73 21-2, 56-8; km 11/73 7; w72 726-9; or 130-2; km 4/72 3; km 6/72 3-4; km 9/72 8; w71 214, 218-19, 313, 413-14
balanced view: w74 568-9, 575-6
barrier of fear: km 1/74 3; km 1/73 4
Bible studies: w75 180-1; km 11/73 3-6; or 121-5; km 1/72 8; km 2/72 8; km 7/72 4; km 11/72 5-6; sg 94; km 5/71 4; km 7/71 3
business territory: km 5/73 8; km 6/73 3-4
children: or 130
conduct: km 8/74 8; w73 187-8
discussion: w74 182-8
divisional campaigns: yb75 153-4
effectiveness: km 7/74 4; sg 99; km 8/71 4
elders: km 11/75 3; km 9/74 7
encouraging others to begin: km 1/74 3
endurance: w71 119-20
enthusiasm: w73 460
exposing false teachings: w74 35, 37
friendliness: km 7/74 4
group witnessing: or 119-20; km 6/71 4
house-to-house witnessing: yb76 35-8, 99, 160, 182; w74 241-2; or 114-20
importance: w75 183-4; km 11/75 3; w74 183, 188, 241-2, 332-6, 568-9; w72 423; km 5/71 4
improving: sg 96-9
informal witnessing: w75 40, 318; km 2/75 3-4; w74 185-7, 337-8; km 3/74 4; km 8/74 8; w72 400-3; sg 80-2; km 12/71 4
information marching: yb75 160-1
interested persons search for truth: w75 42
introductions: km 5/74 8; km 6/73 4
inviting new ones: or 128-30
isolated territory: w75 43; g75 2/8 25-6
Jesus set example: w73 21-2, 270-3; or 112-13; w71 78; g71 12/22 9-10
Kingdom News: km 3/75 4; km 3/74 1; km 9/73 1, 7-8
lands: yb76 259; yb75 5, 30, 257; w73 23, 40; w72 27; pm 254; yb72 33; w71 24, 81, 504
language barrier: km 1/74 3-4
legal rights: km 8/71 3-4
letter writing: sg 87-8
literature offers: or 116-17
Bibles: km 6/72 4
magazine distribution: km 6/74 3; or 117-18; km 4/71 4

making more time for: km 8/75 7-8; km 11/75 1, 3
manners: km 7/75 4
meetings for field service: km 8/74 7; km 10/72 8
during circuit overseer's visit: km 12/75 8
methods: yb76 172-3, 215; or 113-26, 131-2
modern beginning: yb75 39-40, 45-6, 85-6, 124-5, 133-4
moral qualifications: or 128-30
not-at-homes: or 118-19; w71 219-20; km 10/71 8
leaving literature: km 6/74 3
objections: w74 3-4; km 6/74 4; w73 548; g72 8/8 7; sg 92-4; km 1/71 4
overcoming apathy: w74 444-6
overcoming obstacles: g75 2/8 24-6; km 4/75 1; w74 537-8
pausing for refreshments: w74 576
phonographs: yb76 111-12, 120, 137, 151; yb75 155-60
prejudgment: km 3/75 4
preparation: sg 39; km 3/71 4; km 7/71 4; km 11/71 7
presentations: km 4/75 2; km 5/75 1; km 7/75 4; km 9/75 8; km 11/75 3; km 12/75 8; km 5/74 1; km 7/74 2; km 10/74 8; km 12/74 1, 4; km 4/73 4; km 6/73 1; km 10/73 8; km 11/73 7; km 12/73 2; km 9/71 2; km 12/71 2
prisons: km 9/75 1
reaching prison inmates: km 4/74 4
proper motive: w74 59-60, 183
purpose: w74 37, 241-2; tp 67; km 11/73 7; w72 277, 280; w71 611
quotas not means of measuring zeal: w75 312
reaching householder's heart: km 7/75 4
reporting: km 7/74 4; km 1/73 4; or 126-8; km 4/71 3
beginning: yb75 124
request not to call anymore: km 6/74 4
return visits: w75 178-80; km 1/75 4; km 3/75 1, 4; km 4/74 4; or 121; km 1/72 8; km 2/72 8; km 8/72 4; w71 220-1
scheduling time for: km 5/75 1
service reports (annual): yb76 22-32, 258-9; w75 23-8; yb75 24-32, 257-8; w74 26-31; yb74 23-32, 254-5; w73 23-8; yb73 23-32, 255-6; w72 22-5, 27, 493; yb72 33-41; w71 23-9
serving where need is greater: km 1/74 4; or 134-5
sincerity: km 7/74 4
sound cars: yb76 135-7; yb75 157-8
stopping to rest: w74 576
street witnessing: yb76 141; km 8/75 8; km 9/75 8; yb75 162-4
tact: km 3/72 4; sg 70-2
telephone: km 7/73 4
temporary pioneers: km 4/75 4
territory coverage: km 1/74 3-4; km 6/74 3; or 73-4, 118-20; km 11/72 8
rurals: km 6/75 3
training new publishers: yb75 227-8; km 5/74 7; w73 531-5
under ban: yb75 18-20; yb74 132-3, 139, 141-3, 155-6, 159; w72 137-8
unfavorable territory: km 1/73 4
use of Bible: km 2/75 4; km 9/75 8; km 12/75 7; km 2/74 8; or 114, 116; yb72 85-6; sg 122-9
use of booklets: km 10/75 1, 8
use of questions: km 4/75 4
war zone: w74 521
witnessing to—
children: km 12/75 8; km 2/73 8
Eskimos: w75 43
"hippies": km 2/73 8
Indians: w75 206
men: km 12/75 8
relatives: km 2/75 3-4; w74 185-6; or 111; km 11/71 8
women: km 12/75 8
working with circuit overseer: km 1/73 3
zeal: w75 311-13

Experiences

actress: g75 5/8 4; w74 605; w73 358
Adventists: g74 5/8 20; yb72 173, 183
agnostic: g71 6/22 21-2
airplane drops literature: w74 141
airplanes: g75 2/8 25-6
ancestor worship: yb73 240-1
apartment house: yb73 39; yb72 101-2
artist: g73 5/8 11
atheist: g74 1/22 21; g71 4/8 3-7
athletes: g75 2/8 29
Australian outback: w75 677-80
Baptists: w73 391; yb73 40; g73 2/22 9-10; w71 551-2
baron: yb74 71-2
black revolutionary: w74 711-14
blind ones learn truth: w74 411; w73 468
blind Witnesses: g72 2/22 20; g71 12/22 4
body builder: g73 5/22 21-4
bookstore: yb74 49-50
boxer: g74 4/8 27
Buddhists: w75 43; yb74 53-4; w73 467-8; g73 7/22 23
bus group: yb72 63-4
calling at every home: w74 142
Catholic opposition: yb73 47, 51-2; w72 148-50, 282-5
Catholic priests: w74 342; yb74 18-19; g74 5/8 20; yb73 39-40; g73 5/22 23-4
Catholics accept truth: yb76 9-10, 12; w75 391-2; g75 3/8 28; g75 11/8 21-3; w74 38, 343, 521, 746-7; yb74 18-19, 21; g74 1/22 21; g74 2/8 11; g74 2/22 7; g74 5/8 20; g74 12/22 10; w73 391-2, 551; w72 285; yb72 62, 102, 203-4; g72 10/8 23; w71 221-2; g71 6/22 20-1
child insists on quitting church: yb74 248
children seek truth: w73 318, 734-5
church members quit to become Witnesses: yb74 37, 41-2, 248; g74 3/8 22
clergymen: w75 478, 650; w74 411; yb74 37, 41-2; g74 3/8 22; g74 5/8 20; w73 392, 509-10; yb72 48, 194; g71 7/22 20
common-law marriage rejected: w73 487
commune dwellers: w75 325-6
Communists accept truth: w75 247; g73 2/22 24; w72 71, 281-2
conscience motivates: w73 357-9
deaconess: w73 628
demon influence: w74 328; g74 2/22 4-6; g74 7/22 9; g74 11/22 7-12; g72 6/8 27-8; w71 709; g71 9/22 8
difficulties endured: yb72 47, 51-4, 58-60, 97-9
disgusted with religion: w73 626-7; g73 6/8 26
divine support: yb72 53-4, 103
doctors: w75 206, 265-6; w74 365-6; g74 5/8 26
drug pushers: g74 4/8 28; g74 10/8 26-7; g73 12/22 26
drug users: w75 246, 325-6; w74 342; g74 5/8 8; g74 10/22 11; g74 11/22 10-12; g73 2/8 15; g73 4/22 26-8; g73 7/22 7; g73 12/8 9-15; g72 3/8 23; g72 3/22 16; g72 9/22 26
drunkard: g74 11/22 26; g73 8/22 6-7
effect of kindness: w75 127
effect of one magazine: yb74 70; g73 9/22 14; km 10/73 1, 8
entertainers: w74 142, 605; g74 3/8 21-2; g74 9/8 7; w71 532-3
evolution: w75 440, 443-4; g71 4/8 3-7
Evolution book: w75 440, 444
family opposition: w74 39, 342; yb74 6-7; w73 502, 734-5; yb73 241; g73 1/22 15-16; g73 7/22 7; g72 5/22 24; w71 574-5
family quarrel: yb76 11-12
family united: g74 2/8 11; g74 4/22 16
festival singer: g74 2/8 24-6
fetishism: yb74 6; g74 3/8 21; w73 486; g71 7/8 19
fetish priestess: g75 7/22 24-6
film showing: yb72 102-4
former criminals become Witnesses: w75 40, 245-6, 650; g75 4/22 21-3, 25-6, 28; g75 7/8 29; g75 10/8 19-20; g74 4/8 27-8; g74 10/8 26-7; yb73 16-17; g73 4/22 24-6; g73 8/22 7; w72 454
former opposers accept truth: w74 38-9, 143, 342; yb74 129; g74 1/22 21; g74 3/8 20; w73 475, 502; yb73 56-7; g73 8/8 22; w72 318-19; w71 533-4; g71 8/8 13-15
fortune-tellers: w75 266
funerals: w74 283; g74 3/22 19; g71 3/8 7
gamblers: g75 3/8 28; w74 587-8; g74 10/22 11
group witnessing: yb72 63-4
guest worker: g73 3/22 21-2
Gypsies: g73 1/8 9-12
handbills: w74 510; yb74 89; km 12/73 3
handicapped persons: g75 8/8 26; g75 10/22 19-20; w74 342; g74 5/8 26; g74 10/8 26; w73 765-6; yb73 232; g73 5/8 11; w72 221; g72 2/22 20
happiest moment: g73 7/22 19
Hindus: w74 644; g74 7/22 9-10; g73 7/8 16-21; g72 1/22 24-6
"hippies": w75 43; g75 3/8 28; w74 643-4; g74 11/22 8-12; yb73 11; g73 4/22 27-8; w71 574-5
honeymoon preaching: yb74 73
hospital: yb73 39, 204
housecar: w74 208; g73 12/22 12-13

illiterate persons: w74 410-11; w73 111-12; g72 2/8 24
images abandoned: w75 761; yb75 13, 21; g73 12/22 12; yb72 65; g72 1/22 24-6; g72 5/22 24
immorality rejected: w74 606; w73 626, 631-2; g73 8/22 7-8, 15
informal witnessing: yb75 15-16, 19-20; w74 126, 159, 445, 648; yb74 20-1; g74 9/22 12; w73 391; g73 5/22 22; g73 7/22 7; w71 221-2
interest aroused by opposers: w73 509-10
interested persons search for truth: w75 734-5; yb75 21; yb74 35; w73 507-9, 626-7; yb73 144; w72 541; yb72 67, 147-8; g71 6/22 20-1
interested persons search for Witnesses: g74 6/22 16; g74 11/22 11; yb72 145, 147; w71 383; g71 1/22 26
interested persons study with each other: yb75 23
isolated territory: w75 247; yb75 23; w74 141-3, 474, 648-9; yb74 232-3; g74 11/8 25-6; g73 12/22 12-13; km 2/73 4-5
Jews: w73 519; g71 1/8 24
juju: yb74 6; g71 7/8 19
Kingdom News: w75 392; yb75 6-7, 12, 17, 22, 253; km 2/74 1; km 11/74 1
King Sobhuza: yb76 112, 219-20; w74 474
lawyer: km 9/75 1; w74 366
learn language: g74 1/22 20; g74 11/8 26
lepers: yb73 68
letter writing: g75 1/22 30
literature found: yb74 41; km 2/74 1
Mafia member: w75 40
magazine distribution: km 2/74 1; w72 511; yb72 79-80; w71 220
maid rejects adultery: g72 9/22 26
Malawi woman hides fleeing Witnesses: g75 6/8 4
marriage saved: w74 317
marriages legalized: yb75 7; w74 648; g74 1/22 20-1; g74 2/8 25; g74 4/8 28; g74 9/8 7; w73 626, 631-2; yb73 72-3; g73 8/22 7; yb72 185; g72 10/8 24; g71 9/22 23
Masons: g74 10/8 28
megaphones: yb73 157-9
mental illness overcome: w75 244-5; g75 4/22 20
mercenary: w73 679
Methodists: w73 443-4
military personnel: w74 342-3; g74 10/22 11; yb73 236; g73 8/8 19-22; w72 222; yb72 204; g71 6/22 21-2
Moslems: w75 734-5; g74 4/8 27; yb74 6-7; yb73 12-13; g73 1/22 16; w72 221-2; yb72 100-1, 202; g72 2/8 5-8
multiple sclerosis victim: g75 8/8 26
musician: w75 671
mutineers' descendants: g75 1/22 30
not-at-homes: yb73 14; w71 219-20
nuns: g75 1/22 12-13; w74 746-7; g74 2/22 7; w73 551, 628; g73 2/8 14; g73 9/22 14
nurse: g75 10/8 20-1
occultism: w74 328; w73 487
office buildings: w74 364-6
older persons: w74 342; yb74 43-4; g74 3/8 21-2; yb73 228-9, 251-2; g73 2/8 14; w72 284-5; yb72 53, 66, 101; g72 2/8 24; g72 5/22 24; w71 368-9; g71 11/8 26
overcoming obstacles: yb75 14, 23, 63-4, 134; w74 141-3, 283-5, 587-8; g74 11/8 26; w73 445-7, 507-11, 761-2; yb73 39, 248-9; g73 5/8 11; g73 12/22 12-13; yb72 101-2, 211
overcoming opposition: w75 127; yb75 163-4; yb74 59, 63, 104-5; g74 3/8 20; g74 5/8 20; w73 583, 679; w72 70-1; yb72 202, 241
patience: w73 583
Pentecostals: yb72 176
perseverance: w74 38-9; w73 762-3; yb73 14; yb72 102
physical benefits: w75 247
place of employment: g73 2/22 24
policemen: yb74 9; yb73 161-2, 193; w72 70, 381; yb72 244; w71 542-3
politicians: w75 266; g75 11/8 21-3; yb72 145, 147
polygamy rejected: g75 12/8 13-17; g74 3/8 20-1
pornographer: w72 125
prayers answered: yb76 12-14; w75 42, 326, 413; yb75 21, 134-5; g75 5/8 4-5; g75 10/22 21; km 6/75 1; w74 712; g74 1/8 11; g74 2/22 4, 7; g74 3/22 7; w73 468, 626-8, 679, 760; yb73 18-19; km 7/73 4; km 12/73 3; w72 146, 155, 338, 389-90; g72 3/8 23; w71 383
prisons: w75 40; yb75 112, 176-7; g75 4/22 21-8; g75 10/8 19-20; g75 12/22 18; yb74 129, 190-1; g74 4/8 27-8; yb73 244-5; g73 12/22 26; w72 283; yb72 157-8; g72 7/8 20; g72 9/22 26; w71 508; g71 8/8 14
  prisoner "furloughed": g75 5/22 29
prostitutes: yb76 10-11; w75 285; w74 38-9; g73 2/8 14-15; g73 8/22 8
psychologist: g75 10/8 19; g74 9/22 12
return visits: w71 220-1
school: g74 5/22 26; w73 187-8, 467-8; w72 381-2; g72 6/8 24; g71 3/22 20
seamen: yb73 34-5
seeking "escape": g74 4/8 26-7
self-control blessed: g73 6/22 19
serving where need is greater: w74 208; w73 509-11, 573-4; g73 12/22 11-13; w72 542; yb72 51-4, 57-73; w71 85
sheepherder's wife: g71 5/8 7
skyscrapers: w74 364-6
slide showing: yb74 18
smoking habit broken: w73 453-5; yb72 65
smuggler: w72 125
sound car: yb75 158; yb73 47-8, 118, 154-7; w72 534
spared political persecution: yb74 36, 38
spiritualists: g72 3/8 8-11
sportsmen: g71 9/22 6-8
street witnessing: yb75 18, 163-4; km 10/73 1
suicide prevented: w75 488-9; g75 8/8 26; g75 10/8 22; g75 10/22 21; w74 4, 644; yb74 190-1; w73 325, 766; w72 284-5, 390; g72 11/22 19; w71 507
superstition overcome: w73 701
tact: yb72 241
telephone: km 7/73 4
tracts: yb74 69, 71-3; g74 10/8 28
trading for literature: yb76 253; yb75 153
Truth book: yb75 7, 21, 23; w74 31, 649, 711-12; g74 1/22 21; g74 3/22 7; g74 11/22 10-11; g73 7/22 7
truth transforms lives: w75 40, 245-6, 285, 392-3, 538, 559, 650; yb75 9, 14; g75 4/22 28; g75 10/8 19-20; g75 10/22 21-2; w74 38-9, 343, 587-8, 606; yb74 19; g74 1/22 20-1; g74 2/8 11, 24-6; g74 3/8 20-2; g74 3/22 7; g74 4/8 26-8; g74 7/22 9-11; g74 8/8 6-7; g74 10/8 26-8; g74 10/22 11; g74 11/22 10-12, 26; w73 29-30, 502-3, 626-7, 631-2, 670, 766; yb73 10-11, 15-17, 243; g73 1/8 11-12; g73 2/8 14-15; g73 5/22 21-24; g73 12/8 9-15; g73 12/22 26; w72 125, 453-5; g72 3/8 23; g72 3/22 16; g72 4/8 25; g72 8/22 11-12, 23; g72 9/22 26; g72 10/8 23-4; w71 209, 532-3, 763; g71 2/8 13-16
"underground" activity: yb74 113-14; yb72 85-8, 93, 136, 139-41, 155-6, 163
village accepts truth: g74 1/22 20-1
wagons: yb73 218
weapons rejected: g72 10/8 23-4
witnessing by boat: w74 649; g74 6/22 15-16
witnessing during revolution: g74 5/8 25-6
witnessing in far north: w75 43; w74 141-3
witnessing to relatives: yb75 8; g74 10/22 11; w73 583
women's liberationist: w74 387-93
worldly parents ask Witnesses to train children: w75 763
youthful Witnesses: yb75 13-14, 16; yb74 59, 63; km 8/73 4; g72 6/8 24; w71 368-9, 531-2; g71 4/8 23
  (SEE ALSO CONGREGATION PUBLISHERS, PIONEERS, TEACHING, TERRITORY)

FIG(S)

fig-shower: w72 766
Jesus cursed tree: w72 95-6

FIJI

demon activity: g73 12/8 23
discussion: g73 12/8 20-3
Jehovah's witnesses: yb76 14-15, 24-5; yb75 24-5; w74 207, 649; yb74 24-5; yb73 24-5; g73 12/8 23; yb72 34-5; w71 20-1
  preaching directed by Fiji branch: w74 646-9
population: yb73 24; yb72 34

religion: g72 8/8 30

FILMS
(SEE MOTION PICTURES)

FINES
Christian view of paying: w75 223-4

FINGERPRINTS
g71 1/22 31

FINISHED MYSTERY, THE (Book)
banned: yb75 95-7; yb73 107-8; g73 6/8 16; w72 148
censored: yb75 119
distribution: yb75 94
release: yb75 90-1; ka 313, 347; w72 147
ZG edition: yb75 125-6

FINLAND
Conference on Security and Cooperation in Europe: g75 9/22 29; g75 11/8 3-7
Jehovah's witnesses: yb76 24-5; w75 333-5; yb75 15-16, 24-5; w74 141-3; yb74 24-5; w73 628; yb73 24-5; g73 2/22 24; g73 9/22 16; yb72 34-5
population: yb73 24; yb72 34
religion: g72 8/22 17-18
superstitions of Laplanders: g75 2/8 26

FIRE(S)
Argentina: g72 4/8 29
arson: g75 6/8 30; g74 4/8 31
false alarms: g74 1/8 30
firefighter's experiences: g71 12/8 12-17
fire sticks: g72 2/22 23
forest: g74 12/8 30; g72 10/8 31
France: g71 11/22 3
Japan: g74 1/22 31
ships: g72 2/8 12-16
symbolic: sl 295-6, 306-7; w74 652, 666; ts 107-9, 118-23; ka 156-8; w71 670
tall buildings: g74 2/8 23; g73 1/22 30; g72 12/8 30
United States: g74 2/8 30; g74 4/8 31; g72 10/8 31; g71 12/8 12-17
walking on: g73 12/8 23
"wall of fire" (Zec 2:5): pm 158-61
window gates: g75 7/22 29

FIREWOOD
shortage: g75 11/22 30

FIREWORKS
Chinese ceremonies: ts 61-3; g74 8/8 30

FIRST AID
burns: g74 9/22 8; g73 7/22 12
choking: g73 12/8 30
heart massage: g73 7/22 10
mouth-to-mouth resuscitation: g73 7/22 8-12
new procedures: g73 12/22 31

FIRSTBORN
Jacob: po 93-5
Joseph: po 96-7, 99-102
  not same line as kingship: po 101-2
Levites exchanged for: g72 3/8 28

FIRSTFRUITS
barley harvest: w75 603
congregation of God: ka 106
Jesus Christ: w75 603

FISH
aquarium: g72 9/22 13-16
benefits to man: g75 11/8 17
blood: w73 224
disease: g72 8/22 31
egg-laying habits: g71 7/8 4
electricity: g72 8/22 31
extinction: g74 5/8 30
food from sewage: g72 8/8 31
food production: g71 11/8 16-19
food value: g72 12/22 9
found in deep water: g74 10/8 29
hunting equipment: g75 11/8 19-20
natural antifreeze: w75 715
number of varieties: ts 145
Peru: g73 2/8 31
playfulness: g75 10/22 26
pollution kills: g71 4/22 10
'prehistoric': g72 6/8 29
protective equipment for survival: g75 11/8 18-19, 29
shortage: g74 2/22 23-4; g74 3/22 30; g73 7/22 29
"sixth sense": g75 11/8 19
slime: g72 1/22 30
symbolic: kj 393-6
wetlands: g75 2/8 15
(SEE ALSO MARINE LIFE)

FISHER, G. H.
yb75 90-1, 93, 104, 106, 111, 116

FISHING
Africa: g72 6/8 25-6
commercial: g74 2/22 23-4; g74 3/22 30
Iceland: g71 1/22 9
methods: g73 11/8 10
overfishing: g74 7/22 7
territorial waters: g74 2/22 24

FLAGS
discussion: g71 9/8 12-15
worship: w75 217; w71 117

FLAG SALUTE
Africa: g73 12/8 29
Bible view: w74 62-3; w71 489; g71 9/8 14-15
Brazil: yb73 81-3
conscience: w75 217
Court cases (U.S.): yb75 169-70, 172; w72 760; g73 1/22 29-30; g72 7/8 11-12; w71 722; g71 9/8 14-15
experiences:
  mob invades Kingdom Hall: yb75 169-70
  Witnesses attacked for not saluting: yb75 183, 188
  Witness student excused: g72 9/8 7-8
first public mention by Witnesses: yb75 168-9
Germany: yb74 117
schools:
  expulsion of students: yb75 11, 169; yb73 81-3; w72 760; w71 118
South Africa: yb75 11
standing while others salute: w75 217
swastika: g75 2/22 22
Zambia: yb72 249-53
(SEE ALSO IDOLATRY, NEUTRALITY)

FLEAS
g74 10/22 23

FLOCK
"one flock": w74 287; w73 732-3

FLOOD (Noachian)
angels that sinned: po 71-4, 77-8
confirmation: g75 6/8 6-8; g75 11/22 29; g73 1/22 24
date and length: sl 290-1; w71 410
description: w71 169; te 129-30
discussion: g75 6/8 5-8
effect on earth: g75 6/8 6, 7; g72 4/8 10-11
expression of God's justice and wisdom: w75 665-6
global: g75 6/8 6, 7; w74 664-5
legends: g75 6/8 8; g75 11/22 29
pre-Flood rebellion: w72 651-2; g71 4/22 23
pre-Flood warning: w75 10, 748-9; po 73, 173; ka 333
  allowed Noah time to have offspring: w75 750; po 73
prophetic significance: w75 83, 748-9; g75 6/8 8; w74 665-8; po 71; w71 169; te 130
purpose: po 74; w71 168; te 127-8
rainbow following: g75 1/22 13
tree survival: w73 84-5
water canopy: po 75
where water went: g75 6/8 8
why Noah was told one week before: w75 10-11
writing before the Flood: w71 409-10
(SEE ALSO BIBLE AUTHENTICITY, NOAH)

FLOODS
Argentina: g74 5/22 7-8; yb72 99-100
Brazil: g74 5/22 29; g74 7/8 24-6; g71 5/8 29
causes: w74 735; g74 7/8 25-6
effect on earth: po 76
Honduras: g74 12/22 21-6
Hong Kong: g72 8/8 29
Mexico: g73 10/22 30; g72 6/22 30-1
Nicaragua: yb72 178-9
Philippines: yb73 21; g72 10/8 30
United States: g73 6/22 14-17; g72 4/8 29; g72 8/8 24-6; w71 298
(SEE ALSO DISASTERS)

FLOWERS
African: g75 2/8 20-3
chrysanthemum: g71 7/8 14-15
poppy: w72 596
purpose: w71 325
varieties: g71 1/8 19
(SEE ALSO PLANTS)

FLY
g75 7/8 25-6; g72 9/8 11

FOOD
additives: g72 2/8 29; g72 3/22 29; g72 4/8 31; g71 3/8 29; g71 3/22 29
apples: g75 2/22 31; g74 9/22 7; g73 5/22 15; g73 9/22 23-4; g72 1/22 18
Argentina: yb72 82, 89
badea: g73 1/22 13
bamboo: g71 5/8 11
bananas: g71 5/8 11
basic requirements: g73 8/22 4
beans: g74 9/22 4-5
bean sprouts: g73 11/22 20
beef: g74 10/22 24-6; g72 10/8 30

blood used: g71 10/22 31
Bolivia: g71 6/8 23
bread: g73 2/22 25-6
canned goods: g74 9/8 29
carrot: g73 3/22 23
cereals: g74 10/22 30
cheese: g72 11/8 19-20
Chile: g72 3/22 25-6
chirimoya: g73 1/22 13-14
coconut: g71 5/8 11; g71 6/22 25-6
cooking: g75 3/8 9-11; g74 2/8 17-19; g74 9/22 5-6
corn: g75 12/8 30; g72 7/22 6-7; g71 11/22 20; g71 12/22 29
cost: g75 8/22 29; w74 341; g74 3/8 29; g74 5/8 9; g74 7/22 3-4; g74 8/22 29, 31; g74 9/8 29; g73 2/8 29
cost for family: g73 4/22 30; g73 5/8 23; g73 6/8 29; g73 9/22 30; g73 11/22 9-11
cutting costs: g75 4/8 20-3; g73 8/22 3-5; g73 11/22 30
dandelions: g74 9/22 6
diet: g74 2/8 17; g74 9/22 3-7; g73 1/22 4; w72 413; g72 6/8 31; g72 12/22 8-11; g71 7/22 31
  effect of: g72 1/8 30; g72 6/8 18; g72 7/8 30; g71 2/22 31; g71 9/22 30
  old age: g72 1/22 20-2
  pregnancy: g72 8/8 23
digestion: g71 3/22 16-20
distribution: g74 10/8 5-6
drying to preserve: g75 8/8 18
during famine: g74 9/22 6-7
earth's potential: g75 2/8 30; g75 7/22 30; ts 135-6
earth's supply enlarged: g71 11/22 20
eggs: g73 4/8 23; g72 10/22 31; g71 1/8 16
fat: w72 190-1
figs: w72 766
fish: g74 2/22 23-4; g74 8/8 14-15; w73 224; g73 10/8 7; g71 11/8 16-19
food poisoning: g74 9/22 6; g73 3/8 10; g72 2/8 30
formed as body parts: g72 1/8 29-30
frankfurters: g72 3/22 29
freezing: g75 8/8 18
frozen: g75 5/8 31
garlic: g72 2/8 30-1
Germany: g72 1/8 29-30
gleaning by elderly: g75 8/22 29
gluttony: w74 167-8
Greek: g75 3/8 9-11
guaba: g73 1/22 14
high-yield grain: g71 3/22 29
home canning: g75 8/8 17-18, 29
horseradish: g71 3/8 30
Iceland: g71 1/22 10
insects: w75 464
Japan: g74 8/8 13-16; g73 2/8 22
Korea: g73 5/22 17-18
Lapps: g72 6/22 23
lentils: g72 12/22 11
malnutrition: g71 2/22 31; g71 7/22 31
meat: g74 9/22 3-5; w72 544; g72 3/22 29; g72 4/8 31; g71 5/22 29
milk: g75 11/22 30-1; g73 7/8 12-15
mushrooms: w72 596; g71 8/8 30
naranjilla: g73 1/22 13
oats: g72 7/22 6
  oatmeal: g74 2/8 17
ocean food chain: g75 11/8 17
offerings to idols: w72 563-5; g72 8/22 5-7
orange: g72 3/22 29
organic: g72 1/22 31; g71 7/22 30
overeating: g71 2/22 6
packaging: g73 9/8 21-4
papaya: g73 1/22 14
pet food: g74 8/8 29
potato: g72 7/22 6; g71 11/22 20
poultry: g71 3/22 29
power failure: g74 3/8 19
processing: g74 10/22 30
production: g74 10/8 5; g74 12/8 10
  increasing: g74 11/8 29-30; g71 10/8 11; g71 11/8 16-19
  statistics: g72 10/22 6
  use of energy: g74 6/8 29
proper view of: w73 145
proteins: g74 2/8 17; g74 9/22 4-5
prune: g71 5/8 23
purchasing: g74 3/8 29; g74 10/8 31; g73 8/22 3-5; g71 3/8 8-9
radiation in: g75 5/22 31
ready-mixed: g74 10/8 31
recipes: g74 8/8 13-14, 16; g74 10/22 24-6
religious prohibition of certain foods: w75 300-1
rice: g75 4/8 21; g74 8/8 13-14; g74 9/22 5; g73 12/8 24-6; g72 7/22 3-4, 7-8
salad: g73 11/8 21-3
sauerkraut: g74 12/22 20
seafood: g72 3/22 25-6; g72 5/22 26
shortage: g75 2/22 7-11; w74 195-7; g73 5/22 30; g73 6/8 29; g73 6/22 3-6, 10-12, 16-17, 30; g73 7/8 29; g73 7/22 29; g73 10/8 5-7, 21
  coping with: g75 2/22 11; g74 9/22 3-7
soybeans: g75 2/8 30; g74 2/8 17; g74 9/22 5; g73 9/8 30
spices: g73 11/8 23; g72 2/22 30-1
sprouted seeds: g75 12/22 25-6
sugar: g72 9/8 30
  maple: g73 2/22 11-13
  substitutes: g72 3/22 29; g71 8/22 31
sunflower seeds: g72 1/22 18
surplus destroyed: g71 12/22 30
tamarindo: g73 1/22 14
tomato: g73 1/22 13; g72 1/22 18
vegetables: g75 2/8 30
vitamins: g74 9/22 5-6; w72 63-4; g72 11/22 30
water in: g72 1/22 18
watermelon: g72 1/22 18
weeds: g74 9/22 6-7
wheat: g74 9/8 29; g72 7/22 3-6, 8-9
(SEE ALSO COOKING, DIET)

FOOD SHORTAGES

Afghanistan: g73 2/8 29; g73 6/22 4
Africa: g75 2/22 9-10; g74 3/8 5-8; g74 7/22 4, 6; g73 6/22 4; g73 10/8 6-7
Bangladesh: g75 2/22 9
beef: g72 10/8 30
causes: w75 195-6, 248; g75 1/22 29; g75 6/8 31; g75 6/22 29; w74 196-7; g74 7/22 3-7; g74 10/8 5-6; g74 11/8 29-30; tp 13-15; g73 6/22 6-12; g72 12/22 8-11
  unequal distribution: g74 12/8 8-9
Christian view: w75 634; g75 2/22 8, 11; w74 40, 248-9
coping with: g74 9/22 3-7
difference in today's crisis: g75 2/8 7
discussion: w75 195-6; g75 2/22 7-11; g73 10/8 5-7, 21
effects of: g75 2/22 10-11
ethics of nations: w75 261; g75 1/22 29; g75 5/8 29
farmers' problems: g75 6/22 9-13
fish: g74 2/22 23-4; g73 7/22 29
grain: g74 5/22 29; g74 6/8 31; g74 6/22 6; g74 11/22 29
hoarding: g74 6/22 5, 29; g74 10/8 29
human milk: g74 7/8 13
India: g75 2/22 9-11; g74 7/22 7; g73 6/22 3-4, 7-9; g73 9/22 29; g73 10/8 6-7; w72 615; g72 7/22 3
Iraq: g75 2/22 9
Ireland: g72 7/22 6
meat: g73 7/22 29
nations stockpiling: g74 1/22 6
Nigeria: g75 2/22 9
old people: g75 5/8 30
predictions for future: g75 2/8 30; g75 3/8 4; g75 3/22 29; g75 4/8 30; w74 195-6, 243; g74 2/8 29; g74 4/8 29; g74 5/8 29; g74 6/22 5-6, 29; g74 7/22 3-7, 30; g74 10/22 29; g74 11/8 10, 29; g74 11/22 29; tp 13-14, 82; g73 6/22 5-6, 16-17; g73 9/22 29; g73 10/8 5-7; g73 11/8 29; g72 7/22 3, 10-12; g71 10/8 7, 28, 30
religion: g73 6/22 8-9
solution: w75 196; ts 134-7; g73 6/22 13; g72 7/22 12-13
Soviet Union: g73 10/8 6
statistics: ml 23; w74 295; g74 7/22 3-6; g73 6/22 4-5; g73 7/22 29; g72 7/22 11; g71 10/8 7, 17
symbolic representation: w74 358
technology fails to solve: w74 40, 197; g73 6/22 7, 10
United States' role: g74 7/8 29; g74 7/22 4
weather's effect: g75 3/8 3-4

Quotations

a permanent crisis threatening hundreds of millions: w75 195
by 1985 worldwide famines: tp 14
climate change indicates major crop failures: g75 3/8 4
doubtful whether critical food situation ever so world wide: g75 2/8 7
drastic rise in the death rate through starvation: w72 615
500 million starving in less developed lands: g74 7/22 5

food crisis a 'can't win' dilemma: g75 2/8 30
food will become political weapon: g74 10/22 29
governments today have no policy such as Joseph taught Pharaoh: w75 196
half the human family desperately short: g72 10/22 15
hungry multiplying twice as fast as well fed: tp 13
indefinite, if not permanent, shortages: g74 7/22 5
in 1973 close to having 50-60 million die: g74 7/22 5
millions on brink of starvation: g74 9/22 3
new era of short supplies, hungry people: g74 7/22 4
things much worse than when we wrote *Famine—1975!*: g75 2/22 29
undernourished as before W. W. II: g74 11/8 29
world grain supplies expected to decline: g74 7/22 6
(SEE ALSO FAMINE, LAST DAYS)

FOOT
unit of measure: g74 8/8 19

FOOTBALL
life stories of professional players: g75 9/22 16-21

FOOTNOTES
Bible: w73 702

FORBIDDEN FRUIT
garden of Eden: g72 4/8 27-8

FOREHEAD
marking: w72 48-54, 635-8; kj 164-6, 174-81, 208-9

FOREKNOWLEDGE
Jehovah's: po 94; ts 58-9; g74 7/8 27-8

FOREORDINATION
1914: po 174-7
144,000: po 157, 164

FOREST(S)
Amazon: g74 7/8 25-6; g72 7/8 29
benefits: g73 6/8 9-11
dangers of stripping: g74 7/8 25-6
discussion: g73 6/8 9-11
fires: g74 12/8 30; g73 4/22 30; g72 10/8 31
firewood: g75 11/22 30
insects: w71 326
logging: g71 12/22 17-19
ruined by man: g71 2/22 30

FORGIVENESS
basis: w74 494-8; w72 600; w71 270-2, 276, 632
confession: g74 11/8 27-8
discussion: w75 38-41
examples: w75 39-40; w74 495, 503-5; w72 707-8
Jehovah's: w75 38-41; w74 495-6, 498; ts 188-9; w73 100; w72 118-20, 430-6; w71 236-7
for murder: g75 11/22 28
seeking: w72 335
toward others: w74 148-9, 154, 497-9, 503-5; g74 5/22 27-8; w72 708; w71 102-3, 574, 579-80; te 63-6
toward those guilty of sexual immorality: w75 755-6

FORNICATION
avoiding: w73 31-2, 74-5; w71 594
Bible view: g74 1/22 27-8; g74 2/8 9; w73 561-2, 593; tp 146-50; w72 219-20; g72 2/8 20; g72 4/22 20
children: g72 2/8 17, 19
clergy view: g75 11/22 30; g72 4/22 18-19; w71 451; kj 158; g71 5/22 30
contraceptives for youths: g75 7/8 30
definition: g74 2/8 9; w73 575, 593; w72 31, 767-8
effects: g75 6/22 29; tp 147-9; g73 1/22 28
Greek word: w74 160, 703-4; w73 575; tp 147, 149-50; g73 9/22 27; g73 11/22 27; w72 31
homosexuality: w72 767-8
physical dangers: g74 1/22 28; g72 2/8 17-20
prevalence: g74 8/22 31; g73 5/8 4; g73 6/8 30; g72 2/8 17, 19; g72 6/22 30; g72 8/22 8-12; g72 9/22 30; g72 12/8 7; w71 452; g71 11/22 29
rock music: w75 390
sin against one's own body: g71 1/8 4
spiritual: w72 356-7; kj 117-21
(SEE ALSO MORAL BREAKDOWN, PORNEIA)

FORTUNE-TELLING
Bible view: g75 3/22 27-8; g75 8/8 5-6; ts 76-8, 87
discussion: g75 8/8 3-6
experiences:
fortune-teller learns Bible truth: w75 266; g75 3/22 28
methods: g75 8/8 3-5; ts 86

FOSSILS
dinosaur: g75 6/8 7
evolution: g75 6/22 30; g75 12/8 30; g74 4/8 29; g74 9/22 19-22; g74 11/22 30
frozen mammoth: g73 8/22 31
mammoth in China: g74 4/22 31
"prehistoric" men: g73 10/22 18-21
sudden appearance of life: g74 9/22 20-1; g74 11/22 30; g73 10/22 17-18

FOUNDATION(S)
apostles: w71 747
congregation of God: w72 719
Jesus Christ: pm 188

FOUR
Bible use of number: pm 142

FOUR HUNDRED YEARS OF AFFLICTION
po 106, 108

FOX
playfulness: g75 10/22 26

FRANCE
air pollution: g71 12/8 29
alcoholism: w74 451, 453; g71 6/22 3-5; g71 8/22 26
carnival: g73 3/8 5-8
Catholic church: w75 651; g75 3/22 16-18; w74 745-7; g74 11/22 31; g73 9/8 3-4, 6-7; g73 12/8 17; w71 355-6; g71 7/22 3-10
Lourdes shrine: g75 4/22 31
crime: g75 11/22 4
disaster: g71 11/22 3
Jehovah's witnesses: yb76 15, 24-5; yb75 16, 24-5; w74 745-7; yb74 24-5; w73 634; yb73 12-13, 24-5; g73 9/22 16; w72 221-2; yb72 34-5; g72 5/22 24; w71 17, 90-1, 368; g71 7/22 10
population: yb73 24; yb72 34
Protestants: w74 745
religion: w75 323; w74 745-7
solar furnace: g72 10/8 26
tunnel to England: g74 5/22 31
unemployment: g75 3/22 8
weapons: g72 10/8 10, 29
wine: g74 12/22 30

FRANZ, FRED W.
comment on 1975: yb75 256
conventions: yb74 57
dedication of farm building: w73 314
Gilead graduations: w75 285, 672; g75 11/8 26; w74 286, 670; w73 284, 647; g73 5/8 25; g73 11/8 26; w72 286; g72 5/8 26; w71 287-8, 670
lectures: yb75 201, 203, 211, 213-16, 226, 246
service tours: yb76 14, 42; w75 169; g75 2/8 29; km 3/75 1; km 4/75 1; km 12/74 1; yb73 64, 76-7, 195-7, 245-6, 250; yb72 74-5, 145, 174, 227-8; km 2/71 1

FRAUD
business: g74 12/8 29; w71 765
"dats": g71 9/22 31
embezzlement: g75 11/8 29

FREEDOM
Adam and Eve: gc 12, 14; w71 499
attaining: ts 190; tp 133-4; w71 431-3; g71 5/22 7-8
experience: w74 391-3
Christian freedom: w74 370; ts 190; w73 141-2, 144
discussion: g72 7/8 9-12
efforts to undermine: g71 12/22 11-12
limitations: gc 11-12; g72 8/22 3-4
maintaining: g71 12/22 12-13
religious:
Declaration of Helsinki peace conference: g75 11/8 6
Witnesses establish: g72 7/8 9-12
women's liberation movement: w74 387-93
world's view: w74 369-70, 562
effect: g75 11/22 31

Of Worship
Canada: g75 3/8 20-8; g72 7/8 10
flag salute: g72 7/8 11-12; g71 9/8 14-15
Greece: w75 547-52; g75 9/22 29; g75 12/8 17-21
Portugal: w75 169-71; g75 2/8 29
United States: yb75 172, 178-80

FREEDOM FOR THE PEOPLES (Booklet)
yb75 138

FREEMASONRY
g74 10/8 28

FREE WILL
Adam and Eve: g74 10/8 12
each person: w74 344; ts 82; g74 4/8 16; g74 7/8 27-8; w73 441-2; g73 10/8 26; w72 265-6; w71 638-9
Jehovah not force some to be evil: po 94, 102

FRENCH GUIANA
Jehovah's witnesses: yb76 26-7; yb75 26-7; yb74 26-7; yb73 26-7; yb72 36-7
population: yb73 26; yb72 36

FRIEND, MAXWELL G.
yb75 141, 200

FRIENDLINESS
field service: km 7/74 4

FRIENDS
Bible students: km 8/71 3
Christians: w75 123
discussion: w73 421-4
Jehovah: w74 309-10; w73 424; tp 128-9; w71 6; te 119
Jesus Christ: w74 371-2; w73 424
keeping: g74 7/8 3-4; w73 599-600; w71 223
love for: w72 739-40; g72 2/8 3-4
proving ourselves: w74 310; g72 5/8 23
selecting: w74 247; w73 157-8, 422-4; w71 6-7; te 119-22
unrighteous riches: w73 63-4
with world: tp 127-31

FROG
kokoá: g75 3/22 14

FROM PARADISE LOST TO PARADISE REGAINED (Book)
yb76 192, 252; yb75 217; g72 8/8 19

FRUIT(S)
apples: g75 2/22 31
beverages: g75 4/8 23; g74 7/22 20
Eden's forbidden: g72 4/8 27-8
Kingdom expressions: w72 91
preserving: g73 9/22 23-4
trees: g73 9/22 21-3; w71 325
tropics: g73 1/22 13-14
(SEE ALSO FOOD, TREE)

FRUITS OF SPIRIT
congregation: w71 664
cultivating: w74 116-17
kindness: w75 675-6
love: w73 691
mildness: g75 11/22 12; g71 7/8 28
self-control: g75 11/22 12
(SEE ALSO HOLY SPIRIT)

FRUSTRATIONS
causes: g74 1/22 8; g74 8/8 3-4
discussion: w72 483-4
police: g75 11/22 6-8
relief from: g74 4/8 9-13; g74 8/8 4-7

FUELS
black market: g74 1/8 29
cattle dung: g75 11/22 30
charcoal: g71 5/8 30
coal: g74 1/8 4; g72 8/8 15-16, 18-19
conserving: g74 1/22 22-3
firewood: g75 11/22 30
fuel cells: g72 8/8 29
gasoline: g74 4/8 3; g71 6/22 30
natural gas: g74 1/8 5, 29; g72 8/8 16, 18
oil: g74 1/8 3-8, 29; g74 2/8 29; g74 2/22 16-22; g72 4/8 29; g72 8/8 17-18
peat: g75 2/8 30
propane gas: g71 1/8 31
shortage: g74 1/8 3-8, 29; g74 8/22 22-3; g73 1/22 30; g73 12/22 29, 31; g72 10/22 29
effects: g74 1/8 6-8, 29; g74 2/22 20, 29; g74 4/8 30
tires: g72 6/22 30
waste products: g73 1/22 30; g71 11/22 29
wood: g73 12/22 29
(SEE ALSO GAS)

FULL-TIME SERVICE
blessings: w73 446-7
many years: yb74 74, 95, 240, 247; w73 765
pioneers: km 10/75 7; w74 283-5; km 5/74 3-4, 6; w73 761-3, 765; km 2/73 3-6; km 5/73 3-6
(SEE ALSO BETHEL FAMILY, MISSIONARIES, PIONEERS)

FUNDAMENTALISTS
view of Bible: w71 676
Witnesses not: w74 629

FUNERALS
attire: g74 12/8 27
Buddhism: ts 61-2
burning paper items: ts 61-4
experiences: yb75 176; w74 283; g74 3/22 19; g74 12/8 28; g71 3/8 7
mourning: ts 61-2; g74 12/8 26-8
rites: ts 61-4; g74 12/8 26-7
suicides: w75 448
universal custom: ts 22
wakes: g74 12/8 26
who may perform: km 11/73 8
(SEE ALSO DEATH)

FUNGUS
infections: g75 9/8 7-8

FURNACE
solar: g72 10/8 26

FURS
trapping: g72 12/22 21-3

FUSION RELIGION
Constantine: sl 213, 235

FUTURE
animals no concept of: ts 18-21
Bible prophecy: g74 4/8 7-15; g73 1/22 7-9; w71 467-73
children's: w75 451-3
Christian view: w75 374-80; w74 375-80
human predictions: g74 4/8 3-6; g74 9/8 29; g73 1/22 5-7; g73 11/22 6-7; w71 108, 468-9; g71 4/22 20; g71 7/8 29
speculation: w75 380
worldly view: w75 6, 57; w74 375
(SEE ALSO PROPHECY)

GABON
Jehovah's witnesses: yb76 10-11, 24-5; yb75 24-5; yb74 24-5; w73 529; yb73 24-5; yb72 34-5; w71 251-4
population: yb73 24; yb72 34

GABRIEL
appearances: w72 621; dn 11

GADARENES
w73 287

GALAXY
discussion: g75 6/22 17-19
likened to an atom: g71 8/8 4
most distant, yet observed: g75 8/22 31

GALLIO
w74 80

GALLSTONES
discussion: g71 5/22 25-6

GALLUS, CESTIUS
withdraws army from Jerusalem: w74 426, 683; ka 300-1; g72 10/8 20; g71 12/8 6

GAMBIA
Jehovah's witnesses: yb76 30-1; yb75 30-1; yb74 7, 30-1; yb73 28-9; yb72 38-9
population: yb73 28; yb72 38

GAMBLING
Australia: w74 579
Bible view: w74 582-3, 588; g74 10/22 27-8; w73 30; w72 593-4
bingo: g74 6/22 13; g74 10/22 27-8
Britain: g75 4/22 30
churches: g75 1/8 31; g75 2/8 30; w74 580, 586; g74 4/8 29; g74 4/22 29; g74 10/22 27, 30; g74 11/8 12-13; g74 11/22 30; g73 6/22 30-1; g73 11/22 30; g71 11/8 30
compulsive: w74 581-4
discussion: w74 579-88
effects: w74 135, 580-6; g74 6/22 13; w72 593-4; g71 8/22 29; g71 11/8 3
experiences:
gamblers become Witnesses: w74 584-8; g74 10/22 11
lucrative jobs given up: w73 411
extent: w74 579-81
free tickets for prizes in "drawings": g75 7/8 28
Gamblers Anonymous: w74 583
greyhound racing: g75 10/22 31
illegal: w74 579-80, 585
laws of probability: g75 3/22 21
lotteries: g75 2/8 30; g75 7/8 27-8; w74 579-80
numbers betting: w74 585
on choice for archbishop: g74 6/8 30
playing cards: g75 6/22 27-8
prize tickets: w73 127
public support: g71 11/8 29-30
roulette wheel: g75 3/22 21
sports: w74 580
superstition: w74 586-7
United States: w74 135, 579-81
during Las Vegas flood: g75 8/22 31

GAMES
Bible games: g72 6/22 14-16
chess: g73 1/22 6; g73 3/22 12-14
competition: g73 3/22 13-14
of chance: g74 10/22 27-8
Olympics: g73 2/22 13-15; g72 10/22 29
participation: g72 11/22 9-11
polo: g72 10/22 25-6

selection: g73 3/22 14; g72 6/22 13-14
(SEE ALSO ENTERTAINMENT)

GAMMA GLOBULIN
w74 351

GANDHI, MAHATMA
w75 251; w73 762

GANGS
juvenile delinquency: g74 2/8 5
member becomes Witness: g73 5/22 21-4

GARBAGE
crisis: g73 10/8 30
disposal: g72 11/8 16-17
electricity from: g74 4/22 29
highways paved: g72 2/8 29-30
New York city: g74 11/22 31
paper production: g72 2/22 31; g72 5/22 30
quantity collected: g75 7/22 30
recycling: g71 4/22 21
statistics: g72 11/8 16
strike of collectors: g71 2/8 21-3
use in gardening: g72 11/8 16-18; g71 10/22 29-30
wasted food: g74 6/22 29

GARDEN OF EDEN
authenticity of Bible account: ts 29-30; pm 8-12
blessings: w73 77-8
destruction: pm 11, 17; w71 617; nc 13
discussion: po 37-8, 41, 48
entry of sin: ts 30-4; w72 621; pm 15-17; dn 10; g72 5/22 13; te 39-41
food: po 49-50
location: w71 539-40
name: po 54
paradise: po 37-8, 41, 48; pm 9-12, 15-17; w71 615-17; te 180; nc 9-13
tree of knowledge of good and bad: ts 31; g72 4/8 27-8
tree of life: ts 17

GARDENS
African flowers: g75 2/8 20-3
discussion: g74 5/22 9-12
fertilizer: g74 5/22 10-11
harvest: g74 5/22 12
mixed culture: g71 5/22 17-20
soil: g74 5/22 10
vegetable: g75 4/8 22; g74 5/22 9-12
giant plants: g75 12/22 30
watering: g74 5/22 12
(SEE ALSO PLANTS)

GARLIC
g72 2/8 30-1

GAS
carbon monoxide: g73 2/22 23; g72 2/22 12, 29
chlorine: g72 3/8 14
elements: g72 3/8 14
gasoline: g74 2/22 31; g74 4/8 3; g74 8/8 10; g71 6/22 30
improving gas mileage: g75 7/22 9-10
shortage: w74 243; g73 5/8 29; g73 6/8 3-4; g73 7/22 30; g73 12/8 30
stations close: g74 11/8 31
helium: w71 292
natural: g75 11/22 30; g74 1/8 5; g74 6/8 29
oxygen: g71 7/22 12
propane: g71 1/8 31

GATHERINGS
(SEE SOCIAL GATHERINGS)

GAUMATA (Artaxerxes)
stopped temple building: pm 192

GECKO
lizard: g72 11/22 11

GEHAZI
w74 404-6

GEHENNA
Bible translations: ts 110
discussion: ts 110-17; w73 237-8, 246; bi8 1355-6
historical background: sl 274-5; ts 111, 113-15; w73 237; g72 11/8 6-7; bi8 1355-6
occurrences in Bible: ts 111-12
religious leaders: ts 116, 181-2
salted with fire: w71 670
symbolic: sl 275; ts 111, 115-16; w73 237-8, 246
(SEE ALSO LAKE OF FIRE, SECOND DEATH)

GEMS
diamonds: g74 7/22 24-6; g72 5/8 31; g72 7/8 29

GENEALOGY
Jesus Christ: w74 105-6; ka 58, 61-2, 71

GENERATION
gap between generations: w75 156; w74 261-7, 270
length: sl 7
"this generation" (Mt 24:34; Lu 21:32): gc 22; g75 7/8 29; g71 10/8 16, 26

GENEROSITY
discussion: w74 120-2; g74 12/22 4-6; w72 312-14
examples: w75 318; yb75 209-10; w74 120-1, 535; g74 6/8 18-19
ways to show: w75 318; w74 154, 500; g74 12/22 5-6
when wrong: w74 122

GENES
heredity: g74 2/8 16; g73 2/8 5-6
mutations: g73 10/22 12-15
"recessive": w75 72-4

GENESIS (Book)
Adam and Eve: ts 30
authenticity: w71 50
clergy view: g74 8/22 10
compilation: w71 409-10
effect of rejecting book of: w71 410
factual: ts 29-30

GENETICS
chromosomes: g73 10/22 11-13
genetic code: g71 9/8 5-7
incestuous marriages: w75 72-4
race variations: w73 515-17; g73 2/8 5-6
selective breeding: g73 10/22 16-17

GENTILES
baptism: w72 691-4
called to Kingdom: w74 17; po 164-8; w71 655
Jesus' balanced view: w74 464
view of rabbis: w74 463-4

GENTILE TIMES
(SEE APPOINTED TIMES OF THE NATIONS)

GEOGRAPHY
accuracy of Bible: g72 1/8 27-8

GEOLOGY
determining age: g73 5/8 19; g72 4/8 15
knowledge incomplete: g73 5/8 19
record of rocks: g73 5/8 19
sudden appearance of life: g74 9/22 29

GERMANY
airport: g73 1/22 22-4
automobiles:
prevention of theft: g75 7/22 31
avant-garde music: g75 4/8 31
bankruptcies: g74 11/8 30
Berlin: g71 5/22 21-4
carnival: g73 3/8 5-7
concentration camps: g72 4/22 23
conditions after World War II: yb74 217-19, 234
customs: g73 1/8 26
description: g73 1/22 22-4
economy: yb74 234-5; g73 8/22 30; w72 616; g71 7/8 29
employment: g73 3/22 20-1
food: g72 1/8 29-30
"guest workers": yb74 65, 241; g73 3/22 20-2
highways: g72 6/8 3-4
inflation: w75 567
Jehovah's witnesses: yb76 26-7; yb75 16, 24-5; w74 38, 676; yb74 24-5, 65-253; km 10/74 1; w73 442; yb73 13-14, 24-5; g73 3/22 22; g73 9/22 16; w72 511, 541; yb72 34-5, 44; g72 6/8 29; w71 16-17, 732; g71 1/8 13-15; g71 3/22 4
conventions: yb74 236-9, 248-52; g72 10/22 18
foreign-language congregations: yb74 241-2
kindness to Jews: g75 2/22 22
persecution: w75 85, 424-5; g75 2/22 22; yb74 100, 102-5, 108-28, 131-204, 210-12, 238; w73 377-8, 399; yb73 120, 123, 126-7; w72 143-4, 395-9, 525, 631; yb72 97; g72 4/22 22-3; w71 16, 117, 425, 489-90, 494; g71 1/8 13-14
reconstruction of witness work: yb74 212-17
medicine: g72 7/8 30
military service: g71 1/8 13-15
moral breakdown: g73 4/22 6; g71 12/22 30
Nazism: g75 2/22 17-23; g73 1/22 5-6; g72 4/22 16-17
euthanasia program: w75 294
murder of Jews: w75 294
pollution: g71 7/8 29
population: yb73 24; yb72 34
railroad: g71 7/22 30
rating of its products: g75 10/22 30
religion: w75 364, 400; g75 2/22 17; g75 5/8 29; yb74 66, 68, 94; g74 3/8 30; g72 4/22 13-17; g72 8/8 30; w71 407; g71 3/22 3-4
Cologne Cathedral looted: g75 12/22 30
ships: g72 5/22 18-19
soldier: g73 8/8 19-22
Thirty Years' War: g72 4/22 13; g71 6/22 16-19
trial of war criminals: g71 3/8 30
West Berlin: yb74 24-5
World War II: g75 2/22 17-23;

g72 4/22 16-17; g72 10/8 7; g72 12/8 30-1
clergy responsibility: g75 7/8 30

GERMANY (East)
Berlin: g71 5/22 21-4
Jehovah's witnesses: w74 250; yb74 221-32; w72 71; g72 7/8 20; w71 17, 542
persecution: w75 425-6; yb74 223-232

GERMS
disease: w74 132

GESTURES
public speaking: sg 127, 132-3

GETHSEMANE
location: w75 367

GET-TOGETHERS
discussion: w72 403-4; g72 6/22 13-16

GHANA
customs: g71 10/22 5-8
description: yb73 141, 171
independence: yb73 181
Jehovah's witnesses: yb76 26-7; w75 763; yb75 6-7, 26-7; yb74 9-10, 24-5; yb73 24-5, 141-89; g73 9/22 14-15; w72 381; yb72 34-5; w71 125-6
printery (Watch Tower): yb74 9; g73 9/22 14-15
moral breakdown: g71 5/22 30
population: yb73 24; yb72 34
religion: yb73 141-4

GIBEAH
selfishness of people: w75 359

GIBRALTAR
description: g71 10/22 25-6
Jehovah's witnesses: yb76 28-9; yb75 28-9; yb74 28-9; yb73 28-9; yb72 38-9
population: yb73 28; yb72 38

GIDEON
example for Christians: km 8/73 2
judge: w74 278
refused kingship: po 122; w71 743

GIFTS
attitude toward giving: w75 740; g74 10/22 28; g74 12/22 3-6; g73 11/22 24, 26; g73 12/22 3-4, 7; w71 284, 345-6, 414-15; te 143-6
children: w74 741; g73 12/22 7; w71 345-6; te 143-6
Christmas: w75 739-40; g74 12/22 3-4; g73 12/22 3-4, 7
customs vary: g71 10/22 5-6
practical: g74 12/22 5
use of natural: w74 530-2; w73 109; w71 444

GIFTS FROM GOD
abilities: w74 531-2, 534
appreciation for: w73 155-9
discernment of inspired utterances: w71 503
discussion: w73 372-3; w71 501-5
end of miraculous: w75 95; w74 447; g74 4/22 27-8; g74 12/22 27-8; w71 294, 503-5
faith: w71 502, 504
gifts in men: w75 667-8, 726-7; w74 620; hu 20; w71 748-53
healing: w71 502, 504
knowledge: w71 502-3
miraculous: w74 447; g74 4/22 27; g73 8/8 5-6
how imparted: w75 95
prophesying: w71 502-4
speaking in tongues: g74 12/22 27-8; g73 8/8 5; g72 11/8 7; w71 503-4
speech: sg 5; g71 2/22 7-10
wisdom: w71 502-4

GIFTS OF MERCY
discussion: w71 414-15; g71 8/8 27-8

GIHON
river: w71 540

GILBERT AND ELLICE ISLANDS
Jehovah's witnesses: yb76 24-5; yb75 24-5; yb74 24-5; yb73 24-5; yb72 34-5
population: yb73 24; yb72 34

GILEAD
Israelite occupants: w74 286
meaning of name: g74 5/8 25

GILEAD SCHOOL
appreciation for training: g75 11/8 25-6; w74 475; w73 663, 764; g73 5/8 26; g73 11/8 25
assignments of students: km 12/75 8; g72 11/22 24-6
curriculum: g75 11/8 25; g72 5/8 25
entrance requirements: or 144
experiences:
encouraging others to attend: w74 337
58th class: g75 5/8 25
59th class: km 6/75 1
foreign students: yb73 131
German missionaries: yb74 240-1
graduate statistics: yb75 201-2; g75 5/8 25; km 12/75 8; g73 5/8 25-6; g72 11/22 25-6; g71 5/8 26
languages taught: km 12/75 8
length of course: g75 11/8 25
locations: yb75 200-1
name: g71 5/8 25
opening: yb75 200-1; w73 399; yb72 256; g71 5/8 25
purpose: w74 670; g72 11/22 24-5; w71 82, 288; g71 5/8 25

Graduations
15th class: w72 478
50th class: w71 287-8; g71 5/8 24-6
51st class: w71 669-70; g71 11/8 24-6
52nd class: w72 286; g72 5/8 25-6
53rd class: w72 702-3; g72 11/22 25-6
54th class: w73 284; g73 5/8 25-6
55th class: w73 647; g73 11/8 25-6
56th class: w74 286; g74 5/8 25-6
57th class: w74 670; g74 11/8 24-5
58th class: w75 285; g75 5/8 24-6
59th class: w75 671-2; g75 11/8 24-6
(SEE ALSO MISSIONARIES)

GIRAFFE
discussion: g71 12/8 10-11

GIRLHOOD
change to womanhood: w73 520-3

GIVING
discussion: g74 12/22 3-6

GLACIERS
description: g73 8/22 26-7
glacier theory: g75 3/8 30; g75 6/8 7

GLANDS
ductless: g74 1/22 14; g72 6/22 17-20
pineal: g74 2/8 16
thymus: g74 2/8 16

GLASS
stained: g75 8/8 29-30

GLEANING
modern-day: g75 8/22 29; g75 12/8 30

GLIDERS
kite gliders: g75 5/22 30-1

GLUTTONY
Bible view: tp 158
discussion: w74 167-8

GOALS
failure to attain: w71 328-9
how attained: g73 1/8 4-8
personal: g74 8/22 6-8; km 5/73 2
setting purposeful: g74 8/22 6-8
youth: w75 463; g75 9/22 22-5; w72 274-6

GOATS (Symbolic)
parable of sheep and goats: ka 263, 284-91
characteristics: w74 250, 651
destruction: w74 652

GOD
application of term to Jesus: w75 63; w74 730; g72 5/22 28
atheism: g74 10/8 4; g74 12/8 30; w73 452
believing in: w73 451-2
cares about mankind: gc 3-31; g74 10/8 5-8, 17-22; w72 658-9; g72 10/22 4-16
comments on God's existence:
Newton, Isaac: g75 8/22 26; w74 643
Elohim: w73 702; bi8 1352
Father: w74 447-8
fear of: g72 9/8 28
friendship with: w73 457-62
'God is dead': tp 58
imitating: w74 146-56
Jehovah's title: bi8 1352
judgments: w75 664-6
knowing: w75 113-19; w72 37-40, 197, 469; g72 4/22 28; w71 265-6, 392, 539
man must not forget: te 91-4
man not forgotten by: g72 10/22 9-12
man's dependence on: w72 425-30
man's desire to worship: g75 5/8 3-4; g75 6/22 4
man's need of: g72 10/22 3-16
misconceptions: g74 1/22 17; w73 131-3; w72 508
Christendom: w71 408, 676
Judaism: g73 5/22 27-8
nations collide with: w72 31; w71 611-31; nc 3-29

nearness of: w72 521-32
Person: w74 220
proof of existence: w75 113-14; gc 8; ml 6-7; g75 4/8 8-9; g75 6/22 18; w74 643; g74 5/22 22; g74 10/8 8; w73 35-8; w72 388; pm 147; g72 10/22 4-8; w71 152, 325-7, 613; nc 4-5; g71 7/22 17-18; g71 8/8 3-7; g71 8/22 11-12; g71 9/8 7
proof of Godship: g73 1/22 7
requirements for pleasing: w73 63-4; g73 5/22 27-8; w72 250-1, 454-5, 475; or 14-18; pm 251-2; w71 37; g71 4/22 29
seeing: g71 8/22 28
seeking: w73 429-42
time: po 7-8; w73 579-83
way of approach to: g74 1/22 18-19; g73 5/22 27-8
wisdom of, in dealing with mankind: g71 6/8 12-14
(SEE ALSO JEHOVAH)

GODLY DEVOTION
discussion: w75 119-25
"sacred secret" (1 Ti 3:16): w75 286

GODPARENTS
Catholic church: w72 511-12

GODS (Goddesses)
Amaterasu: kj 156
Anath: w74 457-8
Apollo: w72 586; kj 157
Artemis: w72 586; kj 157
Atropos: ts 10
Babylon: ts 28-9
Bacchus: kj 150
Birappa: g72 12/22 15-16
Buddha: g71 1/8 21-2
Clotho: ts 10
Communism: w72 741
democracy: w72 741
derive from one source: ts 28-9
Diana: w72 586
Edom: po 95
El Tio: g71 8/22 15-16
Good Luck: w72 594
Greece: ts 28-9; w71 509-10
Huari: g71 8/22 15-16
humans in power: w75 227; g72 3/22 6
India: g72 12/22 15-16; w71 101
Kali: g72 1/22 24-5
Krishna: g75 11/8 10
Kumari: g75 6/22 30
Lachesis: ts 10
Liberty: w72 741
Marduk: w72 745; kj 224
Mars: kj 258
Materialism: w75 231-2
Molech: bi8 1355; kj 258
nationalism: w72 754
Perun: yb72 126
political State: w75 227-32
Rome: ts 28-9
Satan the Devil: w72 624-5, 629-30; dn 16-18, 26-7; g71 5/22 5
science: w75 231
Supay: g71 8/22 15
Svarog: yb72 126
Tammuz: w72 572; kj 149-52
"Unknown" gods: w73 429-33

GOD'S "ETERNAL PURPOSE" NOW TRIUMPHING FOR MAN'S GOOD (Book)
public talks: km 9/74 3-5
release: yb75 255

GOD'S KINGDOM OF A THOUSAND YEARS HAS APPROACHED (Book)
public talks: km 9/73 3-6
release: yb75 251

GOD'S ORGANIZATION
(SEE JEHOVAH'S ORGANIZATION)

GOG
destruction (Re 20:9): ka 154-8
discussion: kj 349-68
identified (Eze 38): sl 257, 368; yb75 215; w73 293-4, 343-4; kj 349-54, 394-5
attack: sl 257-63; w75 303-4; po 22-3; w73 293-7, 344-5; kj 357-62, 368-72, 382
time of attack: w73 295-6
identified (Re 20:8): ka 152-3
"Gog and Magog": w74 347-8
(SEE ALSO SATAN THE DEVIL)

GOLD
buying: g74 4/22 29
mining: g73 9/8 29
role in finance: g73 12/22 20-2
United States Treasury: g73 12/22 21-2; g71 8/22 5; g71 10/22 22-3
value per ounce: g74 3/8 29; g71 8/22 4; g71 10/22 21

GOLDEN AGE, THE (Magazine)
banned: yb74 115
distribution: yb75 124-6; yb72 132
editor: yb75 123
name changes: yb75 123
No. 27: yb75 126, 129; yb73 109
release: sl 101-2; yb75 122-3; w74 507; w73 398; ka 192-3, 233; pm 298; kj 64-5, 83
German: yb74 93
street distribution: pm 298
(SEE ALSO AWAKE!)

GOLGOTHA
location: w75 367

GONORRHEA
how spread: w75 48; g75 5/8 5, 8
physical effects: g75 5/8 7-8; g74 1/22 28; g73 3/8 29; g73 6/8 30; g72 2/8 18; g72 7/22 30
statistics: g75 5/8 5-6; w74 14, 424; g74 1/8 30-1; g74 4/22 30; g74 8/8 30; g73 5/22 30; g73 6/8 30; g72 10/22 31; g72 12/8 29; g71 3/22 30; g71 7/8 31; g71 8/22 29
(SEE ALSO VENEREAL DISEASE)

GOOD
doing good to others: te 111-14
Jehovah: w75 542
returning, for evil: g72 3/8 11

GOODNESS
discussion: w75 476-8
distinction between goodness and righteousness: w73 473

GOOD NEWS
definition: w74 330
discussion: w74 329-40; w73 680-3, 686-8, 690, 693; w71 301-8
disinterest in: g72 8/8 5-7
Era of:
beginning: po 85-6
expanded: w74 331
Greek word: w74 335-6
importance: w74 332-6
preaching: w75 681; sl 343; w74 37, 331-8, 568-9, 646-9; w73 658-61; or 3-7; w71 76-89
source: w74 329
"this good news of the kingdom": w74 4, 332, 334; w73 681-3, 687-8, 690, 693; ka 297-8, 307-8; w72 366; or 3-7; pm 100-1; w71 78-82, 302, 308, 466, 753-4

GOODWILL
persons of: w72 375-80
steps to becoming: w72 378-80; w71 237
"year of" (Isa 61:2): w72 368-74; w71 31

GORILLA
g74 8/8 20-3

GOSPELS
harmonious: g71 12/22 6, 8
spurious: g73 8/22 31

GOSSIP
telephone: g75 2/22 30

GOVERNING BODY
First Century
appointment of elders: or 59
appointment of seven assistants: w71 748
decisions: or 10
location: w71 759
members: w71 81, 686-7, 727, 748, 756, 759, 761
role in organization: w71 81
Modern-Day
activities: w74 206; yb74 62, 64, 257
appointment of elders: w75 86; yb75 248-9; or 61-3, 69
appointment of members: w71 727
beginning: w71 760-1
chairmanship: yb75 250
governments cannot dissolve: sl 261
identified: w71 81
members: yb73 257; w72 458
names of: w75 60
unjustly imprisoned: pm 370-1
membership enlarged: w75 60
presiding overseer: yb73 257
proper view of: w72 272
purpose: w72 703-4; w71 727
recommendations sent to: km 9/74 7
relation to Watch Tower Society: yb74 257; or 10-11; w71 81, 755-62
role in organization: w72 590, 755
rotation: yb75 249-50; yb73 257; w71 669-70, 759, 761-2
(SEE ALSO FAITHFUL AND DISCREET SLAVE, REMNANT)

GOVERNMENTS
blame religion: g74 7/22 29
corruption: w74 67; w71 299-300, 630
decline of confidence in: g75 12/8 30
democracy: g75 3/22 3-4; g75 6/22 29-30; g75 9/8 29; g72 3/8 30-1
Greece: g75 6/8 25-6
desirable: w72 611-12
dictatorships: g75 3/22 3-4
discussion: g75 3/22 3-6
exist at God's permission: w72 266-7
failure of human: w75 611; og 3; g75 3/22 3-4; w74 5, 547-51, 611-

16; ts 153-4; hu 3-5, 9-11; g74 6/22 4-10; g74 7/22 29; g74 9/8 5; g74 10/8 5-6, 15-17, 29; g74 11/22 16, 20; g74 12/8 9-11; g74 12/22 29; g73 2/8 30; g73 10/8 23-5; g73 11/8 3-6; w72 228-9, 231-3, 579-80, 612-16; g72 3/8 5-7; g72 10/22 13; w71 67-8, 165-6, 197, 299-300, 625-6, 630, 741; g71 9/8 30; g71 10/8 18-19
instability: w74 492
fate of human: w72 583; w71 623-4; nc 26-8; g71 8/22 9-10; g71 10/8 23
kinds: pm 14; w71 681
kingdom of God: w75 239, 260-2, 621-3, 632-5; og 24-9; g75 3/22 5-6; g75 4/8 11-14; w74 106-8; g74 8/22 27; w72 580-3; pm 224-5; w71 3-5, 165-7, 281, 286, 568-71, 634-5; te 159; g71 10/8 22-4
earthly administration: w74 292-4
ruler: w74 68-70
leaders distrusted: g74 3/22 6; g73 10/8 12; g73 11/8 3-5; g72 8/22 29
obedience to Caesar's: yb75 238; g74 2/22 27-8; tp 135-9; w72 266-9, 640; te 135-8
people's responsibility: w71 629-30
rise of: g71 6/8 20
symbolic representations: sl 217-18, 297-8, 304; pm 223-4
Theocracy: w71 681, 711, 714, 741-7
world government: w75 260-2, 615-16, 623; og 11, 13, 27-9; g74 6/22 9; g73 2/8 30; g73 10/8 14, 28-9; w72 611-12; w71 68, 197-8; g71 10/8 22-3
(SEE ALSO INDIVIDUAL COUNTRIES BY NAME)

GRAFFITI
prevalence: g74 8/22 3-4; g73 3/22 6; g73 7/8 30

GRAHAM, BILLY
attitude toward homosexuality: w75 560
Lausanne missionary conference: g74 12/8 12-13
neutral view on ordination of women: w75 560
politics: w75 560
salary: g72 10/8 30

GRAMMAR
Greek: g72 5/22 27-8
anarthrous nouns: w75 702-4
improving: sg 57-8
origin: g71 2/22 7-10
(SEE ALSO LANGUAGE)

GRANDPARENTS
honoring: g75 10/22 28

GRASSHOPPER
"ears": w75 560
jumping: g74 10/22 23

GRATIAN
Roman emperor: w72 626

GRATITUDE
how to express: w73 297-9; te 43-6

GRAVE
Greek and Hebrew words: w71 707-8; bi8 1353

GRAVITATION
w72 265

GREAT BRITAIN
abortion: g73 5/8 29
alcoholic beverages: g73 12/8 30
alcoholism: g75 2/8 16; g72 9/22 30
automobiles: g71 12/22 31
belief in God: g74 12/8 30
child mistreatment: w75 327
Church of England: w75 263; g75 4/8 24-6, 31; g75 5/22 15; g75 6/8 30; g74 8/8 30
prayer for British pound: g75 8/22 29
crime: g74 5/22 29; g73 8/8 31; g73 10/8 11; w72 614; g71 5/22 30
description: yb73 89
divorce: g74 4/22 4
doctors:
women: g75 11/22 31
drugs: g73 12/8 5; g71 1/8 30
economy: g74 4/8 4; g74 5/8 9-12; w72 616
energy crisis: g74 5/8 9-10
entertainment: g75 3/22 29
flag: g71 9/8 13
gambling: g75 4/22 30
government: g74 5/8 9-12
historic homes: g75 8/8 29
history: w72 444
illiteracy: g74 7/8 30
Jehovah's witnesses: yb76 24-5; g75 4/8 26; yb75 24-5, 88-90, 160-1; yb74 24-5; yb73 24-5, 88-141; yb72 34-5; g72 10/8 23; w71 508, 665-7, 721; g71 5/8 16
conventions: g75 10/22 16
"lost" tribes of Israel: w72 440-4
money: g71 4/8 30
moral breakdown: w75 327; g75 7/22 30; g74 4/22 5; g72 2/22 29-30; g72 8/22 9; g71 8/8 30-1
"Opium War": g75 5/8 9-12
police: g73 8/8 31
population: yb73 24; yb72 34
prisons: g73 10/22 31; g72 1/8 6-7; g71 10/8 30
Quebec, Canada: g75 3/8 16-17
rating of foreign products: g75 10/22 30
religion: g75 1/8 30; g75 4/8 24-6; g75 6/8 30; g74 12/8 30; g72 2/8 29; g72 8/8 30; g71 5/8 4; g71 5/22 29; g71 10/8 31
Roman occupation: g71 12/22 20
smoking: g71 12/22 30
sports:
violence: g75 6/22 29
strikes: g71 2/8 21-3
subways: g71 6/22 31
suicide: g71 11/8 30-1
three-day workweek: g74 11/8 30
tunnel to France: g74 5/22 31
unemployment: g75 3/22 8; g72 1/8 29; g72 4/8 29
United States: g74 2/8 30
women live longer: g74 10/22 31
working mothers: g74 1/22 31
world power: w71 717-18, 720-4, 728
World War II: yb73 119, 123
youth: g72 5/22 30

GREAT CROWD
clarification of understanding: sl 201, 332; yb75 156; ka 266-9; w72 50, 637-8, 721; pm 78; kj 178
come out of tribulation: w74 172; w72 376-7
earthly prospects: po 182-3; kj 307
evidence "great tribulation" near: w75 84-5
family-like arrangement: w73 107-8
fulfillment of prophecy: w74 572-3
gathering: ka 278-83; pm 173-4; w71 658-9; kj 319-21
holy spirit: w74 312-13; g74 8/22 28
identified: ka 266-9, 271; or 110; pm 78-9; kj 178
judgment: w74 280
marked in forehead: w72 50-1, 638
never die: ts 164-6
"new earth": sl 324-5, 358; w75 85; w72 239-40
perfection: ka 34-5
pictured by—
"mixed company" out of Egypt: po 181
Noah's sons and their wives: w74 666-8
sheep: w74 626
ten men: w74 628
proper attitude: w74 591
protection by Jehovah: w74 171-2, 758-9, 765-6
relation to remnant: w74 591; po 182-4; ka 276-83; kj 208-9, 307-8, 347, 381-2
spiritual paradise: sl 110; w74 668-9
spiritual security: w74 724, 758-9, 766
survive Armageddon: w73 678; ka 27-9, 399-401, 408-9
temple service: w72 607, 721-3, 753
unity: w74 623; hu 27
wave palm branches: w72 722
white robes: w72 608
(SEE ALSO OTHER SHEEP)

GREAT TRIBULATION
attack on God's people: w75 88
when begins: w75 88
(SEE ALSO ARMAGEDDON, TRIBULATION)

GREECE
ancient beliefs: po 40; ts 10, 26, 43-4, 96; g72 11/22 15, 17-18; w71 509-10; bi8 1366
Babylonian influence: ts 28-9, 44
burial permit: w75 71
food: g75 3/8 9-11
government: g75 6/8 25-6
ancient: g75 6/8 25; w71 742
constitution: w75 547-8
Greek Orthodox Church: w75 548-51
history: g72 1/22 13-17
Jehovah's witnesses: yb76 26-7, 32; yb75 16, 26-7; km 3/75 1; yb74 24-5; yb73 24-5; yb72 36-7; w71 678
conventions and special meetings: w75 547-52; g75 6/8 26; g75 9/8 29

marriages recognized by State: w75 548; g75 9/8 29; g75 12/8 17, 20-1
persecution: w75 71; g75 6/8 25; g75 12/8 17-21
marriage: w75 71
philosophy: g72 11/22 17-18
population: yb73 24; yb72 36
symbolic representation: w71 714-15
telephone conversations: g75 2/22 30
world power: po 132; w71 715-16

GREED(INESS)
discussion: w72 723-5
examples: w74 63, 197, 205, 404-6, 582; g74 4/8 19; g74 5/8 19; g74 6/8 25-6; g74 7/22 26; g74 9/8 4; g74 11/22 29; w73 30
results: w74 407; g74 10/8 6

GREEK
Bible translation: w74 361
grammar: g72 5/22 27-8
anarthrous nouns: w75 702-4
koiné or common: po 132-3; w73 581
philosophy adopted by Christendom: w75 55-6, 173

GREEK ORTHODOX CHURCH
Bible: w73 602
clergy: g74 10/22 13-14, 30

GREEK SCRIPTURES
(SEE CHRISTIAN GREEK SCRIPTURES)

GREENLAND
Jehovah's witnesses: yb76 24-5; yb75 24-5; yb74 24-5; yb73 11-12, 24-5; yb72 34-5
population: g75 10/8 30; yb73 24; yb72 34

GREEN REVOLUTION
g72 7/22 3-13, 29; g72 12/22 10

GREETINGS
disfellowshiped persons: w74 465, 468; km 11/74 4
greeting cards: g71 2/8 30
handshaking: g73 1/8 25-6

GRENADA
Jehovah's witnesses: yb76 24-5; yb75 24-5; yb74 24-5; yb73 24-5; yb72 34-5
population: yb73 24; yb72 34

GRIEF
enduring: g75 5/8 22-3
mourning for the dead: g74 12/8 26-8
overcoming: g74 12/8 28-9
(SEE ALSO MOURNING)

GROH, JOHN O.
w75 190

GROUND
curse on: w75 664-6

GROWTH
physical: w73 86-9; w72 112-13; g72 12/22 8
spiritual: w75 90, 92; w72 31; w71 605-6, 661-5

GRUDGES
w74 441; w72 707-8
(SEE ALSO FORGIVENESS)

GUADELOUPE
Jehovah's witnesses: yb76 26-7; yb75 26-7; yb74 26-7; yb73 24-5; w72 338, 532; yb72 36-7
population: yb73 24; yb72 36

GUAM
Jehovah's witnesses: yb76 26-7; yb75 26-7; yb74 26-7; yb73 26-7; w72 125; yb72 36-7
population: yb73 26; yb72 36

GUARD
private security guards: g75 9/22 30

GUATEMALA
Bible in many languages: w74 394
description: yb73 189-90
Jehovah's witnesses: yb76 26-7; yb75 26-7; yb74 26-7; g74 6/22 15-16; yb73 26-7, 189-209; yb72 36-7
Lake Izabal: g74 6/22 15-16
population: yb73 26; yb72 36
volcanoes: g75 11/22 24-5

GUERRILLAS
experience: g71 3/8 13-15
terrorism: g71 6/8 17-20

GUESTS
behavior of good: w74 61; g73 3/22 6; g73 11/22 13-15; g72 9/8 26
discussion: w73 599-600
entertainment: w72 403-4; g72 6/22 13-16
preparation for: g73 11/22 14
treatment of: g73 11/22 13-14

GUIDANCE
Bible a sound guide: g75 10/8 8-29
divine: w74 344
failure of worldly: g75 10/8 6-7
need of proper: g75 10/8 3-7; g73 10/8 13-16; g71 1/22 3-4

GUINEA, REPUBLIC OF
Jehovah's witnesses: yb76 30-1; yb75 30-1; yb74 8, 30-1; yb73 30-1; yb72 40-1
population: yb73 30; yb72 40

GUM ARABIC
g74 12/8 31

GUNS
accidents: g75 11/22 12, 29
availability: w74 102; g73 4/22 11, 29; g72 12/8 30
discussion: g72 7/8 21-3
employment carrying: w73 127-8
laws to control sale: g72 7/22 29
missing: g73 11/8 31
self-defense: g75 9/8 28; g75 11/22 12, 29; g75 12/8 28
youth: g73 2/22 30
(SEE ALSO WEAPONS)

GUYANA
beverages: g74 7/22 20
Jehovah's witnesses: yb76 26-7; yb75 26-7; yb74 26-7; g74 11/8 17; yb73 26-7; w72 478-9; yb72 36-7; g72 1/22 25-6; g72 2/22 12
population: yb73 26; yb72 36

GYMNASTICS
career abandoned: g71 9/22 6-8

GYPSIES
experience: g73 1/8 9-12
sea gypsies: g75 9/22 13-15

HABAKKUK (Book)
discussion:
chapter 3: w73 746-60

HABAKKUK (Prophet)
discussion: w73 746

HABITS
borrowing: g71 12/8 23-4
tobacco: w71 670-2

HADES
Greek conception: w73 237
Hebrew equivalent: ts 94-5; w73 237; g72 11/8 6; bi8 1353, 1361
'hurled into lake of fire': ts 118-19
meaning of term: ts 94-5, 98; w73 236-7; g72 11/8 6; bi8 1361
misconceptions: ts 95, 98; w73 236-7; g72 11/8 6-7
occurrences in Greek Scriptures: ts 94-5; bi8 1361
use of word in *New World Translation:* bi8 1361
(SEE ALSO GEHENNA, HELL)

HADRIAN
statue discovered: g75 9/22 30-1

HAGGAI (Prophet)
name: pm 25, 48

HAGRITES
w74 286

HAIR
barbering: g72 11/8 12-14
care: g72 11/22 22-3
factory workers: g72 8/22 30
head: w73 138-41; w72 666-7; g71 6/22 24
lice: g73 2/8 31
men: w72 666-7; g72 5/8 16, 31
spray: g72 10/22 30
style: w73 138-41; g72 8/22 30
wigs: g72 2/22 13-15
women: w72 666-7

HAITI
Jehovah's witnesses: yb76 26-7; yb75 26-7; yb74 26-7; yb73 26-7; yb72 36-7
population: yb73 26; yb72 36

HAM (Noah's Son)
shamed Noah: po 83

HAMAN
death: w71 182
nationality: w71 177
plotted death of Jews: w71 178
prophetic drama: w71 172-85
prophetic significance: w71 177

HANDBILLS
use by Witnesses: yb75 18; km 5/75 3; w74 510; km 6/74 3; km 12/73 3; or 105, 119

HANDBREADTH
unit of measure: g74 8/8 19

HANDICAPPED
causes: w74 319-20
consideration for: g73 6/22 29
experiences:
accept Bible truth: w75 559; w74 342; g74 10/8 26; g73 5/8 11; w72 221; g72 2/22 20
copes with paralysis: g75 2/22 12-16
Jehovah rewards faith: w74 702

participation in field service: w73 765-6; yb73 232; g73 5/8 11
worked at convention: g74 11/8 20
Jehovah "appoints": w74 319-20
proper view: g73 6/22 28-9; w71 262; g71 12/22 4
sight: w72 547; g72 5/8 17-20

HANDS
handshaking: g73 1/8 25-6
symbolic: w74 757

HAPPINESS
basis for: w73 157, 326-7; w72 207-8, 215-16, 243-4, 259-60; g72 2/8 3-4
contributing factors: g75 6/22 3-5; w74 205; g74 8/8 5-7; w73 137, 139, 156-7; tp 109-10; g73 7/22 19; g72 5/8 3-4; w71 345-6, 534-5; te 143-6; g71 9/22 3-6
discussion: w75 643-6
field service: w74 575-6
New Order: tp 109-10
Sermon on the Mount: w75 644-6; g71 6/8 27-8; g71 6/22 27-8; g71 7/8 27-8; g71 7/22 27-8; g71 8/8 27-8; g71 8/22 27-8; g71 9/8 27-8; g71 9/22 27-8; g71 10/22 27-8
(SEE ALSO JOY)

HARE KRISHNA
experience: g74 11/22 9

HARLOT(S)
symbolic: g72 10/8 22; kj 238-63

HAR-MAGEDON
(SEE ARMAGEDDON)

HARP OF GOD, THE (Book)
yb75 128

HARVEST
barley:
sheaf of firstfruits: w75 603
congregation of God: po 171-2
Jesus' illustration: w75 594, 596, 599
vegetables: g74 5/22 12
wheat:
two loaves of leavened wheat bread: w75 601-2

HATE
discussion: g72 9/22 3-4
effect on health: g74 2/22 11
examples: w72 707
for Christ: w73 649-53, 657
for Christians: w74 650-1; w73 656-61
godly: w74 442-3
hating bad: w74 153, 442-3
meaning of term: w74 442
murder: w74 675-6; w72 707
overcoming: w72 708; g72 9/22 4
when proper: w74 153, 442-3; w73 100; g72 9/22 3

HAWAII
earthquake: g73 6/22 30
Jehovah's witnesses: yb76 26-7; yb75 11, 26-7; km 2/75 3; km 6/75 1; yb74 26-7; yb73 14-15, 26-7; yb72 36-7; km 12/72 3, 5
life expectancy (males): g75 10/22 30
music: g73 6/8 12-14
population: yb73 26; yb72 36
proportion of unmarried women to men: g75 4/22 31
surfing: g73 7/22 17-18

HEAD
hair: w73 138-41; g71 6/22 24
headaches: g72 8/8 8-12

HEAD COVERING
women: w72 446-7

HEADSHIP
husband's responsibilities: w75 153-4; w74 117-18, 392-3; tp 139-40; g72 5/22 13-14; w71 582-3
New Order: w74 393; w73 368-9
recognition by children: tp 140-2
recognition by women: w75 154-5; w74 118; w73 255; tp 140-1; w72 270-1, 445-7; g72 2/22 7-8; g72 5/22 13-14; g72 9/22 27-8
theocratic: w73 255, 368-9; w72 266, 272-3, 729-31, 755-7

HEADSTONE
pm 188-90, 198-201

HEALING

"Faith Healing"
Bible view: w74 326-7; g72 11/8 7
discussion: g75 6/22 5-8
exposed: g75 6/22 6-8; w74 624; g73 8/8 28
Lourdes shrine: g75 4/22 31
money asked: w74 624
pagan practices: w73 697-701

Physical
acupuncture: g72 7/22 30; g72 9/8 12-16
after Armageddon: g75 10/8 23-4; ts 138-9; g74 9/8 23; kj 392-8
electroshock treatment: g72 9/22 30
herbs: g72 10/22 31
miraculous: w71 502, 504; te 43-4, 87-9, 107-9, 112-13
prayer: g75 9/22 4
performed by Jesus: sl 66-8; w73 365-6; te 43-5
prayer: w74 137-8
(SEE ALSO DOCTORS, MEDICINE, SURGERY)

Spiritual
anointed: w74 253
discussion: w74 758
great crowd: w74 406-7

HEALTH
acupuncture: g72 9/8 12-16
air pollution: g71 4/22 8, 13; g71 6/8 9-11
alcoholic beverages: g73 8/8 25; g71 6/22 4-5; g71 7/22 30
apples: g74 9/22 7
application of Bible principles: w72 195-6
backaches: g75 1/8 30; g73 8/8 23-5
bacteria: g73 3/8 9-11
bad breath: w72 414; g71 9/8 24-6
breast-feeding: g75 9/22 30
care of: w74 524; w72 412-15
climate change: g72 3/8 30
colds: g73 12/22 8-10
cosmetics: g75 9/8 29
deodorants: g74 3/8 25-6
diet: g74 9/22 3-7; g74 10/22 26; g73 1/22 4; g73 12/22 9; w72 413; g72 1/8 30; g72 6/8 18; g72 7/8 30; g72 12/22 8-11; g71 4/8 29; g71 9/22 30
disease prevention: g74 12/22 12; g73 1/8 21-2; g73 12/22 9-10; g72 6/8 17-20; g71 7/22 25; g71 9/22 18-19
effects of faith: g74 9/8 30
emotional ills: w75 255
emotions affect: g74 2/22 10-11; g74 5/22 27-8; g74 8/22 17-19; w73 291-2; g73 11/8 12; g73 12/22 10; w72 195-6; g72 8/8 11; w71 163-4
epilepsy: g71 8/8 20-3
exercise: g75 2/22 30-1; g74 2/22 11, 31; g74 9/8 23; g73 7/8 3; g73 8/8 23-5; g72 6/8 19-20; g72 8/22 12
experience:
effects of Bible truth: w75 247
fatigue: g74 2/22 8-11
first aid: g74 9/22 8
food: g73 8/22 4; g72 1/22 31; g71 7/22 30
food additives: g71 3/8 29
food poisoning: g73 3/8 10
food shortages: g74 9/22 3-7
gallstones: g71 5/22 25-6
headaches: g72 8/8 8-12
heart: g75 7/22 21-2; g75 12/22 29; w71 133
hormones: g74 1/22 13-16
horseradish: g71 3/8 30
laughter: g72 1/8 3-4
margin of safety: g73 4/8 20-3
massage: g73 9/8 24-6
mental: w75 759; g75 4/22 3-21; g73 9/22 17-20
Mosaic law health measures: w75 133-5
nervous breakdown: g74 8/22 16-19
noise affects: g72 1/22 30; g72 2/8 30; g72 8/22 30; g72 9/22 30
obesity: w74 133, 167-8; g74 4/22 21-2
old age: g72 1/22 20-3
overeating: w74 167-8; g74 9/22 3-4; g73 8/22 5; g71 2/22 6
perfection: g75 10/8 23-4; w74 134; w73 412-15
population growth threat: g71 1/8 30
posture: g73 8/8 24
potassium: g74 4/22 24
reducing devices: g72 12/22 31
relaxation: g74 8/22 18; g73 7/8 3-4
sin: w74 134
sleep: g75 9/22 31; g74 2/22 9; w72 414-15; g72 9/22 30
smoking: g74 2/22 30; g74 5/22 18-19; g74 11/22 30; g73 1/22 19; g73 8/22 17-20; g73 12/22 9; g72 4/8 31; g72 7/22 30; g72 9/8 31; g72 11/22 31
sprouted seeds: g75 12/22 25-6
stress: g75 1/22 30-1; g75 2/22 30-1; w74 524; g71 11/8 30-1
superstition hinders: g74 6/22 31
teeth: w72 414; g72 7/8 21-3

tongue: g73 1/22 17-19
unprocessed foods: g74 10/22 30
viruses: g73 12/22 8-9
vitamins: g74 2/22 9; g72 11/22 30; g71 6/8 10-11
water:
in pipes overnight: g75 11/22 31
water pollution: g71 7/22 29
Witness view of health matters: w75 415
world problem: g74 6/8 30-1
(SEE ALSO DISEASE, HUMAN BODY, MEDICINE)

HEARING
animals': g75 6/8 19-20
discussion: g75 6/8 17-20; g71 8/22 10
Greek word: w72 159-60
hazards: g73 8/22 31; g72 2/8 30; g72 8/22 30; g71 11/8 30
jellyfish: w75 560
loud music: g74 3/22 31
protection of: g75 6/8 20
rock music: g75 10/22 31; g72 4/8 30; g71 2/8 30; g71 11/8 30
snakes: g75 6/8 19
(SEE ALSO DEAF, EARS)

HEART
ability under stress: g73 4/8 21-2
at birth: g73 7/8 7-8
attacks: g75 2/22 30-1; g75 7/22 16-22; g75 10/22 29; g75 12/22 29; g74 1/8 31; g74 2/8 29; g74 9/8 23; g73 7/22 8-10; g73 9/22 29-30; g72 6/8 17, 19; g72 10/8 31; g72 11/8 30-1; g72 12/22 30
massage: g73 7/22 8-10; g73 9/8 25-6
Bible use: w72 695-6; w71 134
care: g75 7/22 21-2; g74 9/8 23; g73 5/22 31; g73 6/22 27; g72 6/8 17-20; w71 133; g71 2/22 29
circumcision: sl 34; w71 442-4
diet: g72 1/8 30; g72 6/8 18; g72 7/8 30
discussion: g75 7/22 16-22; w71 133-52
disease: w75 634; g75 10/22 29; tp 20; g73 2/22 30; g73 7/8 3; g72 3/22 19; g72 6/8 17; g71 2/22 29; g71 3/8 10; g71 4/22 31; g71 10/8 11
effect of stress: g75 10/22 29
effects of evil: w71 138, 143-4
faith exercised: w72 695-6
giraffe: g71 12/8 10
Greek word: w71 135
guarding: g75 1/8 6; w74 153; w71 133-4, 145, 147-52; g71 8/22 27-8
heartbeat: g73 11/22 19
Hebrew words: w71 135
mind: w71 134-42; sg 74-5
motivation: w73 287; g73 11/22 27; w71 134-9; sg 74-5
pulse: g74 7/22 14
pumping: g75 7/22 18; g74 7/22 14; g74 10/8 7; g72 1/8 3-4; g72 6/8 19; w71 133; g71 1/22 15
purity: g71 8/22 27-8
smoking: g71 8/22 29
soft water: g71 10/22 31
surgery: g75 11/22 29; w74 720; g74 6/22 18-20; g73 2/8 19, 29; g72 6/8 30; g72 6/22 29; g71 11/8 6-7
teaching so as to reach: w74 338-9; sg 73-8
transplants: g72 7/8 28; w71 135-6; g71 11/22 31
treacherousness: w71 139-42
wholeheartedness: w71 146-52
work capacity: g74 7/22 14

HEAT(ING)
boring by: g72 2/8 30
home: g74 1/22 22-3
sun: g72 10/8 26

HEAVEN
evidence of heavenly hope: w75 106
Paul's vision: sl 131-4
requirements for entry: g73 5/8 6
symbolic: w72 231-8; w71 511-12
who go to: g74 8/22 27; w73 730-3; g73 5/8 5-7

HEAVENLY JERUSALEM
(SEE JERUSALEM ABOVE)

HEAVENS
symbolic: sl 217-18, 297, 304-5, 310, 322-4

Physical
creation: w71 43-4
mysteries: g74 1/8 12-15
perishable: w71 480
reflect Jehovah's glory: g71 8/8 3-5
water canopy: po 75
(SEE ALSO ASTRONOMY, SOLAR SYSTEM, UNIVERSE)

Righteous
new heavens: po 186-7; g74 8/8 11; w71 635

Wicked
composition: g75 8/22 28; w71 479, 511
destruction: sl 323-4, 356-7; w74 95, 666; po 186; pm 67-71; w71 511-12

HEBREW
Adamic language: w74 43
alphabet: g71 9/8 20
numbers: g71 9/8 20
poetry: g73 2/8 27-8

HEBREWS (Book)
background: w73 213-18
discussion: w73 213-18
purpose: w73 42
summary of contents: w73 43-9
time written: w73 45; pm 330

HEBREW SCRIPTURES
divine name: pm 388
(SEE ALSO BIBLE, BIBLE MANUSCRIPTS, BIBLE TRANSLATIONS)

HEDONISM
g72 1/22 26

HEGAI (Eunuch)
w71 175

HELL
belief in fiery torment: w74 145; w73 132-3, 232-3; g73 7/22 27; yb72 54-5; g72 11/8 6-7; w71 627-8, 646
Christendom: ts 89-91
not good motivation to serve God: w75 58; ts 89-90, 98
pagan: g75 4/22 30; ts 88-90, 96
results: ts 89-90, 96
source of: w75 56; ts 96
unreasonable: g75 10/22 7
Bible view: ts 90-1, 93-5
clergy: w73 132
condition: w73 231-41; g72 3/8 17
discussion: ts 88-98; w73 227-47; g73 7/22 27-8
experiences:
witnessing to believers: g73 2/22 9; km 3/73 4
Gehenna: ts 110-17; w73 237-8, 246; bi8 1355-6
Greek and Hebrew words: ts 92, 94-5; w73 233-4, 236-7; g72 3/8 17; g72 11/8 6-7; bi8 1353, 1361
"limbo": ts 91-2
release from: w73 232-47
rich man and Lazarus: ts 98-110; w73 236-7
survey on belief: g73 5/8 5

HEMOPHILIA
g75 2/22 30

HEMORRHOIDS
g75 1/8 25-6

HENSCHEL, MILTON G.
Gilead graduations: w75 671; g75 5/8 26; w73 647; g73 11/8 26; g72 5/8 25-6
service tours: yb76 65, 166-8, 170-1, 173, 186, 188-92, 197-8, 253; km 7/75 1; km 8/75 1; yb75 211-12; yb74 39, 46-7, 56, 216; km 7/74 1; yb73 13, 69-70, 76, 130, 168-9, 174-5, 178-9, 185, 195, 203, 205, 233, 242; yb72 82-3, 91-3, 105, 138-9, 155, 164, 168, 202, 210-12, 224, 229, 240, 248; km 3/71 1

HEPATITIS (Jaundice)
babies: g72 6/22 29
blood transfusions: g75 6/8 29; g74 5/22 18-20, 30; g74 6/22 17, 19, 21; g74 10/22 30-1; g73 5/22 31; g73 7/8 31; g72 3/8 30; g71 2/8 30-1; g71 3/22 13; g71 4/22 30; g71 5/22 30; g71 6/22 8; g71 7/22 30-1
discussion: g72 5/8 21-3
hemophilia treatment: g75 2/22 30
pierced ears: g74 6/8 30
seafood: g74 1/8 31
treatment by light: g71 12/22 30

HERALD OF THE MORNING (Magazine)
yb75 36-8; w73 395

HERBS
use in "bush medicine": w73 697-8, 700
value: g72 10/22 31

HEREDITY
genes: g74 2/8 16
incestuous marriages: w75 72-4
overweight: g74 4/22 22

HERMON (Mountain)
transfiguration: w74 78

HEROD AGRIPPA I
sl 222

HEROD AGRIPPA II
sl 222

HEROD ANTIPAS
birthday party: te 123-5
Jesus' appearance before: w75 8; sl 222

HERODIANS
sl 222-3

HEROD THE GREAT
attempted murder of child Jesus: sl 222
Jerusalem besieged: pm 272
HEROIN
connection with marijuana: g74 5/8 5, 30
deaths: tp 160; g73 12/8 6
drug addiction: w73 179; g73 12/8 6, 11; w72 596; g71 3/22 30-1; g71 4/8 18
traffic in: g73 3/22 30; g73 12/8 6
(SEE ALSO DRUGS, NARCOTICS)
HERO WORSHIP
athletes: g73 5/22 29-30
HEZEKIAH
aqueduct: g73 1/8 13
reign: w71 394-5
HIBERNATION
g72 1/8 20
HICCUPS
g72 2/8 30
HIDDEKEL
river: w71 540
HIEROGLYPHICS
g71 11/22 24-6
HIGHER CRITICISM
computers: g72 1/22 27-8
Pentateuch: g73 3/22 16-17; g72 2/22 27-8
proper view of: w74 181
view of Bible: g73 3/22 16-19; w71 324
(SEE ALSO BIBLE AUTHENTICITY)
HIGH PRIEST
Aaron: ka 103-5; pm 175-6
atonement day: w74 176
Israel: w74 157
Jesus Christ: w74 157-9, 251; w73 308-12; ka 87-93, 96, 102-3; pm 176, 179, 181-5
Joshua: pm 176-85
prophetic significance of Israel's: w74 251; ka 103-6
sign of dedication: ka 104
turban: pm 402-3
(SEE ALSO PRIESTS)
HIGHWAYS
garbage in pavement: g72 2/8 29-30
grooves: g71 6/8 30
hallucinations: g74 3/22 11
safety: g73 10/22 31
United States: g72 6/8 4; g71 4/22 17
HIJACKING
g73 3/8 30
HIKING
dangers of mountain: g75 9/22 29
discussion: g73 8/22 24-7
HIMMLER, HEINRICH
yb74 174, 195-7, 202, 205, 211
HINDI
number speaking: g75 11/8 29
HINDUISM
Babylonian influence: ts 44-5
beliefs: w74 624; ts 9, 36-7; g74 1/8 18-19; g74 1/22 17; g74 7/22 8-10; w73 604; g73 7/8 16-21; g72 2/22 19
desire for "escape": g75 11/8 9-10
caste: g75 11/8 9
customs: g74 7/22 8-11
dances: g71 12/8 25
discussion: g75 11/8 8-11
effect of: g73 6/22 8-9
experiences: yb76 256-7; yb75 13; w74 644; g74 7/22 9-10; g73 7/8 16-21; g72 1/22 24-6
fire walking: g73 12/8 23
gods:
living-child goddess: g75 6/22 30
meditation: g75 11/8 10-11
membership: sl 206; g74 7/22 8; w71 14
rosary: w74 259
similarities to Catholicism: g74 7/22 8-9
"thali": g74 7/22 10-11
yoga: g75 2/22 27-8
HINNOM
discussion: ts 111, 113-15
location of valley: ts 113; bi8 1355
'low plain of fatty ashes' (Jer 31:40): ts 113
symbolic: ts 111, 113-15
(SEE ALSO GEHENNA)
"HIPPIES"
experiences: w74 643-4; g74 11/22 8-12; yb73 11; w71 574-5
"Jesus people": g72 11/8 3-8
HIPPOCRATES
g72 12/22 23
HIPPOPOTAMUS
g73 11/22 30-1
HISTORY
African: g74 12/22 18
ancient: g74 4/8 22-6
ancient Near East: w73 644; g72 1/22 13-17; w71 381-2
Asia: w72 444
Catholic papacy: g71 5/8 12-16
dates often unreliable: g72 5/8 28
difficult to establish facts: g74 12/22 16
discussion: g74 4/8 22-6
epitome of Bible: w75 579-88
Europe: g73 1/8 16-19; g72 6/8 12-16; g72 9/22 21-5; g71 6/22 16-19
industry: g71 4/22 14-17
modern-day witnesses of Jehovah:
United States: yb75 34-256
North America: g73 2/22 4-5; g71 5/22 13-16
proper view of: g74 12/22 19
purpose of Bible's: po 65
rewriting: g74 12/22 16-18
sources: g74 4/8 22-5
South America: g71 1/22 20-3
superiority of Bible's: g74 4/8 25-6; g74 10/8 9-10; g74 12/22 19
theories regarding: g74 12/22 18-19
world since 1914: w71 299
HITLER
automobile swindle: w75 241
church support: g75 2/22 19-20; yb74 66, 112-13
euthanasia program: w75 294
oath of obedience to: g75 7/22 27-8
promises: yb74 211; ka 8-9; g73 1/22 5-6
rise to power: yb74 65-6
Roman Catholic Church:
concordat: w75 398; g72 4/22 16
Vatican support: g75 2/22 17-23; g72 4/22 16-17; g71 12/8 3-4
statements on—
clergy: g75 2/22 20
conscience: w75 209
swastika: g75 2/22 22
tactics: w73 515
Thousand-Year Plan: ka 7-9
Witnesses persecuted by: g75 2/22 22; yb74 108-28, 132-90, 193-204, 210-12, 238; w72 395-9; g72 4/22 22-3
Witnesses send warning: yb75 174; yb74 110-11, 136-9, 155, 161
Witnesses' victory over: yb74 210-12, 216, 238, 249-51
(SEE ALSO NAZISM)
HITTITES
discussion: w71 348-9
HOBBIES
memorizing Bible facts: g75 9/22 25-6
oil painting: g74 5/8 21-3
sewing: g73 8/22 9-12
stamp collecting: g71 7/8 20-3
HOLIDAYS
Bairam (Moslem): w74 742
birthdays: te 123-6
Carnival: g74 5/22 31; g73 3/8 5-8
Christian view: w74 739-41; g74 2/8 27-8; g73 12/22 6-7
Christmas: w75 739-40; w74 739-41; g74 12/22 3-4; yb73 212; g73 1/8 28; g73 12/22 3-7; g72 10/22 29; te 126; g71 6/22 23-4; g71 8/22 16
discontinuance of religious holidays after Babylon's destruction: sl 245
Easter: g75 4/22 29; g73 1/8 28
Halloween: g71 12/22 30
May Day: g74 2/8 27-8
Mother's Day: g74 2/8 27-8
New Year: w74 32
"official" holidays: g73 8/8 30-1
St. Valentine's Day: g74 2/8 27-8
Witnesses adjust view of: yb75 147
HOLLAND
(SEE NETHERLANDS)
HOLY (Holiness)
meaning of term: w73 741; tp 163; w72 595; or 154
HOLY CONTRIBUTION
kj 400-2
HOLY ONES (Saints)
torment false worshipers: ts 122
HOLY PLACE
Christendom's: w75 741-4
right condition: w71 711-28
HOLY ROMAN EMPIRE
Hitler's plan: ka 8-9

g, Awake!; **ka**, God's Kingdom of a Thousand Years; **kj**, "The Nations Shall Know that I Am Jehovah"; **km**, Kingdom Ministry; **or**, Organization; **pm**, Paradise Restored—By Theocracy!; **po**, God's "Eternal Purpose"; **sg**, Theocratic School Guidebook; **sl**, Man's Salvation out of World Distress!; **te**, Listening to the Great Teacher; **tp**, True Peace and Security; **ts**, Is This Life All There Is?; **w**, Watchtower; **yb**, Yearbook. **Complete list on page 6.**

HOLY SPIRIT
active force: w74 421-3; kj 43
aid to faithfulness: w74 64, 415, 479
aid to living morally clean life: w74 489
aid to speaking: w74 414-15
anointing: w75 105-8
asking for: w74 115-16; w72 329-30
begetting: g74 8/22 27; w73 730, 732
Bible writing: w75 141-6; g72 2/8 27-8; w71 228-9; sg 15-17; g71 11/8 27-8
born of water and spirit: g74 8/22 27
discussion: g71 3/22 27-8
fruitage: w71 664
grieving: w74 422
heavenly life: w73 730, 732
helper (paraclete): w74 422-3; w71 461-2; g71 3/22 27-8
miraculous gifts: w71 501-5
on "great crowd": w74 312-13
on Jesus Christ: sl 176-7
operation on congregation: w73 110
other sheep: g74 8/22 28
Pentecost: po 158-9; w71 398-9
personalized: g71 3/22 27-8
prayer: w74 115-16; w73 405
receiving: w74 340; km 3/74 1
religious "ecstasy" no evidence of: g75 5/22 27-8
relying on: w74 314
remembrancer: w74 414-15
sealing: w72 636
sin against: w75 460; ts 181-2
speaking in tongues: g74 12/22 27-8
teacher: w74 414-15
Trinity: w74 363, 421-3
witness bearer: w72 562-3
(SEE ALSO SPIRIT)

HOLY YEAR
discussion: w75 397-400
frequency: sl 205
1933: w75 397-8
1950: w75 398-9
1975: w75 390, 397, 399-400; sl 205; g75 2/22 29; g72 3/8 29

HOME BIBLE STUDIES
(SEE BIBLE STUDIES)

HOMEMAKING
bookkeeping: g71 6/22 13-15
cleaning: g74 5/8 13-15; g74 12/22 7
cutting expenses: g75 8/8 16-18; g74 12/22 7
organization: g74 5/8 13-15
schedule: g74 12/22 7
training children: g72 5/8 5-8; g71 9/8 8-11

HOMES
basement: g74 9/8 13-14
bookkeeping: g71 6/22 13-15
can openers: g72 2/8 30
care of: g74 5/8 13-15; g74 12/22 7
Christian atmosphere: w74 311-17
cleanliness: km 1/75 3
closets: g74 9/8 13-14
construction: g72 10/22 28; g71 1/8 23-4
cutting expenses: g75 1/8 7-8; g71 3/8 8-10
fire: g71 12/8 14-16
generation gap: w74 261-7, 270
heating: g74 1/22 22-3
Iceland: g71 1/22 8-9
indoor gardens: g72 7/8 13-15
log cabin: g75 11/8 31
mobile: g72 3/22 12-15; g71 11/22 13-16
nursing: g73 1/22 12
organization of: g74 5/8 13-15
ovens: g71 9/8 30
painting rooms: g74 3/22 15-16
plants: g72 7/8 13-15
power failure: g74 3/8 17-19
precautions with cleaners: g75 12/22 30; g71 12/8 31
protection against theft: g75 11/22 14; g73 4/22 8, 14-15
repairs: g74 7/8 17-20; g74 12/8 7
rocking chair: g74 11/8 22-3
storage: g74 9/8 12-14
temperature: g74 1/22 23
uninvited calls: g71 12/22 9-13
water beds: g72 3/22 29-30

HOMESICKNESS
discussion: g72 7/22 14

HOMOSEXUALITY
attempt to justify: w73 356; g71 5/22 5-6
Bible view: w74 483-6; w73 355-6; tp 149-50; w72 734-5; g72 4/8 23; g72 4/22 20; g72 12/8 7
cause: g75 10/8 17
changing from: w74 486-9
clergy view: w75 560; w74 483, 493, 562; g74 4/22 30; g74 5/22 29; g74 7/8 29; g74 9/22 30; w73 355-6; g73 2/22 7; g73 5/22 29; g73 7/8 31; g73 8/8 29; g73 10/8 15, 31; g73 11/8 29; g73 12/8 29; g72 4/8 22-3; g72 4/22 18-20; g72 6/8 29; g72 6/22 30; g72 8/8 30; w71 451, 557; kj 158; g71 5/8 5-6, 30-1; g71 6/8 30; g71 7/22 4-5, 9; g71 10/8 31; g71 11/8 30
dangers: w75 364
discussion: w74 483-9
divorce: w71 31-2
effects: w74 483-4
experience:
  truth overcomes: w74 487-8
fornication: w72 767-8
Greek word: tp 149
homosexual churches: g74 2/8 30; w73 355; g73 5/22 29
homosexual synagogue: w74 135
Jesus' view: w74 484-6
legalization: g72 8/8 30
lesbianism: g75 3/8 31; w74 390-1
marriage: g75 3/8 31; g73 8/8 29; w71 451; g71 6/8 30; g71 7/22 4
marriage illegal: g75 2/22 30
misconceptions: g72 5/22 29
overcoming: g73 11/8 29-30
prevalence: g72 4/8 22; g72 8/8 30
prisons: g75 3/8 31; g72 1/8 9
sodomy: w74 485
venereal diseases: g73 4/22 31; g72 8/22 29
YMCA: w74 684
(SEE ALSO MORAL BREAKDOWN)

HONDURAS
description: g72 4/8 26
Hurricane Fifi: g74 12/22 21-6
  relief sent: g74 12/22 26; km 11/74 1
Jehovah's witnesses: yb76 16-17, 26-7; yb75 26-7; yb74 26-7; g74 12/22 22-6; w73 134-5; yb73 26-7; g73 3/8 14; w72 222; yb72 36-7; w71 679
population: yb73 26; yb72 36
war: g72 4/22 14

HONESTY
balanced view: g74 12/8 5-6
business dealings: w75 291-3; g74 3/8 27-8; g74 12/8 6; w73 316; w71 127-8, 765-7
discussion: w74 245-7; g74 12/8 3-6; w73 316-18
employees: w75 698; w74 151; g74 3/8 28; w73 316; tp 118-19; g71 4/8 13
examples: w75 293, 489, 763; yb75 6; g75 3/8 15; w74 39, 205, 411-12, 516, 555; g74 3/8 28; g74 11/8 20; g74 12/8 3, 5; w73 358-9, 597-8, 633; g73 7/22 29; g73 11/8 19; w72 318, 381; yb72 241-2; g72 10/22 22; w71 191, 388, 533; g71 4/8 13; g71 10/22 15-16
importance: g75 2/22 31; g75 3/22 30; w74 246-7; w72 36
lost items: w74 204-5; g74 10/22 30
public welfare: w73 316-17
schoolchildren: w75 699
speaking truth: g74 12/8 4; w73 597-8; tp 114-16
types of honesty: g74 12/8 3-6; w73 316-18

HONG KONG
crime: g75 1/8 29; g71 2/22 30
disaster: g72 8/8 29; g71 10/22 29
discussion: g73 7/8 22-5
Jehovah's witnesses: yb76 26-7; yb75 12-13, 26-7; yb74 26-7, 44-7, 49-51, 56-64; yb73 26-7; g73 7/8 25; w72 221; yb72 36-7
marriage: g71 4/8 24-6
materialism: g74 9/22 9
population: yb73 26; yb72 36
religion: yb74 45; g74 2/22 30; g73 7/8 24-5; g72 3/22 17-18; g72 8/22 5
Treaty of Nanking: g75 5/8 11

HONOR
husband toward wife: w74 212
Jehovah: g72 3/22 19
parents: g75 10/22 27-8; g72 3/22 19

HONORARY TITLES
Bible view: w75 726; kj 303-4
minister: w75 730-1
Rabbi: w75 726

HOPE
aid to endurance: ts 174-5
basis: w75 80-6; w74 643-5; w73 643-6; g73 10/8 27
Bible gives: w73 765-6; g73 10/22 29
discussion: w75 80-6
effect of lack: g74 10/8 23; g72 9/8 31
evidence of heavenly: w75 106
examples of having: w74 643-4
in Jehovah: w74 701
meaning of term: w72 617; dn 3-4
"of his glory" (Col 1:27): w73 692-3
physical benefits: w75 80, 247; g75 8/8 26; w72 195
strengthening: w74 645-6
worldly view: w75 80

HOREB (Mountain)
po 109-10

HORMONES
body's defense system: g72 12/22 20
discussion: g74 1/22 13-16
use for mental illness: g75 4/22 13

HORNS
small horn (Da 8:9): w71 715-17, 720, 724
symbolic: pm 141
ten (Re 17:12, 16): g75 2/8 8-9

HOROSCOPE
w74 716; g73 11/22 3-5

HORSE(S)
bells: pm 402-3
black (Re 6:5): ts 162
eyes: g71 7/22 19
mustangs: g71 9/22 31
odds against evolution producing: g75 3/22 23
racing: g74 7/8 30
red (Zec 1:8): pm 127-8
riding: g72 10/22 24-6
symbolic: pm 127, 222-3, 225-8
use in witnessing: yb75 62-3

HORSEMEN
Revelation 6: w74 355-9; ts 161-2
symbolic: pm 127-8

HORSE RACING
g72 10/22 26

HORSERADISH
g71 3/8 30

HOSPITALITY
appreciation for: w75 360
customs vary: g71 10/22 6
discussion: w75 359-60; km 9/75 7; w73 372, 599-600; g73 11/22 13-15
displaying: w74 440
examples: w75 359-60; yb74 43-4
opportunities for: w75 360
social gatherings: km 7/74 3

HOSPITALS
blood donors: g71 3/8 29
blood transfusion liability: g73 2/22 29
blood transfusions: g74 6/22 21; g71 8/22 31
 form: g71 7/22 31
breast-feeding in: g74 7/8 14-16
childbirth: g74 6/8 21-3
cost for hospitalization: g71 10/22 31
 China: g75 12/8 31
experiences in witnessing: yb73 39, 204
infections: g72 5/8 29
mentally ill: g73 9/22 17-18
mistakes: g71 2/22 29
negligence: g73 2/8 11-12
violation of patients' rights: w75 759; g74 3/22 20-1; g74 6/8 23-4; g71 11/8 7-9
(SEE ALSO DOCTORS, MEDICINE, SURGERY)

HOUSE(S)
apartment: g74 9/8 14
basement: g74 9/8 13-14
closets: g74 9/8 13-14
construction: g71 1/8 23-4
 failure to keep pace with need: g74 8/8 30-1
cost of buying: g75 7/22 30
cutting expenses: g75 1/8 7-8
fire: g71 12/8 14-16
household hints: g74 12/22 7
household organization: g74 5/8 13-15
housing problems: g72 10/22 15
Iceland: g71 1/22 8-9
Jehovah's: te 155-8
log: g75 11/8 31
mobile homes: g72 3/22 12-15; g71 11/22 13-16
overcrowded: g74 2/8 30
painting:
 with brush or roller: g74 3/22 15-16
 with spray gun: g75 8/8 30
repairs: g74 7/8 17-20; g74 12/8 7
rocking chair: g74 11/8 22-3
storage in: g74 9/8 12-14
United States: g74 2/8 30
water beds: g72 3/22 29-30

HOUSE-TO-HOUSE PREACHING
adaptability: or 115-16; sg 150, 172-5
attitude of publisher: km 7/75 4; w73 21-2; w72 726-9; or 130-2; km 4/72 3; km 6/72 3-4; km 9/72 8; w71 214, 218-19, 313, 413-14
Bible precedent: or 56
discussion: or 114-20
effectiveness: km 7/75 4; sg 99; km 8/71 4
experiences:
 apartment house: yb73 39; yb72 101-2
 not-at-homes: yb73 14; w71 219-20
group witnessing: km 6/71 4
importance: w74 241-2; km 5/71 4
improving: sg 96-9
introductions: km 5/74 8
legal rights: g71 12/22 9-13; km 8/71 3-4
literature offers: or 116-17
 Bibles: km 6/72 4
magazine distribution: or 117-18
manners: km 7/75 4
methods: or 114-20, 122, 131-2
modern beginning: yb75 39-40, 45-6
not-at-homes: or 118-19; w71 219-20; km 10/71 8
objections: g72 8/8 7; sg 92-4
prejudgment: km 3/75 4
preparation: sg 39; km 3/71 4; km 7/71 4
presentations: km 9/71 2; km 12/71 2
publisher's appearance: sg 184-7; g71 7/22 26
purpose: w74 241-2; w71 611
reaching householder's heart: km 7/75 4
reporting: or 126-8; km 4/71 3
tact: km 3/72 4; sg 70-2
territory coverage: or 73-4, 118-20; km 11/72 8
 rurals: km 6/75 3
training new publishers: yb75 227-8; km 5/74 7
under ban: w72 137-8
use of Bible: km 2/75 4; km 9/75 8; km 12/75 7; or 114, 116; sg 122-9
use of questions: km 4/75 4
witnessing to—
 children: km 12/75 8
 men: km 12/75 8
 women: km 12/75 8
working in pairs: or 120
(SEE ALSO FIELD SERVICE)

HOVERCRAFT
g73 11/22 21-3

HOWE, JUDGE HARLAN B.
yb75 105, 107-8, 116-17

HUMAN BODY
adaptation: g71 10/22 3
adenoids: g74 2/8 16; g72 6/8 31
adrenals: g74 1/22 14; g73 4/8 20-1
aging process: g75 1/8 27; g71 2/22 13-15
air pollution's effects: g71 6/8 9
amniotic sac: g74 2/8 13-14
appendix: g74 2/8 16; g72 12/8 30
arteries: g74 7/22 14-15
artificial body parts: g75 1/22 30; g73 12/22 24-6
back: g73 8/8 23-5
bacteria: g74 7/22 13; g73 3/8 11
bad breath: g71 9/8 24-6
balance: g73 1/8 31
blood: g74 5/22 18-19; g74 7/22 12-15; g74 12/8 17; g73 4/8 22; w72 412; g72 7/8 28; g72 12/22 17-18; g71 3/8 16-18
 chart showing cells: g74 7/22 13
blood vessels: g74 7/22 14-15
blushing: g74 3/22 12-14
body-building: g73 5/22 21-4
bone marrow: g74 7/22 12
bones: w72 412
brain: w75 263, 684; g75 8/22 30; ts 17-18; g74 12/8 16-21; tp 105; g72 2/8 30; g72 8/8 30-1; g72 12/8 31; g71 8/8 21-2
breast: g71 11/8 31
breathing: w72 414; g72 1/22 11; g71 9/22 16-19
can live forever: w74 375; ts 17-18; g73 11/22 19; g71 2/22 12-15
capillaries: g74 7/22 15
care: w74 524; g74 8/22 19; w72 412-15; g71 6/8 9-11; g71 7/22 24-6
cells: g74 10/8 7; g72 10/22 7-8; g71 3/8 16-18, 26; g71 8/8 5-6; g71 9/8 5-7
chemistry: g71 7/22 11
circulatory system: g74 7/22 12-15; w72 387
cleanliness: g74 3/8 25; g71 7/22 24-6
coping with limitations: g75 6/22 3-5
creative capacity: w75 263
digestion: g72 1/8 4; g71 3/22 16-20
discussion: g73 4/8 20-3; g72 12/22 17-20
DNA: g71 2/22 12-13; g71 8/8 6; g71 9/8 5-7
ductless glands: g74 1/22 14; g72 6/22 17-20
ears: g73 4/8 21; g71 8/22 10; g71 9/22 30
evidence of Creator: g74 2/8 15-16; g74 3/22 14; g73 4/8 20-3; g72 10/22 7-8; g72 11/8 23

exercise: g75 2/22 30-1; g74 8/22 7; g74 9/8 23; g73 7/8 3; g72 6/8 19-20; g72 8/22 12
eyes: g73 4/22 30; w72 388
face: g72 6/8 30; g71 10/22 31
Fallopian tubes: g74 2/8 12-13
fatigue: g74 2/22 8-11
feet: g72 3/22 22-4
feminine hygiene: g74 3/8 26
first aid: g74 9/22 8
gallbladder: g72 2/22 29; g71 5/22 25-6
growth: w73 86-9
gums: g72 7/8 21-3
hair: g73 2/8 31; g71 6/22 24
headaches: g72 8/8 8-12
hearing: g72 4/8 30; g71 8/22 10; g71 11/8 30
heart: g74 7/22 14; g74 9/8 23; g74 10/8 7; g73 4/8 21-2; g73 11/22 19; g72 6/8 17-20; w71 133-4; g71 1/22 15; g71 10/22 31; g71 11/22 31
hiccups: g72 2/8 30
homeostasis: g74 1/22 14
hormones: g74 1/22 13-14
hypothalamus: g74 1/22 14
immunity of: g74 2/8 16; g72 12/22 17-20
inner clock: g71 2/22 30
intestines: g73 4/8 21; g71 3/22 16-20
iron: g74 7/22 12
kidneys: g73 4/8 20; g72 9/22 30
laughter: g72 1/8 3-4
lice: g71 11/8 31
limb restoration: g72 9/22 31
liver: w74 452; g73 4/8 21; g72 1/8 3-4; g72 10/22 8; g71 6/8 10-11; g71 6/22 5
lungs: g73 4/8 20; g72 9/8 31; g72 10/22 30; g71 3/8 26; g71 6/8 8; g71 9/22 16-19
margin of safety: g73 4/8 20-3
metabolism: g74 4/22 22
mouth: g71 9/8 24-6
muscles: w72 412
nervous system: g74 8/22 16-19; g72 10/22 8
nose: g75 7/8 6
ovaries: g73 4/8 21
paired organs: g73 4/8 20-1
pancreas: g73 4/8 21
perspiration: g74 3/8 24-5
pineal gland: g74 2/8 16
placenta: g74 2/8 13-14
potassium: g74 4/22 24
pulse: g74 7/22 14
race variations: g73 2/8 5-7
relaxation: g74 8/22 18; g73 7/8 3-4
resistance to disease: g74 9/8 20, 22-3; g74 10/8 7; g74 12/22 12
RNA: g71 9/8 5-6
skin: g72 2/8 31; g71 1/8 17; g71 1/22 11
sleep: g75 9/22 31; w72 414-15; g72 9/22 30
sneezing: g71 3/8 6
speech: g74 12/8 21; g73 1/22 18-19
sperm: g74 2/8 12-13
spleen: g73 4/8 22; g71 3/8 16-18
sprain: g74 9/22 8
stomach: g74 2/8 17; g73 4/8 21; g71 3/22 17
strain: g74 9/22 8
stress: w74 524
sweat glands: g74 3/8 24
tallness: g75 5/22 29; g75 6/8 29
taste: g73 1/22 19
teeth: g73 1/22 31; w72 414; g72 2/8 30; g72 7/8 21-3; g71 9/8 24-5
temperature: g75 12/8 25-6
thymus gland: g74 1/22 14; g74 2/8 16
thyroid: g74 1/22 14; g73 4/8 21
tongue: g73 1/22 17-19
tonsils: g74 2/8 16; g72 6/8 31; g71 1/22 15; g71 7/8 31; g71 11/22 30
transplanting parts: w75 519; w74 684; g74 12/22 12; w73 254; g72 6/8 30; g72 7/8 28; g71 11/8 9
twilight's effect: g71 3/8 22
uterus: g74 2/8 12-16
veins: g74 7/22 15
voice: g72 1/22 10-12; sg 64-5; g71 3/8 18
water: g72 1/22 18
water needed: g73 4/8 23
weight loss: g74 4/22 21-4; g72 8/22 12; g72 12/22 31
womb: g74 2/8 12-16
"wonderfully made": w75 712
worth: g74 12/8 31
yawning: g71 3/8 26
(SEE ALSO HEALTH, PARTS BY NAME)

HUMILITY
all need: w74 317
children: w71 200; te 106
discussion: w75 297-9; w74 103-4, 401-13; g73 3/8 3-4; w72 201-4
displaying: w74 315-17, 439-40
examples: w75 721-2, 724; w74 300, 401-3, 405-6, 408, 410-12; g74 10/22 19-20; g73 3/8 3-4; w72 201, 602; te 27-9
gestures denoting: w74 532
how attained: w74 408-9
"humble" jobs: w75 297-9
keeping, despite advancement: g74 10/22 19-20
marriage: w74 410
meaning of term: w74 408
mock humility: w74 213
others as superior: w74 299-300, 316
overseers: w75 721-8; w74 103-4, 367-8; w72 201-4, 287, 756-7
value: w74 180, 409-10, 412-13; w73 114-16; g73 3/8 3-4; w72 505-6; w71 580, 606-7
(SEE ALSO MEEKNESS, MILDNESS)

HUMOR
value of sense of: g75 7/22 13-14

HUNGARY
Catholic church: w74 341
inflation (1946): w75 567
Jehovah's witnesses: w72 71; w71 209

HUNGER
causes: g75 5/8 29; g73 6/22 6-12; g72 12/22 8-11
Christendom's view: w71 419-22
green revolution: g72 7/22 3-13, 29
old people: g75 5/8 30
prevalence: g73 2/8 29; w72 615-16; g71 10/8 7
proper attitude when suffering: g73 6/22 12-13
statistics: g72 7/22 11
(SEE ALSO FOOD SHORTAGE, STARVATION)

HUNTING
aborigines: g72 2/22 22-4
boomerang: g72 2/22 24
pandas: g73 11/22 18-19

HURRICANES
Dominican Republic: yb72 143
Honduras: g74 12/22 21-6
United States: g72 8/22 13-16; w71 611

HUSBAND
appreciation for wife: w75 16; g74 5/8 13-14
avoiding adultery: w73 538-40
care for sick: w71 516
communication with wife: w75 485-6; w74 305-11; g72 8/8 3-4
consideration for wife: w75 153, 314; w74 45-6, 90, 155, 212; g74 2/8 25; g74 4/22 9-12; g74 5/22 4-5; w72 575-6, 740; g72 5/22 12-15; w71 204-6
disfellowshiped: w74 470-1
divided household: km 8/75 7; w71 204-6
enduring drunkenness of: w75 287
experiences:
  aiding unbelieving: yb75 19; km 11/72 6
  alcoholism: g71 6/22 8
  opposition from, overcome: w74 39; yb73 243; w72 71; yb72 221; g72 3/22 15; g72 4/8 25; g72 9/22 26; w71 202, 204, 209, 211, 533, 679-80
  wife's opposition overcome: w71 205-6
headship: w75 153-4, 433-4, 484-5; w74 392-3, 410; g74 4/22 9; w72 270-1, 445-7; g72 2/22 7-8; g72 5/22 13-14; w71 30
humility: w74 316
Jehovah: w72 78-80; kj 118, 241-2, 248-9, 251-2
Jesus Christ: tp 139-40
love for wife: w75 153; w74 45-6, 317, 392; g74 4/22 10-11; g72 1/8 4
marriage dues: g74 4/22 10-11; w72 767
nagging: g71 3/8 10
prayer: g74 5/22 4
refuses to support family: km 9/73 8
responsibilities: g74 5/22 5
runaways: g75 10/22 29
to be 'as though they had no wives' (1 Co 7:29): w75 351-2
unbelievers: g74 4/22 9; w71 287
unbelieving wife: w71 204-6
violent: w75 286-8; g75 9/8 29-30; km 9/73 8
(SEE ALSO FAMILY, FATHER, PARENTS)

HYBRIDS
grain: g71 10/8 11

HYDROGEN
g72 10/22 7

HYDROGEN BOMB
power from atoms: g71 8/8 30

HYKSOS
discussion: w71 381-2

HYPNOTISM
ban in Israel: g75 11/8 29
dangers: g75 11/8 29
discussion: g74 9/8 27-8

HYPOCRISY
Christendom: w71 549
examples: g74 4/22 15

ICE
Antarctica: g72 8/22 16
characteristics: g72 1/22 19; g71 7/22 12
freezing dead: g71 8/22 30
icebergs: g72 2/8 11
massage: g73 9/8 26

ICELAND
description: g71 1/22 8-11
Jehovah's witnesses: yb76 26-7; yb75 26-7; yb74 26-7; yb73 26-7; yb72 36-7
population: yb73 26; yb72 36
territorial waters: g74 2/22 24
volcano: g73 3/22 30-1; g73 5/22 19-20

IDOLATRY
Bible view: w74 395-6; g74 2/8 27-8; g73 1/8 27-8; g73 5/22 28; w72 250-1, 539-40; g72 8/22 6-7; te 139-42
Christendom: w74 459; w72 538-9; yb72 112-13; kj 103, 119, 146, 156-61
covetousness: g73 11/22 28
creature worship: yb74 174-5; g72 7/8 6, 8
demonism: w74 396, 588; g74 2/22 4-5
discussion: w72 295-6; g72 8/22 5-7
Enosh's day: po 67-8
experience:
destruction of idols: w75 761
fetishes: w74 395-6
flag salute: g71 9/8 12-15
food offered to images: w72 563-5; g72 8/22 5-7
gambling: w74 588
Hinduism: g73 7/8 16-18
Israelites: w74 457-9; po 111-12; w72 42-3, 74, 295, 509, 537-8, 572; kj 25, 28, 30, 98-9, 101-2, 115-19, 145, 147-51, 154-6, 167-8, 239-40, 249
juju: w75 761; w73 172
ornaments: w72 295-6
relative worship: w74 395-6; g73 12/22 6
Roman Catholic Church: g75 1/8 23; w74 395-6; g73 2/22 29-30; g73 8/8 28; yb72 173-4, 194; g72 7/22 23
(SEE ALSO IMAGES)

IGNATIUS
w72 670

ILLEGITIMATE BIRTHS
discussion: g72 8/22 8-12
experiences: g72 8/22 8-12
illegitimate child can serve God: w74 224
New Zealand: g74 8/8 30
rock music: w75 390
schools: g71 8/8 30-1
statistics: w75 390; g74 3/22 31; g74 4/22 4, 5; g74 8/22 31; w72 218-19; yb72 184; g72 8/22 8-9; g72 9/22 29; g72 10/22 30; w71 452
(SEE ALSO ABORTION, ADULTERY, FORNICATION, MORAL BREAKDOWN)

ILLITERACY
Bible view: w74 592
experiences:
active Witness: g72 2/8 24
progress of former illiterates: w73 111-12
problems faced by illiterates: yb73 180
statistics: g75 7/8 31; w74 592; g74 6/22 5; g74 7/8 30; g74 12/8 10; g72 12/8 31
television: g74 9/8 8
Watch Tower reading schools: yb76 173, 175, 185; yb75 202; yb74 39-40; g74 7/22 16; w73 111-12; yb73 73-4, 159-60, 181-2; w71 157; g71 4/8 22-3
(SEE ALSO READING, SCHOOLS)

ILLUSTRATIONS
Jesus' use: w74 429-30; w73 17-18; sg 169
number of parables: w75 589
purpose of parables: w75 593-4
teaching with: g75 1/8 11-12; g74 1/8 25; g74 12/22 15; km 11/74 4; sg 52-3, 168-71
using pictures in publications: km 11/74 4
value: w74 429-30

Bible Illustrations (Parables)
choosing prominent places: w71 199-200; te 103-6
dragnet (Mt 13:47-50): w75 593, 596, 599-601
grand evening meal: w72 214-15
king that canceled large debt: w72 550-1; w71 102-3; te 63-6
leaven hidden in dough: w75 589-92, 597, 601-4; sl 209-15
lost sheep: te 115-16
marriage feast:
bride: w74 686-7, 690, 700
discussion: w74 686-700
few chosen: w75 108, 286; w74 636, 698-9
king: w74 686-7
man without marriage garment: w74 636, 696-9
marriage garment: w74 696-7
son: w74 686, 690
those first invited: w74 636, 687-90, 694-5
those from roads outside: w74 695-6
two notifications to come: w74 636, 691-3
when first invited: w74 636, 688-90
minas: w73 633-4, 710-21; ka 213, 215
distant land: w74 61
man of noble birth: w74 61
purpose: w74 541
ten minas: w74 61
ten slaves: w74 61; w73 713, 715, 717
wicked slave: w73 719-21
mustard seed: w75 589-90, 595-8, 600-1, 604-5; sl 206-9
identity of planter of: km 11/75 4
neighborly Samaritan: w71 413; te 36-8; g71 8/8 27
pearl of high value: w75 21, 594
Pharisee and tax collector: te 147-9
prodigal son: w74 462; w72 432-5, 568
rich man (Lu 12:16-21): te 91-4
rich man and Lazarus: ts 98-110; g73 6/8 7
sheep and goats: w74 625-8, 651-2; ka 258, 262-66, 269-72, 281, 284-92; w71 457; g71 8/8 28
sower (Mt 13:3-23): w72 90-1, 287; or 108-9; w71 31
talents: ka 212-40, 247-56, 258; w72 207-8
ability: w74 542
beginning of fulfillment: w74 542-3
belongings: w74 541-2; ka 216-18
five-talents class: w74 542
man traveling abroad: w74 541
master's return: w74 557
purpose: w74 540-1
reward to faithful slaves: w74 558-9
slaves: w74 542, 558
wicked slave: w74 589-91; ka 247-55
ten virgins: w75 593; ka 169-83, 189-206, 211
bridegroom: ka 171
discreet virgins: w74 506, 508-9
discussion: w74 430-2, 477-80, 505-9
door closed: w74 508-9
foolish virgins: w74 506, 508-9; ka 195-7, 199-204
lamps: w74 478-9, 506
oil: w74 479, 506, 508; ka 178-9, 195
purpose: w74 430; ka 176
significance of number: w74 478; ka 170
slept: w74 479-80, 506-8
treasure hidden in a field: w75 594
two sons (Mt 21): w72 213
wheat and weeds (Mt 13:24-30, 36-43): w75 594, 596, 599; sl 207-8; yb75 33; w74 477, 480; w71 501-2; pm 101-5, 362-3
(SEE ALSO PROPHETIC DRAMAS)

IMAGE (Nebuchadnezzar's Dream)
discussion: w75 620-1; sl 310-13; og 23-4; w71 619-24; nc 18-27
meaning of: pm 375-6

IMAGE OF THE BEAST
identified: w75 743; w73 676; w71 723-4; kj 256, 258, 363-4
scarlet-colored wild beast: w75 743
(SEE ALSO BEASTS)

IMAGES
Bible view: w74 395-6; po 111-12; g74 2/8 27-8; g73 1/8 27-8; g73 5/22 28; w72 250-1; g72 8/22 6-7; te 139-42
Catholic church: yb72 112-13, 173-4, 194
churches imitate pagans: w74 491
demonism: w74 396; g74 2/22 4-5
discussion: g72 8/22 5-7
experiences:
Bible truth frees worshipers: yb75 13, 21; g74 2/22 5, 7; yb72

65, 194; g72 1/22 24-6; g72 5/22 24; g72 12/22 15-16
fetishes: w74 395-6
Hinduism: g73 7/8 16-18
Holy Blood: g72 7/22 23
Kali: g72 1/22 24-5
Mary: g73 1/8 27-8; g73 2/22 29-30; g73 8/8 28
Nebuchadnezzar's: w72 141; te 139-42
ornaments: w72 295-6
relative worship: w74 395-6; g74 2/8 27
"Saint" Peter: g75 1/8 23
(SEE ALSO IDOLATRY)

IMITATING
false gods: w74 144-6
Jehovah: w74 146-56

IMMEDIATELY
Bible use of term: w74 750

IMMERSION
(SEE BAPTISM)

IMMIGRATION
Australia: g71 3/22 21-3
New Zealand: g71 2/8 29

IMMORALITY
avoiding: w74 61, 564; w73 31-2, 74-5, 538-40, 590-6; w72 287; w71 150-1; g71 10/22 3-4
Bible view: w74 484-6; g74 1/22 27-8
congregation's attitude toward sexual immorality: w75 755-6
results: g75 1/8 4-5; g75 6/22 29; w74 758; ts 14; g74 8/8 4; g74 9/8 21
rock music: w75 390
Soviet Union: g75 8/22 30-1
television: g75 6/22 28; w74 563, 565; g74 9/8 9
truth overcomes: w74 606; w73 502-3; g73 8/22 6-8, 15
(SEE ALSO ADULTERY, FORNICATION, MORAL BREAKDOWN)

IMMORTALITY
Bible use of the word: ts 111

IMMORTALITY OF THE SOUL
Babylonians: w73 605
Bible view: g75 10/22 5-6; ts 37-43; g74 6/8 28; w73 230-1, 550; g73 6/8 5-8; g73 7/22 27-8; g72 11/8 6; w71 47-8
Buddhism: g74 1/8 16, 19
Catholic church: w73 550
clergy see error: w75 56, 357; g73 5/8 5; g72 4/8 30; g71 3/8 28; g71 8/8 26
extent of the belief: ts 36-7
false claims: w75 356; ts 35-7, 43-6, 89, 91-2; g72 11/8 6; w71 47-8; g71 3/8 28
Greeks: w75 55; g75 10/22 6; ts 43-4; g73 6/8 5
Hinduism: ts 36-7; g74 1/8 19
illogical: ts 45-6
Plato: g73 6/8 5
resurrection: g71 3/8 28
scriptures misapplied to support:
Genesis 35:18: ts 42-3
1 Kings 17:21: ts 42-3
Luke 23:43: g73 6/8 6-7
Acts 20:10: ts 42-3
source of belief: w75 55-6, 744; ts 43-5
transmigration: ts 55-60

IMMUNITY
human body: g72 12/22 17-20

IMPALEMENT
archaeological evidence: g71 2/22 30
Jesus Christ: g74 9/22 27-8; w71 249; bi8 1360-1
modern reenactment: g74 6/8 30

IMPERFECTION
cause: gc 14-17; ts 34-5; g74 10/8 12-13
effect on mind: w73 511-12
overlooking: w74 437-8; w73 323-4, 334-5; w72 439-40
why earthly resurrected imperfect: w74 607-8
why imperfect race allowed to exist: ts 59
(SEE ALSO PERFECTION, SIN)

IMPROMPTU SPEAKING
sg 61-2

INCENSE
symbolic: ka 108; w71 284-5

INCEST
discussion: w75 72-7
effects of: g73 6/22 29; g72 12/22 29-30
genetic dangers: w75 72-4
laws against: w75 74-5
Lot and daughters: w72 319-20
marriages prohibited under Mosaic law: w75 73

INDIA
abortions: g75 8/22 4
atomic weapons: w74 550
blindness: g72 6/22 16
blood racket: g74 2/22 30
caste conflicts: g73 9/8 30
crime: g74 11/8 29
customs: g74 7/22 8-11
dances: g71 12/8 25
disease: g74 12/22 30
economic conditions: w75 68; g74 1/22 7; g74 12/8 10; g72 11/8 29
famines: g75 2/22 9-11; g74 7/22 4, 7; g73 6/22 3-4, 7-9; g72 7/22 3
food: g74 3/22 31; g73 2/22 31; g73 5/8 29; g73 5/22 30; g72 7/22 4, 8-11
fuel: g75 11/22 30
government: g74 1/22 7
gurus: g73 7/8 18
Jehovah's witnesses: yb76 26-7; yb75 13, 26-7; km 4/75 1; yb74 20-1, 26-7; g74 7/22 11; w73 761-4; yb73 16-17, 26-7, 111; w72 327; yb72 36-7; g72 8/8 22-3; w71 15, 667-8
Kasi tribe: g74 1/22 20
marriage: g72 8/8 20-3
Moslem-Hindu conflict: w73 764
music: g74 8/8 24
oil costs: g74 7/22 7
population: g74 6/22 8; g74 7/22 6; yb73 26; yb72 36; g72 7/22 10; g71 6/8 29
rats: w74 624
religion: g73 7/8 16-21; g72 12/22 15-16; w71 101
animal worship: g75 9/22 30; w74 624; g74 1/22 20
Buddhism: g74 1/8 16-19
Hinduism: g74 7/22 8-11
living-child goddess: g75 6/22 30
"Saint" Xavier: g75 4/8 30
suicides: g72 3/8 30
wealth: g74 3/22 31

INDIANS
American: g75 1/22 31; g71 5/22 16; g71 12/8 29
Australia: g72 2/22 21-6
Brazil: g72 6/8 21-3
Canada: g75 2/8 26; w74 141
changing view of: g74 12/22 16-17
Choco: g71 9/22 20-1
Cuna: g71 9/22 21-2
Ecuador: g71 9/8 19-20
Guaymi: g71 9/22 22-3
Mayan: w74 394
Totonacos: g75 7/22 11-12

INDIFFERENCE
family circle: w74 675

INDONESIA
divorce: g74 4/22 4
Jehovah's witnesses: yb76 26-7; yb75 26-7; km 4/75 1; yb74 26-7; yb73 26-7; yb72 36-7
persecution: yb76 17
population: yb73 26; yb72 36
religion: g72 2/22 17-20

INDULGENCES
w75 55; ts 64, 66-8; g72 3/8 16-17

INDUSTRY
discussion: g75 8/22 17-20
labor unions: g74 6/8 13-15
Orville Wright's comment on: g75 8/22 19
pollution: g71 4/22 15-19
rise of: g71 4/22 14-15
shortages of raw materials: g74 11/22 16-20
spying: g73 7/8 9-11
(SEE ALSO BUSINESS, EMPLOYMENT)

INFALLIBILITY
popes: w72 643-4; g72 9/8 20; g71 3/8 30; g71 5/22 29

INFANT
baptism: g74 3/22 27-8
death: g74 12/8 9
feeding: g73 7/8 12-15
nursing: g74 7/8 13-16
(SEE ALSO BABIES)

INFANTILE PARALYSIS (Polio)
w74 132-3

INFECTION
g73 12/8 15

INFLATION
causes: w75 3-4; g75 1/22 19; g75 5/22 4; w74 14-15; g74 1/22 4, 6-7; g74 9/8 30; g73 10/8 8-10; g73 11/22 11; g73 12/22 17-22
coping with: w75 4-6; g75 4/8 20-3; g75 8/8 16-18
discussion: g74 1/22 3-8; g73 11/22 8-12; g73 12/22 17-23
dishonesty accompanies: g75 2/22 31
economists' fears: g75 6/22 30; g75 7/22 29
historical examples: w75 567; g74 1/22 6
increase: g75 1/22 20; g75 2/8 6; g75 8/8 29; g74 1/22 3, 5; g74 8/22 29; g73 9/8 29; g73 10/8 7-10; g73 10/22 30; g73 11/22 8-11, 29; g71 10/8 4

Japan: g74 6/8 25-6
results: w75 3, 5-6; g75 1/8 29; g75 5/22 3-4; g75 7/22 30; g75 8/8 29; w74 14-15; yb74 101; g74 9/8 31; g73 11/22 8-12; g73 12/8 29; g73 12/22 20, 22-3; w71 470; g71 7/8 29; g71 8/22 7-9
world wide: g75 2/8 6; g74 1/22 3-5; g74 6/22 30; g74 11/22 30; g73 11/22 10-11, 29
(SEE ALSO MONEY)

INFLUENCE
right: km 12/71 4

INFLUENZA
g72 1/8 30; w71 406; g71 3/8 3-6; g71 10/8 16
(SEE ALSO SPANISH INFLUENZA)

INFORMAL WITNESSING
appropriate occasions: w75 318; w72 400-3
discussion: sg 80-2; km 12/71 4
experiences:
places of employment: w73 187; w71 221-2
prisons: w75 40
to relatives: km 2/75 3-4
(SEE ALSO FIELD SERVICE)

INFORMATION MARCHING
yb75 160-1

INHERITANCE
discussion: w73 494-500

INHIBITIONS
discussion: g71 9/8 3-4

INQUISITION
Catholic histories of: g74 12/22 17
Catholic institution: g72 9/22 21-5
Peru: g71 1/22 20-3
(SEE ALSO ROMAN CATHOLIC CHURCH)

INSECT(S)
benefits: g72 9/8 9-11
bioluminescence: g73 2/8 17; g71 11/8 20
building ability: g71 10/22 18-20
burglar alarms: g71 2/8 19
chirping: g75 10/8 31
controlling: g73 9/22 22-3
courtship and mating: g71 9/8 21-2
discussion: g72 9/8 9-11
evidence of Creator: w71 326-7
eyes: g71 7/22 19; g71 9/8 23
flight: g71 9/8 23
forests: w71 326
harmful: g73 8/22 30; w71 326-7; g71 5/22 20
hearing: g75 6/8 19-20
jumping: g74 10/22 23
light's effects: g71 7/8 15
navigation: g75 2/8 29
number of species: ts 146; g72 1/22 23
pollination of plants: g72 9/8 9
size: g71 12/22 26
smelling: g72 8/22 31
soil: g72 2/22 12; w71 326-7; g71 5/22 17-18

List by Name
ant: g75 4/8 30; g75 9/22 29; g72 6/22 30; g72 10/22 8; g72 11/22 21; g71 10/22 18, 20
aphids: g72 9/8 10
bee: w75 560; g75 1/22 29; g75 5/22 23; g74 4/8 21; g72 3/22 31; g72 10/22 7; g71 3/8 11; g71 10/22 18-19
beetle: g72 9/8 10; g72 11/22 20; g71 12/22 26
butterfly: g75 3/22 14; g72 11/22 21
caddis fly: g71 10/22 19
codling moth: g73 9/22 23
cricket: g75 6/8 19-20; g75 10/8 31; g74 10/22 23; g71 2/8 19
dragonfly: g71 9/8 21-3
firefly: g73 2/8 17; g71 11/8 20
flea: g74 10/22 23
fly: g75 7/8 25-6; g72 9/8 11
glowworm: g73 2/8 17
grasshopper: w75 560; g75 6/8 19; g74 10/22 23
ichneumon fly: g71 10/22 20
katydids: g75 6/8 19-20
lice: g71 11/8 31
locust: w75 464; g74 10/22 23; g71 6/8 29
maggot: g72 12/22 30
moth: g75 3/22 13-14; g72 8/22 31; g72 9/8 10; g71 7/8 15; g71 10/22 18-19; g71 12/22 26
railroad worm: g73 2/8 17; g71 11/8 20
screwworm: g72 11/8 30
spider: g75 5/22 20-3; g71 10/22 19
termite: w75 464; g71 10/22 19-20
tumblebug: g72 11/22 20-1
wasp: g71 10/22 20
(SEE ALSO ANIMALS, BIRDS, MARINE LIFE)

INSECTICIDES
bees: g75 1/22 29
boric acid: g72 11/22 31
dangers: g73 1/22 30; g73 9/22 22-3; g72 5/8 30; g72 7/8 30
DDT: ts 147-8; g72 8/8 31; g71 1/8 8; g71 4/22 11-12; g71 9/22 29
garlic: g72 2/8 30-1

INSOMNIA
g75 3/8 12-14

INSPIRATION
evidence of Bible's: w75 133-40; g75 10/8 8-9; g72 2/8 27-8; w71 228-9; sg 15-17
manner: w75 141-5; fu 5

INSTINCT
animals: ts 18-20

INSTRUMENTS
(SEE MUSIC)

INSURANCE
arson: g75 6/8 30
automobile: g74 3/22 9; g73 12/22 30
life: g75 3/22 21
unemployment: g75 3/22 8-9

INTEGRITY
aids to keeping: yb75 190, 208-9; w74 249-50, 373, 479, 529-30, 532, 534, 538-9; yb74 226-8; w73 40-51; w72 30, 121-4, 133-9, 145-6; w71 112-14, 527-30
discussion: w72 140-6; w71 524-35
examples:
Bible accounts: sl 58-61, 78-9, 89; w72 123, 140-3, 523-4; g72 9/8 7; g72 12/8 24-5; w71 110-12, 120, 487-8, 530-1
early Christians: w72 142-3; g72 12/8 20; w71 118, 488-90
modern-day Witnesses: yb75 183-4, 186-90, 208-9, 223-4; km 6/75 1; w74 56, 373; yb74 54-6, 59-60, 63, 115-26, 163-4, 166-9, 172-4, 180-90, 194, 196-7, 202-4, 208-12, 224, 226-31; w73 172-3, 376-9, 571-3; w72 143-4, 381, 397-8, 520-1, 524-5, 531-2, 631; yb72 97, 150-3, 156-8, 160-2; g72 6/8 24; g72 12/8 10-13, 15-17; w71 114, 117-18, 489-90, 494-5, 531-4; g71 1/8 25-6; g71 8/8 13-15; g71 10/22 4, 28
pre-Flood: po 80-1
importance: g75 3/22 30; w74 603; po 80-1; w72 36; w71 202-3, 524-5
testing: w74 169-72; yb74 252-3; g72 12/8 24-5; w71 485-91
weakening influences: w73 69-75; w72 144-5; w71 525-7

INTELLIGENCE
computers fail to have: w74 555
human brain: g74 12/8 16-21
IQ scores: g74 5/22 30
worship of intellect: w74 756
(SEE ALSO MIND)

INTERCOURSE
(SEE SEXUAL INTERCOURSE)

INTEREST(S)
moneylending: g72 3/8 3
rates: g75 5/8 30
youth: w72 157-8

INTERFAITH
Bahai: g74 1/22 17-18
Bible view: g75 11/22 22-4; w74 631; g74 1/22 18; g73 5/22 28
Christendom: g75 11/22 21-2; w74 273; g74 1/22 17

INTERFERON
g72 12/22 19-20

INTERNATIONAL BIBLE STUDENTS ASSOCIATION
British corporation: yb73 96
(SEE ALSO WATCH TOWER BIBLE AND TRACT SOCIETY OF PA.)

INTERPRETATION
clergy: g74 8/22 9-11

INTESTINES
g75 2/8 19; g73 4/8 21; g71 3/22 16-20

INTOLERANCE (Booklet)
yb75 173-4

INTRODUCTION
house-to-house preaching: km 5/74 8
public speaking: sg 46-7, 113-16

IODINE 131
g75 5/22 31

IRAN
carpets: g74 2/22 25-6

earthquake: g72 6/8 29; g71 4/8 11
Jehovah's witnesses: yb76 26-7; yb75 26-7; yb74 26-7; yb73 26-7; yb72 36-7
population: yb73 26; yb72 36

IRAQ
famines: g75 2/22 9
Jehovah's witnesses: yb76 26-7; yb75 26-7; yb74 26-7; yb73 26-7; yb72 36-7
population: yb73 26; yb72 36
ruins of Babylon: w75 294

IRELAND
Belfast: g74 11/22 13-15
Catholic-Protestant conflict: g72 10/8 14; g72 10/22 29
clergy: g74 8/22 30; g74 11/22 5
Dublin: g74 11/22 13
electricity: g71 5/8 17-19
food shortage: g72 7/22 6
internal problems: g74 1/22 29; g74 11/22 14-15; g73 4/22 29-30; g73 7/8 29; g72 4/22 14; g71 6/22 19
Jehovah's witnesses: yb76 26-7; yb75 26-7; w74 517-21; yb74 26-7; w73 28-9; yb73 26-7; g73 1/22 16; g73 8/22 14; yb72 36-7, 45
population: yb73 26; yb72 36
religion: w74 360; g74 12/8 15; g72 11/22 29; w71 407, 484
war: w74 360, 517-21; g74 8/22 30
  children: g74 7/8 30-1
  deaths: w75 445
wool: g73 2/8 24-6

IRENAEUS
w72 670-1

IRON
g74 11/22 17

IRREPREHENSIBILITY
discussion: km 11/75 3

ISAAC
Abraham attempted to sacrifice: w72 503
line of promised "seed": po 91-3
name: w71 58
prophet: po 98

ISAIAH (Book)
Dead Sea Scrolls: g73 3/22 19; g72 6/22 6, 8
discussion: g73 3/22 18-19
number of writers: g73 3/22 18-19

ISH-BOSHETH
po 124

ISHMAEL
not "seed": po 91; g73 8/22 28-9
"seed" afflicted by: po 106

ISLAM
(Also called Mohammedanism)
Bairam: w74 742
beliefs: g73 8/22 28-9, 31; g73 9/8 14; yb72 200
  hell: g73 7/22 27
birth control: g74 11/22 29
deaths on pilgrimage to Mecca: g75 10/8 30
experiences:
  Moslems accept truth: w75 734-5; yb73 12-13; g73 1/22 16; w72 221-2; yb72 100-1, 202
  witnessing to Moslems: g72 2/8 5-8
Ishmael: g73 8/22 28-9
membership: w71 14
rosary: w74 259
Soviet Union: g73 4/8 14-15
witnessing to members: yb72 200-1

ISLANDS
coral: g72 10/22 28
Jehovah's witnesses: w71 18-21
  experiences of missionaries: g74 11/8 25-6
  preaching in Pacific: w74 646-9
Kodiak Island: g72 1/8 18-19

ISOLATED TERRITORY
efforts to work: yb75 226-7
moving to: w71 85-8
number in United States: km 8/75 8

ISRAEL(ITES)
assembly at Mt. Sinai: po 109-10, 112-14
assembly in Moab: w73 585-9; w72 502-3
Baal worship: w74 457-9; w73 586-9
Bible view of current events: w75 387-9
bloodguilt: w73 305-7
business: w71 765-6
captivity in Babylon: w72 723-4
  restoration from: po 130-1; ts 158-9; g74 4/8 13-14; w73 219-21, 249-51; w72 300-1, 305-7, 724; pm 28-32; g72 3/8 28; w71 649; kj 299-300
captivity in Egypt: w72 38-40; w71 381-2
  exodus: po 108-9; g74 4/8 26; w73 365; w72 40; pm 59-60
  length: po 108
cast off: w74 127-8, 693-4; g74 10/8 19; w71 683-4
child training: w75 759; w71 361-2
cities of refuge: w73 303-5
conventions: w71 392-6
copper mining: w75 112
corruption: w74 35-6
dancing: w72 567
dedicated to God: w71 555
Diaspora: w73 582
disobedience: w74 63; w73 90-2, 586-9; w72 356-8; w71 121, 147, 556, 558, 618; kj 28-31, 86-8, 115-19, 198-9, 238-52, 288; nc 14-16
division into two kingdoms: w72 309; kj 28, 69, 239-41
entering Promised Land: po 120-1; w71 121, 393; kj 115
fasts: pm 235-6; w71 536-7
fatherless boy: w74 82-3
festivals: po 115, 117
government: w71 681-5, 742-6
idolatry: w74 457-9; po 111-12; w72 42-3, 74, 295, 509, 537-8, 572, 752; kj 145, 147-51, 167-8, 239-40, 249, 288
illegitimate child: w74 224
impartiality of Jehovah: w74 68; g74 10/8 18-19
Jehovah's mercy: w74 460-2
Jehovah's wife: ts 104-5
Jehovah's witnesses: or 132; w71 652-3
Jerusalem's destruction (70 C.E.): w74 680-3, 693-4
Jeshurun: po 119
kings: po 100-2; w73 59-61; pm 118-20, 214-15; w71 393-5
  request human: po 122-3; w71 743-4
Law covenant: g74 10/8 20; w73 580-1; kj 198-9
  capital punishment: g75 11/22 26-7; g74 7/22 27-8
  crime and compensation: g72 1/8 14-16
  dietary laws: w72 190-1
  health: w74 134
  keeping perfectly: po 117-18
  release from Law: ts 104-5
  returning lost items: w74 204-5
  uncleanness: pm 108-10
  unsolved murders: g75 11/22 27
life in ancient: w71 312
map:
  exodus from Egypt: w73 752
marriage: w72 82-3, 86-8
"Messianic" nation: po 98-9
music: w75 30
older men: w71 684-5
opportunity to become "kingdom of priests": w74 688, 694-5
poor: w75 70
prayer: g74 1/8 9
priesthood: w74 156-7; po 114-16, 118; w72 489
  not nation of priests: po 114, 157-8
prophetic significance: g74 4/8 10-14; kj 85, 216-17
prophets: w74 35-6
prosperity: g71 11/22 27-8
rejected as God's "congregation": po 159
relation to Jehovah: w74 68, 597-8, 687; po 109-10, 112-14, 117-19; g74 10/8 18-19; w73 752; tp 63-5; kj 118-19, 240-2
religion: w72 74
religious bondage: w72 560-1
sabbath observance: g74 4/8 9-10
separateness from other peoples: w74 325
spiritual: sl 32-5, 108-10, 115-18, 127-9, 139, 143; w74 126-8, 600, 696-7; po 159-64, 171, 181; w73 747-9; pm 44-52, 101, 144-6, 251-8; w71 430; kj 306-11, 313, 315, 318-20, 342-3, 346-8, 352-61, 380-1
  Christendom's hatred: sl 226-7
  disciplinary experiences: sl 144-5
  Gog's attack: sl 257-63; kj 357-62, 368-72, 382
  lamed by Babylon the Great: sl 150
  liberation from Babylon the Great: sl 158
tax collectors: w74 139-40
temptations: w74 63
ten "lost" tribes: w72 440-4; kj 340, 345
weddings: w74 430-1
why chosen by God: g71 6/8 13-14
wilderness journey: w73 752; w72 73-4; w71 121, 147; kj 23-4
work: w72 490

Northern Kingdom
Assyrian domination: w71 672
calf worship: w72 295; kj 240
discussion: kj 238-43
exile by Assyrians: w72 74; kj 340
Oholah: kj 238-46

Republic
Arab opposition: g72 11/8 9
armaments:
  cost per person: g75 10/22 30

attitude toward Jesus: g74 12/22 17
Bible view of restoration: w74 14; w73 747
crime: w75 263; g75 4/22 29; g73 4/22 6
description: g72 1/8 27-8
desert farming: g71 9/22 30
establishment: kj 352
Ethiopian Falasha sect: g75 7/8 30
government: w71 682
Hadrian's statue discovered: g75 9/22 30-1
Har-Magedon: w74 230, 232
hypnosis ban: g75 11/8 29
Jehovah's witnesses: yb76 17-18, 26-7; yb75 26-7; yb74 22, 26-7; yb73 26-7; g73 1/22 16; yb72 36-7; g71 11/8 12-15
photographs: w74 78-9
pollution: g73 2/22 31; g71 9/8 30-1
population: yb73 26; yb72 36
religion: g72 2/22 30
ostracism: g75 10/8 31
touring: w74 77-80
Wailing Wall: w75 248
war with Arabs: g74 10/22 16-17; g74 11/8 5

ISRAEL OF GOD
Adam Clarke's commentary on: kj 68
beginning of: w71 747; kj 352
discussion: w74 126-8; po 159-61
identified: w71 430
(SEE ALSO CONGREGATION OF GOD)

ISSUE OF UNIVERSAL SOVEREIGNTY
clarification of belief: yb75 191-2
final test: w74 347-8
modern-day announcement of issue: w74 725
origin of issue: sl 61-2; fu 16-17; w74 595-6; yb74 252-3; g74 10/22 7-8; tp 47-54; w71 267-8, 539
reason issue not settled at once: g74 10/8 14; w73 196-7; tp 53-7; g72 10/22 11-12; g72 12/8 24-5; w71 268-9, 487-8
settlement: w74 345-8; po 185-6, 191; ka 409; pm 382-3, 393; w71 244
upholding the issue: w75 619, 622; og 21, 26-7; w74 169-70, 597, 603-4, 724-6; w73 144-5, 295-6; tp 133
(SEE ALSO JEHOVAH)

IS THE BIBLE REALLY THE WORD OF GOD? (Book)
yb75 222

IS THERE A GOD WHO CARES? (Booklet)
km 10/75 1, 8; km 12/75 1

IS THIS LIFE ALL THERE IS? (Book)
presenting, in field service: km 5/75 4
public talks: km 9/74 3, 5-6
release: yb75 255

ITALY
art thefts: g71 6/22 31
automobile thefts: g71 11/8 29
birth control: g71 5/8 29
Catholic church: w74 424, 456; g74 9/22 13-15; g74 11/22 31; g72 4/22 30; g72 7/8 31
children's view of churches: g75 8/22 29-30
Holy Year (1933): w75 397-8
Holy Year (1950): w75 397-8
Holy Year (1975): w75 390, 397, 399-400
Communism: g75 8/8 29
crime: g75 11/22 4
divorce: w75 364; w74 424; g74 5/8 30; g74 9/22 13-15
entertainment: g75 3/22 29
Jehovah's witnesses: yb76 26-7; w75 40, 285; yb75 17, 26-7; g75 4/8 29; w74 80; yb74 26-7; w73 634, 663-6; yb73 17, 26-7; w72 510-11; yb72 36-7, 44; w71 17, 278-9
mayor accepts truth: g75 11/8 21-3
kidnapping: g75 5/22 6
Lateran Treaty: w75 364
orphans: g71 6/8 30-1
politics: w75 364; g75 8/8 29; g75 11/8 21-3
population: yb73 26; yb72 36
prostitution: w71 452
religion: g75 2/8 31
saints: g75 4/8 30
snakes: g75 5/22 30
spiritism: g71 7/8 29-30
terrorism: g71 6/8 18
tower of Pisa: g75 5/22 29
Venice: g75 11/22 29-30
view of Holy Year (1975): g75 2/22 29
vipers: g72 10/22 30
World War II: g72 10/8 7

IVORY
Chinese: g73 8/8 14
demand: g75 11/8 30

IVORY COAST
fishing: g72 6/8 25-6
Jehovah's witnesses: yb76 26-7; yb75 7, 26-7; yb74 8-9, 26-7; yb73 18-19, 26-7; yb72 34-5; w71 125
population: yb73 26; yb72 34

JAAZANIAH
kj 147-8, 167, 194-5

JABEZ
w73 647; g73 11/8 26

JACKAL
sl 151-2

JACOB (Israel)
attitude: w73 496-8
discussion: po 93-101; w73 496-500
foreknown: po 94; ts 58-9
Jehovah's blessing: po 93-5
lameness: w73 498
love for Joseph: w74 500
prophet: po 98, 100-1
prophetic significance: sl 224
purchase of burial plot: w75 735-6

JADE
Chinese: g73 8/8 13-14

JAEL
discussion: w73 112-13

JAILER
experience: g71 8/8 13-15

JAMAICA
Jehovah's witnesses: yb76 26-7; yb75 26-7; yb74 26-7; yb73 26-7; yb72 36-7; g72 4/8 25; w71 369, 522-3
population: yb73 26; yb72 36

JAMBRES
kj 12-13

JAMES
brother of Jesus: w75 221-2; w74 19
Jesus' post-resurrection appearance: w75 222
brother of John: w75 222
son of Alphaeus: w75 222

JAMES (Book)
discussion of faith: w74 19-22, 24-5

JAMES I
sponsor of English Authorized Version: kj 304-5

JANNES
kj 12-13

JAPAN
abacus: g71 11/22 17-20
abortions: g74 6/22 7-8; g73 12/22 31
agriculture: g75 8/22 18
armaments:
cost per person: g75 10/22 30
atheist: g74 1/22 21
automated supermarket: g75 8/22 29
bankruptcy: g75 12/8 30
birds: g72 3/8 30
bonsai trees: g71 6/8 15-16
centenarians: g74 2/22 30
Christmas: g74 1/22 31
city financial problems: g75 12/8 30
cooking: g74 8/8 13-16
crime: g75 4/22 31; g71 10/22 11
description: yb73 209-11, 222, 243, 246; g73 2/8 20-3
disasters: g74 1/22 31
earthquakes: g75 4/22 29
economy: g75 11/22 31; g74 1/22 3; g74 6/8 25-6; g74 11/22 19-20; g73 11/22 10-11, 29; g71 10/22 9-11
education:
teacher regrets militaristic: w75 715
family: w74 261
food: g74 8/8 13-16; g74 8/22 31; g73 2/8 22
health: g72 11/8 30-1
Hiroshima: yb73 221, 242-3
Jehovah's witnesses: yb76 26-7; yb75 13-14, 26-7; km 2/75 3; yb74 18, 26-7; w73 54-5; yb73 26-7, 209-55; g73 9/22 11-12; w72 410; yb72 36-7, 44; g72 6/8 24; g72 9/8 7-8; km 12/72 4-5; w71 15-16; sg 96; g71 1/22 26
printery (Watch Tower): g73 9/22 11-12
juvenile delinquency: g75 3/8 29
language: g73 9/22 12
martial arts: g75 12/8 28-9

mineral resources: g74 11/22 16-17, 19
moral breakdown: g73 3/22 30; g71 10/22 10-11
noise of city life: g75 4/22 31
oil: g74 1/8 5-6; g74 6/8 25
pearls: g74 9/8 24-6
pollution: g71 10/22 10
population: yb73 26; yb72 36
prisons: g75 11/22 31
railways:
items lost in trains: g75 7/22 31
rating of its products: g75 10/22 30
recording to prevent crying of babies: g75 5/22 30
relations with China: g72 11/22 29
religion: yb73 210-14, 222
rise of: g71 4/8 11
snowmen: g71 1/8 20-2
solar energy: g72 10/8 26
stature of people increased: g73 2/22 31
Taiwan: g73 7/22 21-2
time spent watching television: g75 11/8 30
Tokyo: g73 4/8 30; g71 10/22 29; g71 11/22 30
air pollution: g72 10/8 10-11
traffic accidents: g71 10/22 10
typhoon: yb73 227-8
when judged civilized: g71 4/8 11
youth: g73 9/22 30

JEALOUSY
examples: g75 4/8 29; w74 501-2
ungodly:
avoiding: w74 439

JEBUS
po 125

JEBUSITES
pm 266

JEHOIACHIN (Jeconiah)
cursed: ka 62
reign: pm 118-20; kj 94

JEHOIAKIM (Eliakim) (King of Judah)
tributary to Babylon: kj 94, 245

JEHOSHAPHAT (King of Judah)
respect for Bible: w73 202-3

JEHOVAH
Adonay: bi8 1352
all-powerful: w74 726-7
alone at one time: po 26
anger: ts 187-8; w71 357-60
'appoints deaf, blind': w74 319-20
appreciation for: w73 67-8, 554; ka 400-1, 410-11; w72 212; w71 265-76, 553-4; te 185-6
appreciation for servants: w75 17-18, 713-14; w74 574-5
approachable: w74 367-8
belief in existence: w73 451-2
blessing: w72 400-6
cares about mankind: w75 17; gc 3-31; w74 120-1; g74 10/8 5-8, 17-22; w73 195-7; tp 59-62, 64-5; w72 369-70; g72 9/8 3-4; g72 10/22 4-16; w71 325-7, 709
clergy rejection: w71 408
communication with creatures: po 44-5; tp 60
communication with Jesus: w74 307
compassion: w75 517-18; w74 281-2; ts 123-4
counsel: w74 614; po 19; hu 7
Creator: w74 593-4; po 15, 26-7, 33-42; g74 1/22 9-11, 13; g74 2/8 15-16; w73 35-6; g73 3/8 29; g72 10/22 5-8; sg 5; te 15-18
dependable: w75 82
destroys wicked: w75 636-8; w74 663-6, 668; ts 187-8; tp 38-43
discipline: w74 82; w73 227-9; tp 112-13
discussion: w75 227-40
Elohim: po 36; bi8 1352-3
endurance: g74 4/8 17; w73 100-1
eternal: w74 375-6; w71 480
eternal purpose: po 12-13, 187-8
eyes: pm 166, 199, 203
faithful: w74 152, 528-9, 534-7
Father: w74 447-8; po 26-7, 33-4, 40; w71 583, 633
of Jesus: g72 3/22 7-8; g71 12/22 5-8
fear of: w74 179; w73 491, 750, 753-4; g72 9/8 28; w71 357-60; g71 9/8 4
feelings: g75 1/22 22
foreknowledge: po 94; ts 58-9; g74 7/8 27-8; w71 466-7
forgiveness: w75 38-41; g75 11/22 28; ts 188-9; w73 100; w72 430-6; w71 270-2, 276
Friend: w74 339; w73 157, 457-62; tp 128-9
generosity: w74 120-1, 154; w72 312-13
glory: w72 152; kj 47, 185-6
God of Jesus Christ: w75 238
God of peace: tp 23, 45
goodness: w75 476-7
goodwill of: w72 368-74
hate: w74 153
history: g74 12/22 19
honoring: g72 3/22 19
humility: w74 409; g73 3/8 4; w72 201
Husband: w73 141; w72 78-80; kj 241-2, 248-9, 251-2
imitating: w74 121-2, 146-56, 211; w73 99-101
impartial: w74 68; g74 10/8 18-19; tp 63-5
invisible: w72 101; te 17
Judge: w73 341-3; tp 61-2; w72 552
God's past judgments: w75 664-6
justice: w75 116-17, 665-6; w74 384, 495-6, 499; ts 33-4; g74 7/22 27-8; w73 195-7; tp 43, 45; g73 7/8 27-8; w72 102; w71 631-3; kj 40, 282-4
kindness: w74 120-1
King of Israel: w72 43-4
kingship: w74 346; ka 148
knowing: w75 113-19; g75 1/8 28; w74 147-8, 339, 566; tp 166-7, 170-1; w72 37-40, 197, 469; g72 4/22 28; w71 265-6, 392, 539
Kyrios: bi8 1352
Lawgiver: w72 35-6
Life-Giver: g73 10/22 25-6
light: w74 560-1, 572; w71 436
listens: w74 436
long-suffering: w75 750-1; w74 495; g74 4/8 17
love: w75 520-6; g75 1/22 22; w74 120-1, 146-7, 190-1, 370-1; w73 67-8, 133, 138, 227-8, 252-3, 458; tp 121-3, 166-7; w72 102, 304; g72 2/8 4; w71 75, 325-7, 357-8, 360; kj 40
love for: w74 151; w72 304, 739; te 183-6
loving-kindness: w71 275, 631-3
lowly ones cherished: w73 105-16
loyalty: w73 585; w71 515-16
man's obligation to: w73 297-9
memory: ts 173-4; w71 708
mercy: w75 39-40, 115-17, 517-18; sl 115-17; w74 370-1, 460-3, 467-8, 495-9; w73 105-6, 147, 197, 303-5; g73 7/8 28; w72 73-4, 430-6, 549-50; w71 411, 566-7; g71 8/8 27-8
miracles: w72 38-40; w71 291-4
name: fu 8-10; w74 433; po 14-17; w73 259-61; g73 3/22 27-8; w71 387-91, 465; kj 7-8, 11-12, 14-21, 25-7, 32-5, 313, 315-16, 371, 406-7; te 19-22
African Bibles: yb73 142-3
American Standard Version: w71 391
Christendom's views: g73 3/22 27-8
Christian Greek Scriptures: w73 259; yb73 142-3; w71 453-5; bi8 1358-60
Declaration: w72 54-7
emphasized in literature from 1926: yb75 149; w74 764; ka 238-40; w71 651
experiences: w75 326; yb73 172-3
Ezekiel (Book): w72 75, 155
Hebrew numerals: g71 9/8 20
Hebrew Scriptures: g74 1/22 19; g73 3/22 27-8; w71 387
hidden by religious leaders: fu 9-10; pm 389; w71 627, 649
hidden by superstitious Jews: w71 389-90, 454
importance: w74 728-9; w72 748
incorporated in other names: w71 58
Jah: w71 453
Jesus' use: w73 259; w71 455; te 19-20
"knowing": w74 434
Lachish Letters: w74 79
Lingala versions: g73 1/22 26
making for himself: po 17-23
meaning: w74 728-9; po 16; w71 387
music: g71 3/22 10
New English Bible, The: g73 3/22 27-8
New World Translation: bi8 1352-5, 1358-60
"not known" to Abraham: w72 72-3
oaths in: w73 59-62
occurrences in Bible: w73 259; w72 155; w71 229, 387; kj 53; sg 17
on cover of *Watchtower:* w74 764
people for: w71 654-9
preaching work: w72 728
profanation: w72 31, 55; w71 646-9
pronunciation: po 16; g73 3/22 27-8; pm 388-9; w71 389, 391; bi8 1357
respect for: w73 260-1; w72 31; w71 645-59
Rotherham's view: g73 3/22 28
sanctified: w73 222-3; w72 75; kj 323-6, 328
Septuagint: w71 389-91, 454; bi8 1357-8

taking in worthless way: yb72 113; w71 645-6
Tetragrammaton: po 16; km 9/74 8; g73 3/22 27; pm 388; w71 389-91, 454-5; bi8 1352, 1354-5, 1357-8
upholding: w73 260-1
vindication: w72 56
walking in: w73 31; yb73 4-5, 260-1
Yahweh: g73 3/22 27-8
nations collide with: w72 31; w71 611-31; nc 3-29
nearness of: w72 521-32
New Jerusalem's temple: w72 720
not forgetting: te 91-4
not "plan" human history: po 66, 94, 102
not slow: w72 4, 246-7
not source of what is bad: w75 657
obedience to God: w73 146, 148, 430-6; w72 429-30
oneness with Christ: w74 525-7
ownership: km 8/75 1; w74 593-9, 604
patience: sl 300-2; w74 495; g74 4/8 17; tp 58-9; g73 3/8 4; w72 246-7, 308-12
Peacemaker: g71 9/8 27
permits evil: gc 3-21; w74 643-4; g74 4/8 16-17; g74 10/8 14-17; w73 195-7; tp 46, 52-7; g72 10/22 10-12
Person: w74 220
personality: w74 495, 497, 499
pictured by Abraham: po 162, 180
power: w73 750, 752-5; w72 102; pm 392-3; kj 40
praise: te 107-10
presence: w72 710-11, 714, 716-17, 719-21; w71 712
promises: w75 81-7, 700-2; g75 1/22 13; g74 4/8 15-18; tp 98-9; w72 241-5
proof of existence: w73 35-8; w72 388; pm 147; w71 613; nc 4-5; g71 8/8 3-7; g71 8/22 11-12; g71 9/8 7
proof of Godship: g73 1/22 7
Protector: yb76 64-5; w74 169-72, 203, 722-34, 752-4, 757-8, 760-6; yb74 207-10; g74 12/22 23, 25; w73 173; ka 399-401, 404-5, 407-10; kj 24-5, 358, 379
Provider: w74 189-91; w73 765; tp 116-18; kj 23
punishment: w73 228-9
purpose: w75 81-7, 96; w74 597-8, 614, 616, 658-62, 669; po 11-15, 19, 34, 48-9, 60-1, 64, 102, 180, 187-8; hu 7, 12-13; tp 62; w72 169-71
epitome of 6,000 years: w75 584-8
to sanctify himself: po 23
qualities: w75 234-5; fu 11-12; w74 574; w72 102; kj 39-40
revealed by Jesus Christ: w75 117
ready to help: w75 517-18
reasons for serving: w75 227-40; w73 67-8, 297-9
refuge: w75 636-9; w74 726-9, 731-4, 752-4, 759, 765
'regrets making man' (Ge 6:6): po 74
relationship with: w75 18, 51, 305-11, 352; fu 31-2; w74 212, 309-10, 339, 371-2, 415, 433-8, 496-7, 602-3; g74 12/8 21; w73 210-11, 457-62, 490-1; tp 186-90; or 13-18
reliance on: tp 116-18; sg 50
requirements for life: w73 63-4; w71 64, 633-9
requirements for pleasing: w74 340, 344; w73 63-4, 451-2; tp 95-7; g73 5/22 27-8; w72 99-100, 209-10, 250-1, 454-5, 475; or 14-18; pm 251-2; w71 37; g71 4/22 29
'residing with': w74 639-40
respect for: w72 266, 272-3
rest: po 189
resurrects Christ: w73 350-1
return to: w72 430-6; pm 92-106
rewards from: w71 92-4
righteousness: w72 365
Ruler: w72 580; w71 681-2, 711, 742-7; kj 326
Sabbath day: po 189-90
Savior: w74 190-1; po 17, 24-5; w73 755-6, 759; ka 399-401, 404-10
"secret place of": w74 724
seeing: g71 8/22 28
seeking: w73 429-42
self-control: w71 360
service to: w73 67-8; or 107-32
Shepherd: or 53; kj 293, 299, 302-4, 310-11; te 116-18
Source of peace: tp 178-9
sovereignty: w75 614-18, 622-3, 657-663; sl 59-63, 81, 126, 253, 267-8, 271, 279-81, 344-7, 354, 368; og 10-18, 26-9; w74 725-6; pm 382-3, 393; w71 244, 267-8
Spirit: w72 101
stability: w71 350-1
Sustainer: w74 190
Teacher: sg 49, 53-4
temple: w71 711-13
thoughts higher than men's: g73 1/22 27-8
throne: w72 716-17, 721
time: w74 56-7, 163, 644-5; po 7-8; w73 579-83
titles: w72 172; w71 389, 391
Almighty: w74 726-8, 731
God: bi8 1352
Lord: bi8 1352-3
Most High: w74 726-8, 731
Prince of princes: w71 716, 720
torment: ts 123-4; w73 227-9
trueness: w75 82; w74 753-4
trust in: w75 420-1, 700-2; w74 701-2, 730-1, 754, 766; g74 12/22 22-3, 25
truthfulness: g74 4/8 15
unchangeable: w71 350-1
undeserved kindness: w74 189-91
unselfishness: w73 99-100
visions of: w72 101-4, 152-3
voice: w74 298
waiting upon: w73 474-7
way of approach to: w73 176-81, 186-7; g73 5/22 27-8
weather control: pm 283-5, 398-9
wisdom: w75 665-6, 715; w73 163-4; w72 102; kj 40
dealings with mankind: g71 6/8 12-14
hardiness of life testifies to: g71 8/22 11-12
words stolen: pm 212-14
works: w72 486
worship: w75 227-40; w73 67-8; g73 5/22 27-8
exclusive devotion required: w75 380-2
(SEE ALSO GOD)

JEHOVAH (Book)

release: ka 266-7

JEHOVAH-SHAMMAH

kj 401-6

JEHOVAH'S ORGANIZATION

appreciating: w73 396, 400-7, 460-1
identified: kj 51-4
no organizational symbol: km 9/74 8
progressive in understanding: w74 52-3
spiritual security: w74 753-4, 757-63
symbolic representation: kj 48-51

Capital

New Jerusalem: w75 490-2; w72 720; pm 149-53

Universal

Ezekiel's vision: w72 151-5; kj 35-54, 89
identified: w72 154-5
mankind: pm 148
members: w72 78-80; pm 148
symbolic representation: w72 153-4; pm 224
wife of Jehovah: po 61, 79
woman of Genesis 3:15: po 60-1, 64, 79
(SEE ALSO ANGELS, CONGREGATION)

JEHOVAH'S WITNESSES

adjustments in view: yb75 147-9; w72 498-505
advocate Kingdom: yb75 234-7
appreciation for: w73 401-7; g73 10/8 30; w72 542
assembly halls: km 4/75 4; g74 6/8 16-20
attitude toward opposers: g72 12/8 26-7; w71 491-2
attitude toward work: w73 187, 328-9; g73 9/8 11; w72 206-11
baptism report: yb76 3, 23, 31; w75 18-19, 23, 27, 86; yb75 5, 31, 254, 257; km 5/75 1-2; w74 15, 26; yb74 4, 23; km 11/74 1; w72 50; yb72 42-3; g72 10/22 23; w71 24, 562; kj 179
beliefs: w74 629-31; g74 11/8 19, 21; g73 9/8 13-14; w72 8-9, 644; yb72 9-10; w71 676-7
benefits enjoyed: w73 49-51; g71 9/22 3-6
benefit to community: w75 631; g75 4/8 18-19; w73 153-5; w72 346-7; g72 12/8 21; w71 423-6
Bible:
view and use: w74 629, 631-2, 637, 768; g74 9/8 6-7; w72 169; w71 91, 465, 676-7
business agreements: w73 287-8
Christendom's attitude: yb73 117-19; w72 574-5, 749
chronology of: w75 63-4
clergy opposition: yb76 35-7; yb75 95-7, 101-2, 109, 154-5, 180-1,

183, 191; yb74 36-8, 40, 58, 100, 103-4, 108, 112-13; w73 119-20, 172, 379; yb73 39-41, 47, 51-2, 58-9, 61, 63, 151-9, 191, 201; w72 60, 147-50, 283-5; yb72 105-6, 127, 131, 133, 138, 140, 150-1, 153-4, 160-1, 178, 185-8, 225, 235, 237, 241-2; g72 10/22 17-18; w71 18, 252, 287, 508; g71 11/8 13-15
commendation: w75 217-18, 316; g75 1/22 30; g75 3/8 15; g75 4/8 18-19, 23-4, 29; w74 411-12, 456, 516; g74 2/8 10; g74 3/22 7; w73 37-8, 442; g73 4/8 17; g73 7/22 23; g73 8/22 30; w72 125, 381, 542, 555; w71 598; g71 10/22 17
clergy: w75 759; g75 4/22 25, 28; g75 5/22 16-17; g73 2/22 8; w72 423-4; g72 6/8 16; g71 1/8 24, 29; g71 9/22 12
convention (quotes): w75 171; w74 44, 632, 635, 637-9; yb74 239, 251; g74 3/8 29; g74 9/8 6; g74 11/8 17-21; g74 12/8 4-5; w73 38, 453, 456, 486, 629-32; g73 3/8 11; g73 11/8 14-17, 20; yb72 41-2, 246; g72 10/22 17-19, 21-3; w71 123; g71 3/22 26; g71 10/22 13-15
press: w75 631; w74 149, 152, 632, 645-6; g74 7/22 30; g74 9/8 6-7; g74 9/22 31; g74 10/8 29; w73 38; yb73 198, 230; g73 4/22 22-5; g73 10/8 30; w71 13-14, 91, 595-9, 601; g71 10/22 13-15
prison officials: g75 4/22 23-4, 28
school textbook: g74 9/22 30
commission: w71 423-6
Communist lands: g73 4/8 17-19; yb72 45
conduct of, impresses outsiders: w73 187-8
congregations: w75 27; yb75 3, 5, 30-2, 258; g74 6/8 16; w72 8, 333; yb72 9, 43
foreign-speaking, in the United States: km 7/75 4
number of new ones: km 8/75 8
when to divide: km 7/75 4
different from other religions: w74 629-31
different from world: w73 187-8
disinterest in: g72 8/8 5-7
drugs: w73 336-8, 340-3
evolution theory: g73 10/22 28
exposure of false religion: w75 127-8; yb75 55, 94-5, 97-8, 126, 135-7, 155, 181, 228-9, 235; yb73 162
faith: g75 12/22 16-19; w74 393, 572-3; w73 691-2
financial support: g75 9/8 25-6; w74 282; g74 6/8 18-19; g74 10/22 28; w73 297-9, 508; g73 11/22 29; or 148-54; w71 506-7
flag salute: w75 217; g75 2/22 22; yb73 81-3; g73 12/8 29; g72 7/8 11-12; w71 489, 722; g71 9/8 14-15
generosity: yb74 105; g74 6/8 18-19
governing body: w75 60; yb74 257; w73 537; w72 703-4, 750; or 10-11, 59, 61-3, 69; w71 669-70, 727
growth: yb75 212, 254; w74 15, 206; g74 3/8 20; g74 5/8 25; g74 7/22 16; yb74 254; km 4/74 1; km 6/74 1, 3; w73 41, 221, 313-15, 459; ka 252, 283; g73 4/8 18; g73 5/22 18; g73 9/8 4; g73 9/22 9-16; km 6/73 1; w72 211, 313; yb72 43-5, 242; w71 88; kj 319-21, 330-1; g71 1/8 29; g71 5/8 26
statistics: yb74 4-5, 23; g73 6/8 30-1
handicaps coped with: g75 2/22 12-16
happiness: w75 60; w72 260
health matters: w75 415
honesty: w75 293; g75 3/8 15; w74 516, 555; g74 11/8 20; g74 12/8 4-6; w73 358-9, 597-8; tp 118-19; g73 4/22 23-5; g73 7/22 29; g73 11/8 19
hope: w73 692-3
identification cards: km 6/75 3
interfaith: w74 631
Israelites: or 132; w71 652-3
jury duty: w73 190-1
kindness to German Jews: g75 2/22 22
Kingdom Halls: g72 8/22 19-23
lands preaching in: yb76 23; w75 23-7; yb75 5, 30, 257; w74 15, 26; yb74 5; w73 23, 40; yb73 23, 256; w72 27, 340, 342, 457; pm 254; yb72 33; w71 24, 81; kj 179
languages in which Bible study aids printed: yb75 32; pm 254; yb72 256
legal contributions toward religious liberty: yb75 172, 178-80; g74 9/22 30; g74 12/8 22-5; g72 7/8 9-12
legal recognition:
Portugal: w75 169-71; g75 2/8 29
Spain: w75 456
legal rights: yb76 37, 44, 124-5; yb75 172, 175, 179-80, 208; km 8/71 3-4
literacy: g75 3/8 15
love for brothers: yb75 209-10; km 3/75 3-4; w74 39, 443, 569-71, 635; yb74 61, 207; g74 12/22 23-6; w73 403, 691; g73 3/8 14, 16; g73 6/22 15; g73 8/22 16; g73 11/8 20; or 183-4; w71 463-4
love for people: w74 141-3, 241-2, 338, 631; g74 12/22 24-6; w73 627-9; tp 121-4, 131
"marked" person: w73 318-20
materialism: g73 8/22 14-15
meetings: w74 15; w73 253-4; w72 406-12; or 91-107
when attendance exceeds seating capacity: km 7/75 4
mercy toward brothers: km 3/75 2
military service: yb75 101, 103; g74 12/8 22-5; g72 4/22 22-3; g71 1/8 13-15
misrepresentation: yb72 236
clergy: yb72 138, 140, 153-4, 160, 178, 185-6, 225, 237
press: yb73 107-8, 117, 122, 125, 161; yb72 160
modern history: w73 394-400; ka 186-93, 206-10, 232-40, 245-6, 251-2; g73 6/8 16-26
Afghanistan: yb72 209-13
Angola: yb76 198-208
Argentina: yb72 46-125
Ascension Island: yb76 230-1
Australia: yb76 5-6
Austria: yb76 6
Barbados: yb76 6
Belgium: yb76 6-7
Bolivia: yb76 7-8
Botswana (Bechuanaland): yb76 180-1, 213-16
Brazil: yb73 33-88
British Isles: yb75 88-90; yb73 88-141
Burma: yb76 8
Canada: w75 41-2
Central African Republic: yb76 9; yb74 34-41
China: yb74 41-4, 46-9, 51-6, 59-60, 63
Congo: yb76 9-10
Cyprus: yb76 11
Czechoslovakia: yb72 126-41
Dahomey: yb76 11-12
Dominican Republic: yb72 143-71
El Salvador: yb76 12-14
Fiji: yb76 14-15
Gabon: yb76 10-11
Germany: yb74 65-253
Ghana: yb73 141-89
Greece: yb76 32
Guatemala: yb73 189-209
Honduras: yb76 16-17
Hong Kong: yb74 44-7, 49-51, 56-64
Indonesia: yb76 17
Israel: yb76 17-18
Japan: yb73 209-55
Kenya: yb76 105-7
Lesotho (Basutoland): yb76 159-60, 194, 209-13
Luxembourg: yb76 34-47
Macao: yb74 57-8
Malagasy Republic (Madagascar): yb76 114, 198
Malawi (Nyasaland): yb76 20-1, 75-6, 118-20, 151-3, 168-71
Malaysia: yb76 19
Mauritius: yb76 112-13, 177-8, 197-8
Mozambique: yb76 19-21, 98, 115-18, 178
Newfoundland: yb76 47-67
Nicaragua: yb72 172-95
Norway: yb76 21
Pakistan: yb76 21-2; yb72 196-209, 211-13
Portugal: yb76 31-2
Rhodesia (Southern Rhodesia): yb76 82, 122-6, 167-8
St. Helena: yb76 110-11, 181-3, 196-7, 230
São Tomé: yb76 198
South Africa (and neighboring territories): yb76 67-242
South Vietnam: yb76 15-16
South-West Africa: yb76 103, 111-12, 146-8, 222-5
Sri Lanka (Ceylon): yb76 242-57
Swaziland: yb76 112, 179-80, 194-5, 217-21
Syria: yb76 18-19
Tahiti: yb76 14; km 4/75 1
Taiwan: yb72 214-34
Tanzania (Tanganyika): yb76 106-7, 160-1
Tonga: yb76 15
Uganda: yb76 121
United States: yb75 34-256
Zaïre (Belgian Congo): yb76 22, 175-7
Zambia (Northern Rhodesia): yb76 126-34, 155-9, 171-5; yb72 234-54
Zululand: yb76 136
moral standards: w74 218, 340; g74 9/8 6-7; g74 10/8 29; yb74 239; w73 144-5, 287, 336-43, 357-9;

yb73 72-3; g73 2/22 9-10; g73 4/22 22-8; g73 8/22 6-8, 15; or 154-82; g72 10/22 21; w71 452-3
maintaining: yb72 170-1, 184-5, 230-2, 238, 246
name: yb76 108; sl 109-10; yb75 149-51; po 179; yb73 112, 218; ka 238-40; w72 637, 751; pm 364; w71 651, 757; kj 66, 172, 319-20
blessings resulting from: w75 84
resolution adopting: ka 239-40
names applied to: yb75 150
neutrality: yb76 18, 20-2; yb75 119, 205-8; w74 517, 519-21, 631; g74 11/8 29; w73 28-9, 264-6, 538; yb73 98-100, 162-4; g73 3/8 18-19; g73 8/22 13-14; pm 334; yb72 124; g72 4/22 22-3; w71 466, 489-90, 720
no clergy-laity distinctions: w74 630-1
older persons: g75 11/8 16; w73 400-1
peace: g74 2/8 26; pm 90-1
persecution: w75 622; sl 260-1, 340, 368-70; og 26-7; yb74 33, 212; w74 201-2, 207, 218, 373; yb73 127; w72 340; pm 73, 370-4; yb72 44-5; w71 464, 489-90, 622-3, 720-2; nc 24-5
Argentina: yb73 7; yb72 61-2, 82-8, 105-6, 109-11
Australia: w73 53; w72 534-5
Belgium: w73 572-3
Botswana (Bechuanaland): yb76 146; yb74 17
Brazil: yb73 49-56, 58-9, 62-7, 79-84
Cameroon: yb74 11; w73 529-30; yb73 19-20; w71 157
Canada: yb75 95-6; g75 3/8 16-22; w74 284-5; g73 6/8 16-26; w72 144, 148-51; g72 7/8 9-10; w71 22
China: yb74 53-6, 59-60; g74 7/8 9; w72 521, 524-5, 532
Colombia: w72 282-5
Communist lands: yb74 53-6, 59-60, 223-232; w72 71
Cuba: w71 19, 678; g71 10/22 28
Czechoslovakia: yb72 127, 132-6, 138-41
Dominican Republic: yb72 151-63; w71 18, 343
East Germany: w74 250; yb74 223-232; g72 7/8 20
Ethiopia: yb75 7-8; yb74 12-13
Fiji: w71 20-1
Gabon: yb76 10-11; w73 529; w71 251-4
Germany: yb75 174; w74 202, 676; yb74 100, 102-5, 108-28, 131-204, 210-12, 238; w73 377-8, 399; yb73 120, 123, 126-7; w72 143-4, 395-9, 525, 631; yb72 97; g72 4/22 22-3; w71 16, 117, 425, 489-90, 494; g71 1/8 13-14
Ghana: yb74 9-10; yb73 151-66, 168-70, 172-8
Great Britain: yb73 98-100, 117-35; w71 721
Greece: w75 71; g75 6/8 25; g75 12/8 17-21; w71 678
Guadeloupe: w72 532
India: w73 763-4
Italy: w73 664-5
Japan: yb73 214-21; w71 15-16
Kenya: yb74 12; g73 9/22 30
Korea: w71 14; g71 8/8 13-15
Lesotho (Basutoland): yb76 146
Liberia: w73 172-3
Lithuania: g73 5/22 29
Luxembourg: yb76 35-41
Macao: yb74 58
Malagasy Republic (Madagascar): w71 89-92
Malawi (Nyasaland): yb76 20-1, 84-5, 88, 236-8; w75 341; yb75 10; g75 12/8 3-12; g75 12/22 15-19; km 12/75 1-2; w74 218; yb74 15; w73 264-8; yb73 22-3; g73 1/8 29; g73 3/8 17-24; yb72 45; g72 7/8 20; g72 11/22 29; g72 12/8 9-28; w71 111
Mauritius: yb76 113
Mozambique: yb76 19-21, 116-17, 178
Newfoundland: yb76 51, 53, 55, 57-64
Nicaragua: yb72 178, 185-90
Nigeria: g74 3/8 20; w72 520; w71 157
Pakistan: yb72 199
Philippine Republic: w71 20
Poland: w71 490
Portugal: w75 170
Rhodesia (Southern Rhodesia): yb76 100, 154-5
Russia: w74 218; g73 4/8 17-19
Singapore: w72 341-9
Solomon Islands: g75 6/22 14
South Africa: yb76 83, 89, 98-102, 138-9, 141-6, 162, 188; yb75 11
Sri Lanka (Ceylon): yb76 244
Swaziland: yb76 146
Taiwan: yb72 215-26
Tanzania (Tanganyika): yb76 106; yb74 13-14
Togo: yb74 10-11
Turkey: w74 218; g74 2/8 29; g73 3/22 15; g73 6/8 29; g73 9/8 12-16
Uganda: yb74 13
United Arab Republic: w72 525; w71 114, 117-18
United States: yb75 95-110, 116-17, 141, 153-4, 163-4, 169-73, 175-91; w73 117, 120-2, 661; g72 7/8 10-12; w71 379, 520-1, 722, 730
Zaïre (Belgian Congo): yb74 14
Zambia (Northern Rhodesia): yb76 96; g73 3/8 19-21; yb72 235-40, 242, 245, 247-50
positive outlook: g74 9/8 6
preaching: w74 3-4, 123-5, 141-3, 183-8, 241-2, 332, 334, 337-40; g74 3/8 20; w73 744; tp 83, 87; g73 9/22 6-9, 16; w71 331-2
far north: g75 2/8 24-6
training for: yb75 227-8; w73 531-5
preaching methods: g73 3/22 22; g73 4/8 25; w72 277, 280, 400-3, 424; or 113-26, 131-2
prejudice against: g72 8/8 6
printing activities: w73 313-15, 538; g73 9/22 7-16
prophecies announced: w71 467-73
qualifications to be a Witness: km 3/74 4; or 128-30
race: g75 4/8 19; w74 712-14; w73 518-19
relief work: yb76 11, 16-17, 20-1; yb75 209-10; g75 4/8 18-19; yb74 216-17; g74 12/22 26; w73 95-6, 134-5, 267-8; yb73 95; g73 3/8 13-16, 19-20; g73 6/22 15; or 149-50; yb72 99-100, 137, 179, 225-6, 252-3; g72 8/8 26; g72 8/22 15-16; w71 424-5; g71 3/22 25
sedition charge disproved: yb73 162
separate from world: w73 137-40, 146, 264-6; tp 120-1, 124-31
service reports (annual): yb76 22-32; w75 23-8; yb75 24-32, 257-8; w74 26-30; yb74 23-32; w73 23-8; yb73 23-32, 255-6; w72 22-5, 27, 493; yb72 33-41; w71 23-9
settling difficulties: w73 331-5, 703-4; w72 464-7; or 155-9
six millenniums of: w75 581-4
spiritual condition: w74 667-8; w73 221-3
taxation: g74 9/8 15-16
tobacco: w74 71, 223-4; w73 338-43, 453-5; g73 8/22 20
unity: ml 29; w74 44, 207, 712-14; g74 9/8 6-7; g74 10/8 22; g74 11/8 21; w73 37-8, 68, 281, 283, 331, 400-1; yb72 246-7; g72 2/8 26; w71 122-7; kj 343-4, 346-8; g71 3/22 24-6; g71 4/8 20-3
unselfishness: yb74 105
use of literature: g74 9/22 30
use of time: w71 312-13
why people attracted to: w73 626-9, 632
youths: g75 1/22 30; yb74 234; g74 2/8 10; g74 9/22 31
zeal: g74 6/8 19-20; w73 446-7; g73 7/22 6; w72 211, 423-4

Statements by Others

allegiance only to Jehovah: w71 489, 677
areas where Witnesses are strongest are now more trouble-free: yb72 246
balanced view of man and environment: g73 3/8 31; g74 6/22 11
bursting with good qualities: g72 4/22 23
can produce answer to all [Bible] questions: sg 95
churches getting emptier but Witnesses increasing: w75 41
civilized people . . . as in paradise: w74 149; g74 9/8 6
cover the earth with witnessing: g73 9/22 7; w72 211
doctrines of Witnesses based on Bible: w71 465
each a fortress, destroyed but never taken: w72 515; g71 10/22 4
exemplary family discipline: g73 4/22 23
family units obvious in homes of African Witnesses: yb72 246
follow the apostolic method of going from house to house: w75 759
form a community of trust: w75 764
genuine regard for all races: w73 518
heroic steadfastness to convictions: w72 631
high morals, eliminate tribal discrimination: w74 218; g73 10/8 30

high standards of morality, honesty: g73 4/22 22
if all lived by Witnesses' creed bloodshed and hatred would end: w71 463
if Baptists believed the way Witnesses believe: g73 2/22 8
if more people were like Witnesses there would be fewer criminals: g75 4/22 23
if owned chain of stores would hire Witnesses to run cash registers: g75 4/22 24
if they were only people in world we would not have to bolt doors: g75 3/8 26
know Bible so well: w71 465
large number of highly creative children: w75 217-18
magazines are nice and even interesting: g75 4/8 29
model citizens: g75 12/22 16; g73 3/8 18
most honest people in Germany: w74 152
Nazis unable to master: yb74 210-11
new Witnesses study Bible harder than most Christians: sg 12
place emphasis on honesty and moral purity: g75 3/8 27
races intermingle, everyone smiling: g74 9/8 7
redeeming criminals and drug addicts: g75 4/22 25, 28
revival of primitive Christianity: g72 4/22 22
rocks in a sea of mud: w71 494
Soviets infuriated by activity: g73 4/8 17
still obey God before man: g73 3/8 24-5
submitted to trials patiently and with peculiar gladness: w71 425
take advantage of every occasion to witness: w75 759
their principles remind us of the early Christians: w71 489
very certain, governed by Bible: g74 9/8 6
withstood Nazi camps because uncompromising faith: yb74 211
Witnesses can trust both kin and fellow Witnesses: g75 3/8 15
Witnesses have real principles: w75 44
Witnesses prepared to organize new order: g74 9/8 6; g73 11/8 14-15
Witnesses recognize Bible as wholly, literally and exclusively true: sg 95
zealous: w72 211, 423-4
(SEE ALSO CONVENTIONS, FIELD SERVICE, MEETINGS)

JEHOVAH'S WOMAN
remnant's relationship: w72 78-80

JEHU (King of Israel)
discussion: g73 4/8 27-8
rewarded by Jehovah: w75 713

JEPHTHAH
vow: w74 278

JEREMIAH (Prophet)
commission: kj 101
faith: w72 140; w71 364-5
period of prophesying: kj 101-2
qualities: km 12/73 2

JEROME
Apocrypha: w75 414
comment on supremacy of one overseer: w75 730

JERUSALEM
Allenby captures: pm 371
bloodguilt: w73 123-6
Castle of Antonia: w75 366-7
climate: w75 365
cooking pot (figurative): w73 123-5; w72 677; kj 195-7, 267-70
David captures: po 125
description: w75 365-7; w74 78-9; g72 11/8 11
destruction (607 B.C.E.): w73 60-1, 92, 125-6, 148-9; w72 42-5, 470-1, 587, 677, 744-5, 764-6; pm 136, 162, 235-6; g72 3/8 27; g72 5/8 27-8; kj 99, 105-11, 124, 137, 169-70, 188-90, 198, 201-2, 205-6, 218, 220-3, 254, 261-3, 273, 279, 285-6, 289, 351-2, 383
  time of the end: po 173
destruction (70 C.E.): w75 138-40, 742; sl 19, 20, 22; ml 21-2; w74 425-9, 680-3, 693-4; w73 710; ka 294-6, 302-3; w72 372, 625, 629, 748; pm 365; dn 18, 25; g72 10/8 20-1; kj 135, 210, 233, 316, 351; te 33-4; g71 12/8 5-6
  Jesus' prophecy concerning: w74 681-3
  time of the end: po 172-3
discussion: w75 365-7
elevation: w75 365
flight of Christians: w75 340-1; ml 22; w74 426; g74 11/8 11; w72 108-9; g72 10/8 20-1; g71 12/8 5-6
garden tomb: w75 367
gates: pm 155
Golgotha: w75 367
"holy place": w75 741
Jebus: po 125
Jehovah's temple: w75 365-6
Jesus' prophecy concerning: w75 138-40
maps: w75 366; pm 156
Mount of Olives: w75 367
Mt. Zion: w72 171-2
Oholibah: w73 90-2; kj 238-41, 243-63
photograph: w74 79
pictures—
  Christendom: w75 742; w74 717-18; po 173; ka 305, 315, 395; w72 45, 324, 472-3, 764; kj 111-13, 140-1, 146, 161-2, 173, 175-6, 189-90, 210, 216, 238, 268-71, 277-8, 286, 343, 359
  kingdom of God: ts 157, 159-60; pm 128-30, 278
pools: w75 367
population: pm 155, 160
potter's field: w75 367
Queen Helena's palace: g75 11/8 30
rebuilding after destruction in 70 C.E.: w72 300-1, 305-7
restoration beginning in 537 B.C.E.: w72 746; pm 22-43, 134-6; w71 396; kj 115, 206, 316
Roman armies withdraw in 66 C.E.: w75 138; w74 426, 683; ka 300-1; g72 10/8 20; g71 12/8 6
Roman domination: w75 7-8
seventy-year desolation: ts 158-9; w72 745-6; pm 131-6, 237; g72 5/8 27-8; kj 115, 122, 130, 206
'treading down': kj 232-5
Wailing Wall: w75 248
walls rebuilt (455 B.C.E.): sl 321; g71 12/8 8

JERUSALEM ABOVE
identified: ts 127; w73 141
spiritual children: sl 94

JESHURUN
po 119

JESUITS (Roman Catholic Order)
discussion: g74 7/8 10-12; g71 11/22 9-12

JESUS CHRIST
adopted by Joseph: po 142
ancestry: w74 105-6, 618; hu 15-16
anointing: po 144-5; ka 64-6, 105; w71 242, 713
appreciation for: w71 265-76
ascension: po 155; w73 711-12; g72 9/22 5-8
attitude toward drugs: w73 182-3, 337
attitude toward Gentiles: w74 463-4
attitude toward homosexuality: w74 484-6
attitude toward persecution: w73 653-5; w72 176-8; w71 109-10, 492-3, 495-6
attitude toward politics: w75 236-7; g74 11/22 6
attitude toward poor: w75 69-70
attitude toward Scriptures: pm 8-12
attitude toward tax collectors: w74 463-4
avenger of blood: w73 308
baptism: w74 603; po 144; w73 5, 274; w72 175-6, 379, 601, 606, 623, 686-7, 715-16; dn 16; te 184
begetting: w74 222
betrayal by Judas: pm 321-5
birth: w74 739-40; po 135-41; w73 3-4; ka 58-63; w72 369-70; te 23-5; g71 12/22 5-8
  angelic messages: po 135-6, 138-9
  born perfect from imperfect mother: w72 621; dn 10-11; w71 272; g71 12/22 7
  date: g75 12/22 27-8; po 139-40; ka 63; g73 12/22 4-5
  place: po 139
  "star": po 140, 142-3; g73 12/22 5
  why 400 years since Malachi: w73 581-2
  "wise men": po 142-3; g74 12/22 4; g73 12/22 5
body pictured by Memorial loaf: g73 9/8 5
Bridegroom: ka 171
burial: sl 76-7
came at right time: w73 580
care for congregation: w74 117-18
Chief Agent of life: w73 104; w72 680-701; w71 30
childhood: w73 4-5; w71 366; te 155-7
Christendom's attitude: g71 1/8 29
cleansed temple (30 and 33 C.E.): w73 6-7, 18-19
coming again: w75 9-11
coming on clouds: w74 751

comparison with Moses: po 147-51
compassion: w74 281
conception: w74 68-9; po 136-8; ts 128-9; w72 621; dn 11
confidence in followers: w74 300
courage: w74 522
covenants for kingdom: po 161
created: w75 175-6; w74 526-7; w73 132
criticism of religious leaders: g74 11/22 28
"day and hour" of great tribulation: w75 768
death: w75 619; sl 76-7; og 19; w73 3, 20, 766-8; w72 256, 517; pm 12-13; g72 2/8 7-8; w71 235, 440; te 163-6
 accursed on stake: po 151-2
 date: w73 766-8; pm 340
 drugged wine: w71 249
 earthquake: w75 639-40
 events just preceding: w73 18-20; w72 527-8; w71 273-4, 397; te 163-6
 manner: po 151-2; g74 9/22 27-8; g72 2/8 7; bi8 1360-1; te 165-6
 memorialized: te 167-70
 significance: w72 237; g72 10/22 14
 time in tomb: w73 766-8
dedication: w72 686-7
depicted as created "Wisdom": w75 511-12
disciples: w74 600-3; w73 6-8, 14, 16, 269-73; w72 107; w71 438; te 55-8
discussion: w75 249-51; g73 3/8 27-8
disowned himself: w74 601, 603
endurance: w75 54; w73 15, 655-6; g71 1/22 27
exaltation since resurrection: g75 1/22 23; w74 601; ka 70-1; g73 7/22 4; pm 152-3; w71 275
executioner: ka 163-4
existence confirmed by non-Christian historians: w75 249-50; g72 2/8 8
Father: w75 623; sl 361, 365; og 29; w74 157, 200, 251; ts 167; w73 466; ka 133-4; w71 431-2
fig tree cursed: w72 95-6
firstborn: w73 262-3
forgave sins: g74 11/8 28; te 87-90
foundation cornerstone of Zion: pm 188
'friend of sinners': w74 140, 464
friends he chose: w71 6-7; te 119-21
fulfilled prophecies: w74 105-6; po 131-2, 144-5, 151-3; w73 37; w72 174-8, 241-2; pm 270-2, 321-4, 339-41, 355-8; w71 96, 242-3; g71 12/22 27
genealogy: w74 105-6; ka 58, 61-2, 71
God's qualities revealed by: w75 117, 305, 307-8
hated by world: w74 522; w73 649-53
head of congregation: w72 755-7
High Priest: w74 157-9; ts 140; w73 216-17, 308-12; ka 87-93, 96, 102-3; pm 87-8, 176, 179, 181-5; w71 570
 cessation: w73 311-12, 543
historicity of: w75 237, 249-51
honoring: w74 739-41
humility: w74 409; g73 3/8 4; w72 201; te 27-9
imitated Jehovah: w74 149
immortality: w71 480
inherited earth: w74 662
integrity tested: sl 78-9, 89; w74 69-70, 222; w73 653-6; w72 621-2, 624, 627; dn 11-13, 16-18, 22; g72 12/8 24; w71 110, 272-4, 530-1
Jehovah is the God of: w75 238
Jehovah's spiritual temple: w74 221-3, 252-3; ka 93-112; w72 606-7; pm 87-8; w71 712-13
Jews reject: w74 692; w73 652-3, 709, 716; pm 366-7; w71 273-4; g71 12/8 3-6, 9
Josephus' comments on: w75 249
joy: w74 559
Judge: sl 179-82; w74 277-9, 398; ka 119, 136-7, 140-2
kingship: g75 4/8 12-14; w74 68-70, 105-6, 238, 356-7, 398, 618; po 136, 152; ts 127, 130, 140, 152-5, 160-1; hu 16; w73 61, 709-11, 716; ka 163-5; tp 66; w72 171, 180-1, 463, 580-2; pm 230-1, 367-70; g72 10/22 15-16; w71 5, 238-42, 281-2, 635; kj 232-5, 356-7, 364-5; te 159-62
knowing: w75 117-18
Lamb: sl 70, 254, 267; pm 151-2
"last Adam": w71 275
Law covenant: w73 580-1; w72 127, 685-8; or 91; g72 11/22 6
love for followers: w74 371-2; w73 458; w72 580-1
love for mankind: g75 1/22 23; w74 371
lowliness: ts 154-5
loyalty: fu 18
main events of earthly life: w73 3-20
marriage: w74 431, 686-7, 690
Mediator: po 159-61; w73 198-9; w72 685-8; g72 2/8 5-6
meekness: w74 662
Memorial emblems: w72 166
mercy: w74 494, 497; w71 412-13
Messiah: sl 26; w74 69, 105-6; po 131-2, 135-6, 138-41, 144-5, 151-3; g73 9/8 27-8; w72 241-2, 654-5; g71 12/8 6-9; g71 12/22 27-8
Messianic "Servant": sl 66, 69, 88-9
Michael: w74 191-2; po 137-8, 155; w71 269-70
ministry: w74 59-60, 336; km 5/74 3; w73 5-20, 269-73, 650-1, 654, 767-8; w72 422-3; or 112-13; w71 9, 78, 260, 396-7, 422-3, 456-7; g71 12/22 27-8
miracles: w75 251; sl 66-8; w74 134; po 149-50; g74 4/8 11-12; w73 6, 8-13, 17, 365-6; tp 106-7; g73 3/8 27; w72 448; g72 10/22 14; w71 293-6, 439; te 43-5, 59-62, 67-70, 83-6, 87-8, 112-13; g71 12/22 27-8
 those performed in Capernaum: w75 669-70
Moslem legend: g72 2/8 7
name: w74 729; po 139, 141; w73 102-4, 287; w72 237; pm 388; w71 58, 241, 455, 654
Napoleon's comments on: w75 250
Nazarene: po 143
new covenant: po 159-61; pm 276-7
obedience: w74 222
offspring: sl 80-1
oneness with Jehovah: w74 525-7
owner: w74 598-9
persecution: w74 522
physical appearance: sl 50; w73 6
pictured by—
 Aaron: pm 176
 Ahasuerus: w71 172-3
 Boaz: w72 77
 Cyrus: kj 300
 David: po 125; w73 168
 Elimelech: w72 77, 79-80
 High Priest Joshua: pm 176, 230
 Melchizedek: w74 158-9; po 155; ts 130; ka 88-93, 102-3; pm 186-7, 231, 401
 Moses: w74 297; po 110-12, 147-51; g72 2/8 5-6; w71 242
 Noah: w74 666-8
 sheaf of firstfruits of barley harvest: w75 603
 two olive trees (Zec 4): pm 206
 Zechariah: w75 554; pm 314
 Zerubbabel: w75 454-5; pm 120-3
politics: ka 66-7, 76; g71 5/8 4
prayers: w74 137; g74 1/8 9; w72 527-8; sg 77-8
prehuman existence: w74 69, 526-7; ts 128-9; w73 262-3; g73 3/8 27-8; w72 580; g71 12/22 6-7
presence: w75 633-5; sl 286-8; w74 255, 397-400; ka 167-9, 187-8, 205-11, 259-61; g73 7/22 3-6; w71 237-40
presentation at time of baptism: w72 686-7
Prince of Peace: tp 45; w71 198; g71 9/8 27
prophet: sl 25-6; w74 425-6, 428-9, 681-3; po 150-1; g74 5/8 17-19; g73 1/22 8-9; g71 12/8 5-6
 successor not needed: g74 1/22 18
publicity avoided: g71 12/22 27-8
public reading: w73 204
purpose in coming to earth: w74 222; w73 466
qualities: g75 4/8 12; w74 69-70; w73 6-7, 9, 21-2, 263; ka 114-15, 139-42; tp 66; g73 1/22 4; g73 3/22 4; w72 303, 313; w71 275, 439
Rabbi: w75 726
ransom: w75 431-2; g75 4/8 10-11; g75 10/8 25; w74 70, 121, 200, 278, 370-1; ts 138; w73 262, 277, 381-3, 543; w72 175, 235-8, 375, 517, 607-8, 685-8; g72 2/8 6-7; g72 9/22 7-8; w71 269-76, 712-14; kj 388-98; g71 12/22 7
rejected as king: w72 654-5
relationship with Jehovah: w75 306-9
relatives: w75 220-3; km 2/75 3; w71 75
resurrection: w73 239, 248, 350-1; w72 238; te 171-4
 appearances after: w75 222, 479; ts 169-70; g73 7/22 4-5; w72 159-60; w71 398; te 173

body disposed of: po 155
date: po 153; w73 766-8; w72 622; pm 341; dn 13
evidence: sl 27-9; g75 5/8 30; ts 168-9; w72 242; g72 2/8 8
faith in: w75 54; w74 17-19
spirit: w75 478-9; po 154-5; w73 711-12; g73 7/22 4-5; w72 622; dn 13; g72 9/22 7
spirits in prison: w71 607-8
survey of Catholics as to whether Jesus is "really living": w75 651
time: po 153
revelation: g73 7/22 6
ride into Jerusalem: pm 271-2
rider of white horse: w74 356-7
rock-mass foundation of congregation: w74 600
role in creation: w75 175-6; w74 594; w72 486; w71 480
role in God's purposes: w74 179-80, 199-200, 598; po 156-7; w73 261-3, 277
"root of Jesse": sl 197
rulership: w72 627-8, 631; dn 22-24, 29
sabbath issue: w73 10-11, 17
sacrifice: w74 254; ts 138-9, 165
Samaritans: w71 159-60
Seed of Abraham: w74 330; po 180; tp 64-5; g73 8/22 28-9; w71 301-2
Seed of God's woman: w75 81-6, 619; og 19; w74 106; po 134-8; ts 129; w73 580; g72 10/22 13-15; w71 301-2
Sermon on the Mount: w75 251; g75 4/22 19; w73 11-12; w71 396, 638; g71 6/8 27-8; g71 6/22 27-8; g71 7/8 27-8; g71 7/22 27-8; g71 8/8 27-8; g71 8/22 27-8; g71 9/8 27-8; g71 9/22 27-8; g71 10/22 27-8
servant: sl 35-42
Shepherd: w73 168-9; or 53, 55; pm 315-25; kj 297, 305-7, 310-11
sinless: w74 70
Son of David: po 136
Son of God: w74 730; po 136-7; w73 388-9; g72 3/22 5; te 23-6
Son of Man: w75 479; w74 748; ts 154; w72 580; g72 2/8 6-7; kj 55
sign of: w74 748, 750-1
Sprout (Branch): sl 175; pm 187, 230
subject to Jehovah: w74 311, 525-7; w73 388-9; g73 2/22 28; g73 3/8 28; w72 294, 734; g72 3/22 7-8; w71 649-50; g71 12/8 4
sufferings: sl 58, 62-3, 68-9, 78, 82, 88-9; w74 601; po 138, 146-7; ts 139; w72 176-8; w71 272-4
symbolic "twig": sl 175
Talmud comments on: w75 249
taxation: w74 140
Teacher: w74 429-30; w73 12, 17-19, 270-3; w72 105-7; sg 49, 53-4; te 7-10
temptation by Satan: w75 619; og 20-1; w74 722-3; po 145-6; w73 5; w72 624-5, 627; dn 16-18, 22; w71 38-9; te 51-4
tomb: w75 367
transfiguration: w74 296-9
trial: w75 8; w73 652; ka 85; g73 9/8 16; w71 110, 340; te 163-5
truth: w74 36; w71 461
unselfishness: w73 139
use of divine name: po 147-8; w73 259, 543; w71 455; te 19-20
use of illustrations: w75 589, 593-4; w74 429-30
victory over world: w74 61; w73 648-56
wisdom: w72 105-6
witness borne to Jesus: w71 95-6
Word of God: w75 63, 173-5; w74 306-7; w73 263, 524; bi8 1362-3
world's attitude toward, if returned in flesh: g75 3/22 30
yoke: w73 277
(SEE ALSO KINGDOM)

"JESUS PEOPLE"
discussion: g72 11/8 3-8

JEWELRY
"cross and crown" pin: yb75 148
pearls: g74 9/8 25

JEWELS
diamonds: g74 7/22 24-6; g72 5/8 31; g72 7/8 29
pearls: g74 9/8 24-6

JEWS
alcoholism: w75 560
attitude toward Gentiles: w74 463-4
attitude toward Jesus Christ: w75 8; w74 692; g74 12/22 17; pm 366-7; g71 12/8 3-6, 9
beliefs:
regarding Messiah: g73 9/8 27-8; g71 12/8 6-9
cantor: g71 11/8 12-15
captivity in Babylon: w72 723-4, 745
restoration from: po 130-1; w72 300-1, 305-7, 500, 724; pm 28-32; g72 3/8 28; w71 649; kj 299-300
cast off: w74 127-8
chronology: w75 63-4
Diaspora: w73 582
disunity: g72 2/22 30
divine name: w71 389-90
Ethiopian Falasha sect: g75 7/8 30
experiences: w71 574-5; g71 1/8 24; g71 11/8 12-15
fasting: pm 234-9; w71 536-7
invitation to Kingdom: po 162-4
Jerusalem's desolation (607-537 B.C.E.): g72 5/8 27-8
Jerusalem's destruction (70 C.E.): w74 425-9, 680-3, 693-4; ka 294-6, 302-3; w72 372; kj 135, 210, 233, 316, 351; te 33-4; g71 12/8 5-6
marriage: g74 5/22 29-30; g71 8/22 30
modern-day return to Palestine: w73 747; kj 59, 67
music: g73 1/8 29
persecution: w75 294
population statistics: g73 2/8 31
revolts against Rome: po 133; kj 351
spiritual: w74 126-8; w73 747-9
synagogue: g73 1/8 29
tradition: w72 560-1
witnessing to: ka 265-6
Witness kindness to German Jews: g75 2/22 22
(SEE ALSO HEBREW, ISRAEL, JERUSALEM)

JOB
endurance: w72 647-8
integrity: sl 58-61; w72 554-5; g72 12/8 24-5; w71 112, 487, 565-6
self-justification: g73 2/8 4

JOB (Book)
authenticity: w75 133

JOHN (Apostle)
characteristics: w71 435
relatives: w75 222
scroll eaten: w72 253; kj 75-6

JOHN (First Book)
time and place written: w71 435

JOHN (Second Book)
time and place written: w71 435

JOHN (Third Book)
time and place written: w71 435

JOHNSON, PAUL S. L.
yb75 89-91, 93; yb73 101-6

JOHN THE BAPTIST
beginning of ministry: po 143
death: te 123-5
food in wilderness: w75 464
pictured at Malachi 3:1: po 143
pictured by Elijah: ts 57-8; w71 239
prepared way for Jesus: g75 4/8 28; w71 239
relationship to Jesus: w75 222

JOKES
"practical": g71 9/22 31

JONAH (Book)
authenticity: w75 709-10; g73 3/22 17-18
clergy view: w75 710
writer: w75 710

JONAH (Prophet)
clergy view: w75 710
discussion: w75 709-12; km 5/74 2
lessons from Jonah's experience: w75 711-12
qualities of: w75 710-11
reproved by Jehovah: w72 213-14
swallowed by fish:
clergy view: g74 8/22 9-10

JONATHAN (Son of Saul)
love for David: w73 421-2; w72 740

JONES, STANLEY ERNEST
yb75 208

JOPPA
discussion: g72 1/8 27

JORDAN
Jehovah's witnesses: yb76 26-7; yb75 26-7; yb74 26-7; yb73 26-7; yb72 36-7
population: yb73 26; yb72 36

JORDAN RIVER
pollution: g73 2/22 31

JOSEPH (Jesus' Foster Father)
adoption of Jesus: po 142
ancestry: w75 220-1; ka 62
children by Mary: w75 221; po 142
death: w75 221
engagement to Mary: w75 221
Passover in Jerusalem: w75 221-2
poor materially: w75 221

JOSEPH (Son of Jacob)
biographical sketch: w74 500-4
conscience: w75 209-11
dreams: w74 501-3

food administrator: w75 196; w71 381
Potiphar's wife: w72 220-1
prison: w74 502-3
qualities: w74 500, 502-5; w72 707-8; w71 411-12
sold into slavery: w74 501-2; po 97; g72 2/22 28

JOSEPHUS, FLAVIUS
accuracy: w74 425; g74 4/8 24
comments on—
Alexander the Great: g74 4/8 24; g72 1/22 16
Apocrypha: w75 414
conscience: w75 209-10
Hyksos: w71 381-2
Jerusalem's destruction (70 C.E.): w75 139; w74 425, 427-8; g72 10/8 21
Jesus Christ: w75 249; w72 242
Theocracy: w71 681
Titus: w75 139
withdrawal of Roman armies (66 C.E.): g72 10/8 20

JOSHUA (Jeshua) (High Priest)
prophetic significance: pm 176-84, 186

JOSHUA (Judge)
respect for law of God: w73 202

JOSIAH (King of Judah)
events of reign: w73 203; w71 363-4, 395; kj 101-2, 155

JOY
basis: tp 109-10
integrity brings: w71 530-5
Jehovah's service: w74 575-6; w71 553-8; km 11/71 7
unselfishness brings: g72 12/22 3-4
(SEE ALSO HAPPINESS)

JUBILEE
g74 4/8 10; g74 10/8 21-2; tp 102-3

JUDAH
person:
relations with Tamar: w73 383-4

Southern Kingdom
desolation: w72 745, 765; kj 32, 57, 109-11, 115-22, 130, 206, 215-16, 220-3, 230-1, 289, 312, 314-15, 322, 336
exile in Babylon: kj 31-2
Oholibah: w73 90-2; kj 238-41, 243-63

Tribe
kingly tribe: po 100-2
union with Ephraim: kj 343-5
(SEE ALSO ISRAEL)

JUDAISM
beliefs: w73 213-16
cantor becomes Witness: g71 11/8 12-15
decline in membership: g74 8/8 29-30
decline in synagogues: g74 5/8 30
destruction: sl 240-1
divisions: g74 5/8 30; g72 2/22 30
evolution theory: g74 7/8 22-3
failure: w71 740
gambling in synagogues: g74 11/8 12-13
homosexuality: w74 135, 483
Jesus Christ: g73 9/8 27-8
mixed marriages: g74 5/22 29-30; g71 8/22 30
money-raising: w74 524; g74 11/8 12-13; g71 7/22 29-30
music: g73 1/8 29
part of Babylon the Great: sl 238
rabbis: g72 8/22 30; g72 9/8 30; g71 1/8 24; g71 8/22 30; g71 11/8 13-15
Soviet Union: g73 4/8 15
synagogue attendance: w74 15
war: g72 4/22 6, 15
(SEE ALSO JEWS, ZIONISM)

JUDAS ISCARIOT
betrayal of Jesus: pm 321-5; w71 427, 438; te 152-3
dishonesty: w71 426-7; te 151-3; g71 5/22 10
disloyalty: w75 109
sin of, unforgivable: w75 459-60

JUDE (Judas, Brother of Jesus)
Bible writer: g71 11/8 27

JUDGE(S)
Bible times: w74 277-8
discussion of Israel's judges: ka 121-4
elders: w75 92-4
Gideon: w74 278
Israel: w74 204-5
Jehovah: w72 552
Jephthah: w74 278
Jesus Christ: w74 277-9
worldly: w74 655; w73 117, 120-2, 703; yb73 120-1, 133-4; yb72 151; g71 11/8 5-6, 8
(SEE ALSO COURTS, LAW)

JUDGMENT
basis: w75 93-4; w72 471-2; w71 631-3
Christ's presence: w74 557-9, 626
criticizing religious beliefs: g74 11/22 27
day of Jehovah: w74 49-56; ts 187-8; w73 543
elders as judges: w75 92-4
God's past judgments: w75 664-6
Jehovah as judge: w74 495-9; g74 3/8 4
Jesus as judge: w74 277-9
mercy: w74 495-500, 504-5; w72 551-5
nonbelievers as individuals: w75 94
not judging brother: w74 437-8
not judging individuals: ts 182; g74 11/22 27
prejudice affects personal: w75 92-3; w71 323-4
religious leaders: ts 116, 181-2
resurrected persons: w74 277-80; ts 182-6
sheep and goats: w74 626-8

JUDGMENT DAY
basis for judgment: ts 182-5; ka 120-2, 128-31
discussion: ts 182-6; ka 117-21, 124-42, 136-9, 145-6
evildoers executed: ka 138
judges: ka 117-19, 124-5, 131, 136-7, 139-42
length: w74 277
mercy: w74 505; w72 551-2
misconceptions: w74 277
Sodom and Gomorrah: g75 10/22 13
those affected: sl 246; w74 278-80; ts 183

JUDICIAL COMMITTEE
appealing decisions: or 178-9
attitude toward sexual immorality: w75 755-6
committee matters: or 78
confession to: w73 351-2; w72 437-8
confidential matters: w71 223-4
congregation records: km 2/74 8
consulting elders: w73 542-3
disfellowshiping: w73 594, 703; or 170-9; w71 383-4
domestic problems: km 9/73 8
hearings: or 164-5
members: w72 604; or 78, 159
reporting wrongdoing: km 10/74 7; w72 465, 467; or 181
reproof:
no "terms": km 5/73 8
not restrict preaching: km 12/74 4
right view of: w73 703
service committee: or 78
signing letters on behalf of body of elders: km 8/75 6
unbaptized wrongdoers: km 10/75 8
use of Kingdom Hall: w74 276; km 11/73 8
(SEE ALSO OVERSEERS)

JUDICIAL DECISIONS
by elders: w75 92-3
discussion: w73 190

JUDO
Bible view: g75 12/8 28-9

JUJU
experiences:
black magic fails to harm Witnesses: g75 7/22 26; w74 716
fear of the dead: ts 70-2
juju celebrations: w75 761

JUPITER
planet: g75 8/22 13-14; g74 5/22 30; w72 291

JURY
attractive plaintiffs sway: g75 4/8 30
serving on: w73 190-1

JUSTICE
Israelite society: g74 7/22 27-8; g72 1/8 14-16
Jehovah: w75 116-17; kj 282-4
Jehovah's actions toward Adam and Eve: ts 33-4
man's failure: w75 163-4; g75 2/22 5-7; w74 708-10, 714; g74 8/8 8-9, 11; w72 763; g72 1/8 13-14
New Order: w75 164
symbolic representation: w72 102; kj 39-40
unbalanced justice: g71 3/22 29

JUSTIFICATION
after final earthly test: po 190-1

g, Awake!; **ka**, God's Kingdom of a Thousand Years; **kj**, "The Nations Shall Know that I Am Jehovah"; **km**, Kingdom Ministry; **or**, Organization; **pm**, Paradise Restored—By Theocracy!; **po**, God's "Eternal Purpose"; **sg**, Theocratic School Guidebook; **sl**, Man's Salvation out of World Distress!; **te**, Listening to the Great Teacher; **tp**, True Peace and Security; **ts**, Is This Life All There Is?; **w**, Watchtower; **yb**, Yearbook. **Complete list on page 6.**

congregation of God: w74 252; ka 110-11; w72 518-19, 608
other sheep: w74 96; w72 520

JUSTINUS (Justin Martyr)
idols: w74 48
infant baptism: g74 3/22 28
neutrality: w74 47
sabbath: g72 11/22 7

JUVENILE DELINQUENCY
adult responsibility: g74 8/22 4-6
contributing factors: w75 37; w74 262-3, 267, 270; g74 8/22 4-6; g74 9/22 31; g73 10/22 24; w72 457; g71 10/22 11
examples: g75 7/8 30; g75 11/22 5; g74 11/8 10; w73 552-3, 557-9; g73 6/22 31; g72 5/22 30; g72 7/8 31; g71 3/22 30; g71 9/8 29; g71 12/8 30
experience: g73 12/8 9-15
father not necessarily at fault: km 7/75 3
gangs: g74 2/8 5; g72 2/22 29-30
girls: g73 9/8 30
Japan: g75 3/8 29
narcotics addiction: g73 12/8 3-5, 7-14
schools: g75 5/22 29; g74 2/8 4-6; g74 8/22 3-6; g72 2/22 29-30; g72 4/22 30; g71 4/22 31
statistics: w75 439; g74 11/8 29; g73 10/22 24; g72 6/8 29-30; g71 12/8 30
vandalism: g74 8/22 3-6; g73 3/22 5-6; g71 4/22 31
(SEE ALSO MORAL BREAKDOWN, YOUTH)

KARATE
Bible view: g75 12/8 28-9
dangers: g75 4/8 30; g74 3/8 16
experience:
karate expert accepts truth: w74 654

KELLER, HELEN
g75 10/22 4

KENNEDY, JOHN F.
g73 5/22 3-4

KENYA
drought: g71 5/22 31
ivory demand: g75 11/8 30
Jehovah's witnesses: yb76 26-7, 105-7; yb75 7, 26-7; w74 207; yb74 11-12, 26-7; yb73 26-7; g73 9/22 30; yb72 36-7, 44; w71 85, 157-8
marriage: w73 151
population: yb73 26; yb72 36

KEY(S)
key of death: w73 239-40, 243
key of Hades: w73 239-40, 243
"Key 73": w73 742-4

KIDNAPPING
discussion: g75 5/22 6-9
skyjacked: g74 5/22 13-16
statistics: w74 244

KIDNEYS
description: g73 4/8 20
dialysis machines: g74 9/22 29
discussion of Bible usage: w75 479-80
disease: g74 7/8 30
stones: g75 1/22 25-6
transplants: w75 519; g72 9/22 30

KILLING
animal that kills a man: w75 639

KIND (Genesis)
discussion: g73 10/22 8-9, 11, 15-18, 21
variations within: g73 10/22 8-9, 16-17

KINDNESS
consideration for older persons: g75 5/22 26
discussion: w75 675-6; w74 120-2
examples: w75 127, 675-6; g75 2/22 22; g75 6/8 4; w74 120-1; yb74 99; g74 3/22 21; w72 221-2, 318-19; yb72 60, 117; te 36-8
lacking in world: g75 7/22 29; g74 7/22 30
proper response to unkindness: g75 6/8 3-4
rewards: w75 676
(SEE ALSO LOVE, LOVING-KINDNESS)

KING(S)
Jehovah: w74 346; po 119; w72 43-4; w71 743-7
Jesus Christ: w74 238, 346, 356-7; ts 127, 130, 153-5; w72 171, 180-1, 463; pm 230-1; w71 5, 238-42, 281-2, 635; kj 232-5, 356-7, 364-5; te 159-62
nation of Israel: po 100-2, 122-4, 127-9; w71 743-4
number of years: po 127
prophecy giving kingship to Judah: po 100-2
"of the north": g74 2/22 22
"of the south": g74 2/22 22
rule one hour (Re 17:12): g75 2/8 8-9
seven (Re 17:10): w74 606-7

KING, HAROLD
yb75 208-9

KING, WILLIAM MACKENZIE
g75 7/8 31

KINGDOM
accomplishments: w74 345-6
advocating:
Jehovah's witnesses: yb75 234-7
not seditious: yb73 162
appreciation for: w75 21-2
demonstrating: w71 131-2
blessings to earthly subjects: w75 261-2; fu 21-5; gc 23-8; g75 4/8 13-14; w74 291-4, 377-8; ts 133-4, 136-40, 142-3; g74 4/8 9-15; g74 6/22 10-11; g74 8/8 11; g74 9/8 23; g74 10/8 17, 21-2; w73 78-9; tp 7-8, 43-5, 101-10; g73 4/22 18-21; g73 10/8 25-9; g73 11/22 12; w72 496, 580-2; g72 5/22 17; g72 7/22 12-13; g72 10/8 18-19; g72 10/22 15-16; w71 5, 36-7, 100-1, 245-6; g71 4/22 25-7; g71 10/8 23-5
calling members: w71 568-70
Christendom a fake "kingdom of the heavens": w75 597-601, 604-5; sl 208
Christendom rejects: w74 614-15; hu 8-9; w73 615-16, 620; dy 12-13, 21; w72 625-7; dn 18-22
covenant with David: po 126-9, 136, 142
desirability of: w71 165-7
discussion: w75 361-3, 685-97; g75 4/8 11-14
earthly representatives: sl 361-4; ts 132
establishment: w75 621; sl 243; og 24-5; w72 180-1; pm 71-2
announced: w74 331-4; w71 68-9, 467-8, 560
physical facts in evidence: ts 160-3
time: sl 41-2, 103-4, 190; w74 236-7, 356-7, 398, 622, 630; po 174-7; ts 155, 159-60; hu 25; w73 645; ka 164-5, 210, 228; w72 180, 351-2; pm 331, 368-9; kj 232-5, 346, 353-4
why tribulation followed: ts 163
'from founding of world': w74 288
"fruits of the kingdom": w72 91
government: w75 239, 260-2, 622-3; og 25-9; g75 3/22 5-6; g75 4/8 11-13; w74 5, 106-8, 625, 629-30, 712-13; w73 389, 634; w72 580-3; pm 224-5; g72 10/22 16; w71 3-5, 165-7, 198, 281, 286, 568-71, 634-5; te 159; g71 10/8 22-4
earthly administration: w74 292-3; ts 132
handed over to Jehovah: w75 623; og 29; w74 604; ts 131; ka 148
heavenly: w74 690, 735-6; ts 160; g74 8/22 27-8; w73 616; w71 4-5
communication with earth: ts 132
importance: w75 623; yb75 151-2; og 28; w74 376
'inheriting the kingdom': w74 626; g74 8/22 28; w73 495; ka 272
Jehovah's universal: pm 224, 376-8
'kingdom drawn near': ts 128, 155
King Jesus Christ: w75 262; g75 4/8 12-14; w74 68-70, 106-8; ts 127, 130, 160-1; w73 61; w72 171, 180-1, 580-1, 627-8, 631; dn 22-24, 29; w71 5, 198, 238-42, 281-2, 635; kj 232-5, 354, 356-7, 364-5; te 159-62
language: ka 49-50
members: w75 687-9; g75 4/8 11-12; w74 106-8
misconceptions: w74 296; w73 689-90
nations shaken by preaching of: w75 361-2
"new heavens": w75 261; sl 322-3, 355-8
not in heart: w73 689-90
opposition to: sl 253
parables concerning: w75 589-605
pictured by—
copper mountain: pm 224-5
David's kingdom: w71 744
Jerusalem: ts 157, 159-60; w72 631; pm 128-30, 278; dn 29
male child (Re 12:5): po 177
split Mt. of Olives (Zec 14:4): pm 378-9
stone (Da 2:34): sl 312-18; pm 375-6; w71 620-4; nc 19-28
prayer for 'coming' of: w75 261
princes: w72 581-2
proclamation:
first century: w74 685
purpose: w75 81-6; ts 131-3; w71 99-101, 131; g71 4/22 23-5
reality of: w71 166-7
refuge: w75 604-8, 685-97
rejection: w71 99-100, 132
repentance with regard to: w75 751
rule over congregation: w73 458-9
seeking first: w75 565; yb75 8, 62; fu 26-7; w74 250, 569, 653-5; g74 8/8 5-7; w73 436-8; w72 135-6; g72 10/22 16; kj 358-9
seizing: w72 90-2

"stronghold" (Zec 9:12): w73 30-1; w72 630-1; dn 27-9
subjects: w71 571
supporting: w73 721
"this good news": w75 681; w73 681-3, 687-8, 690, 693; ka 297-8, 307-8; w72 366; pm 100-1; or 3-7; w71 78-82, 302, 308, 466, 753-4
(SEE ALSO 1914, SIGN, THOUSAND-YEAR REIGN)

KINGDOM FARM
sale of portion: yb75 244
threat to destroy: yb75 182-3
(SEE ALSO WATCHTOWER FARMS)

KINGDOM HALLS
Africa: yb72 243
attendants: or 105; km 3/72 4
cleanliness: km 1/75 3
construction: yb76 184, 212, 253-4; km 11/75 1; km 6/74 3; g72 8/22 19-23
  building committee: or 104
  disagreements: w74 437-8
  rate of: g73 9/22 9
contrast to churches: w74 491, 630; w71 564
description: g72 8/22 19
discussion: yb75 166-7; or 103-5
experiences: w71 167
  building: yb74 8; g72 8/22 20-3
  child urges father to attend: g74 7/22 23
  first visit: w74 510; g74 2/8 11; g74 6/8 4; w73 627-9; g72 1/22 25; w71 534, 552; g71 9/8 17-18
  reporter comments on: g74 9/8 7
  wedding talk convinces woman of truth: w75 245
financial support: km 6/74 4; w73 298; km 10/73 8; or 149; w71 506-7
first use of term: yb75 167; yb73 15
invitation to attend: w71 402-3
library: or 81; km 5/72 4
maintenance: or 104; km 7/71 4
meeting times: km 11/75 1; km 8/74 8
no smoking: km 11/73 7
remodeling: km 6/74 3
sign: yb72 145, 147
Singapore closes: w72 344-5
telephone number listing: or 105
use for funerals: km 11/73 8
use for weddings: km 6/75 4; w74 275-6; km 11/73 8
when attendance exceeds seating capacity: km 7/75 4
  (SEE ALSO CONGREGATION, MEETINGS)

KINGDOM MINISTRY
beginning: yb75 86
use in service meeting: w72 759; or 97

KINGDOM MINISTRY SCHOOL
attendance statistics: km 5/75 4
beginning: yb75 202; km 5/75 4
efforts to attend: yb73 75, 136-7
purpose: w73 399-400

Countries
Argentina: yb72 115-16
Brazil: yb73 75-6
Germany: yb76 45; yb74 234
Great Britain: yb73 136-8
Guatemala: yb73 204, 207
Italy: w73 665
Japan: yb73 251
Nicaragua: yb72 190-1
South Africa: yb76 221
Taiwan: yb72 229-30, 232
United States: km 12/74 1; km 1/71 1
Zaïre Republic: g72 1/8 21, 24
Zambia: yb72 247

KINGDOM NEWS (Tract)
announcement of work (1973): yb75 252
experiences with: w75 392; yb75 6-7, 12, 17, 22, 253; km 3/75 4; km 11/74 1
No. 1: yb75 97-8
No. 2: yb75 98
No. 3: yb75 98
No. 16: yb75 252; km 9/73 1, 7-8; km 12/73 1
No. 17: yb75 252; km 1/74 1; km 2/74 1; km 3/74 1; km 12/73 1
No. 18: yb75 252; km 4/74 1, 3; km 8/74 1
No. 19: km 10/74 7
No. 20: km 5/75 1
No. 21: km 10/75 1

KINGDOM OF GOD
(SEE KINGDOM)

KINGDOM SCHOOLS
United States: yb75 170-1; w72 760

KINGDOM, THE HOPE OF THE WORLD, THE (Booklet)
yb75 151-2

KING OF THE NORTH
god of fortresses: w72 741
identified:
  Communist: g71 7/8 9

KISSING
idols: w74 536
single persons: w74 12-13

KITE
discussion: g73 3/22 24-6
hang gliding: g75 5/22 30-1

KNORR, NATHAN H.
background: yb75 195-6
conventions: yb75 211, 213-18; km 8/74 1; w73 456
dedication of farm building: w73 314-15
elected president: yb76 148; yb75 195-6; yb72 120
Gilead graduations: w75 285, 672; g75 11/8 26; w74 286, 670; g74 5/8 25; w73 284, 647; yb73 258; g73 5/8 25-6; g73 11/8 26; w72 205, 286; g72 5/8 26; w71 287, 669-70; g71 5/8 25-6; g71 11/8 25
lectures: yb75 201, 203, 211, 213-18, 246
Mexico branch office: g74 7/22 16
service tours: yb76 14, 16, 43, 45, 65, 166-8, 170-1, 173-4, 185-6, 188-90, 192-3, 233-4, 236, 248, 251; w75 169; yb75 211-12; g75 2/8 29; km 3/75 1; km 4/75 1; km 8/75 1; km 11/75 1, 2; yb74 46-7, 56-7, 61, 216, 244-6; km 1/74 1; km 10/74 1; w73 54; yb73 7, 13, 15, 17, 19-22, 64-5, 69-70, 76-7, 84, 86, 130-1, 135-6, 168-70, 174-5, 177-8, 183-7, 195-7, 199-200, 202-3, 232-3, 239-40, 250; km 1/73 1; km 5/73 1; km 7/73 1; yb72 74-9, 82-3, 88-93, 114-17, 121-2, 138-9, 145, 155, 165, 174, 177, 192-3, 202, 208, 224, 226-7, 232, 240, 242, 246; km 2/72 1; km 3/72 1; km 4/72 1; km 7/72 1; km 12/72 1; w71 20; g71 4/8 29; km 4/71 1
talk to missionaries: yb72 119-20

KNOWLEDGE
accurate: w74 178-82
compared to food: sg 20
"complete" (1 Co 13:10): w75 95-6
how acquired: w74 114-15, 179-82; w71 137; sg 19-29, 33-8
"increases pain" (Ec 1:18): g72 9/8 27-8
"knowing" Jehovah: w75 113-19; sl 191-7, 204; w74 433-8, 566
"knowing" Jesus Christ: w75 117-18
loss because of death: ts 25
miraculous gift: w71 502-3
need: w74 17
New Order: ts 145-8, 150
potential for increasing: ts 145-8, 150
science's: w75 101-2
value: w74 177-8; g74 9/22 11; w73 156; w71 287
(SEE ALSO EDUCATION, STUDY)

KODIAK ISLAND
bear: g72 1/8 18-20

KORAN (Quran)
reading championships: g75 4/22 30
teachings: g75 4/22 30; g73 8/22 28-9

KOREA
blood transfusions: g75 3/22 29; g72 3/8 30
Cheju Island: g74 11/22 24-6
description: g73 5/22 16-18; g72 11/8 15
etiquette course for travelers: g75 7/8 30-1
hair: g73 7/22 31
Jehovah's witnesses: yb76 26-7; w75 264-6; yb75 14, 26-7; yb74 18-19, 26-7; g74 11/22 26; yb73 26-7; g73 5/22 18; w72 382; yb72 36-7; km 12/72 6; w71 14-15, 188-90; g71 5/8 26; g71 8/8 13-15
Korean war: w71 188-9
language: g74 11/22 25
population: yb73 26; yb72 36
religion: g73 5/22 18
way of life: g73 5/22 16-18
women divers: g74 11/22 24-5

KU KLUX KLAN
Catholic membership: w75 631

KUWAIT
income per person: g75 7/22 31
Jehovah's witnesses: yb76 26-7; yb75 26-7; yb74 26-7; yb73 26-7; yb72 36-7
population: yb73 26; yb72 36

KYRIOS
bi8 1352

LABOR PAINS
childbirth: g72 11/22 13, 16

LABOR UNIONS
corruption: g74 6/8 13-14
oaths: g75 7/22 28
strikes: g74 8/22 30; g71 2/8 21-3; g71 9/22 25-6
violence: g74 6/8 14-15

LACQUER WARE
discussion: g71 7/22 23

LAETRILE
g74 9/8 22

LAITY
clergy-laity distinctions: ka 375-8; w71 330-1
preaching: g74 12/8 14-15

LAKE OF FIRE
discussion: w74 381-4; ts 117-19; ka 156-8
symbolic: w74 381-2, 652; ts 118-19; ka 285-6
(SEE ALSO GEHENNA, SECOND DEATH)

LAMB
Lamb of God: pm 151-2; kj 389
use of term in Revelation: ts 130

LAMENESS
figurative: sl 150

LAMPS
Bible times: w74 506
symbolic: w74 478-9

LAMPSTAND(S)
golden (Zec 4:2): pm 193-4, 203-6
symbolic: pm 205

LAND
amount cultivated: g74 6/22 10
amount per person: g75 4/22 30; ts 134-5; g71 5/22 29
lost: g71 10/8 11
most expensive: g74 4/22 31
population concentration: g74 6/22 10
sinking: g75 10/22 30
(SEE ALSO EARTH, SOIL)

LANGUAGE(S)
Adam: g71 2/22 8
African: g75 5/22 17-19
angels: w73 524; g71 2/22 8
Arabic: g74 12/8 30
Bible translations: w74 394; w72 388; g72 12/8 29
brain: g75 8/22 30
child's ability to learn: g74 10/22 30
Chinese: g75 5/22 9-13
complexity of ancient: w73 526
confusion: w75 666; w74 41-2; w73 525-6; w72 428; sg 5; g71 2/22 8-9
discussion: w73 524-30; g73 8/22 21-3; g72 12/22 12-14
English: g75 1/8 29; g73 2/8 30; g73 4/22 31; g73 8/22 21-2; g72 12/22 12-14; g71 7/22 10; g71 12/22 20-3
families of: w73 525-6; g72 12/22 12-14; g71 2/22 9-10
French:
patois: g72 9/8 21
German: g72 12/22 13-14
God's new order: w74 43-4; w73 530; ka 49-50; g71 2/22 10
grammar: sg 57-8; g71 2/22 9
Greek: g72 5/22 27-8
Guatemala: w74 394
Hebrew: w73 525; g71 9/8 20
Japanese: yb73 209-10
Lao: g72 12/22 13-14
learning new one: g74 8/22 6-7; g72 7/22 13-14
  experiences while learning: g74 8/8 12
Lingala: g73 1/22 25-6
number in world: w75 464; w73 524; g71 2/22 8
number speaking popular ones: g75 11/8 29; w73 530
144,000 in heaven: w74 42; ka 49
origin: w75 464; g71 2/22 7-9
"primitive" peoples': w75 464
pure language: w74 42-4; w73 528-30; w72 248-9
Quechua: g75 9/22 31
Spanish: g74 8/8 12; g72 7/22 13-14
students' ability to use: g75 12/22 30
Swahili: g75 2/22 26
Thai: g72 12/22 14
useful languages for scientists: g75 8/8 30-1; g73 4/22 31
word exchange: g73 8/22 21-3

LAOS
Jehovah's witnesses: yb75 30-1; yb74 30-1; yb73 30-1; yb72 40-1; g71 2/22 24-6
population: yb73 30; yb72 40
religion: g71 2/22 23-6

LAPLAND
people of: g72 6/22 20-3
superstition: g75 2/8 26

LASER
diamond: g72 7/8 29
lighthouse: g72 2/22 31
watchmaking: g72 8/22 30

LAST DAYS
awakeness: w73 56-8; g71 11/22 4
beginning: g75 10/8 13; w74 165; po 174-7; g73 1/22 8; w72 582
discussion: w74 3-4; tp 72-89; w72 3-4
economics: g74 1/22 8
endurance: w73 40-1
of Jewish system (70 C.E.): w74 680-3, 693-4; po 172-3
ridiculers: sl 285-90, 293, 298-300
sign of last days:
  as days of Noah: w75 10-11; km 7/75 2
  as lightning: w74 750
  chart on features: tp 82-3
  composite: w75 633; g73 10/8 20-2
  earthquakes: w75 634-5; w74 72-4, 243; g74 5/8 17-19; tp 83; g73 3/8 12-16; g73 10/8 21; w72 339; g72 10/8 16; w71 69, 406; te 177
  false prophets: ka 320-2
  food shortages: w75 634; g75 2/22 8; w74 195-7; w74 243; ts 162; tp 82; g73 6/22 3-6, 10-12; g73 10/8 5-7, 21; w72 339, 615; g72 10/8 15; w71 69, 406; te 177
  generation: w75 632, 635; gc 22; g75 7/8 29; w72 582-3; g72 10/8 15
  lack of natural affection: w75 327
  lawlessness increasing: w75 635; g75 11/22 15; w74 99-101, 244; tp 17-19, 83; g73 10/8 10-11, 21; g72 10/8 16; w71 406; te 178
  lovers of pleasures: g75 3/22 29; g72 1/22 26
  men faint out of fear: w75 635; g75 4/8 15; w74 656; w71 69
  persecution of Christians: w72 340
  pestilences and diseases: w75 634; w74 131-3; ts 162; tp 82; g73 10/8 20-1; g72 10/8 16; w71 69, 406; g71 3/8 4
  preaching of this good news of kingdom: w75 635; w74 4; ka 307-8; tp 83, 87; g72 10/8 16; w71 69, 80-2, 466
  reason "sign" needed: w74 398-400
  separation of "sheep" and "goats": w74 625-8; g73 7/22 5-6
  signs from heaven: km 7/75 2; w74 40
  signs in sun, moon and stars: w75 276; ka 322-6
  wars: w75 274, 633-4, 684; g75 10/8 13; ts 162; tp 80-2; g73 10/8 16-17, 20; w72 339; g72 10/8 15; w71 69, 406; te 177

Quotations
1914 punctuation-mark of twentieth century: g75 10/8 13
1914, turning point: g73 10/8 17
since 1914, security and quiet have disappeared: w71 69
since 1914, world has character of international anarchy: w71 69
this decade is like no other the world has known: g75 3/8 30
today's upsets compare with time of change during World War I: g75 4/22 29
universal sense of apprehension: g75 4/8 15
(SEE ALSO CHRIST'S PRESENCE, 1914)

LATERAN TREATY
w75 364

LATIN AMERICA
arms race: g74 11/8 6
Catholic church: g74 4/22 20; g74 11/22 4; g71 7/22 7-8
religion: g74 9/8 29
terrorism: g71 6/8 18

LAUGHTER
discussion: g75 7/22 13-15; g72 1/8 3-4
mistakes of others: g73 1/22 3-4

LAUSANNE CONGRESS
g74 12/8 12-15

LAW(S)
benefits of God's: gc 12
blood: g74 5/22 19-22
calling at homes: g71 12/22 9-13
capital punishment: g72 1/8 6, 15-16; g72 4/22 31
cases involving Society: g74 9/8 15-16
Christian view of courts: w73 703-4
conscience: w75 114; w73 30, 36-7; w72 556-9
creation: w72 35, 264-5; g72 10/22 4-8; w71 554-5; g71 8/8 4-5
defiance of law: w72 261-4; g71 2/22 16-18
discrimination against women: g72 5/22 6

field service: km 8/71 3-4
gun-control: g72 7/22 29
Hammurabi: w75 115
incest: w75 73-6
inherited rule of conduct: w72 588
Israel (ancient): w74 204-5; w72 127; g72 1/8 6, 14-16
Jehovah's superior: w75 115-17; w74 40; w72 36
judicial decisions: w73 190
jury duty: w73 190-1
law and order: g72 10/22 5
Law covenant: w72 127, 287-8; w71 416
crime and compensation: g72 1/8 14-16
uncleanness: pm 108-10
meaning of term: w73 189; w72 563
obedience: te 136-8
patients' rights: g74 5/22 19-20
peace through: w74 40
probability: g75 3/22 20-3
sex education: g72 1/22 3-9
United States: g74 9/8 30
wills: g71 12/22 14-16
Witness contributions: yb75 172, 178-80, 208; g74 9/22 30; g74 12/8 22-5; g71 9/8 15
Witness lawyers: yb75 178

Quotation

human laws derive force from God's law: g72 10/22 10
(SEE ALSO COURTS, SUPREME COURT DECISIONS)

LAW COVENANT
(SEE COVENANTS)

LAWLESSNESS
(SEE CRIME, JUVENILE DELINQUENCY, MORAL BREAKDOWN, SIN, VIOLENCE)

LAZARUS (Jesus' Friend)
resurrection: w71 708-9; te 67-70
clergy disbelief: g75 3/22 30-1

LAZARUS (of Parable)
discussion: ts 98-110
prophetic significance: ts 103

LAZINESS
Bible view: w75 588; w74 589, 591; g74 2/8 9; w72 205-6, 208-9, 485; g72 7/8 23

LEAD
metallic element: w71 292
poisoning: g74 12/22 29

LEAGUE OF NATIONS
Anglo-American support: w72 189; kj 60, 351
clergy support: w74 135; w72 189, 626; dn 21; w71 560; kj 60-1
"disgusting thing": ka 314
eighth world power: sl 237; ka 310, 314-15; kj 351
establishment: kj 65
failure: sl 237; w73 617; dy 16; g72 10/8 6; kj 73
National Council of Churches: w72 189, 198; pm 138; kj 60-1
symbolic representation: sl 244; yb75 203; w71 718; kj 256
Witnesses' attitude: sl 146; w74 508; ka 197-8; w72 198; w71 469, 560, 718

Quotations

Christian means of attaining peace: w75 260
political expression of God's kingdom: w75 274; kj 60
world sick of war . . . solid framework for League: w74 357-8
(SEE ALSO BEASTS, UNITED NATIONS)

LEARNING
ability of children: w72 112
benefits: w72 156-7
God's truth: w73 55
human brain: g74 12/8 17-21
Source: w72 105

LEATHER
shoes: g71 8/22 17-19

LEAVEN
Jesus' parable of, hidden in dough: w75 589-92, 597, 601-4; sl 209-15
Pentecost: w75 601-3
symbolic: w75 591-2, 597, 601-4; sl 209-14

LEBANON
cedar trees: w75 541
description: g71 11/8 10-11
food: g73 2/22 25-6
Jehovah's witnesses: yb76 26-7; yb75 26-7; g75 5/8 4; yb74 26-7; yb73 26-7; yb72 36-7; w71 542
population: yb73 26; yb72 36

LEEWARDS-ANTIGUA
Jehovah's witnesses: yb76 28-9; yb75 26-7; yb74 26-7; yb73 26-7; yb72 36-7
population: yb73 26; yb72 36

LEGAL CASE
between Christians: w73 703-4

LEISURE TIME
average person's use of: g73 10/8 31
discussion: w71 311-15

LENSES
discussion: g71 7/22 16-19

LENT
Catholic church: g73 3/8 5-6
fasting: g73 3/8 5-6

LEPROSY
experience: yb73 68
lepers healed by Jesus: te 43-5
Naaman: w74 402-3; te 107-9

LESBIANISM
g75 3/8 31; w74 390-1
(SEE ALSO HOMOSEXUALITY)

LESOTHO
description: g71 7/22 26
Jehovah's witnesses: yb76 30-1, 159-60, 194, 209-13; yb75 30-1; yb74 30-1; yb73 30-1; yb72 40-1
population: yb73 30; yb72 40

"LET GOD BE TRUE" (Book)
experience with: yb74 51
release: yb75 211, 239

LETTERS
business: g75 2/8 30; sg 85-7
discussion: sg 84-90
experience:
witnessing by: g75 1/22 30
need of writing: sg 85, 88
protest Witness persecution: yb75 210; yb74 136-8, 157-60; g73 3/8 26; yb72 110-11
Society: km 2/74 8
to Society on personal problems: km 10/74 8
use in witnessing: sg 87-8

LEVI (Son of Jacob)
disqualified as to 'line of seed': po 96-7

LEVIRATE MARRIAGE
(SEE BROTHER-IN-LAW MARRIAGE)

LEVITES
age for beginning service: g72 3/8 27
firstborn exchanged for: g72 3/8 28

LIBERATION
women's: g72 5/22 3-17

LIBERIA
Jehovah's witnesses: yb76 28-9; yb75 8, 28-9; w74 39; yb74 8, 28-9; w73 172-4; yb73 28-9; yb72 38-9; g72 3/8 10-11; w71 123-4
population: yb73 28; yb72 38
spiritism: g72 3/8 8-11

LIBRARIES
books reduced to cards: g71 1/22 31
Kingdom Halls: or 81; km 5/72 4
Nineveh: w72 314-16

LIBYA
Jehovah's witnesses: yb76 26-7; yb72 36-7
population: yb72 36

LIE(S)
Bible view: w74 58, 246-7, 314; w73 597-8; tp 114-16; w71 309-10; te 71-4
detector tests: g72 12/8 30
examples: g75 7/22 30; w73 597-8; w71 524-5; te 71-4
exposing: w74 35-7
first: ts 80; w72 178, 426-7
liar: w71 436
living a lie: w74 247
marriage: w71 539
public officials: w71 306
(SEE ALSO DISHONESTY, MORAL BREAKDOWN)

LIECHTENSTEIN
Jehovah's witnesses: yb76 30-1; yb75 30-1; yb74 30-1; yb73 30-1; yb72 40-1
population: yb73 30; yb72 40

LIFE
appreciating its value: ts 15-16; g74 2/8 16; g74 7/22 28; w73 325-30, 488-90; tp 155-65; yb73 3; g71 1/8 25-6
belongs to Christians: w71 352
Chief Agent of: w73 104; w71 30
"come to life" (Re 20:5): w74 7, 95-6, 608
differing views on: ts 7-16
discussion: w75 328-31; ml 3-31; w73 325-30
disregard for human life: g74 10/8 23
early Christians' view: w71 344
earth's zone of: g71 4/22 5

evolution's effect on: ml 12-14
goals: g74 8/22 6-8
hardiness of: g71 8/22 11-12
interdependency: g73 7/8 7
life-span: g75 1/8 27-8; ts 17-26, 143-4; g74 3/22 26; g74 12/8 9; ka 7; g73 11/22 19; w71 471
effects of short: ts 6, 9, 13-15
Hawaii: g75 10/22 30
not 'chemical accident': w74 720
outer space: g73 5/22 3, 6, 11-15
proper pace: g73 7/8 3-4
purpose: ml 4, 14, 18, 30; g75 5/8 3-5; w74 657, 659-60, 662, 669; w73 326-30
search for: g74 11/22 7-12
quality of: g74 9/8 3-6
improving: g74 9/8 5-7
requirements: w73 325-30; w72 454-5; w71 64, 132, 477-8, 633-9; te 187-90
sacred: w75 639; g75 11/22 26-8; g74 5/8 27; w73 300-2; w71 344
satisfaction in: w75 54-61; g75 5/8 3-5; g74 8/8 3-7
scientists' claims: g71 9/8 5-7
scientists unable to create: g75 12/8 21; g72 10/22 7-8
Source: w73 36, 163-4, 325, 488; tp 155-6; w71 44
uncertainty of present: ts 5-6, 8, 13-14
using, to serve Jehovah: w74 369-74, 378-80; g74 8/8 4-5; g71 9/22 3-6
waters of: ts 165
when begins: w74 509; g74 2/8 13; tp 156; g73 12/22 27
worldly views on origin: ml 9-10; g74 9/22 20; g73 10/22 9-12

LIFE EVERLASTING
Adam and Eve: po 43-4, 54-5; ts 17
basis: w73 380-3; w72 496; g71 2/22 15; g71 7/8 4
discussion: w74 376-8
evidence man designed to have: ts 17-26
first opportunity: ka 129
great crowd: ts 164-6
love: ts 149-50
not boring: ts 144-50
physical potential: w74 375; ts 17-18; g74 3/22 26; tp 104-6; g73 11/22 19; g72 6/8 6-7; g71 2/22 12-15
potential for learning: ts 145-8, 150
requirements: w74 602-3; w73 63-4, 75-82; w71 64, 132, 477-8, 633-9; te 187-90
test proving worthiness: w74 346-7
why desirable: w73 329

LIFE EVERLASTING—IN FREEDOM OF THE SONS OF GOD (Book)
yb75 256

LIFE FORCE
ts 49-53; g72 8/8 27-8
(SEE ALSO SPIRIT)

LIFE-SPAN
discussion: g75 1/8 27-8; ts 17-26, 143-4
human potential: w74 375; ts 17-18; g74 3/22 26; tp 104-6; g72 6/8 6-7; g71 2/22 12-15
modern-day man: g75 3/8 7-8; g73 1/22 9-10; g72 9/22 30; w71 471; g71 4/22 31
effects of short: ts 6, 9, 13-15
poor nations: g74 12/8 9
palmistry predictions of: g75 2/8 29
smoking: g71 2/8 31
trees: w73 82-5
women live longer: g74 10/22 31

LIFE STORIES OF JEHOVAH'S WITNESSES
Banda, Florentino: w73 507-11
Bangle, Aleck: w71 519-23
Blackwell, Victor V.: w73 117-22
Brickell, R. Bennett: w72 533-6
Callaway, Neal L.: w71 473-6
Cannon, Ruth: w71 277-80
Carvajalino, Finda, Felisa and Ines: w72 281-6
Catanzaro, Angelo: w75 205-7
Charuk, John: w73 170-4
Cotterill, Richard S.: w71 665-8
Cuffie, Rose: w72 476-9
Dickmann, Heinrich: w72 395-9
Fredianelli, George: w73 661-6
Glass, Kathryn: w71 341-4
Goodman, Claude S.: w73 760-5
Hardin, Emily: w71 729-32
Hoffmann, Oskar: w75 533-5
Klukowski, Jennie: w72 57-60
Kwazizirah, Gresham: w72 661-5
Lounsbury, Grace: w74 283-5
MacDonald, Janet: w72 146-51
Mikkelsen, Herman: w72 758-62
Nisbet, George: w74 473-6
Ott, Carlos: w71 215-18
Pallari, Väinö: w75 333-5
Prior, Beulah: w73 443-7
Schrantz, Emile: w73 570-4
Seliger, Ernst: w75 423-6
Steele, Don and Earlene: w71 186-90
Thompson, Adrian: w73 52-5
Woodworth, Harold P.: w71 377-80
Wrobel, Paul: w73 376-9

LIGHT
benefits to man: g72 2/8 10-11; g72 10/8 25-8
colors: g75 1/22 14-16; g71 6/22 9-12
effect on creatures: g71 7/8 15
effect on plants: g72 2/8 10; g71 7/8 13-15
goggles intensify: g72 8/8 29
insects: g71 11/8 20
jaundice cure: g71 12/22 30
lasers: g72 2/22 31; g72 7/8 29; g72 8/22 30
power: g72 10/8 25-8
sensed without eyes: g73 7/22 31
source: g71 6/22 9
speed: g72 2/8 9
spiritual: w74 560-1, 572
walking in: w74 561-4, 569-71
sun: g72 10/8 25-8; g71 3/8 21-2
symbolic: w74 477-8, 756; pm 381-2; w71 436
telescopes: g71 8/8 30
theories about: g75 1/22 15-16
twilight: g71 3/8 21-2

LIGHT (Books)
release: w71 181-2
use in Japan: w73 54; yb73 225

LIGHTHOUSE
laser: g72 2/22 31

LIGHTNING
volcanic eruptions: g75 11/22 25

LIMITATIONS
coping with human: g75 6/22 3-5

LION
characteristics: g75 10/22 25; po 100-1; g73 10/22 26
decline in numbers: g75 12/22 30
food before the Flood: w75 606
Judah compared to: po 100-1
symbolic: w74 762-3; kj 39-40
zoo guard: g72 9/22 30-1

LIP(S)
movement while reading: g75 2/22 30

LISTENING
children: g74 11/22 21-2
improving habits: g74 11/22 21-3; sg 25-7
meaning of term: g74 11/22 21
meetings: sg 24-9
overseer: g74 11/22 22-3
taking notes: g74 10/8 30-1
to disturbed persons: g74 11/22 23

LISTENING TO THE GREAT TEACHER (Book)
appreciation for: w73 563-4
experiences with: g74 12/22 22; km 8/73 4; km 8/72 3
printing: w75 519
release: yb72 42; w71 599
use in field service: km 8/72 3-4

LITERATURE
best sellers: g71 4/8 19-20
congregation funds: or 151-3
contributions: w74 3
effect of World War I: g75 1/8 29
experiences:
hidden from opposers: yb75 100-1
medical: g72 1/8 26
ministerial servant: or 151-2
obscene: g74 5/8 29
older Watch Tower publications: km 11/74 3
ordering: or 151
proper care of: km 11/74 3
reporting placements: or 126
selectivity in reading: w74 112, 153; w73 590, 595; g73 1/8 5
trading: yb72 112
United States:
foreign-language literature shipments: km 7/75 1
use in witnessing: g74 9/22 30; or 116-19
beginning: yb75 39, 45-6, 64, 124-8, 134
worldly magazines: g71 11/8 29
(SEE ALSO READING, WATCH TOWER PUBLICATIONS)

LITHOGRAPHY
printing: g72 8/22 24-6

LITTERING
causes: g74 11/22 31
cost: g71 6/8 20
moon: g73 2/8 31
problem: g71 4/22 21

LITTLE FLOCK
(SEE CONGREGATION OF GOD)

LIVER
human body: g73 4/8 21; g72 1/8 3-4; g72 10/22 8; g71 6/8 10-11

LIVING CREATURES
cherubs: w72 102; kj 38, 45-6

LIZARDS
gecko: g72 11/22 11
LOANS
Bible view: w71 526-7, 766-7
LOCKS
protection of home: g75 11/22 14; w74 515
LOCUSTS
eaten as food: w75 464
invasion: g71 6/8 29
LODESTONE
g75 6/8 24
LOG CABIN
g75 11/8 31
LOGGING
discussion: g71 12/22 17-19
LONDON, ENGLAND, CONVENTION (1926)
resolution: yb73 111
LONDON MANIFESTO
(SEE MANIFESTO)
LONELINESS
campaign to combat: g71 12/22 10
causes: g74 6/8 3-4
remedy: w73 156-7; w71 262-3
LONG-SUFFERING
in preaching: w74 444, 446
Jehovah: w75 750-1
ways to show: w74 154-5, 315
"LOOK! I AM MAKING ALL THINGS NEW" (Booklet)
experiences with: w75 181
LOOSE CONDUCT
discussion: w73 574-6
Greek word: w73 574-6
LOOTING
archaeological sites: g72 1/22 30
attitude: g73 9/22 31
disaster victims: g74 6/8 10; g74 7/22 30; g73 3/8 15
LORD
Adon: bi8 1353-4
Adonay: bi8 1352
Kyrios: bi8 1352
(SEE ALSO JEHOVAH, JESUS CHRIST)
LORD'S DAY
discussion: w74 356-7
LORD'S EVENING MEAL
(SEE MEMORIAL)
LORD'S PRAYER
clergy view: w73 689
discussion: te 49-50
kingdom come: w73 689-90
personal application: g74 6/8 7; w73 436-7
LOS ANGELES, CALIF., CONVENTION (1923)
ka 264-5
LOT
kindness: w75 676
sons by daughters: w72 319-20
LOTTERIES
Bible view: g75 7/8 27-8
churches: g75 2/8 30; g73 12/22 30
free tickets for prizes in "drawings": g75 7/8 28
number of countries operating: w74 579
United States: g75 2/8 30; w74 579-80
LOVE
baby's need of: g74 6/8 22
believes, hopes and bears all things: w74 441-2; w72 132
benefit to individuals: g74 6/8 4; w73 291-2; g72 2/8 3-4
"builds up": w73 291-2
children's need of: w72 457; g72 1/8 30; g72 5/22 10-11; g72 7/22 29; g72 9/8 30; g72 10/22 30
child training:
retarded children: g75 6/22 23
Christian requirement: g75 1/22 23-4; w73 371-2
command: w73 441
cooling off: sl 13; w74 682; w73 691
covers sins: w75 342-8; w72 739
cultivating: w75 527-8; w73 371-2; w71 516
discussion: w75 336-48, 520-32; g75 1/22 21-4; w74 438-42; w73 291-2; tp 166-77; w72 131-2, 739-40
endures all things: w74 442
examples:
Bible accounts: w75 337
modern-day: yb75 209-10; g75 1/22 23; w74 443, 676; yb74 99, 105, 207; g74 3/22 21; g74 5/22 8; g74 7/8 26
family: g73 1/22 3-4; w72 131-2
fear thrown outside: w73 210-11
for Christian brothers: w75 341-2; g74 12/22 23, 25-6
for enemies: g73 2/22 15
forgiveness: g75 1/22 24
for Jehovah: g75 1/22 23; g75 7/22 4; w73 252-4; w72 304, 739
for neighbor: g75 7/22 3-4; w74 120-5, 409, 676; g74 7/8 4; g74 10/8 24; tp 171-5; w72 69, 726-9; or 111-12; te 35-8
for people of world: g75 1/22 24; g74 12/22 24-6; tp 121-4, 131, 173-5
for relatives: w71 74-5
fruit of the spirit: w73 691
Greek words: w75 338; g75 1/22 22; w72 131; g72 2/8 3-4
health: g74 5/22 28
husband and wife: w74 439; g74 4/22 6-7, 10-12; w72 740
identifies true religion: or 183; w71 463-4
in marriage: g74 5/22 4-5
in the congregation: w75 509-10, 526-32; w74 569-71; km 3/74 3; w73 371-2; tp 168; w72 17-19; or 183-4; yb72 23-6; w71 75; te 82
Jehovah: w75 520-6; g75 1/22 22; w74 146-7, 153-5, 190-1, 370-1; w73 67-8, 227-8, 252-3; tp 166-7; w72 304; g72 2/8 4; w71 75, 357-8, 360, 437-8
Jesus Christ: g75 1/22 23; w74 371-2
lack in world: tp 169-71
long-suffering and kind: w74 439; km 3/74 3; w72 131-2
medicinal value: g74 5/22 28
mental health: g75 4/22 16, 18
"new commandment": w75 520-1; tp 168; w71 191
New Order: ts 149-50
not become provoked: w74 440
not behave indecently: w74 440
not brag, not puffed up: w74 439-40
not jealous: w74 439; km 3/74 3; w72 132
not keep account of injury: w74 441; w72 132, 739
not look for own interests: w74 440; w72 132, 287
'perfect love': w74 151
potential growth of: ts 149-50
rejoices with truth: w74 441
romantic love: g75 1/22 21-2
symbolic representation: w72 102; kj 39-40
taught by God to love: w75 339
unifying force: w71 305
widening out: w74 120-5
"LOVE FEASTS"
yb75 58
LOVING-KINDNESS
discussion: w73 584
trait of Jehovah: w71 631-3
LOWLY(INESS)
God cherishes: w73 105-16
lowliest one of mankind: ts 152-5
mental attitude: w73 114-16
of mind: w74 401, 403, 407-9
examples: w74 401-3, 405-6, 408, 410-12
meaning of term: w74 408
LOYALTY
definition: w73 584-5
discussion: km 6/75 3-4; w73 584-96
examples:
Bible accounts: fu 18; w74 535-7; w73 588-9
modern-day Witnesses: yb74 52, 55-6, 59-60, 163-4, 166-9, 172-4, 180-90, 231
Jehovah: w73 585; w71 515-16
manifesting: w71 516
oaths: w73 62-3
to Christ: w73 104
to friends: w73 421
to Jehovah: fu 16-17; w74 172, 219, 345, 348, 530; w73 589-93, 596; w72 739; pm 350-5; w71 116-18
to Jehovah's organization: w74 153, 413
LOYALTY (Booklet)
yb75 168-9
LSD
g74 5/8 5, 7-8; g74 11/22 7-8, 10; g73 12/8 6, 11-13; g72 1/22 29; g72 2/22 30; w71 247; g71 4/8 18
(SEE ALSO DRUGS)
LUBRICANTS
"jojoba" shrub: g75 7/22 30
sperm whale oil: g75 7/22 30
LUCIFER
identified: w73 209
LUCK
"beginner's luck": w74 582, 588

god of Good Luck: w74 588; w72 594

LUKE (Book)
authenticity: g71 12/22 6-8

LUKE (Physician)
Bible writer: g71 3/8 25; g71 4/8 27-8

LUNGS
cancer: g74 9/8 17-18, 20, 23
effect of smoking: w75 12; g75 12/22 30; g73 1/22 19; g72 7/22 30; g72 9/8 31
function: g73 4/8 20; g71 6/8 8; g71 9/22 16-19
hair spray effects: g72 10/22 30
yawning: g71 3/8 26

LUTHER, MARTIN
beliefs: g72 3/8 17-19
excommunication: g72 3/8 18
ninety-five theses: g72 3/8 17
Reformation: w72 199
view of Bible: g74 8/22 11

LUTHERAN CHURCH
baptism: g72 3/8 18-19
beliefs: g74 8/22 9-11; g72 4/8 30
Catholic church: w74 273; g72 3/8 16
clergy: g74 8/22 8-12; g72 1/22 5, 29; g72 8/22 18; w71 215
decline: g72 8/22 17; g71 12/22 31
disunity: g74 3/22 29; g74 8/22 8-12; g72 1/22 30; g71 10/22 30
experiences:
minister becomes Witness: w74 411; w72 327
failure: g74 6/8 31
homosexuality: w74 483; w73 356
membership: g71 11/8 30
morals: w71 451
nudity: g71 5/8 29
opposition to Witnesses: yb72 140
revolution: g72 4/22 17
theological schools:
Concordia: g74 8/22 8-12; g74 11/8 30
war: g75 2/22 19-20; g72 4/22 6-8

LUXEMBOURG
Jehovah's witnesses: yb76 28-9; 34-47; yb75 28-9; yb74 28-9; g74 12/22 10; w73 573-4; yb73 28-9; yb72 38-9; g72 9/22 26; w71 211-12
languages: yb76 45-6
population: yb76 34; yb73 28; yb72 38
religion: yb76 34; g74 12/22 8-10

LUXURIES
w75 172

MACAO
Jehovah's witnesses: yb76 26-7; yb75 26-7; yb74 26-7, 57-8; yb73 26-7; yb72 36-7
population: yb73 26; yb72 36

MACCABEES
Apocrypha: g75 1/22 28
Judas Maccabaeus: g74 6/8 27
not restore Davidic kingdom: po 175

MACHINES
adding: g72 6/22 3

MACMILLAN, A. H.
yb75 72-4, 76-7, 79-80, 82-3, 90, 93, 104-9, 111-16, 121-3, 150-1, 206

MADEIRA
Jehovah's witnesses: yb76 28-9; yb75 28-9; yb74 28-9; yb73 28-9; yb72 38-9
population: yb73 28; yb72 38

MADISON SQUARE GARDEN
1939, New York convention: yb75 180-2

MAFIA
book *The Mafia Mystique:* g75 3/8 30
former member accepts truth: w75 40
murder of member in synagogue: g74 11/8 12

MAGAZINE DISTRIBUTION
beginning: yb75 124-5
discussion: or 117-18; km 4/71 4
experiences:
effect of magazines: w72 511
effect of one magazine: km 2/74 1
return visits: yb72 102; w71 220
street witnessing: yb72 79-80
subscription expiration slips: km 2/74 1
subscriptions: km 2/74 2; km 4/74 1; km 1/72 6
"extra" magazines for congregation: km 8/75 8
leaving at not-at-home: km 6/74 3
magazine bags: yb75 162-3
ministerial servant: or 151
older copies: km 11/74 3
presentations: km 9/74 8; or 117
reports: w75 27; yb75 32, 257-8; km 1/75 1; w74 30; yb74 31-2; yb73 31; w71 25
routes: or 118; km 4/71 4
service director: yb75 125
street witnessing: yb75 162-4; km 8/75 8
subscriptions: w75 27, 178; yb75 32; km 1/75 1; km 7/74 1; w73 27; yb73 31; km 12/73 4; km 8/72 4; w71 25; km 9/71 3; km 12/71 3-4
expiration slips: km 4/75 1; km 4/73 4
first campaigns: yb75 125, 162
obtaining: km 1/72 3-6
personal: km 4/73 1; km 10/73 7; km 2/72 8
presentations: km 12/74 4
rate changes: km 7/71 1
(SEE ALSO FIELD SERVICE)

MAGAZINES
advertising: g74 3/8 9
circulation cut: g72 1/8 29
decline in religious: w75 327; g75 3/8 30; g73 2/8 29; g73 9/22 7-8; g72 12/22 30; g71 4/8 29
immoral: w73 539-40
In the Light of Truth (*A Luz da Verdade*): yb73 41-2
medical: g72 1/8 26
publications ceased: w75 327; g73 1/22 29; g72 1/8 29; g71 11/8 29
Sunday newspaper: g75 2/8 30
youth: g72 10/8 30-1

MAGGOTS
accident victim: g72 12/22 30
Gehenna: ts 114

MAGIC
"black": g75 7/22 26; w73 484
books: g74 2/22 5-6
discussion: w73 483-4
Egyptian religion: g74 9/8 28
hypnosis: g74 9/8 27-8
magical healing: w73 697-701
"psychic" tested: g74 12/8 29

MAGNETISM
use of, in ancient weapons detection: g75 6/8 24

MAGOG
identified (Eze 38-9): yb75 215; w73 293-4, 343-4; kj 354, 368, 370, 395
destruction: kj 370-1
identified (Re 20:8): ka 152-3
destruction (Re 20:9): ka 154-5

MAGUEY
discussion: g73 5/22 25-6

MAHLON
name: w72 78

MAIL
(SEE LETTERS, POSTAL SYSTEM)

MAILBOX
g75 10/22 30

"MAKE SURE OF ALL THINGS; HOLD FAST TO WHAT IS FINE" (Book)
preparation of talks: sg 41-2

MALACHI (Book)
time and place written: kj 183

MALAGASY REPUBLIC
Jehovah's witnesses: yb76 28-9, 114, 198; yb75 28-9; yb74 28-9; yb73 28-9; yb72 38-9; w71 89-92
population: yb76 114; yb73 28; yb72 38

MALARIA
California outbreak: g71 5/22 30
unconquered: g75 8/22 31; w74 132

MALAWI
constitution: g75 12/8 5; g72 12/8 28
education: g73 1/8 29
false "Watchtower movements": yb76 118-19, 152
Jehovah's witnesses: yb76 30-1, 75-6, 118-20, 151-3, 168-71; yb75 9-10, 28-9, 210; g75 6/8 4; yb74 15, 28-9; yb73 22-3, 28-9; yb72 38-9, 45; g72 7/8 20; w71 111
persecution: yb76 19-21, 84-5, 88, 120, 168-70, 236-8; w75 341; g75 12/8 3-12; g75 12/22 15-19; km 12/75 1-2; g74 6/22 25; w73 264-8; g73 1/8 29; g73 8/22 30; g72 11/22 29; g72 12/8 9-28
Malawi Congress Party membership card: g75 12/8 4, 7
population: yb73 28; yb72 38
religion: yb76 70-4
uprising in 1915: yb76 80-1

MALAYSIA
Jehovah's witnesses: yb76 19, 28-9; yb75 28-9; km 4/75 1; yb74 20, 28-9; yb73 28-9; yb72 40-1
population: yb73 28; yb72 40
religion: g75 4/22 30

MALI
Jehovah's witnesses: yb76 30-1;

yb75 30-1; g75 1/22 24; yb74 30-1; yb73 30-1; yb72 38-9
population: yb73 30; yb72 38

MALNUTRITION
causes: g75 6/22 29; g71 2/22 31
children: w74 132; g74 10/8 5; g73 10/8 7
effects: g73 6/22 9-10
statistics: g74 10/8 15
United States: g71 7/22 31
widespread: w72 615
(SEE ALSO FOOD SHORTAGES, NUTRITION)

MALTA
Jehovah's witnesses: yb76 24-5; yb75 12, 24-5; yb74 24-5; yb73 24-5; yb72 34-5
population: yb73 24; yb72 34

MALVINAS ISLANDS
Jehovah's witnesses: yb76 24-5; yb75 24-5; yb74 24-5; yb73 24-5
population: yb73 24

MAMMOTHS
g75 6/8 7

MAN
body composition: po 39
breast cancer: g74 12/22 29
capabilities: w75 263
changing from boyhood: w73 86-9
clothing: g71 3/22 29
concept of time: ts 18-21
created to continue living: ts 16-26
creation: w74 594; po 33-42; ts 30; w73 77-8; g73 4/8 20-3; g71 4/8 7
dependence on God: w72 37, 425-30; g72 10/22 3-16; w71 35
designed for life on earth: w72 291-4
dominion over animals: w75 606-8; w74 594-5
evolutionist's prediction: w71 56-7
free moral agent: g74 4/8 16; w71 499
hair: g72 5/8 16, 31
image of God: w74 146, 307; po 37; g74 10/8 23; w73 488; tp 47; g73 10/22 27; w72 170, 445, 543
length of existence on earth:
end of 6,000 years: w75 579
moral sense: g74 3/22 14
need for a sound guide: g75 10/8 3-7
need to worship God: g75 6/22 4; w74 144; g74 12/8 21; w73 488-9; w72 388
proportion of unmarried men to women: g75 4/22 31
purpose of existence: w73 326-7
races: g74 10/8 9; g73 2/8 5-7
responsibility for worldwide suffering: g74 10/8 5-6, 8, 15-17
rhythms: w72 291-3
soul: po 38-40; ts 38-41
speaking ability: sg 5
sterilization: g73 1/8 29; g72 7/8 30
strength: g72 5/22 9
superiority over beasts: po 42; ts 18-21; g74 3/22 13-14; g73 10/22 19, 24-5; g73 11/22 19; w72 515; g72 1/22 10; g72 6/8 6-7; g72 7/8 5-6; g71 1/22 3-4; g71 3/8 11-12
"wonderfully made": g72 10/22 8
work: w72 487

MANASSEH (Son of Hezekiah)
events of reign: kj 101-3
repentance: w75 39; g74 6/8 6-7; w72 434

MANATEES
g75 8/8 30

MANIFESTO
Christ's return: w71 621; nc 20-1

MAN IN LINEN
coals of fire: kj 184-90
discussion: w72 41-54, 633-638
identified: w72 635-6; kj 208-9
marking work: w72 48-54, 633-8; w71 183; kj 164-6, 171-81
prophetic significance: w72 46-8
understanding clarified: kj 171-2

MANKIND
causes of problems facing: g75 4/8 6-7
end of 6,000 years of existence: w75 579
end of 6,000 years of history: w75 579
God's dealings: tp 121-3; g71 6/8 12-14
God's purpose: w74 659-62, 669; po 33-4, 40-1, 45, 48, 54-5, 61-2, 64; g73 2/8 7; w71 35-7
God's universal organization: pm 148
one family: g74 6/22 27; w72 69
perils confronting: w75 259; g75 3/22 29; g75 4/8 3-5; w74 5, 51, 550-1; g74 1/22 4-8; g74 3/22 3-6; g74 5/22 29; g74 6/22 3-8; g74 8/8 10-11; w73 37, 583; g73 10/8 3-15, 20-2, 30; g73 12/8 30; g72 7/8 29; g72 9/8 3-4; w71 57, 67-8, 108; g71 1/22 30; g71 4/22 3-5, 13-14, 18-19; g71 7/22 29; g71 8/22 31
races: w73 515-18; g73 2/8 5-7
solution to problems of: w75 260-2; g75 3/22 30; g75 4/8 9-14

MANNA
miracle: w71 293

MANNERS
bad: w74 675
congregational: w74 440
lack in world: g74 9/8 4
travelers': g75 7/8 30-1

MAN OF LAWLESSNESS
destruction: w75 270-1; ka 393-7
development: w75 167-8, 201-2, 253-4
discussion: w75 201-4, 252-4, 269-71; ka 370-97
identified: w75 202, 254; sl 212-13; po 170; ka 374-5, 378, 380-1
'mystery of lawlessness': w75 252-3
presence: w75 254; ka 388-93
"restraint" against: w75 252-3; ka 384-8
(SEE ALSO APOSTASY)

MAN'S SALVATION OUT OF WORLD DISTRESS AT HAND! (Book)
public talks: km 9/75 3-6
release: w75 627

MANTON, JUDGE MARTIN T.
yb75 118

MANUSCRIPTS
(SEE BIBLE MANUSCRIPTS)

MANUS ISLAND
Jehovah's witnesses: yb76 28-9; yb75 28-9; yb74 28-9; yb73 28-9; yb72 38-9
population: yb73 28; yb72 38

MAPLE SUGAR
discussion: g73 2/22 11-13

MAPS
Africa:
drought area: g74 7/22 4
Argentina: yb72 49
Assyrian Empire: bi8 1371
Brazil: yb73 36
Central America: g74 12/22 21
cities of refuge: w73 303
Czechoslovakia: yb72 129
Israelite exodus from Egypt: w73 752
Jerusalem:
during ministry of Jesus and apostles: w75 366
time of the return (455 B.C.E.): pm 156
Jesus' ministry: w73 14-15
map making: g73 2/22 30
Palestine:
time of Persian Empire: pm 260
Persian Empire: bi8 1371
U.N. member nations: w74 549
Valley of Hinnom: ts 113

MARDUK (Merodach)
w72 745; kj 224

MARGAY
g75 3/22 14-15

MARIJUANA
g75 1/22 31; g75 6/8 30; w74 394; g74 3/8 31; g74 3/22 30; g74 5/8 5-6; g74 10/8 30; g74 10/22 11; g74 12/8 29-30; w73 177-9, 182-3, 186-7; tp 160-1; g73 5/22 30; g73 7/8 30; g73 7/22 7; g73 9/22 30; g73 12/8 6-7; g72 2/8 30; g72 6/22 31; g72 7/8 30; g72 10/8 31; w71 247-8, 250, 526; g71 2/8 20; g71 3/8 30; g71 4/8 17-18; g71 5/22 30; g71 6/22 30; g71 11/22 29
(SEE ALSO DRUGS, NARCOTICS)

MARINE LIFE
aquarium: g72 9/22 13-16
diminishing: g74 2/22 23-4
effects of pollution: g74 2/22 24; g71 4/8 29; g71 4/22 10-11, 30; g71 6/22 30
egg-laying habits: g71 7/8 4; g71 8/22 26
electricity: g72 8/22 31
extinction: g74 5/8 30
fishing: g74 2/22 23-4
food from sewage: g72 8/8 31
hunting equipment: g75 11/8 19-20
knot-tying fish: g71 6/22 15
life on the ocean floor: g75 11/8 20
light-producing creatures: g75 11/8 19; g73 2/8 16-19

museum: g74 3/8 23
natural antifreeze: w75 715
number of species: ts 145
pesticides: g71 1/8 31
plants: g75 11/8 17; g71 1/8 8
playfulness: g75 10/22 25-6
protective equipment for survival: g75 11/8 18-19
seashells: g75 11/22 25
"sixth sense": g75 11/8 19
speed: g74 2/22 12-14; g72 1/22 30
training: g73 1/22 20-1

List by Name

angler fish: g73 2/8 16
barnacle: ts 146-7
barracuda: g74 2/22 14; g72 1/22 30
carp: g71 11/8 17-18
catfish: g71 11/8 17
clam: g71 4/22 30
coelacanth: g72 6/8 29
cone shells: g75 11/22 25
coral: g72 10/22 27-8
diatom: g75 11/8 18
dinoflagellates: g73 2/8 16-17
dolphin: g74 2/22 13; g73 12/22 15
firefly fish: g73 2/8 18
fireworm: g73 2/8 19
flatfish: g75 11/8 29
hagfish: g71 6/22 15
halibut: g74 3/22 30
jellyfish: w75 560
lantern fish: g73 2/8 16
mackerel: g75 11/8 18
manatee: g75 8/8 30
milkfish: g71 11/8 17
Moses sole: g75 11/8 29
octopus: g74 2/22 13; g71 2/22 31
otter: g73 1/22 20; g71 3/8 31
oyster: g74 9/8 24-6; g71 8/22 26; g71 11/8 18
polar bear: g73 1/22 21
porpoise: g73 12/22 15
salmon: g71 8/22 26; g71 11/8 18
sea cucumber: g75 11/8 18-20
sea hare: g71 8/22 26
seal: g75 10/22 25-6; g75 11/8 17; g73 1/22 20-1
sea lion: g73 1/22 21; g72 12/22 31; g71 1/8 31
sea snake: g75 3/22 31
sea urchin: g71 3/8 31
shark: g75 11/8 18, 20, 29; g74 2/22 13
shrimp: g71 11/8 18
snail: g73 1/8 20-2
squid: g74 2/22 13-14
starfish: g72 10/22 8
swordfish: g71 6/22 30
trout: g71 11/8 18
tuna: g74 2/22 13
turtle: g71 12/8 30
whale: g75 7/22 30; g75 10/22 25; g74 3/8 23; g73 2/22 19; g73 12/22 13-16
wrasse: g72 11/8 30
zooplankton: g75 11/8 17
(SEE ALSO ANIMALS, BIRDS, INSECTS, OCEANS)

MARIOLATRY
Bible view: g73 1/8 27-8
decline: g73 2/22 29-30
"Mother of God": w75 539-40
practices: w75 12
prayers: g75 1/22 27; w74 259-60, 396

MARK (Book)
Dead Sea fragment: g72 12/22 27-8
discussion (Mr 16:9-20): g73 8/8 6-7
style: g73 8/8 6-7

MARK (John Mark)
Bible writer: g71 3/8 25
relationship with Paul: w75 344-6

MARKET
supermarkets: g74 11/8 30-1

MARK ON FOREHEAD
Ezekiel 9: w74 57-8; w72 48-54, 287, 635-8; kj 164-6, 174-81, 208-9

MARRIAGE
Abel: w75 75
Abraham: w75 75-6
Adam and Eve: po 45-7; g74 1/22 27; pm 9-10
adultery:
avoiding: w73 538-40; tp 146-7
confessing: g74 11/8 27; w73 351-2
forgiving: w74 511-12
Africa: w73 151-5
age statistics: g72 4/8 29; g72 12/8 3; g71 11/22 31
anniversary: w71 735-6
arranged: g72 8/8 20-3
basis for happiness: g75 9/22 27-8; g74 4/22 6, 10, 16; w72 36, 131-2, 259-60, 270-1, 287; g72 2/22 5-8; g72 5/8 3-4; g72 9/22 27-8; w71 223; g71 2/8 14-15
Bible view: w75 151-3; w72 454; g72 12/8 5-6
bride price: w73 151-2; g71 10/22 7-8; g71 4/8 24-6
Cain: w75 75
Catholic church: g72 5/8 9-12
celibate marriage: w75 295-6
ceremony: g74 5/22 3-6; w73 153-4, 694-6
children: w72 108-9
common-law: yb74 39
communication: w75 485-6; w74 305-11; g72 8/8 3-4
concubines: w73 152-4
consensual: g75 4/8 29; yb72 184-5; g71 2/8 13-14
contraceptives: w75 159-60; w73 255-6
courtship: w74 8-13, 607
customs: yb76 215; w74 8-9, 430-1; w73 151-5; g72 8/8 20-3; g71 4/8 24-6; g71 10/22 7-8
sea gypsies: g75 9/22 15
death dissolves: ts 179
discussion: w75 483-6; g74 5/22 3-6; w73 151-5; g72 2/22 5-8; g72 12/8 3-5; g71 2/8 13-16
disfellowshiped mate: w74 470-1; or 173, 176
divided households: km 8/75 7; w74 314-17, 441-2; g74 4/22 9
divine origin: g74 1/22 27; g72 5/22 12
divorce: w75 286-8, 483; g75 3/22 30; g75 9/22 27-8; w74 8-9, 511-12, 671-2, 703-4; g74 1/22 31; g74 4/22 3-4; tp 150-1; w72 31-2, 766-8; g72 2/22 5; g72 4/8 29; g72 12/8 29; w71 309-10; g71 4/8 30; g71 4/22 31; g71 11/22 31
engagement:
breaking of, unilaterally: w75 382-4
experiences:
adultery rejected: g72 9/22 26
Bible truth unites: w75 484-5; g75 10/8 21-2; w74 317, 643-4; g74 7/22 9-10; g74 9/8 7; g73 9/22 28; w72 455; g72 4/8 25; g72 10/8 23-4; w71 202, 204-6, 209, 211-12, 376; g71 4/8 23
consensual marriage rejected: g71 2/8 13-16
marriages legalized: yb75 7; w74 648; yb74 8-9; g74 1/22 20-1; g74 2/8 25; g74 9/8 7; yb73 72-3, 182-3; yb72 185; g72 10/8 24; g71 9/22 23
faithfulness: w74 152
feast (Mt 22): w74 685-700
garment in Bible times: w74 696
homosexuality: g75 2/22 30; w72 31-2
husband's role: w75 153-4, 484-5; g74 4/22 9-12; tp 175-6; g73 9/22 27-8; g72 2/22 7-8; g72 5/22 13-14
husbands to be 'as though they had no wives' (1 Co 7:29): w75 351-2
incest: w75 72-7; g74 6/22 28
in Kingdom Hall: km 11/73 8
interracial: w73 735-6
Israelites: w74 430-1; w72 82-3, 86-8
jealousy in "open marriage": g75 4/8 29
Jehovah: g74 5/22 3-4
Jesus Christ: w72 108-9
Jewish view of mixed: g71 8/22 30
legal requirements: w73 154, 735; g72 8/22 3
lies: w71 309-10, 539
loneliness: g74 6/8 4
love: g74 5/22 4-5; w72 131-2, 287; g72 2/8 3
marriage counselors: g75 12/8 30-1
monogamy: w75 151-2
Noah's grandsons: w75 76
"one flesh": po 47; g74 5/22 4
"only in the Lord": g75 9/22 28; w74 607; w73 73, 476-7; w72 273, 364-5
'past bloom of youth' (1 Co 7:36): w74 703
polygamy: g75 3/8 15; g75 12/8 13-17; w73 151-5; yb73 143, 167; w72 366; w71 158; g71 10/22 7
clergy view: w75 200
experiences: yb76 180; g74 2/8 25; w73 154; yb72 243; w71 124-5
prayer: g74 5/22 4
preparation: w75 152; w74 8-13; w73 696
problems: w74 435-6; g74 4/22 3-12; g72 2/22 5-6; g72 5/8 3-4; w71 579
psychology: w74 308
purpose: po 45-6
reasons people marry: g73 9/22 26
registration:
Greece: g75 6/8 25
remarriage: w74 511-12, 671-2
resolving problems: g74 4/22 5-12; w73 153-5; g73 9/22 27-8; km 9/73 8; g72 8/8 3-4
respect for powers of procreation: w75 158-60

resurrected ones: ts 178-80
separation: w75 286-8, 575-6; w72 382-4
sex relations: w74 436, 703-4; g74 4/22 4, 6-7, 10-12; w73 352; tp 153; w72 575-6, 734-6; g72 2/22 6, 8
singleness: w74 379-80, 703; w73 476-7; w72 107-8; g72 5/8 4, 12; g72 12/8 5-8
swapping mates: g73 8/8 29; g71 7/22 30
teen-age: w74 9, 703
"trial marriage": w73 152-3
tribulation in the flesh: w75 152
trust: w73 478
violent husband: w75 286-8; g75 9/8 29-30
vows: w74 275; w71 309-10
wedding ring: w72 63
wife's role: w75 154-5, 484-5; g74 4/22 5-9; tp 176-7; g72 2/22 8; g72 5/22 6-7, 10-11; g72 9/22 27-8
worldly views: g74 12/22 29-30
youth: w75 461-2; g72 12/8 3-5

MARRIAGE FEAST (Illustration)
bride: w74 686-7, 690, 700
discussion: w74 686-700
few chosen: w75 286; w74 698-9
king: w74 686-7
man without marriage garment: w74 696-9
marriage garment: w74 696-7
son: w74 686, 690
those first invited: w74 687-90, 694-5
  notifications: w74 691-3
those from roads outside: w74 695-6

MARROW
food: w72 63-4

MARS
planet: g75 8/22 14; g74 5/22 30
  description: g73 5/22 9-11
  life possibility: g75 2/8 29; g75 8/8 31; g73 5/22 11
  pictures of: g73 5/22 10; g72 7/8 29
  travel to: g75 2/8 29; g74 8/22 15; g73 5/22 9-10; g72 1/22 29; g71 11/22 8

MARSHALL ISLANDS
Jehovah's witnesses: yb76 26-7; yb75 11-12, 26-7; yb74 26-7; yb73 15, 26-7; yb72 36-7
population: yb73 26; yb72 36

MARSHES
(SEE WETLANDS)

MARS HILL
(SEE AREOPAGUS)

MARTIN, R. J.
yb75 104, 111, 116, 123, 129, 145; ka 245-6

MARTINIQUE
Jehovah's witnesses: yb76 26-7; yb75 26-7; yb74 26-7; yb73 26-7; w72 381; yb72 36-7
population: yb73 26; yb72 36

MARTYR, JUSTIN
(SEE JUSTINUS)

MARX, KARL
ml 13

MARY (Jesus' Mother)
ancestry: w75 220, 222
children: w75 221-2, 296; po 142
conception of Jesus: w75 220; w74 68-9; po 136-8; ts 128-9; w72 621; dn 11; w71 439; te 24; g71 12/22 5-6
discussion: w75 295-6
engagement to Joseph: w75 221
Jesus' birth: w71 272; te 23-5; g71 12/22 5-8
Jesus' view: w75 540; w74 259-60, 362
personality: w74 295
reward: w71 439-40
virginity: w75 295
(SEE ALSO MARIOLATRY)

MASADA
Jews capture (66 C.E.): w74 425
Roman conquest (73 C.E.): w72 625; dn 18; kj 351

MASORETES
Masorah: bi8 1352-3

MASORETIC TEXT
Masorah: bi8 1352-3

MASS
attendance statistics: g75 7/22 31; g72 10/22 29; g72 12/22 30
Catholic view: g71 11/22 11-12
changes in: g75 3/8 30-1; g74 11/8 30; w71 644
money making: g74 10/22 29; w71 709; g71 8/22 13-14
sports events: g75 6/8 29
tortillas: g71 9/22 31

MASSAGE
discussion: g73 9/8 24-6

MASTURBATION
w74 160; w73 564-9; tp 152; w72 92-4; g72 12/8 7

MATERIALISM
advertising: g74 3/8 9
Bible view: w74 113, 605; g74 9/22 10-11; w73 408; tp 116-18; g71 11/22 27-8
Bible warnings: w75 50-1, 493-5; w73 57-8; g73 6/22 13; w71 470, 573; g71 10/22 11
causes: w72 299-300
Chinese: g74 9/22 9-10
comments about: g71 4/22 30
counteracting: w75 50-1; w74 380, 701; w73 57-8; w72 303-4; g72 3/8 3-4; w71 151, 563
dangers: g75 9/22 8; ts 14; g74 9/22 10
discussion: w75 561-75; w73 155-9
effect on family: g74 9/22 9-10
effect on one's relationship with God: w74 419-20, 701
effect on one's thinking: w74 112-13; g74 8/8 3-4; w73 155-9; g72 3/8 4; g71 3/22 30
effect on one's worship: w75 231-2; w74 59; w73 502; w71 557
effect on society: g74 9/8 3-4; g74 11/22 17-18, 20
effect on youth: w73 155-9
examples:
  Bible accounts: w74 404-6; w72 300
  modern-day: yb74 235; g74 8/8 3-4; g74 9/22 9-10; g72 3/8 3; w71 526-7
experiences in resisting: w75 185, 264-6; yb75 8; w74 403, 653-5; yb74 59; g74 2/8 26; g74 8/8 6-7; g73 8/22 14-15; km 2/73 5-6; km 5/73 5-6; g72 5/8 4; g71 10/22 11
not bring happiness: w75 51; g72 5/8 3
'not using world to full' (1 Co 7: 31): w75 91
television: g74 9/8 9
worship of: w75 231-2

MATERIALIZATION
angels that sinned: ts 83-5
Jesus Christ: ts 169-70; w73 248

MATHEMATICS
abacus: g71 11/22 17-20
African: g75 5/22 17-19
children's knowledge of multiplication: g75 7/22 30
Egyptian: g71 2/8 10
"new math": g71 2/8 9-12
numerical systems: g71 2/8 11-12
proof of God's existence: g74 5/22 22; g71 8/8 5
use of, in everyday living: g75 9/22 29

MATRIARCHAL SOCIETY
girl from, accepts truth: g75 8/22 21-4

MATTER
atomic structure: g73 11/22 23; g72 3/8 12-15; g71 6/8 29

MATTHEW (Apostle)
Bible writer: g71 3/8 25
tax collector: w74 139-40

MATTHEW (Book)
authenticity: g71 12/22 6-8

MATTHIAS
apostle to replace Judas: w71 319-20

MATURITY
discussion: w74 109-14; w71 661-5
spiritual:
  advancement after attaining: w75 92; w74 114-19
  aiding others to attain: w74 338-40
  attaining: w74 110-12; w72 31; w71 661-5
  dangers to: w74 112-14
  identifying: km 2/75 1; w74 109-10
  importance: w71 605-6

MAURITANIA
Jehovah's witnesses: yb76 30-1; yb75 30-1; yb74 30-1; yb73 30-1; yb72 40-1
population: yb73 30; yb72 40

MAURITIUS
Jehovah's witnesses: yb76 28-9, 112-13, 177-8, 197-8; yb75 28-9; w74 475-6; yb74 28-9; g74 5/8 20; yb73 28-9; yb72 38-9

g, Awake!; **ka**, God's Kingdom of a Thousand Years; **kj**, "The Nations Shall Know that I Am Jehovah"; **km**, Kingdom Ministry; **or**, Organization; **pm**, Paradise Restored—By Theocracy!; **po**, God's "Eternal Purpose"; **sg**, Theocratic School Guidebook; **sl**, Man's Salvation out of World Distress!; **te**, Listening to the Great Teacher; **tp**, True Peace and Security; **ts**, Is This Life All There Is?; **w**, Watchtower; **yb**, Yearbook. **Complete list on page 6.**

persecution: yb76 113
population: yb73 28; yb72 38

MEALS
conversation: sg 79-80
prayer: w72 334
suggested dishes: g73 12/8 24-6

MEAT
additives: g72 4/8 31
amount consumed: g74 9/22 3
Argentina: g71 5/22 29
beef:
consumption: g74 7/22 6
cuts of: g74 10/22 24
ways to serve: g74 10/22 24-6
blood: w72 544
buying: g74 8/22 31; g74 9/22 5; g73 8/22 4, 30
dangers of eating too much: g74 9/22 3-4
fat: w72 190-1
grain needed to produce: g74 7/22 6
offered to idols: w72 563-5

MEDIATOR
Jesus Christ: po 159-61; w73 198-9; w72 166, 685-8; g72 2/8 5-6
Moses: po 109-10; w72 682-3; g72 2/8 5-6
(SEE ALSO JESUS CHRIST)

MEDICINE
acupuncture: g72 7/22 30; g72 9/8 12-16; g71 7/8 31
advancement: g74 3/22 23
ancient: w75 134-5
antibiotics: g73 12/22 9; g72 4/8 30-1; g71 3/22 29; g71 8/22 12; g71 11/22 30; g71 12/8 31
antiseptics: g71 2/8 30
aspirin: g73 12/22 9; g72 2/22 29; g72 10/22 30; g71 1/22 30; g71 5/22 30
birth-control pills: g74 1/22 15
cancer: g74 9/8 17, 21-2
charcoal: g72 10/22 30
colds: g73 12/22 9-10
cortisone: g74 1/22 16
costs: g72 12/8 31
dangers: g74 1/22 15-16; g73 1/22 30; g73 2/22 10; g72 7/22 31; g71 4/22 30; g71 8/8 31; g71 10/8 7
warning list ignored: g71 2/8 31
DES: g74 1/22 16
diagnosis errors: g71 6/22 22
diet pills: g71 9/22 30
health care problems: g74 6/22 31; g73 1/22 31
herbs: g72 10/22 31
hormones: g74 1/22 13-16
ineffective: g72 9/8 30; g71 2/8 30-1
insulin: g74 1/22 15
love: g72 10/22 30
medical literature: g72 1/8 26
mercury: g71 2/8 30
minipill: g74 1/22 15
pain-killing drugs: g73 2/22 10
penicillin: w72 387; g71 4/22 30
placebo: g71 11/22 30
plasma volume expanders: g74 6/22 18-21
psychosomatics: w73 291-2
satellite relays medical advice: g72 2/8 29
serums: w74 351-2
silicone: g71 11/8 31
sleep-inducing drugs: g72 2/8 23; g72 10/22 30
television: g71 12/22 31
tranquilizers: w75 246; g72 5/8 30-1; g71 2/8 31
vaccinations: w74 132, 351
wine: g73 12/22 10; g71 7/22 30
(SEE ALSO DOCTORS, DRUGS, HOSPITALS, SURGERY)

MEDITATION
Buddhism: g74 1/8 16-19
demons: g74 1/8 19
Hindu: g75 11/8 10-11, 29
importance: w72 404-5, 522-4
prayer: g74 6/8 6
transcendental meditation: g75 11/8 10

MEDITERRANEAN SEA
symbolic: pm 384-6

MEDO-PERSIA
rulers: w72 349-51
world power: w71 715

MEEKNESS (Mildness)
discussion: w74 103-4
elders: w74 103-4
meaning of term: g71 7/8 27
meek inherit the earth: w74 662; g71 7/8 27-8
'seeking' (Zep 2:3): ts 188
value: w74 180
(SEE ALSO HUMILITY)

MEETINGS
applause: km 4/72 4
appreciation for: w75 20; w73 404; yb73 241; w72 407, 410; w71 678-80
assisting others to attend: yb76 182; km 12/74 3
attendance statistics: w74 15
attendants: or 105; km 3/72 4
being on time for: km 8/74 7
benefits: w75 62, 317; km 7/75 1, 3; w74 115, 567; w73 205, 253-4, 533-5; tp 187; w72 407-8; w71 400-2
chairman: km 12/73 4
child attendance: w75 61-2; w73 671-2; or 92-3; w71 555; te 157-8
reluctant children: w75 319-20
child behavior: sg 27
child commendation: km 4/75 3
comments by new ones: km 4/75 4
congregation book study: km 9/74 7-8; or 100-1; km 5/72 3
cottage meetings: yb75 43-4
discussion: w72 406-12; or 91-107
disfellowshiped persons: w74 469-70; km 11/74 4
early Christians: or 91-2; w71 396-400
effort to attend: yb76 182; w75 246, 489; yb75 43; g75 1/22 24; w74 647; yb73 20-1; yb72 95-6, 99; g72 5/22 24; w71 678-80
experiences:
attendances in war zone: w74 518-19
early modern-day: yb76 78-9, 244-5; yb75 43-4
first attendance: w74 510; g74 6/8 4; w73 627-9; yb72 55; g72 1/22 25; w71 167, 221, 534, 552; g71 9/8 17-18
impressed by love: w73 519
talk impresses boy: w73 29
husbands sitting with wives: yb76 97
importance of attendance: w75 62; w74 412, 566-8; w73 48, 253-4; w72 133-4, 406-8; w71 149, 586
invitation to attend: w71 402-3
Jesus attended: te 156-7
meetings for field service: km 10/72 8
ministerial servants' privileges: km 2/75 4
older men (elders): or 63-70
with circuit overseer: km 8/74 7
overtime: km 7/72 4
participation: w73 255; w72 134, 411, 696; or 92, 100; sg 91-2, 189; g71 9/8 3
paying attention: w72 410-11; w71 149; sg 24-9
prayer: w72 334-5, 411; or 92; km 1/72 8
prayer and testimony meetings: yb75 43-4, 133
preparation: w74 115; km 12/74 3-4; w72 408-9; sg 91-2
presiding: w72 757
public meetings: km 6/73 4; km 12/73 4; or 95-6; km 2/71 7-8
purpose: w73 253
regularity in attending: w74 567-8
service meeting: km 12/74 3; km 10/73 7; or 97-8; km 9/72 7; sg 178; km 8/71 4
small congregations: w72 447; or 102-3
songs: w72 411
Theocratic School: yb75 197-9; w73 533-5; w72 460-1; or 98-100; yb72 77; sg 8-13, 96-9; km 12/71 3
times of: km 11/75 1; km 8/74 8; or 103
during circuit overseer's visit: km 12/75 8
under ban: yb74 134-6, 139, 143-5, 152; w72 136-7; yb72 86-93
Watchtower study: yb75 133; w72 134, 460; or 93-4; yb72 73, 76-7; km 6/72 4; w71 73
welcoming strangers: w72 409-10; km 10/71 7
when attendance exceeds seating capacity: km 7/75 4
woman's role: w73 255
(SEE ALSO CONVENTIONS)

MEGIDDO
area around, not symbolic Har–Magedon: w75 387-8
picture: w74 229
prophetic significance: w74 77, 230-2
strategic importance: w75 515; w74 77, 231-2
(SEE ALSO ARMAGEDDON)

MELCHIZEDEK
prophetic significance: w74 158-9; po 88-90, 155; ka 88-93, 102-3; pm 186-7, 231, 401

MEMORIAL (Lord's Evening Meal)
annual observance: w73 175
determining whether to partake: w75 105-8
discussion: w73 198-200; km 3/73 3-4; w72 165-7; g72 3/22 27-8; te 167-70
emblems:
bread: w72 166; g72 3/22 27-8
significance: te 170
wine: w72 166; g72 3/22 27-8
significance: te 170

encouraging attendance: w75 165; km 3/73 3-4
experiences: yb74 143-5, 221; km 3/72 1; w71 343
fasting: w71 537
invitation: w75 165; w74 199-200; w72 167; w71 195-6
Jesus institutes: w71 397; te 167-70
only Christian celebration: pm 253
partakers: w75 105-8; yb74 31-2; w72 166-7; te 170
planning for: km 3/74 3-4
reasons for commemorating: w74 199-200; w73 198-200; km 3/73 3-4; w71 196
time of observance: w73 175

List by Year

1917: yb75 94
1919: yb75 94; pm 202, 253
1970: w71 25; kj 334
1971: pm 253; yb72 254
1972: w73 23, 27; yb73 30
1973: w74 30-1; yb74 31-2; w73 639; km 7/73 1
1974: w75 27-8, 44; yb75 31-2, 258-9; km 6/74 1; km 7/74 1
1975: yb76 23, 31, 47, 67; sl 330

MEMORY
animals: ts 19-20
dead forgotten: ts 23
Jehovah: ts 173-4; w71 708
man: ts 18-21; g74 12/8 16-21
loss of: g74 12/8 20
memorizing Bible facts: g75 9/22 25-6
older persons: g74 12/8 18
reading to remember: sg 19-24

MEN OF GOODWILL
steps to becoming: w71 237

"MEN OF GOODWILL" DISTRICT ASSEMBLY
Africa: w71 122-7, 155-8; g71 3/22 24-6; g71 7/8 23
Brazil: g71 4/8 20-3

MENOPAUSE
g74 1/22 15

MENSTRUATION
g74 2/8 13; w73 479; w72 293, 575-6

MENTAL ILLNESS
after heart surgery: w74 720
animals: g73 6/8 31
causes: w75 255; g75 4/22 3, 7-10, 13-14, 21
children: g75 4/22 6-7; g75 6/22 20-3; g73 9/22 29
contributing factors: g75 4/22 3-4; g75 11/22 31; g73 9/22 18, 20, 29; g72 4/22 30
depression: g75 4/22 5-6
discussion: g75 4/22 3-21
drug therapy: g75 4/22 11-12
effect of Bible knowledge: w75 244-5; g75 4/22 19-21; g72 8/22 23
effect of faith: g74 9/8 30
electroshock treatment: g75 4/22 11; g73 9/22 18; g72 9/22 30
experiences in overcoming: g75 4/22 20
help from elders: g75 4/22 20-1
home care: g75 4/22 19; g73 9/22 17-20
hormone treatment: g75 4/22 13
institutional care: g73 9/22 17-19
listening to disturbed persons: g75 4/22 16
need for love: g75 4/22 16, 19
nervous breakdown: g74 8/22 16-19
neuroses: g75 4/22 5
nutrition: g75 4/22 13-14
psychotherapy: w75 255; g75 4/22 12, 15-19; g71 9/22 23
schizophrenia: g75 4/22 4, 6, 8, 16; g74 7/22 31
statistics: g75 4/22 4; g73 10/8 12; g71 7/8 30-1
vitamin treatment: g75 4/22 14
(SEE ALSO PSYCHIATRY)

MERCURY
antiseptics: g71 2/8 30
planet: g75 8/22 13; g74 5/22 30
pollution: g72 5/8 30; g71 4/8 29

MERCY
basis: w73 30; or 166-7
discussion: w74 460-6, 472-3, 493-505; w72 549-55; w71 411-15, 539, 566-7; g71 8/8 27-8
disfellowshiped persons: w74 460-8, 472-3
examples: w74 494-5, 498-9, 503-5
extending: w75 755-6; w74 46, 494-500, 503-5
Jehovah: w75 115-17, 517-18; sl 88-9, 115-17; w74 370-1, 460-3, 467-8, 495-9; w73 105-6, 147, 197, 303-5; g73 7/8 28; w72 73-4, 430-6, 549-50
Jesus: w74 494, 497
meaning of term: w74 497; w72 549
not condoning sins: w75 755-6; w74 493-6
practicing: km 3/75 2; w74 497-500

MERCY KILLING
discussion: g74 5/8 27-8
Nazi euthanasia program: w75 294

MESSAGE OF HOPE (Resolution)
yb75 137

MESSIAH
ancestry: w74 105-6; po 83, 85, 88-90, 95, 100-2
Bethlehem: po 123, 127
counterfeits: w74 682; ka 296-7, 320-2
discussion: g73 9/8 27-8
identified: w74 235-6; po 135-6, 138-41, 144; w72 241; g71 12/8 8-9; g71 12/22 27-8
Israel "Messianic" nation: po 98-9
Jehovah's 'eternal purpose': po 60, 64, 102, 129, 156-7
Jews' beliefs: w73 716; g73 9/8 27-8; w72 654-5; g71 12/8 6-9
kings of Judah: kj 220
meaning of term: po 8, 60; w71 241
pictured by "sprout": sl 173, 175
pictured by "twig": sl 173, 175
prophecies: po 123, 125-7, 129, 146, 151-3; ts 154-5; g73 9/8 27-8; w72 241-2
prophecy of 70 weeks: po 131-2, 144-5; g73 9/8 28; g71 12/8 6-9
resurrection: sl 27-9
'seed of woman': po 60
"Servant": sl 88-9
transformation: sl 30-1, 38, 42, 45-7
why came when he did: w73 580-2
(SEE ALSO JESUS CHRIST)

METALS
aluminum: w74 102; g74 11/22 18-19
cadmium: g71 9/8 31
copper: w75 112; g74 11/22 18-19; pm 225
gold: g71 8/22 4-5
iron: g74 11/22 17
lead: w71 292
price increases: w74 102; g74 11/22 18-19
recycling: g71 8/8 30
steel: g74 11/22 18
tin: g74 11/22 18-19

METEORS
g75 4/8 8; g74 5/22 31; g73 7/8 5-6

METHADONE
Bible view: w73 336-8, 340
deaths: g73 9/8 30-1

METHODIST CHURCH
abortion: g71 10/22 30
attitude toward Bible: g71 9/22 15
church magazine: w75 327
church program: w71 643
clergy: g74 12/22 30; w71 330, 451; g71 9/22 15; g71 10/8 31; g71 11/8 30
experiences: w73 443-4
admiration for Witnesses: g72 6/8 16
couple quit because of immorality in: g74 10/8 28
members become Witnesses: g71 3/8 7
minister becomes Witness: g71 7/22 20
witnessing to members: yb72 57
failure: g74 7/22 30; g74 8/8 30; w72 366; g71 9/8 31
homosexuality: g74 5/22 29; w73 356
membership: w75 323; g75 6/8 30; g74 8/8 30; g73 1/22 30; g71 10/8 31
morals: g75 1/8 31; g74 9/8 30; g73 2/22 7; g72 4/22 18-19
Wesley's Chapel: g75 4/8 25

METHUSELAH
knew Adam, Noah: po 70

METRIC SYSTEM
g74 8/8 17-19

MEXICO
adobe houses: g71 1/8 23-4
ancient civilization: g72 4/22 11
disasters: g73 10/22 30; g72 6/22 30-1; g72 7/22 29; g72 11/22 29; g71 7/8 29
epidemic: g72 8/8 29
gasoline: g74 2/22 31
history: g71 5/22 15-16
International Women's Conference: g75 8/22 29; g75 9/8 30

Jehovah's witnesses: yb76 28-9; w75 247, 649-50; yb75 21, 28-9; yb74 28-9; yb73 28-9; yb72 38-9
new building: g74 7/22 16
jumping beans: g73 9/22 25
life-span: g72 9/22 30
manatees: g75 8/8 30
piñata: g71 6/22 23-4
population: yb73 28; yb72 38; g72 1/22 9
religion: g71 6/22 23-4
Taijin flyers: g75 7/22 11-13
typhoid: w74 132

MICAH (Prophet)
location of home town: w72 742
name: w72 743
outlook: w74 378
time of prophesying: w72 742

MICHAEL
archangel:
identified: po 137-8, 155; w71 269-70
'stands up': w74 191-2
"time of distress": w74 191-2

MICHELANGELO
g75 1/8 22-3

MICRONESIA
g74 11/8 25-6

MICROPHONE
public speaking: sg 68-9

MICROSCOPES
discussion: g74 1/22 12-13
electronic: g72 9/8 29

MIDDLE EAST
Bible prophecy: w75 387-9

MIDIANITES
women ensnare Israelites: w73 585-9

MIDWIFE
experience:
delivery at home: g74 6/8 22-3
history: g72 11/22 13-16

MILDEW
g74 9/8 13-14

MILDNESS
benefits from exercising: g75 11/22 12; w74 180; g72 3/22 15; w71 208-10
discussion: w74 103-4; g71 7/8 27-8
elders: w74 103-4
fruit of the spirit: g71 7/8 28
(SEE ALSO HUMILITY)

MILITARY SERVICE
alcoholism: g73 11/8 30
Australia: g73 5/8 31
Catholics during World War II: g75 2/22 18-23
chaplains: g75 2/22 19, 21; w71 644
civilian work as substitute for: g74 12/8 23
clergy view: g75 2/22 18-23
conscientious objection: yb75 101; yb73 22, 79-81, 98-100, 120-2, 124, 162-3; g71 1/8 13-15; g71 3/22 29
cost and size statistics: g74 2/8 30; tp 14; g73 9/8 29; g73 12/22 18; g71 8/22 6-8
court case regarding Witness exemption: yb73 133-5
drug abuse: g73 12/8 4
early Christians: g73 5/8 23; g72 4/22 21-2
experiences:
military personnel: w74 342-3; yb73 236; w72 222; yb72 204; g71 6/22 21-2
Witnesses refuse: yb75 11; km 6/75 1; w74 373; yb74 118-19, 123-4; w72 520
morale difficulties: g73 6/22 30
pioneers exempt (Germany): g71 1/8 13-15
prestige declines: g71 2/8 29
South Africa: yb76 236
Witnesses during World War I: yb75 119
Witnesses during World War II: yb75 205-7
Witnesses exempted: yb75 208; w74 604-5; g74 12/8 22-5
(SEE ALSO NEUTRALITY)

MILK
human: g75 11/22 30; g74 7/8 13, 15-16
iodine 131: g75 5/22 31
sleep aid: g75 11/22 30-1
yogurt: g75 2/8 19

MILLENNIAL DAWN (Book)
w73 396

MILLENNIUM
meaning of term: ka 13
(SEE ALSO THOUSAND-YEAR REIGN)

MILLIONS NOW LIVING WILL NEVER DIE
book: yb76 90; yb75 127; yb73 109
lecture: yb76 90; yb75 127; yb74 88-90; yb73 109-10

MINAS
Jesus' parable: w74 61, 541; w73 710-21; ka 213, 215
monetary value: w73 713
ten slaves: w73 713, 715, 717
wicked slave: w73 719-21

MIND
attitude: g74 12/8 21
bad thoughts: w73 511-12
body: g74 12/8 20-1
creative capacity: w75 263
developing: g74 12/8 21
discussion: g74 12/8 16-21
effect on physical health: g74 2/22 10-11; g74 6/8 29
"force actuating": w74 210, 312
guarding: w74 112-3; w73 178-9, 186-7, 511-12, 595
heart: w71 134-42; sg 74-5
IQ scores: g74 5/22 30
'making over': w74 110-11, 210
memory: g74 12/8 16-21
"mental regulating": g74 2/8 8-9
mind of Christ: w74 209-11, 213
open mind: w74 180
peace of mind: w74 178
proper use: g74 12/8 17-18, 21; w73 178-9, 186-7, 477-9
psychosomatics: g71 11/22 30
soundness of: w74 523
thinking clearly: g73 1/8 3-8
transforming: w74 312; w71 138, 543-4

MINERALS
diamonds: g74 7/22 24-6
potassium: g74 4/22 24
shortages: g74 11/22 16-20
treatment for mental illness: g75 4/22 14
United States: g74 1/22 6

MINING
Bible mention: w71 640
copper: w75 112; g75 1/8 18-20; g73 7/8 25-6
diamonds: g74 7/22 25-6
diseases: g74 11/8 30
union corruption: g74 6/8 13

MINISTER(S)
discussion: w75 728-34
Greek word: w75 716-22, 728-31; w71 456
ordination: w75 732-4
proper view of English word: w75 731-4
(SEE ALSO CLERGY, OLDER MEN, PRIESTS)

MINISTERIAL SERVANTS
accounts: or 151-3
appointment: yb75 248-9; km 8/75 3; km 8/73 3; w72 21, 599; yb72 30; sg 191
congregation book study conductor: km 1/75 4
discussion: w72 20-1, 25-7; yb72 29-33
duties: w72 25-6; or 68-9, 73-4, 81, 104-5, 151-2; yb72 31-2
filling vacant positions: km 11/72 7
gifts in men: w75 667-8
Greek word: w75 720-1; or 58; w71 690, 692
literature: or 151-2
magazines: or 151
moving to another congregation: km 1/75 4; km 8/75 5-6; km 6/73 3
ordination: w75 732-4
parts on meetings: km 2/75 4
public talks: km 2/75 4; km 6/73 4
qualifications: yb75 248; w73 469-72; w72 21, 126, 287; or 60-1; yb72 29-30
age: km 8/75 3
time interval since baptism: km 8/75 3
removal: km 8/75 3-4; km 6/73 3
reproof: w72 126
responsibilities: w71 223-4
shifts in assignments: km 8/75 5
teaching: km 1/75 4
(SEE ALSO OVERSEERS, SERVANT)

MINISTRY
discussion: or 107-32; w71 456-9, 539, 602-3
early Christians: w73 51; w71 330, 457-8
Greek word: w75 716-22
Jesus Christ: or 112-13; w71 456-7; g71 12/22 27-8
(SEE ALSO FIELD SERVICE, JEHOVAH'S WITNESSES)

MIRACLES
childbirth: g73 7/8 7-8
clergy disbelief: g75 3/22 30-1
discussion: w71 291-4
end of miraculous gifts: w74 447
extrasensory perception (ESP): w74 323, 326; g74 4/22 27
Jehovah: w72 38-40
Jesus Christ: w75 251; sl 66-8; g74 4/8 11-12; w73 6, 8-17; w72 448; w71 293-6, 439; te 43-5, 59-62, 67-70, 83-8, 112-13; g71 12/22 27-8

those performed in Capernaum: w75 669-70
Lourdes, France: g73 8/8 28
Mary's conception of Jesus: po 136-8; ts 128-9
purpose: w74 447; ts 59; w71 294
reason for belief: g74 1/8 14-15; g74 4/8 25-6; w71 291-4
science: w75 251; w71 292

"MIRACLE WHEAT"
yb75 70-1

MISHNAH
divine name: w71 390

MISSILES
arms race: w75 487; g74 11/8 3-4
statistics: g72 10/8 10
(SEE ALSO WEAPONS)

MISSING LINKS
search for: g71 8/8 30

MISSIONARIES
appreciation for: yb74 63-4; yb73 228, 230
attitude toward assignment: w74 670; yb74 62-3, 240; w73 171; yb73 224; g73 11/8 25-6; yb72 108-9
blessings: g74 11/8 25-6; w73 171-4; g73 5/8 25-6
Christendom's: yb76 75; w75 285; g75 1/8 30-1; g75 3/8 15; w74 656, 677; g74 12/8 14-15; yb73 142-3, 248; g73 8/8 29; g73 12/8 21; g72 6/8 23
become Witnesses: yb74 41-2
China: g75 9/22 21
circuit overseer's visit:
pioneer meeting: yb72 109
discussion: or 143-5
endurance: w73 664-5; yb73 223, 225-8, 231, 235, 237-8, 243, 248, 251-2; w72 479; g72 2/22 11-12
examples in Bible: w74 336-7
experiences:
during revolution (Dominican Republic): yb72 167-8
during Vietnam War: g73 11/8 26
learning new language: g74 8/8 12
service: yb76 247, 249; w75 671; yb74 47-53; g74 5/8 25-6; g74 11/8 25-6; w73 171-4, 663-6; yb73 15, 20, 69-70, 196-203, 223-35, 237-45, 247-9, 251-2, 255; w72 60, 478-9; yb72 111-14, 143-6, 149, 222-4; km 11/72 6; w71 85, 343-4, 475; g71 2/8 25-6
financial support: g74 11/8 25; or 145
German: yb74 240-1
importance of love for people: w74 670
influence: g73 5/8 25-6; yb72 114
language study: yb73 225-7, 229, 234-5, 237-8; yb72 108, 205-6, 226-7
missionary homes: yb74 49-50; yb73 196-7, 203-4, 207, 224-5, 227-34, 237-8, 240-4, 249, 255; yb72 145-6, 149, 172, 175, 177-80, 182, 201, 203, 206, 226, 228-9, 232-3
number: yb76 23; yb75 258; yb74 255; yb73 32
persecution: yb74 53-6, 59-60; w73 172-3, 664-5; w72 342-8; yb72 161-2, 178, 252
(SEE ALSO GILEAD SCHOOL)

MISTAKES
acknowledging: g73 2/8 3-4; w72 643-4; w71 659, 661
overlooking others': g73 1/22 3-4

MOAB(ITES)
destruction: w75 421-3
god of: w72 684-5
location: w75 421
women ensnare Israelites: w73 585-9

MOBS

List by Country

Australia: w72 534
Brazil: yb73 63
Canada: w74 284; w72 148
Czechoslovakia: yb72 138
Dominican Republic: yb72 162
Great Britain: yb73 118, 121
Italy: w73 664-5
Newfoundland: yb76 58
Nicaragua: yb72 179, 186
South Africa: yb76 102, 136-7
United States: yb75 99, 163-4, 169-70, 182-90; w73 661; w72 761; w71 520-1, 722, 730
(SEE ALSO BANS, PERSECUTION)

MODERATION
alcoholic beverages: g73 8/8 25; g71 8/22 26
eating: w74 167-8; g74 9/8 23

MODESTY
discussion: w74 532
dress: w75 500; w74 118-19; g74 3/8 16; w72 757
example: g74 10/22 19-20
exhibiting: w72 756-7

MODULATION
public speaking: sg 160-3

MOHAMMEDANISM
(SEE ISLAM)

MOLECH
god: bi8 1355; kj 258

MOLECULES
protein: g71 4/8 6

MONEY
bankruptcy: g72 3/8 3; g71 2/8 29; g71 3/22 30; g71 4/8 30
banks: g75 6/8 9-13; g71 5/22 29
bartering: g74 1/22 30-1
borrowing: w71 526-7, 766-7
cost of: g75 5/8 30
budgeting: w75 4-6; g74 8/22 7; g71 3/8 8-10; g71 6/22 13-15
coins: g74 3/22 30
cost of printing paper: g75 7/8 31
credit cards: g75 5/8 29-30; g71 2/8 29
debt in world: g75 6/8 11
decimal currency: g71 4/8 30
defined: g75 1/22 17
devaluation: g73 4/8 29; g73 5/8 22-3; w71 470; g71 2/8 29; g71 8/22 3-9; g71 10/22 23-4; g71 11/22 31
discussion: w75 568-75; g71 8/22 3-10; g71 10/22 21-4
disease-causing germs on: g75 7/22 31; g72 5/8 30
dollar: g74 3/8 29; g74 5/8 29; g73 7/8 29; g73 11/22 9-10; g73 12/22 20-2
funds for philanthropic causes: g71 5/22 29
gold coins: g74 4/22 29
gold standard: g73 12/22 20-1; g71 8/22 4-5; g71 10/22 21-3
Great Britain: g71 4/8 30
home bookkeeping: g71 6/22 13-15
inflation: w75 3-6, 567; g75 1/22 19; w74 14-15; yb74 101; g74 1/22 3-8; g74 11/22 30; g73 10/8 8-10; g73 11/22 8-12; g73 12/22 17-23; w71 470; g71 7/8 29; g71 8/22 7-9; g71 10/8 4
interest: g72 3/8 3
International Monetary Fund: g71 8/22 4-8; g71 10/22 21-3
Kuwait:
income per person: g75 7/22 31
lending: w71 526-7, 766-7
love of: w75 569; g75 10/22 31
military spending: g73 12/22 18; g71 8/22 6-8
mina: w73 713
money lust a cause of economic woes (quote): g75 10/22 31
never made a man happy (quote): w75 570
not bring happiness: g74 9/22 10
Papua New Guinea: g75 7/22 23
proper use: w74 419-20
proper view: w75 568-9; w74 380; g74 1/22 8; g74 9/22 10-11
religious fund-raising: g74 11/8 12-13; w72 419-20; w71 505-7; g71 7/22 29-30; g71 8/22 13-14
saving: w75 5-6; g75 8/8 16-18; g74 9/8 30-1
shell money: g75 7/22 23
silver: g74 4/22 29
Solomon Islands: g75 7/22 23
stock market: g74 2/8 30; g74 8/22 30; g74 11/8 29
system failing: g75 6/8 12-13; w74 14-15, 492; g74 1/22 3-5, 8, 30-1; g74 8/8 29; g73 11/8 29; g73 11/22 8-12; g73 12/22 21-3
when valueless: w72 419-22

MONGOLISM
g75 6/22 20-3

MONKS
Roman Catholic: g74 6/22 31; g73 4/8 29
(SEE ALSO NUNS, PRIESTS, ROMAN CATHOLIC CHURCH)

MONOTONY
causes: w71 349-50

MONSOONS
g75 3/8 4-5

MONTH
February:
formerly 30 days: g71 1/8 26

MONTSERRAT
Jehovah's witnesses: yb76 28-9; yb75 28-9; yb74 26-7; yb73 26-7; yb72 36-7
population: yb73 26; yb72 36

MOON

age: g73 5/22 6
description: g73 5/22 5-8
discussion: g73 5/22 4-8
distance from earth: g72 10/22 4
heat: g72 1/22 30
influence on earth and its life: g75 3/8 30; w72 293
litter left on: g73 2/8 31
origin: g74 8/22 14
possibility of life on: g73 5/22 6
quasimoon: g71 11/22 30
reflects light: g73 5/22 8
revolution around earth: g72 10/22 4
rocks from: g74 8/22 14; g73 5/22 8; g72 7/8 29; g71 11/22 8
stood still: g74 1/8 14-15
symbolic: w74 528
travel to: w75 612; og 6; w74 295; g74 8/22 13-16; g73 1/22 29; g73 5/22 4-7; w72 294, 586; g72 7/8 29; g72 10/22 4-5; w71 40; g71 1/8 5; g71 5/8 30; g71 9/22 29; g71 11/22 5-8
(SEE ALSO ASTRONOMY)

MORAL BREAKDOWN

abortion: w75 248
airplane hijackings: g71 6/8 18
arson: g75 6/8 30
attitude toward: w74 389, 392; g74 3/22 4; w73 144; g73 3/22 3-4; g73 4/22 12-13, 30; g73 9/8 5, 7; g71 5/22 30
bombings: g71 4/22 30
burglary: w74 515; g73 4/22 14-15; g72 4/8 3; g72 5/8 30; g72 8/22 29; g72 9/22 30; g72 12/8 31; g71 6/22 30-1
business: g75 7/8 29; g73 4/22 10; g71 2/8 4-5
cargo thefts: g75 5/8 30; g71 6/22 31
causes: w75 36-7; g75 1/8 3-5; w74 100-1, 144-6, 262-3; ts 13-14; g74 3/22 4-6; g74 9/8 9-11; w73 178-9; g73 1/8 30; g73 3/22 3-4; g73 4/22 9-14, 30; g73 10/22 24; w72 262-4; g72 1/8 10, 12; g72 8/22 9; g71 1/22 17-19; g71 10/22 11
cheating: g73 1/8 29; g73 11/8 29
cheating in school: g71 6/22 30
child mistreatment: w75 327
churches: g75 1/8 4; w71 451-2; g71 5/22 7; g71 7/8 30; g71 10/22 30
clergy: w74 100-1, 562; g74 11/22 30; g74 12/22 29-30; g73 2/22 7; w72 453; g72 1/22 29; g72 4/8 22-3; g72 4/22 18-20, 30; g72 6/22 12, 30; g72 8/8 30; g72 9/22 29; g72 12/8 29; w71 451, 557, 628; kj 158-9; g71 5/8 5-6, 30-1; g71 5/22 30; g71 6/8 30; g71 7/8 30; g71 7/22 4-5, 9-10; g71 10/8 31; g71 11/8 30
colleges: g74 11/8 31; g73 2/22 29; g73 11/22 30; g72 8/8 30; g71 6/8 5-6
comments on: w72 261-2; g72 3/8 30-1; g72 7/22 29; g71 6/22 31; g71 8/22 31; g71 9/8 30; g71 10/8 17
crime statistics: w75 35-6; g75 1/8 30; g75 1/22 31; g75 3/22 29, 30; g75 5/8 30; g75 5/22 30; g75 6/8 30; g75 10/22 29; g75 11/22 3-7, 29; w74 99, 102, 341; g74 3/8 30; g74 5/22 29; g74 6/22 30-1; g74 8/8 29; g74 11/8 29; g73 1/8 30; g73 3/8 29; g73 4/22 4-6; g73 9/22 31; g73 10/8 10-11, 21; g73 11/8 30; g73 12/8 30; g72 2/8 31; g71 5/22 30-1; g71 6/8 29; g71 8/8 30; g71 10/8 5; g71 10/22 30; g71 12/8 30
women: w75 464
embezzlement: g75 11/8 29
employee dishonesty: g75 11/8 29-30; w74 341; tp 18; g73 7/22 29; g72 5/22 30; g72 6/22 31; g72 8/22 29; w71 306, 524-5; g71 4/8 13, 29; g71 7/8 29; g71 10/8 13
foretold: w71 587-8
fornication and adultery: g75 6/22 29; w74 389; g74 2/22 31; g74 4/22 4-5, 13; w73 74-5; g73 1/22 28; g73 2/8 30; g73 6/8 30; g73 8/8 29; g73 9/8 24; w72 218-21, 767-8; g72 2/8 17, 19; g72 4/22 18-19, 30; g72 6/22 30; g72 8/22 8-12; g72 9/22 30; g72 12/8 7; kj 158; g71 7/22 30; g71 9/8 29; g71 11/22 29
gambling: g75 8/22 31; w74 135, 579-85; g71 8/22 29; g71 11/8 3, 29-30
homosexuality: w74 390-1, 684; g74 2/8 30; w73 355-6; w72 767-8; g72 4/8 22-3; g72 4/22 18-20; g72 5/22 29; g72 6/8 29; g72 6/22 30; g72 8/8 30; g72 8/22 29; kj 158; g71 5/22 5-6; g71 6/8 30; g71 7/22 4-5, 9-10
illegitimacy: g74 3/22 31; g74 4/22 4-5; g74 8/8 30; g74 8/22 31; w72 218-19; yb72 184; g72 8/22 8-11; g72 9/22 29; g72 10/22 30-1; w71 452; g71 8/8 30-1
increase: g74 6/22 30-1; g74 10/8 30; g74 11/22 29; g73 1/8 30-1; g73 4/22 3-9; w72 263-4; g72 3/22 3-4; g72 6/22 31; g71 2/8 29-30; g71 4/22 30; g71 5/22 30-1; g71 6/8 4-6, 17-20; g71 7/22 30; g71 10/8 5, 30; g71 10/22 30; g71 11/8 29
kidnapping: g75 5/22 6-9
labor unions: g74 6/8 13-15
looting: g74 6/8 10; g74 7/22 30; g73 3/8 15; g73 9/22 31; g72 1/22 30
lying: g75 7/22 30
motion pictures: g73 3/22 4; g71 1/22 16-17; g71 11/8 29
murder: w74 99; g74 6/22 31; g74 9/8 4, 10, 30; g73 3/8 30; w72 480; g72 1/8 15; g72 9/22 4; g71 5/8 31; g71 8/22 29
narcotics: g73 12/8 3-8; w72 339-40; g72 4/22 31; g72 5/8 30; g72 7/8 30; g72 8/22 3-4; g72 9/8 29; w71 247-51; g71 3/8 30; g71 4/8 16-18; g71 5/8 30; g71 5/22 30; g71 6/8 6; g71 6/22 29-30; g71 7/8 30; g71 9/8 29; g71 10/8 7-8, 28, 31; g71 11/22 29; g71 12/22 30
"new morality": g75 6/22 29
organized crime: g75 3/8 30
permissiveness: g75 1/8 3-5
pickpockets: g71 11/8 3
police: g72 3/22 3
assaults on: g71 2/22 16-18
strike: w72 261
politics: g75 11/8 21-2; g73 1/8 30; g73 11/8 3-5
pornography: g75 12/22 29; yb73 10-11; g73 5/8 4; g72 12/8 29; g71 1/22 16-19
prisons: g72 1/8 8-9
prostitution: g72 3/22 30; w71 452; g71 6/8 29
rape: g75 2/22 30; w74 99; g74 1/8 30; g74 3/8 13, 16; g73 4/8 30; g71 10/22 30
results: g73 3/22 11
runaways:
adults: g75 10/22 29
schools: g74 2/8 4-6
shoplifting: g75 3/22 7; g75 6/22 30; g74 1/22 7; g73 4/22 4, 7-8; g73 12/8 30; g72 3/22 30; g72 7/22 30-1; g72 12/8 30; g71 1/8 30; g71 1/22 29; g71 9/22 30; g71 11/22 29
number per year: g75 9/8 31
small town: g74 7/8 30
Soviet Union: g75 8/22 30-1
stealing: g75 8/8 29-30; g75 10/8 30; g75 12/22 30; g74 5/8 29; g74 7/8 31; g74 12/8 5; g74 12/22 30; w73 451; tp 18; g73 2/22 29; g73 3/8 15; g73 3/22 30; g73 4/22 4, 7-8, 10-11; g73 5/22 29; g73 11/8 30; pm 210-14; w71 306; g71 4/8 13, 29; g71 7/8 29; g71 10/8 31; g71 11/8 3
"stealing time": g75 3/8 29
tax-evasion: w72 451-2
truck hijackings: g71 6/22 31
unnatural sex acts: w75 48; w72 734-6
vandalism: g75 2/8 29-31; g75 5/22 29; g74 8/22 3-6; g71 4/22 31
venereal disease: g75 7/22 29; w74 424; g74 3/22 31; g74 4/22 30; g74 8/8 30; g74 9/22 30; g73 5/8 4; g73 9/22 30-1; w72 219, 339; g72 2/8 17-20; g72 10/22 31; kj 158-9; g71 1/8 30; g71 1/22 29; g71 3/22 30; g71 5/8 30; g71 7/8 31; g71 8/22 29; g71 9/8 29; g71 12/8 30
wife beating: g75 9/8 29-30
youth: w75 37, 390; g75 3/8 29; g75 5/22 29; g75 9/8 30; w74 262-3, 267; g74 1/22 31; g74 2/8 4-6; g74 8/22 3-6; g74 9/8 10; g74 11/8 10; w73 136, 552-3, 558-9; g73 2/8 30; g73 3/22 30; g73 5/8 30; g73 10/22 24; w72 218-21; g72 2/22 29-30; g72 6/8 29-30; g72 9/22 30; w71 517; g71 1/22 23; g71 3/22 30; g71 6/8 29; g71 9/8 29; g71 10/22 11
rock music: w75 390; g75 7/22 29; g72 5/22 23; w71 403-4
(SEE ALSO CRIME, JUVENILE DELINQUENCY)

MORALS

Bible's standards: w74 483-6; w73 574-6; w72 35-6; w71 451-3
challenge of principles: w72 515-16, 548
Christendom: w74 562-3; g74 5/8 30; w71 451-2
Common Catechism: g75 5/22 29
Christian standard: g75 1/8 5-6; w74 10-13, 340; g74 5/8 30; w71 119
evolution's effect on: g73 10/22 21, 24
importance to Christians:

w74 340; w73 69-75, 589-96; w72 583
need of a guide: g74 4/22 13-14
personal: g72 3/22 3-4
rock music's effect on: w75 390
television's effect on: g74 9/8 9; g73 3/22 3-4

MORDECAI
name: w71 175
prophetic drama: w71 172-85

MORIAH (Mount)
w74 79

MORMONS (Latter-day Saints)
evolution theory: g74 7/8 23
racism: w74 656; g74 12/8 30

MOROCCO
Jehovah's witnesses: yb76 28-9; yb75 8, 28-9; yb74 28-9; yb73 28-9; yb72 38-9
population: yb73 28; yb72 38

MORRISON, ROBERT
w74 744-5

MOSAIC LAW
(SEE COVENANTS)

MOSES
age: g73 1/22 10
anointing: po 107-8
Bible writer: g73 3/22 16-17; g72 2/22 27-8; w71 228, 409-10; sg 16
circumcision of his son: w75 415-16
comparison with Jesus: po 147-51
example of faithful service: w73 158, 452; km 8/73 2; w71 572-3; g71 1/22 28
mediator: po 109-10; w72 682-3; g72 2/8 5-6; kj 25
Mt. Sinai: po 109-10
name: kj 13
offered himself as leader: po 107
plagues on Egypt: w74 333; kj 16-19
prophetic significance: po 110-12, 147-51; g72 2/8 5-6; w71 242
Psalm 91: w74 722
sent to Egypt: w71 650; kj 14-15; te 20-1
slow of tongue: w73 531
spoke with God face-to-face: w74 310
transfiguration: w74 297

MOSLEMS
(SEE ISLAM)

MOST HOLY
Babylonians invade: kj 135
contents: w72 745
dimensions: w72 710
symbolic: ka 99-100; w72 711, 716-17, 719, 721
when entered: w74 176, 221-3

MOTHER
dedicated son: w72 446-7
experiences:
integrity: w71 532
pioneering: yb72 53-4; w71 339
role in child training: w75 434, 436; w74 85; tp 176; km 2/73 8; w72 270-1; g72 5/22 6-7, 10-11; w71 104; g71 9/8 8-11
secular work: g74 1/22 31
(SEE ALSO CHILDBIRTH, CHILD TRAINING, WIFE)

"MOTHER OF GOD"
w75 539-40

MOTHS
g74 9/8 14; g75 3/22 13-14
(SEE ALSO INSECTS)

MOTION PICTURES
churches: g71 10/22 30
clergy: g71 3/8 31
crime and morals: g75 1/8 30; g74 3/8 15; g73 4/8 31; w71 606; g71 1/22 16-18; g71 10/22 30; g71 11/8 29
decline: g72 1/8 30
influence of: w73 144; g73 3/22 4
selectivity in attending: w74 153; g74 3/8 31
Watch Tower Society's films: yb75 231-2; yb72 102-4, 183, 226, 228, 243, 245

List by Name
"God Cannot Lie": yb75 232; yb73 207
"Happiness of the New World Society: yb76 197; yb73 203
"Heritage": yb75 232
"Photo-Drama of Creation": yb76 34-5, 48-9, 82, 244; yb75 58-60; yb73 96-8; yb72 131; w71 377
"Proclaiming 'Everlasting Good News' Around the World": yb75 231
"The New World Society in Action": yb76 191, 195, 197; yb75 231-2; yb73 179
"The Sorrow and the Pity": w72 515

MOTIVE
heart: w71 134-9; sg 74-7
importance of proper: w73 138-9
self-examination: w74 566
understanding others' motives: w73 478-9

MOTORCYCLES
accidents: g75 5/8 30; g74 9/22 31
dangers: g72 11/22 30-1
sales: g74 9/22 30-1

MOTORS
g72 8/8 29-30

MOUNTAINS
climbing: g75 7/22 30
copper: pm 222-5
highest, measured from center of earth: g75 10/8 31
hiking: g75 9/22 29
Sherpa village: g75 11/22 17-21
"survival" hideaway in: g75 10/22 31
symbolic: sl 217, 297-8, 304, 313, 320; pm 223-4, 374-80

List by Name
Andes: g75 3/22 26
Carmel: w74 79
Chimborazo: g75 10/8 31
Everest: g75 7/22 30; g75 9/8 29
Gilboa: g72 11/8 11
Hermon: w74 78
Himalayas: g75 11/22 17-21; g74 2/22 31
Moriah: w74 79
Mount of Olives: w74 79; pm 377
Tabor: g72 11/8 11
Telescope Peak: g71 2/8 7
Vesuvius: g71 2/8 20
Whitney: g71 2/8 7
Zion: po 89; ts 130

MOURNING
'better to mourn': ts 15-16; g74 12/8 27-8
cuttings upon the flesh: g74 12/8 27
death of loved ones: g74 12/8 26-8
discussion: g74 12/8 26-8
funerals: ts 22, 61-2
"happy are those who mourn": g71 6/22 27-8
wakes: g74 12/8 26
wearing black: g74 12/8 27
(SEE ALSO DEAD, DEATH)

MOUTH
bad breath: g71 9/8 24-6

MOUTH-TO-MOUTH RESUSCITATION
g73 7/22 8-12

MOVIES
(SEE MOTION PICTURES)

MOVING
discussion: g75 7/8 16-19
emigration: g71 12/8 21-3
principles of packing: g75 7/8 17-18
South America: g72 7/22 13-16

MOZAMBIQUE
independence: g75 8/8 31
Jehovah's witnesses: yb76 20-1, 30-1, 98, 115-18, 178; yb75 9-10, 28-9; yb74 15-17, 28-9; w73 266-8; yb73 28-9; w72 390; yb72 38-9
persecution: yb76 19-21, 178
population: yb76 114; yb73 28; yb72 38
refugees: g75 12/8 3, 5, 7; yb74 15-17; g74 6/22 25; w73 266-8; g73 3/8 19, 23-34; g73 8/22 30

MULTIPLE SCLEROSIS
discussion: g72 2/22 9-12
truth gives hope to victim of: g75 8/8 26

MURDER
abortion: g75 6/8 30; g73 12/22 28; g71 2/22 29
Bible definition: g74 5/8 27
Bible penalty: g75 11/22 10, 26-8; g74 7/22 27-8; w73 300-8; w72 480
by friends and relatives: g75 11/22 4-5
causes: w75 36; g75 4/22 31; g73 3/8 30; w72 707
children: g72 12/8 30
demonism: g75 5/22 30
examples: g75 11/22 8-10; g72 1/8 15
forgiveness possible for: g75 11/22 28
legal case over fetus death: g75 6/8 30
"mercy killing": g74 5/8 27-8
"plea bargaining": g75 11/22 9-10
pollution: g71 4/22 24
ritual: yb76 160, 194
Satan: ts 80

g, Awake!; **ka**, God's Kingdom of a Thousand Years; **kj**, "The Nations Shall Know that I Am Jehovah"; **km**, Kingdom Ministry; **or**, Organization; **pm**, Paradise Restored—By Theocracy!; **po**, God's "Eternal Purpose"; **sg**, Theocratic School Guidebook; **sl**, Man's Salvation out of World Distress!; **te**, Listening to the Great Teacher; **tp**, True Peace and Security; **ts**, Is This Life All There Is?; **w**, Watchtower; **yb**, Yearbook. **Complete list on page 6.**

statistics: g75 11/22 3-7; w74 99; g74 6/22 31; g74 7/22 30; g74 9/8 4, 30; g73 3/8 30; g72 9/22 4; g72 10/8 30; g71 5/8 31; g71 8/22 29
unsolved, in ancient Israel: g75 11/22 27
victims: w75 36
youth: g74 9/8 10
(SEE ALSO CRIME, MORAL BREAKDOWN)

MURMURING
Bible examples: w71 147

MUSEUMS
Leningrad, Soviet Union: g74 2/8 31
Museum of Sea, Venezuela: g74 3/8 23
Oregon Museum of Science and Industry: g75 4/8 29
Taiwan National Palace Museum: g73 8/8 12-15
thefts: g75 4/8 29

MUSHROOMS
poisonous: w72 596; g71 8/8 30

MUSIC
ancient Israel: w75 30
avant-garde: g75 4/8 31
Beethoven: g74 8/8 24
childbirth aided by: g75 7/8 30
communication: w74 302
composing: g74 8/8 24-6
conductor breaks arm: w72 547
congregation singing: w75 29-31
country: g75 8/22 30
decline in quality: g72 7/22 31; g71 5/22 11-12
decline of classical: g73 3/8 30; g71 9/8 30
dirges: w73 746
discussion: w74 301-4
dissonance: g72 5/22 20-1
divine name in: g71 3/22 10
effect on animals: g71 12/22 29
effect on musicians of loud: g75 4/8 31
effect on people: w74 262, 301-4; w72 569; w71 403-4
electronic: g72 5/22 22
elements of: g74 8/8 25-6
experiences:
career rejected: g74 2/8 24-6; g73 2/8 15
Kingdom song: w75 31
folk music: g71 3/22 9-12; g71 9/8 19-20
Handel: g74 8/8 24
Hawaiian: g73 6/8 12-14
hearing loss: g74 3/22 31
improvisation: g74 8/8 24-6
India: g74 8/8 24
instruments: g73 6/8 13-14; g71 2/22 20-3; g71 9/8 19
jazz: g74 8/8 26; g72 5/22 21
Vatican radio: g75 8/8 29
Kingdom song recordings appreciated: w72 405
Lesotho buses: g71 7/22 26
listening: g72 11/22 10-11
modern: ts 13; g72 5/22 20-3
national anthem: w74 62-3
obscene lyrics: g75 8/22 30
orchestra credited: g72 2/22 4
Peru: g72 3/8 20-3
reflects despair: w75 57; ts 13
rock 'n' roll: w75 390, 504; g75 6/8 30; g75 7/22 29; g75 10/22 31; w74 262, 303-4; g74 6/22 13-14; g73 2/8 15; w72 567-9; g72 4/8 30; g72 5/22 21-3; w71 403-4; g71 2/8 30; g71 3/22 12; g71 11/8 30; g71 12/22 29
selectivity: w74 303-4
song festival: g71 5/22 11-12
tape recordings pirated: g71 1/22 29
theme: sg 135
theocratic: w75 29-31; yb74 96-7
United Nations: g72 3/8 5
use in religion: g74 11/8 30; g73 1/8 29; g72 10/8 29; w71 403, 643-4; g71 3/8 29

MUSK OX
g74 8/22 24-6

MUSSOLINI, BENITO
Catholic church: w75 364

MUSTARD SEED (Illustration)
w75 589-90, 595-8, 600-1, 604-5; sl 206-9

MUTATIONS
evolution theory: g75 6/8 30; g74 9/22 22-4; g73 2/8 6; g73 10/22 12-15

MYSTERY
'mystery of lawlessness': w75 252-3
"sacred secret": po 156-7, 166-8

MYTHS
attributed to Bible wrongly: g75 10/8 10-11
Babylonish origin: ts 27-9
distortions of Bible account: w72 428
Greek: ts 26; w71 509-10; bi8 1366

NAAMAN
discussion: w74 402-4, 406
healed of leprosy: w72 602; te 107-9

NABONIDUS CHRONICLE
discussion: w71 315-16

NAGGING
g71 3/8 10

NAMES
Africa: g72 5/8 31; g72 7/8 24-6
Bible: w71 58-9
good name with Jehovah: w74 532-3
Greek word: w73 103
Jehovah: fu 9-10; w74 433, 728-9; g73 1/22 26; g73 3/22 27-8; w72 31, 54-7, 748; pm 388-9; yb72 113; w71 387-91, 453-5, 465, 627, 645-59; kj 7-8, 11-12, 14-21, 25-7, 32-5, 53, 313, 315-16, 323-6, 328, 371, 406-7; te 19-22; g71 9/8 20
Jesus: w73 102-4, 287; w72 237; pm 388; w71 455, 654
meaningful: w71 58-9
value of good name: ts 15-16; w73 156-7, 287; w72 517; w71 387-8, 645-6

NAOMI
name: w72 77
prophetic drama: w72 76-90

NAPOLEON BONAPARTE
comments on Christendom's missionaries: g75 9/22 21
comments on Jesus Christ: w75 250

NARCOTICS
addiction: g74 6/22 13; g73 12/8 3-15; g72 9/8 29; w71 247-51; g71 1/22 30; g71 4/8 16-18; g71 5/22 30; g71 7/8 30; g71 10/8 7-8, 28, 31
Bible view: g74 5/8 4-8; w73 287, 336-8, 340-3; tp 160-2; w71 248-51
cocaine: g73 4/8 30
cost: g73 9/22 29; g73 12/8 3, 6
crime: g73 4/22 9; g73 12/8 3-4, 6, 11-12
dogs: g72 2/8 31
effects: g74 7/8 30; g73 12/8 3-4, 6-7, 9, 11-13; g72 5/8 30; g72 6/22 31; g72 8/22 3-4; w71 247-8; g71 2/8 20; g71 4/8 17-18; g71 5/22 30; g71 6/22 30; g71 7/8 30; g71 11/22 29
heroin: tp 160; g73 12/8 6, 11; g72 5/8 30; g71 3/22 30-1; g71 4/8 18; g71 6/22 29; g71 10/8 31
LSD: g74 5/8 5, 7-8; g73 12/8 6, 11-13
marijuana: w74 394; g74 3/8 31; g74 3/22 30; g74 5/8 5-6; g73 5/22 30; g73 12/8 6-7; g72 2/8 30; g72 6/22 31; g72 7/8 30; w71 247-8, 250, 526; g71 2/8 20; g71 3/8 30; g71 4/8 17-18; g71 5/22 30; g71 6/22 30; g71 10/8 7; g71 11/22 29
opium: g75 5/8 10-11; w72 444
trafficking: g72 9/8 29
youth: g74 2/8 5-6; g74 5/8 3-8; g73 12/8 3-5, 7-15
(SEE ALSO DRUGS, MORAL BREAKDOWN)

NATHAN (Prophet)
reproof of David: g72 7/8 7

NATIONAL ANTHEM
Bible view: w74 62-3
Britain: w75 614; og 9
(SEE ALSO FLAG SALUTE)

NATIONAL COUNCIL OF CHURCHES
comments on politics: g73 12/22 29
laymen: g71 4/8 29
League of Nations: w74 135; w72 189, 198; pm 138; w71 560; kj 60-1
politics: g74 1/22 29
problems: g74 1/22 29
woman secretary: g73 12/22 29
(SEE ALSO WORLD COUNCIL OF CHURCHES)

NATIONALISM
beginning: w74 597
Bible view: w75 496-8
early Christians: w75 497
experience:
former military man accepts truth: g74 10/22 11
flag salute: w75 217; g71 9/8 12-15
increase: g73 2/8 30
Jehovah's witnesses: w74 734; g73 8/22 13-14
national entities always look after themselves: w75 516
Olympic Games: g73 2/22 13-15; g72 10/22 29
results: w75 612; og 5; g75 3/22 4, 29; w74 734; g74 4/8 19, 31; g73 10/8 13; g71 3/8 13-14
symbolic representation: w74 733-4
World War I: g73 6/22 10-11
World War II: yb75 182

Quotations

divides humanity into mutually intolerant units: w75 496

many problems due to narrow nationalism—'my country, right or wrong': w75 496

(SEE ALSO FLAG SALUTE, NEUTRALITY, PATRIOTISM)

NATIONS

Christian neutrality: w72 753

collision with God: g73 10/8 22-5; w72 31; w71 611-31; nc 3-29

destruction: w71 623-6; nc 26-8

fight against God: w71 622-3; nc 24-5

industrial:

problems: g75 8/22 17-20

interdependence among: w75 613; og 7

issue of world domination: w71 614-15; nc 6-8

Kingdom-preaching shakes: w75 361-2

poor nations: g74 12/8 8-11

post millennium: ka 152-3

treaties made: w71 299-300

when judged civilized: g71 4/8 11

Quotation

refuse an authority that can tell them what to do in the international arena: w75 516

(SEE ALSO APPOINTED TIMES OF THE NATIONS, GOVERNMENTS, "THE NATIONS SHALL KNOW THAT I AM JEHOVAH"—HOW?)

NATURE

Greek word: w73 140-1

learning from: ts 146-7

(SEE ALSO CREATION)

NAVIGATION

birds: w75 71; g75 2/8 29

insects: g75 2/8 29

NAZARETH

Jesus' hometown: po 143; g72 11/8 11; te 111-12

NAZISM

Catholic church: g72 4/22 16-17; g72 8/8 30; g71 12/8 3-4

concordat: w75 398

suppression of book on role in World War II: w75 715

clergy responsibility: g75 7/8 30

concentration camps: yb74 118-19, 193-208

euthanasia program: w75 294

Gestapo: yb74 138, 140-1, 143-8, 150-60

Himmler: yb74 174, 195-7, 202, 205, 211

Hitler: ka 8-9; g73 1/22 5-6; g71 12/8 3-4

mass murder: w75 294; yb74 205-7

persecution of Witnesses: yb75 174; g75 2/22 22; yb74 108-28, 132-90, 193-204, 210-12, 238; w73 572-3; w72 143-4, 395-9; yb72 134-6; g72 4/22 22-3

racism: w73 515

Thousand-Year Plan: ka 7-9

Vatican aids escape of Nazis: w75 48

Vatican view of atrocities: g75 2/22 17-23

Witness victory over: w75 85; yb74 210-12, 216, 238, 249-51

youth: w71 370

(SEE ALSO CONCENTRATION CAMPS, HITLER, PERSECUTION)

NEATNESS

km 1/75 3

NEBUCHADNEZZAR

conquest of Ammon: w73 61-2; kj 235-6

divination: w73 60; kj 224-6

dream image: w75 620-1; sl 310-13; og 23-4; pm 375-6; w71 619-24; nc 18-27

dream tree: po 176; ts 152-3, 156-9; tp 74-6

Hebrews thrown into furnace: w72 141; te 139-42

image made for worship: w72 141; w71 116-17

insanity: w73 644-5; ka 9-11

Jerusalem, siege and destruction, 609-7 B.C.E.: w73 60-1; w72 470-1, 587, 745, 764-5; g72 3/8 27; kj 96-7, 105-11, 128, 137-9, 163-4, 261-3, 266-7, 285-6, 351

recognition of Jehovah: w73 645-6

rewarded for destroying Tyre: w75 714

siege of Tyre: pm 263

worship of Marduk (Merodach): kj 224

NEBUZARADAN

g72 3/8 27

NEEDLE

infections: g73 12/8 15

NEGEB

w74 624

NEGLECT

religion: g72 9/22 25

NEGROES

examples of prejudice against: w74 707-10

hair style: g72 8/22 30

segregation: g73 2/22 4-5

NEIGHBOR

fear of: w74 201-3

love for: g75 7/22 3-4; w74 120-5, 409, 676; g74 7/8 4; g74 10/8 24; w72 69, 726-9; or 111-12; te 35-8

NEPAL

Jehovah's witnesses: yb76 26-7; yb75 26-7; yb74 26-7; yb73 26-7; yb72 36-7

pollution: g74 2/22 31

population: yb73 26; yb72 36

Sherpas: g75 11/22 17-21

NEPHILIM

discussion: po 73-6

identified: w72 651-2

meaning of term: po 74; w72 651

NERO

Christians in household: w72 592

persecution of Christians: g72 6/8 13

NERVES

breakdown: g74 8/22 16-19

NERVOUS SYSTEM

human body: g74 8/22 16-19; g72 10/22 8; g72 11/8 23

starfish: g72 10/22 8

NEST(S)

birds: g71 6/22 12; g71 7/22 13-15

NETHERLANDS

crime: g73 12/8 30

history: g72 9/22 21-5

imports: g74 11/22 19

Jehovah's witnesses: yb76 28-9; yb75 28-9; yb74 28-9; yb73 28-9; yb72 38-9; g72 4/8 24; w71 376

military service: w74 604-5; g74 12/8 22-5

population: yb73 28; yb72 38

rains: g75 1/22 29

religion: g75 6/22 31; g74 9/8 31; g73 3/22 31; g73 9/8 4-5; g72 4/8 21-4; g72 9/22 21-5; g71 7/22 4-5, 8

Witkars: g75 2/22 24-5

women: g72 5/22 4

NETHERLANDS ANTILLES (Curaçao)

Jehovah's witnesses: yb76 28-9; yb75 28-9; yb74 28-9; yb73 28-9; yb72 38-9

population: yb73 28; yb72 38

NETHINIM

prophetic significance: sl 162, 167

NEUTRALITY

Bible view: w75 496-8; w74 62-3; w73 741; w71 307-8, 465-6

examples:

modern-day: yb76 18-22, 211, 213, 218-19, 236, 251; yb75 11, 205-8; w74 517-21, 604-5; yb74 10, 14, 115-19, 123-4, 163, 166-8, 183, 186-9, 196, 198, 204-5, 230; g74 11/8 29; g74 12/8 22; w73 28-9, 264-6, 411, 476; g73 3/22 15; g73 12/8 29; w72 520, 532; yb72 124; g72 4/22 22-3; w71 187, 489-90, 532; g71 12/22 24

issue clarified: w74 734, 762; w71 720

maintaining: w71 151

violators of Christian: w72 124

Witnesses during World War I: yb75 97, 101, 103, 119; yb74 82-3; yb73 98-100

Witnesses during World War II: sl 188; yb75 182, 205-7; w74 734; yb73 162-4; w72 753; pm 334; w71 721-2

(SEE ALSO MILITARY SERVICE)

NEVIS

Jehovah's witnesses: yb76 28-9; yb75 28-9; yb74 28-9; yb73 26-7; yb72 38-9

population: yb73 26; yb72 38

NEW BRITAIN

Jehovah's witnesses: yb76 28-9; yb75 28-9; yb74 28-9; yb73 28-9; yb72 38-9

population: yb73 28; yb72 38

NEW CALEDONIA

Jehovah's witnesses: yb76 24-5; yb75 24-5; w74 648-9; yb74 24-5; yb73 24-5; w72 390; yb72 34-5

population: yb73 24; yb72 34

g, Awake!; **ka**, God's Kingdom of a Thousand Years; **kj**, "The Nations Shall Know that I Am Jehovah"; **km**, Kingdom Ministry; **or**, Organization; **pm**, Paradise Restored—By Theocracy!; **po**, God's "Eternal Purpose"; **sg**, Theocratic School Guidebook; **sl**, Man's Salvation out of World Distress!; **te**, Listening to the Great Teacher; **tp**, True Peace and Security; **ts**, Is This Life All There Is?; **w**, Watchtower; **yb**, Yearbook. **Complete list on page 6.**

NEW COVENANT
(SEE COVENANTS)

NEW EARTH
administration: kj 404-6
land division: kj 399-401
nucleus: sl 358
significance of term: w75 261, 747, 752; sl 324-5; w74 292; g74 4/8 12; g74 8/8 11; w73 360-1; w72 238-40, 287; g71 4/22 23

NEWFOUNDLAND
Jehovah's witnesses: yb76 28-9, 47-67; yb75 28-9; yb74 28-9; yb73 28-9; yb72 38-9
population: yb76 47; yb73 28; yb72 38

NEW GUINEA
air travel: g73 4/8 24-6
betel nut: w74 742
Jehovah's witnesses: yb76 28-9; yb75 28-9; yb74 28-9; yb73 28-9; yb72 38-9
population: yb73 28; yb72 38
trees: g72 3/8 26

NEW HEAVENS
significance of term: w75 261, 747, 752; sl 321-3; g74 4/8 12; g74 8/8 11; w73 360-1; w72 231-8; g71 4/22 23

NEW HEBRIDES
Jehovah's witnesses: yb76 24-5; yb75 24-5; w74 649; yb74 24-5; yb73 24-5; yb72 34-5
population: yb73 24; yb72 34

NEW IRELAND
Jehovah's witnesses: yb76 28-9; yb75 28-9; yb74 28-9; yb73 28-9; yb72 38-9
population: yb73 28; yb72 38

NEW JERUSALEM
comes down out of heaven: ka 150
discussion: w75 490-2; pm 149-53
identified: w74 599
temple: w72 720
(SEE ALSO CONGREGATION OF GOD, KINGDOM)

NEW ORDER (Jehovah's, After Armageddon)
blessings: w75 88-90, 263, 683; gc 28; w74 4; ts 133-4, 136-40, 142-3; g74 3/22 6; g74 4/8 9-15; w73 78-9, 363-4; tp 43-5, 101-10; g73 4/22 19-21; g73 10/8 25-9; w72 227, 240, 243-5, 496; g72 4/22 26-7; g72 5/22 17; g72 6/8 7-8; g72 7/22 12-13; g72 10/8 18-19; te 179-82; g71 4/22 25-7
death no more: ts 137-9, 164-6; tp 104-6
freedom from crime: w75 35-8
freedom from injustice: w75 164
freedom from want: g74 4/8 12; tp 102-4; g73 11/22 12; kj 397
healing of handicapped: ts 138-9
health: gc 25-6; g75 10/8 23-4; w74 134; ts 137-9; g74 4/8 11-12, 15; g74 5/8 28; g74 9/8 23; w73 412-15; tp 104-7; g73 4/22 21; g71 10/8 25
land distribution: w75 379; g74 6/22 10
land produce: ts 135-7; g74 6/22 10-11
no food shortage: w75 262; gc 25; ts 134-7
peace: gc 23-4; w74 240; g74 4/8 9-13; tp 7-8; g71 10/8 24
perfection: ts 139-40, 144, 165-6; g74 4/8 14; g73 10/8 26-7; w71 500, 539
pollution eliminated: g74 6/22 10
resurrection: w75 89-90, 262; fu 24; gc 26-7; ka 120-2, 125-31; tp 107-8; g72 6/8 7
righteousness: w75 261-2; w74 293-4
security: fu 21-5; g75 11/22 16; w74 101, 240; g74 4/8 9-13; tp 102-4
unity: w74 623; hu 28
Christ as King: w75 262; w72 463
discussion: w75 745-58; w72 227-40, 243-5, 247-9
education: w74 293-4; ts 144-50
evidence that near: w74 51-3
government: w74 292; ts 132; w73 425-8; w72 273; w71 634-5; g71 10/8 22-4
inheritance: w73 495
initial conditions: w73 364, 366-70
knowledge: ts 145-8, 150
language: w73 530; ka 49-50; g71 2/22 10
laws: g72 1/8 17
love: ts 149-50
meaning of term: w71 347
"new earth": w75 747, 752; w73 292, 360-1; w72 238-40; g71 4/22 23
New Order society: w71 347
not boring: ts 144-50
overpopulation no problem: ts 134-7; g74 6/22 10-11; tp 108-9
peace with animals: w75 606-8; ts 142; ka 144-5
perfection: ts 139-40, 144
personality changes: w73 366-7; ka 142-3, 145-6
pollution eliminated: g71 4/22 25-8
preparing for life in: w75 378-9, 752-8; w73 75-82, 360-76; w72 247-51, 273; w71 633-5
princes: ts 132; ka 131-6, 153-4
questions concerning: w73 361-2, 371
requirements for life: w75 751-8; tp 111-19
unintentional sin: ts 139-40
value of hope in: g75 2/22 4, 11
wicked removed from: ts 185
work: g75 10/8 26-7; w72 463; g71 4/22 26-7; g71 10/8 24-5
(SEE ALSO KINGDOM, PARADISE)

NEW PERSONALITY
(SEE PERSONALITY)

NEW SONG
discussion (Ps 98:1): w73 622-3; dy 25-8
identified: w73 401

NEWSPAPERS
computer: g71 10/22 30
editing: g73 12/8 31
foreign-language: g72 4/8 29
Jehovah's witnesses:
comments on growth: yb75 21
comments on Witness conduct: w74 149, 152, 632, 635, 637-9, 645-6; g74 3/8 29; g74 9/8 6-7; g74 10/8 29; g74 11/8 17-21; g74 11/22 31; g74 12/8 4-5; yb73 198, 230; w71 13-14, 91, 595-9, 601; g71 3/22 26; g71 10/22 13-15
misrepresentation: yb73 107-8, 117, 122, 125; yb72 160
persecution criticized: yb72 186, 188-90
use by: yb73 152, 161, 193; g71 5/8 16
Witness interviewed: g74 11/8 29
publication ceased: g72 9/22 31
religious news: g75 5/8 29
Sunday magazines: g75 2/8 30
use in witnessing: yb74 70, 74
Watch Tower Society's syndicate: yb75 46-7

NEWTON, ISAAC
book *The Religion of Isaac Newton:* w75 651
discoveries: w75 651
statements on God's existence: g75 4/22 17; g75 8/22 26; w74 643

NEW WORLD
(SEE NEW ORDER)

NEW WORLD BIBLE TRANSLATION COMMITTEE
yb75 219; w74 767-8

NEW WORLD TRANSLATION OF THE HOLY SCRIPTURES
divine name: bi8 1352-5, 1358-60
features: w74 361-2
French: yb75 16
German edition: yb74 247; yb73 9, 13; g72 6/8 29
languages: yb75 220-1
presenting, in field service: km 5/75 4; km 11/75 4
release:
first portion (Greek Scriptures): yb75 213, 219
one-volume (1961) edition: yb75 220
1971 Revision (large-print edition): yb72 42; w71 608; g71 10/22 15
translation committee: w74 767-8
(SEE ALSO BIBLE TRANSLATIONS)

NEW YEAR'S DAY
w74 32

NEW YORK CITY
(SEE UNITED STATES OF AMERICA)

NEW ZEALAND
climate: g75 10/8 30
Fiordland National Park: g75 9/8 21-3
illegitimacy: g74 4/22 4-5; g74 8/8 30
immigration: g71 2/8 29
Jehovah's witnesses: yb76 28-9; yb75 12, 28-9; km 4/75 1; yb74 28-9; w73 52-3; yb73 28-9; w72 319, 533; yb72 38-9; g72 9/22 26
juvenile delinquency: g71 9/8 29
population: yb73 28; yb72 38
religion: g74 8/8 30

NICARAGUA
description: yb72 171-3, 177, 179-81
earthquake: w75 341-2; w73 95-6, 134-5; g73 2/8 29; g73 3/8 12-16
Jehovah's witnesses: yb76 28-9; yb75 21-2, 28-9; yb74 28-9; yb73 28-9; g73 3/8 13-16; yb72 38-9, 172-95; w71 679, 732; g71 5/8 26

population: yb73 28; yb72 38
religion: yb72 173-4
stump processing: g74 11/8 23

NICENE COUNCIL
Constantine: kj 103
Constantine summoned: g73 1/8 17
spiritism possibility: g71 2/22 26
Trinity adopted: g73 1/8 16-17

NICODEMUS
w73 7

NIGER
Jehovah's witnesses: yb76 28-9; yb75 28-9; yb74 28-9; yb73 28-9; yb72 38-9
population: yb73 28; yb72 38

NIGERIA
census: g74 6/8 11-12
crime: g74 9/22 31
deaths from auto accidents: g75 2/22 31
drug abuse: g74 12/8 29
famines: g75 2/22 9
Jehovah's witnesses: yb76 28-9; w75 760-3; yb75 8-9, 28-9; w74 206; yb74 11, 28-9; g74 3/8 20; km 3/74 1; w73 171-2; yb73 19, 28-9; g73 9/22 15; w72 318-19, 520; yb72 38-9, 44; km 12/72 4-5; w71 12-13, 155-7; g71 7/8 18-20, 23; g71 9/8 17-18
 printery (Watch Tower): yb74 11; g73 9/22 15
languages: w75 760
moral breakdown: g71 11/8 29
polygamy: w75 200
population: w75 760; g74 6/8 11-12; yb73 28; yb72 38
religion: w75 263; g72 3/8 31; g71 9/8 16-18; g71 10/22 29
 Moslems die on pilgrimage: g75 10/8 30
robbers executed: g71 6/22 31
soil erosion: g74 5/8 29-30
transportation: g72 3/8 24-6

NIMROD
aims: w74 41, 597
Apollo identified with: kj 157
city builder: ka 22-3; w72 428, 653
hunter: w75 580; w72 573; w71 648
rebel: w74 41; w72 572
Tammuz identified with: w72 572-3; kj 150-2
used by Satan: po 84

1914
"appointed times of the nations": sl 8, 41, 198, 316; w74 163-5; po 174-7; ts 155; w73 645; tp 74-6; g73 10/8 17-18; w72 187-8; pm 72, 74, 129, 331-2, 368; kj 57-8, 73, 105, 345-6, 352-3, 356-7
 end of times: w75 661
changes since: g73 6/22 10-12; g73 10/8 16-17, 20-22; g71 1/22 11; g71 10/8 15-17
end of seven times: w73 645; ka 186, 259-61; tp 74-6
 C. T. Russell: yb75 37
Kingdom's establishment: sl 41-2, 103-4, 190, 316; w74 236-7, 356-7, 398, 622; hu 25; w73 645; ka 164-5, 210, 228; g73 10/8 17-18; kj 232-5, 346, 353-4
 advance announcement: yb76 79-80, 82; yb75 75; w73 402; g73 1/22 8; g73 10/8 17-18; w71 68-9, 467-8, 560
 chronology: po 174-7; g73 10/8 17-18
 world events in 1914: yb74 78-9; g73 10/8 16-17, 20
preaching: yb75 85
time of the end: w75 750; g74 4/8 17-18; tp 73-8; g73 6/22 10-12; w72 582-3; g72 10/8 15
views of individual Witnesses during 1914: yb75 72-4
world conditions before: g73 10/8 16; g73 12/8 28; w71 467; g71 10/8 14-15
world population: ka 257

Quotations

age of insecurity began: tp 77
a mortal change: w75 684
calm world of yesterday vanished: tp 77
century of peace sharply came to an end: g71 10/8 15
day the world went mad: tp 84
end of optimism and confidence: g73 10/8 16
first total war: g73 10/8 20
great divide in world history: g71 10/8 15
look out for 1914: yb75 75; g75 4/8 15; g73 10/8 17; w71 468
1918, Horsemen of Apocalypse active: ts 162
1914, end of one epoch and the beginning of another: g75 4/8 15
1913, last normal year: w71 560
prophecy on war literally fulfilled: tp 80
punctuation-mark of the twentieth century: g75 10/8 13
security and quiet have disappeared since: w71 69
since 1914 predetermined march to disaster: g73 10/22 27
since 1914, world has character of international anarchy: w71 69
turning point: w74 165; tp 77; g73 10/8 17; g71 10/8 15
ushered in century of Total War: w75 633; ml 23
year world, as it was known then, came to an end: g75 10/8 13
 (SEE ALSO CHRONOLOGY, KINGDOM, LASTS DAYS, SIGN)

NINEVEH
desolation foretold by Bible: w75 137
destruction: g72 6/22 28; kj 245
Jonah: w72 213-14
library: w72 314-16
'rises up in judgment': g75 10/22 13
 (SEE ALSO ASSYRIA)

NIRVANA
Buddhism: g74 1/8 17-18
meaning of term: g73 7/8 18

NITROGEN
cycle: g71 1/8 6
water pollution: g72 7/8 29-30

NIUE
Jehovah's witnesses: yb76 24-5; yb75 24-5; yb74 24-5; yb73 24-5; yb72 34-5
population: yb73 24; yb72 34

NOAH
ark construction: w74 23, 380; w72 488; w71 168; te 128
 time involved: w75 10; ka 333
ark discovery claims: g75 9/8 17-21
dedicated: w72 699
different from world: sl 291-2; w74 664; w72 651-2
discussion: po 71, 81-3
faith: w75 748-9; w74 23-4; po 71, 81
faithfulness: tp 94; w72 488-9; km 11/72 5; w71 634
intoxication: po 83
living conditions in ark: w75 752
name: po 71, 82
preacher: w75 748-9
prophetic significance: w74 666-8
rainbow: g75 1/22 13
time before Flood to have offspring: w75 750
time of the end in day of: po 73, 173
why told of Flood one week before: w75 10-11
wives of grandsons: w75 76
 (SEE ALSO FLOOD [NOACHIAN])

NOISE
effect on man: g75 4/22 31; g72 1/22 30; g72 2/8 30; g72 8/22 30; g72 9/22 30; g72 12/22 29; g71 10/8 6, 30
 rock concerts: g75 10/22 31
effect on unborn babies: g75 8/22 30

NORFOLK ISLAND
Jehovah's witnesses: yb75 28-9; yb74 28-9; yb73 28-9
population: yb73 28

NORTH AMERICA
history: g71 5/22 13-16
Indians: g71 5/22 16
Jehovah's witnesses: yb75 20-2; w71 21-2

NORTHERN RHODESIA
 (SEE ZAMBIA)

NORWAY
child survives forty-minute submergence: g75 8/22 31
Jehovah's witnesses: yb76 21, 28-9; yb75 28-9; w74 141-2; yb74 28-9; yb73 28-9; yb72 38-9; g72 3/22 16; km 11/72 6
population: yb73 28; yb72 38
women: g72 5/22 4

NOSE
marvel of human: g75 7/8 6

NOSTRADAMUS
predictions: g73 1/22 5

NOTE TAKING
sg 43

NUCLEAR REACTORS
g74 8/22 22; g73 2/22 20-3, 30; g72 2/22 31

NUCLEAR WEAPONS
(SEE ATOMIC WEAPONS)

NUDISM
Bible term "naked": w74 20
church play: g75 5/22 30
church service: g75 6/22 30-1; g71 5/8 29

NUMBERS
Hebrew manuscripts: ka 208-9
Jehovah's name: g71 9/8 20
symbolic: sl 242

List by Number
four: pm 142
seven: pm 399-400
ten: sl 242; ka 170
seventy: pm 399-400

NUNS
alcoholism: g74 7/22 29
celibacy: g75 1/22 9
decrease in number: g75 1/22 7-9; g75 2/8 31; g75 11/8 29; g74 6/22 30
discipline: g75 1/22 10-11
discussion: g75 1/22 7-13
drugs: g74 7/22 29
experiences:
admit church not true: w72 281
former nuns accept truth: g75 1/22 12-13; w74 746-7; g73 2/8 14; g72 6/22 12-13; g72 7/22 17-26
leaving convent: g75 1/22 7-12; g75 2/8 31; g74 4/22 18; g72 3/22 29; w71 330, 484
lottery: g73 12/22 30
number world wide: g75 1/22 8; g75 11/8 29
problems: g75 1/22 9-12; g75 2/8 31
shortage: g74 7/8 12; g71 9/22 10
(SEE ALSO ROMAN CATHOLIC CHURCH)

NURSE(S)
abortions: g75 8/22 5; g74 8/8 30; g73 3/22 11; g72 6/8 30; g71 12/8 31
discussion: g73 2/8 8-13
experience:
nurse learns truth: g75 10/8 20-1
negligence: g73 2/8 12
shortage: g72 7/8 30
training: g73 2/8 10-11

NUTRITION
discussion: g74 9/22 3-7
neglect: g75 6/8 31
role in mental illness: g75 4/22 13-14
sprouted seeds: g75 12/22 25-6
(SEE ALSO DIET, HEALTH)

OATHS
discussion: g75 7/22 27-8
Jehovah's: kj 316
keeping: w72 29-30
labor unions: g75 7/22 28
'loyalty': w73 62-3
passports: g75 7/22 28; g72 10/8 29
Zedekiah: w73 59-61; pm 214-15

OBEDIENCE
Bible examples: tp 92-4; te 33-4
children toward parents: g75 10/22 27; w73 670-2; w72 362-4; te 31-4
discussion: g71 1/8 3-4
Jehovah's law: w73 430-6; w72 429-30; g71 1/8 3-4
laws of Caesar: te 135-8
older men (elders): w72 464-5
required of Christians: w73 142, 144-6
test on Adam and Eve: fu 14-15; po 43-4, 56-9; ts 30-4; g74 10/8 11-12
(SEE ALSO DISOBEDIENCE, INTEGRITY, SIN)

OBJECT AND MANNER OF THE LORD'S RETURN (Booklet)
yb75 36

OBJECTIONS
answering: sg 92-4
"I believe in Jesus": g75 11/8 28
"I'm busy": km 6/74 4; km 3/72 4
"I'm not interested": km 6/74 4; g72 8/8 7
"Our family always gone to same church": g73 11/8 27-8
"Why call at my door? I have a religion": w74 3-4
request not to call anymore: km 6/74 4
sign: no religious calls: km 6/74 4
(SEE ALSO FIELD SERVICE)

OBLIGATIONS
discussion: w72 451-2; g72 8/22 4

OBSTACLES
challenge of: w72 547-8

OCCULTISM
Bible view: w75 52-3; w74 325, 328, 715-16; ts 76-8, 87; g74 9/8 28
Catholicism: g75 5/22 30
charms: w74 715-16
discussion: w74 323-8
hypnotism: g74 9/8 27-8
interest in: w74 166
practices connected with: w75 52-3; g75 2/22 27-8; ts 76, 86
(SEE ALSO SPIRITISM)

OCEANS
beaches: g71 8/22 20-2
color of: g72 8/8 26
discussion: g75 11/8 16-20
evaporation: w71 350
exploration: g75 2/22 30; g74 10/8 29
fishing: g74 2/22 23-4
floor: g75 11/8 20
food chain: g75 11/8 17
light penetration: g72 8/8 29
Pacific:
South American fault line: g75 3/22 26
pollution: g75 1/8 30; g75 7/8 10; g74 2/22 24; g73 4/8 30; g73 11/22 29-30; g72 10/8 11; g71 1/8 7-8; g71 4/22 10-11, 30; g71 9/22 29; g71 12/8 29
"red tide": g75 11/8 18
seashells: g75 11/22 25
survival in: g73 6/22 17-19
territorial waters: g74 2/22 24; g74 9/22 30
waves: g74 8/8 11; g71 8/22 21-2
(SEE ALSO MARINE LIFE, SEAS)

OCTOPUS
poisonous: g71 2/22 31

OFFENSE
forgiveness: w71 574

OHOLAH
discussion: w73 90-1; kj 238-43

OHOLIBAH
discussion: w73 90-2; kj 238-41, 243-63

OIL
Abu Dhabi: g75 12/8 31
Alaska:
pipeline: g75 6/22 29
China: g75 9/8 31
consumption: g74 1/8 4, 6-7; g74 2/8 29; g74 2/22 16-17; g74 6/22 29; g73 6/8 3-4; g72 8/8 17-18
cost: g74 1/8 7-8; g74 2/22 20; g74 5/8 10; g74 7/22 7; g74 8/8 8-11; g74 11/22 20; g74 12/8 10-11
crisis: g75 2/22 29; g74 1/8 3-8, 29; g74 2/22 19-22, 29; g74 5/8 9-10
depth: g75 1/22 30
discussion: g74 2/22 16-22
drilling: g75 1/22 30
economic problems: g74 11/22 30
from coal: g74 4/22 29
grease: g74 7/8 30
import: g74 1/8 6-8; g74 11/22 19
India: g74 7/22 7
Japan: g74 6/8 25
microorganisms: g72 3/8 29
Middle East: g74 2/22 17-22; g73 6/8 4; g72 8/8 18
North Sea: g75 3/22 31
origin: g73 5/8 30
pipelines: g72 4/8 29
political power: g74 2/22 16-22
poorer countries: g74 3/22 30; g74 12/8 10-11
production: g73 6/8 3-4
profits: g75 4/22 29; g74 8/8 8-10
refineries: g74 2/8 29; g73 6/8 4
reserves: g74 2/22 17
search for: g73 7/8 29-30
shortages: g74 8/8 9-10; g74 11/8 31
Soviet Union: g75 7/22 30
sperm whale: g75 7/22 30
spill pollution: g74 1/8 30
symbolic: w74 479; ka 178-9, 195; pm 204
tankers: g75 1/8 30; g75 6/22 31
United States import: g74 1/8 5-8; g74 2/22 16, 19-20; g74 8/8 9-10; g73 10/8 9
wasted: g74 11/22 30
whale: g73 12/22 15-16

OIL PAINTING
discussion: g74 5/8 21-3
life story of a famous artist: g75 7/8 12-16

OKINAWA
description: g72 2/8 25-6
Jehovah's witnesses: yb76 28-9; yb75 28-9; yb74 28-9; yb73 28-9, 235-7; yb72 38-9; g72 2/8 26; g72 4/8 25; g72 6/8 27-8; w71 679
lacquer ware: g71 7/22 23
population: yb73 28; yb72 38

OLD AGE
ability to learn: w74 424; g74 12/8 18; g73 1/22 9; g73 4/8 31
boredom: g74 2/22 10
cancer: g74 9/8 19
care for older persons:

g75 5/22 24-5; w74 570; km 11/74 3; w71 516
cause of: g75 1/8 27; g73 1/22 11; g72 1/22 20; g71 2/22 13-15
changing religion: g73 11/8 28
climate change: g72 3/8 30
consideration for older persons: g75 5/22 25-6; km 11/74 3; km 3/72 3; w71 518
coping with food costs: g75 8/22 29
discussion: g73 1/22 9-12; g72 1/22 20-3
employment: g74 9/8 30; g72 11/8 30
examples of longevity: g74 2/22 30; g73 1/22 9-10; g72 3/22 30
experiences:
  active Witnesses: w74 285, 537-8; yb74 234; yb73 228-9, 251-2; yb72 53, 66, 101, 107-8; g72 1/22 23; g72 2/8 24; w71 339
  older persons learn truth: yb75 15, 22; w74 342; g74 3/8 21-2; g73 2/8 14; g73 11/8 28; w72 284-5; g72 5/22 24; w71 368-9, 415; g71 1/8 28; g71 4/8 23; g71 11/8 26
faithfulness: w74 533, 537-8
homes: g73 1/22 12
myths concerning cause: ts 26-9
number of elderly persons: g75 11/8 30-1
problems of older persons: g75 5/22 24
progeria (disease): g71 2/8 30
respect for: g74 9/8 30; km 11/74 3; km 3/72 3
retirement: g75 11/8 12-16; g73 11/22 30; g71 12/22 3-4
(SEE ALSO LIFE-SPAN)

OLDER MEN (Elders)
accepting suggestions: w74 300, 318
all "preside": w75 471
ancient Israel: w74 204-5; w71 684-5
appointment: w75 86, 732-3; km 8/75 3; km 8/73 3; w72 19-20, 31, 458; or 61-3, 69; yb72 26-9; w71 688-90, 699-701
  beginning of modern-day: yb75 248-9
approachable: w74 367-8
attitude toward fellow elders: w75 529
attitude toward responsibility: w75 474, 668; km 4/72 3
balance needed: w75 368-74
balancing shepherding with field service: km 11/75 3-4
benefits of arrangement: w75 471; yb75 250
benefits to congregation: w75 86
Bible study overseer: w72 460; or 76-7
branch overseer: or 89-90
care for brothers: w74 103-4, 111-12, 306, 316, 434-6; tp 188
chairman: w75 472-3
circuit overseer: km 8/75 6; w72 461-2; or 82-7
city overseer: or 82
confidence in: w75 764-6
confidential matters: km 7/75 3
congregation book study conductor: w72 461; or 81-2
congregation meetings: km 12/74 3
congregation records: w74 368
conscience of body of: w75 219
consciences: w72 591, 599
consulting each other: km 10/74 7-8; w73 542-3
counseling others: w75 268, 371-2, 530; w74 61, 435-6; w73 374, 503-5, 541-3; or 159-64
  marital problems: w75 287
discussion: w75 465-75; km 8/75 3-6; w72 9-21, 25-7; or 53-70; yb72 10-33; w71 603-4, 690-701
district overseer: w72 462; or 87-9
duties: w73 205; w72 20, 590; or 55-8; yb72 28; km 9/71 3-4
early Christian congregation: w75 729-30; w72 755; w71 685-92
effect of broken engagement: w75 382-4
elder arrangement announced: yb72 42; w71 603-4
elders' meetings: w75 472-4; or 63-70
  following through on decisions: km 12/75 6
  topics for consideration: km 12/75 4-6
elected: yb76 56, 83; yb75 39, 164-5
equality: w74 408; w72 10, 31; or 63; yb72 11-12; w71 691
example: w74 306; km 8/74 7; w73 138-9, 141, 374-5
field overseer: w72 460-1; or 73-6
filling vacant positions: km 11/72 7
gifts in men: w75 667-8
Greek word: or 54-5; w71 685, 695
handling difficulties: w72 604; or 159-80
handling of disfellowshiped ones: w74 467-70, 472
harmony as a body: w75 668
Hebrew word: w71 684-5
helping others to qualify: km 12/75 6; w73 506-7
humility: w75 530, 721-8; w74 103-4, 300, 316, 367-8, 571; km 3/74 3; w73 541-3; w72 201-4, 287, 756-7
interest in children: km 4/75 3
judgments of: w75 92-4
listening: w74 435-6
making comparisons: w74 269-70
making decisions: w75 372-4
meeting with circuit overseer: km 12/75 3-4; km 8/74 7
mentally-ill persons helped by: g75 4/22 20-1
minister: w75 728-34
moving to another congregation: km 1/75 4; km 8/75 5-6; km 2/73 7; km 6/73 3
no salary: or 150
not imposing their conscience on others: km 6/75 4
obedience to: w73 141-6; w72 464-5
overseers: w72 9-10, 13-14; or 54-8; yb72 10-11, 17-18; w71 603, 689-90
presiding overseer: w72 459-60; or 70-3
  annual report: km 8/75 5
  mailing address: km 8/75 4
proper view of: w75 529; w74 265-6; km 3/74 3; or 11
proper view of ability: w74 530-1
qualifications: km 3/75 3; yb75 248; km 8/75 3; w73 469-74; w72 10-19, 459; or 58-63; yb72 12-26
  ability to exhort and reprove: w72 15-17; yb72 20-3
  children in subjection with seriousness: w72 13-14, 126; yb72 17
  fine testimony from outsiders: w72 14-15; yb72 18-19; g71 5/22 10
  hospitable: w72 11; yb72 13-14
  husband of one wife: w72 11; yb72 13
  irreprehensible: w72 10-11; yb72 12-13
  moderate in habits: w72 11; yb72 13
  not a drunken brawler, smiter, belligerent, nor lover of money: w72 13; yb72 15-16
  not newly converted: w72 14; yb72 18; g71 5/22 10
  orderly: w72 11; yb72 13
  presiding over household in fine manner: w72 13, 126; yb72 16-17
  qualified to teach: w72 11-12; yb72 14-15; w71 752
  reasonable: w72 13; yb72 15-16
  sound in mind: w72 11; yb72 13
  (see also list under Overseers)
recommendations for: w75 93; km 8/75 3, 6
recommendations of those previously reproved or disfellowshiped: km 8/75 6
removal: km 8/75 3-4; km 9/74 7; km 6/73 3
  little time in field service: km 9/74 7
rotation: km 8/75 4; km 7/73 2; km 8/73 3
service committee: km 8/75 6
shepherds: w73 39, 142
submission to Christ: w72 755-7
symbolic representation: w71 751-2
Theocratic School overseer: w72 460-1; or 79-81
transition with new service year: km 8/75 4-5
varying gifts: w73 373
visiting others: w75 475; w73 600
Watchtower study conductor: w72 460; or 78-9
ways elders teach: km 5/75 4
zone overseer: or 90
(SEE ALSO OVERSEERS)

OLDER PERSONS
(SEE TWENTY-FOUR OLDER PERSONS)

OLIVES, MOUNT OF
height: pm 377
location: w75 367; w74 78-9
symbolic: pm 374-80

OLIVE TREE(S)
after Flood: w73 84-5

illustration in Romans 11: w74 696
two (Zec 4): pm 204-7

OLYMPIC GAMES
contrast with assembly: yb74 251-2
discussion: g73 2/22 13-15
failure: g72 10/22 29
religious connection: g73 2/22 15
1896: g72 10/8 30
1968: g72 10/8 30

OMENS
g73 11/22 5-7

ONAN
w73 255-6

144,000
early Christians' persecution: w72 415-16
"executed with ax": w73 740-1; ka 32-3
Jews first opportunity: w74 694-5
literal number: g73 5/8 7
selecting: w74 478
twenty-four elders: w73 62
(SEE ALSO CONGREGATION OF GOD)

OPIUM
smoking: g75 5/8 11
wars: g75 5/8 9-12; g74 7/8 5

OPPOSITION
(SEE PERSECUTION)

OPPRESSION
human governments: w74 616-17; hu 13-14
Negroes in United States: w74 707-10

ORCHARDS
g73 9/22 21-4

ORDERLINESS
Bible view: km 10/75 7; w73 472
shown in creation: w73 35-6; w72 265; g72 10/22 5; g71 8/8 3-7

ORDER OF TRIAL (Booklet)
yb75 175, 178-9

ORDINATION
from God: kj 66-7
of women:
Billy Graham's neutral view: w75 560
who are ordained ministers: w75 732-4

ORGANIZATION
Bible view: w73 393
God's earthly: w74 52-3, 281-2, 753-4, 757-63
of home: g74 5/8 13-15
(SEE ALSO CONGREGATION, JEHOVAH'S ORGANIZATION)

ORGANIZATION FOR KINGDOM-PREACHING AND DISCIPLE-MAKING (Book)
governing body: yb73 257
questions for baptismal candidates: yb75 254
release: yb75 249; w72 605; g72 10/22 20

ORGANIZATION OF AFRICAN UNITY
g74 6/22 23-6

ORIGEN
statement on infant baptism: g74 3/22 28

ORPAH
prophetic significance: w72 80

ORPHANS
Italy: g71 6/8 30-1

ORTHODOX CATHOLIC CHURCH
clergy: g72 5/8 10
membership: sl 206

OSTRACISM
g75 10/8 31

OSTRICH
discussion: g72 2/22 16

OTHER SHEEP
clarification regarding baptism of: yb75 156
gathering: ka 278-83
great crowd: yb75 156; ka 266-9, 271; pm 79, 173-4; kj 177-8, 319-20, 347
holy spirit: g74 8/22 28
identified: w74 287-8; w73 200; w72 637-8; or 109-10; kj 173-4, 177-81, 307
inherit kingdom: g74 8/22 28; ka 272
justification: w72 520
Memorial: w73 200
not born again: g74 8/22 28
pictured by Jonadab: yb75 156
pictured by men in Jerusalem that sigh and cry: kj 173-81
relation to remnant: w74 627-8; ka 276-83
servants in congregations: yb75 166
(SEE ALSO GREAT CROWD)

"OUIJA" BOARD
dangers: g75 2/8 11; w74 166, 326; g74 2/22 6; g73 6/8 27-8; g71 5/8 30; g71 12/22 30
discussion: g75 2/8 10-11; g73 6/8 27-8
origin: g73 6/8 27
sales: g75 2/8 10
source of messages: g75 2/8 10-11; g75 8/8 5-6

OUR KINGDOM SERVICE
(SEE KINGDOM MINISTRY)

OUTLINES
preparation and use: g74 12/22 14-15; sg 44-9, 59, 61, 140-2

OVEN
microwave: g71 9/8 30

OVERCONFIDENCE
thinking one is exception: g71 11/8 3-4

OVEREATING
effects: g71 2/22 6

OVERSEERS
accepting responsibility: km 4/72 3
accepting suggestions: w74 300, 318
appointment: w75 732-3; yb75 165-6, 248-9; km 8/75 3; w72 19-20, 31, 458; or 61-3, 69; yb72 26-9; w71 689-90, 699-701; sg 191
approachable: w74 103-4, 367-8
balance needed: w75 368-74
Bible study overseer: w72 460; or 76-7
branch overseer: or 89-90
circuit overseer: km 5/75 3-4; km 8/75 6; w72 461-2; or 82-7
city overseer: or 82
congregation book study conductor: w72 461; or 81-2
congregation meetings: km 12/75 5; km 12/74 3; or 71-2
congregation records: w74 368
consciences: w72 591, 599
consulting each other: km 10/74 7-8; w73 542-3
counseling others: w75 371-2, 530; w74 435-6; w73 141, 145, 374, 503-5, 541-3; or 159-64
counselors: w71 347
dealing with others: km 3/75 3; w74 103-4, 306, 316, 434-6
discussion: or 53-70
district overseer: w72 462; or 87-9
duties: w72 20; or 55-8; yb72 28; km 9/71 3-4
equality: w74 408; w72 10, 31; or 63; yb72 11-12; w71 691
example: w74 306; km 8/74 7
field overseer: w72 460-1; or 73-6
filling vacant positions: km 11/72 7
handling difficulties: w74 435-6; w73 503-5, 541-3; km 9/73 8; w72 15-17, 604; or 58, 159-80; yb72 20-3
handling of disfellowshiped ones: w74 467-70, 472
Hebrew and Greek words: w75 730; w72 9; or 54-5; yb72 10; w71 689-91
humility: w75 530, 721-8; w74 103-4, 300, 316, 367-8; km 3/74 3; w72 201-4, 287, 756-7
Kingdom Ministry School: km 5/75 4
listening: w74 435-6; g74 11/22 22-3
making decisions: w75 372-4
meetings: or 63-70
meeting with circuit overseer: km 12/75 3-4; km 8/74 7
no salary: or 150
obedience to: w73 145; w72 464-5
older men: w72 9-10, 13-14; yb72 10-11, 17-18; w71 689-90
presiding overseer: w75 472-3; w72 459-60; or 70-3
annual report: km 8/75 5
mailing address: km 8/75 4
pride: w74 300
proper view of ability: w74 530-1
qualifications: yb75 248; w73 469-74; w72 10-19, 459; or 58-63; yb72 12-26
ability to exhort and reprove: w72 15-17; yb72 20-3
children in subjection with seriousness: w72 13-14, 126; yb72 17
fine testimony from outsiders: w72 14-15; yb72 18-19; g71 5/22 10
hospitable: w75 468; km 9/75 7; w72 11; yb72 13-14
husband of one wife: w75 467; w72 11; yb72 13
irreprehensible: w75 467; km 11/75 3; w73 470; w72 10-11; yb72 12-13
lover of goodness: w73 473
loyal: w75 469-70; w73 473

moderate in habits: w75 467; w72 11; yb72 13
not drunken brawler, smiter, belligerent nor lover of money: w75 468; w72 13; yb72 15-16
not greedy of dishonest gain: w73 470-1
not newly converted: w75 469; w72 14; yb72 18; g71 5/22 10
not self-willed: w75 725-6
old enough: w75 467; km 8/75 3
orderly: w75 468; km 10/75 7; w73 472; w72 11; yb72 13
presiding over household in right manner: w75 542; km 7/75 3; w73 471; w72 13, 126; yb72 16-17
qualified to teach: km 5/75 4; w74 530-1; w73 472-3; w72 11-12; yb72 14-15; w71 752
reasonable: w75 707-8; km 3/75 3; w73 473; w72 13; yb72 15-16
sound in mind: w72 11; yb72 13
reaching out for office: km 8/75 3; km 12/75 6; w74 539; w73 475; w72 10, 21; yb72 12, 30-1; w71 691, 698; sg 191
removal: km 8/75 3-4; km 9/74 7
respect for: km 3/74 3; w71 527
responsibility to assist others: km 5/75 4; km 10/74 8; w73 374-5, 503-7; tp 142; km 6/71 3-4
rotation: km 8/75 4; km 7/73 2
shepherds: w73 39, 142
stewards: w74 531-2
symbolic representation: w71 751-2
Theocratic School overseer: km 5/74 8; w72 460-1; or 79-81
vacancy in one of the five principal positions: km 8/75 4
Watchtower study conductor: w72 460; or 78-9
ways overseers teach: km 5/75 4
zone overseer: or 90
(SEE ALSO MINISTERIAL SERVANTS, OLDER MEN)

OVERSIGHT
congregation: w72 456-62

OVERWEIGHT
g74 4/22 21-4; g74 9/22 3

OWNERSHIP
disown oneself: w74 600-1
Jehovah's: w74 593-9, 604
Jesus': w74 598-9, 601-2

OXYGEN
forests supply: g72 7/8 29
gas: g72 10/22 7; g71 7/22 12
prevalence: g71 12/22 23
production by Amazon jungle: g75 3/8 8

OYSTER
g74 9/8 24-6

PACKAGING
food: g73 9/8 21-4

PAGANISM
Christendom: w74 742; g74 2/8 28; g74 4/22 30; g74 7/22 8-9; w72 63; g72 2/22 30; g71 8/22 15-16; g71 9/22 30-1
Vatican: g75 1/8 21-3
(SEE ALSO CHRISTENDOM, INDIVIDUAL RELIGIONS BY NAME, NAMES OF SPECIFIC HOLIDAYS)

PAIN
drilling teeth: g73 1/22 31
pain-killing drugs: g73 2/22 10

PAINT
poison: g71 7/8 29; g71 7/22 29
spray gun: g75 8/8 30

PAINTING
oil: g74 5/8 21-3
painting rooms: g74 3/22 15-16

PAINTINGS
life story of a famous artist: g75 7/8 12-16
principles for buying: g75 6/22 24-6

PAKISTAN
description: yb72 195-6, 205
disasters: g75 2/22 29; g71 1/8 29
Jehovah's witnesses: yb76 21-2, 28-9; yb75 28-9; km 4/75 1; yb74 21, 28-9; yb73 28-9; yb72 38-9, 196-209, 211-13
population: yb73 28; yb72 38, 195; g71 10/8 11
religion: yb72 195, 200

PALATINE GUARD
g75 5/22 13-17

PALAU
Jehovah's witnesses: yb76 26-7; yb75 26-7; yb74 26-7; yb73 15-16, 26-7; yb72 36-7
population: yb73 26; yb72 36

PALESTINE
British rule: w71 717
climate: g75 3/8 6
description: w74 77-80
map: pm 260
modern events and Bible prophecy: w75 387-9
Negeb: w74 624
(SEE ALSO ISRAEL)

PALM(S)
coconuts: g71 6/22 25-6
date: g71 2/22 15
waving symbolic: w72 722

PALMISTRY
g75 2/8 29

PANAMA
birds: g72 3/8 26
Indians: g74 1/22 20-1; g71 9/22 20-3
Jehovah's witnesses: yb76 28-9; yb75 28-9; yb74 28-9; w73 29-30; yb73 28-9; yb72 38-9; g71 9/22 22-3
population: yb73 28; yb72 38
religion: w71 740
rice: g73 12/8 24-6
wildlife: g71 3/8 19-20

PANDA
g73 11/22 16-19

PAPAYA
g73 1/22 14

PAPER
cost: g73 5/8 31
garbage: g72 2/22 31; g72 5/22 30
radioactive, used to trap illegal printers: g75 9/8 30
shortage: g74 4/8 30-1
wood chips: g72 1/22 30

PAPUA NEW GUINEA
independence: g75 12/22 22-4
intertribal fighting: g75 12/22 30
Jehovah's witnesses: yb76 28-9; yb75 28-9; g75 12/22 24; yb74 28-9; yb73 28-9; yb72 38-9
money: g75 7/22 23
population: yb73 28; yb72 38

PARABLE
(SEE ILLUSTRATIONS)

PARADISE
ancient Israel: w73 219-21
definition: tp 100
discussion: g75 12/22 3-12; pm 7-21, 396-408
earthly, after Armageddon: w75 623; sl 90; gc 23-8; og 28; w74 6-7, 291-4, 661-2, 668; po 188-90; ts 133-43; w73 78-9, 412-15, 425-8, 624-6; ka 35-6, 142-6; tp 100-10; dy 28-30; w72 227, 240, 243-5, 463; g72 4/22 26-7; pm 18-21; kj 392-407; te 179-82; g71 4/22 22-7
peace between man and animals: w75 606-8
evildoer: sl 90; w74 6; ka 35, 121; pm 12-13, 395; w71 255-6
garden of Eden: g75 12/22 6; po 37-8, 41, 48-50, 54; w73 77-8; w72 621; pm 9-12, 15-17; dn 10; w71 615-17; kj 114; te 180; nc 9-13
heavenly: sl 90
spiritual: w75 696-7; sl 91, 110-12, 130-7, 203-4, 258-9; yb75 260; w74 191, 634-5, 667-9; w73 221-3, 283, 459, 468-9; pm 396-7; kj 309-10, 328, 330-4, 343, 354-5, 381-2, 387
beautifying: sl 182
personality of residents: sl 184-8, 191-4, 197, 203-4
residents: sl 169-70, 334
(SEE ALSO NEW ORDER, THOUSAND-YEAR REIGN)

PARADISE RESTORED TO MANKIND—BY THEOCRACY! (Book)
public talks: km 9/72 3-6
release: w72 606; g72 10/22 20

PARAGUAY
Jehovah's witnesses: yb76 28-9; yb75 28-9; g75 1/22 12-13; yb74 28-9; yb73 20, 28-9; yb72 38-9, 123-4
official languages: g75 9/22 31
population: yb73 28; yb72 38

PARALYSIS
experience: g75 2/22 12-16

PARAN
discussion: w73 751-2

PARCHMENT
w74 553

PARENTS
abuse of children: g75 5/22 31; g73 1/22 30; g73 9/8 29-30
appreciation for: w72 732-4; w71 107, 532

appreciation for children: w75 14-15
authority over children: w73 318
communication with children: w74 89-90, 92-3, 261-3, 267-72; g74 11/22 21-2
companionship with children: w74 270-1; g74 2/8 10; g74 7/22 22-3; w73 559-60, 562; sg 80
confidence of children: w73 559-60, 562; w72 31, 163-4, 259-60; g72 4/8 4; w71 587-92
custom of blessing children: w73 447-8
death of children: g71 12/8 28
disciplining children: w75 14-15; g74 2/8 8; g74 4/22 14-15; w73 556-8; w72 740; w71 555-6, 588-9, 592
drugs: g74 5/8 3-8; w73 182-7; g72 8/22 30
early training of children: g75 12/22 30; w74 267-8; g74 2/8 7-8; w73 670; g73 2/22 17-19; g71 9/8 8-11
encouraging children: g74 1/8 24
evolution theory: w71 41-2
example for children: w74 245, 263; g74 4/22 15; w73 184-5, 451; w71 370-2, 583, 589; g71 9/8 29; g71 12/8 30
experiences:
  blood-transfusion case (Austria): g72 9/22 17-21
  opposition to truth: w71 369, 533; g71 7/22 20
  school discussion: g71 3/22 20
  training of children: g71 2/22 11
  unbelieving, accept truth: km 5/72 4
failure of worldly guidance: g75 10/8 6-7
fallacy of permissiveness: w75 71; g71 5/22 30
family merit and family responsibility: w72 360-5, 543
future of children: w75 451-3
honor due: g75 10/22 27-8; g72 3/22 19
household chores for children: g71 9/8 8-11
Israel: w71 361-2
learn by listening to children: g75 7/8 30
love toward children: w74 269, 741; g74 4/22 15-16; g74 7/22 22-3; w72 457; g72 7/22 29
obedience of children: w72 362-4, 732-3; g71 3/22 8
privilege to have children: g74 11/8 11
religious training of children: km 7/74 4; w73 532-3, 535-6, 553-64; w72 360-3; km 1/72 7-8; w71 104-7, 170-1, 585-6, 599; sg 37-8; te 5-6; km 5/71 3-4
respect for: w72 732-4; w71 518
responsibilities toward children: w75 14-15, 314; g75 5/8 21; w74 81-94, 267-72; g74 2/8 7-11; g74 3/22 9-11; g74 8/22 4-6; g74 12/22 6; w73 553-64; w72 51-2, 109-11, 360, 364; g72 8/8 4; w71 361-2, 369-72, 581-92; g71 3/22 7-8
rights: w72 359
sex education for children: g74 2/8 9; g74 4/22 13-14; w71 589
teaching proper habits, attitudes to children: g75 6/8 14-16; w74 267-72; g74 2/8 7-11; g74 4/22 13-16; w73 184-5, 556, 561-2; g73 8/8 31; w72 452; g71 7/22 26
time with children: w74 270-1
toys' value for children: g71 1/8 9-12
unbelieving: km 5/72 4
(SEE ALSO CHILD TRAINING)

PARKS

New Zealand: g75 9/8 21-3
Rhodesia: g75 2/8 20-1
statistics: g73 5/8 31

PAROCHIAL SCHOOLS

(SEE SCHOOLS)

PAROUSIA

(SEE CHRIST'S PRESENCE, PRESENCE)

PARTIES

(SEE SOCIAL GATHERINGS)

PASSION

'bloom of youth' (1 Co 7:36): w74 703
reason for marriage: w73 595-6
self-control: w74 12-13; w73 593, 595-6; w72 218-21

PASSOVER

celebration in Egypt: te 167-8
Jesus observed: te 167-8
lamb: w72 681
time of observance: w73 175

PASSPORTS

oaths: g75 7/22 28; g72 10/8 29

PASTORAL WORK

yb75 85-6

PATIENCE

Bible accounts:
  Jehovah's: sl 300-2; w72 308-12
demonstrating: w74 155; w73 474-7; w72 504-5
discussion: g73 3/8 3-4
examples: w73 499
listening: g74 11/22 21-3

PATRIARCHAL SOCIETY

Jacob's sons: po 99
power of patriarchal head: w75 117

PATRIOTISM

clergy: kj 153
flag salute: w74 62-3; g72 7/8 11-12
flag worship (experience): yb75 205
(SEE ALSO FLAG SALUTE, NATIONALISM, NEUTRALITY)

PAUL (Saul)

apostle to the nations: w71 319-20
Areopagus (Mars Hill): w73 429-33; w72 119; w71 323-4
Bible writer: w73 42, 45; g71 3/8 25; g71 11/8 28
biographical sketch: w72 405
calling: w74 658-9
congregations established: w72 512
conversion: w72 159-60; w71 154, 320; te 77
discussion: w73 285-6
disposition: w75 676; w73 285-6; w72 565-6
dispute with Barnabas: w75 344-6
example to elders: w75 721-2, 724; w73 375
faced wild beasts: w74 216
method of ministry: w72 216-17
missionary tours: w71 79, 83-4, 88
persecution of Christians: w72 562; w71 153-4, 486; te 75-7
qualities: w74 522-3; w73 285-6; w72 215-17, 275, 297, 303; or 133; w71 573
source of missionary assignment: w75 672
'thorn in flesh': w71 262
vision: sl 131-4
voyage to Rome: g71 4/8 27-8
zeal: w73 285-6

PAUSING

public speaking: sg 119-21

PEACE

acquiring: g72 10/8 23-4
among men: w72 67-9; g72 10/8 18-19; g72 11/22 29; kj 347-8; g71 10/8 24
animals and man: w75 606-8
Conference on Security and Cooperation in Europe: g75 9/22 29; g75 11/8 3-7
congregational: yb76 260-1; w75 758; w73 331-5; pm 90; kj 308
discussion: g74 4/8 4-8, 12-14; w73 330-5, 675, 677; tp 5-13; w72 67-9; g72 10/8 3-19
failure of man's efforts: w75 445; w74 40; g74 4/8 5-7; g74 6/8 30; w73 330; tp 9-13; g73 3/22 29; g73 8/8 30; w72 613; g72 3/8 5-7; g72 10/8 3, 4; w71 197, 299, 468-9; g71 10/8 12-13, 19, 23
God's kingdom: tp 7-8
League of Nations: w74 135
mental: w74 178
obstructors to: w73 675, 677; tp 11-20
peaceable persons happy: w71 372-4; te 131-4; g71 9/8 27-8
"peace and security": w75 682; g75 2/8 9; g75 11/8 7; w74 244, 552; g74 4/8 4-8, 20; tp 89; g72 10/8 9, 14-18
personal: w73 331-5, 679
source of lasting peace: w74 40, 135; g74 4/8 8-9; w73 330-1, 679; tp 178-9; g72 10/8 18-19; w71 100, 245-6; g71 9/8 27
treaties: g74 4/8 5-7; w71 299-300
United Nations: w74 135, 547-52; g72 3/8 5-7
years of peace: g73 3/22 29; w71 299-300; g71 4/22 20

Quotations

first time in 45 years without a war, but real peace elusive: w75 445
first time world has known complete peace since 1931: g75 7/8 29
world authority needed: w75 516

PEARL

discussion: g74 9/8 24-6
diving: g74 9/8 25
Jesus' parable of pearl of high value: w75 594

PEAT

fuel: g75 2/8 30

PELATIAH

w72 678; kj 194, 201-2, 204

PELLA

w74 426

PENGUIN

discussion: g75 12/22 20-2

PENICILLIN

g74 12/22 12; w72 387

PENTATEUCH
discussion: g73 3/22 16-17; g72 2/22 27-8
published in Russia: w75 487

PENTECOST

33 C.E.
beginning of Christian congregation: po 158-60; w72 688-90; w71 746, 755-6; kj 333, 352
conversions to Christianity: w71 10
faithful and discreet slave: w75 46
gift of tongues: g74 12/22 27-8; w73 526-7
outpouring of spirit: ka 105-6; w71 398-9, 683, 745-6
Peter's talk: w73 526-7

PENTECOSTALS
experience in witnessing to: yb72 176
minister becomes Witness: w72 679
snake-handling: g73 8/8 5
view of television: w75 327

PEOPLES FRIEND, THE (Booklet)
yb75 139

PEOPLES PULPIT (Tract)
yb75 45-6

PEOPLE'S PULPIT ASSOCIATION
yb75 52-3

PERCEPTION
"seeing": g73 7/22 3

PERFECTION (Completeness)
Adam and Eve: gc 11-12; w71 499-500, 539
as Jehovah: w74 151, 155
Bible uses of term: w73 211; w71 498
Christian standard: w72 30; w71 565-8
discussion: w71 497-500, 565-8
earthly heirs of New Order: ts 137-40, 144, 165-6; g73 10/8 26-7; w71 500, 539
gradual process: w74 607-8; ts 139-40
faithful persons: w71 565-6
Jesus Christ: w71 500
limited: gc 11-12; w71 565
meaning of term: w74 150-1; w71 497
not granted upon earthly resurrection: w74 607-8
perfect activity: g71 9/22 3-6

PERFUME
g73 12/22 14; w72 667-8

PERMISSIVENESS
discussion: g75 1/8 3-6
fallacy of parental: w75 71

PERSECUTION
apostles: w74 214-16
attitude toward: w75 22-3; yb75 108, 110; yb74 212; w73 268; w72 178-80; g72 12/8 26-7; w71 115-16, 264, 491-6; g71 1/22 27-8; g71 9/22 28; g71 10/22 4, 27-8
causes: w74 201-2, 207; w71 154; te 78; g71 9/22 27; g71 10/22 27
Communist lands: w74 373; w72 71, 144; yb72 45
conduct before officials: w71 541-3; sg 94-5
discipline: sl 144-5
discussion: w72 140-6; w71 720-2
divided households: km 8/75 7; w73 501-2; w71 201-13
early Christians: g75 12/8 4; w73 42-3, 46; w72 136, 142-3, 415-16; g72 12/8 20; w71 213, 447, 485-6, 488-9, 716
effect on witness work: yb74 14, 52-6, 129-48, 150-60; yb73 164-5; yb72 85-8, 116
enduring: w75 22-3, 85, 331-3; yb75 183-4, 186-90, 208-9; g75 12/22 16-19; w74 202-3, 219-20, 249-50, 442; yb74 55-6, 59-60, 63, 163-4, 166-9, 172-4, 180-90, 194, 202-4, 207-12, 226-31; w73 173, 572-3; g73 3/8 25-6; w72 133-46; or 185-7; w71 112-21, 496-7, 584; g71 1/22 27-8; g71 9/22 28
trust in Jehovah: w74 702
experiences:
baptisms: w74 342; yb74 145-6
brother hung, rope breaks: yb75 188-90
burial permit denied: w75 71
children taken from parents: yb74 119-21, 125, 186-90
clergy incite: yb76 18-19, 35-7, 53, 55, 57-8, 83, 88, 94, 96, 98-100, 102, 106, 113, 116-17, 120, 138-9, 141-3, 151-2, 168-70, 183, 188, 206, 220, 244; yb75 95-7, 101-2, 109; yb74 40, 58; g74 5/8 20; yb73 117-18, 152-7; yb72 105-6, 127, 131, 133, 138, 140, 153-4, 160-1, 185-8, 225
effect on persecutors: yb74 159-60, 169
faithful until death: w74 373; yb74 166-8, 174, 180-9
family opposition overcome: yb76 9, 19; w74 342; yb74 6-9; yb73 241; g73 1/22 15-16; g72 5/22 24; g72 12/22 5-7; w71 533-4, 574-5, 679-80
former opposers accept truth: w74 39; yb74 129; g74 3/8 20; w73 502; yb73 56-7; w72 318-19; w71 533-4; g71 8/8 13-15
Memorial: yb74 143-5
mob violence: yb76 136-7; yb75 182-90
new ones endure: yb74 118-19, 145, 166-8, 189; w73 661; w72 70-1; yb72 202
prisons: yb74 226-30
remaining in assignment: yb74 53-6; w73 664-5
remaining neutral in war zone: w74 519-21
solitary confinement: w74 250; yb74 226-8
tarred and feathered: yb75 99-100
traitor: yb74 178-9
tribal chief defends Witnesses: yb73 163-4
foretold: w75 622; sl 368-70; og 26-7; w74 171; w73 657-8; w72 133, 143, 340; w71 485-6, 491
preparing for: w74 248-50, 339-40
prisons: yb75 176-7; yb73 215-19, 221; w72 283, 521, 524-5, 532; yb72 152-3, 156-8, 160-1, 217-18; g72 1/8 8-9; w71 508; g71 8/8 13-15; g71 10/22 28
results: w71 115-16, 490-1
significance: w71 622-3; nc 24-5
why permitted: w74 169-70; w73 267-8; g72 12/8 24-6; w71 111-12, 172-8, 485-91, 539

List by Countries
Angola: yb76 204-8
Argentina: yb73 7; yb72 61-2, 82-8, 105-6, 109-11
Australia: w73 53; w72 534-5
Belgium: w73 572-3
Botswana (Bechuanaland): yb76 146, 195-6; yb74 17
Brazil: yb73 49-56, 58-9, 62-7, 79-84
Cameroon: yb74 11; w73 529-30; yb73 19-20; w71 157
Canada: g75 3/8 16-22; w74 284-5; w72 144, 148-51; g72 7/8 9-10; w71 22
China: yb74 53-6, 59-60; g74 7/8 9; w72 521, 524-5, 532
Colombia: w72 282-5
Communist lands: w72 144
Cuba: w71 19, 678; g71 10/22 28
Czechoslovakia: yb72 127, 132-6, 138-41
Dominican Republic: yb72 151-63; w71 18, 343
East Germany: w75 425-6; w74 250; yb74 223-32; g72 7/8 20
Ethiopia: yb75 7-8; yb74 12-13
Fiji: w71 20-1
Gabon: w73 529; w71 251-4
Germany: w75 85, 424-5; yb75 174; w74 202, 218, 676; yb74 100, 102-5, 108-28, 131-204, 210-12; w73 377-8, 399; yb73 120, 123, 126-7; w72 143-4, 395-9, 525, 631; yb72 97; g72 4/22 22-3; w71 16, 117, 425, 489-90, 494; g71 1/8 13-14
Ghana: yb74 9-10; yb73 151-66, 168-70, 172-8
Great Britain: yb73 98-100, 117-35; w71 721
Greece: w75 71; g75 12/8 17-21; w71 678
Guadeloupe: w72 532
India: w73 763-4
Indonesia: yb76 17
Italy: w73 664-5
Japan: yb73 214-21; w71 15-16
Kenya: yb76 105-6; yb74 12
Korea: w71 14; g71 8/8 13-15
Lesotho (Basutoland): yb76 146
Liberia: w73 172-3
Luxembourg: yb76 35-41
Macao: yb74 58
Malagasy Republic: w71 89-92
Malawi (Nyasaland): yb76 20-1, 84-5, 151-2, 168-70, 236-8; w75 341; yb75 10; g75 12/8 3-12; g75 12/22 15-19; km 12/75 1-2; w74 218; yb74 15; w73 264-8; yb73 22-3; g73 1/8 29; g73 3/8 17-24; g73 8/22 30; yb72 45; g72 7/8 20; g72 11/22 29; g72 12/8 9-28; w71 111
Mauritius: yb76 113
Mozambique: yb76 178
Newfoundland: yb76 51, 59-64
Nicaragua: yb72 178, 185-90
Nigeria: g74 3/8 20; w72 520; w71 157
Pakistan: yb72 199

Philippine Republic: w71 20
Poland: w71 490
Portugal: w75 170
Rhodesia (Southern Rhodesia): yb76 94, 100, 128, 154-5
Russia: w74 218
Singapore: w72 341-9
Solomon Islands: g75 6/22 14
South Africa: yb76 89, 98-102, 136-7, 141-6, 162, 188; yb75 11
Spain: w75 456-7
Swaziland: yb76 146, 179-80, 218-21
Taiwan: yb72 215-26
Tanzania: yb74 13-14
Togo: yb74 10-11
Turkey: w74 218; g74 2/8 29; g73 3/22 15; g73 9/8 12-16
Uganda: yb74 13
United Arab Republic: w72 525; w71 114, 117-18
United States: yb75 95-110, 116-17, 153-4, 163-4, 169-73, 175-91; w73 117, 120-2, 661; g72 7/8 10-12; w71 22, 379, 520-1, 722, 730
  Georgia: yb75 175-6, 178-9
  Illinois: yb75 183-4
  Indiana: yb75 186-8
  New Jersey: yb75 141, 173-4, 176-7
  Oklahoma: yb75 185-6
  Texas: yb75 188-90
Zaïre: yb76 22; yb74 14
Zambia (Northern Rhodesia): yb76 96, 127-33, 156-7, 172-5; yb72 235-40, 242, 245, 247-50
(SEE ALSO BANS, MOBS)

PERSEVERANCE
discussion: w72 274-6
examples: w72 701; yb72 102

PERSIA
standards: g71 9/8 13
(SEE ALSO IRAN)

PERSONALITY
disposition can be changed: w74 311-12, 516; g74 8/8 4-5; w72 117, 247-9; w71 543-4
effect of organ transplants: w75 519
factors that mold: w72 113-14
Jehovah's: w75 664-6
new: w74 58, 111, 210-14, 312, 314-15; g74 4/8 20-1; g74 8/8 4-5; g74 12/8 21; w73 596; w72 49-50; w71 444-5, 586
old: w71 585-6
personality clashes: w75 508-11
residents of spiritual paradise: sl 184-8

PERSUASION
g75 1/8 9-12

PERU
armaments: g74 11/8 6
earthquakes: g75 3/22 26; g71 4/8 11
economy: g74 1/22 3
fish industry: g73 2/8 31
food shortage: g72 10/8 30
Inquisition: g71 1/22 20-3
Jehovah's witnesses: yb76 28-9; yb75 28-9; w74 208; yb74 28-9; yb73 28-9; g73 2/22 24; g73 12/22 11-13; yb72 38-9
music: g72 3/8 20-3
population: yb73 28; yb72 38
religion: g73 12/22 12
second official language: g75 9/22 31
spiritism: w73 698

PESTICIDES
(SEE INSECTICIDES)

PESTILENCE
Armageddon: w73 753
cholera: g73 10/22 30
discussion: w74 131-4
Spanish influenza: w75 634; tp 82; g71 3/8 3-6
statistics: w75 634; sl 10; g74 1/22 30
symbolic: w74 733-4, 755-8

PETER (Cephas) (Apostle)
characteristics: w74 213
death: w71 768
denial of Jesus: w74 437
miracle performed by: w71 235
never in Rome: w72 669-71
not chief of apostles: w72 729-30
release from prison: te 100-1
travels: w72 669-71

PETER (First Book)
background: w73 341-2
time written: w73 21

PETER (Second Book)
authenticity: g71 2/8 27-8
writer: g71 2/8 27-8

PETITIONS
Argentina: yb72 110
Brazil: yb73 65-6
Dominican Republic: yb72 158-9
release of Watch Tower officials from prison (1919): yb75 115-16
suppression of *Finished Mystery:* yb75 98

PETS
discussion: g72 7/8 3-8
fish: g72 9/22 13-16
large dogs: g75 7/8 31
number: g72 5/8 31
ratio to human population: g74 8/22 31
sterilization: w73 159

"PETTING"
w73 593; g71 5/8 28

PHARAOH
inscriptions: g75 5/8 29
Necho(h): g74 10/22 17

Time of Exodus
challenged Jehovah: w75 230
plagues: w72 39-40; kj 16-19

PHARISEES
beliefs: w72 551, 560-1
exposed: w74 36
Jesus' illustrations: ts 102-3, 106-9; te 147-9
self-righteousness: ts 103
sin against holy spirit: w75 460; ts 181-2

PHILIP
evangelizer: w74 336; w72 690-1; w71 752-3
source of missionary assignment: w75 672

PHILIPPIANS
Christians in Caesar's household: w72 592

PHILIPPINE REPUBLIC
customs: g73 8/8 17-18
description: g73 8/8 16-18; g71 5/8 11
floods: yb73 21; g72 10/8 30
food: g73 9/22 29; g72 12/22 10; g71 5/8 11
Jehovah's witnesses: yb76 28-9; w75 127, 391-3; yb75 14, 28-9; g75 9/22 14-15; yb74 28-9; yb73 20-1, 28-9; g73 9/22 15-16; w72 125; yb72 38-9, 44; km 12/72 5-6; w71 20, 206, 474-6, 679; g71 6/8 24-6
  printery (Watch Tower): g73 9/22 15-16
peoples: g73 8/8 16-17
population: yb73 28; yb72 38
priests in politics: g74 1/22 29-30; g74 11/22 4-5
religion: g72 7/22 20-1; g71 2/8 16-19
  Catholicism and occultism: g75 5/22 30
rice farming: g72 7/22 4, 7
sea gypsies: g75 9/22 13-15

PHILISTINES
destruction: w75 421-3

PHILOSOPHY
Babylonian influence: ts 44-5
doctors of (Ph.D): g75 4/8 29-30
Epicurean: g72 11/22 17-18
existentialism: w73 452
Greece: g72 11/22 17-18
influence on Christendom: w75 173; ts 96
Stoic: g72 11/22 17-18
worldly: g75 11/22 31; w74 756; g74 9/8 3-4; g71 10/8 9-10

PHONOGRAPH
records: g73 3/8 30; w72 405
use in field service: yb76 38, 53, 57, 60-1, 111-12, 120, 137, 151; yb75 155-60, 198; yb73 48, 63, 113-14, 119-20, 157; yb72 172

PHOTO-DRAMA OF CREATION
book: w72 476
description: yb75 58-60; w73 397
showings: yb76 34-5, 49, 82, 244; w74 283; yb74 79-80, 83, 87, 93-4, 96; yb73 96-8; yb72 131; w71 377

PHOTOGRAPHY
crystals: g71 8/8 30

PHOTOSYNTHESIS
ts 147; g72 2/8 10; g72 10/22 6-7

PHYLACTERY
w73 191-2

PHYSICS
g74 1/8 12, 14

PICKPOCKETS
g73 4/22 17

PIGEONS
navigation of homing: w75 71; g71 6/8 29
problems in cities with: g74 12/8 30

PILATE
archaeology confirms existence: g72 1/8 28; w71 340
discussion: w75 7-8
trial of Jesus: w71 340

PILES
discussion: g75 1/8 25-6

PILGRIMAGES
discussion: g73 8/8 26-8
India (experience): g74 11/22 8-9

PILGRIMS (Watch Tower Representatives)
discussion: yb76 50; yb75 48-51
number:
1894: yb75 48
1917: yb75 85
work revived: yb75 124

PIÑATA
discussion: g71 6/22 23-4

PIONEERS
appreciation: km 2/71 5-6
Bible examples: w74 336-7
blessings: w75 187-9; w73 118-19; w72 58-9; yb72 53; km 12/72 5-6
colporteurs: yb76 91-2, 245-6; yb75 39-40, 61-4, 86; yb74 87; yb73 91, 93, 217-18, 220
difficulties endured: w73 761-2; yb73 54-5; yb72 47, 51-4, 58-60, 97, 197-8, 215-16
discussion: w75 183-9; km 10/75 7; km 5/73 3-6; or 135-40; km 2/72 3-6; km 12/72 3-6; w71 334-9; km 2/71 3-6
divine support: w73 118; yb72 53-4, 198; w71 337
effect on children: w75 188
encouraging others: km 5/73 6; km 12/72 4
entire family: w75 186; yb73 53-5
family cooperation: w75 187; km 2/73 5; km 12/72 5-6
fathers: w75 186-8; km 12/72 5-6; w71 339
Great Britain: yb73 112-15, 121, 129, 139-41
increase: km 5/74 3
many years in service: w74 283-5; yb74 74, 95; w73 509-11, 765; yb72 47, 53; w71 339; km 2/71 5
mothers: w75 188; km 2/73 3-4; km 2/72 4-6; w71 339
number: w75 27; yb75 32, 258; km 10/75 7; yb74 32, 255; km 2/74 7; km 5/74 3; km 8/74 1; w73 27; yb73 32, 255-6; yb72 255; w71 25, 334; km 2/71 3
older persons: w75 186; w74 285, 537; w73 511; w71 339
personal organization: w71 336
physical benefits: km 2/72 4; km 2/71 6
proper viewpoint: km 5/74 3-4, 6; km 2/73 3-6; km 5/73 3-6; w71 214
requirements: km 5/74 4; or 136-7; km 2/72 3; w71 336; km 2/71 3-4
retired persons: g75 11/8 16
secular work: w71 337
special pioneers: yb75 32, 258; km 2/75 3-4; or 141-3
suggestions for success: w71 335-8
temporary pioneers: w75 189, 443; km 2/75 3; km 4/75 4; km 6/75 1; km 2/74 7; or 140-1; km 2/72 3-4, 6; km 1/71 3; km 2/71 4-5; km 6/71 4
youths: w75 186-7, 443; yb73 55; km 5/73 3-6; km 2/71 5-6
(SEE ALSO FIELD SERVICE, MISSIONARIES, TEMPORARY PIONEERS)

PIPE(S)
smoking: g75 12/22 30
water in, overnight: g75 11/22 31

PIRACY
airplanes: g71 6/8 18

PISHON
river: w71 540

PITCAIRN (Island)
Jehovah's witnesses: g75 1/22 30

PLACENTA
g74 2/8 13-14

PLAGUES (Blows)
"deadly plague" (Re 6:8): w74 358-9
Egypt:
first (water to blood): w72 39; kj 16-17
second (frogs): w72 39; kj 17
third (gnats): w72 39; kj 17
fourth (gadflies): w72 39; kj 18
fifth (pestilence on animals): kj 18-19
seventh (hail): w72 39-40
tenth (death of firstborn): po 108; w72 40; kj 19
importance of Moses' announcing: w74 333
seven (Re 16): yb75 236
fourth: w74 756

PLANETS
discussion: g75 8/22 12-16
possibility of life on other: g73 5/22 3, 6, 11-15
radiation: g73 11/22 4

List by Name

Earth: g75 3/8 30
Eros: g75 8/22 14-15
Jupiter: g75 8/22 13-14; g74 5/22 30; g73 5/22 12; w72 291
Mars: g75 2/8 29; g75 8/22 14; g74 5/22 30; g73 5/22 9-11; g72 1/22 29; g72 7/8 29
Mercury: g75 8/22 13; g74 5/22 30
Saturn: g75 8/22 15-16
Venus: g75 8/22 12-13; g75 12/22 29; g74 5/22 30; g73 5/22 11-12; g72 9/8 29; g71 3/8 30-1
(SEE ALSO ASTRONOMY, SOLAR SYSTEM, UNIVERSE)

PLANTS
disease: g74 3/8 29; g72 7/22 6-7
dried: g72 7/8 15
evidence of Creator: w71 152
fertilizing: g72 7/22 7; g72 10/22 7
flowers: w71 325
African: g75 2/8 20-3
chrysanthemum: g71 7/8 14-15
timing mechanisms: w73 579
varieties: g71 1/8 19
gardens: g74 5/22 9-12
growth: g72 10/22 6-7
homes: g72 7/8 13-15
indoor gardens: g72 7/8 13-15
light's effects: g71 7/8 13-15
microscopic: g74 1/22 9-10
mixed culture: g71 5/22 17-20
ocean plants: g75 11/8 17
photosynthesis: ts 147; g74 1/22 10; g72 2/8 10; g72 10/8 25; g72 10/22 6-7
poisonous: g72 8/8 31
purify water: g75 4/22 29-30
seeds:
sprouted: g75 12/22 25-6
shrubs: g75 5/8 29
terrarium: g72 7/8 15
tropics: g72 3/8 26
twilight's effect: g71 3/8 22
vegetables: g74 5/22 9-12
giant plants: g75 12/22 30
watering: g74 5/22 12
wild food: g74 9/22 6-7

List by Name

algae: g74 1/22 9-10
bamboo: g73 1/8 22-4; g71 5/8 11
banana: g71 5/8 11
bean: g71 5/22 18-19
black gram: g73 11/22 20
bulrush: g75 4/22 29-30
cactus: g72 7/8 15; g72 9/8 10
carrot: g71 5/22 20
cattail: g74 9/22 7
coca: w72 594
corn salad: g72 9/22 31
dandelion: g74 9/22 6
diatoms: g74 1/22 9-10; g71 1/8 8; g71 4/22 11
fennel: g71 5/22 19
jojoba shrub: g75 7/22 30
Klamath weed: g72 9/8 10-11
kohlrabi: g71 5/22 20
leek: g71 5/22 20
lettuce: g71 5/22 20
maguey: g73 5/22 25-6
nettle: g74 9/22 6
oat: g72 7/22 6
phytoplankton: g75 11/8 17
poppy: w72 596
radish: g71 5/22 20
ragweed: g71 7/8 14
rice: g72 7/22 3-4, 7-8
savoy: g71 5/22 19
seaweed: g72 3/22 25-6
Sedum telephium: g71 7/8 14
spinach: g71 5/22 18
Spirogyra: g74 1/22 10
tobacco: g71 7/8 13
Volvox: g74 1/22 10
wheat: g72 7/22 3-6, 8
wormwood: g71 5/22 19
(SEE ALSO TREE)

PLASMA VOLUME EXPANDERS
advantages over blood: g74 6/22 19, 21; g73 6/8 15
dextrose solution: g74 6/22 18-20
doctors' use of, for their loved ones: g75 7/8 30
research: g74 6/22 22
Ringer's lactate solution: g74 6/22 19-21; g73 2/8 19; g71 6/8 31
saline solution: g75 8/8 19; w74 524; g74 6/22 19, 21
seawater: g73 6/8 15
synthetic blood: g73 7/8 31; g72 6/22 29-30
(SEE ALSO BLOOD TRANSFUSION)

PLASTIC(S)
g74 12/8 30-1

PLAY
animals: g75 10/22 24-6

PLAYING CARDS
g75 6/22 27-8

PLEASURE
lovers of: g75 3/22 29; g72 1/22 26
wise view of: w74 373-4; g72 3/8 4

PLUMBING
repairs: g74 7/8 18-19
PNEUMONIA
g74 12/22 11-12
POETRY
Adam: w74 308
Hebrew: w73 188, 190; g73 2/8 27-8
POISE
public speaking: sg 181-4
POISONS
accidental poisonings: g71 5/8 29; g71 12/8 31
carbon monoxide: g73 2/22 23
first aid: g74 9/22 8
food poisoning: g72 2/8 30
home canning: g75 8/8 29
fumes from mixed cleaners: g75 12/22 30
insecticides: g73 1/22 30; g72 5/8 30; g72 7/8 30; g72 8/8 31; g71 1/8 8; g71 4/22 11-12; g71 9/22 29
kokoá frog: g75 3/22 14
mushrooms: g71 8/8 30
paint: g71 5/8 29; g71 7/8 29; g71 7/22 29
pencils: g71 7/22 29
pet food: g74 12/22 29
plants: g72 8/8 31
poultry feed: g71 3/22 29
serums: w74 351
treatment: g72 10/22 30
POLAND
doctors:
women: g75 11/22 31
Jehovah's witnesses: w71 490
POLICE
assaults on: g71 2/22 16-18
assist Witnesses: yb75 185; yb74 126-7
comments on Witness conduct: w72 381
corruption: g75 11/22 6, 8; g72 3/22 3
dangers: g74 7/8 29
detective work: g75 11/22 8-9
dishonesty: g74 10/22 30
experiences: yb73 161-2, 193; w72 70; yb72 105-6, 244; w71 542-3
New York City veteran officer: g75 11/22 5-10
fingerprinting: g71 1/22 31
frustration: g75 11/22 6-8
lack of confidence in: g74 4/22 29-30
methods: g73 4/22 8, 12
murder of: g75 11/22 7
New York city: g75 9/22 30
personal appearance: g72 10/8 31
private: g75 5/22 30; g73 3/8 30
refuse to protect Witnesses: yb75 185, 188
strike: w72 261; g71 2/22 18
POLIOMYELITIS
w74 132-3; g71 1/22 15
POLITICS
Bible view: w75 357-8; w74 679-80; g74 11/22 6; w73 549; w71 465-6; g71 5/8 4
a protection: w75 697
bragging: g74 12/22 30
Catholic church: g74 11/22 3-5; w73 549; g73 6/8 23-5; g73 9/8 3-6; g73 11/8 7; g73 12/8 16-19; w72 367; yb72 142-3; g72 2/22 30; g72 4/22 6-11, 14-17, 30; g72 6/22 9-10, 24-6; g72 12/22 29; w71 740; g71 2/22 3-6; g71 7/22 6-8; g71 8/22 29
Christendom: g73 1/22 29; g73 4/8 29; g73 6/8 16-19, 23-5; g73 12/8 16-19, 29; w72 340, 366-7, 573-4; g72 3/8 19; g72 4/22 3-11, 14-17; g72 7/8 31; g72 12/22 29; kj 152-3, 296-8; g71 1/8 29; g71 5/8 3-4; g71 12/8 3-4
missionaries of: g75 9/22 21
clergy: w74 101; g74 11/22 3-6; w73 675; g73 6/8 16-19, 23-5; g73 9/8 3-6; g73 11/8 7; w71 644; g71 5/8 3-4
corruption: g75 11/8 21-2; g73 1/8 30; g73 6/22 7; g73 11/8 3-5; w71 299-300
experiences:
politicians accept truth: w75 266; g75 11/8 21-3
school: g72 9/8 7
failure of leaders: w75 241-3
instability: g74 7/22 29
Jesus Christ: g74 11/22 6
leaders distrusted: g72 8/22 29
symbolic representation: w75 227-9
view of worldly people: g73 10/8 31
POLLUTION
abolition: ts 147; g73 9/8 23-4; w72 355-8; g71 4/22 22-7
air: sl 11; g75 12/22 8-9; g73 8/8 31; w72 614; g72 1/22 29; g72 3/8 29; g72 6/8 3; g72 7/22 29; g72 8/8 15-16, 18-19; g72 9/8 29-30; g72 10/8 10-11; g71 1/8 6-7; g71 4/22 6-8; g71 6/8 9-11; g71 10/8 6; g71 10/22 10; g71 12/8 29
cities: g74 9/8 20
deaths: g74 8/22 30-1
cadmium: g71 9/8 31
cancer: g75 10/22 30; g74 9/8 20
causes: g75 7/8 10-11; g75 12/22 9; g71 4/22 14-19
control problems: g73 2/22 30; g71 4/22 20-2; g71 10/22 10
cost to remedy in U.S.: g72 10/8 30
DDT: ts 147-8; g71 4/22 12
definition: tp 15
discussion: g75 7/8 8-11; g71 1/8 5-8; g71 4/22 3-29
earth: sl 11; g74 8/22 29; g73 9/8 23-4; w72 355, 613; g71 4/22 3-30; g71 10/8 6
ability to recover from: g75 12/22 4-7
effect on wildlife: g73 5/8 18
God not to blame: g75 7/8 8-11
mercury: g73 1/22 30; g72 5/8 30; g71 4/8 29
noise: g72 1/22 30; g72 12/22 29; g71 10/8 6, 30
ocean: g75 1/8 30; g75 7/8 10
oil spill: g74 1/8 30
plastic: g73 5/22 30; g73 9/8 23
prevention: g71 1/8 8
radioactivity: g73 5/22 30; g72 9/22 9-12
recycling: g71 4/22 21
results: g74 1/8 30; tp 16; g72 3/8 29-30; g71 4/22 13-14
returnable bottles: g73 9/8 23
soil: g71 4/22 11-12
solid wastes: w72 613
solutions: g75 12/22 9-11; tp 44-5
suggestions to reduce: g71 4/22 28
threat to mankind: g74 10/8 6; tp 15-17; g73 11/22 29-30; g72 10/8 10-11; kj 158; g71 4/22 3-5, 13-14, 18-19
underground: g71 8/8 31
water: sl 11; g74 2/22 24; g73 2/22 31; g73 4/8 30; g73 7/22 30; g73 9/8 30; g73 11/22 29-30; w72 613-14; g72 5/8 29; g72 7/8 29-30; g72 8/22 31; g72 9/22 31; g72 10/8 11; g71 1/8 7-8; g71 4/22 8-11, 30; g71 7/8 29; g71 7/22 29; g71 9/8 30-1; g71 9/22 29; g71 10/8 6; g71 12/8 29
bulrushes used to control: g75 4/22 29-30
why continues: g73 3/8 31
POLO
game: g72 10/22 25-6
POLYCARP
martyrdom: w72 416
POLYGAMY
Africa: g75 3/8 15; g75 12/8 13-17; yb74 34; g74 1/22 21, 25; w73 151-5; yb73 143, 167; w71 158; g71 10/22 7-8
Bible view: g71 10/22 7
clergy view: w75 200, 762; g74 12/8 15; w72 366; g72 4/8 30
experiences:
rejected to conform to Bible truth: yb76 185; g75 12/8 13-17; g74 1/22 21; g74 2/8 25; g74 3/8 20-1; yb72 243; w71 124-5
(SEE ALSO MARRIAGE)
POLYNESIA
Jehovah's witnesses: w74 647-8
PONAPE
Jehovah's witnesses: yb76 26-7; yb75 26-7; yb74 26-7; yb73 26-7; yb72 36-7
population: yb73 26; yb72 36
PONTIFEX MAXIMUS
bishops of Rome: ka 382-3; w72 626; dn 19-20
Constantine: sl 208-9, 235; w72 625-6; dn 19-20
pagan origin: g75 1/8 24
(SEE ALSO POPES)
POOR
governments fail: w72 579-80
nation of Israel: w72 579
needs satisfied: w72 580-1
POPES
apostolic succession: g71 11/22 11
birth-control ban: g71 1/8 30
celibacy: g75 5/8 27
Communist leader visits: g71 1/8 29
corruption: g71 5/8 12-16
decline of influence: g75 9/8 25
demonstration against: g71 7/22 29
divinity claims: w75 203; ka 380
infallibility: w74 273, 720; ka 380; g72 9/8 20; g71 3/8 30; g71 5/22 29
military organizations: g75 5/22 13-14
morals: g71 11/22 11
Nazi atrocities: g75 2/22 17-23
Palatine Guard: g75 5/22 13-17

papal primacy: w74 742
rivalry among: g71 5/8 12-16
statements on—
  celibacy: g75 5/8 27
  church crisis: g74 4/22 18
  Communism: g72 10/8 7
  Nazi atrocities: g75 2/22 17-19
  peace: g72 10/8 8
  United Nations: g73 2/8 29
  war: g75 2/22 19; w71 407
  world unity: w72 47
titles: w75 203; g75 1/8 24
travels: g71 2/8 16-19
Treaty of London: kj 59

List by Name

Alexander II: g71 5/8 13
Benedict IX: g71 5/8 12-13
Benedict XIII: g71 5/8 15
Clement II: g71 5/8 13
Clement V: g71 5/8 13
Clement VII: g71 5/8 14
Damasus: ka 383
Gregory VI: g71 5/8 12-13
Gregory IX: g71 1/22 20
Gregory XI: g71 5/8 13
Gregory XII: g71 5/8 15
Honorius II: g71 5/8 13
Innocent IV: g71 1/22 20
John XXIII: g71 5/8 15
Julius II: g75 5/22 13
Leo III: g73 5/8 15; w72 573
Leo X: g72 3/8 16, 18
Martin V: g71 5/8 15
Paul III: g75 1/8 24
Paul VI: w75 400; g75 2/22 17; g75 5/8 27; g75 5/22 14-16; w74 295, 720, 742; g74 3/22 29; g74 4/22 18, 29; g74 10/22 29; g74 11/22 31; w73 614, 707-8; g73 2/8 29; g73 12/8 16; g73 12/22 29; w72 47; g72 1/22 31; g72 3/8 29; g72 3/22 9-11; g72 5/8 9, 11; g72 6/22 10; g72 7/22 30; g72 10/8 8, 9; g71 2/8 16-19; g71 5/8 12, 16; g71 7/22 29; g71 10/8 29
  question to, "Why don't you forbid Catholics to take part in wars?": w71 407
Pius XI: w73 708; yb73 117-18; g72 10/8 7
Pius XII: g75 2/22 17-23
Sylvester III: g71 5/8 12-13
Urban II: g72 4/22 12, 14
Urban VI: g71 5/8 14
(SEE ALSO ROMAN CATHOLIC CHURCH, VATICAN)

POPULATION

area required for world, at one location: g75 4/22 30
birth rate: g74 11/8 9
Christendom: kj 317
cities: g73 4/8 30; g71 12/22 16
  growth compared to rurals: g75 9/8 30
distribution in world: g74 6/22 4; g73 4/8 30
earth's food supply: g75 2/8 7, 30; g74 6/22 6-7, 29; tp 109; g71 11/22 20
increase: g75 2/8 3-5; g75 2/22 30; g74 1/22 7; g74 4/8 6-7; g74 6/22 3-4; g74 7/22 5-6; g74 11/22 16; ka 282; tp 108; g73 10/8 7; w72 616; g72 1/22 9; g72 2/8 29; g72 7/8 26; g72 7/22 10; g72 10/8 11; g71 1/8 30; g71 4/22 16; g71 6/8 29; g71 10/8 11, 17
Jews: g73 2/8 31
land area used: g71 4/22 17
land per person: g75 4/22 30; ts 134-5
1914: ka 257
number of elderly: g75 11/8 30-1
poor desire children: g74 10/8 29
poor nations: g74 12/8 9
reasons for increase: g74 6/22 3-4, 7-8; g74 10/8 29
religious: ka 282
threat of overpopulation: g75 4/8 30; g74 4/8 6; g74 6/22 3-8; g74 11/8 9-10; tp 13-14; w72 616; g72 7/8 26; g72 10/8 11
  doctor's advice for dealing with: g75 6/8 30
total in human history: tp 108
world: sl 11; g75 2/8 3-5; g75 2/22 30; g75 5/8 31; g74 4/8 6-7; g74 7/22 5-6; g74 11/22 16; ka 282; tp 13; g72 10/8 11; kj 318; g71 1/8 30

Quotation

vegetable diet could support fifty billion people: g75 2/8 30

PORCELAIN

g73 8/8 13-14

PORNEIA

w74 160, 485-6, 671, 703-4

PORNOGRAPHY

Bible view: w75 756; g73 11/22 27-8
clergymen: g74 12/22 31; g72 12/8 29; g71 7/8 30
crime: g74 3/8 15; g73 4/22 30
Denmark: yb73 10-11
derivation of word: w72 767
discussion: g73 5/8 4; g73 11/22 27-8; g71 1/22 16-19
experiences: yb73 10; w72 125
link with organized crime: g75 12/22 29
movies: g73 4/8 31; g73 5/8 4
(SEE ALSO MORAL BREAKDOWN)

PORTUGAL

aqueducts: g73 1/8 13-15
Catholic church: g73 6/22 31
Jehovah's witnesses: yb76 28-9, 31-2; yb75 17-18, 28-9; g75 2/8 29; km 3/75 1; yb74 28-9; km 7/74 1; yb73 28-9; w72 390; yb72 38-9; g72 9/22 26; km 12/72 4, 6; w71 542-3
  legal recognition: w75 169-71; g75 2/8 29
population: yb73 28; yb72 38

PORTUGUESE GUINEA

Jehovah's witnesses: yb74 28-9; yb73 28-9; yb72 38-9
population: yb73 28; yb72 38

POSTAL SYSTEM

advertising on stamps: g72 3/8 29
history: g71 7/8 20-1
mailbox use: g75 10/22 30
rare stamps: g71 7/8 23
stamp collecting: g71 7/8 20-3
(SEE ALSO LETTERS)

POTASSIUM

g74 4/22 24

POTS

widemouthed cooking: pm 403-5

POTTER'S FIELD

location: w75 367

POVERTY

aiding the needy: w72 579-83
ancient Israel: w75 70; w72 579
causes: w75 68-9
Christendom's view: w75 69; w71 419-22
discussion: w75 67-70
India: w75 68
"poor always with you": w75 69-70
prevalence: w75 67-8; w74 550; g74 12/8 9-10; w72 615-16; g72 5/22 16; g72 12/8 31; g71 10/8 7
problems of poor nations: g74 12/8 8-11
right view of situation: w75 70; w74 420, 439
United States: w75 67-8; g74 8/8 29; g73 11/22 8-9

POWER

discussion: g73 2/22 20-3; g72 8/8 13-19
failure of electric: g74 3/8 17-19
growth of Communist: g75 7/22 5-7
Jehovah gives: w74 522
production: g72 1/22 18-19; g72 2/22 31; g72 8/8 15; g72 9/22 9-12; g72 10/8 25-8; g71 5/8 17-19; g71 8/8 30
sources of: g75 2/8 30; g74 8/22 20-3; g72 8/8 16, 29; g72 10/8 25-8; g71 4/22 26
symbolic representation: w72 102; kj 39-40
uncanny power: g75 8/8 5
windmills: g75 9/22 30

PRAISE

right view: g72 2/22 3-4

PRAYER

acting in harmony with: w74 212; w72 330
addressing God as Father: w74 447-8
Aladura beliefs concerning: g71 9/8 16-18
Amen: w72 334; g72 11/22 27-8; te 47-8
answered: yb76 12-14; w75 42, 326, 334, 413, 424; yb75 21, 134-5; g75 2/8 25; g75 5/8 4-5; g75 10/22 21; km 6/75 1; w74 712; yb74 177, 191, 194; g74 1/8 9-11; g74 2/22 4, 7; g74 3/22 7; g74 12/22 23; w73 760; yb73 18-19; g73 3/8 25-6; km 12/73 3; w72 146, 155, 338, 389-90; g72 3/8 23; km 11/72 6; w71 383
Bible studies: sg 77-8
children: g72 11/22 27-8; te 47-50
congregation: w75 413; w72 334-5, 411; or 92; km 1/72 8; km 9/72 8
discussion: w75 401-13; g75 9/22 3-4; w74 136-8; g74 1/8 8-11; g74 6/8 5-7; w72 328-38, 389-90; g72 8/22 27-8; te 47-50; g71 2/22 27-8
disfellowshiped persons: w71 383-4
early Christians: g74 6/8 7

faith: w75 402-3; w74 136; g74 6/8 5
fear cast out: w74 116; w73 210-11
field service: w73 405; w72 330
for miraculous healing: g75 9/22 4
holy spirit's role: w74 115-16, 415; w73 405-6
husband and wife: g74 5/22 4
importance: w74 115-16; g73 3/8 25-6; w72 134-5, 329-30, 404; or 187; w71 586; g71 2/22 27-8
improving quality: w74 116, 136-8
in the name of Jesus: w73 104; g72 8/22 28
Israelite: g74 1/8 9
Jehovah not reproaching: w74 318
knowledge: w74 136
Lord's Prayer: w74 235; g74 6/8 7; g72 11/22 27-8; te 49-50
mealtime: w75 301; w72 334
meaning of term: g72 8/22 27
meditation prior to: w75 411, 413
need of: w73 367-8
not hindering: w74 212
offered to the right one: w74 729; g72 8/22 28
overcoming bad habits: w73 454-5
personal benefits: w74 149, 409; w73 174; w72 329-30, 335-6, 531-2
posture: g74 1/8 10-11; w72 335; te 48-9
power of: yb74 136, 176-7, 185
practices of worldly religions:
  Buddhism: w74 259
  Catholicism: g75 1/22 27; w74 259-60; ts 64-8; g72 8/22 27-8
  for British pound: g75 8/22 29
  prayer book: g74 6/8 5
  "prayer breakfasts": g75 3/22 30
  purgatory: ts 64-9
  repetitious: w74 259-60; ts 66-7; g74 6/8 5
praise: g71 2/22 28
primary requirement: w74 136
'problem of what to pray for' (Ro 8:26): w75 121-2
Psalms: g71 1/22 5-8
regularity: w74 211; g74 1/8 11; w72 328-38, 404, 527-9
right manner: w74 137-8, 729; g74 1/8 10-11; g74 6/8 5; w72 389; g72 8/22 27-8; g72 11/22 27-8; w71 150; sg 78; g71 2/22 28
right matters: yb75 199-200; w74 136-8; g74 1/8 9-10; g74 6/8 5-7; w73 474; w72 135, 330-1, 335-7; w71 586; te 49-50; g71 2/22 27-8
  enemies: g71 1/22 6-7
  fellow Christians: w74 137, 702; g74 6/8 7; g72 8/22 27-8
  forgiveness of sins: w74 137-8; w72 335
  for strength: w74 249; g74 6/8 6-7; g73 3/8 25-6; w72 329, 522
  God's kingdom: w74 137
  God's spirit: w72 329-30, 757
  personal needs: w71 263
  personal problems: w75 118; w74 137-8
  sanctification of God's name: w74 137
  sickness: w74 137-8; g74 6/8 6
Scriptural examples: w75 405; w74 137-8, 249; g74 1/8 9-10; g74 6/8 5-7; w72 328-9, 389, 527-8; sg 77-8; g71 2/22 27
silent: w74 136; g74 1/8 11
spirituality: w74 211-12
thanksgiving: g74 6/8 6; w72 332-3

PREACHING

adaptability: w74 185-7; or 115-16; sg 150, 172-5
attitude of Witness: km 7/75 4; w74 60, 124-5, 183-4, 568-9; km 1/74 4; w73 21-2, 56-8; tp 173-5; w72 726-9; or 130-2; km 4/72 3; km 6/72 3-4; km 9/72 8; w71 214, 218-19, 313, 413-14
Australian outback: w75 677-80
balanced view: w74 568-9, 575-6
Bible studies: or 121-5; km 1/72 8; km 2/72 8; km 7/72 4; km 11/72 5-6; km 5/71 4; km 7/71 3
by fine conduct: w74 187; km 8/74 8
children: or 130
Christian obligation: yb76 258; g75 1/22 24; w74 183; km 5/74 3; g73 9/22 5-6
despite world's hatred: w73 658-61
discussion: w74 182-8; w71 701-3
divisional campaigns: yb75 153-4
early Christians: w74 61, 183, 185; w73 681-3, 687-8, 717-18; g72 11/8 8
effectiveness: km 7/74 4; sg 99; km 8/71 4
encouraging others to begin: km 1/74 3
endurance: km 4/75 1; w71 119-20
exposing falsehood: w74 35, 37
friendliness: km 7/74 4
group witnessing: or 119-20; km 6/71 4
house-to-house: yb76 70, 99, 160, 182; w74 241-2
importance: w74 183, 188, 241-2, 332-6, 568-9; w72 423; km 5/71 4
improving: sg 96-9
informal: yb76 17, 21, 87; w75 40, 318; w74 185-7, 337-8; km 3/74 4; w72 400-3; sg 80-2; km 12/71 4
information marching: yb75 160-1
introductions: km 5/74 8
isolated territory: w75 43, 247; g75 2/8 25-6; w74 141-3
Jesus set example: km 5/74 3; w73 21-2; or 112-13; w71 78; g71 12/22 9-10
lands: yb76 259; yb75 5, 30, 257; w73 23, 40; w72 27; pm 254; yb72 33; w71 24, 81, 504
language barrier: km 1/74 3-4
legal rights: km 8/71 3-4
literature offers: or 116-17
  Bibles: km 6/72 4
magazine distribution: or 117-18; km 4/71 4
making more time for: km 8/75 7-8
manners: km 7/75 4
methods: yb76 5, 35-8, 50-5, 57, 59-63, 65, 74, 79, 82-3, 91, 99, 102-3, 108-10, 137-8, 155, 172-3, 215; w74 185-7; or 113-26, 131-2
modern beginning: yb75 39-40, 45-6, 85-6, 124-5, 133-4
moral qualifications: or 128-30
nations shaken by Kingdom: w75 361-2
not-at-homes: or 118-19; w71 219-20; km 10/71 8
leaving literature: km 6/74 3
obstacles: w75 42-3, 677-9; g75 2/8 24-6; km 4/75 1; w74 537-8; yb73 248-9
overcoming apathy: w74 444-6
overcoming objections: w74 3-4; km 6/74 4; g72 8/8 7; sg 92-4; km 1/71 4
personal appearance: km 8/74 8; sg 184-7; g71 7/22 26
phonographs: yb76 38, 51, 53, 55, 57, 60-1, 111-12, 120, 137, 151; yb75 155-60
preparation: sg 39, 50-1; km 3/71 4; km 7/71 4; km 11/71 7
presentations: km 4/75 2; km 5/74 1; km 7/74 2; km 12/74 1, 4; km 9/71 2; km 12/71 2
prisons: w75 40, 649-50; g75 4/22 21-8; g75 10/8 19-20; km 9/75 1; km 4/74 4; yb72 157-8; w71 508; g71 8/8 14; g71 10/22 28
proper motive: w74 59-60, 183
purpose: w74 3-4, 37, 241-2; w73 329; tp 67; km 11/73 7; w72 277, 280; w71 611
quotas: w75 312
reaching householder's heart: km 7/75 4
reporting: or 126-8; km 4/71 3
request not to call anymore: km 6/74 4
responsible for others' lives: w74 123-4
return visits: km 1/75 4; or 121; km 1/72 8; km 2/72 8; km 8/72 4; w71 220-1
service reports (annual): yb76 22-32, 258-9; w75 23-8; yb75 23-32, 257-8; w74 26-31; yb74 23-32; w73 23-8; yb73 23-32, 255-6; w72 22-5, 27, 493; yb72 33-41; w71 23-9
sign: no religious calls: km 6/74 4
sincerity: km 7/74 4
sound cars: yb76 57, 135-7, 159; yb75 157-8
street witnessing: yb76 42-3, 141; yb75 162-4; km 8/75 8; km 9/75 8
tact: km 3/72 4; sg 70-2
territory coverage: km 6/74 3; or 73-4, 118-20; km 11/72 8
  rurals: km 6/75 3
"this good news of the kingdom": w74 332, 334; ka 297-8, 307-8; tp 83, 87; w72 366; or 3-7; pm 100-1; w71 78-82, 466, 753-4
to—
  children: km 12/75 8; km 2/73 8
  Eskimos: w75 43; g75 2/8 26
  "hippies": km 2/73 8
  Indians: w75 206
  men: km 12/75 8
  relatives: km 2/75 3-4; w74 185-6; or 111; km 11/71 8
  schoolmates: yb76 6
  women: km 12/75 8
tobacco users: km 7/73 4; km 11/73 7
training new publishers: yb75 227-8; km 5/74 7
under ban: yb76 10-11, 59-64, 144-5, 154-5, 157, 159, 194-5; yb75 18-20; w74 285; yb74 20, 112-15, 132-3, 139, 141-3, 155-6, 159; w72 137-8
"underground" activity: yb72 85-8, 93, 136, 139-41, 155-6, 163
use of airplanes: g75 2/8 25-6

use of Bible: km 2/75 4; km 9/75 8; km 12/75 7; km 2/74 8; or 114, 116; yb72 85-6; sg 122-9
use of letters: g75 1/22 30; km 6/74 3; sg 87-8
use of questions: km 4/75 4
use of telephone: km 7/73 4
war zone: w74 521
zeal: w75 311-13
(SEE ALSO FIELD SERVICE)

PREDESTINATION
Bible view: po 94, 102; g74 7/8 27-8; w73 488
Jacob and Esau: ts 58-9

PREGNANCY
abortion: w75 191-2; w74 509; g74 1/22 15-16; g74 2/8 13; g73 2/8 12-13; g73 3/22 8-11; g72 1/22 4; g72 3/22 30-1; g72 5/8 31; g72 5/22 8; g72 6/8 30; g72 7/22 30; w71 484; g71 2/22 29; g71 4/8 30; g71 6/22 29-30; g71 7/8 30; g71 7/22 19; g71 9/22 30; g71 12/8 31
affected by—
alcoholism: g75 7/22 29-30; g75 9/8 30; w74 453; g74 1/8 31
coffee drinking: g75 12/8 31
diet: g72 8/8 23; g71 4/8 29
drugs: g74 2/8 14; g73 6/22 28; g72 10/22 30; g71 2/8 31
herpes-virus (venereal disease): g74 10/8 29-30
insecticides: g72 7/8 30
measles (rubella): w75 191-2
smoking: g75 12/8 31; g74 2/8 14; g74 4/22 30; g74 5/22 31; g73 2/8 30; g73 6/22 29; g73 8/22 19-20; g72 6/22 30; g71 2/22 29; g71 5/8 29
syphilis: g74 2/8 14
artificial insemination: g74 8/8 27-8
before marriage: g74 8/22 31
biological description: g74 2/8 12-16
cesarean section: w75 159
experiences:
abortion rejected: w75 192, 266; g74 8/22 23
fetus: g71 7/22 19
sensitivity to noise: g75 8/22 30
hormone injections: g74 1/22 13, 15
long: g71 7/22 30
rights of unborn: g72 2/22 30
tubal: w75 191
weight gain during: g72 5/22 29
'woe to pregnant women': g74 11/8 11; w72 108-9
youths: g71 2/22 30
(SEE ALSO CHILDBIRTH)

PREJUDICE
causes: w73 537
overcoming in one's own life: tp 171-3; w71 323-4, 763
racial: w74 708-9, 711; g74 3/22 29; w73 515-19, 536-7, 735-6; tp 171-3; g72 9/22 4; w71 763
religious: w71 323-4
(SEE ALSO RACIAL PREJUDICE)

PREMARITAL RELATIONS
prevalence: g72 12/8 7
worldly view: g73 10/8 30-1
(SEE ALSO SEXUAL INTERCOURSE)

PREPARATION
field service: sg 39, 50-1; km 3/71 4; km 7/71 4; km 11/71 7
meetings: w72 408-9; km 9/72 7; sg 91-2
public speaking: sg 39-43, 50-1, 97-8, 152, 154, 179-80; km 12/71 3

PRESBYTERIAN CHURCH
decline: g75 9/8 30; g73 7/8 29; g73 11/8 29
divisions: g71 10/22 30
evolution theory: g73 10/22 22
experiences: yb73 41, 173, 191
failure: g75 9/8 30; g73 11/8 29; w72 366
financial condition: w74 524
homosexuality: w73 356
membership: w74 492; g74 3/22 29-30; g73 9/22 3; g71 5/8 3
merger rejected: g72 7/22 30
ministers: yb73 158-9; g73 7/22 29; w71 643, 675-6
moral condition: g72 4/22 18-19; g72 7/22 30; w71 451
Sunday schools: w74 555

PRESENCE
discussion: w74 397-400; ka 167-9, 187-8, 205-11, 259-61; g73 7/22 3-6
Greek word: sl 287-8; w74 399-400; ka 168-9; bi8 1364
Jehovah's: w72 710-11, 714, 716-17, 719-21
Jesus Christ's: w75 10-11; sl 286-8; w74 255, 397-400; ka 167-9, 205-11, 259-61; g73 7/22 3-6
misconceptions: w74 397
(SEE ALSO CHRIST'S PRESENCE)

PRESENTATIONS
field service: km 4/75 2; km 5/75 1; km 6/75 3; km 7/75 4; km 9/75 8; km 11/75 3; km 5/74 1; km 7/74 2; km 10/74 8; km 12/74 1, 4; km 4/73 4; km 6/73 1; km 10/73 8; km 11/73 7; km 12/73 2; km 9/71 2; km 12/71 2
adaptability: km 12/75 8

PRESIDING OVERSEER
annual report to Society: km 8/75 5
attitude toward others: w74 408
chairman of meetings of the elders: w75 472-3
change from "congregation overseer": w74 407-8
congregation book study: km 12/72 8
duties: km 12/75 6; w72 459-60; or 70-3
experience:
concern for congregation: w72 459
mailing address: km 8/75 4
(SEE ALSO OVERSEERS)

PRESSURES
coping with: w74 524; ts 189-90; g74 8/8 3-7
discussion: w73 501-3; g71 10/8 3-29
economic: w75 3-6, 12; w73 502
family opposition: w73 501-2
immorality: w73 502-3
kinds: g75 11/22 31; w74 561, 563-4; w71 584-5
not yielding to wrong: w74 519-20, 522-3
trusting in Jehovah: w74 701-2

PRESUMPTUOUSNESS
King Saul: w71 479

PRIDE
Bible view: w74 412
dangers: w74 299-300
definition: w74 299
effects: w74 409; yb74 212; g74 5/22 27; w73 437; g73 3/8 3-4; g71 5/22 10
overcoming, in one's own life: w74 299-300, 408-9, 411

PRIEST(S)
Catholic:
admission about church: w75 650; w74 747
admits clergy corruption: g74 2/22 29
admits Jehovah God's name: g74 4/22 20
admits Witnesses have truth: g74 4/22 20; g71 9/22 12
admits Witnesses love God more: w74 342
admits Witnesses publish truth: g74 8/8 29
alcoholism: g72 7/22 30
beliefs: yb74 18-19
celibacy: w74 102; w73 549; g72 5/8 9-12; g71 11/22 12
complain against lavish churches: g74 6/22 30
condone immorality: g74 5/22 29; g72 4/8 22-3; g72 4/22 19; w71 557
decrease in number: w75 684; g75 3/8 23-4; g74 6/22 30
discredit Bible: g74 6/8 30; g74 7/8 30
discussion: g75 3/22 16-19
dress in black: g75 5/22 29
encourage study with Witnesses: w74 143; yb72 194
favorably impressed by Bible truth: w74 143; g74 4/22 20
fighting: g74 2/22 30; g74 10/22 31
guerrilla warfare: g74 11/22 4-5
homosexuality: g74 4/22 30; g73 12/8 29
immorality: w74 38; g74 8/22 30; w72 281; g72 4/8 22; g72 5/8 9-10; g72 6/22 12; g71 7/22 4-5, 9-10
Jesuits: g74 7/8 10-12
lack accurate Bible knowledge: w75 650
lack interest in Bible: w73 547-8
lack interest in parishioners: yb73 18; g73 12/22 29
leave church: g73 12/22 29
marriage: g71 6/8 30; g71 8/8 24-5
motion pictures: g71 3/8 31
number world wide: ka 392
opposition to Witnesses: yb75 180-1, 183; g74 5/8 20; yb73 39-40, 63, 117-18, 152-3, 157; w72 148-50, 283-5; yb72 105-6, 127, 138, 150-1, 153-4, 160-1; w71 18

politics: w74 166, 217, 244; g74 1/22 29-30; g74 7/8 11-12; g74 11/22 3-5; g73 9/8 3-6; w72 367; g72 2/22 30; g72 6/22 9-10, 25; g72 11/22 29; w71 408, 644, 740; g71 2/22 3-6; g71 7/22 6-8
problems: g75 3/22 16-18; g74 7/8 10-12; g71 8/8 25
quitting: g75 3/8 23-4; g75 3/22 16-18; g75 6/22 31; w74 15, 102; g74 3/8 30; g74 4/8 30; g74 4/22 18; g74 7/8 10, 12; g73 7/8 29; g73 12/8 29; w72 214; g72 4/8 21, 30; g72 6/22 10-11; g72 8/22 30; w71 408, 484; g71 1/22 31; g71 5/8 29-30; g71 8/8 24-5; g71 8/22 13
rebellion: g74 4/22 18-19; g74 9/22 14-15; g72 6/8 29; g72 6/22 29; g72 7/8 31; g72 12/8 29
refuse to preach about God: g73 9/8 3-4
shortage: w74 456; g74 11/22 31; g74 12/22 8; w72 214, 367; g72 4/8 21, 30; g72 6/22 10; g72 8/8 30; g72 11/22 30; w71 408, 484, 739-40; g71 2/8 16-17, 30; g71 2/22 30; g71 4/8 30; g71 8/22 13, 30; g71 11/8 30; g71 12/22 30
why some continue: g74 5/8 30; g74 12/22 9
women: g71 2/8 30
congregation of God: w74 251-4, 690; ka 107-12, 116; pm 88, 103-5
discussion: w74 156-9
Israelite:
end of: w74 681
family of Aaron: po 114-15, 118
functions: w74 156-7; w72 489
high priest: w74 157, 251; pm 175-84
installation: w74 251; po 118; ka 104, 107
Levite assistants: po 114
prophetic significance: w71 283
purpose: ka 87-8
Urim and Thummim: w74 157
Jesus Christ: w74 157-9; w73 308-12; ka 87-93, 102-3; pm 87-8, 176, 179, 181-5; w71 570
juju: ts 70-2
kingdom of: w74 688, 694-5
Melchizedek: w74 158; ka 89-90
purpose: w74 156-7

PRIESTHOOD
congregation of God: ka 107-12, 116
discussion: w74 156-9
Israelite: w74 156-7
Aaron's house: po 114-15, 118; pm 175-6
installation: po 118; ka 104, 107
length of time it operated: pm 176
official services: w72 489
prophetic significance: ka 87, 103-12; pm 186-7; w71 283
separate from kingship: po 114-15
Melchizedek: w74 158; ka 88-90
purpose: w74 156-7

PRINCES
discussion: ka 131-6, 153-4
Hebrew word: ka 135
identified (Ps 45:16): sl 361-4; w74 292; g73 5/8 7; w72 581; kj 404-5
when first identified: yb75 213-14
identified (Isa 32:1): w73 427-8; kj 404-5
Jehovah God: w71 716, 720
misconception regarding 1925: yb75 146
qualifications: ts 132
role in God's new order: sl 364; w74 292-3; ka 131-6, 153-4; kj 404-6

PRINCIPLES
application of Bible's: w74 311-17; w73 37-8; w72 195-6
in business: w75 291-3
challenge of moral: w72 515-16, 548
guide for Christians: g75 10/8 15-22; w72 589-90
Witnesses commended for: w75 44

PRINTING
first, from movable type: g74 8/8 7
Jehovah's witnesses: yb75 32, 128-30, 259; km 8/74 1; km 10/74 1; g73 9/22 7-16
Argentina: yb72 106-7
lithography: g72 8/22 24-6
religious: g74 9/8 16

PRISONS
baptisms in: g75 4/22 21-2, 28
Christian conduct: yb75 206, 208; g75 12/22 18
church members: g75 4/22 27; g74 2/22 31; g73 11/8 30; g71 6/8 30
discussion: g72 1/8 5-17
effects: g72 5/22 30
experiences:
asked to teach other prisoners the Bible: g75 12/22 18
"furloughed" after becoming Witness: g75 5/22 29
jailer of Witnesses accepts truth (Korea): g71 8/8 13-15
prisoner institutionalized all his life accepts truth: g75 4/22 28
prisoners accept truth: w75 40
prison inmates taken to assembly for baptism: g75 4/22 26
released because became Witness: g74 4/8 27-8
failure: g75 4/22 24; g74 4/22 30; g73 4/22 10-12, 30; g73 10/22 31
fine or imprisonment: w75 223-4
flogging: g74 12/22 31
history of: g72 1/8 5-7
holding meetings: g75 4/22 25-8; yb75 206
homosexuality: g75 3/8 31
inmates increase: g71 10/8 30
inmates pay for crimes: g73 1/22 29
numbers in: g74 10/22 30
preaching in: w75 649-50; yb75 112, 176-7, 206; km 9/75 1; yb74 13, 190-1; g74 4/8 27-8; km 4/74 4; yb73 244-5; w72 283; yb72 157-8; g72 7/8 20; g72 9/22 26; w71 508; g71 8/8 14; g71 10/22 28
rehabilitation: g75 4/22 24-8; g75 7/8 29
solitary confinement: yb74 226-8; w72 521, 524-5, 532
"spirits in prison": w71 607-8
Taiwan: yb72 217-18
United States:
Angola, Louisiana: g75 4/22 21-8
Burgaw, North Carolina: g75 4/22 28
Norfolk, Massachusetts: g75 4/22 28
pardons: yb75 207
vandalism: g73 12/8 30
Watch Tower Society's officers: yb75 104-9, 111-12, 115-17
Witnesses in Communist Chinese: yb75 208-9; yb74 56
Witnesses maltreated: yb73 216-19, 221
(SEE ALSO CONCENTRATION CAMPS, PERSECUTION)

PRIZES
tickets for, in "drawings" to advertise: g75 7/8 28

PROBABILITY
laws of: g75 3/22 20-3

PROBLEMS
causes: ml 14-16, 18-19
help with personal: km 10/74 8
mankind's: ml 3-4
causes: w75 259-60; g75 4/8 6-7
description: w75 259; g75 4/8 3-5
discussion: w75 259-62; g75 4/8 3-19
solution: w75 260-2; g75 3/22 30; g75 4/8 9-14
marital: w75 286-8

PROCLAMATION—A WARNING (Resolution)
distribution: yb75 136

PROCRASTINATION
w75 588; w73 101

PROCREATION
respect for powers of: w75 158-60

PRODIGAL SON
discussion: w72 432-5
Jehovah's mercy: w74 462

PROGRESS
benefits of, now: w75 92
making progress: w75 87-92

PROMISES
breaking: w73 59-62
God's: w75 700-2
keeping: w72 28-30

PRONUNCIATION
Bible names: w71 59
public speaking: sg 56, 146-9

PROPAGANDA
effects: g73 1/8 3
prevalence: g73 1/8 5

PROPHECY
Bible authenticity: w75 136-40; sl 289
fulfillment: yb76 79-80, 82; w75 3, 81-6, 136-40; yb75 247; ml 20-5; g75 10/8 13-14; w74 72-4, 163-5, 195-7, 243, 355-9, 425-6, 428-9, 572-3, 645, 681-3, 717-18; po 19-22, 151-3, 158-9; ts 152-63; g74 4/8 13-17; g74 5/8 17-19; w73 37, 211-12, 220-1; ka 294-329; g73 1/22 7-9; w72 172-8, 180-1, 241-2, 499-501; w71 467-73; kj 31; g71 10/8 26; g71 12/8 5-9
Ammonites: w75 421-3
Moabites: w75 421-3
Philistines: w75 421-3
Jesus Christ: w71 95-6

man's attempts: g73 1/22 5-7
Middle East current events: w75 387-9
seven times: ts 155-60
seventy weeks: po 131-2, 144-5; g71 12/8 6-9
source: w71 466-7
when understood: w75 95-6
why God uses symbols: ts 151-2
(SEE ALSO BIBLE AUTHENTICITY, FUTURE)

PROPHESYING
gift of spirit: w71 502-4
witness borne to Jesus inspires: w71 95-6

PROPHETIC DRAMAS
discussion: w72 502-4

List by Name
Abraham, Isaac: w72 503
Mordecai, Esther: w71 172-85
Ruth, Naomi, Boaz: w72 76-90, 503-4

PROPHETS
behavior: w71 575-6
false: g73 11/22 6-7; pm 353-5
purpose: w74 297
true, identified: pm 355

PROSPERITY
Israel: g71 11/22 27-8
kingdom of God: w72 582-3

PROSTHESIS
g73 12/22 24-6

PROSTITUTION
clergy: g75 1/8 31; g74 9/22 30
convention in church: g74 9/8 30
disease: g74 9/8 21
efforts to control: g73 3/22 29; g72 3/22 30
employment: w72 591-2
experiences: w75 285; w73 29-30; g73 2/8 14-15
former living-child goddesses: g75 6/22 30
France: g73 7/22 30-1
Italy: w71 452
religious: kj 238-63
runaways: g71 6/8 29
truth overcomes: g73 8/22 8
(SEE ALSO FORNICATION)

PROTECTION
angelic: yb75 187-90
Bible examples: w72 632-4
crime: g75 11/22 4, 11-16
dogs for: g74 7/22 17-19
great tribulation: w75 377-8; w74 170-2, 318, 667-8
guns for: g75 11/22 12, 29
Jehovah's: yb76 64-5; w75 376-8; sl 350; yb75 260-1; w74 169-72, 203, 722-34, 752-4, 757-8, 760-6; yb74 134-6, 140-1, 147-8, 207-10; g74 12/22 23, 25
self-defense: g75 9/8 27-8; g75 12/8 28-9
separateness from world a: w75 697

PROTEIN
discussion: g72 12/22 8-11
probability of a molecule arising by chance: g71 4/8 6
sources of: g74 9/22 4-5; g73 8/22 4; g72 12/22 11
(SEE ALSO GREEN REVOLUTION)

PROTESTANTISM
beginning: w74 273; g72 3/8 16-19
church attendance: w74 15
clergy: yb72 48; g72 11/8 29; w71 408
contributions: g72 10/22 29
disunity: g72 7/22 30; w71 298
evangelizing: w74 492
evolution theory: g74 7/8 22
membership: sl 206; g72 10/22 29
morals: g72 4/22 18-20
politics: g73 12/22 29
Spain: g75 2/22 29
view of papacy: w74 273
violence: g72 4/22 17
war: w75 445; w74 360; g72 2/22 30; g72 4/22 6-10, 13-15, 17; g72 10/22 29; g71 6/22 16-19

Quotations
end of Protestantism soon a reality: g72 8/22 17
Protestants are tired and confused: g71 10/8 29
(SEE ALSO CHRISTENDOM, CHURCH)

PROVERBS
discussion: w73 489-94

PRUNE
discussion: g71 5/8 23

PSALMS (Book)
acrostic: w73 188
discussion of 91st: w74 722-34, 752-66
discussion of 116th: w75 302-4, 328-31
discussion of 119th: w73 188-90
Hallel: ka 410
prayer: g71 1/22 5-8
prophetic: g71 1/22 5
superscriptions: w72 61-2
superstitious uses: g71 1/22 5-6
why beneficial: g71 1/22 7-8
writers: w74 722

PSYCHIATRY
Bible truth superior: g75 4/22 19-21; g72 8/22 23
Christian view: w75 255-6; g75 4/22 17-18
clergy replaced by psychiatrists: g75 8/22 25-6
hypnotism: g74 9/8 27-8
inconsistencies: g74 10/22 29-30
nervous breakdown: g74 8/22 16, 18
psychiatrists' view of God: g75 4/22 17; g75 8/22 26
religious faith: g74 9/8 30
sexual behavior: w75 255; g75 4/22 17-18
Sigmund Freud: w75 255; g75 4/22 13; g74 10/22 5
suicide: g75 4/22 17; g72 12/8 29
treatment of mental illness: w75 255; g75 4/22 15-19; g73 9/22 17-20
use of astrology: g72 11/8 29
value: g75 8/22 25-6
witch doctor: g73 4/8 29
(SEE ALSO MENTAL ILLNESS)

PSYCHOLOGY
experiences:
psychologist attributes former criminal's change to Witnesses: g75 10/8 19-20
psychologist finds truth: g74 9/22 12
psychologist observes Bible help a family: g75 10/8 19
failure: g75 8/22 26; g71 12/8 30-1
marriage: w74 308

PSYCHOSOMATICS
w73 291-2

PSYCHOTHERAPY
mental illness: g71 9/22 23

PUBLIC DECLARATION
baptism: w72 694-8

PUBLICITY
Jesus avoided: g71 12/22 27-8

PUBLIC MEETINGS
advertising: or 96
beginning of weekly: yb76 161-2; yb75 199
chairman: km 12/73 4; or 66, 72, 95-6
chart talks: yb75 44, 50
class extension work: yb75 47-8
discussion: or 95-6
experience: w73 29
locations: or 96
ministerial servants: km 2/75 4
number: yb72 255
prayer: or 92, 95-6; km 9/72 8
qualifications of speaker: km 6/73 4
V. D. M. questionnaire: yb75 86-7
speakers: or 95; km 9/72 3; km 2/71 7-8
subjects: km 9/72 4-6; km 10/71 3-6
when no speaker: km 6/73 4
(SEE ALSO MEETINGS)

PUBLIC SPEAKING
accuracy of statement: sg 110-11
argumentation: sg 151, 153-8
audience contact: sg 138-40
body of talk: sg 47-8
clear, understandable: g74 12/22 13-15; sg 111-13, 172-3
coherence: sg 149-53
conclusions: g74 12/22 15; sg 48-9, 175-7
confidence and poise: sg 181-4
congregations: w71 701-3
conversational quality: sg 144-6
enthusiasm: g72 9/8 17-20; sg 163-5
experience:
first talk: yb72 80
extemporaneous: sg 58-63, 120-1, 145, 162-3
feeling: sg 165-7
fluency: sg 142-4
gathering material: sg 42-3
gestures: sg 127, 132-3
grammar: sg 57-8
hearts reached: sg 73-8
illustrations: g74 12/22 15; sg 52-3, 168-71
impromptu: sg 61-2
informative material: g74 12/22 14; sg 108-11
introductions: sg 46-7, 113-16, 123-5
lisping: w75 198-9

main points made to stand out: g74 12/22 14-15; sg 135-8
manuscript reading: sg 31-2, 120, 122-3, 139
material adapted for field service: sg 172-5
microphone: sg 68-9
modulation: sg 160-3
outline:
  preparation of: g74 12/22 14-15; sg 44-9, 59, 61
  Society provides first: yb75 199
  use of: sg 140-2
pausing: sg 32, 119-21, 123, 127
personal appearance: sg 184-7
preparation for delivery: sg 39-43, 50-1, 97-8, 152, 154, 179-80
pronunciation: sg 56, 146-9
questions: sg 52, 124, 157-8
quotations: sg 155-6
reading from Bible: sg 32-3, 40, 122-9, 146
repetition: g74 12/22 15; sg 53, 127, 130-2
scripture application made clear: sg 128-9
sense stress: sg 126-9, 158-60
stuttering: w75 198
summary of speech qualities: sg 106-7
teaching: sg 49-50, 52-4
theme: sg 114-15, 133-5, 152-3
timing: sg 177-81
use of notes: sg 138-42
voice improvement: g72 1/22 10-12; sg 63-8
volume: sg 116-19
word choice: sg 6-8, 54-7

PUBLIC WELFARE
(SEE WELFARE)

PUBLISHER
(SEE CONGREGATION PUBLISHERS)

PUBLISHER'S RECORD CARD
or 127

PUERTO RICO
Jehovah's witnesses: yb76 28-9; yb75 28-9; yb74 28-9; yb73 28-9; yb72 38-9; g72 5/8 17-20; km 11/72 6; w71 343-4; g71 12/22 4
population: yb73 28; yb72 38

PULPIT
proper view of term: w75 734

PUNCTUALITY
meetings: km 8/74 7

PURGATORY
Catholic definition: g74 6/8 27
Catholic statements: w75 56
Christendom: w75 55; w71 709-10
indulgences: w75 55; ts 64, 66-9
pagan concepts of: w75 55; ts 62, 64
prayer: ts 64-9
refutation: g74 6/8 27-8
(SEE ALSO IMMORTALITY OF THE SOUL)

PURIM
w71 185

PURPOSE
experiences:
  search for purpose in life: g75 5/8 4-5; g74 11/22 7-12
Greek word: po 11-12
harmonizing life with Jehovah's: w74 657-9, 664-5, 669
Jehovah's: w75 81-6, 96; w74 658-62, 669; po 11-15, 19, 34, 48-9, 60-1, 64, 102, 180, 187-8
  epitome of 6,000 years: w75 584-8
life:
  need for purpose: g75 5/8 4-5
  setting goals: g74 8/22 6-8

PURSUING MY PURPOSE IN LIFE
(SEE LIFE STORIES OF JEHOVAH'S WITNESSES)

QATAR
Jehovah's witnesses: yb76 26-7; yb75 26-7; yb74 26-7; yb73 26-7; yb72 36-7
population: yb73 26; yb72 36

QUAKERS
morals: g72 4/22 18-20

QUALITY(IES)
Jehovah's: fu 11-12
use of: w71 444

QUARRELS
results: g73 9/22 31

QUEBEC, CANADA
Catholic church: g75 3/8 17-19, 23-7; g74 2/8 29; g72 2/22 30; g71 8/8 29; g71 10/22 29
  parochial schools: g75 2/22 30
disaster: g71 7/22 21-2
discussion: g75 3/8 16-28
Duplessis, Maurice: g75 3/8 18-22, 26
Jehovah's witnesses: w75 42; g75 3/8 16, 18-23, 25-8; w74 142-3, 284-5; g74 11/8 18; yb73 10; w72 144, 148-51
  conventions: g75 3/8 16
maple sugar: g73 2/22 11-13

QUEEN OF SHEBA
'raised up in judgment': g75 10/22 13

QUESTIONS
attitude about unanswered: w72 504-5
baptismal candidates: or 19-52
Bible, answered: w72 498-501
improving answers: sg 90-6
locating the answers: sg 35-6
use in field service: km 4/75 4
use in teaching: g74 1/8 25-6; w72 115-16; sg 51-2, 76, 124, 157-8
writing to Watch Tower Society: km 2/71 8

RABBAH
conquest by Nebuchadnezzar: w73 61-2; kj 235-6

RABBI(S)
attitude toward Witnesses: g71 11/8 13-15
beliefs: g72 9/8 30
homosexual synagogue: w74 135
Jesus Christ called: w75 726
meaning of term: w75 726
view of mixed marriages: g71 8/22 30
Witnesses commended by: g71 1/8 24
woman: g72 8/22 30
(SEE ALSO CLERGY, JUDAISM)

RABBIT
greyhound racing: g75 10/22 31

RACES
all related: g74 6/22 27; g74 10/8 9
Bible view of segregation: w73 517-18, 537
intermarriage: w73 735-6
meaning of term: w73 516; g73 2/8 5
origin: w73 515-17; g73 2/8 5-6
"superiority": w73 735
variations: w73 515-18; g73 2/8 5-7

RACIAL PREJUDICE
absence among Witnesses: yb75 10-11; w74 443, 712-14; g74 9/8 6-7; w73 37, 518-19, 537, 679; ka 51-2; g71 10/22 12-13
  picture in *National Geographic:* g75 11/8 29
churches: w74 713
discussion: w73 515-19, 536-7, 735-6
effects: w74 675; g72 9/22 4
enduring: w73 475-6
examples: w74 707-10
experiences:
  Bible truth overcomes: w73 679; w71 763
  black revolutionary accepts Bible truth: w74 707-14
Mormons: w74 656; g74 12/8 30
remedy: tp 171-3
United States: yb75 237; w74 707-10

RADIATION
cancer: g74 9/8 21
cosmic rays: g73 7/8 5; g73 11/22 4; g72 4/8 8
sun: g75 4/8 8; g71 6/22 9

RADIO
Australia: g71 7/8 25-6
chain broadcasts by Watch Tower Society: yb76 102; yb75 138, 143-4, 151-2
first broadcast by Watch Tower Society: yb75 139-40
misreport about Bethel: yb73 107-8
national broadcast—'cease mobbing Witnesses': yb75 184
petitions regarding use by Watch Tower Society: yb75 155
radio astronomy: g71 11/22 30
silence: g71 7/8 25-6
use by Witnesses: yb76 109; yb73 47, 111-13, 201, 236; yb72 48
  opposed: yb75 154-5
Vatican: g75 8/8 29
WBBR: yb75 140-2, 144
"White" network: yb75 144

RADIOACTIVE CLOCK
carbon 14: g72 4/8 5-20
fallibility: g72 4/8 7-19; g71 4/8 31; g71 5/8 31

RADIOACTIVITY
dangers: g72 9/22 9-12
fallout decreases: g72 1/8 30
food contamination: g75 5/22 31
radioactive paper used to trap illegal printers: g75 9/8 30
radioactive wastes: g71 4/22 30

RADIOCARBON CLOCK
(SEE RADIOACTIVE CLOCK)

RADIOISOTOPES
g75 5/22 31

RAGE
w72 196

RAHAB
faith: w74 24-5

RAILROADS
accidents: g72 11/22 29
Argentina: yb72 51
convention trains: yb75 57-8
Europe: g72 3/8 30
Honduras: g72 4/8 26
Japan:
items lost on trains: g75 7/22 31
locomotives: g74 3/22 30
new trains: g72 11/8 30; g71 7/22 30
steam engines: g74 3/22 30

RAIN
acidic: g74 8/8 31
amount: g75 1/22 29
discussion: g73 7/8 6-7
pollution's effects: g72 3/8 29
record: g74 7/8 25

RAINBOW
discussion: g75 1/22 13-16
first: g75 1/22 13-16; po 82
significance: kj 47
theories to explain: g75 1/22 14-16

RANSOM
appreciating: w73 466-9
Author: w72 375; w71 304
benefits: w75 431-2; w74 254, 278; ts 137-9; w73 381-3, 464-9; g73 10/8 27; w71 276; kj 390-8
discussion: w75 429-32; g75 4/8 9-11; w73 464-9; w71 269-76
expression of God's love: w73 67-8
Greek word: w73 465
illustrations to help explain: g75 4/8 10
Jesus' blood: w72 607-8; w71 712-14
Jesus' role: sl 87; g75 4/8 10-11; g75 10/8 25; w73 277; w72 175, 235-8, 517, 685-8; g72 2/8 6-7; g72 9/22 7-8; w71 272-5
Mosaic law: w75 429-30
murderers: g75 11/22 28
ownership of mankind: g75 10/8 25; w74 121, 370-2, 598-9
paid for all mankind: w74 370; po 188
price required: w75 430-1; g75 1/8 27-8; g75 10/8 25; w74 121; po 116; ts 138; w72 236-7; w71 271-2
purpose: w74 70, 121, 370
relation to water of life: kj 387-8
religious denial: yb75 37
requirements for benefits: w74 370
(SEE ALSO JESUS CHRIST, SACRIFICES)

RAPE
college campuses: g74 1/8 30
conduct if threatened: g75 2/22 30; g75 11/22 14; g74 3/8 13-16; g73 4/22 16-17
contributing causes: g74 3/8 15-16; g74 8/22 29; g73 4/22 15-16; g71 10/22 30
experiences: g74 3/8 13-16
statistics: w74 99; g74 3/8 13; g74 8/22 29; g73 4/8 30

RAPTURE
w74 255, 397

RAT
control: g72 10/22 31; g71 5/22 31
India's "holy" rats: g75 9/22 30; w74 624
problem for cities: g75 3/8 30
resistance to poisons: g71 12/22 31
statistics: g75 6/8 29; w74 624; g71 5/22 31

RATTLESNAKE
g71 5/8 31

READING
Bible: w74 179-80; w71 62, 105; sg 21, 23, 32-3, 122-9, 146; km 1/71 4
statistics: w75 200
Bible view: w74 592
children: g74 2/8 4, 9-10; g71 10/22 30
value of reading aloud to them: w75 519; g75 12/22 30
decline as pastime: w74 273
discussion: sg 19-24, 29-33
eye movements: g75 12/8 23
improving: g75 12/8 22-4; w71 70-1; sg 21-4
lip movement: g75 2/22 30; g75 12/8 23-4
many read poorly: w74 592
public: w73 201-7; km 6/72 4; sg 29-33, 40; km 1/71 4
schools not teaching effectively: g74 2/8 4
selectivity in reading material: w74 112, 153; sg 20
speed: g75 12/8 24; w71 70-1; sg 22
thinking while: g75 12/8 24
value: w73 201-7; w71 733-4; sg 23-4
Watch Tower reading schools: w75 763; yb75 202; w74 410-11; yb74 7-8, 16; g74 7/22 16; w73 111-12; yb73 73-4, 159-60; yb72 240; w71 12, 157; g71 4/8 22-3
Witness children commended: g75 12/8 22

REASONABLENESS
demonstrating: g75 1/8 10-11
discussion: w75 707-8; km 3/75 3; w73 473-4
field service: w74 576; km 3/72 4
older men (elders): w72 591, 599

REBEKAH (Rebecca)
tactics regarding Isaac's blessing: po 94

REBELLION
Adam and Eve: w74 595-6; ts 31-4
angelic: w72 427-8
Catholic priests: g72 6/8 29; g72 7/8 31
examples: w72 261-2; kj 95-7, 100-3, 226-9
in family, not necessarily father's fault: km 7/75 3
"man of lawlessness": w75 167, 252-4
youth: g74 2/8 4-5; w73 136

REBIRTH
discussion: ts 53-60; g74 8/22 27-8

RECHABITES
symbolic mark: w72 634

RECONCILIATION
with Jehovah: w74 127-8; tp 179-86; w72 376-80

RECORDS
(SEE PHONOGRAPH)

RECREATION
Bible view: w74 373-4; km 7/74 3; w71 280
discussion: g72 11/22 9-11
experience: w71 280
family: w71 314
get-togethers: w72 403-4; g72 6/22 13-16
large social gatherings: km 7/74 3
oil painting: g74 5/8 21-3
ways time used: w74 273
youth: w75 461
(SEE ALSO ENTERTAINMENT, SOCIAL GATHERINGS)

RECYCLING
benefits: g75 6/22 29
metal: g71 8/8 30
paper: g72 5/22 30
sewage: g73 1/22 30; g71 10/22 29; g71 11/22 29-30
waste: g71 10/22 29-30

RED SEA
destruction of Egyptians: sl 367-8; po 109; w72 681; kj 19-21
flatfish: g75 11/8 29
Israelite crossing: sl 367; g74 4/8 26; w73 365; w72 681
trees: w73 84

REFORMATION
Czechoslovakia: yb72 126
Eighty-Year War: g72 9/22 21-5
England: w72 199; kj 69
Luther, Martin: w72 199; g72 3/8 16-19; kj 69
(SEE ALSO PROTESTANTISM)

REFUGE
city of refuge: g75 11/22 26-7
false: w75 595-604, 690-3
Jehovah: w75 636-9; yb75 260-1; w74 726-9, 731-4, 752-4, 759, 765
kingdom of God: w75 604-8, 685-97

REFUGEES
camp at Sinda Misale: g75 12/22 17-19; g73 3/8 19-21
Mozambique camps: yb75 9-10; yb74 15-17
supplies given by Witnesses: w73 267
Vietnamese: km 7/75 1

REGISTRATION
Selective Service requirements: g75 5/22 31

REGRET
Jehovah: po 74

REHABILITATION
artificial limbs: g73 12/22 24-6
criminals: g75 4/22 21-8; g75 7/8 29

REINCARNATION
Bible view: g75 4/8 27-8; ts 53-60
Buddhism: ts 53, 56; g72 2/22 18-19

experience:
  believer in accepts truth: g74 11/22 7-12
extent of belief: g75 4/8 27
Hinduism: w73 604

RELATIVES
Jesus': w75 220-3
marriage to near: w75 72-7
murder victims: w75 36
putting God first: w75 381-2
witnessing to: km 2/75 3-4

RELICS
"holy tunic": g73 8/8 26-7
worship: g75 12/22 14; g73 8/8 26-7; w72 416

RELIEF
needy brothers: or 149-50
modern-day examples: yb76 11, 16-17, 20-1, 211-12, 237-8; yb75 209-10; yb74 216-17; g74 3/8 7; g74 5/22 8; g74 7/8 26; g74 7/22 30; g74 12/22 26; km 11/74 1; w73 95-6, 134-5, 267-8; yb73 95; g73 3/8 13-16, 19-20; yb72 99-100, 137, 179, 225-6, 252-3; g72 8/8 26; w71 424-5; g71 3/22 25

RELIGION
changing one's: g74 4/8 20; g73 11/8 27-8; g71 1/8 27-8
criticism proper: w75 127-8; g74 11/22 27-8
demand for books on: w75 48
freedom of religion:
  Declaration of Helsinki peace conference: g75 11/8 6
Hebrew word: yb75 225
meaning of term: yb75 161, 225
need of mankind: w74 144; g74 12/8 21; w72 388
newspaper coverage of: g75 5/8 29
not all acceptable to God: g75 4/8 16-17; g74 1/22 18-19; g73 9/22 4-5; g73 11/8 27-8
standard for judging: w74 540, 543; w73 387-8; tp 23, 36; g73 11/8 28; w72 99-100
statistics: w71 14
youth: g72 11/8 3-8

False Religion
assault upon: yb75 228-9, 235; w73 675-6; yb73 162
"charity" drives: g73 11/22 24-6
Communism: w73 707-8
destruction: w75 682; w74 51-4; ts 116-17; g74 4/8 19-20; w73 676; g73 12/8 19-20; w72 45, 51-3; g72 4/22 24-7; w71 101, 471-2; kj 113, 115-27, 129, 216-19
development:
  Greece: w71 509-10
  post-Flood: w72 428
  spread from Babylon: ts 27-9, 44-5; w71 509-10
discussion: g72 4/22 3-28
efforts to unite: g75 11/22 21-2
esteem drops: w75 200, 364; g75 1/8 30; g75 2/8 31; g75 7/22 8; g74 1/22 30
failure: g73 9/22 3-5
friendship with world: yb74 56; g74 10/8 17; g74 11/22 3-6; g74 12/8 13-14; g73 8/8 20; g73 12/8 16-18, 29; w72 639
influence over mankind: w74 360; tp 22
origin of myths: ts 27-9
politics: g73 12/8 16-20, 29; g73 12/22 29
religion a disease of the world (quote): g75 9/8 30
results: g73 9/8 3-7
  failure to change lives: w74 324; g73 2/8 23
  moral collapse: g74 9/8 5; g72 4/22 18-20; g71 5/22 7
  war: w72 748-9, 760; g72 4/22 5-17; g72 10/22 29; w71 483; g71 6/22 16-19
separation from: w75 692; g75 4/8 16-17; w74 181, 564-5; ts 187; g74 2/8 27-8; g74 12/22 9-10; g72 4/22 27-8
"snare and racket": yb75 160-1
Soviet Union: g73 4/8 3-19
ways gain money: ts 68, 70, 72
writers for: g74 9/8 30

True Religion
exposes false religion: w75 127-8
exposing falsehood: w74 35-7
proof of identity: w75 325-6; g75 4/8 17-19; g74 1/22 18-19; w73 387-90; g73 9/22 5-9; w71 463-72
results: po 4-6
  morality: w73 389-90
way of life: w75 643-6; w74 84-5, 630
(SEE ALSO WORSHIP)

REMNANT

Jewish
first century C.E.: w74 695, 698-9
return from Babylon: w72 172-3, 746-7, 750; pm 56-8, 247-8; kj 299-300, 340-1

Modern-Day Spiritual
calling: w73 731-3
cleansing: pm 110-13
commission: or 109; kj 171-81, 189-90
condition:
  captivity to modern-day Babylon: yb75 109-11; kj 207-8, 313, 315, 324, 379
  compromise (1917-19): yb75 119
  fear of enemy: pm 99-100
deliverance from captivity: w74 508, 731; w73 167, 221-3; ka 315; w72 173, 725; pm 161-2, 172, 293, 348-50; kj 208, 300-1, 325-32, 342-3, 346, 354, 380-1
evidence of anointing: w75 105-6
evidence of God's approval: yb75 121-2; w74 557-8, 621; hu 22-3; w73 221-3, 459; ka 355-7; pm 243-5; kj 309-11, 318-23, 326-34, 379-82
faithful and discreet slave: ka 342, 345-57; w72 755; or 9-11; w71 462-3, 750, 754
gathering: w72 173; pm 159-60, 232
history: w73 394-400; ka 186-93, 232-40, 245-6, 251-2
Jehovah's protection: w74 753-5, 758-9
loyalty to God: w73 740-1; pm 350-5
make God's name known: po 179
need for alertness: w74 432
number remaining: ka 283; yb73 30
persecution: po 178-9; ka 189-90; w72 198, 280; pm 73, 370-4; kj 62-3, 82-3, 91-2, 300, 315, 318-19, 326
pictured by—
  Elisha: w74 406-7
  Ezekiel: w72 155, 188-90, 197-200, 252-5, 278-80; kj 53, 58-72, 78-92, 275-8, 286, 290-2
  Haggai: pm 49-52
  lampstand: pm 205
  Naomi, Ruth: w72 77
  Noah's wife: w74 666-8
  "ten slaves" (Lu 19:13): w73 715, 717-19
  two witnesses (Re 11:3): yb75 103-4; pm 46-7
pictures applying to or including the remnant: w74 506-9; w73 715, 717-21; ka 169-83, 189-204; pm 359-60
relationship to universal organization: w72 79-80
replacements for unfaithful: w75 108
requirements: w73 199-200
resurrection: w74 254-6, 558-9; w73 251-2
revival for work: yb75 120-2, 124; w74 506-8; w73 251-2; w72 278; pm 102-6, 114-15, 157-61, 172-3; kj 82-5
some on earth after great tribulation: w74 765-6; w73 623; ka 401, 406, 411; dy 26
spiritual security: w74 723, 731-2, 753, 755, 758-9, 765
temple-building: w72 750-2
(SEE ALSO CONGREGATION OF GOD)

REPAIR
home: g74 7/8 17-20; g74 12/8 7

REPENTANCE
aid to ones showing: or 159-68
angels' joy over: w72 431
discussion: tp 181-3; w72 118-20, 436-40; or 14-18
examples: w74 504; or 15-16
exhorting disfellowshiped to: w74 468-9, 472
for sexual immorality: w75 755-6
Greek word: w72 118, 439
how demonstrated: w74 469, 602; tp 181-3, 185; w72 120, 287, 437-9, 543; or 166-7; pm 342-3
Jehovah encourages: w74 461-2; w73 441-2; w72 430-6; kj 282-5
John's baptism: w72 431
mind and heart: w74 343
with regard to Messianic kingdom: w75 751

REPRODUCTION
respect for powers of: w75 158-60

REPROOF (Reproving)
defined: w75 267-8
giving: w72 466; or 165-70
Jehovah: w74 461
ministerial servants: w72 126
no "terms": km 5/73 8
not "probation": km 3/75 4; km 5/73 8
not "put on": km 3/75 4
one reproved may still preach: km 12/74 4
overseers: w72 15-17; or 165-70; yb72 20-3
public: w72 438; or 168-70
restrictions: km 3/75 4
when reproved one moves: km 3/75 4
wrongs some years ago: km 10/72 8

REPTILES
Bible mention: w73 447

number of varieties: ts 145

REPURCHASE
marriage by: w72 82-3, 86-8

RESENTMENT
overcoming: w72 759

RESOLUTIONS
seven (1922-1928): pm 167-8, 294
1922, Cedar Point, Ohio, "A Challenge": yb75 135-6
1923, Los Angeles, Calif., "A Warning": sl 161-2; yb75 136
1924, Columbus, Ohio, "Indictment": yb75 136; yb74 100-1; yb73 150; w72 148; kj 83-5
1925, Indianapolis, Ind., "Message of Hope": yb75 137
1926, London, Eng., "A Testimony to the Rulers of the World": yb75 137; yb73 111
1927, Toronto, Canada, "To the Peoples of Christendom": yb75 137-8
1928, Detroit, Mich., "Declaration Against Satan and for Jehovah": yb76 102; yb75 139; w74 764
1931, Columbus, Ohio, "A New Name": yb75 149-50; kj 172
Columbus, Ohio, "Warning from Jehovah": yb75 151-2
1936-7, protests to Hitler regime: yb74 155-7, 161
1938, appointment of servants by governing body: yb75 166
1945, Witness survivors of Nazi concentration camp: yb74 208-9
1946, Cleveland, Ohio, asks pardon for 4,000 imprisoned Witnesses: yb75 206-7
1948, Prague, Czechoslovakia: yb72 139
1950, New York, N.Y.: yb75 234
1953, New York, N.Y.: yb75 215
1956-7, protest to Bulganin: yb75 234-5
1958, New York, N.Y.: yb75 235; yb74 233
1963, "Everlasting Good News" Assembly: yb75 235-6
1971, "Divine Name" District Assembly: w72 54-7; g71 10/22 15
1972, Malawi *vs.* Witnesses: g72 12/8 14-15, 18
1973, "Divine Victory" International Assembly: w73 637-8, 722-5
1974, "Divine Victory" International Assembly: yb75 236-7
(SEE ALSO DECLARATIONS)

RESPECT
breakdown in: w72 261-2
children's, for parents and others: w74 90-1; g74 12/22 6; w72 163-4, 270-1, 732-4
family members: w74 46
for Jehovah: w72 272-3
Jehovah's name: w72 31; w71 645-59
theocratic authority: w72 271-3
wife for husband: g74 4/22 8-9; w72 270-1; g72 9/22 27
worldly authorities: w72 263-70

RESPIRATION
mouth-to-mouth resuscitation: g73 7/22 8-12

RESPONSIBILITY
avoiding: w72 212-18
community: w71 235-6, 629-31
individual: w73 441-2; g73 9/8 7; w71 631-3
overseers (older men): km 4/72 3
parents, toward children: w72 109-11
proper view: w72 451-2

REST
man's need: w72 414-15, 490
(SEE ALSO SABBATH, SLEEP)

RESTORATION
Jews, from Babylon: w72 300-1, 305-7, 500
"times of restoration" (Ac 3:21): w71 233-46, 287

RESURRECTION
basis for hope: gc 27; g75 10/22 8-9; w74 278-9; po 188; ts 167-9, 172-4; g74 12/8 28; w73 238-49, 382; tp 106-8; g73 6/8 8; w72 195, 240; g72 6/8 7-8; g72 8/8 28; w71 246, 296, 708-10; te 86; g71 12/8 27-8
"better" (Heb 11:35): ts 174-5
Biblical examples: g75 10/22 8-9; ts 167-8; w73 239, 247-8; w71 295-6, 708-9; kj 335; te 83-6
children: ts 180-1; w72 448; w71 295-6; te 83-6; g71 12/8 28
discussion: g75 10/22 8-13; ts 166-86; w73 231, 238-49; w71 708-10
early Christian belief: w73 248
earthly: kj 390-1
  body given: w75 89-90; w74 96, 607-8; ts 170-3; w73 248-9, 726-7
  first to be raised: w75 90
  raised imperfect: w75 90; w74 607-8
  time of: w74 6, 95; w73 382-3
evidence of pre-Christian belief: w73 235, 241-3
evildoer: ka 121
faith in: w75 53-4
"first" (Re 20:6): ts 183; w73 727-9; ka 36-42
  misconceptions: w73 728; ka 37, 41
God's memory: ts 173-4; w73 249
heavenly:
  body given: w75 89; ts 169-70; w73 248
  time of: w74 255-6, 558-9; ka 242-4
Jesus Christ: sl 27-9; w73 239, 248, 350-1; w72 238; te 171-4
  appearances after: w75 479; ts 169-70; g73 7/22 4-5; w71 398; te 173
  body disposed of: po 155
  date: w72 622; dn 13
  evidence: sl 27-9; g75 5/8 30; ts 168-9; w72 242
  faith in: w74 17-19
  spirit: w75 478-9; po 154-5; w73 711-12; g73 7/22 4-5; w72 622; dn 13; g72 9/22 7
  survey of Catholics as to whether Jesus is living: w75 651
  time: w73 766-8
judgment of resurrected ones: w74 278-80, 293-4; ts 182-6; ka 120-2, 125-31, 133-4; w72 240
marriage: ts 178-80
of judgment (Joh 5:29): ts 182-6
of life (Joh 5:29): ts 186
orderly: w73 246, 382-3
questions concerning: ts 176-7, 180, 182
rapture: w74 255
re-creation: ts 171-3
"righteous and unrighteous": w74 278-80; w73 638; ka 120-2, 125-8, 130
same person: w75 89-90; g75 10/22 10-11
value of hope in: w75 53-4; g75 2/22 4; w74 644
views of heathen: g73 6/8 8
who will be resurrected: sl 363; w74 279-80; ts 176-7, 180-4; w73 210, 232-47

RETALIATION
g74 5/22 27-8

RETARDATION
g75 6/22 20-3

RETIREMENT
disadvantages: g75 11/8 14; g74 1/8 30; w73 328-9; g73 11/22 30
discussion: g75 11/8 12-16
health: g75 11/8 14
Jehovah's witnesses: g75 11/8 16
keeping busy: g75 11/8 15-16
preparing for: g75 11/8 12-14
use of time: g71 12/22 3-4

RETURN
Bible use of term: ts 51-2

RETURN VISITS
answers to questions: sg 35-6
calling back soon: w75 178-80
car groups: km 6/71 4
developing interest in truth: km 4/74 4
experiences:
  calling back soon: w75 179
  formerly interested ones: km 2/74 2
  magazine placements: yb72 102; w71 220
  perseverance: yb73 14; yb72 102
  publisher neglects to return: w71 221
expiration slips: km 4/73 4
need: w75 178-9; km 10/71 8
number: w75 23, 27; yb75 31-2, 257; w74 26; yb74 31; w73 23; yb73 23; w72 50
opposite sex: km 8/72 4
pastoral work: yb75 85-6
preparing for: km 1/75 4
purpose: or 121-2; km 1/72 8; km 2/72 8
reporting: or 126-7
subscriptions: km 2/74 1-2
use of Bible: km 2/75 4
(SEE ALSO FIELD SERVICE)

REUBEN (Son of Jacob)
birthright: po 96

RÉUNION
Jehovah's witnesses: yb76 28-9;

yb75 28-9; yb74 28-9; yb73 28-9; yb72 38-9
population: yb73 28; yb72 38

REVELATION (Book)
horsemen of chapter 6: w74 355-9
theme: w73 612; dy 5

REVOLUTION(S)
Argentina: yb72 104-5
Christian view: w74 714; g74 11/22 6
church support: w74 244; g74 11/22 4-5; g73 12/8 17-18, 29; w71 740; g71 7/8 30; g71 7/22 6-7
Cyprus: g71 3/8 13-15
discussion: g71 6/8 17-20
Dominican Republic: yb72 142, 165-8
experience:
black revolutionary accepts Bible truth: w74 707-14
green: g73 2/22 29; g72 7/22 3-13, 29; g71 10/8 11
Industrial Revolution: g71 4/22 14-17

REWARDS
for serving Jehovah: w75 77, 79; g75 1/22 23; w74 558-9, 574; ts 125-6; w71 92-4

RHINOCEROS
discussion: g72 6/8 9-11
Sumatran, endangered: g75 8/8 29
surgery on: g75 4/22 30

RHODESIA
flowers: g75 2/8 20-3
Jehovah's witnesses: yb76 28-9, 82, 122-6, 153-5, 167-8; yb75 9, 28-9; yb74 15, 28-9; yb73 28-9; yb72 38-9
persecution: yb76 100, 128
opposed by African nations: g74 6/22 25-6
population: yb73 28; yb72 38
religion: g73 6/8 30; w72 340
trees: g75 2/8 21-2

RICE
g74 8/8 13-14; g73 12/8 24-6; g72 7/22 3-4, 7-8

RICHES
Bible view: w74 419-20, 544; g74 9/22 10-11; tp 117-18; w72 491; g71 11/22 27-8
discussion: w75 561-75
spiritual: w75 572-3
use of material riches: w75 565; w74 419-20
unable to save religious leaders: kj 131-4
unrighteous: w73 63-4
(SEE ALSO MATERIALISM, WEALTH)

RICHES (Book)
release: yb75 148

RICH MAN
Jesus' illustration (Lu 12:16-21): te 91-4
"rich men" (Jas 5:1): w71 447-8

RICH MAN AND LAZARUS
Christendom's views: ts 98-9, 109
death, symbolic: ts 103-7
discussion: ts 98-110
literal application unreasonable: ts 98, 100-2, 109; g73 6/8 7

RICH YOUNG RULER
w75 566-7

RIDICULE
last days: sl 285-90, 293, 298-300

RIGHTEOUSNESS
gift: w74 599
hunger and thirst for: g71 7/22 27-8
Jehovah: w72 365
ones declared righteous: sl 82-3, 87; w74 252
seeking God's: w74 250, 534; ts 188-9; w73 437, 440-2
(SEE ALSO INTEGRITY)

RIGHTS
discussion: w73 136-46
experiences:
black fights for: w74 709-11
woman fights for: w74 387-91
of unborn: g72 2/22 30
parents': w72 359; g71 9/22 30
patients': g72 9/22 30; g71 11/8 7-9
women's: g72 5/22 3-7, 29

RINGS
demonism: g72 3/8 9
seal ring: pm 119, 122
wedding: w72 63

RIOTS
racial: yb75 237
results: g73 2/8 30
youths: g71 8/8 10-12

RIVERS
deltas: g71 5/22 12
flood control: g73 6/22 14-15
pollution: g75 12/22 6; g73 2/22 31; w72 613-14; g72 8/22 31; g72 10/8 11; g71 1/8 7; g71 7/8 29
symbolic:
Ezekiel chap. 47: kj 387-98
river of water of life (Re 22:1): kj 388, 397
tidal bore: g73 11/8 10
worship of: yb73 141-2

List by Name
Amazon: g75 3/8 8; g73 1/8 31; g73 11/8 10; g72 1/22 18
Chemung: g72 8/22 14
Columbia: g72 7/8 29-30
Congo: g72 11/8 24-6
Dog: g71 11/8 10
Euphrates: w74 230-1; g72 1/22 18; w71 540
Fox: g72 8/22 31
Fuchun: g73 11/8 10
Gihon: w71 540
Hiddekel: w71 540
Jordan: g73 2/22 31
Mississippi: g73 6/22 14-17; g72 1/22 18; g71 5/22 12
Paraná: g71 8/22 23
Pishon: w71 540
Rhine: g72 1/22 18; g71 7/8 29
Susquehanna: g72 8/22 13-16
Thames: g75 12/22 6
Weser: g72 5/22 18-19
Willamette: g75 12/22 6

ROADS
garbage in pavement: g72 2/8 29-30
Roman Empire: w73 582

ROBBERY
(SEE STEALING)

ROBISON, F. H.
yb75 104, 111, 116

ROCKETS
space shuttle: g72 2/22 31
travel to Mars: g72 1/22 29
travel to Venus: g71 3/8 30-1
(SEE ALSO SPACE TRAVEL)

ROCKS
heat boring device: g72 2/8 30

ROD
Bible usage: w74 82; w72 393; kj 127-9

RODRIGUES
Jehovah's witnesses: yb76 28-9; yb75 28-9; yb74 28-9; yb73 28-9; yb72 38-9
population: yb73 28; yb72 38

ROMAN CATHOLIC CHURCH
abortion: w73 419
anticlericalism: yb72 50; w71 740; g71 8/22 14
attendance statistics: w75 651; g75 3/8 24; g75 7/22 31; g75 12/22 30; w74 15; g74 1/8 30; g74 2/8 29; g74 4/22 17; g74 6/22 30; g74 11/22 31; g73 3/22 29; g73 6/22 31; g73 9/8 4; g73 12/22 29
beer licenses: g75 8/8 30
Bible: w73 547-50, 601-3
attitude toward Bible study: w73 547-8
discredit Bible: w74 38; g74 6/8 30; w73 602-3; tp 33; g73 3/22 16-19; g73 5/22 23; w71 676; g71 8/8 26; g71 12/22 5
shortage: g71 9/22 29
bingo: g74 10/22 27
birth control: g74 2/22 29; g74 6/22 8; g74 10/22 29; g74 11/22 29-30; g73 3/8 29; g73 6/22 9; g73 9/22 31; g72 6/22 10; w71 407-8; g71 1/8 30; g71 5/8 29; g71 8/22 14
bishops: g75 1/22 30; g75 2/22 21; w74 592, 742; g74 11/22 30; g74 12/22 29; g73 9/8 29; w72 626-7; yb72 142-3; g72 1/22 29-30; g72 4/22 6-7, 9, 16-17; g72 8/8 30; w71 407, 484; g71 9/8 31; g71 9/22 9; g71 11/22 12
suppress book on church role in World War II: w75 715
Synod of: g72 1/8 30-1; g72 1/22 31; g72 3/22 9-11; g72 5/8 9-12
Boys Town: w75 172
bullfighting: g75 9/8 12, 16
cannibalism: w74 394
cardinals: g75 2/22 18; g71 11/22 10-12
carnival: g73 3/8 5-8
catechism: g75 5/22 29; g74 9/22 29; w71 297-8
celibacy: g75 1/22 9; g75 5/8 27-8; w74 102; w73 549; g73 5/8 30; g72 1/22 31; g72 3/22 9; g72 5/8 9-12; g71 8/8 24-5; g71 11/22 12; g71 12/22 30
changes: g75 3/8 30-1; w74 198; g73 3/22 16-19; g71 7/22 29
chaplains: g75 2/22 19, 21; g73 5/8 30
"charity" drives: g73 11/22 24-5
chart showing teachings: w73 549-50
children's view of churches: g75 8/22 29-30
Church and State: g75 3/8 17-20

clergy-laity distinction: ka 375, 378, 380
Communism: w74 71, 341; g74 3/22 29; g74 4/22 29; g74 11/22 4-5, 30; w73 707-8; g73 4/8 6; g73 6/8 29; g73 12/8 17; g73 12/22 29; g72 10/8 7-9; w71 408; g71 1/8 29; g71 7/22 6-7
concordats:
  Hitler: w75 398; g72 4/22 16
  Italy (Lateran Treaty): w75 364
  Trujillo: yb72 158
confession: w74 198; g74 11/8 27-8; g73 6/8 29; g73 9/8 30; g71 5/22 29; g71 7/22 4
confirmation: w71 170-1
councils:
  Elvira: g75 5/8 28
  Laodicea: g75 1/22 27
  Nicaea (Nicene): g73 1/8 16-17
  Trent: g75 1/22 27; g75 5/8 28
  Vatican II (1962-5): g73 1/8 16
Creeds:
  Athanasian: w73 131-2
criticism of: g74 11/22 27
Crusades: g72 4/22 12-13; g72 10/22 29
deacons: g71 2/22 30; g71 8/22 30
decline: g75 3/8 22-5; g75 10/22 29; w74 166; g74 1/8 30; g74 2/8 29; g74 2/22 29; g74 4/22 17-18; g74 5/8 31; g74 6/22 30; g74 9/22 13, 15; g74 10/22 29; tp 86; g73 1/8 29; g73 3/22 29; g73 4/22 29; g73 5/22 29; g73 9/8 3-7; g73 9/22 3-4; w72 340; g72 1/8 31; g72 2/22 30; g72 3/22 29; g72 4/8 21, 30; g72 6/22 9-11, 29; g72 10/8 12; g72 11/22 30; g72 12/22 30; w71 484, 739; kj 317-18; g71 3/22 3-4; g71 8/8 29; g71 12/22 30
disunity: g74 2/22 29; g74 4/8 30; g74 4/22 17-19, 29; g74 8/8 30; g74 9/8 31; g74 9/22 14-15; g73 1/8 16-19; g73 3/8 29; g73 3/22 31; g73 9/8 4-6; g72 3/22 10-11; g72 4/8 21-2, 24, 30; g72 6/8 29; g72 6/22 9-10; g72 8/8 30; g72 12/8 29; w71 297-8, 355-6, 407-8; g71 5/8 12-16; g71 7/22 6-9, 29; g71 8/22 13-14; g71 11/8 30; g71 11/22 10-12
divorce: w75 364; w74 424; g74 5/8 30; g74 9/22 13-15; w72 597
end of church predicted: g72 6/22 29
evangelizing: w74 492, 720; g74 6/8 30; g74 11/22 30
evolution theory: g74 7/8 22; g73 10/22 22; w71 41, 46-51, 56
excommunication: g72 3/8 18
exorcism: w74 327
experiences:
  Catholics accept Bible truth: g75 3/8 28; w74 38, 746-7; yb74 18-19, 21; g74 12/22 10; w73 551; w72 285; yb72 62, 102, 203-4; g72 6/22 11-13; w71 221-2; g71 6/22 20-1
  nuns accept truth: g75 1/22 12-13; w74 746-7; g73 2/8 14; g72 6/22 12-13; g72 7/22 17-26
  opposition to preaching: yb73 47, 51-2, 117-19; w72 60, 148-50, 282-5; yb72 105-6, 127, 131, 138, 140, 178, 185-8; w71 520
  priest admits Church wrong: w74 747
  priest admits Witnesses have truth: g74 4/22 20; g71 9/22 12
  priests encourage study with Witnesses: yb72 194
  priests lack accurate Bible knowledge: w75 650; g73 5/22 23-4; g71 6/22 21
  priests' opposition to preaching: yb73 39-40, 63, 117-18, 152-3, 157; yb72 127, 138, 150-1, 153-4, 160-1; w71 18
  priest tries to exploit parishioners: w74 648
failure: w75 651; g75 3/8 25, 29; g74 1/22 30; g74 2/8 30; g74 4/22 17-20; g73 3/8 29; g73 9/8 3-7; w72 366-7; g72 1/8 30-1; g72 3/22 11; w71 254; g71 2/8 16-19, 30
friendship with world: w73 614
gambling: g74 2/8 30; g74 4/8 29; g74 10/22 27, 30; g74 11/22 30; g73 6/22 30-1; g73 11/22 30; g73 12/22 30
girl altar servers: g75 3/22 30
godparents: w72 511-12
hell teachings: w75 56; ts 89, 91-2, 95-6; g74 9/22 29; w73 132; g73 7/22 27
Hitler:
  concordat: g72 4/22 16
  Nazi protected: g72 8/8 30
  Vatican support: g75 2/22 17-23; g72 4/22 16-17; g71 12/8 3-4
holidays: yb72 173-4; g71 6/22 23-4; g71 8/22 16
Holy Years:
  1933: w75 397-8
  1950: w75 398-9
  1975: w75 390, 397, 399-400; g75 2/22 29; w74 295; g72 3/8 29
homosexuality: w74 483; g74 5/22 29; g74 7/8 29; w73 356; g73 12/8 29
image worship: g75 1/8 23; yb72 112-13, 173-4, 194; g72 7/22 23
indulgences: ts 64, 66-8; g72 3/8 16-17
infallibility (papal): w74 273, 720; g74 8/8 30; ka 380; g73 5/8 30; g72 9/8 20; g71 3/8 30; g71 5/22 29
influence waning: g75 3/8 22-7; g74 4/22 17-18; g74 12/8 15; g74 12/22 8; g73 5/8 30; g72 4/8 21; g71 1/22 30; g71 2/22 5-6; g71 10/22 29
Inquisition: g74 8/8 30; g74 12/22 17; g72 9/22 21-5; g71 1/22 20-3
Italy: g74 9/22 13-15
Jesuits: g74 7/8 10-12; g71 11/22 9-12
Ku Klux Klan: w75 631
Latin language: g74 12/8 30
Lent: g73 3/8 5-6
Lourdes shrine: g75 4/22 31
Lutheran church: w74 273
Mariolatry:
  decline: g73 2/22 29-30
  liberated woman: w74 295
  "Mother of God": w75 539-40
  practices: w75 12
  rosary: w74 259-60
marriage:
  annulment: g74 9/22 13-14
Mass: w75 651; g75 3/8 30-1; g74 10/22 29; g74 11/8 30; g72 6/22 9; g72 10/8 29; g72 10/22 29; g72 11/8 29; g72 12/22 30; w71 644, 709; g71 8/22 13-14; g71 9/22 31; g71 11/22 11-12
members' comments: g75 3/8 30
membership: w75 254, 400; sl 206; g75 1/8 21; g75 6/8 30; ka 392
members view of Christ's return: g75 3/8 29
military service: g75 2/22 18-23
money-raising schemes: w75 172, 263; w74 295; g74 4/22 29; g74 10/22 29; g74 11/22 30; g73 12/8 29; w71 506; g71 8/22 13-14
morals: g74 2/8 30; g73 9/8 5, 7; g72 4/8 22-3; w71 452
motion pictures: g74 4/8 30
Nazi assignment to report Witnesses: g75 2/22 22
Nazi atrocities: g75 2/22 17-23
Nazi criminals aided: w75 48
Nazi euthanasia program: w75 294
neglects home visits: w75 759
nuns: g75 1/22 7-13; g75 2/8 31; g75 11/8 29; g74 4/22 18; g74 6/22 30; g74 7/8 12; w72 281; g72 3/22 29; g72 7/22 17-26; w71 484; g71 9/22 10
Orthodox Catholic Church: g72 5/8 10
pagan origin of doctrines and practices: g73 3/8 5-8; w72 63
pagan practices allowed: w75 12, 172; g75 5/22 30; w74 742; g74 4/22 30; g74 7/22 8-9; yb73 206; g73 3/8 5-8; g73 12/22 5-6, 12; g72 2/22 30; g72 6/8 23; g71 6/22 23-4; g71 8/22 15-16; g71 9/22 30-1
Palatine Guard of Honor: g75 5/22 13-17
parochial schools: g75 1/22 8; g75 2/22 30; g75 4/22 30; g74 2/22 30; g74 4/22 29; g74 5/8 31; g74 6/22 30; g73 9/8 30; w72 367; g72 1/8 31; g72 1/22 29-30; g72 2/8 29; g71 1/22 30-1; g71 3/22 31; g71 5/22 29; g71 9/22 9-12
persecution of Witnesses: yb76 141-3, 151-2; yb75 154-5, 180-1, 191; g75 3/8 16-22; yb74 58
Peter:
  church claims: w72 669-71
  never in Rome: w72 669-71
pilgrimages: g73 8/8 26-8
politics: g75 3/8 17-20; g74 11/22 3-5; w73 549; g73 12/8 16-19; w72 367; yb72 142-3; g72 6/22 9-10, 24-6; g71 3/8 30; g71 8/22 29
  political activity: g75 10/8 30; w74 166, 244, 679; g73 6/8 23-5; g73 8/8 18; g73 12/8 17-19; g72 4/22 30
  public disapproval: w74 424; w72 340
  within church: g74 9/22 29
polygamy: w75 200; g72 4/8 30
prayers: ts 64-8

g, Awake!; **ka**, God's Kingdom of a Thousand Years; **kj**, "The Nations Shall Know that I Am Jehovah"; **km**, Kingdom Ministry; **or**, Organization; **pm**, Paradise Restored—By Theocracy!; **po**, God's "Eternal Purpose"; **sg**, Theocratic School Guidebook; **sl**, Man's Salvation out of World Distress!; **te**, Listening to the Great Teacher; **tp**, True Peace and Security; **ts**, Is This Life All There Is?; **w**, Watchtower; **yb**, Yearbook. **Complete list on page 6.**

"Glory be to the Father": w74 260
"Hail Mary": w74 260
rosary: w74 259-60
priests:
alcoholism: g72 7/22 30
beliefs: yb74 18-19; g74 6/8 30; g74 7/8 30
celibacy: w74 102; g72 5/8 9-12; g71 11/22 12
complain against lavish churches: g74 6/22 30
condone immorality: g74 4/22 30; g72 4/8 22-3; g72 4/22 19; w71 557
decrease in number: w75 684; g74 6/22 30
discussion: g75 3/22 16-19
dress in black: g75 5/22 29
fighting: g74 2/22 30; g74 10/22 31
guerrilla warfare: g74 11/22 4-5
immorality: w74 38; g74 8/22 30; w72 281; g72 4/8 22; g72 5/8 9-10; g72 6/22 12; g71 7/22 4-5, 9-10
lack interest in parishioners: yb73 18; g73 12/22 29
marriage: g71 6/8 30; g71 8/8 24-5
motion pictures: g71 3/8 31
number world wide: w75 254; ka 392
politics: w74 166, 217, 244; g74 7/8 11-12; g74 11/22 3-5; w72 367; g72 2/22 30; g72 6/22 9-10, 25; g72 11/22 29; w71 408, 644, 740; g71 2/22 3-6; g71 7/22 6-8
problems: g75 3/22 16-18; g74 4/22 18-19; g74 7/8 10-12; g71 8/8 25
quitting: g75 3/8 23-4; g75 3/22 16-18; g75 6/22 31; w74 15, 102; g74 3/8 30; g74 4/8 30; g74 4/22 18; g74 7/8 10, 12; g73 4/22 29; g73 9/22 3-4; g73 12/8 29; g73 12/22 29; w72 214; g72 4/8 21, 30; g72 6/22 10-11; g72 8/22 30; w71 408, 484; g71 1/22 31; g71 5/8 29-30; g71 8/8 24-5; g71 8/22 13
rebellion: g74 4/22 18-19; g74 9/22 14-15; g72 6/8 29; g72 6/22 29; g72 7/8 31; g72 12/8 29
refuse to preach about God: g73 9/8 3-4
shortage: g75 3/8 24; w74 456; g74 11/22 31; g74 12/22 8; g73 4/22 29; w72 214, 367; g72 4/8 21, 30; g72 6/22 10; g72 8/8 30; g72 11/22 29; w71 408, 484, 739-40; g71 2/8 16-17, 30; g71 2/22 30; g71 4/8 30; g71 8/22 13, 30; g71 11/8 30; g71 12/22 30
why some continue: g74 5/8 30; g74 12/22 9
women: g71 2/8 30
problems: g73 3/22 16; g71 10/8 29
processions: yb72 112-13
Protestantism: g72 3/8 16-19; g72 4/22 13
publications discontinued: g71 12/22 30
purgatory: w75 55-6; ts 64-8; g74 6/8 27-8
relics: g75 12/22 14; g73 8/8 26-8
rosary: w74 259-60
saints: w75 112, 487; g75 1/22 27-8; g75 4/8 30; g75 12/22 12-15
scholarship: g73 3/22 16-19
seminaries: g75 3/8 27
survey as to whether Jesus is "really living" today: w75 651
taxes: g74 2/22 27
thefts from churches: g75 12/22 30; g71 7/8 29
tradition: ts 66; g74 4/22 19; w73 550
Trinity doctrine: w74 75; w73 131-2, 550; g73 1/8 16-19; g73 2/22 27-8; w71 355-6
United Nations: w74 135
voodoo: w75 172; g74 1/8 30
war: w75 445; g75 2/22 19-23; w74 360, 679; w73 549; tp 24-5; g73 10/8 15; g73 11/8 30; w72 625-7; g72 4/22 6-17; g72 10/8 7; g72 10/22 29; w71 463; g71 3/8 30; g71 6/22 16-19; g71 8/22 30; g71 9/8 31; g71 11/8 30
book on church role in World War II suppressed: w75 715
Vietnam: w75 400; g75 6/22 30
wealth: w75 263; ts 68; g73 3/22 29; g72 2/22 30; g72 6/8 29; g71 1/22 30; g71 2/8 17; g71 9/22 29
financial reports: g73 9/8 4
Witness successes discussed: w75 759

Quotations

bishops have blood on their hands: g72 4/22 9; g71 9/8 31
bishops supported all wars: w73 549
ceased being Christian, perhaps never were: g74 2/22 29
church adopts customs of people and gives new meaning: g73 12/22 6
church experiencing self-demolition: g71 10/8 29
church has had more bad theology than good: g71 11/22 12
church hindrance to evangelization of Kingdom: w74 720
church not a beacon of light and hope: g75 3/22 16
church not practice what Christ taught: g73 7/8 29
church rationalized wars, even eating dead: w74 394
church sleeps with all regimes: g71 8/22 29
church would deal with Devil himself: w73 708
coming apart of traditional, tightly knit organization of church: g73 1/8 29
duty to participate in politics: g73 9/8 6
faithful no longer afraid to be unfaithful: g74 10/22 29
faltering and incoherent message: g74 1/22 30
if things said in last ten years are true, everything church said for 2,000 years is false: w75 324; g74 6/22 30
internal collapse, faith crisis: g73 9/8 3
last place to look for illumination: g75 1/22 12
many priests no longer believe: g73 9/8 4
morally, intellectually and religiously bankrupt: g72 4/8 30
most dramatic collapse in history: g74 4/22 17
neglect greatest preoccupation of Witnesses—the home visit: w75 759
no church by year 2000: g74 5/8 31
pagan practices sanctified by adoption into church: w74 742
papacy no longer considered a strong moral force: g75 9/8 25
priesthood headed for extinction: g71 11/8 30
priests convey impression they will bless any war: g75 2/22 23
rebellion everywhere, church authorities overwhelmed: g74 4/22 18
secular influence greater than church: g74 12/8 15
she's a whore but she's our mother: g72 12/8 29
Vatican not speak for many Catholics: g74 10/22 29
we profess degenerate religiosity completely different from simple Christianity: g71 2/8 19
where was the church when Nazism was on the rise?: w75 715
(SEE ALSO POPES, VATICAN)

ROMAN EMPIRE
aqueducts: g73 1/8 13-14
army: g72 4/22 12
British Isles: g71 12/22 20
Christians persecuted by: g75 12/8 4; w72 415-16; g72 6/8 13-15; g72 12/8 20; w71 716
control of Palestine: po 133
holidays: w75 740; g73 3/8 7-8; g73 12/22 5-6
Jerusalem's destruction: w75 138-9; w74 426-9, 683, 693; ka 294-6, 300-4; w72 372, 625, 629, 748; pm 365; dn 18, 25; g72 10/8 20-1; te 33-4; g71 12/8 6
moral decay: g72 6/8 14, 16
roads: w73 582
rulers: g72 6/8 12-16; g71 9/8 14, 18
standards: g72 4/22 12; g71 9/8 13
symbol "fasces": ka 32
world power: w71 716-17

ROME
ancient:
aqueducts: g73 1/8 13-14
Arch of Titus: w75 139-40; w74 80
Babylonian influence: ts 28-9
beliefs: ts 96
childbirth: g72 11/22 14-15
Christian congregation: w74 18-19
Colosseum: w74 80
holidays: g74 2/8 28; g74 12/22 4; g73 3/8 7-8; g73 12/22 5-6
roads: w73 582
modern:
Holy Year (1975): w75 390
prostitution: w71 452
shortage of priests: w74 456; g74 11/22 31
Paul's voyage to: g71 4/8 27-8
Peter: w72 669-71

ROSARY
w74 259-60

ROSETTA STONE
g71 11/22 24-6

ROTATION
branch office elders: yb73 257
circuit and district overseers: or 89
congregation book study conductors: or 68
congregation's older men: km 7/73 2; w72 20; or 64, 67, 69, 76; yb72 28-9; w71 693-701
governing body: yb73 257; w71 669-70, 759, 761-2
(SEE ALSO OVERSEERS)

ROYAL PRIESTHOOD
(SEE CONGREGATION OF GOD)

RULERS
Christendom: kj 295-8, 304-5
discussion: w75 241-3; w73 165-9
God's kingdom: w74 68-70; w72 580-2; w71 568-71
Israel: kj 294-6
worldly: ts 153-4
failure: w72 612-19; dn 3-5
subjection to: yb75 238; kj 326

RULERSHIP
divine: w75 243; w74 68; w73 196-7, 615-16; dy 11-13; w72 617-31, 645-58, 680-701; dn 3-30
failure of man's: w75 241-3, 579-81; g74 10/8 5-6, 15-17; g73 10/8 23-5; g73 11/8 3-6; w72 617-19; dn 3-5
Jesus Christ: w74 68-70, 105-6, 398; po 136; ts 140
ownership of earth: w74 594-9, 603-4
supporting Jehovah's: w74 538-9

RUNAWAYS
adults: g75 10/22 29
discussion: w71 525; g71 3/22 5-9
prostitution: g71 6/8 29
wives: g71 4/22 31

RUNNERS
Christian course: w75 493-8

RUSSELL, CHARLES T.
birth: yb75 35
convention trains: yb75 57-8
death: yb76 83-4; yb75 78-9; w74 507; w73 397; yb73 100
debates: yb75 55-6
envisioned 'great work ahead': yb75 76-7
false charges refuted:
immorality: yb75 69-70
"miracle wheat": yb75 70-1
field service recommended: yb75 39-40
first study group: yb75 35-6
funeral: yb75 68, 79-80
Gentile times: yb75 37, 72-3
hellfire doctrine: yb75 55-6
lectures: yb76 76; yb75 53-4, 56-8
ministry: w73 394-7; w71 21-2
newspapers carried sermons: yb76 79; yb75 46-7
not faithful and discreet slave: yb75 88; ka 346-7
opposition from within Society: yb75 65-6
opposition to: yb73 93-4, 191
"Pastor": yb75 36
Photo-Drama: yb75 58-60
religious background: yb75 34-5
search for truth: yb75 34-8
sectarianism: ka 346-7
service tours: yb76 243-4; yb75 42, 56-8, 72; yb74 67, 74-7; yb73 90, 93-7, 213; w71 15, 20
use of material wealth: w75 565
view on chronology: yb75 74
view on 1914: yb75 37, 73-5
wife: yb75 65-70; w72 383-4
writings: yb75 36-41, 76; w74 506-7; yb74 80-1; w73 395-7; ka 186-7, 206-8, 345-6; g73 10/8 18

RUSSIA
(SEE SOVIET UNION)

RUSSIAN (Language)
number speaking: g75 11/8 29

RUSSIAN ORTHODOX CHURCH
clergy: g73 5/22 24
decline: g73 4/8 4-14
relations with Russian government: g73 4/8 4-14; g73 5/22 24
wealth from prayers for dead: ts 68

RUTH (Moabitess)
loyalty: w71 92-3
name: w72 77
prophetic drama: w72 76-90, 503-4

RUTHERFORD, JOSEPH F.
biographical sketch: yb75 81-3
Catholic church: yb75 154-5, 180-1
conventions: yb74 99-100, 151, 154, 161
court actions: yb75 118-19
creature worship: yb75 193
death: yb76 62, 148; yb75 193-4; w73 399; ka 246; yb72 119, 255
debates: yb75 55
early contact with Witnesses: yb75 41, 82
early service with Society: yb75 51, 55, 83
elected president: yb75 80-1
health: yb75 120
"Judge": yb75 81
lawyer: yb75 81, 83
letters: yb74 132-3, 147; w73 396; ka 189-90
misrepresentations answered by: yb75 120
name "Jehovah's witnesses": yb75 149-51
opposition within Society: yb75 87-94, 107
personality traits: yb75 83-5
release from prison and exoneration: yb75 116-18
service tours: yb75 126-7; yb74 77, 87-8, 90-1, 106-7, 151, 154; yb73 109-11, 114
speeches: yb75 120, 122-3, 127, 131, 149-52, 173, 180-1, 192-3; yb74 91-2; ka 234-5
trial and imprisonment: yb75 104-9, 111-15; w73 398; ka 189-90; g71 10/22 28
use of radio: yb75 138-41, 143-4, 154-5, 168-9
writings: yb75 128, 193

RWANDA
Jehovah's witnesses: yb76 26-7; yb75 26-7; yb74 26-7; yb73 26-7; yb72 36-7
population: yb73 26; yb72 36

SABBATH
beginning of observance: g75 2/8 27
Christians: g75 2/8 27-8; g72 11/22 5-8
discussion: g75 2/8 27-8; g72 11/22 5-8
Jehovah's rest: g75 2/8 28; po 52-3, 189-90; g72 11/22 8
beginning of: w75 285
Jesus Christ: w73 10-11, 17; w72 486; g72 11/22 6
number between death and resurrection: w73 766-8
prophetic significance: g74 4/8 11-12; g71 10/8 27
punishment for violation: w73 148-9
purpose: w72 490
sabbath periods:
Jubilee year: g74 4/8 10; g74 10/8 21-2
seventh year: g74 4/8 9-10; g74 10/8 21

SACRED POLES (Asherahs)
w74 457-8

SACRED SECRET
w75 119-20, 286; po 156-7, 166-8; w71 569-70

SACRIFICES
animals: po 115-17
atonement day: w74 175-6; po 115-17
fat of animals: w72 190
grain offerings: w71 284-5
human sacrifices: g72 8/22 5-6
incense offering: w71 284-5
Jesus Christ: g75 4/8 10-11; w74 221-3; po 154-5; ka 96-7; w72 714-16; w71 712-14
benefits: ts 138-9, 165; ka 113
requirements for acceptance: w71 284-5

SADDUCEES
beliefs: ts 177-8

SAFETY
automobile driving: g74 3/22 8-11; g73 1/8 29-30; g73 10/22 31; g72 3/22 30; g72 6/8 4; g71 6/8 30
buildings: g72 12/8 30
children: g71 12/8 30
factory: g72 8/22 30
home:
fire: g71 12/8 14-16
repairs: g74 7/8 18
infants in automobile: g74 1/8 31
skyscrapers: g74 2/8 23
(SEE ALSO ACCIDENTS)

ST. EUSTATIUS
Jehovah's witnesses: yb73 26-7; yb72 38-9
population: yb73 26; yb72 38

ST. HELENA
Jehovah's witnesses: yb76 30-1, 110-11, 181-3, 196-7, 230; yb75 30-1; yb74 17-18, 30-1; yb73 30-1; yb72 40-1
persecution: yb76 183
population: yb73 30; yb72 40

ST. KITTS
Jehovah's witnesses: yb76 28-9; yb75 28-9; yb74 28-9; yb73 28-9; yb72 38-9; w71 280
population: yb73 28; yb72 38

ST. LOUIS, MO., CONVENTION (1941)
yb75 190-3; w74 725

ST. LUCIA
description: g72 9/8 21
Jehovah's witnesses: yb76 24-5; yb75 24-5; yb74 24-5; yb73 24-5; yb72 34-5
population: yb73 24; yb72 34

ST. MARTIN
Jehovah's witnesses: yb76 28-9; yb75 28-9; yb74 28-9; yb73 28-9; yb72 38-9
population: yb73 28; yb72 38

ST. PIERRE & MIQUELON
Jehovah's witnesses: yb76 24-5

SAINTS (Man-made)
cost of sainthood: w75 487
Council of Laodicea: g75 1/22 27
Council of Trent: g75 1/22 27
discussion: g75 12/22 12-15
hoaxes: g75 4/8 30
number of: g75 1/22 27
prayer: g75 1/22 27-8; w74 396
veneration unscriptural: g75 1/22 27-8; g75 12/22 14-15

List by Name
Anthony: yb73 142
Mother Seton: w75 112, 487; g75 12/22 12-13
Xavier, Francis: g75 4/8 30

ST. VINCENT
Jehovah's witnesses: yb76 24-5; yb75 24-5; yb74 24-5; yb73 24-5; yb72 34-5
population: yb73 24; yb72 34

SAIPAN
Jehovah's witnesses: yb76 26-7; yb75 26-7; yb74 26-7; yb73 26-7; yb72 36-7
population: yb73 26; yb72 36

SALADS
discussion: g73 11/8 21-3

SALARIES
statistics: w72 616; g72 10/8 30

SALOME
Zebedee's wife: w75 222

SALT
composition: g75 8/8 19; g72 3/8 14; g71 7/22 12
discussion: g75 8/8 19
fire: w71 670
health: g75 8/8 19; g74 4/22 24; g72 10/22 30
'lose saltness': g74 8/8 16
"salt of the earth": w75 646
seas: g75 8/8 19

SALT SEA
(SEE DEAD SEA)

SALVATION
means of: w74 622; hu 26
"public declaration": tp 184-6
requirements: g75 11/8 27-8; w74 17-19, 602-3; w72 694-701
source: sl 14, 15, 371; po 24-5; w73 463-6; ka 399-401, 404-10
spiritual security: w74 753-4, 757-63
(SEE ALSO RANSOM)

SALVATION ARMY
experience: w71 415
ministers: g72 5/22 30
"rock" music: g72 11/8 29

SAMARIA
conquest by Assyria: kj 238-9, 243, 245, 251, 261
Oholah: w73 90-1; kj 238-43, 261, 263

SAMARITANS
become Christians: w75 104; w72 690-1
beliefs: w75 104
discussion: w75 103-4
identified: w75 103-4
Jesus' preaching instructions: w71 159-60
parable of neighborly Samaritan: te 36-8

SAME
Lapps: g72 6/22 20-3

SAMOA, AMERICAN
Jehovah's witnesses: yb76 24-5; yb75 24-5; w74 648; yb73 24-5; yb72 34-5
population: yb73 24; yb72 34

SAMOA, WESTERN
Jehovah's witnesses: yb76 24-5; yb75 24-5; w74 647-8; yb73 24-5; yb72 34-5
population: yb73 24; yb72 34

SAMSON
foreordained: g74 7/8 28

SAMUEL (Prophet)
not priest: w71 478-9
not speak to Saul after death: ts 75-8

SANCTIFICATION
Jehovah's name: po 23; kj 368

SANCTUARY
right condition: w71 711-28
(SEE ALSO TEMPLE)

SAND
beaches: g71 8/22 20-2

SAN MARINO
Jehovah's witnesses: yb76 26-7; yb75 26-7; yb74 26-7; yb73 18, 26-7; yb72 36-7
population: yb73 26; yb72 36

SÃO TOMÉ
Jehovah's witnesses: yb76 198

SAPPHIRA
lie to Peter: te 72-3

SARAH
faith: w75 281-2
submissiveness: w74 310

SATAN'S ORGANIZATION
demons: po 78; ts 83-5
earthly: w74 732-4
political, pictured by wild beast out of sea: w75 227-30
structure: pm 100
(SEE ALSO DEMONS)

SATAN THE DEVIL
abyssed: w75 622, 682-3; sl 319; og 27; w74 6, 239-40; po 186; g74 10/22 10; w73 344-5; ka 28-9, 42-4; ka 156; kj 370-1, 395
access to heaven: w74 639-40
accusations against God: g74 10/22 7-8
adversary: w72 620; dn 8-9
aims: po 169; w73 144-5, 591; w72 138-9, 628-9; dn 24-5; w71 582; te 42
author of darkness: w74 560-1
bruising in head: po 186, 191; w72 620-3, 631; dn 8-15, 29; g72 10/22 13-15
cast out of heaven: w74 5-6; ts 163; w73 617; ka 29; dy 15-16; w72 628-9; pm 68-70; dn 23-5
deceiver: ts 80-2
demons: po 78; w73 484-5; w72 427-8; g72 6/8 27-8; g71 5/22 3-4, 28
"designs" (2 Co 2:11): w74 466-7
destruction of: ka 154-8
Devil: po 57, 59; ts 81; g74 10/22 7
dragon (Re 12):
persecuted the woman: po 178
third of stars hurled to earth: w72 427
existence doubted: g74 10/22 3-6; g73 12/8 27; w72 623-4; dn 14-17
final attack after 1,000-year reign: w74 347-8; ka 149-54
Freud, Sigmund, view of: g74 10/22 5
god of world: g74 10/22 8-9; w73 739; tp 124-6; g73 11/8 6; w72 624-5, 628-30; dn 16-18, 24-7; g71 5/22 5
Gog (Eze 38-9): sl 257; w73 293-4, 343-4; kj 349-68, 394-5
growing belief in existence: g74 6/22 30
influence on human governments: ml 19; w74 5-6; g74 10/22 8-9; g73 12/8 28
issue of integrity: fu 16-17; tp 53-4; w72 647-58; g72 10/22 11-12; g72 12/8 24-5; w71 111-12, 487-8
issue of universal sovereignty: fu 16-17; g74 10/22 7-8; w73 144-5, 196-7; tp 51-7; g72 10/22 11-12; g72 12/8 24; w71 539
liar: po 56-7, 59; ts 80; w72 178, 232-3, 426-7
Lucifer: w73 209
method of operation on humans: w75 53; w74 325-7, 561, 569, 732-5, 763; ts 80-3; g74 10/22 7-9; w73 176-81, 185-6, 501-3; w72 623; yb72 78, 170-1; dn 14; g71 5/22 3-10
misconceptions: g74 10/22 4-6
murderer: ts 80
origin: w74 325-6; po 55-9; ts 81-2; g74 10/22 7; tp 49-50; g72 6/8 27
original serpent: ts 80-1
proof he is a person: g74 10/22 6-7; g73 10/22 27; g73 12/8 27-8; w72 232, 623-4; dn 16-17
protection from: g74 10/22 9-10
rebellion: w72 262-3
release from the abyss: ka 149-51, 153; w72 273
repentance for having been under sovereignty of: w75 751
resisting: g74 10/22 9-10
'ruler of air': w74 735
ruler of demons: pm 69
Satan: po 57, 59; ts 81; g74 10/22 7; tp 50; w72 262, 647-9; g72 12/8 24

seed of serpent: po 78
similarity of course of king of Tyre: ts 82
storms: w74 735
symbolic representation: w74 732, 763; ts 83
temptation in Eden: fu 15-16; po 55-7, 59-60; ts 79-80; tp 51-2; w72 262-3, 426-7, 620-1; dn 9-10; te 41-2; g71 5/22 6
tempting of Jesus: w74 722-3; w73 5; w72 624-5, 627; dn 16-18, 22; w71 38-9; te 51-4
tormented forever: w74 382-4; ts 117-21; ka 156-8, 285-6, 291
use of false religion: g73 5/22 27-8
weather: w74 735
why allowed to remain: g74 10/22 7-8; g72 10/22 11-12; w71 111-12
wicked sovereign: w75 654-6
world distress: ml 18-20; w74 5-6; w73 617-19; dy 16-18; g73 12/8 28; g71 10/8 20-2
worship of: w75 228-30; g74 10/22 5; g71 5/22 3-10; g71 8/22 15-16, 30; g71 11/8 29

SATELLITES
communication satellites: g74 4/8 30; g72 2/8 29; g71 12/8 19
military: w74 40
Soviet Union: g71 4/22 30
United States: kj 157-8; g71 4/22 30

SATISFACTION
finding, in life: w75 54-61; g74 8/8 3-7

SATURN
planet: g75 8/22 15-16

SATURNALIA
Roman celebration: g74 12/22 4; g73 12/22 5-6

SAUDI ARABIA
death of pilgrims to Mecca: g75 10/8 30
desert sheep farm: g75 11/22 29
execution of assassin: g75 8/8 30
Jehovah's witnesses: yb76 28-9; yb75 26-7; yb74 26-7
oil: g74 2/22 17-20

SAUERKRAUT
g74 12/22 20

SAUL (King)
anointed as king: po 122-3
consulted spirit medium: ts 75-8
disobedience: w75 51-2; w71 479
presumptuousness: w71 479
relationship with David: w71 576
witch of En-dor: w75 52

SCALES
Richter: g74 5/8 16-17

SCARLET-COLORED WILD BEAST
(SEE BEASTS)

SCAVENGERS
insects: g72 11/22 20-1

SCEPTER
symbolic: kj 220-2

SCHEDULE
housework: g74 5/8 13-15

SCHIZOPHRENIA
blood of schizophrenics: g75 4/22 4, 8
contributing factors: g75 4/22 8; g73 9/22 18
dogs help: g74 7/22 31
effect of Bible knowledge: w75 244-5
suicide: g75 4/22 6
treatment: g72 3/8 29
types of: g75 4/22 6

SCHOOLS
cheating: w74 245-6
college: g74 11/8 31; g71 6/8 3-8; g71 6/22 30; g71 12/8 30
counteracting worldly influences: w75 759; g72 9/8 5-8; w71 584-5
discipline: g72 1/8 29
history: g73 5/8 14
Kingdom Ministry School: yb76 221; yb75 202; yb73 75-6, 136-8, 207; yb72 115-16, 190-1, 229-30, 232, 247; g72 1/8 21, 24
Kingdom Schools: yb75 170-1; w72 760
mathematics: g71 2/8 9-12
medical: g74 8/22 31
practical trades: w75 759
Theocratic School: yb76 150, 161; w74 411; w73 111-12; or 98-100; yb72 256
theological: g74 8/22 8-11
TV's effect on students: g75 5/22 31
Watchtower Bible School of Gilead: yb75 200-2; yb72 256; w71 82
Watch Tower reading schools: yb76 173, 175, 185; yb75 202; w74 410-11; yb74 7-8, 16; g74 7/22 16; w73 111-12; yb73 73-4, 159-60, 181-2; yb72 240; w71 12, 157; g71 4/8 22-3

Parochial Schools
Catholic church:
closed: g75 1/22 8; g74 6/22 30; g73 9/8 30; g72 1/8 31; g71 1/22 30; g71 3/22 31; g71 5/22 29; g71 9/22 9-12
decrease in nuns as teachers: g75 1/22 8
enrollment: g74 5/8 31
evolution theory: w71 41, 47
failure: g74 2/22 30; g74 5/8 31; w72 367
money for: g74 4/22 29
non-Catholic students: g72 2/8 29
problems: g75 4/22 30; g72 1/22 29-30
strike: g72 1/8 31
students leaving church: g72 3/22 29
teachers quitting: g71 1/22 30-1
textbooks: g75 2/22 30

Public Schools
ability to use English language: g75 12/22 30
benefits: w72 156-7; w71 733-5
cheating: g73 4/8 31; g71 6/22 30
crime: g72 1/22 31
dangerous to mental health: w75 759
discussion: g75 5/8 16-21; g74 2/8 3-7
disrespect: g74 2/8 4-5
driver's education: g74 3/22 9-10
dropouts: w75 543-4
drug addiction: g74 2/8 5-6; g74 5/8 6-7; g74 12/8 29; g73 12/8 3-5
evolution theory: g74 9/22 17, 26; g73 10/22 6-7; g72 10/22 29; w71 40-2
experiences:
conduct of Witnesses: w72 381-2, 403, 555
flag salute: g72 9/8 7-8; w71 531
honesty: w72 381
military exercises: w71 532
persecution endured: g72 6/8 24; w71 531; g71 10/22 28
pioneering while in school: km 2/71 6
politics: g72 9/8 7-8
religious services in school: w71 531
sports: g72 9/8 8
teacher becomes Witness: w72 541-2
teachers witness to pupils: yb73 224
use of Society's literature: w72 444; g72 8/8 19; km 11/72 6
Witness bus driver: g75 4/8 19
witnessing in school: w75 440-3; g74 5/22 26; w73 187-8; km 8/72 3; w71 732
Witness parents in class discussion: w74 272; g71 3/22 20
flag salute: yb73 81-3; g72 9/8 7-8; w71 118
court cases: yb75 169, 172; g73 1/22 29-30; yb72 251-2
expulsion of students: yb76 241; yb75 11, 169; yb74 9-11; yb73 81-3; w72 760
gangs: g74 2/8 5
high schools: g75 5/8 16-21
illegitimacy: g71 8/8 30-1
juvenile delinquency: g74 9/22 31; g73 6/22 31; g72 2/22 29-30; g72 4/22 30
mathematics: g75 7/22 30
morals: g75 5/8 17, 20
parents' notes to teachers excusing absences: g75 7/22 30
politics: g72 9/8 6-7
party cards: g73 1/8 29
racial problems: g75 3/8 30; g75 5/8 19
reading: g74 2/8 4; w71 733-4
Witness children commended: g75 12/8 22
religious activity: yb76 241; yb75 11
religious holiday activity: w74 741
removing children: w73 184
science education: g75 7/22 30
sex education: g75 1/8 30; g75 5/8 20; g74 2/8 6; g72 1/22 3-9; g71 1/22 29-30
sports: w75 544
student apathy: g74 2/8 3-4
subjects taught: w75 759; g74 2/8 6
teachers: g75 5/8 16-21;

g74 2/8 5; g74 9/8 5; tp 138-9; g72 7/8 31; g71 6/8 3-4
test of Bible knowledge: g75 6/8 29
truancy: g72 5/22 30
use of Society's literature: w72 402
vandalism: g75 5/22 29; g74 2/8 5; g74 8/22 3-6; g71 4/22 31
violence: g75 5/8 17-18; g75 5/22 29; g75 9/8 30; g74 2/8 5; g73 5/8 29-30
Watch Tower Society's view on schooling: w75 542-4; w71 733-5
witchcraft: g71 7/22 29
witnessing in: w72 401-3; w71 95
Zambia: yb72 249-53
(SEE ALSO EDUCATION, KNOWLEDGE, TEACHERS, TEACHING)

SCHROEDER, ALBERT D.
w75 60; yb75 160-1, 200

SCHWEITZER, ALBERT
beliefs: w75 249

SCIENCE
a god: w75 231; w72 584-7; kj 156-8
astrology disproved: w75 715
attempts to create life: g75 12/8 21; g71 1/8 29
attempts to understand rainbow: g75 1/22 14-16
Bible rejected: w71 324
confirmation of faith in Bible: w71 292
astronomy: w75 133
geology: g74 9/22 29
medical science: w75 133-6
dangers created by: g75 6/8 30; g72 10/22 12; g72 12/22 30; w71 561; g71 2/22 29; g71 10/8 3, 11-12
dogmatism of scientists: g74 9/22 18-19, 26
"doomsday clock": g75 2/8 3
effect on faith: g71 9/8 30
entropy: g71 7/8 3-4
evolution theory: ml 9-11; g74 9/22 17-26
facts as differentiated from theories: g71 4/8 6
failure: w75 99-103; g75 2/8 4-5; g75 3/8 30; g75 10/8 7; w74 131-3, 198, 477; g74 9/22 30; w73 483-4; tp 19-20; g72 11/8 30; w71 470-1; kj 158; g71 2/22 29
knowledge decline among students: g75 7/22 30
knowledge incomplete: w75 101-2
order of universe: g75 6/22 18; g71 8/8 3-7
origin of life: w74 720; g74 9/22 20; w73 36; g73 10/22 9-12; g71 9/8 5-7
origin of universe: w75 200
predictions of future: g71 1/8 7
prestige declines: g73 3/22 30; g72 5/22 30
proper view of: w75 101-2
scientists expressing belief in Creator: w75 651; g75 4/22 17; g75 8/22 26; w72 388; w71 152, 292; g71 8/8 4-5
scientists unemployed: g71 1/8 30; g71 2/8 30
useful languages for scientists: g75 8/8 30-1
viewpoint changes: g75 6/22 19; g74 1/8 12-14; g73 10/22 4-6, 19-20, 30
warnings of annihilation: g72 9/8 3; g71 7/22 29; g71 8/22 31; g71 10/8 17, 28
why scientists accept evolution: g75 3/8 31
(SEE ALSO ARCHAEOLOGY, ASTRONOMY, BIBLE AUTHENTICITY, GEOLOGY)

SCOTLAND
Church of Scotland: g74 8/22 12
religion: g71 1/22 29; g71 6/8 30

SCREAMING
discussion: w71 163-4

SCROLLS
disadvantages: w74 553
Ezekiel: w72 200, 278; kj 71-2, 74-7
"flying scroll" (Zec 5:1): pm 208-16
little scroll (Re 10): kj 75-6
opened (Re 20:12): w74 292-4; w73 364; ka 130-1
"scroll of life" (Re 20:12): g72 4/22 26-7

SEA(S)
color of: g72 8/8 26
coral: g72 10/22 27-8
Dead Sea (Salt Sea): pm 384
diving: g74 9/8 25
farming: g74 9/8 24-5; g72 5/22 26; g71 11/8 16-19
food: g72 3/22 25-6; g72 5/22 26
Jesus' power over: te 59-62
Mediterranean Sea: pm 384
mollusks: g75 11/22 25
molten, in temple: w72 295
nations divide among themselves: g74 9/22 30
North Sea: g75 3/22 31
oil under: g75 3/22 31
pollution: g74 2/22 24; g72 10/8 11; g71 1/8 7-8; g71 4/22 10-11, 30; g71 9/8 30-1; g71 9/22 29; g71 12/8 29
seafood diminishing: g74 2/22 23-4
seashells: g75 11/22 25
symbolic: pm 384-6
underwater exploration: g72 8/8 29
waves: g71 8/22 21-2
(SEE ALSO MARINE LIFE, OCEANS)

SEA CREATURES
(SEE MARINE LIFE)

SEAL
mammal: g75 10/22 25

SEAL(S)
foreheads of God's slaves: w72 636

SEA LIONS
whiskers: g72 12/22 31

SEA MONSTER
discussion: w73 447

SEA OF GALILEE
g71 9/8 30-1

SEA SNAKE
g75 3/22 31

SEASONS
"seasons of refreshing" (Ac 3:19): w72 118-20

SECOND ADVENTISTS
yb75 34, 36

SECOND COMING
(SEE CHRIST'S PRESENCE)

SECOND DEATH
continued existence of: w74 383
meaning: w74 239, 382; ka 26, 157-8, 285-6, 290-1
symbolic representation: w74 381-2; ts 118-21
torment: ts 120-1
use after Armageddon: ts 183, 185-6
(SEE ALSO DEATH, GEHENNA)

SECRETARY
man in linen: w72 41-54

SECTARIANISM
w75 166-8

SECULAR WORK
attitude toward: w72 205-9, 269-70, 299; g72 3/22 30; g72 5/8 5; g72 9/22 16; w71 231-2; te 95-8; g71 4/8 12-15; g71 12/8 29
boredom: g72 5/22 31
carrying weapons during: w73 127-8
Christian conduct: w71 223
college graduates: g71 6/8 7-8
experiences:
conduct of Witnesses: w72 381, 510; yb72 241-2; g72 3/8 11
putting Kingdom service first: yb72 79; km 12/72 3-5; w71 680
refusing military or religious work: w71 533-4; g71 12/22 24
witnessing to workmates: w71 221-2
giant corporations: g71 2/8 3-6
giving employer full measure: w71 260; g71 4/8 15
informal witnessing: w72 400-1
stress: g71 11/8 30-1
unemployment: g71 3/22 30
women: g72 5/22 7; g71 3/22 30
(SEE ALSO EMPLOYMENT, WORK)

SECURE FUTURE—HOW YOU CAN FIND IT, A (Booklet)
public talk: km 12/75 1, 8

SECURITY
bulletproof equipment: g75 4/8 29
Conference on Security and Cooperation in Europe: g75 9/22 29; g75 11/8 3-7
discussion: fu 3-32
God's new order: fu 21-5; g75 11/22 16; w74 101
lack in world: g75 11/22 3-4; w74 492; g74 9/8 3; g74 10/8 16
obtaining: fu 25-32; g75 5/22 3-6
private security guards: g75 5/22 30; g75 9/22 30
spiritual: yb75 260; w74 721-9, 733-4, 753-4, 757-63
where found: fu 5-12; g74 8/8 5-7
worldly views: w74 721

SEDITION
Witnesses disprove charges: yb74 38; yb73 162

SEED
of good news: w74 573; w73 680-4, 685-6, 690, 693
symbolic: w73 683-6

SEED OF ABRAHAM
discussion: po 161-8, 180-1; g73 8/22 28-9
faith needed: po 163
Gentiles included: po 164-8

Jesus Christ: w74 330; tp 64-5; g73 8/22 29; w71 301-2
Jews offered first opportunity: po 161-4
relationship to 'seed of woman': po 87
(SEE ALSO CONGREGATION OF GOD, JESUS CHRIST)

SEED OF SERPENT
identified: po 78
(SEE ALSO SATAN'S ORGANIZATION)

SEED OF WOMAN
Bible records line of descent: po 65
blessings to mankind: g72 10/22 15-16
discussion: w75 81-6
genealogy:
- Abraham: po 85, 87
- David: po 89
- Isaac: po 91-3
- Jacob: po 93-5
- Shem: po 83, 85

heel bruised: ts 129; w72 622; dn 13; g72 10/22 13-15
how heavenly "woman" provides: po 134-5, 137
identified: w75 619; og 19; po 151-3; ts 129-30; g72 10/22 13-14; w71 301-2
Messiah: po 60
selection: po 134-5
serpent's head bruised: po 186, 191; w72 623; dn 14-15
"woman" identified: po 60-1; ts 126-7
(SEE ALSO CONGREGATION OF GOD, JESUS CHRIST)

SEGREGATION
absence among Witnesses: w73 37; g71 10/22 12-13
Bible view: w73 517-18, 537
churches: g73 2/22 4-5
schools: g75 3/8 30
United States: g73 2/22 4-5

SEIR
w75 31

SELECTIVE SERVICE
conscientious objection: yb75 101; yb73 22, 79-81, 98-100, 120-2, 124, 162-3
court cases: yb73 133-5
exemption of Witnesses: yb75 205, 208; yb73 80-1, 99; g71 1/8 13-15
registration requirements: g75 5/22 31
Witnesses during World War I: yb75 101-3, 119
Witnesses during World War II: yb75 205
(SEE ALSO MILITARY SERVICE)

SELF-ABUSE
discussion: w73 564-9; tp 152; w72 92-4

SELF-CONTROL
anger: g74 5/22 28; w72 68-9; w71 164
benefits: g75 11/22 12; g72 12/8 7-8
developing: g74 5/22 28
eating and drinking: w74 167-8; g74 4/22 23
examples of: g73 6/22 19; w71 360
examples of loss:
- modern-day: w74 243; g74 3/8 13-16

health factor: g74 5/22 27-8; w72 195-6
masturbation: w73 568-9; tp 152
natural ability: g71 10/22 3
not cowardice: g74 5/22 28
passion: w74 12-13; w73 593, 595-6; w72 93-4; g72 12/8 8
recreation: g73 3/22 4
singleness: w74 61; w73 476-7, 568
thinking: w73 511-12

SELF-DEFENSE
Bible view: yb75 190; g75 9/8 27-8; g75 12/8 28-9; g74 3/8 4
protection against crime: g75 11/22 11-14; g74 3/8 4, 16

SELF-EXAMINATION
w74 562, 566

SELF-INDULGENCE
due to parental neglect: g75 3/8 29

SELFISHNESS
examples: w74 50, 102; g74 6/8 25-6
how manifested: g74 1/22 5; g74 3/8 3-4; g74 5/8 30; g73 10/8 9, 14; g72 2/22 3-4; w71 199-200; te 103-6
results: g75 12/22 9; g74 7/8 4; g74 10/8 16; g72 10/8 13

SELF-RIGHTEOUSNESS
w75 707; w74 213

SEMINARY
beliefs of professors: w74 14; g74 8/22 9-10
beliefs of students: w71 548, 675
closing: g75 3/8 27; g72 4/8 30; g71 8/8 29
discord: g74 8/22 8-11
enrollment: w74 166; g74 6/22 30; g74 8/22 8-9; g74 11/8 30; g72 4/8 30; w71 408, 484; g71 12/22 30
failure: g75 9/8 30; g74 3/8 30; g74 8/22 8-11; g73 7/22 29; w71 739
lose teachers: g74 8/22 8
problems: g74 3/22 29; g74 8/22 8-11; g74 11/8 30; g71 3/8 29
(SEE ALSO CLERGY)

SEMIRAMIS
priestly celibacy traced to: g75 5/8 28

SENEGAL
Jehovah's witnesses: yb76 30-1; yb75 28-9; yb74 6-7, 28-9; yb73 28-9; yb72 38-9; g72 6/8 28; w71 122-3, 127
population: yb73 28; yb72 38

SENSE STRESS
public speaking: sg 126-9, 158-60

SEPARATION
from Babylon the Great: w75 692; g72 4/22 27-8
from world: tp 120-1, 124-31; g72 12/8 20; w71 559-64
- benefits: w75 697

marriage: w75 286-8, 575-6; w74 511; w72 382-4

SEPTUAGINT
Tetragrammaton: w71 389-91, 454; bi8 1357-8
time and circumstances of translation: po 132-3; w71 389, 454
(SEE ALSO BIBLE TRANSLATIONS)

SERAPHS
discussion: po 31-2
subjection to God: kj 49-51
(SEE ALSO ANGELS, CHERUBS)

SERMON ON THE MOUNT
discussion: w73 436-8; g71 6/8 27-8; g71 6/22 27-8; g71 7/8 27-8; g71 7/22 27-8; g71 8/8 27-8; g71 8/22 27-8; g71 9/8 27-8; g71 9/22 27-8; g71 10/22 27-8
summary: w71 396, 638
time given: w73 11-12

Quotations
still our best guide: g75 10/8 15
world's best psychiatry just awkward summation of: g75 4/22 19

SERMON OUTLINES (Booklet)
preparation of talks: sg 41-2

SERMONS
Christendom: g73 1/22 30; g72 5/8 29; g72 12/22 30; w71 408, 643; g71 3/22 4
(SEE ALSO FIELD SERVICE, PRESENTATIONS)

SERPENT
cautious: po 55
curse: po 59
used by Satan: po 55-7, 59-60; ts 80
without limbs: po 42, 55
(SEE ALSO SATAN THE DEVIL)

SERUMS
w74 351-2

SERVANT(S)
Greek word: w75 716-22, 729-31
humility: w75 722-8
ordination: w75 732-4
"superior authorities": w75 719
(SEE ALSO MINISTERIAL SERVANTS, OVERSEERS)

SERVETUS, MICHAEL
death: w74 145

SERVICE
Christian:
- discussion: w75 716-22
- Greek word: w75 716-19
- humility: w75 722-8
- serving physical needs: w75 716-19
- serving spiritual needs: w75 719-20

(SEE ALSO FIELD SERVICE)

SERVICE COMMITTEE
(SEE JUDICIAL COMMITTEE)

SERVICE DIRECTOR
yb75 125, 165; w72 759

SERVICE MEETING
applause: km 4/72 4
concluding comments: km 8/71 4
demonstrations: or 98
discussion: or 97-8

ending on time: sg 178
forerunner of present-day: yb75 43-4, 133
participants: km 2/75 4
preparation and procedure: km 12/74 3; km 10/73 7; or 97; km 9/72 7
"special": km 8/74 2
testimony meeting: w72 759
(SEE ALSO MEETINGS)

SERVICE REPORTS
annual report for world: yb76 22-32; w75 23-8; yb75 23-32; w74 27-30; yb74 23-32; w73 23-8; yb73 23-32, 255-6; w72 22-5, 27, 493; yb72 33-41; w71 23-9
congregation: km 11/72 7
proper view: or 127-8
why kept: or 126-7
(SEE ALSO FIELD SERVICE)

SERVING WHERE NEED IS GREATER
discussion: km 1/74 4; or 134-5; w71 83-9
evangelizing spirit: w74 336-7
experiences:
joys: w74 208; w72 542; yb72 52-4, 59-60, 64; w71 85
overcoming obstacles: yb72 51-4, 57-66
response: yb73 137, 208-9; yb72 182, 193-4
invitation: w71 84-5
modern-day beginning: yb75 226-7
requesting information on: w71 88
Rhodesia: yb75 9
Tonga: yb76 15

SETH
line of descent to promised "seed": po 66
name (meaning): w71 58

SETTLING PERSONAL DIFFERENCES
g74 5/22 27-8; g74 7/8 3-4; km 10/74 7; w73 703-4; w72 465-7; or 155-9; g72 8/8 4; w71 438

SEVEN
symbolic: pm 399-400

SEVENTH-DAY ADVENTISTS
experience: w74 38-9
Watchtower court case: g71 2/8 25-6

SEVEN TIMES
(SEE APPOINTED TIMES OF THE NATIONS)

SEVENTY
Bible use of number: pm 399-400

SEVENTY WEEKS OF YEARS
beginning: g71 12/8 8
discussion: po 131-2, 144-5; g73 9/8 28; g71 12/8 6-9
seventieth:
beginning: po 144
end: po 162-4; pm 256
middle of the week: po 162, 164
(SEE ALSO CHRONOLOGY)

SEWAGE
bacteria: g73 3/8 10
disposal plant: g73 6/22 24
fertilizer: g75 3/8 31; g71 11/22 29-30
fish food from: g72 8/8 31
fuel from: g73 1/22 30
reclamation of water: g71 1/22 29; g71 10/22 29

SEWING
discussion: g73 8/22 9-12
making own clothes: g73 8/22 9-12; g71 5/8 8-10; g71 5/22 29
sewing machine: g73 8/22 10-11

SEX
advertising: g74 3/8 12
Bible view: w74 436, 703; g74 6/22 11; w73 590-6; tp 145-54
child education: g75 1/8 30; g74 4/22 13-14; w73 520-2; g72 1/22 3-9; g72 7/22 29-30; w71 589; g71 1/22 29-30
church film: g71 10/22 30
Commmon Catechism, view of: g75 5/22 29
courtship: w74 11-13
crime: g71 10/22 30
development: w73 87-8
diseases: w75 48; g75 5/8 5-8; w74 424; g73 11/22 29; w72 219; g72 2/8 17-20; g72 8/22 29
group sex: g71 7/22 30
marriage: g74 4/22 4, 6-7, 10-12; w72 734-6; g72 2/8 20
masturbation: w73 564-9; w72 92-4; g72 12/8 7
music: w74 302
perversion: w72 734-6, 767-8; g72 5/22 29; g72 8/8 30; g71 6/8 30
pornography: w75 756; g73 11/22 27-8; g71 1/22 16-19
procreative force: w71 594; g71 5/8 28
purpose: po 48; w71 452
repentance for sexual immorality: w75 755-6
respect for organs: w73 592-4
sterilization: g73 1/8 29
superstition: g72 6/8 9-10
surgical change of: w74 360; g74 6/8 29
swinging sex life: g75 4/22 31
"toying" with sexual immorality: w73 74-5
uncleanness: w73 592-6
"wet dreams": w73 566-7
women as symbols: g72 5/22 7-8
youths: w75 461-2

SEXUAL INTERCOURSE
Adam and Eve: g72 4/8 27
bestiality: w72 32; g72 1/22 5
extramarital: w72 767-8
illicit: g75 4/22 31; g75 6/22 29; g74 6/22 14
repentance for: w75 755-6
incestuous marriages: w75 72-7
married persons: w74 436, 703-4; g74 4/22 4, 6-7, 10-12; tp 153; w72 575-6, 734-6; g72 2/8 20; g71 1/22 19; g71 7/22 30
rock music: w75 390
single persons: g74 1/22 27-8; g74 4/22 13-14; g74 8/22 31; w73 74-5; g73 10/8 30-1; g73 12/8 29; w72 218-21; g72 2/8 17, 19-20; g72 4/22 18-19; g72 8/22 8-12; g72 10/22 30-1; g72 12/8 7; g71 5/22 30; g71 6/8 5-6; g71 9/8 29; g71 11/22 29
unnatural acts: w75 48; w74 424; tp 153; w72 734-6

SEX WORSHIP
Canaanites: w74 457-9
Midianites: w73 586-8
Moabites: w73 586-8
modern-day: w75 231-2
Totonacan Indians: g75 7/22 11-12

SEYCHELLES
Jehovah's witnesses: yb76 26-7; yb75 26-7; yb74 26-7; yb73 26-7; yb72 36-7
population: yb73 26; yb72 36

SHECHEM
place: w75 735-6

SHEEP
figurative: kj 293-307
characteristics: w74 250
"other sheep": w74 287-8; g74 8/22 27-8
shepherding: w73 39; or 53-8; pm 305-6, 310-11, 314-16
straying: km 12/75 7-8
literal:
coyote predators: g75 9/22 31
desert farm: g75 11/22 29
eagle attacks on lambs: g75 7/22 31
shearing: g74 11/8 14-15
sheep ranch: g74 11/8 14-16
shepherd's care: w73 39; or 55, 57
shepherd's voice: w75 432
wool: g74 11/8 14-16
lost sheep (Mt 18:12-14): te 115-16
(SEE ALSO OTHER SHEEP)

SHEEP AND GOATS (Illustration)
basis for separation: w74 250, 626-8; ka 274-8, 286-9; tp 86-7; g73 7/22 6
clarification of understanding: ka 266-9
goats: ka 284-92
everlasting cutting-off: ka 290-1
sheep identified: w74 287-8
sheep inherit kingdom: w74 626; ka 272
time of fulfillment: w74 625-6; ka 258-60

SHEKINAH LIGHT
significance: w72 585; kj 165

SHEM
line of Messiah: po 83
living in Abraham's day: po 83, 85, 92

SHEOL
discussion: ts 92-5; w73 233-5; bi8 1353
Greek equivalent: w73 236-7; g72 11/8 6; bi8 1353
meaning of term: ts 92-3, 95; w73 233-5; g72 11/8 6; bi8 1353, 1361
misconceptions: g72 11/8 6-7
occurrences in Scriptures: bi8 1353, 1361
(SEE ALSO HELL)

SHEPHERDS
care of sheep: w73 39; or 55, 57; te 115-16
rulers: kj 293-301
sheep know voice: w75 432; w73 39
spiritual: w74 281-2
false: w75 553-5; w73 165-6; pm 305-10
gifts in men: w71 751-2

Jehovah: or 53; kj 293, 299, 302-4, 310-11; te 116-18
Jesus Christ: w73 168-9; or 53, 55; pm 315-25; kj 297, 305-7, 310-11
overseers of congregation: w74 434-5; w73 39; or 53-8
Zechariah: pm 305-6, 310-14, 319-20

SHERPAS
g75 11/22 17-21

SHIELD
symbolic: w74 753-4

SHILOH
identified: w72 82
meaning of term: po 101; w72 82

SHINTO
yb73 210-11, 214; w71 14

SHIPS
Bounty: g75 1/22 30
disaster: g72 2/8 12-16; g72 8/8 29
Germany: g72 5/22 18-19
harbor pilot: g75 8/8 20-3
submarines: g73 11/8 31
supertankers: g75 1/8 30
tanker: g75 6/22 31
trade routes: g74 10/22 16, 18

SHIPWRECK
avoiding spiritual: w75 505-11

SHOCK
treatment: g73 7/22 12

SHOES
g73 11/22 29; g72 3/22 23-4; g72 10/22 30; g71 8/22 17-19

SHOPLIFTING
effect on consumers: g73 4/22 4
efforts to combat: g73 4/22 7-8
elderly: g75 6/22 30
increase: g75 3/22 7; g72 3/22 30; g72 7/22 30-1; g72 12/8 30; g71 1/8 30; g71 1/22 29; g71 9/22 30; g71 11/22 29
inflation's effect on: g73 10/22 30
number per year: g75 9/8 31
supermarkets: g73 12/8 30
(SEE ALSO STEALING)

SHRUBS
g75 5/8 29

SHYNESS
w75 197-9

SICKNESS
accident victim awakes from eight-year coma: g75 9/8 30-1
body's resistance: g74 10/8 7
cancer: g74 9/8 17-23
colds: g73 12/22 8-10; g71 1/8 29-30; g71 3/8 30
diabetes: g74 1/22 15-16
discussion: w74 131-4
effect of going to bed at late hours: g75 9/22 31
enduring: w73 476
extent in world: g74 6/8 30-1
fever: g75 12/8 25-7
first aid: g74 9/22 8
hay fever: g74 1/22 16
home care for mentally ill: g73 9/22 17-20
kidney stones: g75 1/22 25-6
nervous breakdown: g74 8/22 16-19
neuroses: g75 4/22 5
pneumonia: g74 12/22 11-12
prayers concerning: w74 137-8; g74 6/8 6
psychosomatic: g71 11/22 30
sin: w74 134
spiritual: w74 756-8, 760; w71 664
why Jehovah permits: ts 59
(SEE ALSO DISEASE, HEALTH, MEDICINE)

SIERRA LEONE
Jehovah's witnesses: yb76 30-1; yb75 10, 30-1; yb74 7-8, 30-1; w73 29; yb73 30-1; yb72 40-1; w71 124-5, 679
name: w71 124
population: yb73 30; yb72 40

SIGHT
figurative: g73 7/22 3

SIGN(S)
Christ's presence: w75 633-5; w74 398-400; ka 165-9, 205-11
Jesus Christ: w71 405-6; te 175-8
last days:
as days of Noah: w75 10-11; km 7/75 2
as lightning: w74 750
chart on features: tp 82-3
composite sign: w75 633; ka 293; g73 10/8 20-2
earthquakes: w75 634-5; w74 72-4, 243; g74 5/8 17-19; tp 83; g73 10/8 21; w72 339; g72 10/8 16; w71 69, 406; te 177
false prophets: ka 320-2
food shortages: w75 634; g75 2/22 8; w74 195-7, 243; ts 162; tp 82; g73 6/22 3-6, 10-12; g73 10/8 5-7, 21; w72 339, 615; g72 10/8 15; w71 69, 406; te 177
fulfillment upon Jerusalem (70 C.E.): sl 22; w74 682-3; po 172-3; ka 294-304; tp 79-80
generation: w75 632, 635; gc 22; g75 7/8 29; g73 4/22 19; g72 10/8 15
lack of natural affection: w75 327
lawlessness increasing: w75 635; g75 11/22 15; w74 99-101, 244; tp 83; g73 10/8 10-11, 21; g72 10/8 16; w71 406; te 178
lovers of pleasures: g72 1/22 26
men faint out of fear: w75 635; w74 656; w71 69
persecution of Christians: w72 340
pestilences and diseases: w75 634; w74 131-3; ts 162; w73 753; tp 82; g73 10/8 20-1; g72 10/8 16; w71 69, 406; g71 3/8 4
preaching of this good news of kingdom: w75 635; w74 4; po 174; ka 307-8; tp 83; g72 10/8 16; w71 69, 80-2, 466
reason Jesus gave "sign": w74 398-400
separation of "sheep" and "goats": w74 625-8; g73 7/22 5-6
signs from heaven: km 7/75 2; w74 40
signs in sun, moon and stars: w75 276; ka 322-6
wars: w75 274, 633-4, 684; g75 10/8 13; ts 162; tp 80-2; g73 10/8 16-17, 20; w72 339; g72 10/8 15; w71 69, 406; te 177
"sign" of Jehovah's sovereignty: sl 126
sign of Son of man: km 7/75 2; w74 748, 750-1; ka 326-8
(SEE ALSO CHRIST'S PRESENCE)

SIGNAL
identified: sl 199-203
raised up: sl 199

SIKKIM
Jehovah's witnesses: yb75 26-7; yb74 26-7; yb73 26-7; yb72 36-7
population: yb73 26; yb72 36

SILOAM
pool: w75 367

SILVER
money: g74 4/22 29

SIMEON
son of Jacob:
disqualified as to 'line of seed': po 96-7

SIMPLICITY
word choice: g73 9/8 20; sg 6-8

SIN
abolition: ts 137-9; g73 10/8 26-7; w71 276; te 90
Adam and Eve: w75 459; fu 14-16; po 56-9; ts 30-4; g74 10/8 12-13; tp 48-52; w72 178; g72 4/8 27-8
against holy spirit: w75 39, 460; ts 181-2
avoiding: w74 496-7; w73 511-12; g73 11/22 27-8; w72 516, 528-31
basis for forgiveness: w75 39-40; g75 4/8 9-11; w74 370, 494-8; ts 138; g74 3/22 28; w73 464-7; w72 687-9; w71 270-2, 276
children: w72 359-60
confession to God: g74 11/8 27-8
confession to judicial committee: km 10/74 7; w72 437-8; or 165
dead acquitted from: w74 607
forgiveness: w75 38-40; w74 494, 497-8; g74 11/8 28; w72 118-20, 335; w71 236-7
freedom from: g73 10/8 26-7; w71 431-3
in heart: g73 11/22 27
inherited: g75 1/8 27; g75 4/8 6; w74 190; po 62-3; ts 34-5; g74 10/8 13; w73 511; w72 359-60, 621; dn 10-11; g72 6/8 7; w71 581-2; g71 12/8 27-8
Jesus forgave sins before his death: g74 11/8 28; te 87-90
kinds of: w74 496-7
Law covenant: po 115-18; w72 287-8
love covers: w75 342-8
meaning of term: g75 4/8 6; w73 464; tp 181-2; w71 30; g71 10/8 19
misconceptions: g73 6/22 28-9
New Order:
gradual elimination: ts 138-40, 165-6
not concealing: km 10/74 7
physical effects: w74 319-20
practicers of: w74 494-6, 512

g, Awake!; ka, God's Kingdom of a Thousand Years; kj, "The Nations Shall Know that I Am Jehovah"; km, Kingdom Ministry; or, Organization; pm, Paradise Restored—By Theocracy!; po, God's "Eternal Purpose"; sg, Theocratic School Guidebook; sl, Man's Salvation out of World Distress!; te, Listening to the Great Teacher; tp, True Peace and Security; ts, Is This Life All There Is?; w, Watchtower; yb, Yearbook. Complete list on page 6.

results: w74 369-70; ts 34-5; g71 10/8 19-20
sickness: w74 134
temptation: w74 63-4
unforgivable: w75 39, 286, 459-60; ts 182
willful: w73 466-7
worldly view: g73 9/8 7

SINAI (Wilderness)
Israelite assembly after exodus: pm 59-60

SINCERITY
insufficient by itself: g73 5/22 27; g73 11/8 27-8; w72 742

SINGAPORE
description: w72 341
flogging criminals: g74 12/22 31
Jehovah's witnesses: yb76 30-1; yb75 30-1; km 4/75 1; yb74 20, 30-1; yb73 30-1; w72 341-9; yb72 40-1
population: yb73 30; yb72 40

SINGING
church choirs: w75 112
congregation meetings: w75 29-31
Israelite worship: w75 30

"SINGING AND ACCOMPANYING YOURSELVES WITH MUSIC IN YOUR HEARTS" (Songbook)
appreciation for: w72 405
benefits of Kingdom songs: w71 404
experiences with: w75 31; w72 479
recordings: w72 405

SINGLENESS
advantages: w74 379-80
Bible view: w74 379-80, 703; w73 31-2; g72 5/8 12; g72 12/8 6
discussion: w72 107-8; g72 12/8 5-8
(SEE ALSO CELIBACY, MARRIAGE)

SKEPTICISM
g73 3/22 16-19; w72 387-8

SKIN
acne: g71 1/8 17-19
antiseptic: g72 2/8 31
description: g71 1/8 17; g71 1/22 11
race variations: g73 2/8 5-7
tattooing: g72 2/8 29

SKY
colors: g71 6/22 11

SLACKS
used by women: w72 671-2

SLANDER
Bible view: w74 247

SLAVE(S)
Christians: w74 370-4; w73 277; ka 339-40; w72 121-2, 697
disown themselves: w74 600-1
sluggish (Jesus' illustration): w74 589-91
subjection to owners: w72 598
to sin: w74 369-70; w71 431-3
unforgiving (Jesus' illustration): w72 550-1; w71 102-3; te 63-6
(SEE ALSO EVIL SLAVE AND FAITHFUL AND DISCREET SLAVE)

SLAVERY
all mankind: w74 369-70
United States: w74 709; g73 2/22 4

SLEEP
accident victim awakes from eight-year "sleep": g75 9/8 30-1
aids: g75 3/8 13-14; g74 6/8 15
amount needed: g74 2/22 9; g72 9/22 30
discussion: g75 3/8 12-14
dreams: g75 1/22 3-6
effect of going to bed at late hours: g75 9/22 31
effect of sleep loss: g75 8/8 31
importance: g74 2/22 9; w72 291-2, 414-15, 490
insomnia: g75 3/8 12-14
positions for backache: g75 6/8 31
sleep-inducing drugs: g72 2/8 23; g72 10/22 30
sleep-inducing foods: g75 11/22 30-1
"wet dreams": w73 566-7

SLIDE PROGRAMS
yb75 232-3; w74 648-9

SLOTH
g71 3/22 15

SMALLPOX
g74 1/22 30; g72 8/22 31; g71 12/22 31

SMELL
selling by means of: g75 7/8 6-8

SMOKE
symbolic: ts 121-2

SMOKING
addiction: g74 7/22 30
advertising: w75 12; g75 5/22 29; g75 10/22 30; g74 3/8 11; g73 10/22 30; w72 595
air pollution: g73 8/22 17-18; g72 1/22 29
associates with congregation: km 11/73 7
Bible view: w73 338-43, 543; w72 594-6; w71 670-2
bishops addicted: g75 1/22 30
blood donors: g75 1/22 30
breaking the habit: w74 510; w73 453-5; g73 8/22 20; yb72 65; w71 671-2
children: g74 2/22 30; g73 9/22 30; g71 1/22 31
cigarettes: g75 5/22 29-30; g75 12/22 30; g73 9/22 31; g72 2/22 29; g72 4/8 31; g71 4/22 30-1
nontobacco: g74 7/8 30
smuggling: g75 5/22 30
doctors: g71 2/22 29
effect on nonsmokers: g74 4/22 30; g73 8/22 17-19; g73 9/22 30; g72 1/22 29; g72 6/22 30
effect on offspring: g75 4/8 30; g75 12/8 31; g74 2/8 14; g74 5/22 31; g73 2/8 30; g73 8/22 18-20; g72 6/22 30; g71 5/8 29
effect on user: w74 168; g74 2/22 30; g74 4/22 30; g74 7/8 30; w73 338-9, 453-5; g73 1/22 29; g73 2/22 23; g73 5/22 30; g73 8/8 30; g73 8/22 17, 19; g73 12/22 9; w72 595-6; g72 2/8 29; g72 2/22 29; g72 4/8 31; g72 6/8 30; g72 11/22 31; g71 1/22 14; g71 2/22 29; g71 11/8 4; g71 12/22 30
blood: g75 1/22 30; g74 5/22 18-19; g71 2/22 29
gums: w75 327; g74 6/8 29-30
heart: g74 2/8 29; g71 8/22 29
life-span: g74 11/22 30; g71 2/8 31; g71 4/22 30
lungs: w75 12; g75 10/22 30-1; g75 12/22 30; g74 5/22 30; g74 9/8 18, 20, 23; g73 1/22 19; g72 7/22 30; g72 9/8 31
strokes: g75 4/8 30
teeth: w75 327
field service privileges: km 7/73 4
former members of congregation: km 11/73 7
government spending to warn of dangers: g75 10/22 30
government subsidy: g75 10/22 30
indifference to consequences: w74 71; g73 10/22 30; g73 12/22 30; g72 7/8 30
infringes on rights: g71 3/8 29
opinions of health authorities: g74 4/22 30; g73 8/22 17-19; g71 2/22 29; g71 11/8 4
opium: g75 5/8 11
pipes: g75 12/22 30
restaurant with nonsmoking room: g75 9/8 30
six months to stop: w73 340
statistics: g74 2/22 30; g74 5/22 30; g73 1/8 31; g73 3/22 31; g73 9/22 31; g72 11/8 29; g71 11/8 4
Witness business establishment: w74 223-4
Witness home: w74 223-4
Witness view of: w74 71
women: w75 12
(SEE ALSO TOBACCO)

SMUGGLING
experiences: yb73 17; w72 125

SNAIL
disease: g73 1/8 20-2

SNAKE(S)
anaconda: g71 3/8 19
cobra: g75 6/8 19; g71 3/8 19-20
handling: g73 8/8 5-7
hearing: g75 6/8 19
Italy: g75 5/22 30
poison: g71 3/8 19-20
python: g71 3/8 19
rattlesnake: g71 5/8 31
sea snake: g75 3/22 31
serpent in Eden: po 55-7, 59-60
vipers: g75 5/22 30; g72 10/22 30
without limbs: po 42, 55
(SEE ALSO ANIMALS)

SNEEZING
effect: g71 3/8 6

SNOW
formation: g71 12/8 30
Japan's snowmen: g71 1/8 20-2
shoveling: g75 2/22 30-1
snowmobiles: g71 1/22 30

SOCIAL GATHERINGS
activities: w72 403-4; g72 6/22 13-16; w71 314
large: km 7/74 3
"marked" person: w73 319
wedding receptions: w73 696

SODOM AND GOMORRAH
destruction: g72 4/8 23
Jehovah's view: g74 10/8 20

Judgment Day: g75 10/22 13
wickedness: w74 485

SODOMY
divorce grounds: w72 767-8
(SEE ALSO HOMOSEXUALITY)

SOIL
bacteria: g73 3/8 10; g73 7/8 7
discussion: g75 8/8 12-15
earthworms: g75 8/8 14
erosion: g74 5/8 29-30
fertilizers: g75 8/8 15; g74 5/22 10-11
insects: w71 326-7
microorganisms: g72 2/22 12
mixed culture: g71 5/22 17-18
pollution: g71 4/22 11-12
types: g74 5/22 10
(SEE ALSO FARMING)

SOLAR SYSTEM
asteroids: g74 1/8 12
Earth:
moon: g74 8/22 13-16; g73 5/22 4-8; w72 293
quasimoon: g71 11/22 30
Eros: g75 8/22 14-15
Jupiter: g75 8/22 13-14; g73 5/22 12
Mars: g75 8/22 14; g73 5/22 9-11
Mercury: g75 8/22 13
meteors: g74 5/22 31
mysteries: g74 1/8 12-13
order: g71 8/8 4-5
Saturn: g75 8/22 15-16
size: g75 6/22 17-18; g74 1/8 12
sun: g75 8/22 16; g74 8/22 20; g71 6/22 9; g71 12/22 29
tenth planet: g74 1/8 12
Venus: g75 8/22 12-13; g75 12/22 29; g73 5/22 11-12; g71 3/8 30-1
(SEE ALSO PLANETS, STARS, UNIVERSE)

SOLDIERS
first-person account: g73 8/8 19-22
hearing damage: g73 8/22 31
venereal disease: g74 3/22 31

SOLOMON
Bible writer: g73 3/22 18
failings: w73 439-40
loss of God's favor: w71 151
reign:
prophetic: w75 83; fu 22-3
temple building: w71 393-4; kj 27
wisdom: g74 10/22 20; w73 489-91

SOLOMON ISLANDS
copper mining: g75 1/8 18-20
Jehovah's witnesses: yb76 28-9; w75 478; yb75 28-9; yb74 28-9; yb73 28-9; yb72 38-9
ban lifted: g75 6/22 14-15
money: g75 7/22 23
population: yb73 28; yb72 38

SOMALIA
Jehovah's witnesses: yb73 26-7; yb72 36-7
population: yb73 26; yb72 36
Suez Canal: g74 10/22 18

SONG OF SOLOMON (Book)
writer: g73 3/22 18

SONGS
Kingdom songs: yb74 227-8; w72 405, 477, 479; w71 404
meetings: w72 411
"new song" (Ps 98:1): w73 622-3; dy 25-8
popular: w71 403-4
"rock" songs: w74 303-4
victory after Har-Magedon: w74 239
(SEE ALSO MUSIC)

SON OF MAN
Daniel: kj 55
Ezekiel: w72 186-7; kj 55
identified: w74 748; ts 154; w72 580; g72 2/8 6-7; kj 55
meaning of term: w75 479
sign of: w74 748, 750-1
(SEE ALSO JESUS CHRIST)

SONS OF GOD
angels: w72 651-3
discussion: po 26-34, 40
humans: w71 431-2
Jesus Christ: g72 3/22 5; te 23-6
peacemakers: g71 9/8 27-8
(SEE ALSO ANGELS)

SOPHERIM
changes made by: bi8 1352-3
extraordinary points: bi8 1356

SORCERY
w74 325-6; ts 76, 86-7; g74 4/22 30; w73 342, 483-6; g71 7/8 29-30
(SEE ALSO SPIRITISM, WITCHCRAFT)

SORROW
enduring: g75 5/8 22-3
(SEE ALSO MOURNING)

SOUL(S)
animals: ts 38-40; bi8 1351
attributes and qualities: w73 726
'cannot kill soul' (Mt 10:28): w75 53, 286; g75 8/8 28; g75 10/22 11
definition: g75 8/8 27; po 39; ts 38-41; g74 1/8 19; w73 230-1; g71 3/8 28
different from spirit: ts 47-51
discussion: g75 8/8 27-8; po 38-40; ts 35-46; w73 230-1
Greek word: g75 8/8 27; ts 37-9; w73 230-1; bi8 1351
Hebrew word: g75 8/8 27; po 39; ts 37-43; w73 230-1; bi8 1351
Hinduism: ts 36-7
'losing' soul: ts 42-3
loving God whole-souled: or 132-47
misconceptions: po 38, 40; ts 35-7, 43-6, 55-6, 59-60, 69-70, 89, 91-2; g74 1/8 16; w73 603-5; g73 6/8 5-6; g73 7/22 27-8; w71 47-8; g71 3/8 28
source of: w75 744; ts 43-5
mortal: ts 37-43, 45-6; g74 1/8 19; g74 6/8 28; w73 208, 230-1; g73 5/8 5; g73 6/8 5-7; g72 11/8 6; g71 3/8 27-8; g71 8/8 26
resurrection: g74 6/8 28; w73 726-7
underneath altar (Re 6:9): g73 6/8 7

SOUND
echolocation: g75 6/8 20
medical uses: g72 12/22 31

SOUND CARS
yb76 57, 135-7, 159; yb75 157-8

SOUTH AFRICA
history: yb76 67-9
Jehovah's witnesses: yb76 30-1, 67-242; yb75 10-11, 30-1; w74 207, 474-6, 644; yb74 17, 30-1; km 3/74 1; yb73 21-2, 30-1; w72 389-90; yb72 40-1, 44; g72 6/8 24; g71 3/22 24-6
persecution: yb76 89, 98-102, 136-9, 162
preaching work among Greeks: yb76 228-9
preaching work among Indians: yb76 232
preaching work among Portuguese: yb76 227-8
languages: yb76 67-9
ostrich farms: g72 2/22 16
population: yb76 67-9; yb73 30; yb72 40
racial segregation: yb76 67, 69, 183-4
religion: yb76 69; g72 8/22 30; w71 740

SOUTH AMERICA
Catholic church: g74 11/22 4
Jehovah's witnesses: yb75 22-3; w71 23
moving to: g72 7/22 13-16
Pacific-Coast fault line: g75 3/22 26

SOUTHERN RHODESIA
(SEE RHODESIA)

SOUTH-WEST AFRICA
Jehovah's witnesses: yb76 30-1, 103, 111-12, 146-8, 222-5; yb75 30-1; yb74 30-1; yb73 30-1; yb72 40-1
population: yb76 103; yb73 30; yb72 40

SOUVENIRS
g73 3/22 6-7

SOVEREIGNTY
discussion: w75 652-63
earth: w75 611-12; og 3, 4; w74 597, 603-4
integrity to Jehovah's: w74 347-8, 538-9, 725-6, 759; w73 144-5; g72 12/8 24-5; w71 487-8
Jehovah's: w75 614-18, 622-3, 657-63; sl 59-63, 81, 126, 253, 267-8, 271, 279-81, 344-7, 354, 368; og 10-18, 26-9; w74 726
nations': w75 361, 611-13; og 3-5, 8
repentance for having been under Devil's: w75 751
universal: sl 61-2; yb74 252-3; g74 10/8 14; g74 10/22 7-8; pm 382-3, 393; g72 10/22 11-12; g72 12/8 24; w71 244, 267-9, 539
(SEE ALSO ISSUE OF UNIVERSAL SOVEREIGNTY)

SOVIET UNION (Russia)
agriculture: g74 6/22 30; g74 7/22 3, 6; g73 1/22 29; g71 7/8 8
alcoholism: g74 4/8 29
armaments:
cost per person: g75 10/22 30
arms race: g74 11/8 3-7
Bible:
Pentateuch published: w75 487
buying on credit: g75 10/22 29

g, Awake!; **ka**, God's Kingdom of a Thousand Years; **kj**, "The Nations Shall Know that I Am Jehovah"; **km**, Kingdom Ministry; **or**, Organization; **pm**, Paradise Restored—By Theocracy!; **po**, God's "Eternal Purpose"; **sg**, Theocratic School Guidebook; **sl**, Man's Salvation out of World Distress!; **te**, Listening to the Great Teacher; **tp**, True Peace and Security; **ts**, Is This Life All There Is?; **w**, Watchtower; **yb**, Yearbook. **Complete list on page 6.**

cancer: g74 5/22 30
college: g74 10/22 31
crime: g74 2/22 29-30
divorce: g73 10/8 11
doctors: g75 4/8 31
  women: g75 11/22 31
energy sources: g75 2/8 30
history: g73 4/8 4-11
industry: g71 7/8 8
Jehovah's witnesses: yb75 234-5; g73 4/8 17-19
  persecution: g73 5/22 29
Kara-Kum desert: g74 12/8 31
longevity: g72 3/22 30
Middle East activity: g74 2/22 21-2
military strength: g74 11/8 3-5; g72 10/8 10; g71 7/8 6-8
moral breakdown: g75 1/8 5; g75 8/22 30-1; g74 1/22 31
nuclear missiles: w75 487
oil: g75 7/22 30; g74 1/8 7-8; g74 2/22 17, 21-2
power growth: g75 7/22 5-7; g71 7/8 5-9
recognition of its post-World War II frontiers: g75 11/8 4
relations with United States: g72 10/8 5-6, 29
religion: g75 4/8 30-1; g75 9/8 30; g74 2/8 31; w73 707-8; g73 4/8 3-19
science: g74 10/22 31
scientists: g75 4/8 31
smoking: g73 1/8 31
space achievements: g73 5/22 3-4, 9-11, 30; g73 8/8 29-30; g71 11/22 6, 8
sports: g72 12/8 30
Stalin: g73 4/8 9
United Nations: w74 548
United States: g74 4/8 5
use of ants to find water: g75 4/8 30
weather: g75 1/22 29
women: g74 7/8 31
youth: g75 1/8 5
(SEE ALSO COMMUNISM)

SOWING
Jesus' illustration: w73 683-6, 688; w72 91, 287
word of Kingdom: w74 573

SOYBEANS
protein: g75 2/8 30; g72 12/22 11

SPACE TRAVEL
accidents: g71 11/22 6
accomplishments: w74 295; g74 4/8 30; g74 5/22 30; g73 5/22 3-12
balloon: g73 7/8 30
Bible view: g73 5/22 12-15; w71 555
blood loss: g74 8/22 15
budget cut: g73 4/8 30
cost: w74 295; g74 8/22 13-14; g73 5/22 4; g71 11/22 7
  mothballed equipment: g75 9/22 29
dangers: g74 8/22 14-15; w72 292-4; g72 7/22 31; g71 5/8 30; g71 11/22 5-7
distances involved: g73 5/22 12
disunity: w71 303
effect on men: g73 11/8 30-1
evidence of God: g73 5/22 6-8, 13
evolution theory: g73 10/22 23-4
finding life in space: g73 5/22 3, 6, 11-15
Jupiter: g73 5/22 12
laws of creation: g72 10/22 4-5
Mars: g74 8/22 15; g73 5/22 9-11; g72 1/22 29; g72 7/8 29; g71 11/22 8
moon: w75 612; og 6; w74 295; g74 8/22 13-16; g73 1/22 29; g73 5/22 4-8; w72 294; g72 1/22 30; g72 7/8 29; g72 10/22 4-5; w71 40; g71 1/8 5; g71 5/8 30; g71 9/22 29; g71 11/22 5-8
nationalism: g73 5/22 3-4
objections to: w74 295; g74 3/22 29; g74 8/22 13-16; g73 5/22 4, 13; g73 10/8 12; g73 10/22 24; w72 294
satellites: g73 8/8 29-30
shuttle: g72 2/22 31
Soviet Union: g73 5/22 3-4, 9-11, 30; g71 11/22 6, 8
"space garbage": g74 3/22 29; g72 11/22 30; g71 4/22 30
ultimate position: w71 4-5
United States: g74 8/22 13-14; g73 1/22 29; g73 5/22 3-6, 9-10, 12-13, 30; g72 2/22 31; w71 303, 555; g71 1/8 5; g71 11/22 5-8
Venus: g73 5/22 11-12; g72 9/8 29; g71 3/8 30-1

SPAIN
bullfighting: g75 9/8 9-12
  life story of a matador: g75 9/8 13-16
Catholic church: g73 8/8 20; g72 2/22 30; g71 7/22 6; g71 11/8 30; g71 11/22 10; g71 12/22 30
  discusses successes of Jehovah's witnesses: w75 759
internal problems: g71 6/8 18
Jehovah's witnesses: yb76 30-1; w75 456-8; yb75 30-1, 210; g75 2/22 29; yb74 22, 30-1; km 7/74 1; yb73 22, 30-1; yb72 40-1, 44; g72 9/8 24; g72 10/22 17-18; w71 202; g71 4/8 29
population: yb73 30; yb72 40
Protestant religions: g75 2/22 29

SPANISH
experiences while learning: g74 8/8 12
language: g72 7/22 13-14
number speaking: g75 11/8 29

SPANISH INFLUENZA
w75 634; w74 358-9; tp 82; g73 10/8 20-1; g72 10/8 16; w71 406; g71 10/8 16

SPECIAL PIONEERS
beginning (1937): yb75 158-9
Bolivia: yb76 7-8
discussion: or 141-3
experiences: yb72 97
  overcoming obstacles: yb74 241
financial support: km 2/75 4; or 143
number: yb75 32, 258; yb74 255; w73 27; yb73 32; yb72 255; w71 25, 335
requirements: km 2/75 3-4; or 142
(SEE ALSO PIONEERS, TEMPORARY PIONEERS)

SPECULATION
unwise: w75 380, 389

SPEECH
apes vocally equipped: g71 3/8 12
clear expression: g74 12/22 13-15
conversation: sg 78-84
experiences while learning new language: g74 8/8 12
freeness of: g74 6/8 5
gift from God: w74 302; sg 5; g71 2/22 7-10
improving: g74 12/22 13-15; g72 9/8 17-20; sg 54-8
injurious: w72 67-8
Jehovah "appoints" speechless: w74 319-20
lisping: w75 198-9
obscene: w74 112; w71 306-7; sg 56
production: g73 1/22 18-19; sg 64-5
"rotten": w74 314-15
slang: sg 56-7
stuttering: w75 198; g75 7/8 19-22
truth: w74 314; sg 5-6
upbuilding: w74 85; km 10/74 7
vocabulary: sg 6-8, 54-7

SPEECH COUNSEL SLIP
reproduction: sg 104-5
use of: sg 100-2

SPEED
craving for: g74 6/22 12
creation's examples: g71 6/8 23
slime on fish: g72 1/22 30

SPICES
benefits: g73 11/8 23
filth: g72 2/22 30-1

SPIDER
g75 5/22 20-3

SPIES
Communist: yb74 223, 229-31
Nazi: yb74 150-1, 178-9

SPIRIT
angels: po 30-3; g73 5/22 14-15; g72 6/8 28
animals: ts 49-50
different from soul: ts 47-51
discussion: ts 47-53, 70-3
Greek word: ts 48-9
Hebrew word: ts 48-50
holy spirit (active force of God): w74 421-3; kj 43
  aid to faithfulness: w74 64, 415, 479
  aid to living morally clean life: w74 489
  aid to speaking: w74 414-15
  anointing: w75 105-8
  asking for: w74 115-16; w72 329-30
  begetting: g74 8/22 27; w73 730, 732
  Bible writing: w75 141-6; g72 2/8 27-8; w71 228-9; sg 15-17; g71 11/8 27-8
  born of water and spirit: g74 8/22 27
  discussion: g71 3/22 27-8
  fruitage: w71 664
  grieving: w74 422; w72 756
  heavenly life: w73 730, 732
  helper (paraclete): w74 422-3; w71 461-2; g71 3/22 27-8
  miraculous gifts: w71 501-5
  operation on congregation: w73 110
  other sheep: w74 312-13; g74 8/22 28
  Pentecost: po 158-9; w71 398-9
  personalized: g71 3/22 27-8
  prayer: w74 115-16; w72 757
  receiving: w74 340; km 3/74 1
  religious "ecstasy" no evidence of: g75 5/22 27-8

relying on: w74 312
remembrancer: w74 414-15
sealing: w72 636
sin against: w75 460; ts 181-2
speaking in tongues: g74 12/22 27-8
teacher: w74 414-15
Trinity: w74 363, 421-3
witness bearer: w72 562-3
identified: ts 49-53
Jehovah God: w72 101
Jesus Christ: ts 169-70; g73 7/22 3-5; g72 9/22 7
life force: ts 47-53; g72 8/8 27-8
mental disposition: g74 12/8 21
misconceptions: ts 47, 70
returns to God: ts 47-8, 50-3
world's: sl 305; w74 735; w73 136-8, 146; tp 128-31; w71 630

SPIRIT BEGOTTEN
(SEE CONGREGATION OF GOD)

SPIRITISM
Africa: g71 9/8 16-18
Argentina: yb72 113-14
astrology: g73 11/22 3-7; g71 10/8 10, 21
Bible view: w75 52-3; w74 715-16; ts 76-8, 87; w73 339, 342-3, 484-6, 699-701; g71 2/8 14; g71 2/22 25; g71 5/22 4-5, 27-8
books on occult: g74 2/22 5-6
Brazil: g74 2/22 3-5
breaking free: ts 86-8; g74 2/22 3-6
bush medicine: w73 697-701
clairvoyants: g74 8/22 29
clergy: g71 5/22 27
connection with drugs: g74 5/8 4-5; w73 179-81, 339, 342-3; tp 161
dangers: g75 10/22 31; w74 324-8; g74 2/22 3-6; g74 4/22 28; w73 179-81, 484-6; g72 4/22 30; g71 5/22 4-5, 28; g71 12/22 30
defense against: w74 328, 715-16; g74 10/22 9-10
demonism: ts 85-8; w73 179-81, 484-6; g71 2/22 25-6; g71 5/22 28
discussion: g74 2/22 3-6; w73 179-81
divination: g75 2/8 29; g75 8/8 3, 5, 6; g74 2/22 5-6; g72 3/8 8-9
dreams: g75 1/22 5-6
evidences of: ts 78, 86, 88
evolution theory: w71 56
examples: w74 323, 328; w73 698-9; g72 6/8 27-8; g71 2/8 14; g71 5/8 30; g71 5/22 27-8; g71 6/22 30; g71 7/8 16-18
exorcising demons: w74 447; g74 10/22 10
experiences:
Bible truth frees from: g75 3/22 28; w74 328; g74 2/22 3-6
causes death: g75 11/8 29
causes illness: w74 328, 396, 715-16; g74 2/22 4-6
demon activity: g74 2/22 3-6; g72 6/8 27-8; w71 710; g71 9/8 16-18; g71 9/22 8
fetish fails to harm Witnesses: g71 7/8 19
fetish priestess accepts truth: g75 7/22 24-6
hears "voices": g75 2/8 11; g74 11/22 7-9
juju: g75 7/22 26; g71 7/8 19
murder: g75 5/22 30
spiritists accept Bible truth: w75 266; g74 2/22 3-4; g74 7/22 9; w73 701
witch doctors accept truth: g72 3/8 8-11; g71 7/8 16-20
extrasensory perception (ESP): w74 323, 326; g74 4/22 27-8; w71 710
fetishism: w74 395-6
fortune-telling: g75 8/8 3-6
Hindu meditation: g75 11/8 10-11
hypnotism: g74 9/8 27-8
investigation of spiritistic manifestations: w74 324, 326
Italy: g71 7/8 29-30
juju: w75 761; w74 716; ts 71-2
King, William Mackenzie: g75 7/8 31
magic: g75 7/22 26; w73 483-4
Nicene council: g71 2/22 26
"Ouija" board: g75 2/8 10-11; g75 8/8 5-6; w74 326; g73 6/8 27-8; g71 5/8 30; g71 12/22 30
practices connected with: g75 2/8 29; ts 86
predictions: g75 3/22 27-8
"psychic" tested: g74 12/8 29
public schools: g71 7/22 29
religious "ecstasy": g75 5/22 27-8
speaking in tongues: g75 5/22 30; g74 12/22 28
spirit mediums: w75 52; g75 3/22 27-8; po 78-9; ts 74-8, 86-7
voodoo: w75 172
water witching: g74 7/22 30
witchcraft: g74 2/22 6; w73 483-6
yoga: g75 2/22 27-8; g75 11/8 29
youths: g74 2/8 6
(SEE ALSO DEMONS)

SPIRITS IN PRISON
identified: w72 427-8; w71 607
imprisonment: ts 84-5
Jesus preached to: w71 607-8

SPIRITUAL FOOD
channel: w75 45-7, 78-9; yb75 237-8
proper view: w74 250; g74 8/8 5-6; w73 493; w72 306

SPIRITUALITY
advancing: w74 315
blessings: w73 49-51
examples of treasuring: w74 702; yb72 70
importance: g74 12/8 21; w73 488-9, 493, 499; w72 306
maintaining: w74 479, 701-2; w73 56-8; yb72 218
man's capacity for: g74 12/8 21
maturity: w71 661-2
spiritual person: w74 209-14, 219-20; w73 463-4

SPIRITUAL NEED
consciousness of: g71 6/8 27-8
prayer: g74 6/8 7

SPIRITUAL SICKNESS
Christendom: w74 756-8, 760
mature Christian can suffer from: w71 664

SPITE
discussion: w71 579-80

SPLEEN
discussion: g71 3/8 16-18

SPOCK, BENJAMIN
g75 10/8 6

SPORTS
accidents: g73 1/8 31
announcers: g74 6/22 13
basketball: g75 2/8 29; g75 6/8 29
Bible view: w75 502-3
bicycle racing: g75 8/8 7-8
boxing: g75 6/8 31; g74 6/8 29; g71 5/8 30
chaplains: g73 3/8 29-30
cheating: g73 1/8 29
college: g72 5/22 31
cost of collegiate: g72 5/22 31
dangers to health: g75 4/8 31; g74 2/22 31; g74 4/22 31; g74 12/22 30
effects: g71 9/22 7
experiences:
basketball player explains why he quit: g75 2/8 29
bicycle racer accepts truth: g75 8/8 7-8
football players accept truth: g75 9/22 16-21
girl gymnast accepts truth: g71 9/22 6-8
Rugby player enters full-time preaching work: w73 52-3
soccer player accepts truth: g71 4/8 23
football: g75 4/8 31; g75 9/22 16-21; g73 3/8 29-30; g72 12/8 30; g71 11/22 29
gambling: w74 580
hero worship: w74 145-6; g73 5/22 29-30; g73 9/8 30; w72 539
highest-paid athletes: g75 6/8 31; g73 9/22 30
hiking: g73 8/22 24-7
hockey: g75 5/8 30; g74 1/22 30; g74 8/8 30
judo: g75 12/8 28-9; g72 9/8 8
karate: g75 12/8 28-9
kite flying: g73 3/22 24-6
Olympics: g73 2/22 13-15; g72 10/8 30; g72 10/22 29
participation: g72 11/22 9
religious: g75 6/8 29; g73 6/8 31
riots at sports events: g74 6/22 13; g73 10/22 30
skiing: g74 3/8 30-1; g73 1/8 31
snowmobiling: g71 1/22 30
soccer: g75 6/22 29
Soviet Union: g72 12/8 30
stock-car racing: g73 9/8 30
surfing: g73 7/22 16-19
swimming: g72 1/22 30; g71 7/8 10-12; g71 8/8 16-19
tennis: g74 12/22 30
ticket "scalpers": g73 7/22 31
track: w71 334
use of blood: g74 8/8 30
violence: g75 5/8 30; g75 6/22 29; g74 1/22 30
witch doctors: g74 7/22 31

SPRAY CANS
inhaling vapors: g72 1/8 30; g71 1/22 29; g71 9/8 30

SPROUT (Branch)
symbolic: pm 185-8, 229-30

SPROUTS
food: g75 12/22 25-6

SPURIOUS TEXTS
Matthew 17:21: w71 537
Mark 9:29: w71 537
Mark 16:9-20: g73 8/8 6-7
Acts 10:30: w71 537
1 Corinthians 7:5: w71 538

SPYING
industrial: g73 7/8 9-11

SRI LANKA (Ceylon)
caste system: yb76 251-2
crisis: g74 6/22 30
dances: g71 12/8 25
grooming: g73 7/22 31
history: yb76 242-3
Jehovah's witnesses: yb76 30-1, 242-57; yb75 30-1; yb74 21, 30-1; g74 5/8 20; w73 762-3; yb73 30-1; yb72 34-5; w71 678-9; g71 12/8 26
languages: yb76 242, 250-1
malaria: w74 132
population: yb73 30; yb72 34
religion: yb76 242-3

STABILITY
importance of: w71 349-51

STALIN, JOSEPH V.
w75 241-2

STAMPS
advertising: g72 3/8 29
hobby of collecting: g71 7/8 20-3

STANDARD(S)
Bible: w72 35-6
thinking by right: g73 1/8 5
worldly: w74 562-3

STARFISH
g72 10/22 8

STARLING
bird: g71 2/22 19

STARS
Andromeda constellation: g75 6/22 18
Arcturus: g71 1/8 8
brightness: g72 2/8 9; g72 12/22 24-6; g71 1/8 8
Coma Berenices constellation: g75 6/22 18
constellations: g75 6/22 18
energy source: g75 8/22 31
galaxies: g75 6/22 17-19; g75 8/22 31; g71 2/22 31; g71 8/8 4
Milky Way: g75 6/22 17-18; g72 9/22 31
number visible: g72 12/22 25
quasars: g71 5/8 29; g71 6/8 29
radiation: g73 11/22 4
"Star of Bethlehem": po 140, 142-3
symbolic:
daystar (2 Pe 1:19): w74 298
seven (Re 1:16, 20): w71 751-2
third hurled to earth (Re 12): w72 427
travel to nearest: g72 2/8 9
(SEE ALSO ASTROLOGY, ASTRONOMY, UNIVERSE)

STARVATION
Africa: g75 2/22 9-11
Bangladesh: g75 1/22 29; g75 2/22 9; g74 11/22 29
Christian view of: g75 2/22 11
effects of: g75 2/22 10-11
ethics of nations: g75 1/22 29; g75 5/8 29; g74 9/22 29
India: g75 2/22 9-11
Iraq: g75 2/22 9
Nigeria: g75 2/22 9
old people: g75 5/8 30
preventing:
finding food: g74 9/22 6-7
weather's effect: g75 3/8 4
(SEE ALSO FAMINE)

STATE
worship of: w75 227-32

STEALING
artworks: g71 6/22 31
automobiles: g73 4/22 11, 17; g71 9/8 29; g71 11/8 29
prevention: g75 7/22 31
banks:
embezzlement and fraud: g74 7/8 31
robberies: g71 1/22 23
Bible examples: w71 426-7; te 151-3; g71 11/8 3
Bible view: w73 316-18; tp 170; pm 210-11; w71 426-7; te 151, 153-4
bicycles: g73 6/22 27
boats: g71 10/8 31
burglary: w74 515
businessmen: g74 3/8 27-8
chart comparing employee theft with shoplifting: w75 291
college thieves: g73 2/22 29
Cologne Cathedral looted: g75 12/22 30
compensation under Law: w75 115-16
employees: w75 291, 293; w74 341; g74 9/8 4; g74 11/8 30-1; g73 5/22 29; g73 9/8 31; w72 614; g72 5/22 30; g72 6/22 31; w71 306; g71 4/8 13, 29; g71 7/8 29; g71 10/8 13
hotel patrons: g75 10/8 30
Jehovah's words: pm 212-14
lost items kept by finders: w74 204-5
museums: g75 4/8 29
parents' example: w73 451
pickpockets: g71 11/8 3
prevalence: w74 341, 515; g74 5/8 29; g74 11/8 30-1; g74 12/8 5; g73 2/22 29; g73 4/22 4-8, 11
priests warned about stealing art: g71 7/8 29
protection against robbery: g73 4/22 14-17; g72 5/8 30
shoplifting: g75 3/22 7; g75 6/22 30; g74 1/22 7; g73 4/22 4, 7-8; g73 12/8 30; g72 3/22 30; g72 7/22 30-1; g72 12/8 30; g71 1/8 30; g71 1/22 29; g71 9/22 30; g71 11/22 29
number per year: g75 9/8 31
souvenirs: g73 3/22 6-7
"stealing time": g75 3/8 29
supermarkets:
cheating by clerks: g74 11/8 30-1
hiring guards: g75 5/8 30
trucks: g71 6/22 31
vandalism: g75 2/8 29-30
windows of stained glass: g75 8/8 29-30
worldly view: g74 12/22 30; g73 3/22 5-7; g73 4/22 10-11, 13
(SEE ALSO CRIME, MORAL BREAKDOWN)

STEAM
bus powered by: g72 3/8 30

STEEL
usage by country: g73 8/22 31
scrap: g74 3/22 30

STEPHEN
martyrdom: w71 153; te 76

STERILIZATION
Bible view: w75 158-60; g74 2/8 16
effect of, on one's congregational responsibility: w75 158-60
increase: g75 9/22 30
male: w75 159-60; g73 1/8 29; g73 3/22 30; g73 4/22 31; g72 7/8 30

STEWARD
Bible times: w73 372
overseers: w74 531-2

STOICS
beliefs: w73 430
discussion: g72 11/22 17-18

STOMACH
human: g74 2/8 17; g73 4/8 21

STONE(S)
cornerstone:
discussion: pm 187-90
identified: pm 188
granite: g72 2/8 30
lodestone: g75 6/8 24
Nebuchadnezzar's dream (Da 2): sl 312-13; pm 375-6

"STONE AGE"
g73 5/8 19-20

STORAGE
home: g74 9/8 12-14

STORES
discount stores: g75 1/8 29
duty-free airport: g75 2/8 30-1
supermarkets: g75 5/8 30; g74 11/8 30-1
Japan: g75 8/22 29

STORK
pm 219

STORMS
causes: w74 735
cyclones: g75 3/22 24-6; km 3/75 4; g71 1/8 29
destructive: g74 6/8 8-9; g72 7/22 29
dust: g74 3/8 8
hail: g72 6/22 30-1
hurricanes: yb72 143; g72 8/22 13-16; w71 611
Jesus' power over: te 59-62
tornadoes: g74 6/8 8-10
typhoons: yb73 227-8; g71 10/22 29

STRANGERS
welcoming at meetings: w72 409-10

STREET WITNESSING
appearance: km 9/75 8
conduct: km 9/75 8
experiences: yb75 163-4; w73 29; yb72 79-80; km 10/71 8
magazine distribution: km 8/75 8
modern-day: yb76 141; yb75 162-3

STRENGTH
obtaining from Jehovah: km 4/72 3

STRESS
adjusting to: g75 1/22 30; g75 9/8 3-6
affects blood-cholesterol level: g75 7/22 21
cause of mental illness: g75 4/22 15
heart disease: g75 10/22 29
modern-day: g75 4/22 7

STRIKES
Bible view: g75 2/22 6-7
effects: g74 11/22 14-15
garbage collectors: g71 2/8 21-3
labor unions: g71 9/22 25-6
parochial schools: g72 1/8 31
police: w72 261; g71 2/22 18
teachers: g72 1/8 31
Witnesses neutral: yb72 238-9

STROKES
drugs: g72 3/22 31
statistics: g73 11/8 31

STRONTIUM 90
g75 5/22 31

STUDENTS
violence: g73 5/8 29-30; g71 8/8 10-12

STUDIES IN THE SCRIPTURES
original name of series: yb75 40
titles of Vols. II-VI: yb75 41
use in field service: yb75 64
Vol. I, *The Divine Plan of the Ages:* yb75 40
Vol. VII, *The Finished Mystery:*
banned: yb75 95-7
censored: yb75 119
release: yb75 90-1
ZG edition: yb75 125-6

STUDY
aids:
note taking: sg 43
underlining: sg 22, 36
Watch Tower publications: sg 35
benefits: g74 8/8 4-5; km 9/74 7-8; w73 201-7, 212, 403-4, 460; tp 186-7; w71 73; sg 38
Bible reading: w71 62, 105; sg 21, 23, 32-5
discussion: w71 60-2, 70-3; sg 33-8
effort required: g75 1/22 23; w74 180-1; w73 122, 205, 212; km 12/73 3
family: w73 205-7; w71 104-7; sg 37-8
importance: w74 115; km 7/74 3; w73 491; km 12/73 3; w72 134
importance of context: w73 207-18
improving interest in: km 7/74 3
meditation: w74 115, 211
motivation: w71 60-1
motive: w74 180; w73 463-4
objective: w74 211; g74 8/8 4-5; sg 34
personal: km 12/73 3; w71 60-2, 70-3; sg 33-8
proper study conditions: w71 71-2
reading: w73 201-7; w71 70-1; sg 19-24
scheduling time: w71 61-2, 105; sg 33-4
Watchtower: w71 72-3, 106; sg 21, 36-7, 92

STUMBLING
avoiding stumbling others: w75 127, 218-19, 300-2, 510, 724; w74 304; w72 564-5, 570-1
avoiding stumbling ourselves: w75 125-7
causes: w74 112-13, 561, 563-4
over imperfection: w72 643-4
over teaching: w72 272, 505-8

STUTTERING
discussion: g75 7/8 19-22
overcoming: w75 198; g75 7/8 20-2

SUBJECTION
head covering a sign of: w72 446-7
manifestation of love: w74 316
man's dominion over animals: w74 594-5
superior authorities: yb75 238; w74 62-3; g74 2/22 27-8
wives: w75 154-5; w74 118, 316-17; g74 5/22 5; w72 445-7; g72 9/22 27-8
women in congregation: w73 255
(SEE ALSO HEADSHIP)

SUBMARINES
atomic: g72 10/8 9-10

SUBSCRIPTIONS
(SEE MAGAZINE DISTRIBUTION)

SUBWAYS
cost to build: g74 11/8 31
London: g71 6/22 31
New York: g74 8/22 3-4

SUCCESS
business: g74 3/8 30

SUDAN
Jehovah's witnesses: yb76 26-7; yb75 26-7; yb74 26-7; yb73 26-7; yb72 36-7
population: yb73 26; yb72 36
Suez Canal: g74 10/22 18

SUETONIUS
g74 4/8 22

SUEZ CANAL
"cleanest waterway": g75 6/22 29
discussion: g74 10/22 16-18

SUFFERING
for righteousness' sake: w71 491-7
Jesus' attitude: w72 176-8
man's responsibility: g74 10/8 5-6, 8, 15-17
prophesied Messiah must suffer: po 138, 146
why permitted: w72 179; g72 10/22 10-12; w71 485-91, 539

SUGAR
amount consumed: g74 10/22 29
food value: g74 10/22 29; g72 9/8 30
maple: g73 2/22 11-13
substitutes: g72 3/22 29; g71 8/22 31

SUICIDE
causes: w75 52; g75 2/22 11; g75 4/22 4, 6; g75 8/8 24-5; g75 11/22 31; g73 7/8 30; g72 2/8 23; g72 3/8 30; g72 9/8 31; g71 3/22 30; g71 6/22 5; g71 11/8 30-1
occultism: g75 10/22 31
Christian view: w75 447-8; g75 8/8 25
college students: g72 6/8 30
crowd encourages: g73 11/22 29
danger to innocent persons: g75 9/22 29-30
demons encourage: w75 52, 447
discussion: g75 8/8 24-5
doctors: g74 2/8 31
funerals: w75 448
psychiatrists: g75 4/22 17; g72 12/8 29
statistics: g75 4/22 4; g75 8/8 24; g73 5/22 31; g73 7/8 30; g72 3/8 30; g72 11/8 30; g71 4/8 30; g71 5/22 30
truth prevents: w75 488-9; g75 8/8 26; g75 10/8 22; g75 10/22 21; w72 284-5, 390; g72 11/22 19; km 1/72 3; w71 507
Witness prevents: w73 766
youth: g75 8/22 30; g73 5/22 31; g72 8/22 30
(SEE ALSO DEATH)

SUITER, GRANT
service tour: yb76 42

SULLIVAN, T. J.
yb75 206; w74 554

SULPHUR
symbolic representation: w74 383

SUN
benefits to man: g72 10/8 25-8; g71 3/22 28
causes sky colors: g71 6/22 11
description: g72 2/8 9-10
discussion: g72 2/8 9-11
energy from: g75 8/22 16; g74 1/8 5; g74 8/22 20-1; g73 7/8 5; g72 2/8 9-10; g72 10/8 25-8; g71 4/22 26; g71 6/22 9
rays cause fire: g73 12/22 30
relation to signs of zodiac: g73 11/22 5
solar battery: g72 10/8 27
solar flares: g73 11/22 31; g72 2/8 10; g72 4/8 8
stability: g71 12/22 29
stood still: g74 1/8 14-15
sunspots: g72 2/8 10
symbolic: w74 528, 756
temperature: g72 2/8 9
twilight: g71 3/8 21-2
water evaporation: g72 2/8 10-11
worship: w72 585-7; kj 154-9
(SEE ALSO SOLAR SYSTEM)

SUNBATHING
cancer: g74 9/8 20-1

SUNDAY SCHOOLS
attendance: w74 555; w72 340; w71 484
Bible knowledge lacking: g75 6/8 29
failure: w74 555
(SEE ALSO CHRISTENDOM)

SUPERIOR AUTHORITIES
benefits of subjection: w72 266-7
Christian's attitude: w74 62-3; tp 135-9; w72 267-9
Christian's obligation: g74 2/22 27-8; w73 142; tp 135-9

clarification of understanding: yb75 238; w72 501-2
God's servants: w75 719
identified: te 137
paying fines to: w75 223-4

SUPERSTITION
Africa: yb76 152; g74 1/22 26; w73 486, 698, 701; g72 6/8 26; g71 9/8 18
bush medicine: w73 697-701
concerning Psalms: g71 1/22 5-6
evil spirits: w73 697, 699-701; g71 2/22 25-6
experiences:
Bible truth overcomes: yb74 8; w73 701
gamblers: w74 586-7
hinders medical aid: g74 6/22 31
Hong Kong: g74 2/22 30; g71 4/8 24, 26
Laplanders: g75 2/8 26; g72 6/22 23
rhinoceros: g72 6/8 9-10

SUPREME COURT DECISIONS
Canada
false arrest (*Lamb v. Benoit*): g75 3/8 22
freedom of worship: g72 7/8 10
liquor license (*Roncarelli v. Duplessis*): g75 3/8 21
Witness statistics: g75 3/8 21
Germany
military service: g71 1/8 13-15
Greece
Witnesses recognized: g75 12/8 17-21
Nicaragua
freedom of worship: yb72 189-90
United States
Bethel home: g71 6/8 26
flag salute: yb75 169, 172; g74 9/22 30; g72 7/8 11-12; w71 722; g71 9/8 14-15
license tax: yb75 172, 179-80
military service: yb75 208; g74 9/22 30
pornography: g71 1/22 17
president contradicts: g71 9/22 29
Zambia
flag salute: yb72 251-2

SURFING
discussion: g73 7/22 16-19

SURGERY
abortions: g73 2/8 12-13; g73 3/22 9-10
acupuncture: g72 7/22 30; g72 9/8 12-15; g71 7/8 31
advancements: g74 3/22 17, 23
appendix: g72 12/8 30; g71 10/22 31
backaches: g75 1/8 30; g73 8/8 24
blood misused: g71 2/8 30
brain tumor: g74 6/22 20
cancer: g74 9/8 21
cesarean section: w75 159
cornea: g73 8/8 30
court orders for: g71 11/8 5-6
cryosurgery: g74 6/22 22
emergency: g73 2/8 9, 13
errors: g73 2/8 12
gallstones: g71 5/22 25-6
heart-lung machine: w74 720; g74 6/22 18
heart operations: g75 11/22 29; g74 1/22 29; g74 5/22 18; g74 6/22 18-20; g73 2/8 19, 29; g72 6/8 30; g72 6/22 29
mental problems after: w74 720
hemorrhoids: g75 1/8 26
hemostasis: g74 6/22 18
hip joint: w75 445
history: g72 11/8 13
hysterectomies: w75 159; g75 5/8 7; g74 8/8 31
life story of surgeon: g74 3/22 17-23
limb restoration: g73 11/8 31; g72 9/22 31
malpractice and mistakes of doctors: g71 2/22 29; g71 11/8 7-8
micro-surgery: g72 12/22 30
neurosurgery: g74 6/22 22
orthopedic: g73 12/22 24-6
precautions to avoid transfusions: g74 6/22 18-22; g72 7/8 30-1
psychosurgery: g75 4/22 12
recoveries without blood: g74 1/22 29; g74 3/22 21; g74 5/22 21-2; g74 6/22 18-21; g73 2/8 19, 29; g72 6/8 30; g72 6/22 29; g72 8/22 29; g71 11/8 6-7
rhinoceros intestinal obstruction: g75 4/22 30
"sex change": w74 360; g74 6/8 29
silk-suture stapler: g75 11/8 30
sterilization: w75 158-60; g74 2/8 16; g74 3/22 23; g73 1/8 29; g73 3/22 30; g72 7/8 30
stored blood used: g72 4/8 29-30
tonsils: g73 7/8 30; g71 7/8 31
transplanting organs:
cancer: g74 1/22 30
hazards: g74 2/22 30-1; g74 12/22 12; g72 6/8 30
heart: g74 5/22 30; g72 7/8 28; w71 135-6; g71 11/22 31
kidney: w75 519; g72 9/22 30
problems: w75 519
without permission: g71 11/8 9
unnecessary surgery: g75 1/8 30; g74 8/8 31; g73 8/8 31; g72 4/8 30; g72 6/8 30-1; g72 9/8 30-1; g72 10/8 31; g71 1/8 31; g71 8/22 30
urologic: g74 6/22 20-1
vibrating scalpel: g74 6/22 22; g72 6/22 30
without blood transfusions: w75 445; g75 11/22 29; g74 5/22 17-19, 21-2; g74 6/22 17-22; g74 12/22 30
(SEE ALSO BLOOD TRANSFUSION, DOCTORS, HEALTH, HOSPITALS, MEDICINE)

SURINAM
bush medicine: w73 699
Jehovah's witnesses: yb76 30-1; yb75 30-1; g75 8/22 21-4; yb74 30-1; yb73 30-1; w72 531; yb72 40-1; g72 4/8 25; w71 679-80; g71 2/8 14-16
matriarchal society: g75 8/22 21-2
population: yb73 30; yb72 40
women: g71 7/8 24

SURTSEY
g75 8/8 13

SURVEYS
(SEE BELIEFS)

SURVIVAL
at sea: g73 6/22 17-19
how to assure: tp 90-7; w72 51-3, 326-7, 372-4
mankind: w74 662, 666-8; g72 9/8 3-4
misconceptions: g75 10/22 31; g72 5/22 30

SWAHILI
g75 2/22 26

SWAMPS
(SEE WETLANDS)

SWASTIKA
g75 2/22 22

SWAZILAND
Jehovah's witnesses: yb76 30-1, 112, 179-80, 194-5, 217-21; yb75 30-1; w74 474; yb74 18, 30-1; yb73 30-1; w72 381; yb72 40-1
persecution: yb76 179-80, 218-21
population: yb76 112; yb73 30; yb72 40

SWEAT
body odors: g74 3/8 24-6
glands: g74 3/8 24

SWEDEN
abortion: g73 3/22 8-11
Bible translation: g71 3/8 23-6
illegitimacy: g74 4/22 4-5
Jehovah's witnesses: yb76 30-1; yb75 18, 30-1; yb74 30-1; yb73 30-1; g73 9/22 16; yb72 40-1; g71 4/8 3-7
moral breakdown: g72 6/22 30; g72 8/22 9; g72 9/22 29
music during childbirth: g75 7/8 30
population: yb73 30; yb72 40
prison: g73 1/22 29
strikes: g71 9/22 25-6
Varberg Castle: g75 8/8 30

SWIMMING
babies: g72 1/22 30
discussion: g71 7/8 10-12; g71 8/8 16-19
drown proofing: g73 6/22 17-19
safety: g73 6/22 17-19

SWINGLE, L. A.
yb75 211

SWITZERLAND
advertising: g75 4/22 29
Jehovah's witnesses: yb76 30-1; yb75 30-1; g75 5/8 4-5; yb74 30-1; yb73 30-1; g73 9/22 16; yb72 40-2
Lausanne missionary conference: g74 12/8 12-15
most expensive land: g74 4/22 31
population: yb73 30; yb72 40
taxes: g74 2/8 30

SWORD(S)
Bible times: w73 159
Jesus' disciples: g75 9/8 28; tp 134
symbolic: w73 159-60; w72 763-6; kj 215-24

SYMBOLISM
use in Bible: w74 629
why Jehovah uses: ts 151-2

SYMBOL OF JEALOUSY
identified (Eze 8:3, 5): w72 509; kj 145-6

SYNAGOGUE
financial problems: g75 9/8 25
money raising: g71 7/22 29-30
music: g73 1/8 29
ruins of Capernaum: w75 671

SYNTYCHE
w75 343-4

SYPHILIS
blood transfusion: g74 2/22 30; g74 6/22 29-30
effect on body: g75 5/8 6-8; g74 2/8 14; g72 2/8 17-18, 20
how spread: g75 5/8 5-6, 8
increase: g75 5/8 6; g73 5/22 30; g72 10/22 31
(SEE ALSO VENEREAL DISEASES)

SYRIA
Jehovah's witnesses: yb76 28-9; yb75 26-7; yb74 26-7; yb73 26-7; yb72 36-7
persecution: yb76 18-19
population: yb73 26; yb72 36

SYSTEMS OF THINGS
end of Jewish (70 C.E.): sl 22; w74 680-3; ka 294-304
present wicked system: w71 634-5
end: w75 621; sl 23-4; og 24; w74 3-4, 665-6, 668; tp 39-43; g73 11/8 6-7; g72 10/8 16-17
needs to be replaced (quote): g75 8/22 20

TABERNACLE
contents: w74 175
copper altar: w74 221; w73 31; ka 97-8, 109
courtyard: w74 174-5, 221-2; w73 31; ka 98, 101, 110-11
curtain between Holy and Most Holy: w72 711, 714
diagram of ground plan: w74 173; ka 93; w72 711
dimensions: w74 174-5
Holy: w74 175, 221-2; w73 31; ka 93-4, 101-2, 108-9, 111
illustration: bi8 1368
incense: w74 222
Jehovah's presence: w74 174-5
Levites' service: g72 3/8 27
Most Holy: w74 175-6, 221-3; w73 31; ka 99-100; w72 711
perfection: w71 498-9
pictures spiritual temple: w72 712-13
prophetic significance: w74 173-4, 176, 221-3; w73 31; ka 93, 98-9
purpose: w74 174
(SEE ALSO TEMPLE)

TACITUS
comment on Jesus Christ: w75 250; g72 2/8 8
comments on early Christians: w74 48
prejudices of: g74 4/8 24

TACT
discussion: sg 69-73
examples:
modern-day Witnesses: yb72 241; g72 3/22 15
field service: km 3/72 4; sg 70-2
meaning of term: sg 69

TAHITI
Jehovah's witnesses: yb76 14, 30-1; yb75 24-5; km 4/75 1; w74 647; yb74 24-5; yb73 24-5; w72 511; yb72 34-5
population: yb73 24; yb72 34
surfing: g73 7/22 17

TAIWAN
Jehovah's witnesses: yb76 30-1; yb74 30-1

TAJIN FLYERS
g75 7/22 11-13

TALENTS
Jesus' parable: ka 212-42, 247-56, 258
beginning of fulfillment: w74 542-3
belongings: w74 541-2; ka 216-18
five-talents class: w74 542
man: w74 541
master's return: w74 557
purpose: w74 540-1
reward to faithful slaves: w74 558-9
wicked slave: w74 589-91; ka 247-55
proper view of abilities: w74 299-300, 531-2, 534

TALKING
tongue: g73 1/22 18-19

TALLNESS
human: g75 5/22 29; g75 6/8 29

TALMUD
comments on—
Jesus: w75 249; g71 12/8 5, 8
work: w72 490

TAMAR
Amnon violates: w72 220
relations with Judah: w73 383-4

TAMMUZ
god: w72 572; kj 149-52

TANZANIA
description: g71 12/22 25-6
elephants: g75 10/22 30
Jehovah's witnesses: yb76 26-7, 106-7, 160-1; yb75 26-7; yb74 13-14, 26-7; yb73 26-7; yb72 36-7
persecution: yb76 106
population: yb73 26; yb72 36

TAOISM
ts 64; w71 14

TAPE RECORDING
piracy: g71 1/22 29

TARTARUS
angels that sinned: ts 85; w72 427; w71 607-8
significance: po 60, 78; ts 84-5; bi8 1366
use in mythology: ts 84; bi8 1366

TASMANIA
parochial schools: g72 1/8 31

TASTE
g73 1/22 19

TATTOO(ING)
removal: g72 2/8 29

TAX(ATION)
Bible times: w74 139-40
Bible view: w74 151-2; g74 2/22 27-8; w73 316-17; tp 136; w72 640; g72 12/8 19; w71 253; te 135-6
British court case: yb73 131-3
churches: w75 364; w71 407; g71 3/22 3-4
conscience: w75 214-15
decision regarding Society property: g74 9/8 15-16
Europe: g74 2/8 30
evasion: g74 2/22 27; g73 5/22 30-1; g73 11/8 29; w72 451-2
increase: g71 10/8 4
Malawi: g72 12/8 19-20
Roman Empire: w74 139-40
United States: g74 2/8 30; g74 2/22 27-8; g74 11/8 30; g73 5/22 30-1; g73 11/8 29; g72 5/22 29; g71 5/22 29

TAX COLLECTORS
discussion: w74 139-40
Jesus' balanced view: w74 464
Matthew: w74 139-40
rabbinical writings: w74 463-4
Zacchaeus: w74 139-40

TAXICABS
discussion: g72 7/8 16-19
Japan: g73 2/8 20

TCHAD
Jehovah's witnesses: yb74 24-5, 38, 40; yb73 24-5; w72 542; yb72 34-5
population: yb73 24; yb72 34
(SEE ALSO CHAD)

TEA
tearooms: g72 11/8 15
use: w72 596

TEACHERS
attitude: g74 1/8 23-4
congregation: w71 333
experience: w73 444-5
gifts in men: w71 752
improving as: g74 1/8 23-6
Japan:
teacher regrets militaristic education: w75 715
Jehovah: sg 49, 53-4
Jesus Christ: w73 12, 17-19; w72 105-7; sg 49, 53-4; te 7-10
secular: g71 6/8 3-4

Parochial Schools
shortage: g71 9/22 10

Public Schools
cheating: g71 6/22 30
dangers: g75 5/8 17-19; g74 2/8 5; g73 5/8 29-30; g72 1/22 31; g72 7/8 31
discussion: g75 5/8 16-21
experience:
becomes Witness: w72 541-2
flag salute: g73 1/22 29-30
lack of concern: g74 9/22 31
morals of teachers: g74 9/8 5
(SEE ALSO EDUCATION, SCHOOLS)

TEACHING
attitude: g74 1/8 23-4
children: g75 5/8 21; g74 1/8 24-5; g73 8/8 31; w72 111-17; g72 5/8 5-8; km 1/72 7-8
unselfishness: g75 6/8 14-16
congregation book study: km 9/74 7-8; km 5/72 3
discussion: g74 1/8 23-6; sg 49-54
elders: w74 530-1
enthusiasm: g74 1/8 24
failure of secular: g74 3/22 30
holy spirit: w74 414-15
home Bible studies: w74 338-40; or 122-5; sg 49-54, 75-8

g, Awake!; **ka**, God's Kingdom of a Thousand Years; **kj**, "The Nations Shall Know that I Am Jehovah"; **km**, Kingdom Ministry; **or**, Organization; **pm**, Paradise Restored—By Theocracy!; **po**, God's "Eternal Purpose"; **sg**, Theocratic School Guidebook; **sl**, Man's Salvation out of World Distress!; **te**, Listening to the Great Teacher; **tp**, True Peace and Security; **ts**, Is This Life All There Is?; **w**, Watchtower; **yb**, Yearbook. **Complete list on page 6.**

listening: g74 11/22 21-2
mildness: g74 7/8 4
overseers: km 5/75 4; w72 11-12; yb72 14-15; w71 752
principles of: g74 1/8 23-6
reaching students' hearts: w74 125, 338-9; sg 75-8
reliance on Jehovah: w74 339, 531; sg 50
simplicity: g74 1/8 24-5; w73 535
use of Bible: km 5/72 3
use of illustrations: g74 1/8 25; sg 52-3, 168-71
use of questions: g74 1/8 25-6; w72 115-16; sg 51-2, 76
(SEE ALSO EDUCATION, SCHOOLS)

TEAROOMS
Korea: g72 11/8 15

TECHNOLOGY
failure: g75 8/22 17-20; g75 10/8 7; w74 40, 51, 197; g74 9/8 30; g74 9/22 30; g73 11/8 31; g73 12/22 29

TEETH
care: w72 414; g72 2/8 30; g72 7/8 21-3
disease: g72 2/8 30
drilling: g73 1/22 31
effect of foods: g71 9/8 24-5
gums: g74 6/8 29-30; g72 7/8 21-3

TELEPHONE(S)
cutting operating expenses: g74 9/22 16
Greece: g75 2/22 30
use in preaching: km 7/73 4; or 118-19

TELESCOPES
Chile: g72 12/22 24-6
largest: g74 12/22 30
lens: g71 7/22 17
problems: g71 8/8 30
radio telescope: g71 11/22 30

TELEVISION
addiction: g75 6/22 26; g74 9/8 11
advertising: g74 3/8 9-12; g74 9/8 9; g73 12/22 30; g71 11/22 21, 23
children: g75 6/22 26; g74 9/8 8-11
crime and corruption on programs: g71 11/22 22-3; g71 12/8 30
discussion: g74 9/8 8-11; g71 11/22 21-3
educational use: g74 9/8 8, 10; g71 11/22 22-3
effect on family life: g75 6/22 26
harmful effects: w75 503; g75 5/22 31; g75 6/22 26; g75 12/22 30; w74 91, 262, 272; g74 2/8 5; g74 9/8 9-11; w73 144; g73 1/22 31; g73 3/22 3-4; g73 4/22 11; g73 12/8 30; g72 1/22 29; g72 5/8 29; g71 1/8 11; g71 3/22 30
Jehovah's witnesses:
use by: w75 43; yb75 232; w74 207
materialism: g74 9/8 9
medicine: g71 12/22 31
number of nations producing programs: g75 8/22 30
number one influence: w74 360
number owning: g74 9/8 8
Pentecostal view of: w75 327
preferred leisure activity: w74 273
preparing for a TV appearance: g75 2/8 31
principles of operation: g71 11/22 21
religious programs: g71 7/22 3-10
satellite transmission: g71 12/8 19
selectivity in programs: w74 112, 153; g74 9/8 10-11; g72 11/22 11, 31
soap operas: g74 9/8 9
talk shows: w74 563
time consumed: w75 503; g75 11/8 30; g74 9/8 8, 10-11; g71 3/22 30; g71 12/8 30
vocabulary: g74 9/8 8-9

TEMAN
place: w73 751-2

TEMPER
control: w71 164

TEMPLE(S)
Ezekiel's vision: w73 380-3; kj 383-92
pagan: w74 490-1

Built by Solomon
altar: w74 221
construction time:
beginning: po 120
end: ka 94
courtyard: w74 252; pm 87
curtain: w72 606; w71 713
destruction: w72 744-5; w71 712; kj 135
Holy: w74 221-2, 252-3; w73 31; ka 93-4, 101-2, 108-9, 111; w72 606-7; pm 87-8, 103-4; w71 713-14
idolatry: w72 42-3
illustration: pm 1-2; bi8 1369
inauguration: pm 53
inner courtyard: w74 221-2; w73 31; ka 98, 101, 110-11; w71 714
copper altar: w73 31; ka 97-8, 109; w72 606, 714-15
molten sea: w72 295
Most Holy: w74 221-3; w73 31; ka 99-100; w72 585, 606, 710-11, 745; pm 84, 87-8; kj 135
pictures Jehovah's spiritual temple: w72 712-13; w71 712
priestly courtyard: w72 606-7
prophetic significance: w73 31; ka 93, 98-9
Shekinah light: w72 585; w71 712
years of existence: w74 173; pm 85

Built by Zerubbabel
building opposed: w75 453-4; pm 30-1
Cyrus' decree: pm 28-32
Darius' decree: pm 196-8
date completed: sl 321; w72 746
discussion: w71 396
foundation laid: sl 166; w72 746
prophetic significance: w73 31; ka 93, 98-9
years of existence: pm 85

Rebuilt by Herod
altar: w72 714
colonnades: w75 365
Court of Gentiles: w75 365-6; w73 31; w72 607, 721
Court of Israel: w75 366
Court of Priests: w75 366
Court of Women: w75 366
date construction began: pm 86
destruction: sl 17-19; w72 747-8
diagram: w72 721; pm 85
Holy: w75 366
illustration: pm 418-19; bi8 1370
Jesus cleansed: w73 6-7, 18-19
Most Holy: w75 366
prophetic significance: w73 31; ka 93, 98-9; w72 721
wall fencing off Jew from Gentile: w75 366

Spiritual
altar: w74 221; ka 97-8, 109; w72 714-16
appreciation for: w75 20
ark of the covenant: w72 606, 710
beginning: w74 221-3; w73 381; w72 606, 713, 715-17; pm 87
builder: kj 274-5, 384
building: pm 231-3
congregation of God: w74 491; w73 440; w72 713, 717-19
courtyard: w75 395-6; w74 221-2, 252; ka 98, 101, 110-11; w72 753
curtain: w74 253; ka 100, 102, 111-12; w72 714, 717-18, 721
discussion: w75 394-6; w74 220-3; ka 93-112; w72 709-23; pm 84-91
God dwells in: w72 606, 751; w71 711-12
great crowd serve at: w72 607, 721-3; pm 80-2, 89-90, 232-3
Holy: w74 221-2, 252-3; ka 101-2, 108-9, 111; w72 716-18
incense: w74 222, 252; ka 102, 108
Jesus' sacrifice: w74 221-3; ka 95-7; w72 714-16; pm 87; w71 712-13; kj 274-5
lampstand: ka 101, 108
loaves of presentation: ka 101-2, 108
Lord's coming to (Mal 3:1): yb75 88
Most Holy: w74 221-3; ka 99-100; w72 716-17, 719, 721, 751
purpose: w74 220
widemouthed cooking pots: pm 403-5

TEMPORARY PIONEERS
discussion: km 2/74 7; or 140-1; km 6/71 4
experiences:
appreciation of privilege: km 6/71 4
congregations: km 12/72 4
fathers: w75 315
joys: km 2/73 4-5
leads to regular pioneering: km 2/72 6; km 2/71 6
mothers: km 2/72 4-6
physically sick: km 2/72 4
response by brothers: km 1/71 3
literature: km 10/71 8
number: km 2/75 3; w73 27; w71 335; km 2/71 4-5
requirements: km 2/75 3; or 140; km 2/72 3; km 2/71 4
youths: km 6/75 1
(SEE ALSO FIELD SERVICE, PIONEERS)

TEMPORARY RESIDENTS (Alien Residents, Strangers)
Christians: w74 760

TEMPTATION
Adam and Eve: fu 14-16; w72 262-3, 426-7
Jesus in wilderness: w75 619; og 20-1; w74 722-3; po 145-6; w73 5; w72 624-5, 627; dn 16-18, 22; w71 38-9; te 51-4
resisting: g75 6/22 28; w74 64, 415; w72 516, 528-31; w71 39, 533, 544
succumbing to: w71 526

'way made out' (1 Co 10:13): w74 63-4, 203

TEN
Bible use of number: ka 170

TEN COMMANDMENTS
part of Law covenant: g75 2/8 27-8
principles continue: g72 11/22 6-8
summary: g71 1/8 3-4
time given: po 110
value recognized by world: g75 10/8 15

List by Number
fourth: g75 2/8 27-8
sixth: g75 2/8 28
seventh: g75 2/8 28
tenth: g75 2/8 28

TEN LOST TRIBES
discussion: w72 440-4

TENSION
discussion: g75 9/8 3-6
remedy: g75 9/8 5-6; w74 524; g74 4/8 9-13

TENT
symbolic: w74 760

TENT OF MEETING
kj 26-7

TERAH (Father of Abraham)
age at Abram's birth: w75 64
worship: g73 11/8 27

TERRITORY
beginning of congregation assignment: yb75 124
businesses: km 5/73 8; km 6/73 3-4; km 3/71 3-4
calling at every home: km 6/74 3
calling on not-at-homes: yb73 14; or 118-19; w71 219-20
field overseer: w72 461; or 73-4
individual assignments: or 118-19
isolated territory: km 8/75 8; km 10/74 1
isolated territory in South Africa: yb76 188, 240-1
language barrier: km 1/74 3-4
new: yb72 51-4, 57-73
regular coverage: km 6/74 3
repeated coverage: yb73 14; km 11/72 8
rural territory: km 6/75 3
sharing with others: w74 440
unworked territory: km 4/73 2-3
unworked territory in Bolivia: yb76 7-8
(SEE ALSO FIELD SERVICE)

TERTULLIAN
statements on—
clergy-laity: ka 377-8
contributions: g74 10/22 28

TEST
Adam and Eve: w74 529-30; po 43-4, 56-9; ts 30-4; g74 10/8 11-12
faithful endurance: w74 169-70, 172, 249-50, 529-30; yb74 115-26; g71 1/22 27-8
following 1,000-year reign: w74 6-7, 345-8; po 190-1; ts 185-6; ka 147-62

TESTIMONY CARD
yb75 160

TESTIMONY MEETING
w72 759

TESTIMONY TO THE RULERS OF THE WORLD, A (Resolution)
distribution: yb75 137

TETRAGRAMMATON
ancient Greek versions of Hebrew Scriptures: bi8 1354-5, 1357-8
ancient Hebrew: po 16
displaying on possessions: km 9/74 8
equivalent in English letters: po 16; w71 389, 454
Kyrios substituted: w71 389-91; bi8 1352
meaning of term: w71 389
New World Translation: bi8 1352-5
occurrences: pm 388
pronunciation: g73 3/22 27
renderings hide divine name: w74 362; w71 454-5
Septuagint: w73 702; w71 389-91, 454; bi8 1357-8
(SEE ALSO JEHOVAH)

TEXTILES
wool: g73 2/8 24-6

THAILAND
Jehovah's witnesses: yb76 30-1; yb75 30-1; yb74 19, 30-1; yb73 30-1; yb72 40-1
population: yb73 30; yb72 40

THALIDOMIDE
deformed babies: g71 2/8 31

THANKS
expressing: w74 190; w73 297-9; te 43-6

THANKSGIVING
expressing to Jehovah: w75 29; ka 410-11
prayer: w72 332-3

THANT, U
warning to nations: w71 68; g71 4/22 4

THEATER
experience:
actress becomes Witness: w74 605

"THE NATIONS SHALL KNOW THAT I AM JEHOVAH"—HOW? (Book)
public talks: km 10/71 3-6
release: yb72 42; w71 605

THEOCRACY
discussion: pm 13-21
Israel: w71 681-3, 742-6
meaning of term: pm 14; w71 681, 711

THEOCRATIC MINISTRY SCHOOL GUIDEBOOK (Book)
purpose: sg 5
release: yb72 42; w71 599
student talks: km 11/72 8
use: sg 98

THEOCRATIC ORGANIZATION
ancient Israel: w71 681-5
appointment of service director: yb75 125
changes in Society charter: yb75 246-7
congregation organization (1938): yb75 166; yb73 116; w71 682, 693, 719, 724-5
discussion: w72 729-31; w71 681-701, 748-55
early Christian congregation: w72 729-31; w71 685-92
elimination of elective elders: yb75 164-6
end of 2,300 days: w71 724-8
governing body: w72 272, 755; w71 81, 686-7, 748-50, 755-62
older men (elders): w71 603-4
structure: w72 458

THEOCRATIC SCHOOL
applause: km 4/72 4
beginning: yb75 197-8; w73 399; yb72 256
Argentina: yb72 77
Brazil: yb73 67
benefits: g75 10/22 15; yb74 234; w73 111-12, 533-5; sg 8-13, 96-9
counsel: km 5/74 8; or 80, 99; km 12/72 7-8; sg 11, 98-108; km 1/71 4
description: w73 534; or 98-100
effects of training: yb76 42, 150, 161; w74 411; w73 534-5; sg 96
enrollment: w73 534; or 80, 98-100; sg 8
instruction talks: km 2/75 4; sg 10
library: or 81; km 5/72 4; sg 11
overseer: w72 460-1; or 79-81; sg 10-11, 103, 107-8
preparation of talks: km 12/74 4; km 4/72 3; sg 39-43, 50-1, 97-8; km 12/71 3
purpose: w73 533-5; sg 9, 13, 96
schedule: km 10/75 3-6; km 10/74 3-6; km 12/74 3-4
sisters enrolled: yb75 198
Speech Counsel slip: or 99; sg 100-2, 104-5
student talks: km 11/72 8; sg 10, 62-3
householder: sg 98
study program: km 12/74 3-4; or 80, 98-9; km 12/72 7-8; sg 9-10
tobacco users: km 11/73 7
written review: or 99-100
(SEE ALSO MEETINGS)

THEOLOGICAL SCHOOLS
beliefs of professors: w74 14; g74 8/22 9-10
beliefs of students: w71 548, 675
closing: g72 4/8 30; g71 8/8 29
discord: g74 8/22 8-11
enrollment: w74 166; g74 6/22 30; g74 8/22 8-9; g74 11/8 30; g72 4/8 30; w71 408, 484; g71 12/22 30
failure: g74 3/8 30; g74 8/22 8-11; g73 7/22 29; w71 739
lose teachers: g74 8/22 8
problems: g74 3/22 29;

g, Awake!; **ka,** God's Kingdom of a Thousand Years; **kj,** "The Nations Shall Know that I Am Jehovah"; **km,** Kingdom Ministry; **or,** Organization; **pm,** Paradise Restored—By Theocracy!; **po,** God's "Eternal Purpose"; **sg,** Theocratic School Guidebook; **sl,** Man's Salvation out of World Distress!; **te,** Listening to the Great Teacher; **tp,** True Peace and Security; **ts,** Is This Life All There Is?; **w,** Watchtower; **yb,** Yearbook. **Complete list on page 6.**

g74 8/22 8-11; g74 11/8 30; g71 3/8 29
(SEE ALSO CLERGY)

THERE IS MUCH MORE TO LIFE! (Booklet)
public talk: km 12/75 1
use in field service: km 10/75 1, 8

THESSALONIANS (Second Book)
background: ka 366-9

"THE WORD"—WHO IS HE? ACCORDING TO JOHN (Booklet)
yb75 229

"THINGS IN WHICH IT IS IMPOSSIBLE FOR GOD TO LIE" (Book)
experience with: w72 511

THINKING
basis for right: g73 1/8 5
concentration: sg 25-7
improving ability: g74 12/22 13-14; g73 1/8 3-8
meditation: w72 522-4
need for words: w73 525
negative: w74 589, 591
on right matters: w74 211; g74 12/8 17-18, 21; w73 477-9
speed: sg 26
training children: w74 91-2

"THIRD WORLD" NATIONS
w74 549, 551; g74 12/8 8-11

THIRST
g74 8/22 29

THIRTY YEARS' WAR
discussion: g71 6/22 16-19
statistics: g72 4/22 13

"THIS MEANS EVERLASTING LIFE" (Book)
yb75 239

THOMAS
Jesus' appearance to: w74 730; g73 7/22 4

THOUGHTFULNESS
w74 46

THOUSAND-YEAR REIGN
beginning: w74 6; ka 16-19
blessings: w74 345; ts 133-4, 136-40, 142-3; g74 4/8 9-15; w73 381-3; ka 81-2, 139-46; tp 101-10; g73 10/8 25-9; pm 18-21
  death no more: ts 137-9, 165-6; ka 159-60; tp 104-6
  freedom from want: tp 102-4; g72 10/22 15-16; kj 397
  healing of handicapped: ts 138-9
  health: ts 137-9; w73 412-15; tp 104-7; kj 392-8
  no food shortage: ts 134-7
  peace: w74 240; ka 52-4, 142-6
  peace with animals: ts 142; ka 144-5
  perfection: w74 608; ts 139-40, 144; ka 159-60; g73 10/8 26-7; w71 500
  personality transformation: ka 142-3, 145-6
  resurrection: w74 608; w73 382-3; ka 120-2, 125-31; tp 107-8; kj 390-1
  righteousness: w74 293-4
  security: w74 240; tp 102-4
  unity: w74 623; hu 28
discussion: w73 364-70; ka 13-19, 30-1, 34-5, 42-4, 48-54, 81-2, 117-22, 124-46
earthly government: w73 425-8
evildoers executed during: w74 294; ts 183, 185; ka 138
final test following: w74 6-7, 345-8; po 190-1; ts 185-6; ka 147-56, 159-62; tp 56-7; w72 273
  number of rebels: ka 151
initial conditions: w73 364, 366-70
judgment period: w74 277-80, 292-4; w73 364, 367; ka 117-21, 124-42, 145-6
kings rule with Christ: w73 739-42; ka 30-1, 48-9, 72-5
literally 1,000 years: w74 7-8; ka 18-19, 42-5
misconceptions: w74 7, 506-7; ka 14, 184-7, 206-11
one language: w74 43-4; ka 49-50
overpopulation no problem: ts 134-7
princes: w74 292-3; ka 131-6
pure language: w74 42
purpose: w74 604; po 187-8; ts 131-3
sabbath: g74 4/8 11-12; g74 10/8 21-2; g71 10/8 27
Satan bound: kj 395
"scrolls": w74 292-4; w73 364; ka 130-1
some anointed on earth: ka 401, 406, 411
unintentional sin: ts 139-40
(SEE ALSO KINGDOM, NEW ORDER)

THREE WORLDS (Book)
yb75 37; w74 506-7; ka 187

THRONE
David's: ka 54-8
Jehovah's: po 127-8; w72 716-17, 721

TIBERIUS CAESAR
beginning of reign: g75 12/22 27; w73 767; g72 6/8 12

TIDAL WAVES
Pakistan: g71 1/8 29

TIDES
Canada, Bay of Fundy: g73 11/8 8-11
discussion: g73 11/8 8-11
France: g73 11/8 11
harnessing: g73 11/8 10-11

TIGER
g73 5/8 30

TILLICH, PAUL
w74 100

TIME
animals not conceive past, future: ts 18-21
calendars:
  adding two seconds: w73 580
International Dateline: g73 12/8 22
leap second: g72 8/8 29
leisure time: w71 311-15
Jehovah: w74 163; po 7-8; g74 4/8 16-17; w73 579-83
Jesus Christ: w73 580-2
Jewish system: w75 63-4
man has concept of eternity: ts 18-21
prophetic period: po 176; ts 155-6; kj 100-3
"stealing time": g75 3/8 29
times long lasting: w71 703-4
wise use: w74 373-4; or 110-12; w71 61-2, 311-15
  youths: w75 462-3
(SEE ALSO CHRONOLOGY)

TIME INDEFINITE
meaning of term: g72 11/22 5-6

TIME OF DISTRESS
w74 191-2; po 184-5

TIME OF THE END
awakeness: w73 56-8; g71 11/22 4
beginning: w75 750; w74 356-7; g73 1/22 8; kj 57-8, 73, 356
chronology to fix beginning: yb75 37; po 174-7; ts 155-9; w73 645
economics: g74 1/22 8
great tribulation (Mt 24:21): po 184-5
Jerusalem: kj 57, 73, 87
Jewish system of things: w74 680-3, 693-4; po 172-3
pre-Flood world: po 73, 173
sign of last days:
  as days of Noah: w75 10-11; km 7/75 2
  as lightning: w74 750
  composite: w75 633
  earthquakes: w75 634-5; w74 72-4, 243; g74 5/8 17-19; w72 339; g72 10/8 16; w71 69, 406; te 177
  food shortages: w75 634; g75 2/22 8; w74 195-7; ts 162; w72 339, 615; g72 10/8 15; w71 69, 406; te 177
  generation: w75 632, 635; g75 7/8 29; g72 10/8 15
  lack of natural affection: w75 327
  lawlessness increasing: w75 635; g75 11/22 15; w74 99-101, 244; g72 10/8 16; w71 406; te 178
  lovers of pleasures: g72 1/22 26
  men faint out of fear: w75 635; w74 656; w71 69
  persecution of Christians: w72 340
  pestilences and diseases: w75 634; w74 131-3, 358-9; ts 162; w73 753; g72 10/8 16; w71 69, 406; g71 3/8 4
  preaching of this good news of kingdom: po 174; g72 10/8 16; w71 69, 80-2, 466
  reason Jesus gave "sign": w74 398-400
  separation of "sheep" and "goats": w74 625-8
  signs from heaven: km 7/75 2; w74 40
  wars: w75 633-4; ts 162; w72 339; g72 10/8 15; w71 69, 406; te 177
(SEE ALSO APPOINTED TIMES OF THE NATIONS, 1914)

TIMOR
Jehovah's witnesses: yb76 28-9; km 7/75 4

TIMOTHY
biographical sketch: te 109-10
calling: w74 658-9
example for youths: w73 157; w72 276
training: w75 157; w72 114

TIN
g74 11/22 18-19

TIRES
discussion: g72 9/8 22-3

TITHE (Tithing)
churches of Christendom: g75 9/8 25-6
discussion: g74 1/8 27-8
Israel: g74 1/8 27

TITLES
(SEE HONORARY TITLES)

TITUS (Roman General)
Arch of Titus: w75 139-40
Jerusalem's destruction: w75 138-9; w74 426-8, 683, 693; ka 302-3; pm 365; g72 10/8 21; kj 351
Josephus' quotation of: w75 139

TOBACCO
advertising: g75 5/22 29; g75 10/22 30; g73 10/22 30
Bible view toward use: w73 338-43, 543; tp 162-3; w72 594-6; w71 670-2
breaking the habit: w73 453-55
dangers: w75 327; g75 4/8 30; g75 12/22 30; g74 2/8 29; g74 2/22 30; g74 5/22 18-19; g74 6/8 29-30; g74 7/22 30; g74 9/8 18, 20, 23; g74 11/22 30; w73 338-9; g73 5/22 30; g73 8/8 30; g73 8/22 17-20; w72 594-6; g72 1/22 29; g72 6/8 30; g71 5/8 29; g71 11/8 4
experiences:
 change employment: w75 763; yb75 9
 stores without tobacco: w75 292
government spending to warn of dangers: g75 10/22 30
government subsidy: g75 10/22 30; g74 5/22 30
production increase: w74 71; g74 5/22 30; g73 11/8 31
sales statistics: g73 3/22 31
why not banned: g72 7/8 30
Witness view of: w73 338-43, 543; km 7/73 4; km 11/73 7
Witness view of growing: w74 456; km 2/74 3-6; w73 409-10
Witness view of selling: km 2/74 3-4, 6
(SEE ALSO SMOKING)

TOBAGO
Jehovah's witnesses: yb76 30-1; yb75 30-1; yb74 30-1; yb73 30-1; yb72 40-1
population: yb73 30; yb72 40
tourism: g72 5/8 15

TOGO
Jehovah's witnesses: yb76 30-1; yb75 11, 30-1; yb74 10-11, 30-1; yb73 30-1; yb72 40-1; w71 126-7
population: yb73 30; yb72 40

TOILETRIES
chemicals: g72 4/8 31

TOKELAU ISLANDS
Jehovah's witnesses: yb76 24-5

TOLERANCE
wrong view of: g71 3/22 29

TOMBS
bodies thrown out of: w75 639-40

TOMTIT
bird: g72 3/22 20-2

TONGA
Jehovah's witnesses: yb76 15, 24-5; yb75 24-5; yb74 24-5; yb73 24-5; yb72 34-5
population: yb73 24; yb72 34

TONGUE
'a fire' (Jas 3:6): ts 112
control of: w71 144
discussion: g73 1/22 17-19
proper use: km 10/74 7

TONGUES, SPEAKING IN
danger: g75 5/22 30
discussion: g74 12/22 27-8
gift of spirit: w71 503-4
Pentecost (33 C.E.): w73 526-7
spiritism: g72 11/8 7, 8

TONSILS
discussion: g71 1/22 15
function: g74 2/8 16
risks from removal: g72 6/8 31; g71 7/8 31; g71 11/22 30

TOOLS
basic: g74 7/8 17

TOPHETH
bi8 1355

TORMENT
belief in fiery: ts 88-90, 96, 98-9; w73 132-3, 232-3; g73 7/22 27
Bible usage: ts 91, 93-4, 119-20; w73 227-30
Gehenna: ts 110-12, 114-15
rich man in torments (Lu 16:23): ts 107-9; w73 236-7
tormented with fire and sulphur (Re 20:10): w74 382-4; ts 117-23; ka 156-8

TORNADOES
Argentina: yb72 100
casualties: g74 1/8 31; g74 4/22 31
discussion: g74 6/8 8-10
ninety in one day: g74 7/22 30

TORTURE
Inquisition: g71 1/22 20-3

TORTURE STAKE
curse upon one hung up: po 151-2
discussion: g74 9/22 27-8; bi8 1360-1
each Christian carries: w74 600-1, 603
Greek word: g74 9/22 27-8; bi8 1360-1

TOURISM
behavior of tourists: g73 3/22 6-7
discussion: g72 5/8 13-16
in the United States: g75 11/22 31

TOWER
CN Tower: g75 6/8 21-4
tower of Pisa: g75 5/22 29
world's tallest: g75 6/8 21-2; g74 8/8 31

TOWER OF BABEL
confusion of language: w75 464, 666; w73 525-6; w72 428; sg 5
construction: w74 490

priest's view: g74 7/8 30

TOYS
dangers: g71 9/8 30; g71 12/8 30
selecting: g74 7/22 22; g71 1/8 9-12

TRACTS
Bible Students' Tracts (*Old Theology Quarterly*): yb75 39
experiences with: yb74 69, 71-3; g74 10/8 28
Kingdom News: g73 11/8 18
 experiences with: yb75 6-7, 12, 17, 22, 253; km 11/74 1
 No. 1: yb75 97-8
 No. 2: yb75 98
 No. 3: yb75 98
 No. 16: yb75 252; km 9/73 1, 7-8; km 12/73 1
 No. 17: yb75 252; km 1/74 1; km 2/74 1; km 3/74 1; km 12/73 1
 No. 18: yb75 252; km 4/74 1, 3; km 8/74 1
 No. 19: km 10/74 7
Peoples Pulpit: yb76 79; yb75 45-6
production: yb75 245
special campaigns: w73 635; km 9/73 1, 7-8; km 12/73 1
The Bible Students Monthly: yb75 85, 94-5

TRADE
United States-Soviet Union: g72 10/8 5, 29
world trade: g75 11/8 30

TRADITIONS
Catholic church: ts 66; g74 4/22 19; w73 550
effects of human: w72 560-1
Flood: g75 6/8 8

TRAFFIC ACCIDENTS
causes: g72 9/22 30; g72 10/8 31; g72 11/22 30
motorcycles: g75 5/8 30; g72 11/22 30-1
Nigeria: g75 2/22 31
statistics: g72 2/22 29; g72 6/8 3-4; g72 9/22 30; g72 11/8 30
value of seat belts: g75 6/8 31
(SEE ALSO ACCIDENTS)

TRAINING
animals: g73 1/22 20-2
children:
 anticipating problems: w74 89-90
 appreciation for: w71 107
 avoiding unfavorable comparisons: w74 269-70
 communication: w74 268-9; g74 11/22 21-2
 congregation meetings: w75 61-2; sg 27
 counsel: w74 89-90, 92-3
 daily routine: w74 84-5
 discipline: w75 14-15, 156-7; w74 82, 92-3, 267-8; g74 2/8 8; g74 4/22 14-15; w71 555-6, 588-9, 592
 drugs: g74 5/8 3-8; w71 249-50
 early: w74 267-8; g74 2/8 7-8; g73 2/22 17-19; w72 111-17; g72 5/8 5-6; w71 104-5
 effect of proper training: g74 7/22 23; w72 403; w71 106-

7, 191, 368; g71 2/22 11; g71 9/22 8; g71 10/22 16
experiences involving Witness children: w75 763; w74 272; g74 2/8 10; w71 368
fallacies to avoid: w75 71; w74 263, 267-72; w72 111, 113-14, 270; g71 5/22 30
father's role: w75 14-15, 156-7
goal: w74 82
good habits: w72 452; g71 7/22 26
home Bible instruction: w75 156-7; w74 84-7; g74 2/8 8-10; km 7/74 4; w72 114-17; km 1/72 7-8; w71 104-7, 170-1; sg 37-8; te 5-6; km 5/71 3-4
household chores: g74 2/8 9; g72 5/8 5-8; w71 312; g71 9/8 8-11
imparting moral values: g74 4/22 13-14
Israel: w71 361-2
love: g74 4/22 15-16
"mental-regulating": g74 2/8 8-9
mother's role: w74 85; w71 104
parental companionship: w75 156-7; w74 270-1; g74 2/8 10; g74 4/22 15-16; g74 7/22 22-3
parental example: w74 263; g74 4/22 15; w71 370-2, 583, 589
parental responsibility: w74 81-94; g74 2/8 7-11; g74 8/22 4-6; w72 51-2, 109-11, 163-4, 360-3; w71 361-2, 367-72
parental unity: w72 270-1
persuasion: g75 1/8 9, 12
reading: g74 7/22 21; sg 23
respect for parents and others: w74 90-1; g74 2/8 4-5; w72 163-4
results of parental neglect: g75 3/8 29; w74 267, 270-1; g74 8/22 4-5; w72 259-60
sex education: g75 1/8 30; g74 2/8 6, 9; g74 4/22 13-14; g72 1/22 8-9; g72 7/22 29-30; w71 589
toys: g71 1/8 9-12
Christians:
effect of proper: g75 1/22 30
home Bible instruction: g75 10/22 14-15
new ones for field service: yb75 227-8; km 5/74 7
trials: w71 108-14
nurses: g73 2/8 10-11
(SEE ALSO TEACHING)

TRAINS
(SEE RAILROADS)

TRANQUILIZERS
w75 246; g75 11/8 30; w74 524; w73 184-5; g72 5/8 30-1

TRANSCENDENTAL MEDITATION
g75 11/8 10

TRANSFIGURATION
w74 78, 296-9, 544

TRANSISTORS
discussion: g71 12/8 18-20

TRANSLATING (Bible)
African languages: yb73 142-3; g73 1/22 26
anarthrous nouns (Greek): w75 702-4
Chinese: w74 744-5
divine name: fu 9-10; w74 362; yb73 142-3; g73 1/22 26
English: w74 743-4
New World Bible Translation Committee: w74 767-8
problems: g72 5/22 27-8; w71 59; g71 3/8 23-6
reasons for: g72 6/22 5-6; g71 3/8 23; g71 12/22 22
responsibility of translators: w74 361-4
Tyndale: w74 743-5
value of: g74 12/8 25
Wycliffe: w74 743

TRANSMIGRATION
Buddhism: g74 1/8 16
extent of belief: g75 4/8 27
Hinduism: g75 11/8 8-9; g73 7/8 17-18
Judaism's belief: g75 4/8 28
refutation: g75 4/8 27-8; ts 53-60; g74 1/8 19
(SEE ALSO IMMORTALITY OF THE SOUL)

TRANSPLANTING
body parts: w74 684; g71 11/8 9
hazards: g74 1/22 30; g74 2/22 30-1; g74 12/22 12; g72 6/8 30
heart: g74 5/22 30; g72 7/8 28; w71 135-6; g71 11/22 31
kidney: w75 519; g72 9/22 30
problems: w75 519
Witness view: w73 254

TRANSPORTATION
automobiles:
accident statistics: g74 5/22 16; g73 10/22 31; g72 2/22 29; g72 6/8 3-4; g72 9/22 30; g71 6/22 3-4; g71 8/22 22; g71 10/22 30; g71 11/8 4
automated: g72 4/8 29
battery-powered: g75 2/22 24-5
driving: g74 12/8 29-30; g73 1/22 29
hitchhiking: g73 2/8 30-1
imports: g71 6/22 29
number: g74 2/22 29; g74 11/8 31; g71 12/22 31
pollution control devices: g73 2/22 30
repairs: g71 6/22 29
safety: g72 3/22 30
seat belts: g73 2/8 30; g73 10/22 31
smoking: g73 1/22 29
speed: g74 11/8 30
tires: g72 9/8 22-3
traffic congestion: g74 11/8 31
U.S. president: g72 10/8 30
aviation:
accidents: g73 2/22 31; g73 4/8 26; g72 2/22 29; g72 7/22 29; g72 12/8 30
airport: g73 1/22 22-4
New Guinea: g73 4/8 24-6
passengers screened: g71 12/22 30
private aircraft: g74 10/8 31
safety: g73 4/8 25-6; g71 8/8 30
bicycles: g74 4/8 30; g73 6/22 25-7
bus: g74 4/8 30; g72 3/8 30
hovercraft: g73 11/22 21-3
mass transit: g74 4/8 30
motorcycles: g74 9/22 30-1; g72 11/22 30-1; g71 12/22 31
Nigeria: g72 3/8 24-6
railroads: yb72 51; g72 3/8 30; g72 11/8 30; g71 7/22 30
subways: g74 8/22 3-4; g74 11/8 31
taxicabs: g72 7/8 16-19
trucks: g74 2/22 29; g71 7/22 30
water:
boats: g72 5/22 18-19

TRANSSEXUAL
w74 360; g74 6/8 29

TRAP
Satan's: w74 732-4

TRAPPING
animals: g72 12/22 21-3

TRAVEL
airplane: g73 1/22 22-4; g73 4/8 24-6; g71 12/22 30
attitude: w73 478
Australia: g72 5/22 25-6
Caribbean: g72 5/8 13-16
Dahomey: g71 1/22 24-6
etiquette: g75 7/8 30-1
Germany: g72 5/22 18-19; g71 5/22 21-4
governments demand neat appearance: g74 7/22 30-1
hitchhiking: g74 8/22 29
Honduras: g72 4/8 26
Israel: g72 1/8 27-8
Japan: g73 2/8 20-3
Lebanon: g71 11/8 10-11
Middle America: g72 9/8 25-6
New Guinea: g73 4/8 24-6
Nigeria: g72 3/8 24-6
organized convention groups: km 9/71 4
Panama: g71 9/22 20-3
Tanzania: g71 12/22 25-6
Zaïre Republic: g72 1/8 21-4

TREASURE
Jesus' parable of treasure hidden in a field: w75 594
laying up in heaven: w75 561-7

TREATIES (Pacts)
broken: g71 10/8 12-13
number: w71 299
Kellogg-Briand Pact: g71 10/8 12-13
London: kj 59
Versailles: kj 59-60, 65

TREE(S)
African: g75 2/8 21-2
age: ts 23-5; g74 3/22 26; w73 82-4; g72 4/8 12
benefits: g75 2/8 23; g73 6/8 9-11; g71 5/8 22
cold-weather trees: w75 715
desert reclamation: g75 7/22 29
discussion: g73 6/8 9-11; g71 5/8 20-3
dwarf: g71 6/8 15-16
Flood survival: w73 84-5
forest: g73 6/8 9-11; g72 7/8 29
fruit: w71 325
kinds: g71 5/8 20
largest: g74 3/22 24-6
logging: g71 12/22 17-19
longevity illustrative: w73 85
lumberjacks: g73 12/8 31
planting: g71 7/22 30
pollination: g71 5/22 20
products from: g74 11/8 23
seeds: g71 5/8 21
stump processing: g74 11/8 23
symbolic: sl 172; po 176; ts 157; w72 765; pm 302-5

tree of Daniel 4: ts 152-60
tree of knowledge of good and bad: po 56-7; ts 31; g72 4/8 27-8
prohibition by God: g74 10/8 11-12
tree of life (Ge 2:9): ts 17
tree-ring chronology: g72 4/8 5, 11-15, 17-19
trees of life (Re 22:2): kj 397-8
tropics: g72 3/8 26
two olive trees (Zec 4): pm 204-7

List by Name

apple: g73 9/22 21-3; g71 5/22 19
bamboo: g71 5/8 11
banana: g72 9/8 21
baobab: g75 2/8 22; w73 82; g73 6/8 11
bo (bodhi): w73 83
cedar: w75 541; g71 5/8 21
coconut: g71 5/8 11; g71 6/22 25-6
coffee: g75 10/22 30
cork oak: g71 9/22 24
fig: w72 95-6
fir: g71 5/8 21
kapok: g71 5/8 11
kauri: w73 84
mangrove: w73 84
maple: g73 2/22 11-12
musanga: w73 85
olive: w73 82, 84-5
palm: g71 2/22 15; g71 6/22 25-6
papaya: g71 5/8 11
pear: g71 5/22 20
pine: w73 82-4; g72 4/8 12-14
prune-plum: g71 5/8 23
redwood: g74 3/22 24-6; g73 6/8 10; g71 5/8 22
sequoia: g74 3/22 24-6; w73 84; g73 6/8 9-10; g71 5/8 21-2
spruce: g71 5/8 21-2
sumac: g71 7/22 23
teak: w73 85
(SEE ALSO PLANTS)

TREE OF KNOWLEDGE OF GOOD AND BAD

not poisonous: ts 31
prohibition by God: g74 10/8 11-12; g72 4/8 27-8
sense of 'knowing good and bad': ts 31

TREE(S) OF LIFE

Eden (Ge 2:9): ts 17

TRESPASS(ING)

discussion: g71 1/8 3-4

TRIAL(S)

Christians subjected to: w75 22-3; w71 108-21, 172-4; g71 1/22 27-8
conduct during: sg 94-5
Jehovah's witnesses: yb75 169, 172, 177-9
Watch Tower Society's officers': yb75 104-8
Jesus' trial: w75 8; ka 85; w71 340; te 163-5
strength from Jehovah: w74 415
training for: w71 108-14

TRIBE

intertribal fighting: g75 12/22 30

TRIBULATION

great crowd come out of (Re 7:14): ka 291-2; w72 376-7; kj 283-4
great tribulation (Mt 24:21): ka 398-9; g72 6/8 8; kj 112-13, 140-1, 146, 159, 161-2, 177, 180-1, 189, 202, 208-9, 256-7, 264, 269, 274-5, 277-8, 281, 290, 292, 298, 302, 307, 309, 359-60, 367-8, 389
at proper time: w74 56-7; w73 583
attack on God's people: w75 88; w74 171
chosen ones: w75 276; w74 749-50; ka 303-4, 315, 318, 328-9
cry of peace and security before: w74 552
cut short: w74 749; ka 318-19
"day and hour": w75 9-11, 277-80, 284, 542, 768
description: w75 758; po 185-6
discussion: w75 272-84
disposal of dead: w73 345-6
evidence that near: w74 51-3
final destruction for some: ts 181
"goats" destroyed: w74 123; ka 289-91
hardships: w75 333, 341; w74 40, 61, 248-9; w73 746, 749, 757-60
issue: po 185
Jerusalem (70 C.E.): w75 273-4, 277-8; w74 425-9; po 172-3; ka 294-304, 323; tp 91-2; w72 629; dn 25-6
material possessions: w75 352, 562-3
modern-day fulfillment: w75 273, 278; sl 316; km 7/75 2; w74 400, 425, 429; w73 293, 296-7; ka 316-19; tp 88-9; g73 4/22 18-19; w72 629; dn 25-6
monetary systems: g74 1/22 8
protection during: w75 377-8; w74 170-2, 318, 667-8, 765-6
right view of: w75 280-4; w74 40; ka 329-31, 336-7
sign of Son of man: w74 748, 750-1; ka 326-8
some flesh saved: w74 749; ts 164-5; ka 318-19, 399
time for exultation: w75 88
"time of distress": w74 191-2; po 184-5
what is destroyed: w73 756-7; ka 398; tp 38-9
when begins: w75 88; w74 170, 379
who preserved: w73 623, 756-7; ka 399, 401, 404-9; tp 90, 95-7; dy 26-7
(SEE ALSO ARMAGEDDON)

TRINIDAD

carnival: g73 3/8 6
Jehovah's witnesses: yb76 30-1; yb75 30-1; yb74 30-1; yb73 30-1; w72 476-8; yb72 40-1
population: yb73 30; yb72 40
tourism: g72 5/8 14-15

TRINITY

Aristotle: w73 465
Athanasian Creed: w75 355; w73 131-2
Buddhism: w74 75-6; g73 2/22 27-8
Catholic church: w74 75; w73 550; g73 2/22 27-8; w72 625; dn 19; w71 355-6
clergy disbelief: w72 294
definition: g73 1/8 16
discussion: w74 75-6; w73 131-2; g73 1/8 16-19; g73 2/22 27-8; g72 3/22 5-8
doctrine opposed by early church fathers: w75 356; g73 1/8 16-19
Elohim: po 36
holy spirit not a person: w74 363, 421-3; g71 3/22 27-8
Jehovah is One and is Supreme: pm 387-8; w71 627
Jesus' God is Jehovah: w75 174-5
Jesus had a beginning: w75 175-6
Jesus inferior to Jehovah: w75 174-5, 356, 540; w74 76, 525-7, 730; w73 132, 388-9; g73 2/22 28; g73 3/8 28; w72 294, 734; g72 3/8 18-19; g72 3/22 7-8; w71 356; g71 12/8 4
official adoption by Christendom: w75 356; g73 1/8 17; w71 31
origin: w75 173
pagan belief in: w74 75-6
scriptures misapplied to support:
Matthew 28:19: w74 422
John 1:1: w75 63, 173-6, 702-4; g72 3/22 6-7; bi8 1362-3
John 8:58: w74 527
John 10:30: w74 525-7
John 14:9: w74 527
John 20:28: w74 730; g72 3/22 6
Acts 20:28: bi8 1363-4
Romans 9:5: g72 3/22 7; bi8 1364
2 Corinthians 13:14: w74 422
2 Thessalonians 1:12: g72 3/22 7
1 Timothy 3:16: g72 3/22 7
Titus 2:13: g72 3/22 7; bi8 1365
1 John 5:7: w75 190-1; bi8 1366
1 John 5:20: g72 3/22 7
symbol on church: g73 1/8 17
view of Isaac Newton: w75 651

Quotations

not directly word of God: w75 355
tool to be used against heretics: w75 355-6

TRUE PEACE AND SECURITY—FROM WHAT SOURCE? (Book)

yb75 251; w74 700

TRUJILLO, RAFAEL L.

yb72 143, 150, 152-3, 158-9, 163-5

TRUK ISLANDS

Jehovah's witnesses: yb76 26-7; yb75 26-7; yb74 26-7; yb73 26-7; yb72 36-7; w71 85
population: yb73 26; yb72 36

TRUMAN, HARRY

yb75 207

TRUMPET(S)

seven, of Revelation 8-11:
first: yb75 135-6
second: yb75 136
third: yb75 136-7
fourth: yb75 137
fifth: yb75 137
sixth: yb75 137-8
seventh: yb75 138-9

TRUST

benefits: w73 478-9
discussion: w75 419-21; g72 4/8 3-4

in Jehovah: w75 420-1, 700-2; yb75 62; w74 249, 701-2, 730-1, 754-5, 757-60, 766; po 24-5; ts 176-7; g74 12/22 22-3, 25; g73 11/8 7
politicians: w75 419; g74 3/22 6; g73 11/8 3-5, 7; g72 8/22 29
when lacking: w74 311; g74 12/8 30

TRUTH
basis for true religion: w72 99-100
benefits: w73 49-51
discussion: w71 460-73
effects: po 4-6; g72 12/22 5-7
experiences:
accepted after efforts to prove wrong fail: yb72 244; w71 551-2
appreciation for: yb72 70
depression overcome: w75 244-5
interested ones search for: w75 734-5; g74 11/22 7-12; yb73 144; yb72 67, 147-8; g71 6/22 20-1
lives transformed: w75 245-6, 559; g75 10/8 19-20; w74 4, 38-9; g74 11/22 10-12; w73 29-30; yb73 10-11, 15-17, 243; g73 1/8 11-12; g73 2/8 14-15; w72 125, 453-5; g72 3/8 23; g72 3/22 16; g72 4/8 25; g72 8/22 11-12, 23; g72 9/22 26; w71 209, 532-3, 763; g71 2/8 13-16
exposing falsehood: w74 35-7
found in simplicity (quote): w75 651
Jesus' bearing witness to: w71 461
love of: g72 2/8 8
misrepresenting: w73 597-8; g73 3/8 31; g72 10/8 30-1
power of: w74 573-4
practicing in life: w74 561-71
price: g72 12/22 7
progressive: w74 572-3; w72 498-505
repetition: w73 49
source: tp 111-12
speaking: w74 245-7, 314; w73 597-8; tp 114-16; sg 5-6; te 71-4, 111-14
worship with: g73 11/8 28

"TRUTH SHALL MAKE YOU FREE, THE" (Book)
experiences with: yb72 79, 144, 147-8, 172-3

TRUTH THAT LEADS TO ETERNAL LIFE, THE (Book)
appreciation for: yb74 62
baptisms since release of: km 12/75 1
best seller: g73 9/22 8
distribution: w75 48; g75 4/8 32; yb72 124; g71 4/8 19-20
experiences with: yb76 227, 230, 255-6; w75 650; yb75 7, 21, 23; g75 10/22 21; w74 31, 649, 711-12; yb74 235-6; g74 11/22 10-11; g73 7/22 7; w72 542
languages: w75 48; yb75 240; g75 1/8 13; g75 4/8 32; w74 700; km 7/73 1
printing: yb75 240; g75 1/8 13; w74 700; g73 9/22 8; km 7/73 1
release: yb75 239-40; yb73 139

TUBERCULOSIS
w74 133

TUMBLEBUG
g72 11/22 20-1

TUMORS
g74 8/8 31; g74 9/8 18-19

TUNISIA
Jehovah's witnesses: yb76 26-7; yb75 24-5; yb74 24-5; yb73 24-5; yb72 34-5
population: yb73 24; yb72 34

TUNNEL
Argentina: g71 8/22 23
Britain-France: g74 5/22 31

TURBAN
kj 228-9

TURKEY
Bosporus Bridge: g74 4/22 25-6
constitution: g73 9/8 14-15
earthquakes: g75 11/8 30
Jehovah's witnesses: km 9/75 8; g74 2/8 29; g73 3/22 15; g73 6/8 29; g73 9/8 12-16; w72 381; g71 11/8 12-15
Military Supreme Court: g73 9/8 12-15
war with Cyprus: g74 10/22 12-15

TURKS AND CAICOS ISLANDS
Jehovah's witnesses: yb76 24-5; yb75 24-5

TURNING AROUND
meaning of term: tp 182-3

TURTLE
ts 24-5; g71 12/8 30

TUTOR
Law covenant: w72 127

TWENTY-FOUR OLDER PERSONS
identified: w73 62

TWILIGHT
discussion: g71 3/8 21-2

TWO-HORNED BEAST
(SEE BEASTS)

2,520 YEARS
(SEE APPOINTED TIMES OF THE NATIONS)

TWO WITNESSES
identified (Re 11:3): pm 46
spirit of life enters them: pm 47-52
wild beast conquers and kills them: pm 46-7

TYNDALE, WILLIAM
w74 743-4

TYPEWRITERS
dance movements: g74 4/8 30
new keyboard: g75 9/8 31

TYPHOID
w74 132

TYPHOONS
Hong Kong: g71 10/22 29
Japan: yb73 227-8

TYRE
king of: ts 82
siege by Alexander the Great: pm 263, 265
siege by Nebuchadnezzar: pm 263
reward from Jehovah: w75 714

UGANDA
Jehovah's witnesses: yb76 26-7, 107, 121; yb75 26-7; yb74 13, 26-7; yb73 26-7; yb72 36-7
marriage: w73 151
population: yb73 26; yb72 36

ULCERS
g74 6/8 29

UNASSIGNED TERRITORY
coverage: yb75 226-7; km 10/74 1
France: w74 746

UNCLEANNESS
Bath-sheba: w73 479
ceremonial: pm 108-10
Greek word: w73 575-6
moral: w74 160; w73 592-6
spiritual: w75 426-9

UNCOVERED (Booklet)
yb75 155

UNDERGROUND
preaching activity: yb74 55, 112-15; yb72 85-8, 93, 136, 139-41, 155-6, 163

UNDERSTANDING
increasing: w74 114-15
meaning of term: w71 137

UNDESERVED KINDNESS
congregation of God: w71 703-4
discussion: w73 371-3
Jehovah to man: w74 189-91; w73 464-6; w72 297-302

UNEMPLOYMENT
Australia: g75 3/22 7-8
Canada: g71 3/22 30
clergy: g72 11/8 29
college graduates: g71 12/22 29
coping with: g75 2/22 4; g75 3/22 8-9; g75 5/8 14-15; g75 7/8 3-6
discussion: g75 3/22 7-9; g75 5/8 13-15
doctors of philosophy: g75 4/8 29-30
effect on people: g75 3/22 8-9; g75 12/22 29
four-day week to prevent: g75 7/22 29
France: g75 3/22 8
Germany: g75 11/22 30
Great Britain: g75 3/22 8; g72 1/8 29; g72 4/8 29
Great Depression: g75 3/22 8
Indonesia: g75 5/8 13
insurance: g75 3/22 8-9
military spending: g75 7/8 30
preference for: g75 11/22 30
proper view: g75 2/22 4; g71 12/22 4
public service employment program: g75 5/8 13
self-employment suggestions: g75 8/22 9-11
statistics: g75 3/22 7; g75 5/8 13; g71 10/8 4, 8-9
temporary pioneering during: km 4/75 4
United States: g75 3/22 7; g75 5/22 3; g75 7/8 3; g75 11/22 30; g71 1/8 30; g71 8/8 31
warning: g71 7/8 29
world: g75 11/8 30

UNION OF SOVIET SOCIALIST REPUBLICS
(SEE SOVIET UNION)

UNITARIAN CHURCH
striptease dancer: g75 6/22 30-1
UNITED ARAB REPUBLIC
Jehovah's witnesses: w72 381-2, 525; w71 114, 117-18
Suez Canal: g74 10/22 16-18
war with Israel: g74 10/22 16-17
(SEE ALSO EGYPT)
UNITED CHURCH
w74 555; g74 8/8 31
UNITED NATIONS
agencies of: w74 547
Anglo-American support: w71 723-4; kj 351
comments by clergy in support: w74 135; g73 2/8 29
comments in support: g74 5/8 29; g74 10/22 29
comments on inabilities: g74 1/22 29; g74 6/22 8; g73 10/8 30; g72 3/8 5-7
Communist China: w74 549; g72 3/8 7; g72 10/8 4, 12; g71 1/8 29; g71 6/22 29; g71 12/8 29
corruption: g73 3/8 20
crime control: g73 1/8 30-1
discussion: w74 547-52; g72 3/8 5-7
"disgusting thing": w75 743-4; w74 718; ka 311-13, 316
eighth world power: sl 237, 271, 318; g75 2/8 8; w74 718; ka 310-13, 317, 394; kj 351
environment conference: g72 9/22 29
establishment: sl 251; w74 547-8; w71 723, 725
failure: w74 611-12; hu 4-5; g74 6/22 8-9; g74 12/8 9; w72 613, 617; dn 4; w71 561
finances: g72 1/8 29; g72 3/8 7; g72 12/22 29
General Assembly: w74 548-9
International Women's Conference: g75 8/22 29
membership: w75 612, 690; sl 9, 237, 339; og 4; g75 5/8 10; g75 7/22 6; w74 548-9, 611; hu 4; g73 11/8 30; w72 626, 741; pm 243, 326; dn 21; kj 351
"peace and security": g75 2/8 9
period of decline: w74 547-9
poor nations: g74 12/8 8-9
problems facing: w74 550-1
purpose: w74 547, 550
religion's destruction: g75 7/22 8; w74 719
rising prestige: w74 550-1
Security Council: w74 548
symbolic representation: w75 743-4; sl 247; g75 2/8 8-9; w74 552, 718; w73 676; g72 10/8 22; w71 723; kj 258, 363-4
United States role: w74 548-9
veto: g72 3/8 5
weaknesses: w74 547-9
(SEE ALSO LEAGUE OF NATIONS)
UNITED STATES OF AMERICA
advertising: g75 4/22 29
agriculture: g74 11/22 29; g71 7/8 8
Air Force Association Convention: g75 11/22 30
airline fatalities: g75 1/22 31
alcoholism: g75 2/8 16-18; w74 451, 453; g72 5/22 31; g72 9/22 30; g71 6/22 3-5; g71 8/22 26
aqueducts: g73 1/8 15
armaments:
cost per person: g75 10/22 30
arms race: g74 11/8 3-7
beverages: g73 1/8 31
Bible reading: w75 200
bicycles: g73 6/22 25-7
birth statistics: g72 4/22 30
business:
big corporations: g75 3/8 29; g75 12/8 30
cancer: g74 1/8 30; g74 1/22 30; g74 9/8 17-18
Catholic church: g74 6/22 30; g71 7/22 7
cities: g71 9/8 29
Communism's growth: g71 7/8 5-9
conditions in: g74 9/8 3-4
Constitution:
Bill of Rights: g72 7/8 10-12
Fourth Amendment: g71 11/8 5
Thirteenth Amendment: g71 11/8 5
crime: w75 35; g75 1/22 31; g75 3/22 30; g75 5/8 30-1; g75 5/22 30; g75 6/8 30; g75 10/22 29; g75 11/8 29-30; g75 11/22 3-11; w74 99, 102, 341; g74 3/8 13, 16; g74 5/22 29; g74 11/22 29; g73 9/22 31; g73 10/8 11, 21; g73 11/8 30; w72 614; g72 4/22 31; g72 6/22 31; g72 8/22 29; g72 10/8 29-30; g71 2/8 29-30; g71 8/8 30; g71 10/22 30
capital punishment: g72 8/22 29
women: w75 464
death statistics: g74 5/22 16
Death Valley: g71 2/8 7-8
debt: g75 5/22 4; g75 6/8 11; g75 9/22 30
decline of confidence: g75 12/8 30
disasters: g74 6/8 8-10; g72 4/8 29; g72 8/8 24-6; w71 611
divorce: g74 1/22 31; g74 4/22 3-4; g74 5/22 3; g74 9/8 4; g73 10/8 11; g72 12/8 29; w71 309; g71 4/8 30
doctors:
women: g75 11/22 31
drugs: g75 2/22 30; g75 11/8 30; g73 2/8 30; g73 12/8 3-6; g71 4/8 16; g71 9/8 29
earthquake: g71 3/22 29; g71 4/8 8-11
economy: g74 3/22 29; g74 11/8 30; g73 1/8 30; g73 4/8 29; g73 5/8 21-3; g73 8/8 29; g73 8/22 30; g73 11/22 8-10; g73 12/22 18-22; g71 10/8 30
agriculture: g74 6/22 29; g74 7/22 3-4; g73 6/22 5-6, 16-17, 30
cost of living: w74 341
cost of raw materials: g74 11/22 18-20
credit cards: g71 2/8 29
distribution of wealth: g74 6/22 9
effect of materials shortage: g74 11/22 16-20
family income: g73 12/8 29
food costs: w74 243; g74 3/8 29; g73 6/22 5, 17, 30; g73 11/22 9-10; g72 10/8 30
foreign investments: g72 6/22 31
inflation: g74 1/22 3, 5; g73 10/8 8-10; g73 10/22 30; g73 11/22 8-10; g73 12/8 29; g73 12/22 18-22
military spending: g75 7/8 30
money: g74 3/8 29; g74 3/22 30; g74 5/8 29; g73 5/8 21-3; g73 7/8 29; g73 12/22 18-22; g72 1/8 29; g71 2/8 29; g71 8/22 3-9; g71 10/22 21-4; g71 11/22 31
national debt: g75 1/22 20; g73 12/22 18; g71 2/8 29
per capita income: w72 616
poverty: w75 67-9; g74 10/8 15; g73 11/22 8-9; g72 5/22 16
rating of U.S. products: g75 10/22 30
recession: g71 1/8 30
stock market: w74 71; g74 2/8 30; g74 11/8 29
emigration: g71 2/8 29
energy consumption: g75 4/8 30
energy crisis: g74 1/8 3-8, 29; g74 2/22 16-20, 29
farms: g74 10/8 30; g73 6/22 16-17; g71 5/22 29
fires: g72 10/8 31; g71 12/8 12-17
fishing: g74 2/22 24
flag: g71 9/8 12, 14-15
food shortage: g74 11/22 29; g73 6/22 5-6, 16-17
fuel shortage: g72 10/22 29
gambling: g75 2/8 30; g75 8/22 31; w74 135, 579-81
gardens: g74 5/22 9
gasoline: g74 7/8 29; g73 6/8 3-4
gold supply: g71 8/22 5; g71 10/22 22-3
government:
clergy in Congress: g73 4/8 29
confidence loss: g72 1/8 29
Congressmen's religions: g73 4/8 29
corruption: g73 9/22 29; g73 11/8 3-5
cost of printing money: g75 7/8 31
crisis: g74 4/8 4
elections: g73 1/8 30
expenditures for defense: g73 12/22 18; g71 8/22 6-8
finances: g75 9/22 30; g73 12/22 18-22; g72 1/8 29; g71 2/8 29; g71 3/22 30; g71 8/22 3-9; g71 10/22 21-4
inauguration: g74 1/22 30; g74 9/22 29; g73 3/8 29
influence growth: g71 6/22 29
president: g73 2/22 31
presidential limousine: g72 10/8 30
president's message: g71 9/8 30
secretary of state's armored car: g75 3/22 29
Supreme Court: g71 9/22 29
handicrafts: g75 1/8 31
health: g75 10/22 29; g74 9/22 3-4; g73 1/22 4; g71 7/22 31
highways: g71 4/22 17
history: g71 5/22 13-16
housing: g74 2/8 30

illegitimate births: g72 8/22 8-9
Indians: g71 5/22 16
industry: g74 11/22 17-20; g71 7/8 8
iron: g74 11/22 17
Jehovah's witnesses: yb76 24-5; yb75 24-5, 34-256; g75 11/8 29; km 5/75 1; km 11/75 1; yb74 24-5, 258; g74 6/8 16-20; km 6/74 1, 3; w73 42; yb73 24-5; g73 2/22 8; yb72 34-5; g72 8/22 19-23
 conventions: w75 94-5, 349-51, 624-30; g75 10/22 16-23; g73 2/8 14-15
 number of congregations: km 11/75 4
 number of new congregations: km 8/75 8
 persecution: yb75 169-73, 175-91; w73 117, 120-2; g72 7/8 10-12; w71 22, 379, 520-1, 722, 730
 service experiences: g73 2/8 14-15; g73 2/22 8-10; w72 338
land area:
 for farming: g74 7/22 7
 per person: g71 5/22 29
 urban development: g71 1/8 7
leisure time: w74 273; g73 10/8 31
life-span:
 Hawaii: g75 10/22 30
mailbox use: g75 10/22 30
metric system: g74 8/8 17-18
military: g75 3/22 30; g74 2/8 30; g73 11/8 30; g73 12/22 18-20; g72 10/8 9-10; g71 2/8 29; g71 6/22 29; g71 7/8 30
mineral resources: g74 11/22 16-20
minerals: g74 1/22 6
moonshine whiskey: g75 11/8 31
music:
 obscene lyrics: g75 8/22 30
newspapers: g72 4/8 29
New York city:
 business dishonesty: g75 2/8 30
 crime: g75 11/22 5-10; g73 1/8 30; g73 11/8 30; g72 4/8 3; g72 7/8 18; g72 9/22 4; g72 10/8 29-30; g71 5/8 30-1; g71 8/22 29
 dog bites: g74 9/8 31
 drugs: g73 9/22 29; g73 12/8 4, 6
 electricity: g72 8/8 13-15
 employment: g75 7/22 29
 financial crisis: g75 7/8 31
 gambling: w74 579-80
 garbage: g74 11/22 31
 graffiti: g74 8/22 3-4; g73 7/8 30
 hospitals: g71 10/22 31
 Jehovah's witnesses: yb75 142; km 9/75 1; pm 254
 pigeons: g74 12/8 30
 police: g75 9/22 30; g72 3/22 3
 pollution: g74 8/22 30-1; g73 9/8 23
 population: g73 4/8 30
 private security guards: g75 9/22 30
 religion: w75 631
 restaurants: g71 9/8 30
 skyscrapers: g74 2/8 21
 vandalism: g75 2/8 29-30
 water supply: g73 1/8 15
 welfare: g73 7/22 24; w72 205; g71 6/22 29
 World Trade Center: g74 2/8 20-3
 young alcoholics: w74 451
number of elderly persons: g75 11/8 30-1
oil: g74 1/8 4-8; g74 11/22 19, 30
oil consumption: g74 6/22 29; g74 8/8 9
oil import: g74 1/8 6-8; g74 2/8 29; g74 2/22 16, 19-20; g74 8/8 9-10; g73 10/8 9
passport oath: g72 10/8 29
pets: g72 5/8 31
pollution: g71 1/8 6-7
population: yb73 24; yb72 34
 Indians: g71 12/8 29
power failure: g74 3/8 17-18
prisons: g72 1/8 5-15
proportion of unmarried men to women: g75 4/22 31
racial prejudice: w74 707-10
relations with—
 Communist China: g74 1/22 30; g73 11/8 30; g71 9/8 29
 Great Britain: g74 2/8 30
 Soviet Union: g74 4/8 5; g72 10/8 5-6, 29
religion: w75 200; g75 1/22 7; g75 11/8 29; w74 360; g74 1/22 30; g73 2/22 3-10; w71 101; g71 7/22 7
 church finances: g75 9/8 24-6
 church membership: w75 323-4; g75 10/22 29
riots: g73 2/8 30
runaways:
 adults: g75 10/22 29
schools: g75 9/8 30
scientists leave: g71 2/8 30
segregation: g73 2/22 4-5
Selective Service registration: g75 5/22 31
sight-seeing: g73 5/8 31
slavery: w74 709; g73 2/22 4
space achievements: g73 1/22 29; g73 5/22 3-6, 9-10, 12-13, 30; g73 8/8 29-30; g72 2/22 31; w71 303, 555; g71 9/22 29; g71 11/22 5-8
sports:
 high-paid athletes: g75 6/8 31
taxes: g74 2/8 30; g74 2/22 27-8; g74 11/8 30; g73 5/22 30-1; g72 5/22 29; g71 5/22 29
television: g75 11/8 30; w74 273, 360; g74 9/8 8-9
Texas High Plains: g75 3/8 29
tourism: g75 11/22 31
transportation: g74 2/22 29
unemployment: g75 3/22 7-8; g75 5/8 13; g75 5/22 3; g75 7/8 3; g71 1/8 30; g71 8/8 31; g71 10/8 4, 9
venereal disease: g73 5/22 30; g71 8/22 29
war: g73 3/22 29
 Indochina: g72 3/8 31
 Vietnam: g73 1/22 29; g72 10/8 3-4; g71 7/22 7; g71 9/8 29
Washington, D.C.: g71 2/8 29-30
 crime: g75 11/22 29
waste: g75 9/22 29; g75 12/8 30; g74 2/22 29
water consumption: g74 11/22 20
weapons: w75 487; g74 11/8 3-6
weather: g75 3/8 3-4
welfare: w72 615-16; g71 1/8 30; g71 3/22 30; g71 6/22 29
what concerns Americans most: g75 7/22 30
women: g75 10/22 29; g75 12/22 29-30
world power: w71 717-18, 720-4, 728

UNITY

barriers: w71 305-8
basis: w74 616; hu 12-13; w71 300-2
Christ's role: w74 618-19; hu 17-18
discussion: w73 280-3; w71 297-308
early Christians: w74 540, 542-3; w71 549-50
family: yb72 246-7
importance: w74 540, 543
Jehovah's witnesses: w74 44, 207, 521, 712-14; g74 9/8 6-7; g74 11/8 21; w73 37-8, 68; kj 343-4, 346-8
 congregational: w73 732-3
 international: g74 10/8 22; w73 281, 283; g72 2/8 26
 interracial: g74 6/8 19; w73 37; w71 122-7; g71 3/22 24-6; g71 10/22 12-13
lack in world: w74 548-9; g74 6/22 8-9, 23-4, 26; g74 11/8 29-30; w71 299-300
lack in worldly religion: g72 7/22 30; w71 297-8
New Order: w74 623; hu 28
with Jehovah:
 Christ's role: ts 131-2

UNIVERSAL ORGANIZATION

(SEE JEHOVAH'S ORGANIZATION)

UNIVERSAL SOVEREIGNTY

clarification of belief: yb75 191-2
issue raised: w75 617-18; sl 61-2; fu 16-17; og 16-18; w74 595-6; g74 10/22 7-8; tp 47-54; w71 267-8, 539
Jehovah's: w75 622-3; og 26-9
reason issue not settled at once: tp 53-7; g72 10/22 11-12; g72 12/8 24-5; w71 268-9, 487-8
settlement of issue: sl 279-81, 345, 347; w74 345-8; po 185-6, 191; pm 382-3, 393; w71 244
"sign" of Jehovah's: sl 126
upholding the issue: w75 615-16, 619; sl 81, 253, 267-8, 271, 344, 368; og 12-15, 21
(SEE ALSO ISSUE OF UNIVERSAL SOVEREIGNTY, JEHOVAH)

UNIVERSE

asteroids: g75 8/22 14-15
"black holes": g74 1/8 14
constellations: g75 6/22 18
discussion: g75 6/22 16-19
elements: g71 12/22 23
galaxies: g75 6/22 17-19; g75 8/22 31; g71 2/22 31; g71 8/8 4
 number of: g75 6/22 17
largest known object: g75 4/8 30
Milky Way: g75 6/22 17-18; g72 9/22 31
mysteries: g74 1/8 12-15
order and unity: g75 6/22 18; g74 5/22 22; w73 35-6; g71 8/8 3-7
pulsars: g74 1/8 14; g72 9/22 31
quasars: g74 1/8 13-14; g71 5/8 29; g71 6/8 29
size: g75 6/22 16-17; g74 1/8 12
solar system: g74 1/8 12-13; g71 8/8 4
 Jupiter: g75 8/22 13-14
 Mars: g75 8/22 14
 Mercury: g75 8/22 13
 Saturn: g75 8/22 15-16

sun: g75 8/22 16; g71 6/22 9; g71 12/22 29
Venus: g75 8/22 12-13; g75 12/22 29; g71 3/8 30-1
stars: g75 8/22 31; g71 1/8 8
theories on origin: w75 200; g75 6/22 19; g75 12/22 29
(SEE ALSO ASTRONOMY, CREATION, SOLAR SYSTEM)

UNKINDNESS
response to: g75 6/8 3-4

UNSELFISHNESS
discussion: g72 12/22 3-4
showing: g74 6/8 10; w73 99-100; g72 5/22 23
teaching children: g75 6/8 14-16

UPPER VOLTA
Jehovah's witnesses: yb76 26-7; yb75 26-7; yb74 9, 26-7; yb73 26-7; yb72 36-7
population: yb73 26; yb72 36

URIM AND THUMMIM
w74 157

URUGUAY
food shortage: g72 10/8 30
government: g72 6/22 24-6
holidays: g73 8/8 30-1
Jehovah's witnesses: yb76 30-1; yb75 30-1; w74 207; yb74 30-1; yb73 30-1; yb72 40-1
population: yb73 30; yb72 40
religion: g72 6/22 24-6

UZZAH
presumptuousness: w73 370

UZZIAH (Azariah) (King of Judah)
cause of leprosy: g71 1/8 4

VACATIONS
wise use: w74 374

VACCINATIONS
babies: g73 2/22 17
Christian view: w74 351
smallpox: g72 8/22 31

VALLEY
Indus Valley: ts 44-5

VALLEY OF GOG'S CROWD
kj 374-5, 377

VALLEY OF HINNOM
discussion: ts 111, 113-15; bi8 1355
Topheth: bi8 1355

VAN AMBURGH, W. E.
yb75 48, 80, 93, 103-4, 106, 111, 116, 201, 246

VANDALISM
causes: g74 8/22 4-6
church: g75 2/8 31
construction sites: g74 6/8 14-15
cost statistics: g74 8/22 4; g73 3/22 5-6
increase: g73 3/22 5-6; g71 4/22 31
injuries from: g74 8/22 3
juvenile delinquency: g74 2/8 5; g74 8/22 3-6; g73 3/22 5-6
New York city: g75 2/8 29-30
schools: g75 5/22 29
(SEE ALSO CRIME, JUVENILE DELINQUENCY, MORAL BREAKDOWN)

VARIETY
congregation: w71 664-5
in living things: g74 9/22 23-4
personalities:
when perfect: ts 144
provided by Jehovah: ts 145-6

VASHTI
w71 173, 175

VATICAN
artworks: g75 1/8 22-4
austerity measures: g75 4/8 29; g75 9/8 24
bad investments: w75 263
birth control: g74 10/22 29
bishops addicted to smoking: g75 1/22 30
Communism: w74 71, 341; g74 11/22 30; g73 12/22 29
concordat with Hitler: w75 398
concordat with Mussolini (Lateran Treaty): w75 364; g74 9/22 13, 15
discussion: g75 1/8 21-4
Helsinki peace conference: g75 11/8 3
mercy killing: w75 294
military organizations: g75 5/22 13-14
Nazi atrocities: g75 2/22 17-19
Nazi criminals aided: w75 48
Palatine Guard: g75 5/22 13-17
radio: g75 8/8 29
St. Peter's: g75 1/8 21-3
Synod of bishops: w74 742; g74 11/22 30; g74 12/8 30; g74 12/22 29
wealth: w75 263
(SEE ALSO POPES, ROMAN CATHOLIC CHURCH)

V. D. M. QUESTIONNAIRE
yb75 86-7

VEGETATION
carbohydrates: g73 7/8 7
design manifests intelligence: w71 152
shrubs: g75 5/8 29
vegetable diet: g75 2/8 30

VENEREAL DISEASES
anal sex: w75 48
cause: w74 14
children: g72 2/8 17, 19; g71 11/8 31
discussion: g75 5/8 5-8; g72 2/8 17-20
gonorrhea: w75 48; g75 5/8 5-8; g75 5/22 31; w74 14, 424; g74 1/8 30-1; g74 1/22 28; g74 4/22 30; g74 8/8 30; g73 3/8 29; g73 5/22 30; g73 6/8 30; g72 2/8 17-18; g72 7/22 30; g72 10/22 31; g72 12/8 29; g71 5/8 30; g71 7/8 31; g71 8/22 29
herpes-virus: w75 48; g75 5/8 5, 7-8; w74 424; g74 10/8 29-30
homosexuality: w75 364; g73 4/22 31; g72 2/8 18; g72 8/22 29
increase: g75 5/22 31; g75 7/22 29; w74 14; g74 1/22 28; g74 8/8 30; g74 9/22 30; g73 5/8 4; g73 5/22 30; g73 9/22 30-1; w72 219, 339; g72 1/8 29; g72 2/8 17; g72 10/22 31; g71 1/8 30; g71 1/22 29; g71 3/22 30; g71 5/8 30; g71 9/8 29; g71 11/22 29; g71 12/8 30
oral sex: w75 48; w74 424
physical effects: w74 319; g74 10/8 29-30
pornography: g71 1/22 18
soldiers: g74 3/22 31
syphilis: g75 5/8 6-8; g74 2/8 14; g74 5/22 18; g73 5/22 30; g72 2/8 17-18, 20; g72 10/22 31; g71 5/8 30
treatment: g72 2/8 18
(SEE ALSO MORAL BREAKDOWN)

VENEZUELA
economy: g74 9/22 30
Jehovah's witnesses: yb76 30-1; yb75 30-1; yb74 30-1; g74 5/8 25-6; yb73 30-1; yb72 40-1
population: yb73 30; yb72 40

VENGEANCE
Christians: w72 68-9; w71 372-3, 579-80; te 131-3

VENUS
planet: g75 8/22 12-13; g75 12/22 29; g74 5/22 30; g73 5/22 11-12; g72 9/8 29; g71 3/8 30-1

VESPASIAN
w74 426-7

VESTIGIAL ORGANS
g74 2/8 16

VICTORY
Christ's over world: w74 61; w73 648-56
Christians' over world: yb74 252-3; w73 656-61
Divine: w73 611-12, 615-16, 623-4; dy 3-5, 11-13, 28
"Pyrrhic victory": g74 7/8 3

VIETNAM
Catholics in politics: g75 10/8 30; g71 3/8 30
defoliation sprays: g71 2/22 30
Jehovah's witnesses: yb76 15-16, 26-7; yb75 30-1; yb74 19-20, 30-1; yb73 30-1; g73 11/8 26; yb72 40-1
population: yb73 30; yb72 40
religion: g71 8/22 29
war: g72 5/22 7
casualties: g73 1/22 29
Catholics: w75 400; g75 6/22 30
Christendom: g72 4/22 5-9; g71 8/22 30
clergy: g71 7/22 7; g71 9/8 31
cost: g72 10/8 3-4; g71 6/22 29; g71 9/8 29; g71 12/8 29-30
crater holes: g72 10/8 4
crimes: g71 2/22 30
drug addiction: g71 6/8 31; g71 6/22 29
quantity of bombs dropped: w75 634

VILCABAMBA
g75 3/8 7-8

VINDICATION (Books)
sl 143; yb75 156; w72 47, 637; w71 183; kj 52, 65, 171-2

VINDICATION (Jehovah's)
importance: kj 7-8, 378
role of humans: ka 408-9

VIOLENCE
causes: g75 4/8 6-7; g74 6/22 13-14; g74 11/8 30; w73 675; g73 3/22 3-4
Christian's attitude toward: w74 517, 520, 714; g74 3/8 4
cost: g73 11/8 30
entertainment: g74 6/22 13-14; tp 155-6
grounds for divorce: w75 286-8
modern-day world: g75 5/22 8; g75 12/22 30; g74 2/8 5; g74 6/22 30-1; g74 8/8 29; g74 9/8 4, 10, 30; g74 11/22 20, 29; g73 9/8 29-30; g73 11/8 30; g72 5/8 29; g71 2/22 16-18; g71 4/22 30; g71 5/22 30-1; g71 6/8 4-5, 17-20; g71 8/8 10-12
 children: g74 7/8 30-1
 churches: w72 391, 394; g72 4/22 17; w71 420, 740; g71 2/22 3-6, 30; g71 7/8 30
 schools: g75 5/8 17-18; g75 5/22 29; g75 9/8 30
 sports events: g75 5/8 30; g75 6/22 29
protection against: g75 9/8 27-8; w74 518-20
television: g74 9/8 10-11
(SEE ALSO MORAL BREAKDOWN)

VIOLIN
discussion: g71 2/22 20-3

VIPER
g72 10/22 30

VIRGIN(S)
birth of Jesus: g71 12/22 5-8
congregation of God: w74 431-2
Jesus' parable of ten virgins: w75 593; w74 430-2; ka 169-83, 189-206, 211
 bridegroom: ka 171
 discreet virgins: w74 506, 508-9
 door closed: w74 508-9
 foolish virgins: w74 506, 508-9; ka 194-200
 lamps: w74 478-9, 506
 oil: w74 479, 506, 508; ka 178-9, 195
 purpose: w74 430; ka 176
 significance of number: w74 478; ka 170
 slept: w74 479-80, 506-8
mythology: g71 12/22 8

VIRGIN ISLANDS (British)
Jehovah's witnesses: yb76 28-9; yb75 28-9; yb74 28-9; yb73 28-9; yb72 38-9
population: yb73 28; yb72 38

VIRGIN ISLANDS (U.S.)
Jehovah's witnesses: yb76 28-9; yb75 28-9; yb74 28-9; yb73 28-9; yb72 38-9
population: yb73 28; yb72 38

VIRUS
diseases: g73 12/22 8-9; g71 8/8 29
hepatitis: g75 6/8 29
scientists reassemble: g75 12/8 21

VISION(S)
Daniel: kj 49-50, 233-4
Ezekiel: w72 42-54, 101-4, 152-3, 186, 253, 508-10, 585-7, 632-8, 725; kj 36-49, 210-12, 336-43, 383-406
John (book of Revelation): kj 50
Paul: sl 131-4
transfiguration: w74 296-9
young men (Joe 2:28): w71 32
Zechariah: pm 127-46, 153-228

VITAMINS
A: g71 6/8 10
B: g71 6/8 10
C: g74 12/22 20; g73 12/22 10; g72 7/8 21, 23; g72 11/22 30; g71 1/8 29-30; g71 6/8 10-11
D: g71 3/22 28
E: g72 6/8 30; g71 6/8 10-11
K: w75 135
air pollution: g71 6/8 9-11
hyperactivity: g72 8/8 31
needs vary: g74 2/22 9
organic derivatives: w72 63-4
sale regulated: g73 9/22 30
therapy for mental illness: g75 4/22 14
(SEE ALSO FOOD, HEALTH)

VOCABULARY
effect of television: g74 9/8 8-9
English language: g75 1/8 29; g71 12/22 20-3
increasing: sg 55-6
value of good: sg 6-8

VOICE
anatomy: sg 64-5
demons: ts 74, 78, 86-8
discussion: g72 1/22 10-12
Greek word: w72 160
improvement: g72 1/22 10-12; sg 63-8
reflects person: g71 3/8 18
sheep know shepherd's: w75 432

VOLCANOES
benefits: g75 11/22 25; g74 3/22 30
flames: g75 11/22 25
gases: g75 11/22 24-5
Guatemala: g75 11/22 24-5
habitat for animal life: g71 12/22 25-6
Iceland: g73 3/22 31; g73 5/22 19-20
Krakatoa: g75 12/22 4-5
Mt. Vesuvius: g71 2/8 20
Nicaragua: yb72 177-8
predicting eruptions: g71 9/22 31
Zaïre: g75 7/8 22-4

VOLTAIRE
g75 10/8 9

VOLUME
prayer: km 1/72 8
public speaking: sg 116-19

VOLUNTEER SERVICE
assembly halls: g74 6/8 16-20
building branch office: g74 7/22 16
Watch Tower conventions: g72 10/22 21-2

VOODOOISM
w75 172; g74 1/8 30; w73 483, 697-701

VOWS
discussion: w73 606-8
fulfilling vows made: w73 607-8
Jephthah's: w74 278
marriage: w74 275; w71 309-10
Scriptural definition: w73 606-8
wife's vow: w73 607

WAGONS
use in field service: yb73 218

WAITING
upon Jehovah: w73 474-7

WAKES
Bible view: g74 12/8 26
(SEE ALSO FUNERALS, MOURNING)

WALKING
in Jehovah's name: w73 31; yb73 4-5, 260-1
physical: g73 8/22 24-7; g72 3/22 22-3; g72 6/8 20
 injuries from stepping on objects: g75 9/8 31

WALRUS
g74 9/8 30

WAR
Armageddon: g74 11/8 7-8; w73 296-7; w71 623-4; kj 363-8, 372-3, 376-7
casualties: g71 10/8 5
causes: g74 4/8 30; tp 12-13; g72 10/8 13, 17; w71 54-5
children: g74 7/8 30-1
China: w72 444
Christendom's responsibility: w74 217, 517; g72 4/22 7-17; g72 10/8 14; g72 10/22 29; kj 78, 104-5, 152-3, 158, 258-9; g71 8/22 30
Christian view: w74 517, 520; w73 549; g72 4/22 21
clergy:
 support of war: g75 2/22 18-23; g75 7/8 30; w74 217; ts 46; g74 10/22 13-14; w73 549; g73 5/8 23; w72 626-7, 748-9, 760; pm 215-16, 307-8; g72 4/22 5-17; g72 6/8 26; g72 10/8 7; g72 10/22 29; g72 12/8 29; w71 215, 463, 644, 647
cost: tp 14; g73 12/22 18-19; g71 8/22 6-8; g71 10/8 5, 24; g71 12/8 29-30
early Christians: g73 5/8 23; g72 4/22 21-2
effect on society: w75 559
Eighty-Year War: g72 9/22 21-5
end: w71 100; g71 10/8 24
horrors of: g74 10/22 12, 15
Indochina: g72 3/8 31; g72 3/22 31
Ireland: g72 10/22 29
Korea: w71 188-9
number of, since World War II: w75 634
number of wars: g72 3/8 6; g71 4/22 20
"Opium War": g75 5/8 9-12
prayers: yb75 119; g75 2/22 20
religions 'justify': ts 36, 46
sign of last days: w75 633-4
Thirty Years' War: g72 4/22 13; g71 6/22 16-19
Vietnam: g73 1/22 29; g72 4/22 5-9; g72 5/22 7; g72 10/8 3, 4; g71 2/22 30; g71 6/22 29; g71 7/22 7; g71 9/8 29; g71 12/8 29-30
 Catholics: w75 400; g75 6/22 30
weapons: sl 9
 arms race: g74 11/8 3-7; g74 12/8 30; g73 7/8 30; g73 11/8 30; w72 613; g72 10/8 3, 5, 10, 29; g71 7/8 6-8
 church investments: g72 2/22 30
 cost: w75 634; g75 1/8 30; g75 4/8 29; g74 10/8 6; g74 11/8 6-7; g74 12/8 8; g73 9/8 29; g73 10/8 28-9; g72 9/8 29; g72 10/8 3, 4; g71 6/22 29; g71 8/22 6
 destructive power: g74 11/8 4-5; g72 10/8 4, 9-10; g71 7/8 6-7

germ warfare: g73 3/8 10
limitation talks: g74 11/8 3
missiles: w75 487; g72 10/8 10
nuclear: g73 1/8 30
sale: g74 11/8 6; g73 7/22 30
stockpile: w75 487; g74 11/8 3-6
submarines: g72 10/8 9-10
testing: g71 2/8 29; g71 4/22 16, 30; g71 9/8 30; g71 12/22 29
threat to human existence: g72 10/8 4, 10; g71 1/22 30; g71 5/22 31
women: g72 5/22 5-7
worldly comments on: g73 10/8 30; g71 4/22 30
years of war and of peace: tp 11; g73 3/22 29; w71 299-300; g71 4/22 20
(SEE ALSO ARMAGEDDON)

WARFARE (Spiritual)
discussion: w74 753-5, 762-3
equipment: w73 159-60

WAR IN HEAVEN
length: w73 617; dy 15
results: w73 616-19; dy 14-18; kj 353

WARNING
Armageddon's approach: w72 56-7, 726-9
earthquake: g75 4/22 29; g71 2/22 30-1
heeding: w71 611
unheeded (examples): w75 748-9; g75 3/22 24, 26; w71 611; g71 2/8 20

WASHING OF FEET
te 27-9

WASHINGTON, D.C.
Witness convention (1935): ka 267-9; yb73 113; w72 638; pm 78; kj 178
(SEE ALSO CONVENTIONS)

WASTE
fuel: g71 11/22 29
mechanized farming: g75 12/8 30
pollution: g71 4/22 11-12, 21, 28, 30
recycling: g73 1/22 30; g71 10/22 29-30
underground disposal: g71 8/8 31
United States: g74 2/8 31

WATCHES
lasers: g72 8/22 30

WATCHTOWER, THE (Magazine)
Adventist court case: g71 2/8 25-6
"Announcing Jehovah's Kingdom": w74 764
appreciation for: w73 460-1, 563; km 1/72 3-4; w71 94
Catholics quote: w71 254
children's articles: w73 563-4
circulation: g71 4/8 29
distribution: g73 9/22 7
1942-74: yb75 241
experiences with: yb74 41, 70; g74 2/22 5-6; w73 734-5; w72 399; g71 9/22 12
"extra" copies for congregation: km 8/75 8
financing: yb75 38; g75 9/8 26
first issue: yb75 38; w74 507; w73 395; w71 756
printed on Watch Tower presses: yb75 129
format changes: yb75 241
importance of study: w73 460-1
languages:
Afrikaans: yb76 141
Cibemba: yb76 209
German: yb74 67
Portuguese: yb73 38, 41-2, 48-9, 52
Sepedi: yb76 209
Sinhalese: yb76 255
Tamil: yb76 255
Tswana: yb76 209
Zulu: yb76 184
name changes: yb75 241
other sheep: yb75 157
printeries: g73 9/22 10-16
printing while under ban: yb74 113-15, 139-41, 181-2, 201
production: yb75 32, 245; w74 30; yb72 256; w71 29
publication not stopped: yb74 113-15; yb73 124
public reading: km 6/72 4
Russell as editor: w71 756
statement of ownership: w74 669; w73 669; w71 669
study of:
congregational: or 93-4; w71 73
family: w71 106
personal: w71 72-3; sg 21, 36-7, 92
subscription: km 2/72 8
rate: km 7/71 1
use in field service: km 12/74 4
ZG edition (March 1, 1918): yb75 125-6

WATCHTOWER BIBLE AND TRACT SOCIETY OF NEW YORK, INC.
(Formerly called Watchtower Bible and Tract Society, Inc., also People's Pulpit Association)
annual corporation meetings: yb74 259; yb73 259; yb72 259
Bethel home: yb75 243-4
Towers Hotel: w75 631
board of directors: yb74 259; yb73 259; yb72 259
court cases: g74 9/8 15-16
exclusively religious organization: g74 9/8 15-16
factories: yb75 242-3; g73 6/22 21-2; g73 9/22 8-11
legal department: yb75 175
membership: yb74 259; yb73 259
production of literature: yb75 241, 245; yb73 256; yb72 43-4
taxation: g74 9/8 15-16
Watchtower Farms: km 5/75 4; w73 313-15; g73 6/22 20-4
writing to: km 2/71 8

WATCH TOWER BIBLE AND TRACT SOCIETY OF PA.
adjustments in understanding: w72 498-505
annual corporation meetings: yb75 113-14; w74 511, 543; yb74 257-9; w73 500, 540; yb73 257-9; w72 496, 540-1, 702-3; yb72 258; km 8/72 3; w71 725-7, 755-8, 762
Bethel home, South Africa: yb76 186-7, 193
Bible-publishing activities: yb75 213, 218-21; g73 9/22 8; yb72 256; w71 762
board of directors: yb74 258; yb73 258-9; yb72 258; w71 669-70, 757-62
branches: yb76 14, 45, 64, 76, 84, 89, 92-3, 100-1, 135, 161, 166-8, 171, 175, 186-7, 193, 197-8, 226, 233-6, 241, 249-50, 253, 259; w75 27; yb75 30, 257; w73 23; yb73 23, 256; w72 27, 461; yb72 33, 255-6; w71 722, 762
British tax case: yb73 131-3
building programs: w73 315
charter: yb75 40; w71 726-7, 758-60
charter amended: yb75 246-7
electing of officers: yb73 258-9; w71 726
expenses: yb75 258; yb74 255; yb73 256
factories: yb76 186-7, 193; yb75 242-5; w73 538
financial support: w74 282; or 148-9; yb72 255
incorporated (1884): yb76 258; yb75 40; w73 395; w71 757
legal department: yb75 153
membership: yb74 257; yb73 258; g73 9/8 15; w71 726
officers unjustly imprisoned: yb75 104-9, 111-12, 115-17; w72 198, 749; pm 371; w71 22; kj 63
release and exoneration: yb75 116-18
organized (1881): yb75 40
Pittsburgh office: yb75 242
purpose: yb75 40; w74 282; ka 239
relation to governing body: w72 458; w71 755-62
use of radio: yb75 140-4

WATCHTOWER BIBLE SCHOOL OF GILEAD
(SEE GILEAD SCHOOL)

WATCHTOWER FARMS
branch of the Society: km 5/75 4
construction volunteers: w73 315
dedication of new building: w73 313-15
discussion: g73 6/22 20-4
factory: g73 6/22 23-4
farm operations: g73 6/22 23-4
number of workers: yb75 244; km 5/74 4
printing: yb75 244; km 5/74 1, 4; km 4/73 1
purchase: yb75 244
taxation: g74 9/8 15-16

"WATCHTOWER MOVEMENTS"
false: yb76 73-4, 81, 94-7, 118-19, 133, 152, 175-7

WATCH TOWER PUBLICATIONS
appreciation for: km 11/74 3; w73 662
Braille: km 4/75 3
censorship of: yb73 123-4, 127-8
commendation: w71 94

distribution statistics: w75 27, 178; yb75 32, 257-8; km 11/75 1; w73 27; w72 27; yb72 33
experiences:
assembly shipment: yb73 176
interest aroused by literature found: yb74 69
languages: w75 179; yb72 256
literature shipments within the United States: km 7/75 1
older copies: km 11/74 3
production statistics: yb75 32, 241, 245, 259; g75 1/8 13-14; km 5/75 1; w74 26, 30; km 12/74 1; yb73 256; g73 9/22 7-16; yb72 43-4
proper care of: km 11/74 3
proper view of: w74 438
use in study: g74 2/8 9-10

Bibles

1902, *The Emphatic Diaglott:* yb75 213
1942, *Authorized Version:* yb75 218-19
1944, *American Standard Version:* yb75 219
1950, *New World Translation of the Christian Greek Scriptures:* yb76 185; yb75 213, 219
1961, *New World Translation of the Holy Scriptures:* yb75 220
1963, *New World Translation of the Christian Greek Scriptures* (6 languages): yb75 220
New World Translation of the Holy Scriptures (large-print edition): yb75 220
New World Translation of the Holy Scriptures (pocket edition): yb75 220
1971, *New World Translation of the Holy Scriptures* (revised, large-print edition): yb75 220-1; yb72 42; w71 608; g71 10/22 15
1972, *The Bible in Living English:* yb75 221; w72 605-6; g72 10/22 20-1
1974, *New World Translation of the Christian Greek Scriptures,* Japanese: yb75 13
New World Translation of the Holy Scriptures, French: yb75 16

Booklets

1873, *The Object and Manner of the Lord's Return:* yb75 36
1881, *Food for Thinking Christians:* yb75 40; yb73 88-9
Tabernacle Teachings: yb75 40
1898, *The Bible vs. Evolution:* yb75 45; yb73 91
1926, *The Standard for the People:* yb73 111
1927, *Freedom for the Peoples:* yb75 138
1928, *The Peoples Friend:* yb75 139
1931, *The Kingdom, the Hope of the World:* yb75 151-2
1933, *Crisis:* yb74 109-10
Intolerance: yb75 173-4
1935, *Loyalty:* yb75 168-9
1937, *Uncovered:* yb75 155
1938, *Cure:* yb73 115
Face the Facts: yb73 117
1939, *Fascism or Freedom:* yb73 117, 119
Neutrality: yb73 120
1941, *Comfort All That Mourn:* g71 8/8 14
1942, *Jehovah's Witnesses: Who Are They? What Is Their Work?:* yb76 155
1943, *Course in Theocratic Ministry:* yb75 197
Fighting for Liberty on the Home Front: yb73 128
Freedom in the New World: yb73 128
1955, *Christendom or Christianity—Which One Is "the Light of the World"?:* yb75 228
1962, *"The Word"—Who Is He? According to John:* yb75 229
1971, *When All Nations Collide, Head On, with God:* km 10/71 7
1975, *A Secure Future—How You Can Find It:* km 10/75 1, 8; km 12/75 1
Is There a God Who Cares?: km 10/75 1, 8; km 12/75 1
There Is Much More to Life!: km 10/75 1, 8; km 12/75 1

Books

1877, *Three Worlds:* yb75 37; w74 506-7; ka 187
1886, *The Plan of the Ages* (*The Divine Plan of the Ages*): yb75 40; yb74 84
1897, *The Battle of Armageddon:* w74 723
1907, *Daily Heavenly Manna for the Household of Faith:* yb75 147
1914, *Scenario of the Photo-Drama of Creation:* w72 476
1917, *The Finished Mystery:* yb75 90-1, 94-7; yb74 86; w72 147-8, 198; kj 62-3, 318
1920, *Millions Now Living Will Never Die:* yb75 127
1921, *The Harp of God:* yb75 128; yb74 92, 97
1926, *Deliverance:* yb73 111
1927, *Year Book:* w72 158
1928, *Government:* pm 300
1929, *Prophecy:* w72 154; kj 51
1930, *Light* (Books One and Two): w73 54; yb73 225; w71 181-2
1931, *Vindication* (Book One): yb75 156; yb73 112; w72 47, 154, 199, 637; w71 183; kj 52, 65, 171-2
1932, *Vindication* (Book Two): sl 143; kj 65
Vindication (Book Three): kj 65
1936, *Riches:* yb75 148-9
1939, *Salvation:* yb73 119
1941, *Children:* yb75 193
1942, *The New World:* yb73 127
1943, *"The Truth Shall Make You Free":* yb72 79, 172-3
1946, *"Equipped for Every Good Work":* yb76 164; yb75 198
"Let God Be True": yb76 164; yb75 211, 239
1950, *"This Means Everlasting Life":* yb75 239
1951, *What Has Religion Done for Mankind?:* yb75 225; yb72 206
1958, *From Paradise Lost to Paradise Regained:* yb76 192, 252; yb75 217
"Your Will Be Done on Earth": yb75 217
1963, *"All Scripture Is Inspired of God and Beneficial":* yb75 199
"Babylon the Great Has Fallen!" God's Kingdom Rules!: yb75 231
1965, *"Things in Which It Is Impossible for God to Lie":* yb75 239
1966, *Life Everlasting—in Freedom of the Sons of God:* yb75 256
1967, *Did Man Get Here by Evolution or by Creation?:* yb75 239; g74 8/8 30
"Your Word Is a Lamp to My Foot": yb75 254
1968, *The Truth That Leads to Eternal Life:* yb76 227, 255; yb75 239-40; w74 700; yb72 124
1969, *Is the Bible Really the Word of God?:* yb75 222
1970, *Aid to Bible Understanding:* yb75 199
1971, *Aid to Bible Understanding* (Complete): yb72 42; w71 598, 600
Listening to the Great Teacher: yb75 238-9; yb72 42; w71 599
"The Nations Shall Know that I Am Jehovah"—How?: yb72 42; w71 605
Theocratic Ministry School Guidebook: yb72 42; w71 599
1972, *Organization for Kingdom-preaching and Disciple-making:* yb75 249, 254; w72 605; g72 10/22 20
Paradise Restored to Mankind—By Theocracy!: w72 606; g72 10/22 20
Yearbook: w72 158-9
1973, *Comprehensive Concordance of the New World Translation of the Holy Scriptures:* yb75 221, 251; w73 638
God's Kingdom of a Thousand Years Has Approached: yb75 251; w73 638
True Peace and Security—From What Source?: yb75 251; w74 700; w73 638; g73 11/8 18
1974, *God's "Eternal Purpose" Now Triumphing for Man's Good:* yb75 255; w74 639; km 9/74 3-5
Is This Life All There Is?: yb75 255; w74 639; km 9/74 3, 5-6
1975, *Man's Salvation Out of World Distress at Hand:* w75 627; km 9/75 3-6

Magazines

1879, *Zion's Watch Tower and Herald of Christ's Presence:* yb75 38
1919, *Golden Age:* yb75 124-5; kj 64-5, 83
1946, *Awake!:* yb75 241

Monthly Service Instructions

1917, *Bulletin:* yb75 86, 133

Songbooks
1925, *Kingdom Hymns:* w72 477
Tracts
1909, "The Bible Students Monthly" ("Peoples Pulpit") ("Everybody's Paper"): yb75 45-6
1917, "The Bible Students Monthly": yb75 85, 94-5
1918, *Kingdom News* No. 1 ("Religious Intolerance—Pastor Russell's Followers Persecuted Because They Tell the People the Truth—Treatment of Bible Students Smacks of the 'Dark Ages'"): yb75 97-8
Kingdom News No. 2 ("'The Finished Mystery' and Why Suppressed"): yb75 98
Kingdom News No. 3 ("Two Great Battles Raging—Fall of Autocracy Certain. Satanic Strategy Doomed to Failure"): yb75 98
1923, "Proclamation—A Warning to All Christians": yb75 136
1924, "Ecclesiastics Indicted": yb75 136
1925, "Message of Hope": yb75 137
1926, "Testimony to the Rulers of the World": yb75 137
1973, *Kingdom News* No. 16 ("Is Time Running Out for Mankind?"): yb75 252; yb74 252; km 9/73 1, 7-8; km 12/73 1
Kingdom News No. 17 ("Has Religion Betrayed God and Man?"): yb75 252; km 1/74 1; km 2/74 1; km 3/74 1; km 12/73 1
1974, *Kingdom News* No. 18 ("Government by God—Are You for It or Against It?"): yb75 252; km 4/74 1, 3; km 8/74 1
Kingdom News No. 19 ("Is This All There Is to Life?"): km 10/74 7
1975, *Kingdom News* No. 20 ("Would You Welcome Some Good News?"): km 5/75 1
Kingdom News No. 21 ("Your Future—Shaky? or Secure?"): km 10/75 1
use in Volunteer Service work: yb75 45-6

WATCH TOWER PUBLICATIONS INDEX
use in Bible study: sg 35
use of: w72 444

WATCHTOWER STUDY
beginning: yb75 133
Argentina: yb72 73, 76-7
comments by new ones: km 4/75 4
conductor: w72 460; or 78-9
method used: or 93-4
participation: w72 134; sg 91-2
preparation: sg 21, 36-7, 92
readers: km 2/75 4; or 94; km 6/72 4; sg 29-31, 146
(SEE ALSO MEETINGS)

WATER
amount on earth: g71 1/8 7; g71 4/22 8
aqueducts: g73 1/8 13-15
beds: g72 3/22 29-30
composition: g73 7/8 6; g71 7/22 12
consumption in United States: g74 11/22 20
cycle: g72 1/22 17-18; w71 350
density: g74 2/22 13
discussion: g72 1/22 17-19
"drip" irrigation: g75 3/8 29
effect on city level: g72 5/8 29
energy: g74 8/22 21-2
evaporation from ocean: g73 7/8 6-7; g72 1/22 17; g72 2/8 10-11; w71 350
freezing: g72 1/22 19; g71 7/22 12
fresh: w71 350
heat: g71 7/22 12
human body: g72 1/22 18
icebergs: g72 2/8 11
in pipes overnight: g75 11/22 31
membrane purifier: g71 7/8 30
Mt. Everest once under: g75 9/8 29
ocean waves: g74 8/8 11
of life: w73 380-3
pollution: g73 9/22 30; g73 11/22 29-30; w72 613-14; g72 5/8 29; g72 7/8 29-30; g72 8/22 31; g72 9/22 31; g72 10/8 11; g71 1/8 7-8; g71 4/22 8-11; g71 7/8 29; g71 7/22 29; g71 9/22 29; g71 10/8 6; g71 12/8 29
bulrushes used to control: g75 4/22 29-30
power of, in motion: g75 6/8 6, 7
pre-Flood world: po 75
properties of: g72 3/22 24
purifying: g74 1/22 12; g73 6/22 24; g71 7/8 30; g71 10/22 29
purity of Amazon: g75 3/8 8
sewage: g71 1/22 29; g71 10/22 29; g71 11/22 29-30
shortage: g72 5/22 29-30
soft: g71 10/22 31
survival in: g73 6/22 17-19
swimming: g72 1/22 30; g71 7/8 10-12; g71 8/8 16-19
symbolic: ts 165; w73 380-3; pm 383-6; kj 387-98
underground: g74 8/22 21-2
use of ants to find: g75 4/8 30
uses: g72 1/22 18-19

WAY OF HOLINESS
sl 134-7, 154-60, 162-3, 165-7

WAY, THE
discussion: w75 698-9

WBBR
history: yb75 140-2, 144
programs: yb75 141, 144
"White" network: yb75 144

WEALTH
Bible view: g74 9/22 10-11; g71 11/22 27-8
Carnegie statement: w72 491
dangers: w74 419-20
patriarchs: g71 11/22 27
richest countries: g75 7/22 31
unequal distribution: g74 6/22 4-5, 9; g73 11/22 29
(SEE ALSO MATERIALISM)

WEANING
Bible times: g72 11/22 14
discussion: g74 7/8 15
Isaac: w74 684
!Kung tribe: w74 684

WEAPONS
accidents: g75 11/22 12, 29; g72 2/22 29
arms race: g74 6/8 30; g74 11/8 3-7; g74 12/8 30; g73 7/8 30; g73 11/8 30; g73 12/22 19; w72 613; g72 10/8 3, 5, 10, 29; g71 7/8 6-8
availability: w74 102; g72 12/8 30
blessings on: g73 7/8 29
chemical: g74 11/8 5
church investments: g72 2/22 30
convention to exhibit: g75 11/22 30
cost: w75 487, 634; gc 9; g75 1/8 30; g75 4/8 29; g75 8/22 18, 30; g74 2/8 30; g74 10/8 6; g74 11/8 6-7; g74 12/8 8; g73 10/8 28-9; g72 9/8 29; g72 10/8 3, 4; g71 6/22 29; g71 8/22 6
per person: g75 10/22 30
destructive power: g75 8/22 30; g74 11/8 4-5; g72 10/8 4, 9-10; g71 7/8 6-7
detection of, in ancient China: g75 6/8 24
employment carrying: w73 127-8
laws to control sale: g72 7/22 29
limitation talks: g74 11/8 3
missiles: w75 487; g74 11/8 3-5; g72 10/8 10
nuclear: w75 487; g74 11/8 3-4; g73 1/8 30; g72 10/8 9-10; g71 4/22 16, 30
old: g72 12/8 30-1
sale: g74 11/8 6
spiritual: w73 159-60
stockpile: w75 487; g75 8/22 30; g74 11/8 3-6
submarines: g72 10/8 9-10
testing: g71 2/8 29; g71 4/22 16, 30; g71 9/8 30; g71 12/22 29
threat to human existence: g72 10/8 4, 10; g71 1/22 30; g71 5/22 31
youth: g73 2/22 30

WEAR
deterioration of things: g71 7/8 3-4

WEATHER
acidic rain: g74 8/8 31
cause of violent: w74 735
effect on agriculture: g74 6/22 6; g73 6/22 6
forecasting: g73 1/22 5-6
God and: g75 3/8 6
monsoons: g75 3/8 4-5
rains: g75 1/22 29
tornadoes: g74 6/8 8-9
unusual: g75 1/22 29; g75 3/8 3-6; g73 10/8 31
walrus used to predict: g74 9/8 30

WEAVING
carpets: g74 2/22 25-6

WEDDINGS
altar servers: g75 3/22 30
anniversary: w71 735-6
announcements of, at Kingdom Hall: km 6/75 4
apparel: w74 275-6
attending worldly: w74 766-7
Bible times: w74 430-1
ceremony: w74 274-7; w73 694-6
experience:
wedding talk convinces woman of truth: w75 245
India: g72 8/8 20-3
Kingdom Hall use: km 6/75 4; w74 275-6
mass weddings: g73 11/22 31
proper view of: w73 694-6
receptions: w73 696
ring: w72 63
typical wedding talk: g74 5/22 3-6
vows: w74 275
who may perform: km 11/73 8
worldly practices: w74 274-5

WEEDS
nutritious: g74 9/22 6-7
spiritual: w75 594, 596, 599

WEIGHTS AND MEASURES
calorie: g74 4/22 21
candela: g74 8/8 19
carats: g74 7/22 24
English (Customary) system: g74 8/8 17, 19
foot: g74 8/8 18-19
handbreadth: g74 8/8 19
kelvin: g74 8/8 19
kilogram: g74 8/8 18-19
liter: g74 8/8 18
meter: g74 8/8 18-19
metric system: g74 8/8 17-19
Richter scale: g74 5/8 16-17

WELFARE
Bible view: g73 7/22 24-5
cost to finance: g71 1/8 30
eligibility: w73 317
statistics: w72 205, 615-16; g71 3/22 30; g71 6/22 29

WELL
opened (Zec 13:1): pm 345-50

WEST BERLIN
Jehovah's witnesses: yb76 26-7

WESTERN SAMOA
Jehovah's witnesses: yb76 24-5; yb75 24-5; yb74 24-5

WETLANDS
discussion: g75 2/8 12-15
value of: g75 2/8 13-15

WHALE
discussion: g73 12/22 13-16
oil of sperm whale: g75 7/22 30
playfulness: g75 10/22 25
skeleton of: g74 3/8 23

WHAT HAS RELIGION DONE FOR MANKIND? (Book)
ban on: yb72 206
release: yb75 225

WHEAT
Canada: g74 7/22 30
demand for: g74 5/22 29
food: g72 7/22 3-6, 8-9
Jesus' illustration of wheat and weeds: w75 594, 596, 599; yb75 33; w74 477, 480; pm 362-3
price: g74 9/8 29
Texas High Plains: g75 3/8 29

WHEEL(S)
Ezekiel's vision: w72 103; kj 42-5
'of life' (Jas 3:6): ts 112
symbolic: kj 191-3

WHIPPING
punishment: g72 5/22 31

WHOLE-SOULEDNESS
discussion: or 132-47

WICKED
destruction: w75 636-8; w73 344-6; tp 38, 41-3; w72 499-500; w71 631-3; te 102

WICKEDNESS (Evil)
cause: gc 14-18; w73 617-19; dy 16-18; g73 12/8 28
discussion: gc 3-31
effects on people: g74 3/8 3-4; g73 5/8 3-4
proper view: w74 153
soon to end: gc 21-3
symbolic representation: pm 218-21
why permitted: w74 643-4; g74 4/8 16-17; g74 10/8 14-17; tp 46, 52-7; g72 10/22 10-12

WIDOWS
congregation aid: w71 414-15
examples of faith: w74 535
problems faced by: g74 12/8 29

WIFE
avoiding adultery: w73 538-40
communicating with husband: w75 485-6; w74 305-11
'craving for husband': w74 392-3
"deep respect": g74 4/22 8-9
desirable qualities: w74 118-19; g74 4/22 7-9; g74 5/22 5-6; w71 259
disfellowshiped: w74 470-1
divided household: w75 437-8; km 8/75 7; w74 317, 767; w73 475; tp 176-7; w71 201-4, 207-13
duties in home: g74 4/22 8, 12; g74 5/8 14; g74 8/22 7; g72 5/22 6-7, 10-11
attitude toward: g74 5/8 14
experiences:
husband's drunkenness: g72 3/22 15; g71 6/22 8
husband's opposition overcome: w74 39; yb74 6-7; yb73 243; w72 71; yb72 221; g72 3/22 15; g72 4/8 25; g72 9/22 26; w71 202, 204, 209, 211, 533, 679-80
opposition from, overcome: w71 205-6
gaining husband's appreciation: w75 16
head covering: w72 446-7
husbands to be 'as though they had no wives' (1 Co 7:29): w75 351-2
Jehovah's: po 61, 64, 79
Israel: ts 104-5
love for husband: g74 4/22 6-7; w71 259, 516
menstruation: w72 575-6
moral support: w71 259
rendering marriage dues: w72 767
role in marriage: g74 4/22 5-9; g74 5/22 4-6
runaways: g75 10/22 29; g75 12/22 29-30; g74 4/22 4; w72 483-4; g71 4/22 31
secular work: g71 3/22 30
subjection to husband: w75 154, 314, 485; w74 118, 316-17; g74 4/22 7-8; g74 5/22 5; tp 140-1; w72 270-1, 445-7; g72 2/22 8; g72 5/22 13-14; g72 9/22 27-8
unbelieving husband: g74 4/22 9; tp 176-7; w71 201-4, 207-13, 287
undesirable qualities: w75 154; g71 3/8 10
wife beating: g75 9/8 29-30
"wife swapping": g71 7/22 30
(SEE ALSO FAMILY, MOTHER)

WIGS
discussion: g72 2/22 13-15

WILD BEASTS
(SEE BEASTS)

WILDERNESS
Israelites: w72 73-4

WILL
Christian view: w74 372-3; g74 9/8 28
Jehovah's: km 5/74 3-6
legal document: w73 704; g71 12/22 13-16

WIND
energy from: g74 8/22 20-1
Jesus' power over: te 59-62
sun's influence: g74 8/22 20

WINDMILLS
g75 9/22 30

WINE
adulteration: g74 12/22 30; g71 8/22 25
alcohol content: w74 452-4
discussion: g72 2/8 21-2; g71 8/22 24-6
Jesus refused drugged: w71 249
lead poisoning: g71 7/8 29
marriage feast at Cana: w71 439
medicinal value: g73 12/22 10; g71 7/22 30
Memorial: w72 166; g72 3/22 27-8
(SEE ALSO ALCOHOLIC BEVERAGES)

WINTER
clothing: g71 1/22 12-14
deaths: g74 2/8 29
home heating: g74 1/22 22-3
Japan's snowmen: g71 1/8 20-2
snowmobiles: g73 1/8 31
surviving cold: g72 11/8 26

WISDOM
acquiring: w75 15-16; w74 114-15; w73 491-2; w72 422; g72 2/22 8
admitting mistakes: g73 2/8 4
discussion: w72 5-9; yb72 3-10
from above (Jas 3:17): w72 6-8; yb72 4-9
godly: w75 102-3
Jehovah's dealing with mankind: g71 6/8 12-14
meaning of term: w72 5; yb72 3; w71 137
miraculous gift: w71 502-4
personified: w75 511-12; po 28-9; w72 105-6
shown in creation: w73 163-4
Solomon's: w73 489-90
source: g73 8/8 4
symbolic representation: w72 102; kj 39-40
worldly: w75 99-102; w74 210-11, 308, 611-14; hu 3-7; w73 160; g72 9/8 27-8; g71 5/22 6-7
(SEE ALSO KNOWLEDGE)

WITCHCRAFT
Africa: w73 698

Bible view: ts 76-8, 87; w73 484-6, 699-701
clergy use witch doctors: yb76 193
connection with drugs: w73 181
discussion: w73 483-6
examples: w74 323, 328; w73 697-9; g71 7/8 16-18
experiences:
spells fail: g74 2/22 6
witch doctor accepts truth: g72 3/8 8-11; g71 7/8 16-20
increase: w74 323
juju priest: ts 70-2
King Saul: ts 75-8
school: g74 2/8 6; g71 7/22 29
sports: g74 7/22 31
witch doctor: g73 4/8 29
(SEE ALSO SPIRITISM)

WITKARS

g75 2/22 24-5

WITNESSES

ancient Israel: kj 22
"two witnesses" (Re 11:3): yb75 103-4, 109
witnesses for Jehovah: w71 31

WITNESSING

adaptability: w74 185-7; or 115-16; sg 150, 172-5
airplanes: g75 2/8 25-6
appearance: km 8/74 8; sg 184-7; g71 7/22 26
attitude of publisher: km 7/75 4; w74 60, 124-5, 183-4, 568-9; km 1/74 4; w73 21-2, 56-8; w72 726-9; or 130-2; km 4/72 3; km 6/72 3-4; km 9/72 8; w71 214, 218-19, 313, 413-14
balanced view: w74 568-9, 575-6
Bible studies: or 121-5; km 1/72 8; km 2/72 8; km 7/72 4; km 11/72 5-6; km 5/71 4; km 7/71 3
by example: w74 187
children: or 130
Christian obligation: yb76 258; g75 1/22 24; w74 183; km 5/74 3
conduct: km 8/74 8
discussion: w74 182-8
divisional campaigns: yb75 153-4
early Christians: w74 183, 185; w73 681-3, 687-8
effectiveness: km 7/74 4; sg 99; km 8/71 4
encouraging others to begin: km 1/74 3
endurance: km 4/75 1; w71 119-20
exposing falsehood: w74 35, 37
failure of churches: w73 742-4
friendliness: km 7/74 4
group witnessing: or 119-20; km 6/71 4
house-to-house: yb76 35-8, 55, 99, 160, 182; w74 241-2
importance: w74 183, 188, 241-2, 332-6, 568-9; w72 423; km 5/71 4
improving: sg 96-9
informal: yb76 17, 21, 87; w75 40, 318; km 2/75 3-4; w74 185-7, 337-8; km 3/74 4; w72 400-3; sg 80-2; km 12/71 4
information marching: yb75 160-1
introductions: km 5/74 8
isolated territory: w75 43, 247; w74 141-3
Jesus set example: km 5/74 3; w73 21-2; or 112-13; w71 78; g71 12/22 9-10
lands: yb76 259; yb75 5, 30, 257; w73 23, 40; w72 27; pm 254; yb72 33; w71 24, 81, 504
language barrier: km 1/74 3-4
legal rights: km 8/71 3-4
letter writing: g75 1/22 30; km 6/74 3; sg 87-8
literature offers: or 116-17
Bibles: km 6/72 4
magazine distribution: or 117-18; km 4/71 4
making more time for: km 8/75 7-8
manners: km 7/75 4
methods: yb76 5, 50-5, 59-63, 65, 74, 79, 82-3, 99, 102-3, 108-10, 137-8, 155, 172-3, 215; w74 185-7; or 113-26, 131-2
modern beginning: yb75 39-40, 45-6, 85-6, 124-5, 133-4
moral qualifications: or 128-30
not-at-homes: or 118-19; w71 219-20; km 10/71 8
leaving literature: km 6/74 3
objections overcome: w74 3-4; km 6/74 4; g72 8/8 7; sg 92-4; km 1/71 4
obstacles: w75 42-3; g75 2/8 24-6; km 4/75 1; w74 537-8; yb73 248-9
overcoming apathy: w74 444-6
phonographs: yb76 51, 53, 57, 60-1, 111-12, 120, 137, 151; yb75 155-60
presentations: km 4/75 2; km 7/75 4; km 9/75 8; km 5/74 1; km 7/74 2; km 12/74 1, 4; km 9/71 2; km 12/71 2
preparation: sg 39; km 3/71 4; km 7/71 4; km 11/71 7
prisons: w75 649-50; g75 4/22 21-8; km 9/75 1; km 4/74 4; yb72 157-8; w71 508
proper motive: km 7/75 4; w74 59-60, 183
purpose: w74 3-4, 37, 241-2; km 11/73 7; w72 277, 280; w71 611
quotas: w75 312
reaching householder's heart: km 7/75 4
reporting: or 126-8; km 4/71 3
request not to call anymore: km 6/74 4
responsible for others' lives: w74 123-4
return visits: km 1/75 4; or 121; km 1/72 8; km 2/72 8; km 8/72 4; w71 220-1
service reports (annual): yb76 258-9; w75 23-8; yb75 24-32, 257-8; w74 26-31; yb74 23-32; w73 23-8; yb73 23-32, 255-6; w72 22-5, 27, 493; yb72 33-41; w71 23-9
sign: no religious calls: km 6/74 4
sincerity: km 7/74 4
sound cars: yb76 135-7, 159; yb75 157-8
street witnessing: yb76 42-3, 141; yb75 162-4; km 8/75 8; km 9/75 8
tact: km 3/72 4; sg 70-2
telephone: km 7/73 4
territory coverage: km 6/74 3; or 73-4, 118-20; km 11/72 8
rurals: km 6/75 3
"this good news of the kingdom": w74 332, 334
to—
children: km 12/75 8
Eskimos: w75 43; g75 2/8 26
Indians: w75 206
men: km 12/75 8
relatives: km 2/75 3-4; w74 185-6; or 111; km 11/71 8
women: km 12/75 8
tobacco users: km 7/73 4; km 11/73 7
training new publishers: yb75 227-8; km 5/74 7
under ban: yb75 18-20; w74 285; yb74 20, 112-15, 132-3, 139, 141-3, 155-6, 159; w72 137-8
"underground" activity: yb72 85-8, 93, 136, 139-41, 155-6, 163
use of Bible: km 2/75 4; km 9/75 8; km 12/75 7; km 2/74 8; or 114, 116; yb72 85-6; sg 122-9
use of questions: km 4/75 4
war zone: w74 521
zeal: w75 311-13
(SEE ALSO FIELD SERVICE)

WOE

pregnant women (Mt 24:19): w72 108-9

WOMAN (Women)

abortions: g73 2/8 12-13; g72 1/22 4; g72 3/22 30-1; g72 5/8 31; g72 5/22 8; g72 6/8 30; g72 7/22 30; w71 484; g71 2/22 29; g71 4/8 30; g71 6/22 29-30; g71 7/8 30; g71 7/22 19; g71 9/8 29; g71 9/22 30; g71 10/22 30; g71 12/8 31
adornment: w74 118-19
African: g75 12/8 13-14
alcoholism: w74 451, 454
beauty: w73 523
breast enlargement: g71 11/8 31
breast-feeding: g75 9/22 30; g75 10/8 30; g73 7/8 12-15
cancer: g75 9/22 30; g74 9/8 17-18, 20-1
changing from girlhood: w73 520-3
church leaders: g72 8/22 30; w71 644; g71 2/8 30
clothing, cosmetics, hair, etc.: w72 665-8, 671-2; g72 11/22 22-3
crime encouraged: g71 2/22 30
deodorants: g74 3/8 25-6; g72 2/8 30
earrings: w74 318-19
fashions: g71 7/8 24
hair: w73 140; g72 2/22 13-15
making own clothing: g71 5/8 8-10; g71 5/22 29
modesty: w74 118-19; w73 522
conduct when threatened with rape: g75 2/22 30; g74 3/8 13-16; g73 4/22 16-17
congregation privileges: w73 255
consideration for: g72 5/22 12-15
creation: po 46-7; g72 5/22 12
crime: w75 464; g73 9/22 31; g71 8/8 30
discussion: w73 520-3
doctors: g75 4/8 31; g75 11/22 31
drugs: g73 9/22 30
emotional makeup: g74 4/22 11; g72 5/22 10-11
fear: g75 10/22 29
girl altar servers: g75 3/22 30
God's view: g72 5/22 12-13

g, Awake!; ka, God's Kingdom of a Thousand Years; kj, "The Nations Shall Know that I Am Jehovah"; km, Kingdom Ministry; or, Organization; pm, Paradise Restored—By Theocracy!; po, God's "Eternal Purpose"; sg, Theocratic School Guidebook; sl, Man's Salvation out of World Distress!; te, Listening to the Great Teacher; tp, True Peace and Security; ts, Is This Life All There Is?; w, Watchtower; yb, Yearbook. Complete list on page 6.

head covering: w72 446-7
homemaking: g74 5/8 13-15; g74 8/22 7; g74 12/22 7
International Women's Conference: g75 8/22 29; g75 9/8 30
Jehovah's: po 61, 64, 79, 134-5, 137
learning in silence: w73 255
liberation movement: w75 464; w74 387-93; g74 6/8 30; g72 5/22 3-17
nuns: g75 1/22 12
menopause: g74 1/22 15
menstruation: g74 2/8 13; w73 520-1; w72 293, 575-6
Moslem: g75 2/22 29
motherhood: g72 5/22 6-7, 10-11
mountain climbing: g75 7/22 30
ordination of:
Billy Graham's neutral view: w75 560
pregnancy: g75 12/8 31; g74 1/22 13, 15-16; g74 2/8 12-16
proper view of sex: g74 4/22 6-7; w73 521-2
proportion of unmarried, to men: g75 4/22 31
qualities desired by man: g74 5/22 6
rights: g72 5/22 3-7, 29
runaways: g75 12/22 29-30; w74 391; g74 3/8 31; g74 4/22 4
scientists: g75 4/8 31
secular employment: g74 10/8 31; g72 5/22 7; g71 3/22 30
sewing: g73 8/22 9-12
sex symbols: g72 5/22 7-8
smoking: w75 12
stealing: g75 10/8 30
sterilization: g74 2/8 16
submission: w74 118; w72 270-1, 445-7; g72 2/22 8; g72 5/22 13-14
Surinam: g71 7/8 24
symbolic: po 60-1, 79; ts 126-7; pm 218-21
venereal disease: w75 48
war: g72 5/22 5-7
(SEE ALSO MOTHER, WIFE)

WOMB
discussion: g74 2/8 12-16
surgery: g71 8/22 30

WOMEN'S LIBERATION MOVEMENT
causes: w74 388-9
failure: w74 390-1
first-person account: w74 387-93
history: w74 389-90
pride: w74 410
rejects Bible: w74 410; g74 6/8 30

WOOD
dating: g72 4/8 5, 11-15, 17-19
firewood: g75 11/22 30
home repairs: g74 7/8 20
logging: g71 12/22 17-19
lumberjacks: g73 12/8 31
paper production: g72 1/22 30
products from: g75 2/8 23; g74 11/8 23
stump processing: g74 11/8 23

WOODWORTH, CLAYTON J.
yb75 90-1, 97, 104, 106, 109, 111, 116, 123

WOOL
discussion: g73 2/8 24-6
musk ox: g74 8/22 25-6
sheep: g74 11/8 14-16

WORD OF GOD
Jesus Christ: w75 63, 173-5; w74 306-7; w73 524; ka 20; bi8 1362-3

WORDS
advertising: g74 3/8 10-12
clear writing: g73 9/8 17-20
derivation: g73 8/22 21-3
English language: g73 8/22 21-2; g71 7/22 10; g71 12/22 20-3
foul: g74 5/8 31
language exchange: g73 8/22 21-3
pronunciation: sg 56, 146-9
"rotten": w74 314-15
slang: g74 5/8 31; sg 56-7
vocabulary: g75 1/8 29
word choice: g73 9/8 17-20; sg 6-8, 54-7

WORK
attitude toward: g74 8/22 7; g73 7/22 24-6; g73 9/8 8-11; w72 205-11, 269-70, 299, 485-6; g72 3/22 30; g72 5/8 5; g72 11/8 31; w71 231-2; te 95-8; g71 4/8 12-15; g71 12/8 29
beneficial: g75 1/22 30; g74 1/8 30; g74 2/22 30; w73 327-9; w72 487
Bible view: w74 151; g74 2/8 9; g73 4/8 27-8; g73 7/22 25-6; g73 9/8 10-11; w72 485-6
children: g72 5/8 5-8
dead works: w72 700; g72 7/22 27-8
discussion: w72 485-97
efficiency: g74 5/8 14-15; w72 483-4
evidence of faith: w74 19-26, 31
field service: w72 491-5
"good work" (Tit 3:1): w75 317-19
"humble" jobs: w75 297-9
older persons: g75 4/22 30; g74 9/8 30
right motive: w73 506
sabbath: g75 2/8 27-8
secular:
absenteeism: w74 453; g74 4/8 30; g74 7/22 29; g73 9/8 8, 31
boredom: g72 5/22 31
choosing: g73 9/8 10-11
Christian view: g71 4/8 15
decline in productivity: g74 9/8 4
dissatisfaction: g73 8/8 30; g73 9/8 8-11
four-day workweek: g75 7/22 29
giant corporations: g71 2/8 3-6
goals: g74 8/22 7
honesty: g74 3/8 27-8; g74 9/8 4
informal witnessing: w72 400-1
irresponsible workers: g74 7/22 29
labor unions: g74 6/8 13-15
stress: g71 11/8 30-1
three-day workweek: g74 11/8 30
tobacco: km 2/74 3-6
unemployment: g75 2/22 4; g71 3/22 30
unemployment preferred: g75 11/22 30
women: g74 10/8 31
stress: g75 1/22 30
(SEE ALSO EMPLOYMENT)

WORLD
"ancient world": w75 747-50, 752
belongs to Christians: w71 352
changes in fifty years: w74 262-3
Christian separateness: w74 54-5, 733-4; w73 137-40, 146; tp 120-1, 124-31; w72 588-9; g72 12/8 20; w71 559-64; kj 348
benefits: w75 697
comments on moral breakdown: w72 261-2; g72 3/8 30-1; g72 7/22 29; g71 6/22 31; g71 8/22 31; g71 9/8 30; g71 10/8 17
crisis: w75 12; sl 7, 10-15; g75 2/8 3-9; w74 550-1, 656; g74 3/22 3-6; g74 4/8 6, 31; g74 5/22 29; g74 7/8 31; g74 7/22 5; g74 10/8 16, 29; g74 11/22 16, 20, 29; g74 12/22 29; g73 10/8 3-15, 20-2, 30
darkness: w74 560-1
debt: g75 6/8 11
decline of civilization: g74 6/8 29
destruction of: sl 291-2; w74 4, 664-6, 668; tp 37-45; g73 10/8 22-5; g73 11/8 6-7
elementary things of: w71 415-16
'founding of world': w74 287-8, 626-7; g74 7/8 28; ka 273-4; w71 704
friends with: tp 127-31
hatred of Christ: w73 649-53, 657
hatred of Christians: w73 656-61
illiteracy: g75 7/8 31
'not using world to full' (1 Co 7:31): w75 91
population: g75 2/8 3-5; g75 5/8 31; g74 1/22 7; g74 4/8 6-7; g74 6/22 3-4; g74 7/22 5-6; g74 11/22 16; ka 282; tp 108; g72 7/8 26; g72 10/8 11; g71 1/8 30
present wicked:
problems of: w75 259-62
ruler of: g74 10/22 8-9
spirit of the world: w73 136-8, 146; tp 128-31; w71 630
spiritual failure: g74 8/22 30
trade: g75 11/8 30
wisdom: w74 210-11; g72 9/8 27-8
world domination: w71 614-15; nc 6-8

WORLD COUNCIL OF CHURCHES
assemblies: g74 9/8 29; g72 8/22 17
failure: g74 1/22 30
guerrilla support: g74 11/22 5; w71 740; g71 3/8 31
oppression, stand on: g75 12/22 15
political activities: w74 244; g74 9/8 29; w73 675; g73 9/22 4
views: w74 75, 135, 244; w73 708; g73 12/8 18; g71 3/8 31
(SEE ALSO PROTESTANTISM)

WORLD POWERS
first, Egypt: sl 234; w72 38
second, Assyria: sl 234; g72 6/22 27-8
third, Babylon: sl 234
fourth, Medo-Persia: sl 234; pm 117; w71 715
fifth, Greece: sl 234; pm 279; w71 715-16
sixth, Rome: sl 234; pm 279; w71 716-17
seventh, British Empire—United States of America: sl 234, 237, 250, 271, 316; g75 10/8 14; w74 607; pm 279-80; w71 717-18, 720-4, 728

eighth, League of Nations—United Nations: sl 237, 247, 271, 318, 339; ka 309-17, 394; w71 718
symbolic representation: w75 620-2; og 23-5; w74 381, 606-7, 718; ka 310
why Bible speaks of seven: w74 606-7

WORLD TRADE CENTER
g74 2/8 20-3

WORLD WAR I
beginning: yb73 98; w72 351-2, 748; pm 332
casualties: w74 357; tp 82; g71 10/8 16
clergy: w74 217; g73 5/8 23; g73 6/8 17-18; pm 307-8; g72 4/22 14-15; g72 6/8 26
conditions before: yb74 78-9
effects: g75 1/8 29; g74 5/8 29; g73 6/22 10-11; w71 468-9; g71 10/8 15
end: w75 611; og 3; pm 273, 333; kj 59, 63, 73, 78
nations participating: kj 59
percentage of persons who recall: g75 7/8 29
previous wars compared: w75 633
significance: w74 357; tp 77, 80-2; g73 1/22 8; g73 10/8 16-17, 20; g71 10/8 15-17
surprise: g73 7/8 30

Quotations
assumed war was impossible: g73 7/8 30
a universe of concepts was shattered: w75 684
benchmark in evolution of modern America: g75 4/22 29
changed the face of the earth: g71 10/8 15
crucial event in first half of twentieth century: g71 10/8 15
first total war: g73 10/8 20
golden age of peace ended abruptly: g73 1/22 8
great divide in world history: g71 10/8 15
marked end of one epoch and beginning of another: g75 4/8 15
no calculated, advance decision made for global war: g73 1/22 8
terminated longest period of peace: g73 1/22 8
turning point: w74 165; g73 10/8 17; g71 10/8 15
ushered in century of Total War: w75 633; ml 23

WORLD WAR II
attempt to prevent: yb73 115
beginning: yb73 119; w71 719-20
book on Catholic church role in, suppressed: w75 715
casualties: w75 634; sl 9; g75 8/22 18; tp 82; g72 5/22 5; g71 10/8 16-17
United States: g75 11/22 3
clergy responsibility: g75 7/8 30; g72 4/22 15-17
Germany:
Catholics who refused military service: g75 2/22 20-2
postwar trials: g71 2/22 30; g71 3/8 30
Russia invaded: g72 10/8 7
Havana Declaration: yb73 62
number of deaths in wars since: w75 634
number of wars since: w75 634
Roman Catholic Church:
support of Axis Powers: g72 10/8 7
substitute for a German peace treaty: g75 11/8 4
United States: yb73 62
weapons: g72 12/8 30-1

WORM
earthworms: g75 3/22 13
screwworm: g72 11/8 30

WORSHIP
man's desire to worship: g75 5/8 3-4; g75 6/22 4; w74 144; g74 12/8 21; w72 388
not all acceptable to God: g74 1/22 18-19; g73 11/8 27-8
standard for judging: w74 540, 543; w73 387-8; tp 23, 36; g73 11/8 28; w72 99-100
with truth: g74 12/22 10

False Worship
ancestor worship: yb73 240-1; g72 3/22 17-19
animal worship: g72 7/8 6, 8
animism: yb73 141-2
assault upon: yb75 228-9, 235
calf worship: kj 25, 28, 98-9, 240
creature worship: w72 539-40
cross worship: w72 572-3; kj 151-2
destruction: ts 116-17; g74 4/8 19-20; w72 45, 51-3; g72 4/22 24-7; w71 101, 471-2; kj 112-13, 115-27, 129, 217
development:
Greece: w71 509-10
post-Flood: w72 428
Roman Catholicism: kj 159-60
spread from Babylon: ts 27-9, 44-5; w71 509-10
Devil worship: g71 5/22 3-10; g71 8/22 15-16, 30; g71 11/8 29
discussion: g72 4/22 3-28
flag worship: g71 9/8 13-14
friendship with world: g74 11/22 3-6
gods: kj 149-52
images: g73 1/8 27-8; yb72 112-13, 173-4, 194; g72 8/22 5-7; kj 147-8
Materialism: w75 231-2
origin of myths: ts 27-9
relic worship: g75 12/22 14; w72 416
results:
failure to change lives: g73 2/8 23
moral collapse: g74 9/8 5; g72 4/22 18-20; g71 5/22 7
war: g72 4/22 5-17; w71 483; g71 6/22 16-19
river worship: yb73 141-2
separation from: w74 564-5; ts 187; g74 2/8 27-8; g74 12/22 9-10; g72 4/22 27-8
State worship: w75 227-32
sun worship: w72 585-7; kj 154-9
ways gain money: ts 68, 70, 72
(SEE ALSO CHRISTENDOM, CLERGY)

True Worship
duties: w73 136-41
exposing falsehood: w74 35-7
proof of identity: g74 1/22 18-19; w73 387-90; w71 463-72
reasons for worshiping Jehovah: w75 233-40
results: po 4-6
way of life: w75 643-6; w74 84-5, 630

WRIGHT, ORVILLE
letter to Henry Ford, Sr.: g75 8/22 19

WRITING
adapt to audience: g73 9/8 18-19
Bible inspiration: w75 141-9; g72 2/8 27-8; g71 11/8 27-8
clear expression: g73 9/8 17-20
cuneiform: w72 314-16
discussion: g73 9/8 17-20
hieroglyphic: g71 11/22 24-6
Hittites: w71 348-9
letters: g75 2/8 30; sg 84-90
Moses: w71 409-10
pre-Flood: w71 409-10
religious: g74 9/8 30; g74 12/8 29

WYCLIFFE, JOHN
w74 743

X RAYS
dangers: g71 5/22 30-1

YAHWEH
g73 3/22 27-8

YAP
Jehovah's witnesses: yb76 26-7; yb75 26-7; yb74 26-7; yb73 26-7; yb72 36-7
population: yb73 26; yb72 36

YARN
g74 11/8 15-16

YAWNING
benefits: g71 3/8 26

YEAR
prophetic: po 176; ts 156
year of goodwill: w72 368-74; w71 31

YEARBOOK
appreciation for: w73 400-1, 438; w72 158-9
first: w72 158
use: km 12/71 2

YEARTEXT
1971: yb71 323
1972: yb72 260
1973: yb73 260
1974: yb74 260
1975: yb75 260-1

YIDDISH
g73 4/8 15

YMCA
w74 684; g73 7/8 30

YOGA
g75 2/22 27-8; g75 11/8 10-11, 29

YOGURT
g75 2/8 19

YOKE
'take my yoke' (Mt 11:29): or 107-8

"YOUR WILL BE DONE ON EARTH" (Book)
yb75 217

"YOUR WORD IS A LAMP TO MY FOOT" (Book)
yb75 254; km 11/71 8

YOUTH
alcoholic beverages: w73 666-70
associations: w74 93, 271-2; w73 73; w71 562-3, 590
automobiles:
accidents: g73 12/22 30; g71 10/22 30
driving: g74 3/22 8-11
benefits of chastity: w73 521-2; g73 3/22 30
Bible examples to follow: w74 536-7; w72 275-6; w71 362-6, 395
boredom: w72 156-8
Christian conduct: w74 10-13, 264-6; w73 521-2; w72 381-2
secular schools: w72 403, 555; g72 9/8 5-8
clothing: w72 475-6, 665-8
conformity: w72 473-6
congregation:
privileges: w72 203-4; km 2/72 7-8
congregation's interest in: km 4/75 3
cosmetics: w72 667-8
courtship: w74 8-13
dating: w74 10-13; w72 31; w71 593-5
dependability: w74 152-3
desire for independence: w75 61
development: w71 594-5
discipline: w71 659-61
disrespect for authority: g74 2/8 4-5
drugs: g74 5/8 3-8
experience:
Witness persuades gunmen to surrender: g75 1/22 30
field service:
integrity: yb74 117-19; w72 381; g72 6/8 24; g72 9/8 7-8; w71 531-2; g71 10/22 28
opposition by parents: w75 440; yb74 63; w73 318; w71 369; g71 7/22 20
pioneering while in school: w75 186-7
proper dress: g74 9/22 31
religious services in school: w71 531
unbelieving parents: km 5/72 4
witnessing in school: w75 440-3; w74 186-7; g74 5/22 26; w72 401-3; km 11/72 6; w71 732
youths may share: yb73 55; w72 203-4; or 130; km 2/72 7-8; km 10/72 7-8; w71 368-9
friends: w73 421-4
goal for future: w75 463; g75 9/22 22-5; g74 7/8 29; w71 517-19
guns: g73 2/22 30; g73 4/22 29
hair: w72 665-8
honesty: w74 245-7
honor due parents: g75 10/22 27
'idols': w74 145-6
interests: w72 157-8
Israelite: w71 361-2
magazines: g72 10/8 30-1
marriage: w75 461-2; w74 8-13, 703; g72 4/8 29; g72 12/8 3-5; g71 11/22 31
masturbation: w73 564-9; w72 92-4; g72 12/8 7
materialism: w73 155-9
modesty in dress: w73 522
moral breakdown: g73 9/22 30-1; g72 12/8 29; w71 517
alcoholism: g75 2/8 16-18; g75 9/8 30; w74 451, 453; g74 12/8 30
burglary: g72 5/22 30
causes: w74 262-3, 267, 270; g74 4/22 15; w73 73; g73 12/8 30; g71 10/22 11
contraceptives: g75 7/8 30
crime: w75 37, 439; g75 3/8 29; g75 7/8 30; g75 7/22 29; g75 11/22 5; w73 552; g72 6/8 29-30; g71 6/8 29; g71 9/8 29
drug addiction: g74 6/22 13; w73 178-9; g73 4/8 30; g73 12/8 3-5, 7-15; g72 9/8 29; g72 11/8 31; w71 247; g71 1/8 30-1; g71 3/8 30; g71 3/22 6, 30; g71 4/8 16-18; g71 5/8 27-8; g71 9/8 29; g71 12/8 30; g71 12/22 30
effect of marijuana on: g75 1/22 31
illegitimacy: g74 4/22 4-5; w73 552-3; g72 10/22 30-1
immorality: g74 4/22 5, 13; w73 552-3; g73 2/8 30; g73 5/8 30; w72 218-21; g72 2/8 17, 19-20; g72 9/22 30; g72 10/22 30-1; g71 9/8 29; g71 11/22 29
murder: g74 9/8 10
pregnancies: g71 2/22 30
riots: g71 8/8 10-12
rock 'n' roll music: g75 6/8 30; g75 7/22 29; g74 6/22 14; w72 568-9; g72 5/22 23; w71 403-4
schools: g74 2/8 4-6; g72 1/22 31; g72 2/22 29-30; g72 4/22 30; g72 5/22 30; g71 4/22 31
stealing: g71 1/22 23; g71 9/8 29
vandalism: g75 5/22 29; g74 8/22 3-6; g73 3/22 5-6
venereal disease: g75 7/22 29
nutrition: g72 6/8 31
obedience: g75 10/22 27; w73 142-3, 146, 671-2; w71 259-60
parental companionship: w73 523
parents' responsibilities: w74 81-94; g74 3/8 31; g74 8/22 4-6; g72 11/8 30; w71 361-2, 369-72; g71 3/22 7-8
'past bloom of' (1 Co 7:36): w74 703
perseverance: w72 274-6
physical development: w73 86-9, 520-1
proper attitude toward meetings: w75 61-2
proper attitude toward older persons: w74 265-6; w73 475; w71 363, 518
puberty: w73 86-9
recreation: w75 461; g72 11/8 30; w71 315
reliability: w72 28-30
religion: g72 3/22 29; g72 8/22 18; g72 11/8 3-8; g71 5/8 5
remembering Creator (Ec 12:1): km 5/74 6; w71 367-72
respect for parents: w74 91; g74 12/22 6; w72 732-4; w71 518
responsibilities: w73 88-9; w72 28-30
results of parental neglect: g75 3/8 29
runaways: w71 525; g71 3/22 5-9
secular education: g74 2/8 3-7; w72 156-7; g72 9/8 5-6; w71 563, 733-5
self-control: g73 3/22 30
sex: w75 461-2
sex education: g72 1/22 3-9; g71 10/22 30
shyness: w75 197-9
singleness: w74 703; g72 12/8 5-8
smoking: g73 12/22 30; g71 1/22 31; g71 11/8 4
Soviet Union: g75 1/8 5
suicide: g75 8/22 30; g73 5/22 31; g72 8/22 30; g71 4/8 30
television's effect: g74 9/8 10
traits and viewpoints of worldly youths: w74 262-4, 267; g74 2/8 3-6; w73 136, 157; g73 3/8 30; w72 205, 208, 262; g72 4/8 4; w71 517, 525; g71 9/8 3
unemployment preferred: g75 11/22 30
use of time: w75 462-3
viewpoint of churches: g75 3/22 30
viewpoint of God's organization: km 4/75 3
witnessing to: km 2/73 8
(SEE ALSO CHILDREN, CHILD TRAINING)

YUGOSLAVIA
pollution: g73 9/8 30

ZACCHAEUS
w75 564-5; w74 139-40

ZAÏRE REPUBLIC (Formerly called Congo [Kinshasa])
copper mining: g73 7/8 25-6
description: g72 1/8 21-4
false "Watchtower movement": yb76 175-7
food provisions for travelers: g75 7/8 24
Jehovah's witnesses: yb76 30-1, 175-7; yb75 30-1; g75 12/8 13-17; g74 1/22 26; yb74 14, 30-1; yb73 30-1; yb72 34-5, 44; g72 1/8 21, 24
persecution: yb76 22, 176-7
Kisangani: g74 1/22 24-6
language: g73 1/22 25-6
mountain gorillas: g74 8/8 20-3
Nyiragongo volcano: g75 7/8 22-4
people: g74 1/22 24-5
population: yb76 175; yb73 30; yb72 34
religion: yb76 175; w72 340
Zaïre River: g72 11/8 24-6

ZAMBIA
All-Africa Conference of Churches: w74 677-9
description: yb72 234
false "Watchtower movements": yb76 133
government: yb72 249
Jehovah's witnesses: yb76 30-1, 126-34, 155-9, 171-5; yb75 30-1; w74 555; yb74 14, 30-1; yb73 30-1; yb72 40-1, 234-54; g72 12/8 9, 12-13; w71 13-14
persecution: yb76 96, 127-33, 156-7
population: yb73 30; yb72 40
refugee camp: g75 12/8 7; g75 12/22 17-19; g73 3/8 19-21

ZEAL
comments on Witnesses': g73 2/22 8; w72 211, 423-4
discussion: w75 311-16

examples:
  Bible accounts: w74 535-7; or 133
  early Christians: w72 210
  modern-day: w75 315-16; yb75 61-4; yb74 64
preaching work: w75 311-13

ZECHARIAH (Book)
authenticity: pm 94

ZECHARIAH (Prophet)
prophetic significance: w75 554; pm 314
shepherd: w75 553-5; pm 305-6, 310-14, 319-20
visions:
  first: pm 127-41
  second: pm 141-6
  third: pm 153-75
  fourth: pm 176-91
  fifth: pm 192-207
  sixth: pm 208-17
  seventh: pm 217-22
  eighth: pm 222-8

ZEDEKIAH (Mattaniah)
capture: w72 470; kj 108-9, 137-8
chieftain of Israel: kj 221, 228-9
dethronement foretold: po 128-9; w73 59-61; w72 765; kj 229-32
rebellion against Nebuchadnezzar: w73 59-60; w72 676-8; pm 214-15; kj 95-6, 197, 226-9

ZERUBBABEL
ancestry: sl 174; pm 118-20
discussion: sl 321
name: pm 121
prophetic significance: w75 454-5; pm 120-3
Sheshbazzar: pm 29

ZIGGURATS
w74 490

ZION
Jerusalem: w72 171-2
prophecies: w72 181-4

ZION (Mountain)
prophetic significance: po 89; ts 130

ZIONISM
Weizmann, Chaim: kj 59, 67

ZION'S WATCH TOWER AND HERALD OF CHRIST'S PRESENCE (Magazine)
yb75 38; w74 507; w73 395; ka 345

ZIPPORAH
circumcision of her son: w75 415-16

ZODIAC
g75 11/8 30; g73 11/22 4-5

ZONE OVERSEER
duties: or 90

ZONE WORK
yb75 167-8

ZOOS
g74 12/22 31; g73 5/8 18; g72 9/22 30-1

ZOROASTRIANISM
belief in a devil: g74 10/22 5-6
burial of dead: g74 11/8 31

ZULULAND
Jehovah's witnesses: yb76 136

SCRIPTURE INDEX

GENESIS
1:1 w75 200; ml 6; w74 593; po 35; w72 646; w71 43; g71 8/8 7
1:3 w74 306
1:5 sl 294
1:6 sl 290; w74 306; po 75
1:7 po 75; sl 290
1:8 sl 290, 294; po 75
1:9 w74 306
1:11 g75 12/8 30; w73 301; g73 10/22 22; w71 44
1:13 sl 294
1:14 w74 306; g72 2/8 11
1:15 g72 2/8 11
1:16 g73 5/22 8
1:19 sl 294
1:20 sl 290; w74 306; bi8 1351
1:21 w73 447; g73 10/22 22; w71 44
1:23 sl 294
1:24 w74 306; yb72 4/10; w71 44
1:25 g73 10/22 22
1:26 yb75 3/14; w74 306; po 36; w73 488, 524; g73 10/22 27; w72 445, 557, 648, 658; pm 9, 15; kj 39; te 16; g71 10/8 19
1:27 g75 10/22 7; w74 146; po 48; g74 10/8 23; w73 326, 457, 488; tp 47; g73 10/22 27; w72 170, 557, 648, 658; pm 9; w71 615; kj 39; sg 5; nc 10; g71 10/8 19
1:28 w75 664; g75 7/8 8-9; w74 594; po 48; ts 134; g74 6/22 28; w73 159, 624; tp 100, 109; dy 28; g73 7/22 25; w72 245, 648, 658; pm 9; g72 4/8 27; w71 497-8, 615, 742; kj 114; nc 10
1:29 g75 12/22 25; po 50; w73 301; w72 648
1:30 po 50; w73 301; g73 10/22 26; w72 648
1:31 w75 657; sl 294; w72 245, 646, 648; w71 498
2:1 po 52
2:2 po 52
2:3 po 52, 189
2:7 ml 9; g75 10/22 6; po 37-9; ts 38, 41; g74 1/8 19; g74 12/8 20; w73 230, 236; g73 5/8 5; g73 6/8 6; w72 291; w71 45; kj 337
2:8 g75 12/22 6; po 37, 41; w71 498, 615; kj 337; nc 9
2:9 po 41; ts 17; g74 10/8 11; g73 6/8 11; w72 245
2:10 w71 540
2:11 w71 540
2:13 w71 540
2:14 pm 10; w71 540
2:15 w73 327; g73 7/22 25; w72 487; kj 114; g71 4/22 25
2:16 w75 617; og 16; po 43, 50; ts 30; yb74 4/28; g74 10/8 11; w73 434; g73 7/8 27; w72 178, 426; g72 4/8 27
2:17 w75 617; fu 14; og 16; po 43, 50, 62; ts 30, 34; g74 10/8 11; w73 235; tp 54; g73 6/8 6; g73 7/8 27; w72 178, 426; g72 4/8 27; te 40; g71 5/22 6
2:18 po 45; g74 4/22 7, 10; g72 5/22 12
2:19 po 41, 46; w73 524; w71 58
2:20 po 41, 46
2:21 po 47; kj 337
2:22 w74 308; po 47; g74 1/22 27; w73 694; kj 337
2:23 w74 308; po 47
2:24 po 47; g74 1/22 27; g74 4/22 10; g74 5/22 4; yb73 5/29; w72 558
2:25 po 48
3:1 po 55; ts 80; w73 434; tp 51-2; w72 178, 262, 427, 649; w71 267
3:2 po 56; ts 80; tp 52; w72 178, 649
3:3 po 56; ts 80; w73 434, 595; tp 52; w72 178, 649
3:4 fu 16; po 57; ts 80; tp 52; w72 178, 649
3:5 fu 16; gc 14; po 57; ts 80; tp 52; w72 178, 649; yb72 6/19
3:6 po 58; ts 31, 80; yb74 7/22; g73 7/8 27; w72 427, 649; g72 4/8 27; g71 12/8 27
3:7 po 58; w72 222; g71 12/8 27
3:8 yb76 4/6; w75 209; w74 309; po 59; yb74 4/9; w73 433; g71 12/8 27
3:9 po 59; w73 433
3:10 po 59; w73 433; g71 12/8 27
3:11 po 59
3:12 w74 309; po 59; w72 650; g72 4/8 28
3:13 po 59
3:14 po 59; ka 273; w72 620; dn 9
3:15 yb76 2/9; w75 81, 618-20; sl 63; og 18-20, 22-3; w74 106; po 59, 61, 81, 134, 137, 169, 186, 191; ts 126, 129; ka 74, 273, 285; tp 62; yb73 8/22; w72 236, 369, 620; yb72 5/2; dn 9; g72 10/22 13-15; w71 269, 301
3:16 w75 287; po 61; g72 11/22 13, 16
3:17 w75 665; g75 12/22 7; po 62, 71; g73 7/8 28; w72 650; pm 16-17
3:18 w75 665; g75 12/22 7; po 62; g73 7/8 28; g73 7/22 25
3:19 w75 665; g75 10/22 5; po 62; w73 236; g73 6/8 6, 8; g73 7/8 27-8; g73 7/22 25; g71 3/8 27
3:20 po 63; g74 6/22 27; g71 11/22 26
3:21 w74 467; po 63; w72 222, 592; g72 7/8 7; g72 12/22 21
3:22 po 63
3:23 po 63; g74 6/22 28
3:24 po 63; g74 6/22 28; kj 38
4:1 w71 58
4:4 g72 7/8 7
4:5 w73 300
4:6 w73 435, 441
4:7 w73 300, 435, 441
4:9 w73 300; w72 558
4:10 yb74 2/20; w73 236, 300
4:11 w75 665; yb74 2/20; w73 236, 300
4:12 w75 665
4:13 w72 438
4:14 w73 301; w72 438
4:15 w73 301
4:16 w73 435
4:17 g71 11/22 26
4:20 g73 7/22 25
4:21 g73 7/22 25
4:22 g73 5/8 19; g73 7/8 25; g73 7/22 25; g71 7/22 11
4:23 g73 2/8 27; w72 558
4:24 w73 301; w72 558
4:25 po 66; w71 58
4:26 po 66-7; w71 648
5:3 po 66; w71 45
5:4 g74 6/22 28; g71 11/22 26
5:5 ts 34
5:21 po 68
5:22 po 68; w73 702; w72 651; bi8 1352
5:23 po 68; w72 651
5:24 po 69; w72 651; w71 617; bi8 1352; nc 12
5:29 w75 665; g75 12/22 7; po 71, 82
5:31 po 71
5:32 po 71
6:1 po 72; ts 84; w73 180; w72 316, 427, 651
6:2 po 72; ts 84; w73 180; g73 6/8 7, 28; w72 316, 427, 651; w71 509, 607; g71 5/22 4
6:3 w74 663; po 72-3; ts 84; w72 651
6:4 po 73; ts 84; w73 485; w72 316, 651; w71 509
6:5 po 74; w73 485
6:6 po 74
6:7 po 74
6:8 po 74
6:9 yb75 8/25; w74 150, 664; po 71; w72 651, 699; w71 565
6:10 po 71
6:11 w72 651; g71 4/22 23
6:12 g71 4/22 23
6:13 w72 651; g71 4/22 23
6:14 w74 380
6:15 w74 380
7:1 sl 291; w72 659
7:2 w72 659
7:3 w72 659
7:4 yb76 5/13; w75 10, 278; sl 291
7:11 sl 291; g75 6/8 6
7:12 sl 291
7:13 sl 291
7:16 sl 291; km 11/75 1
7:18 g75 6/8 7
7:19 g75 6/8 6
7:21 g75 6/8 7
7:22 ts 49; g72 8/8 27
8:1 w72 659
8:11 w73 84
8:17 w72 659
8:18 kj 377
8:19 w75 606; kj 377
8:20 kj 377
8:21 tp 52; g73 5/8 4; g72 12/22 4; kj 377
8:22 g72 2/8 11; kj 377
9:1 w75 606; w74 41; w72 652
9:2 yb76 5/21; w75 606; w74 594; w72 652
9:3 g73 5/8 27; w72 64, 652; g72 7/8 8, 27
9:4 g75 6/8 27-8; w74 351; w73 511; g73 5/8 27; w72 64, 190, 652; g72 7/8 27
9:5 w75 639; g75 11/22 27; w73 511; w72 652; g72 7/8 27
9:6 g75 6/8 27-8; g75 11/22 27; g74 7/22 27; w73 511; w72 480, 652; g72 7/8 27
9:7 w72 652

9:12 po 82
9:13 po 82
9:14 po 82
9:15 po 82
9:24 po 83
9:25 po 83
9:26 w74 43; po 83
9:27 w74 43; po 83
10:1 kj 150
10:5 w73 526
10:6 kj 150
10:7 w71 540
10:8 ka 23; w72 653; w71 648; kj 150, 152, 157
10:9 w75 580; w74 490; ka 23; w72 573, 653; w71 648; kj 150, 152, 157
10:10 w74 490; ka 23; w72 428, 653; w71 648; kj 150-1, 157
10:11 ka 23; w72 653; kj 150-1
10:12 ka 23; w72 653; kj 150-1
10:15 w71 348
10:20 w73 526
10:22 w71 540
10:29 w71 540
10:31 w73 526
11:1 sl 297; w73 525; ka 23; g71 2/22 8
11:2 w74 490; ka 23
11:3 ka 23
11:4 w75 666; w74 41, 490; ka 23; w72 428
11:5 w74 41; ka 23
11:6 w75 666; w74 41; w73 516, 525; ka 23
11:7 w74 41; yb74 5/27; w73 525; ka 23; g71 2/22 9
11:8 w74 41; ts 27; w73 516; ka 23
11:9 ts 27; w73 525; ka 23; g71 2/22 9
11:26 w75 64
11:27 w72 319
12:2 po 161
12:3 w74 330; po 88, 90, 161, 163
12:5 po 86
12:7 po 86, 105
13:1 w74 624
13:10 g75 12/22 7; kj 312
13:14 w75 676
14:18 w74 158; po 88; ka 89; pm 200
14:20 g74 1/8 27
15:1 w74 754
15:2 yb76 12/29; w75 660; w73 702; bi8 1352
15:8 w75 660
15:12 kj 11
15:13 po 104, 109; g73 8/22 28; w72 38; kj 11
15:14 po 104, 109; g73 8/22 28-9; w72 38; kj 11
15:15 po 104
15:16 po 104; g74 4/8 16; w73 582
15:18 w74 286; po 104
15:19 po 104
15:20 po 104; w71 348
15:21 po 104
16:1 w73 365
16:2 w73 365
16:5 bi8 1356
16:11 po 106; g74 2/8 16
16:12 po 106; g74 2/8 16
17:1 w74 727
17:2 w74 727
17:6 po 87
17:8 g73 8/22 28
17:10 w71 441
17:11 w71 441
17:12 w71 441
17:13 w71 441
17:14 w75 416; w71 441
17:16 po 100; g73 8/22 28
17:17 po 87
17:19 g73 8/22 28
17:23 w71 441
17:24 w71 441
17:25 w71 441
17:26 w71 441
17:27 w71 441
18:3 bi8 1352
18:9 bi8 1356
18:11 w73 247
18:12 w72 446
18:19 w75 118
18:20 g74 10/8 20
18:22 bi8 1353
18:25 g73 7/8 28; w71 388, 631
18:27 bi8 1352
18:30 bi8 1352
18:31 bi8 1352
18:32 bi8 1352
19:7 w75 676
19:17 w75 562
19:18 bi8 1352
19:30 w72 319
19:31 w72 319
19:32 w72 319
19:33 bi8 1356
20:4 bi8 1352
20:6 w73 31
20:7 w73 31
20:11 w75 76
20:12 w75 76; g74 6/22 28
21:8 po 106
21:9 po 106
21:12 w73 496; g73 8/22 29
22:2 g73 8/22 29
22:17 w72 82
22:18 w74 330, 694; po 92, 181; w73 432; g73 8/22 28; w72 82; g72 10/22 13; w71 301
23:3 w71 348
23:4 bi8 1353
23:5 w71 348
23:6 bi8 1353
23:7 w74 62; w73 526; w71 348
23:8 w73 526
23:9 bi8 1353
23:10 w71 348
23:15 w75 735-6
23:16 w75 735-6; w71 348
23:17 w75 735-6
23:18 w75 735-6; w71 348
23:19 w75 735-6
23:20 w71 348; bi8 1353
24:22 w74 319
24:47 w74 319
25:18 w71 540
25:23 po 93; g74 2/8 16; g74 7/8 28; w73 497, 727
25:25 w73 496; w71 58
25:26 w73 496; w71 58
25:27 yb74 8/6; w73 496
25:29 w73 497; g72 12/22 11
25:30 sl 137, 224; w73 497; g72 12/22 11
25:31 sl 224; w73 497; g72 12/22 11
25:32 sl 224; w73 497; g72 12/22 11
25:33 sl 224; w73 497; g72 12/22 11
25:34 w73 497; g72 12/22 11
26:24 w73 496
27:15 po 94
27:16 po 94
27:17 po 94
27:18 po 94
27:19 po 94
27:20 po 94
27:21 po 94
27:22 po 94
27:23 po 94
27:34 w72 438
28:1 w73 497
28:3 w73 497
28:4 w73 497
28:6 w73 497
28:10 w73 497
28:14 po 95
28:19 w73 497
28:20 g74 1/8 27
28:21 g74 1/8 27
28:22 g74 1/8 27
28:23 w73 497
31:3 w73 499
31:30 bi8 1356
31:34 w73 521
31:35 w73 521
31:38 w73 500
31:39 w73 500
31:40 w73 500
32:24 w73 498
32:25 w73 498
32:26 w73 498
32:27 w73 498
32:28 w73 498
33:4 bi8 1356
35:10 po 100
35:11 po 100
35:16 g72 11/22 14
35:17 g72 11/22 14
35:18 ts 42; g72 11/22 14
35:19 g72 11/22 14
35:20 g72 11/22 14
37:2 w74 500; w71 409
37:3 w74 501
37:4 w74 501
37:5 w74 501
37:6 w74 501
37:7 w74 501
37:8 w74 501
37:9 w74 501
37:10 w74 501
37:11 w74 501
37:12 bi8 1356
37:22 w74 501-2
37:25 g72 2/22 28
37:27 g72 2/22 28
37:28 g72 2/22 28
37:29 g72 2/22 28
37:35 ts 91; w73 233; bi8 1353
38:8 w73 255
38:9 w73 255
38:10 w73 255
38:11 w73 383
38:13 w72 666
38:14 w73 383; w72 666
38:15 w73 383; w72 666
38:18 w73 383
38:23 w73 384
38:24 w73 384
38:26 w73 384
38:27 g72 11/22 14
38:28 g72 11/22 14
38:29 g72 11/22 14
38:30 g72 11/22 14
39:7 w72 558
39:8 w72 558
39:9 yb76 4/26, 6/2; w75 210; yb74 7/23; w73 556; w72 558
39:12 w73 556
40:8 w73 548
40:14 w74 503
41:45 w74 503
42:6 w74 62
42:21 w74 504
42:22 w74 504
42:23 w74 504; w73 526
42:24 w74 504
42:38 w73 234; bi8 1353
43:30 w71 412
44:14 w74 62
44:29 bi8 1353
44:31 bi8 1353
45:18 w72 190
46:32 kj 293
46:33 kj 293
46:34 kj 293
47:7 w73 447
49:8 po 100
49:9 po 100
49:10 sl 106; po 100-1, 107, 124; w72 82, 241
49:28 po 99; w72 681
49:29 w72 681
49:30 w72 681
49:31 w72 681
49:32 w72 681
49:33 w72 681

EXODUS

1:16 g72 11/22 14
1:17 g72 11/22 14
1:18 g72 11/22 14
1:19 g72 11/22 14
2:5 kj 13
2:6 kj 13
2:7 kj 13
2:8 kj 13
2:9 kj 13
2:10 kj 13
2:11 kj 14
2:12 kj 14
2:13 kj 14
2:14 kj 14
2:15 kj 14
3:1 po 109
3:12 po 108-9
3:14 w74 527, 728; po 14-15, 108
3:15 w71 650; kj 15
3:16 w71 684; kj 15
3:17 kj 15
3:18 kj 15
4:10 bi8 1352
4:11 w74 319
4:13 bi8 1352
4:16 g72 5/22 28
4:24 w75 415-16
4:25 w75 415-16
4:26 w75 415-16
5:1 w75 230; w72 39; kj 16
5:2 yb76 10/11; w75 230, 239; w74 333; w72 39; kj 16
5:22 bi8 1352
6:2 kj 21
6:3 w72 72; g72 11/8 6; kj 21
6:7 kj 21

6:20 w75 76; kj 13
7:5 kj 16
7:17 kj 17
7:22 kj 17
7:23 kj 17
8:6 kj 17
8:7 kj 17
8:16 kj 17
8:17 kj 17
8:18 kj 17
8:19 w72 39; kj 17
8:20 kj 18
8:21 kj 18
8:22 kj 18
8:23 kj 18
8:24 kj 18
9:7 kj 19
9:16 kj 360
9:18 w72 40
9:19 w72 40
9:20 w72 40
9:21 w72 40
10:1 kj 22
10:2 kj 22
10:23 pm 382
12:3 w72 681
12:4 w72 681
12:5 w72 681
12:6 w73 175; w72 681
12:7 w72 681
12:8 w72 681
12:9 w72 681
12:10 w72 681
12:11 w72 681
12:12 w74 333; w72 681; bi8 1352
12:14 g72 11/22 6
12:17 w73 175; g72 11/22 6
12:18 w73 175
12:24 g72 11/22 6
12:29 w73 175
12:35 g73 8/22 29
12:38 po 181
12:40 po 106, 109
12:41 po 106
12:42 po 109
13:1 w72 687
13:2 w72 687
13:3 yb76 7/6
13:9 w73 191
13:17 w72 530
14:2 kj 19
14:3 kj 19
14:4 kj 19
14:15 sl 367
14:16 sl 367
14:17 sl 367; kj 20
14:18 sl 367; kj 20
14:19 pm 338
14:22 w71 293
14:25 w72 40; kj 20
14:30 w72 681
14:31 w72 681
15:1 w72 61
15:3 sl 369
15:11 bi8 1356-7
15:13 w72 681
15:16 w72 681
15:17 bi8 1352
15:18 sl 369
15:22 w73 365
15:23 w73 365
15:24 w73 365
16:4 w71 293
16:5 w71 293
16:12 kj 23
16:20 w71 293
16:24 w71 293
16:25 w71 293
16:26 w71 293
16:27 w71 293
17:8 kj 25
17:9 kj 25
17:10 kj 25
17:14 kj 25
17:15 kj 25
17:16 kj 25
18:11 bi8 1356
19:1 po 109
19:3 po 110; w72 681
19:4 yb75 6/21; po 110; w72 681
19:5 w74 597; po 110; w73 425; yb73 5/20; w72 681
19:6 w74 688; po 110, 157; w72 681
19:7 w72 682
19:8 po 110; yb73 5/27; w72 685, 700; kj 199
19:12 g71 1/8 3
19:13 g71 1/8 3
20:2 yb72 6/28; g72 11/22 5; w71 742; kj 145
20:3 w75 230; yb72 6/28; w71 742; bi8 1356; kj 145; te 140
20:4 w75 230; w74 62, 395; kj 145; te 140
20:5 w74 62, 395; w72 360, 634; yb72 7/24; w71 116; kj 145, 167
20:6 w72 360
20:7 yb72 6/11; w71 645
20:8 g72 11/22 5; g71 10/8 27
20:9 g72 11/22 5
20:10 g72 11/22 5; g71 10/8 27
20:11 sl 294; g71 10/8 27
20:12 w75 444; w73 85
20:13 g74 5/8 27
20:14 w71 119
20:15 g74 12/8 5; w71 426; te 151
20:22 po 112
20:23 po 112
21:2 w74 319
21:3 w74 319
21:4 w74 319
21:5 w74 319
21:6 w74 319
21:22 g75 8/22 5; w73 420; g73 3/22 11; g73 12/22 28
21:23 g75 8/22 5; po 116; w73 420; g73 3/22 11; g73 12/22 28
21:24 po 116; g73 3/22 11; g73 12/22 28
21:25 po 116; g73 3/22 11
21:28 w75 639
21:29 w75 430; w73 305
21:30 w75 430
21:32 w75 430; sl 54
22:1 yb76 5/24; w75 115; w74 204; g72 7/8 7
22:2 g75 9/8 27; w73 305
22:3 w75 115; w73 305
22:4 w75 115; w74 204
22:9 w74 204
22:18 w75 52
22:19 w72 768
22:22 w74 83
22:23 w74 83
22:24 w74 83
23:1 w72 196
23:2 g75 2/22 6; w72 196; yb72 10/23; w71 563
23:13 w74 458, 715; g74 2/8 27
23:17 bi8 1353
23:20 w74 69; pm 338
23:21 w74 69
23:22 w74 69
23:23 w74 69; pm 338
23:26 w73 85
23:28 w73 702
24:1 w71 684
24:3 po 113
24:6 po 112; bi8 1366
24:7 po 112; yb73 7/16; w72 683, 685, 700; bi8 1366; kj 199
24:8 po 112; w72 683, 700; bi8 1366
24:11 w71 684
24:14 w71 684
25:18 kj 38
25:19 kj 38
25:20 kj 38
25:21 kj 38
25:22 kj 38
25:23 w74 175
25:30 w74 175
25:31 w74 175
25:40 w74 173
26:1 w74 175
26:7 w74 175
26:14 w74 175; g72 12/22 21
26:15 w74 175
26:26 w74 175
26:27 w74 175
26:28 w74 175
26:29 w74 175
26:31 w74 175
26:32 w74 175
26:33 w74 175
26:35 w74 175
26:36 w74 175
26:37 w74 175
27:1 w74 175
27:9 w74 175
27:12 w74 175
27:16 w74 175
27:18 w74 175
27:21 g72 11/22 6
28:30 w74 157
28:43 g72 11/22 6
29:28 g72 11/22 6
29:43 kj 27
29:44 kj 27
29:45 kj 27
29:46 kj 27
30:1 w74 175
30:6 w74 175
31:13 g72 11/22 5
31:17 g72 11/22 5
32:2 w74 319
32:4 g75 11/22 22; g73 12/22 6
32:5 g74 2/8 27; g73 12/22 6
32:7 w74 395; g73 12/22 6
32:18 w74 303
33:2 w74 69
33:18 w75 234; kj 26
33:19 w72 550; kj 26
33:20 w72 101
34:6 yb76 12/16; w75 234; w74 495; g73 7/8 28; w72 550; w71 631; kj 26
34:7 yb76 12/16; w75 234, 459; w74 495; g73 7/8 28; w72 550; w71 631; kj 26
34:9 bi8 1352
34:23 bi8 1354
34:24 po 115
34:27 g72 2/8 27
34:28 w73 190
35:21 w71 137
35:22 w74 319
35:26 w71 137
35:29 w71 137
36:1 w71 498
36:2 w71 498
37:7 kj 38
37:8 kj 38
37:9 kj 38
37:12 g74 8/8 19
39:32 w71 498
39:42 w71 498
39:43 w74 173; w71 498
40:4 ka 102
40:5 ka 102
40:12 ka 107
40:13 ka 107
40:14 ka 107
40:15 ka 107
40:16 ka 107; w71 498
40:21 ka 102
40:22 ka 102
40:23 ka 102
40:24 ka 102
40:25 ka 102
40:26 ka 102
40:27 ka 102
40:28 ka 102
40:34 po 118; w71 498
40:35 po 118; w71 498
40:38 w71 498

LEVITICUS

2:1 w71 284
2:7 w72 191
2:15 w71 284
3:17 w72 64, 190
5:4 w73 607
7:16 w73 607
7:23 w72 190
7:24 w72 190
7:25 w72 190
11:18 w71 59
15:16 w73 87, 567
15:17 w73 87
15:18 w73 479
15:19 w73 479
15:24 w72 575
15:29 w73 479
16:2 w74 175
16:3 w74 176
16:5 sl 65; w74 176
16:6 sl 65; w74 176
16:7 sl 65; w74 176
16:8 sl 65; w74 176
16:9 sl 65; w74 176
16:10 sl 65; w74 176
16:11 w74 176
16:12 w74 176, 222
16:13 w74 176, 222
16:14 w74 176
16:15 ka 99
16:17 w74 175
16:18 ka 97
16:20 sl 65; w74 223
16:21 sl 65; w74 223
16:22 sl 65; w74 223
16:30 w74 175; w71 536
17:10 g72 7/8 27
17:11 g73 5/8 27; w72 190; g72 7/8 27
17:12 g72 7/8 27
17:13 w73 224; w72 190; g72 7/8 27; g71 9/22 8
17:14 w72 190; g72 7/8 27; w71 118
18:5 po 117
18:6 w75 73
18:9 g74 6/22 28
18:16 w75 73
18:18 w75 73
18:19 w72 575
18:20 g74 8/8 28
18:22 w74 485; w73 356; w72 735, 768
18:23 w72 735, 768
18:28 g74 4/8 16
18:29 g74 8/8 28; w72 768
19:11 g74 3/8 27
19:13 g74 3/8 27
19:15 w75 373
19:17 w73 145
19:18 w72 707
19:19 g74 8/8 27; kj 107
19:27 yb74 4/3; w73 140

19:28 w74 318; g74 12/8 27
20:10 w72 768
20:11 w72 768
20:12 w72 768
20:13 w72 768
20:14 w72 768
20:15 w72 768
20:16 w72 768
20:18 w72 575
20:21 w75 73
20:22 g74 4/8 12
20:27 yb76 7/13; w75 52; g75 3/22 28; ts 87
21:5 w73 140
21:12 ka 104
22:21 w73 607; w71 284
22:24 w73 159
23:11 w75 603
23:12 yb76 10/25
23:13 yb76 10/25
23:17 yb76 11/29
23:27 w74 175
24:5 w74 175; w71 284
24:6 w74 175; w71 284
24:8 w72 683
25:2 g74 4/8 10; g71 10/8 27
25:3 g74 4/8 10
25:4 g74 4/8 10; g74 10/8 21; g71 10/8 27
25:5 g74 4/8 10; g71 10/8 27
25:6 g74 4/8 10; g71 10/8 27
25:7 g74 4/8 10
25:8 g71 10/8 27
25:10 g74 4/8 10; tp 102
25:20 g74 4/8 12
25:21 g74 4/8 12
26:16 g75 12/8 25
26:43 sl 125
27:34 w73 189

NUMBERS

3:12 g72 3/8 28
3:13 w72 687; g72 3/8 28
3:22 g72 3/8 28
3:28 g72 3/8 28
3:34 g72 3/8 28
3:39 g72 3/8 28; bi8 1356
4:3 g72 3/8 27
4:30 g72 3/8 27
4:47 g72 3/8 27
6:2 w72 684
6:3 w72 684
6:4 w72 684
6:5 w72 684
6:6 w72 684
6:7 w72 684
6:8 w72 684
7:89 w72 717; kj 165
8:24 g72 3/8 27
9:10 bi8 1356
11:7 pm 217
11:15 bi8 1353
11:16 w71 684
11:24 w71 684
11:25 w71 684
11:29 w73 507
11:32 w74 63
12:12 bi8 1353
13:16 pm 388
13:29 w71 348
13:32 kj 322
14:9 yb76 12/19; w75 376
14:17 bi8 1352
14:34 kj 100
16:30 bi8 1353
16:33 bi8 1353
18:12 w72 190
18:14 w72 687
18:15 w72 687
18:16 w72 687
18:23 g74 1/8 27
18:24 g74 1/8 27
21:30 bi8 1356
22:32 w73 586
25:1 w74 459; w73 588; w72 503, 684
25:2 w74 459; w73 588; w72 503, 684
25:3 w72 503, 684-5, 752
25:4 w72 503, 684
25:5 w72 503, 684
25:6 w72 503
25:7 w72 503
25:8 w72 503
25:9 w73 588; w72 503, 684
27:17 kj 294
27:21 w74 157
29:15 bi8 1356
31:16 w73 586
32:23 w73 539; w72 392; kj 124
35:10 w73 303
35:11 w73 303
35:12 w73 303
35:13 w73 303
35:14 w73 303
35:15 yb74 6/24; w73 303
35:20 g74 5/8 27
35:24 w73 304
35:25 w73 304
35:26 w73 304
35:27 w73 304
35:28 w73 304
35:31 w73 303
35:32 w73 305
35:33 w73 302

DEUTERONOMY

2:9 w72 319
2:18 w72 319
2:19 w72 319
2:37 w72 319
4:2 g73 8/8 7
4:15 w74 173
4:16 w74 173
4:19 w72 585; kj 155
5:3 g72 11/22 5
5:8 w72 250
5:9 g73 5/22 28; w72 250
5:12 g72 11/22 5
5:13 g72 11/22 5
5:14 g72 11/22 5
5:15 g72 11/22 5
5:16 yb76 2/10
5:17 g74 7/22 27
6:4 w73 132, 560
6:5 w73 560
6:6 yb75 2/15; w74 84; yb74 10/8; g74 4/22 16; w73 191, 559-60
6:7 yb76 1/16; yb75 2/15; w74 84; yb74 9/15, 10/22; g74 4/22 16; w73 559-60; yb73 3/29
6:8 w73 191, 559
6:9 w73 191, 559
6:10 w72 245
6:11 w72 245
6:12 w72 245
6:13 g74 12/8 21
7:2 w74 458
7:3 w74 458
7:4 w74 458
7:5 w74 458; g74 2/8 27
7:6 g74 2/8 27; w73 585
7:7 g74 10/8 19; tp 63
7:8 g74 10/8 19; tp 63
7:9 w74 152
7:25 w74 716
7:26 w74 716
8:3 g74 12/8 21
8:9 g73 7/8 25
8:18 g71 11/22 27
10:14 w74 594
10:16 sl 34; yb72 10/19; w71 442
10:17 w74 594; bi8 1354, 1356
10:20 g74 12/8 21
11:13 g75 3/8 6
11:14 g75 3/8 6
11:16 g75 3/8 6
11:17 g75 3/8 6
11:19 yb73 10/30
12:15 w72 190
12:16 w72 64, 190
12:30 g73 12/22 6
12:31 g73 12/22 6
12:32 g73 8/8 7
13:1 g75 1/22 6; g74 4/22 27; g73 11/22 6
13:2 g75 1/22 6; g74 4/22 27; g73 11/22 6
13:3 g75 1/22 6; g74 4/22 27; g73 11/22 6
13:6 w75 381
13:8 w75 381; km 10/74 7
13:9 w75 381; g74 7/22 28
13:10 w75 381; g74 7/22 28
13:11 g74 7/22 28
13:17 w74 716
14:21 km 2/74 6
15:1 g74 4/8 10
15:2 g74 4/8 10
15:3 g74 4/8 10
15:9 w73 407
15:11 w75 70; w72 579
16:4 yb76 4/10
16:6 w73 175
16:16 po 115
16:17 po 115; w71 284
17:12 g72 1/8 16
17:13 g72 1/8 16
17:16 g72 10/22 25
17:18 w73 202
17:19 w73 202
17:20 w73 202
18:5 w73 702; bi8 1354
18:9 w74 715; g74 9/8 28
18:10 g75 8/8 6; w74 325, 715; g74 2/22 6; g74 9/8 28; g73 11/22 6-7
18:11 w74 325, 715; g74 2/22 6; g74 9/8 28; g73 11/22 7
18:12 w74 325, 715; g74 2/22 6; g74 9/8 28; g73 11/22 6
18:14 w74 325, 715
18:15 po 110, 147; w72 685; pm 316; g72 2/8 5; w71 242
18:16 w72 685; bi8 1354
18:17 po 110; w72 685
18:18 w74 297; po 110; g74 1/22 18; w72 685; pm 316; w71 242
18:19 w74 297; g74 1/22 18; w72 685; pm 316; w71 242
19:2 w73 303
19:3 w73 303
19:6 w73 303
19:9 w73 303
19:10 w73 303
19:11 w73 302
19:12 w73 302; w71 684
19:13 w73 302
19:21 po 116; g74 7/22 28; w73 302; yb72 10/17; g72 2/8 6; w71 271
20:13 bi8 1354
20:18 bi8 1354
21:1 g75 11/22 27
21:2 w71 684
21:3 w71 684
21:4 g75 11/22 27; w71 684
21:6 w71 684
21:18 w75 116; w71 362
21:19 w75 116; w71 362, 684
21:20 w75 116; w74 167; yb72 1/10; w71 362, 684
21:21 w75 116; w74 167; yb72 1/10; w71 362
21:22 sl 75; po 151; g74 9/22 28; bi8 1361
21:23 sl 75; po 151; g74 9/22 28; bi8 1361
22:1 w74 204
22:2 w74 204
22:3 w74 204
22:5 w73 140; w72 671
22:8 w73 305
22:9 kj 107
22:15 w71 684
22:16 w71 684
22:17 w71 684
22:18 w72 17; yb72 23; w71 684
22:22 w72 768
22:23 w73 544; g73 4/22 17
22:24 w73 544; g73 4/22 17
22:25 w73 544; g73 4/22 17
22:26 w73 544; g73 4/22 17
22:27 g74 3/8 15; w73 544; g73 4/22 17
22:28 g73 4/22 17
22:29 g73 4/22 17
23:1 w75 158
23:2 w74 224
23:3 w73 589
23:4 w73 589
23:10 g71 4/22 28
23:11 g71 4/22 28
23:12 w75 134; g71 4/22 28
23:13 w75 134; g71 4/22 28
23:14 g71 4/22 28
23:18 w73 607
23:21 w73 607
23:22 w73 607
24:4 bi8 1354
24:9 bi8 1354
24:17 yb75 2/4; w74 83
25:4 ts 123
25:5 w72 83
25:6 w72 83
25:7 w71 684
25:8 w71 684
25:9 w71 684

25:15 w71 565; bi8 1354
26:2 bi8 1354
27:2 bi8 1354
28:9 w74 687
28:10 w74 687; w71 654
28:13 kj 231
28:15 kj 231
28:22 g75 12/8 25
28:36 kj 231
28:43 kj 231
28:44 kj 231
29:1 w72 693
29:4 kj 24
29:5 kj 24
29:6 kj 24
29:29 bi8 1356
30:6 sl 34; w71 442
30:11 w72 693-4
30:12 w72 693-4
30:13 w72 693-4
30:14 yb73 8/5; w72 693-4
30:15 g73 10/8 26
30:19 yb76 11/30; g73 6/8 6; g73 10/8 26
30:20 yb76 11/30; w74 377; g73 10/8 26
31:9 w73 201
31:10 w73 201
31:11 w73 201
31:12 w74 271; w73 201, 461; yb72 2/11; w71 393
31:13 w74 271
31:26 bi8 1354
31:27 bi8 1354
31:29 bi8 1354
31:30 w72 61
32:3 w74 528; bi8 1354
32:4 gc 11; w74 528; w73 133, 316, 441; w71 357, 497
32:6 bi8 1354
32:8 w74 726; w73 432
32:10 pm 166
32:14 w72 190
32:16 w74 396
32:20 w74 396
32:22 bi8 1353
32:39 w75 63
33:1 w73 752; w72 61
33:2 w73 752
33:3 w73 752
33:5 po 119; w71 743
33:17 w72 444

JOSHUA

1:8 g75 2/22 30; g75 12/8 24; w74 148; w73 202; w71 71
2:9 w73 702
2:10 w73 702
2:11 w73 702
5:9 w71 442; kj 192
7:8 bi8 1352
8:35 yb72 5/3
10:12 g74 1/8 15
10:13 g74 1/8 15
10:14 g74 1/8 15
11:3 w71 348
15:8 bi8 1355
18:16 bi8 1355
20:6 w73 304
21:45 yb76 1/17; w75 700
22:22 bi8 1356
22:24 bi8 1360
23:14 yb76 1/25; w75 82; w74 152; g74 4/8 15; w72 29
24:2 g73 11/8 27
24:16 yb72 8/17; w71 558

JUDGES

2:3 w74 457
2:6 tp 102
4:12 w74 232
4:13 w74 232
4:14 w74 232
4:15 w74 232
4:16 w74 232
5:1 w72 61
5:21 w74 232
5:31 w74 232
6:15 bi8 1352
8:14 w71 684
8:16 w71 684
9:27 w74 459
11:12 bi8 1360
13:5 g74 7/8 28
13:8 w73 562; bi8 1352
13:9 w73 562
14:8 g74 4/8 21
14:9 g74 4/8 21
19:15 w75 359
19:18 bi8 1353

RUTH

1:1 w72 78
1:2 w72 78
1:3 w72 78
1:4 w72 78
1:5 w72 78
1:6 w72 80
1:7 w72 80
1:8 w72 80
1:9 w72 80
1:10 w72 80
1:11 w72 80
1:12 w72 80
1:13 w72 80
1:14 w72 80
1:15 yb73 3/5; w72 80
1:16 w72 81
1:17 w72 81
1:18 w72 81
1:19 w72 81
1:20 w72 81
1:21 w72 78, 81
1:22 w72 81, 84
2:1 w72 84
2:2 w72 84
2:3 w72 84
2:4 w72 84
2:5 w72 84
2:6 w72 84
2:7 w72 84
2:8 w72 84
2:9 w72 84
2:10 w72 84
2:11 w72 84
2:12 w72 84; w71 92
2:13 w72 84
3:1 w72 86
3:2 w72 86
3:3 w72 86
3:4 w72 86
3:5 w72 86
3:6 w72 86
3:7 w72 86
3:8 w72 86
3:9 w72 86
3:10 w72 86
3:11 yb73 4/18; w72 86
3:12 yb73 5/1; w72 86
3:13 w72 86
3:14 w72 87
3:15 w72 87
3:16 w72 87
3:17 w72 87
3:18 w72 87
4:1 yb73 6/21; w72 87
4:2 w72 87
4:3 w72 87
4:4 w72 87
4:5 w72 87
4:6 w72 87
4:7 w72 87
4:8 w72 87
4:9 w72 87
4:10 w72 87
4:11 w72 87
4:12 w72 87
4:13 w72 88
4:14 w72 88
4:15 yb73 8/28; w72 88
4:16 w72 88
4:17 w72 88

1 SAMUEL

1:9 w74 173; w72 712
1:13 w74 136
1:20 w74 136
1:24 g72 11/22 14
1:25 g72 11/22 14
1:26 g72 11/22 14
1:27 g72 11/22 14
1:28 g72 11/22 14
2:1 kj 335
2:6 w73 243; bi8 1353; kj 335
2:18 w72 665
2:19 w72 665
3:3 w74 173; w72 712
3:13 bi8 1353
8:4 w71 743
8:5 w71 743
10:8 w71 479
12:24 g72 12/22 7
12:25 g72 12/22 7
13:12 w71 479
13:13 w71 479
13:14 w71 479
15:7 w71 540
16:7 w74 136; w72 665
16:13 w71 243
16:14 g72 11/22 4
16:15 g72 11/22 4
16:16 g72 11/22 4
16:17 g72 11/22 4
16:23 g72 11/22 4
18:1 yb76 1/13; w73 422; w72 740
18:3 w73 422
18:10 w71 575-6
19:20 w71 575-6
19:21 w71 575-6
19:23 w71 575-6
19:24 w71 575-6
20:30 w72 740
23:17 w72 740
24:1 w72 61
24:3 w72 61-2
24:4 w72 62
24:5 w72 556
26:23 w75 17
28:12 ts 75; g73 6/8 7
28:13 ts 75
28:14 ts 75
28:15 ts 75, 77

2 SAMUEL

1:23 g74 2/22 14
2:18 g74 2/22 12
5:3 w71 744
5:19 bi8 1353
5:20 sl 337; bi8 1353
5:21 bi8 1353
5:22 bi8 1353
5:23 bi8 1353
5:24 sl 337; bi8 1353
5:25 bi8 1353
6:6 w73 370
6:7 yb74 11/12; w73 370
6:9 bi8 1353
6:10 bi8 1353
6:11 bi8 1353
6:12 bi8 1353
6:13 bi8 1353
6:14 bi8 1353
6:15 bi8 1353
6:16 bi8 1353
6:17 bi8 1353
7:12 w71 302
7:13 w71 302
7:14 w74 82; kj 220
7:16 w74 68; po 126; w71 242
7:23 w72 681
11:4 w73 479
11:5 w73 479
12:1 g72 7/8 7
12:2 g72 7/8 7
12:3 g72 7/8 7
12:4 g72 7/8 7
12:5 g72 7/8 7
12:6 g72 7/8 7
12:14 bi8 1353
12:23 g74 12/8 26
16:10 bi8 1360
16:12 bi8 1353
19:19 bi8 1356
19:22 bi8 1360
19:24 w73 140
20:1 bi8 1353
22:6 bi8 1353
22:7 w72 712; kj 49
22:8 w72 153; kj 49
22:9 w72 153; kj 49
22:10 w74 255; w72 153; kj 49
22:11 w72 153; kj 49
22:26 yb74 5/2; w73 585
22:28 yb75 9/11; w74 412
22:36 w72 201
23:2 yb76 1/27; w75 144; g72 2/8 27
24:10 w75 210; w72 556

1 KINGS

1:6 w72 740
2:6 bi8 1353
2:9 bi8 1353
2:28 w73 303
2:34 w73 303
3:10 bi8 1352
3:12 w73 490
3:15 bi8 1352
3:26 w74 88; w71 412
3:27 w74 88
4:23 w72 190
4:25 yb76 4/25; fu 23
4:30 w73 490
4:31 w73 490
4:32 w73 490
4:33 w73 490
4:34 w73 490
6:1 w74 507; po 120; ka 207, 209; kj 27
6:37 w72 293
7:26 w72 295
7:46 g71 7/22 11
7:47 g71 7/22 11
8:27 w74 173; yb73 6/17; w72 710
8:46 g73 2/8 3
8:56 w75 82
8:65 pm 53
9:2 kj 27
9:3 kj 27
10:29 w71 348
11:4 w73 439; w71 566
12:16 bi8 1353
12:26 kj 99
12:27 kj 99
12:28 w72 295; kj 99
12:29 kj 99
12:30 kj 99
12:31 kj 99
12:32 kj 99
12:33 kj 99
14:9 w72 295
14:10 w74 363
16:29 kj 28
16:30 kj 28
16:31 kj 28
16:32 kj 28
17:18 bi8 1360
17:21 ts 42
18:21 bi8 1352
19:18 w74 536
20:13 bi8 1354; kj 28
20:22 kj 29
20:23 kj 29
20:24 kj 29
20:25 kj 29
20:26 kj 29
20:27 kj 29
20:28 kj 29

20:42 kj 30
20:43 kj 30
21:8 w71 684
21:10 bi8 1353
21:11 w71 684
21:13 bi8 1353
21:21 w74 363
22:6 bi8 1352
22:19 w74 436
22:20 w74 436
22:21 w74 436
22:22 w74 436

2 KINGS

1:2 w74 459; w72 666
1:3 w74 459
1:7 w72 666
1:8 w72 666
2:13 w72 666
2:14 w72 666
3:13 bi8 1360
5:1 w74 402
5:2 w74 536
5:3 w74 402
5:5 w74 402
5:6 w74 402
5:7 w74 402
5:8 w74 402
5:9 w74 402
5:10 w74 402
5:11 w74 402
5:12 w74 402
5:13 w74 403
5:14 w74 403
5:15 w74 403
5:16 w74 403
5:17 w74 403
5:18 w74 403
5:19 w74 403
5:20 w74 404
5:21 w74 404
5:22 w74 404
5:23 w74 405
5:24 w74 405
5:25 yb75 8/10; w74 405
5:26 w74 405
5:27 w75 570; yb75 8/10; w74 405
6:5 g71 12/8 23
6:17 pm 159
7:6 w71 348; bi8 1352
9:8 w74 363
9:22 w73 342
9:30 w72 668
10:30 w75 713
10:31 w75 713; g73 4/8 28
16:3 w74 144
18:11 kj 30
18:12 kj 30
18:33 g72 6/22 27
19:23 bi8 1352
19:35 kj 367
19:36 kj 367
20:3 w71 566
21:3 w74 144
21:5 w72 434
21:6 w74 144; w72 434
21:16 w72 434; kj 101, 103
22:2 g73 11/22 6
22:3 kj 155
22:8 w73 203
22:13 w73 203
22:20 kj 103
23:3 yb72 3/30
23:5 g73 11/22 6
23:10 bi8 1355
23:25 kj 102
23:26 kj 102
23:27 kj 102
24:3 kj 101
24:4 kj 101
24:18 w72 676; kj 195
24:19 w72 676; kj 195
24:20 w72 676; kj 96, 195, 266
25:1 kj 96, 195, 266
25:2 kj 96, 286
25:3 kj 109, 286
25:4 kj 109, 286
25:5 kj 109
25:8 g72 3/8 27
25:18 kj 67, 170
25:19 kj 170
25:20 kj 170
25:21 kj 170

1 CHRONICLES

1:1 po 66
1:19 ts 27
4:9 w73 647; g73 11/8 26
4:10 w73 647; g73 11/8 26
5:1 po 101
5:2 po 101
5:10 w74 286
5:18 w74 286
5:19 w74 286
5:20 w74 286
5:21 w74 286
5:22 w74 286
6:16 w73 393
6:31 w73 393
6:32 w73 393
12:8 g74 2/22 12
13:12 bi8 1353
14:10 bi8 1353
14:11 sl 337; bi8 1353
14:14 bi8 1353
14:15 sl 337
14:16 bi8 1353
16:1 bi8 1353
16:31 w71 744
17:11 po 126
17:12 po 126
17:14 po 126
19:2 w73 478
19:4 w73 478
24:4 w73 62
28:9 yb72 1/1; w71 146
29:11 w74 240; w73 368
29:23 po 128; w72 630; dn 27; w71 744; kj 220

2 CHRONICLES

7:8 pm 53
7:9 pm 53
7:11 w72 439
10:16 bi8 1353
11:14 kj 99
11:15 kj 99
12:12 w72 439
12:13 w72 439
12:14 w72 439
16:9 yb72 1/7
16:10 w75 647
19:6 w72 464
19:7 yb73 7/26; w72 464
20:6 w71 358
20:7 po 90
20:13 yb72 3/27
20:15 sl 263; w72 753
20:17 ka 155
21:12 w74 298
25:14 po 95
28:3 bi8 1355
30:6 g72 8/8 28
33:6 bi8 1355
33:11 w72 434
33:12 w72 434
33:13 w72 434
33:22 kj 102
33:23 kj 102
33:24 kj 102
33:25 kj 102
34:38 kj 103
35:21 bi8 1360
36:11 w72 676; kj 195, 228
36:12 w72 676; kj 195, 228
36:13 w72 676; kj 195, 228
36:15 w74 154; g73 3/8 4
36:16 kj 188
36:17 kj 188, 289
36:18 kj 188, 289
36:19 kj 188, 289, 314
36:20 sl 125; po 130; w72 351; kj 188, 289, 314
36:21 sl 125; po 130; g72 5/8 27; kj 289, 314, 341
36:22 sl 163; w72 351, 746; g72 5/8 27; kj 289, 341
36:23 sl 163; w73 149, 251; w72 351, 746; g72 5/8 27; kj 289, 341

EZRA

1:1 sl 163; w72 746; kj 341
1:2 sl 163; kj 341
1:3 yb73 5/3; w72 300; kj 341
1:4 kj 341
1:5 w72 301
1:8 pm 29
1:11 pm 29
2:58 w72 725
2:61 g72 3/8 28
2:62 g72 3/8 28
2:63 g72 3/8 28
2:64 g72 3/8 28; kj 329, 341, 347
2:65 kj 329, 341, 347
2:66 kj 341
2:67 kj 341
3:1 sl 166; ts 158; pm 30; g72 5/8 27; kj 329
3:2 sl 166; g72 5/8 27; kj 329
3:3 sl 166; g72 5/8 27
3:4 sl 166; pm 30
3:5 sl 166
3:6 sl 166; ts 158; pm 30
3:8 w72 746; pm 30
3:12 w72 746
3:13 sl 167
4:2 w71 672
4:23 pm 31
4:24 pm 31
5:1 pm 32, 93
6:11 g74 9/22 28; bi8 1360
6:15 sl 321; w72 746
7:6 w71 229; sg 16
8:17 or 110
8:20 or 110
9:6 g74 3/22 14
10:3 bi8 1352
10:14 w71 684

NEHEMIAH

1:11 bi8 1352
2:1 g71 12/8 8
2:6 g71 12/8 8
3:13 ts 113
3:14 ts 113
4:14 bi8 1352
7:4 w73 369
7:26 po 134
7:63 g72 3/8 28
7:64 g72 3/8 28
7:65 w74 157; g72 3/8 28
7:66 g72 3/8 28; kj 329
7:67 kj 329
8:8 w73 204, 206
8:10 w73 460; w72 190
9:17 yb76 7/25
9:36 ts 158
10:39 yb74 4/8; w73 404
11:1 yb74 5/4; w73 369
11:2 w73 369
11:30 bi8 1355
12:43 w74 271

ESTHER

1:1 yb72 1/29; w71 172
1:2 w71 172
1:3 yb72 1/29; w71 172
1:4 w71 172
1:9 w71 172
1:10 w71 173
1:11 w71 173
1:12 yb72 2/8; w71 173
2:7 w71 175
2:10 w71 175
2:11 yb72 3/4; w71 175
2:15 w71 176
2:17 w71 176
2:18 w71 176
2:20 yb72 4/26; w71 176
2:21 yb72 3/17; w71 176
2:22 yb72 3/17; w71 176
2:23 w71 176
3:1 yb72 5/9; w71 177
3:2 yb72 5/31; w71 177
3:6 w71 178
3:7 w71 178
3:10 w71 178
3:11 w71 178
3:12 w71 178
3:13 w71 178
4:1 w71 179
4:16 yb72 7/5; w71 179
5:2 w71 180
5:4 w71 180
5:5 w71 180
6:1 w71 181
6:4 w71 181
6:5 w71 181
6:6 w71 181
6:11 w71 181
7:3 w71 182
7:10 yb72 8/26
8:2 yb72 9/18
8:11 yb72 10/7; w71 184
8:15 w71 184
8:16 w71 184
8:17 w71 184
9:2 yb72 12/8
9:25 w71 185
9:28 yb72 11/16
9:31 w71 185
10:1 w71 185
10:2 w71 185
10:3 yb72 1/16; w71 185

JOB

1:1 w71 566
1:5 bi8 1353
1:6 w74 640; po 27; g73 12/8 27
1:7 w72 648
1:8 w72 648; yb72 4/18; w71 565
1:9 fu 17; w72 648; yb72 2/4; w71 267
1:10 w72 648; w71 267
1:11 w72 648; yb72 6/6; bi8 1353
1:12 w72 648
1:20 w72 648

g, Awake!; **ka**, God's Kingdom of a Thousand Years; **kj**, "The Nations Shall Know that I Am Jehovah"; **km**, Kingdom Ministry; **or**, Organization; **pm**, Paradise Restored—By Theocracy!; **po**, God's "Eternal Purpose"; **sg**, Theocratic School Guidebook; **sl**, Man's Salvation out of World Distress!; **te**, Listening to the Great Teacher; **tp**, True Peace and Security; **ts**, Is This Life All There Is?; **w**, Watchtower; **yb**, Yearbook. **Complete list on page 6.**

1:21 sl 60; w72 648
1:22 sl 60; w72 648
2:1 w74 640; g73 12/8 27
2:3 w74 150
2:4 w74 169; w73 196
2:5 w74 169; w73 196; bi8 1353
2:9 w72 648; bi8 1353
2:10 w72 648
3:17 ts 121
3:18 ts 121
3:19 ts 121
4:15 g75 5/22 27
4:16 g75 5/22 27
7:4 g75 3/8 13
7:9 bi8 1353
7:17 po 67
7:20 bi8 1353
9:4 w73 228
9:6 g74 5/8 19
11:8 bi8 1353
14:13 w73 235; g72 3/8 17; w71 708; bi8 1353
14:15 w75 90; g75 10/22 8
17:13 bi8 1353
17:16 bi8 1353
21:13 bi8 1353
24:1 ml 24
24:14 g74 7/22 27
24:19 bi8 1353
26:6 bi8 1353
26:7 w75 133; g73 7/8 21; w72 646
26:14 g71 6/8 12
27:5 sl 61
28:2 g71 7/22 11
28:5 w71 640
28:28 w75 101; g72 9/8 28; bi8 1352
31:26 g73 5/22 28; w72 296
31:27 g73 5/22 28; w72 296
31:28 g73 5/22 28; w72 296
32:3 bi8 1353
32:6 yb72 2/26
33:22 ts 42
34:14 g72 8/8 27
35:6 w75 713
35:7 w75 713
38:3 w72 646
38:4 g73 2/8 27; w72 646
38:5 g73 2/8 27; w72 646
38:6 g73 2/8 27; w72 646
38:7 po 27; ts 81, 83; g73 5/22 14; w72 427, 646-7
38:12 w74 572; w72 646
38:13 w74 572; w72 646
38:14 w74 572
38:24 g75 1/22 16
38:33 g74 1/8 15
38:39 w71 327
38:40 w71 327
38:41 w71 327
39:18 g74 2/22 14
40:15 bi8 1366
40:23 g72 11/8 25
41:22 bi8 1366
41:23 bi8 1366
42:5 g71 8/22 28
42:7 w72 648
42:8 w72 648
42:10 sl 89
42:12 w73 502

PSALMS

1:2 w73 205
1:3 w75 697; w73 205
2:1 yb76 5/10; w75 620; og 22; w74 398; g74 4/8 19; ka 165
2:2 yb76 5/10; w75 620; og 22; w74 398; g74 4/8 19; w72 181; w71 99
2:3 w74 398
2:4 w74 398; bi8 1352
2:5 sl 232, 348; w74 398
2:6 sl 190, 232; w74 398; w72 181
2:7 w74 158; ka 88
2:8 w75 620; sl 42; og 23; ka 262; kj 306
2:9 w75 620; sl 42, 348; og 23; ka 21, 262; kj 306
2:10 sl 347; w73 283
2:11 sl 347; w73 283
2:12 w75 687; sl 44-5, 347; w73 283; w72 181
4:4 w73 370
4:8 g75 3/8 14
5:4 w74 639
5:5 w74 247; g72 9/22 3
5:6 w74 247; ts 73
6:5 ts 92; bi8 1353
6:9 w72 389
7:10 bi8 1352
8:3 yb76 11/28; w75 18; g74 1/8 15
8:4 yb76 11/28; w75 18, 607; g74 1/8 15
8:5 w75 173, 607; sl 50; bi8 1356
8:6 yb76 8/21; w75 607; w74 594
8:7 w75 607
8:8 w75 607
9:9 w73 399
9:10 yb75 1/15; w74 434
9:17 bi8 1353
10:3 bi8 1353
10:4 g72 10/22 9
10:11 g72 10/22 9
10:13 yb72 1/8
10:16 w74 376
10:17 yb76 1/7; w75 401
11:4 yb73 7/3; w72 712
11:7 w73 467
14:1 yb76 5/25; w73 451; tp 144; w72 128; bi8 1353
14:2 bi8 1353
14:5 bi8 1353
15:1 w74 247
15:2 w74 247; w72 29
15:3 w74 247
15:4 w72 29
16:2 bi8 1352
16:8 yb73 7/28; w72 526
16:10 po 153; w73 238; g72 11/8 6; bi8 1353
16:11 po 153
17:8 yb75 9/19; w74 727
18:5 bi8 1353
18:6 w72 712; kj 48-9
18:7 w72 153; kj 48-9
18:8 w72 153; kj 48-9
18:9 w72 153; kj 48-9
18:10 w72 153; kj 48-9
18:23 w71 565
18:35 g73 3/8 4
19:1 w74 187; w73 554; g73 5/22 8
19:2 w74 187; w73 554
19:3 w74 187
19:7 w74 90; g73 2/8 27; w72 36, 288
19:11 w75 18
19:14 w73 460
20:7 g72 10/22 25
22:1 w72 256
22:10 yb73 11/18; w72 114
22:22 or 92; w71 746
22:23 w71 746; bi8 1354
22:30 bi8 1352
23:1 kj 293
23:4 or 57; pm 311
24:1 g73 2/8 27; w71 43, 307, 616; nc 11
25:4 yb76 2/8; g74 1/8 9
25:5 yb76 2/8; g74 1/8 9
25:8 w71 325
25:9 w75 711
26:1 yb72 6/1; w71 524
26:2 yb76 7/2; w71 524
26:3 w71 527
26:4 yb72 7/12; w71 528
26:5 yb72 7/12; w71 528
26:6 w72 414; w71 528
26:7 w71 529
26:8 yb72 12/30; w71 528
26:9 w71 528
26:10 w71 528
26:11 w71 529
26:12 w74 566; yb73 8/18; w72 406
27:4 yb76 11/4; w73 404; w72 184, 712
27:5 w74 726
27:8 yb74 4/19; w73 368
27:9 w73 368
27:10 km 5/73 5
27:13 bi8 1356
27:14 w73 474
28:8 po 98; w73 756
28:9 po 98; w73 756
29:1 bi8 1357
30:3 bi8 1353
30:5 w71 360
30:8 bi8 1352
31:5 ts 52; g72 8/8 28
31:17 bi8 1353
31:24 yb76 10/22
32:1 w72 600
32:2 w72 600
32:3 g74 2/22 11; w73 229
32:4 g74 2/22 11; w73 229
32:5 g74 2/22 11; w72 600
32:9 g74 3/22 14; w72 273
33:9 sl 289
33:17 g72 10/22 25
33:20 po 126
33:21 po 126
34:7 w73 485
34:11 yb76 3/19
34:13 w72 67
34:14 w72 67
34:15 w74 534
34:18 g74 6/8 4; w72 439
35:17 bi8 1352
35:19 w73 652
35:22 bi8 1352
35:23 bi8 1352
36:2 w74 247
36:6 ts 107
36:9 ml 9; w73 325, 488; g73 10/22 9, 25; w71 44
37:1 w72 499
37:2 w72 499
37:8 w75 647
37:9 w73 476; g73 2/8 27; kj 122
37:10 w74 4; w72 499; kj 122
37:11 yb75 8/12; w74 377, 662; g73 4/22 20; w72 500; g72 11/8 7
37:13 bi8 1352
37:21 w71 127
37:23 w74 574
37:25 w74 535; tp 116
37:28 w73 195
37:29 w74 377
37:31 w73 415; yb72 8/25
37:35 w72 499
37:36 w72 499
37:37 w73 319
38:9 bi8 1352
38:15 bi8 1352
38:22 bi8 1352
39:1 sg 95
39:7 bi8 1352
40:1 w73 476
40:5 g74 6/8 6
40:6 w72 686, 715
40:7 w72 686, 715
40:8 w74 603; w73 327; yb73 2/20; w72 178, 686, 715
40:17 bi8 1352
41:3 g74 6/8 6
43:3 w73 394
44:21 w74 136
44:23 bi8 1352
45:1 w71 635
45:6 w71 635
45:7 w73 285, 460; w71 635
45:13 w74 700
45:14 sl 360; yb75 12/26; w74 700
45:15 sl 360; w74 700; w71 711
45:16 sl 80, 360-4; yb75 213; w74 292; ts 132, 167; w73 200, 427; ka 132, 135; g73 5/8 7; w72 581; w71 635; kj 404
46:1 yb76 10/15; sl 353; g74 1/8 9; yb73 11/2; w72 526
46:2 sl 353; w74 569; w72 526
46:3 sl 353
46:4 sl 353
46:5 sl 353
46:6 sl 353
46:7 sl 353
46:8 sl 281, 353
46:9 sl 281, 353; w71 77; g71 9/8 27
46:10 sl 281, 353
46:11 sl 353
47:6 w75 30
47:7 w75 30
48:6 g72 11/22 14
49:6 w71 271
49:7 w75 431; g75 1/8 27; po 116; ts 138; w73 412; w71 271
49:8 w75 431; g75 1/8 27; po 116; w73 412; w71 271
49:9 w75 431; w73 412; w71 271
49:14 bi8 1353
49:15 bi8 1353
50:9 ts 68
50:10 ts 68
50:11 ts 68
50:12 ts 68

51:superscription w72 62
51:1 w74 138
51:4 w74 138
51:5 w74 138, 200; yb72 5/30; g72 12/22 4; g71 12/8 27
51:6 g74 12/8 4; w72 556
51:7 w74 138; g73 9/8 27
51:10 w74 138
51:11 w74 138
51:14 w74 138
51:15 w74 138; bi8 1352
53:1 bi8 1353
53:2 bi8 1353
53:4 bi8 1353
53:5 bi8 1353
54:4 bi8 1352
55:9 bi8 1352
55:15 bi8 1353
55:21 w74 245
55:22 w75 518; g75 2/22 3; g74 6/8 6; w73 555; yb73 9/8; w72 521
55:23 w73 306
57:superscription w72 61
57:6 w72 61
57:9 bi8 1352
58:5 g75 6/8 19
59:11 bi8 1352
62:8 g74 6/8 5; w72 331
62:11 w72 295
62:12 bi8 1352
63:6 yb73 3/18
64:3 w74 755
64:4 w74 755
64:5 w74 755
65:2 yb76 5/1; w74 367; g74 1/8 9; yb73 1/9
65:4 yb72 3/31
66:10 sl 369
66:11 sl 369
66:12 sl 369
66:18 bi8 1352
67:6 g74 3/22 6; tp 102
67:7 tp 102
68:7 pm 60
68:8 pm 60
68:11 w74 533; bi8 1352
68:12 w74 533
68:17 bi8 1352
68:18 yb75 5/19; w74 620; hu 20; w71 748
68:19 bi8 1352
68:20 bi8 1352
68:22 bi8 1352
68:26 bi8 1352
68:32 bi8 1352
69:4 w73 652
69:6 bi8 1352
69:9 w73 7
69:12 w74 303
71:4 w75 662
71:5 w72 758
71:16 w75 662
72:4 g73 11/22 12
72:12 w74 617; hu 15
72:13 w74 617; hu 15; w72 581
72:14 w74 617; hu 15
72:16 g73 11/22 12
73:2 yb76 3/15; w75 50
73:3 yb76 3/15; w75 50
73:4 w75 50
73:5 w75 50
73:11 w75 50
73:12 w75 50
73:13 w75 50, 124
73:17 w75 51
73:18 w75 51
73:20 bi8 1352
73:23 w75 51
73:24 yb76 7/8; w75 616; og 14
73:25 yb76 7/8; w75 616; og 14
73:27 w75 51
73:28 yb76 4/22, 10/14; w75 51, 616, 662; og 14
74:18 w73 326
74:22 w73 326
75:6 pm 378
75:7 pm 378
77:2 w72 523; bi8 1352
77:7 bi8 1352
77:9 w74 499; w72 549; g72 10/22 10
77:12 w72 523
77:14 g72 10/22 10
78:5 yb76 1/8; w75 434
78:6 w75 434
78:40 w73 227
78:41 w73 227
78:50 ts 42
78:57 w72 439
78:65 bi8 1352
78:69 w74 4
79:12 bi8 1352
80:1 po 29; w72 717; kj 38
82:1 bi8 1356
82:5 ka 117; w71 637
82:6 w75 270; w74 104; bi8 1356
82:7 w74 104
83:18 yb76 11/19; w75 614, 617; og 10, 16; g72 11/8 6
84:11 yb76 3/8; w74 754; w73 173; kj 155
85:10 w73 363
85:11 w74 42; w73 363
85:12 w73 363
85:13 w73 363
86:3 bi8 1352
86:4 bi8 1352
86:5 bi8 1352
86:8 bi8 1352
86:9 bi8 1352
86:12 bi8 1352
86:13 bi8 1353
86:15 yb76 3/17; w75 148; bi8 1352
88:3 bi8 1353
89:11 w71 43
89:27 po 89
89:28 po 126
89:29 po 126; g72 10/22 13
89:30 po 126
89:31 po 126
89:32 po 126
89:33 po 126
89:34 po 126
89:35 po 126
89:36 po 126; g72 2/8 11; g72 10/22 13
89:48 bi8 1353
89:49 bi8 1352
89:50 bi8 1352
90:1 bi8 1352
90:2 yb76 11/10; po 26; ts 81; w73 196
90:3 sl 293
90:4 sl 293; po 7; ka 13; w72 38; kj 8
90:10 sl 7; g72 1/22 20
90:12 g71 8/8 8
90:17 bi8 1352
91:1 sl 334; yb75 7/10, 11/16, 12/4; w74 724, 726, 731; ka 155
91:2 yb75 260, 10/19, 11/26, 12/4; w74 172, 728, 730-1; bi8 1354
91:3 yb75 12/14, 12/18, 12/27, 12/30; w74 172, 731, 733
91:4 yb75 6/8, 6/29, 7/5, 8/2; w74 172, 752-3
91:5 yb75 7/12, 7/19, 7/26, 8/22; w74 172, 754-5
91:6 yb75 7/26, 8/22; w74 172, 754-5
91:7 w75 286, 377; yb75 8/30, 9/7; w74 172, 723, 757
91:8 w74 172, 758; ka 155; yb72 10/26
91:9 w74 759; bi8 1354
91:10 yb75 9/27, 10/4; w74 759-60
91:11 yb75 9/30; w74 722, 760
91:12 yb75 10/11, 10/24; w74 722, 761
91:13 yb75 10/18, 10/31, 11/7; w74 762
91:14 yb75 11/19, 11/30; w74 764
91:15 yb75 11/29; w74 765
91:16 yb75 12/13, 12/31; w74 765-6
92:1 bi8 1354
92:4 bi8 1354
92:5 bi8 1354
92:7 w74 645
92:8 bi8 1354
92:9 bi8 1354
92:14 w74 168, 424
94:20 yb76 127; kj 326
95:1 yb72 4/6
95:2 w71 392
95:3 w71 392; bi8 1356
95:6 yb73 2/17; w72 335; kj 398
95:7 kj 398
95:8 g72 11/22 8
95:9 g72 11/22 8
95:10 g72 11/22 8
95:11 g72 11/22 8
96:1 w75 30; yb74 1/31; w73 401; w71 479, 512
96:2 w75 30
96:5 w74 173; w73 486; yb73 11/28; w72 742, 754; bi8 1356
96:7 bi8 1354
96:8 w71 283; bi8 1354
96:9 bi8 1354
96:10 w73 401; w71 744; bi8 1354
96:13 bi8 1354
97:1 bi8 1354
97:5 bi8 1354
97:7 bi8 1356
97:9 bi8 1354
97:10 yb76 4/7; yb75 8/3; w74 153, 442; yb74 5/10; w72 439; g72 9/22 3; w71 556; bi8 1354
97:12 bi8 1354
98:1 w73 622; dy 25
98:2 w73 622; dy 25
98:3 w73 622; dy 25
98:8 g73 2/8 27
99:1 po 29; yb72 6/2; w71 712
100:3 w73 554
101:superscription w72 62
101:5 w74 247; w73 422
101:6 w74 247, 531; w73 422
101:7 w74 247; w73 422
102:superscription w71 479
102:15 bi8 1354
102:16 bi8 1354
102:24 tp 58
102:25 w71 479-80
102:26 w71 479-80
103:1 w74 134; bi8 1354
103:2 w74 134; bi8 1354
103:3 w74 134
103:4 w74 134
103:5 w74 134
103:6 bi8 1354
103:8 w75 517; bi8 1354
103:9 w75 517
103:10 w74 463
103:13 w74 463; w73 441; g72 2/8 3; w71 566
103:14 yb76 1/4; w75 518; w74 529; w73 441; w71 566
103:19 w74 240; w72 645, 658
103:20 w73 393; tp 49; w72 658
103:21 w73 393; w72 658
103:22 w72 658
104:1 w72 153; kj 48
104:2 w72 153; kj 48
104:3 w72 153; kj 48
104:4 w72 153; kj 48
104:5 g73 5/22 15; w72 659; g72 2/8 11
104:24 w74 189
104:29 ts 49; g72 8/8 27
104:31 w72 659
105:15 po 98
105:17 w74 502
105:18 w74 502
105:37 g73 8/22 29
106:3 w74 205
106:20 w72 295; bi8 1353
106:36 g74 2/22 4
106:37 g74 2/22 4
107:27 w74 452; w72 618; dn 5
109:8 w71 690
109:21 bi8 1352
110:1 w74 236, 331; po 88, 141, 177; ka 71; w72 628, 696; pm 153, 331; dn 23; w71 239
110:2 sl 316; w74 236, 331; po 88, 177; w72 180, 628, 631; pm 331; dn 23; w71 239
110:3 w74 236; po 88; w73 328

110:4 w74 158, 236; po 88, 90, 155; ka 89-90; pm 200
110:5 sl 276; w72 181; bi8 1352
110:6 sl 276; w72 181, 628; dn 23
111:10 yb76 11/18; w74 93, 408; w71 357
114:18 w72 176
115:1 w74 595
115:3 sl 289
115:15 g73 5/22 13
115:16 w74 594; w73 425; g73 5/22 13; w72 291; w71 555; kj 399
115:17 w73 329
116:1 w75 303; ka 400
116:2 w75 303; ka 400
116:3 w75 303; ka 400; w72 176; bi8 1353
116:4 w75 303; ka 400
116:5 w75 303; ka 400
116:6 w75 303; ka 400
116:7 w75 304; ka 402, 404
116:8 w75 304; ts 42; ka 402
116:9 w75 304; ka 402, 405
116:10 w75 304, 328; ka 402-3
116:11 w75 304; ka 402
116:12 w75 329; w73 299; ka 405; yb72 4/30
116:13 w75 329; ka 405; yb72 4/30
116:14 w75 329; ka 405; w72 176
116:15 w75 329; w74 172; ka 407-8; w72 520
116:16 w75 329; ka 407
116:17 w75 330; ka 410-11
116:18 w75 330; ka 410
116:19 w75 330; ka 410
118:22 pm 188
118:23 pm 188
118:26 w74 399
119:8 w73 189
119:9 w73 190
119:11 w73 190
119:36 w73 189; w72 306
119:37 w73 407
119:46 w73 189
119:54 w73 189
119:62 yb76 11/15; w74 211
119:63 yb76 2/11
119:72 g74 8/8 5; w73 189
119:97 w74 85; w73 189, 461
119:99 yb76 5/28
119:100 yb76 5/28; w73 189
119:104 w73 189
119:105 w73 113, 190; g72 12/22 6
119:113 w72 603
119:120 w73 190
119:130 w74 90
119:145 w72 335
119:159 w73 189
119:165 w75 126; w73 189; tp 181
119:176 w73 189
121:1 yb73 3/17
121:2 yb73 3/17
121:4 w74 754
122:1 or 91; yb72 12/21
124:6 yb75 12/12
124:7 yb75 12/12; w74 731; w73 299
124:8 w73 299
126:1 yb72 7/23; kj 300
126:2 yb72 7/23; kj 300
126:3 kj 300
126:4 kj 300
127:1 w73 395
127:3 yb76 3/14; w74 82; g74 11/8 11
130:2 bi8 1352
130:3 bi8 1352
130:6 bi8 1352
132:11 po 126; w72 241
132:12 po 126
132:13 w71 446
136:2 bi8 1356
136:3 bi8 1354
137:7 sl 221
137:8 sl 221
138:1 bi8 1356
138:2 yb72 7/14, 9/29; w71 657
138:6 yb74 10/16
138:8 w71 657
139:1 w73 211, 317
139:8 w71 288; bi8 1353
139:13 g74 2/8 15; g73 12/22 27
139:14 w75 712; ml 12; g72 10/22 8; g71 6/8 8
139:15 g74 2/8 15; g73 12/22 27
139:16 ts 173; g74 2/8 15; w73 726; g73 12/22 27; g71 2/22 15
139:17 g74 2/8 16
139:21 w74 442; g72 9/22 3
139:22 w74 442; g72 9/22 3
140:7 bi8 1352
141:2 w71 285
141:5 w75 269; w72 740
141:7 bi8 1353
141:8 bi8 1352
143:10 yb76 1/11; sg 49
145:8 w74 146, 499; w72 549, 554; w71 411
145:9 yb75 11/23; w74 146, 499; w72 549-50; w71 411
145:18 yb76 1/14; g74 1/8 11
145:20 g73 4/8 17
145:21 te 107
146:3 w75 242, 420; fu 6; w74 701, 730; tp 21; w72 229, 618; dn 5
146:4 w75 242; w74 730; ts 50; tp 21; w72 229; g72 8/8 27; g72 11/8 6
146:5 w74 701, 730; tp 21; w72 229, 619; dn 6
146:6 w74 701; tp 21; w72 229
146:7 w72 229
147:4 g72 2/8 9
147:18 w71 350
147:19 po 119
147:20 po 119
148:3 g72 2/8 9
148:6 ts 34; w71 480
148:12 yb76 12/23; yb73 1/20; w72 401
148:13 yb76 12/23; yb72 4/16; w71 648

PROVERBS

1:5 w72 703; sg 24
1:7 yb75 2/25; w74 179; w73 491; w71 53, 660
1:8 yb76 3/25; w73 141; yb72 2/20; w71 526
1:10 g73 5/8 3
1:11 g73 5/8 3
1:12 bi8 1353
1:22 w74 90
1:23 w74 90
1:30 w72 392
1:32 w73 342; w72 675
1:33 fu 28; w73 342
2:3 w73 491
2:4 w73 491, 538
2:5 w73 491, 538
2:7 w71 529
2:9 w73 491
2:21 tp 38; kj 375
2:22 tp 38; kj 375
3:5 yb75 2/26, 4/28; fu 32; w74 730
3:6 yb76 1/28; yb75 2/26; fu 32; w74 265; w72 272
3:7 yb75 4/28; w73 505
3:9 w73 159, 395, 493
3:10 w73 395, 493
3:11 w73 492
3:12 w73 492; w72 272
3:13 yb76 12/11
3:14 yb76 12/11
3:16 yb76 12/11
3:24 g75 3/8 14
3:25 w75 377-8
3:26 w75 377-8
3:31 g75 12/8 29
3:32 w73 317
4:1 yb76 2/22; w75 14; w73 532
4:4 w73 532
4:5 w75 15
4:7 w75 15
4:10 yb76 9/12
4:12 w71 660
4:13 w75 15; w71 660
4:18 km 2/74 6; w73 394; w72 498, 644
4:20 yb72 9/24
4:21 yb72 9/24
4:23 w74 153, 247; w73 540; w72 112; yb72 4/9; w71 133; g71 11/8 4
4:24 w74 247
4:25 yb72 9/20; w71 337
4:26 w71 337
4:27 yb72 9/20; w71 337
5:1 yb75 7/3; w72 644
5:2 yb75 7/3; w72 644
5:5 bi8 1353
5:18 w72 735
5:19 w72 735
6:6 g73 9/8 10
6:16 w74 153, 247; w72 603
6:17 w74 153, 247
6:18 w74 153
6:19 w74 153
6:20 yb76 9/23; w73 561
6:23 w74 410; w71 661
6:24 w73 523
6:25 w73 523
6:27 g71 5/8 28
6:28 g71 5/8 28
6:29 w73 31
7:2 w73 191
7:3 w73 191
7:23 w75 699
7:26 tp 154
7:27 bi8 1353
8:12 w72 486
8:13 w74 179, 408; g72 9/22 3; g71 9/8 4
8:20 w73 505
8:22 w75 511-12; w74 69; po 28
8:23 po 28
8:24 w75 511-12; po 28
8:25 w75 511-12; po 28
8:26 po 28
8:27 po 28
8:28 po 28
8:29 po 28
8:30 w74 69, 311, 594; po 28; w72 486
8:31 w74 69; po 28; w71 270
8:35 w72 105-6
8:36 w72 106
9:8 w73 423
9:9 w73 504
9:10 g72 11/22 18; w71 53, 357
9:18 bi8 1353
10:2 w74 722
10:7 yb74 10/14; w73 210, 287
10:9 w74 246
10:12 yb76 11/13; w74 441; w73 371; w72 739
10:15 w74 419
10:22 g73 4/22 21
10:23 w73 492
11:2 w75 100; w74 532
11:4 yb76 3/9; w75 6; w73 159
11:22 w73 523
11:25 g72 11/22 4
11:27 w72 368, 374
11:28 g74 1/22 8
12:1 yb76 1/2
12:8 w73 542
12:10 w73 159; g72 7/8 7
12:13 w74 246
12:15 w73 141
12:18 w73 504
12:19 w74 247
13:10 w73 542
13:12 w73 474
13:18 w74 266
13:19 w73 492
13:20 yb75 12/7; w74 93; w73 492; yb73 1/1; w72 5, 196; yb72 3
13:21 w72 393; kj 129
13:22 w72 245
13:24 g74 2/8 8; g74 4/22 15; w73 557; tp 175; w72 270
14:6 w73 491
14:8 w73 492
14:15 g74 3/8 10; w73 504; yb73 3/21
14:20 w73 422
14:21 w72 583
14:30 w74 524; w72 196; yb72 2/7; g72 12/22 20

14:32 yb72 6/29
15:1 g75 11/22 12; w74 268; g74 3/8 4; g74 5/22 27; g72 3/22 15
15:2 w73 493
15:3 yb75 4/16; w74 529; yb74 4/21; w73 317, 555; w72 267
15:5 yb76 5/4; w75 15
15:8 w73 493
15:11 bi8 1353
15:12 w73 423
15:14 w73 504
15:17 tp 110; w72 68
15:19 w74 182
15:22 w75 708, 766; w73 542; w72 203
15:23 g75 1/8 10
15:24 bi8 1353
15:28 g75 12/8 24; w74 104; w73 504
15:29 yb76 5/14; w73 493; yb73 5/11
15:30 w73 493
15:31 w74 266
15:32 w74 266
15:33 w74 266
16:3 po 18
16:4 po 18, 77
16:7 w73 157
16:9 yb72 9/3; w71 141; sg 75
16:14 w72 742
16:18 w71 181
16:20 w73 493, 504
16:21 g75 1/8 10; w73 504
16:23 g75 1/8 11; w73 504
16:25 tp 113
16:27 w74 269
16:31 g72 1/22 22
16:32 g74 5/22 28; w72 68
17:1 w72 68
17:9 w74 441
17:17 yb76 11/3; w74 89; w73 157, 421; w72 740
17:18 w71 767
17:20 w74 246
17:22 g74 8/22 19; g73 12/22 10
17:24 g72 9/8 27
17:25 yb73 7/9
17:27 w73 542
18:1 w75 155; w74 181; g74 6/8 4
18:9 g73 7/22 25
18:10 fu 12; w74 729; w73 485; w72 395
18:11 w74 419, 544
18:13 w73 504
18:15 w73 504
18:17 g75 1/8 10; w73 504
18:22 yb76 7/12
18:24 w73 157, 421
19:1 w73 157; ka 127
19:6 w73 422
19:11 g74 3/8 4
19:17 w74 500; w73 494
19:20 w71 660
19:21 yb75 3/1; w74 614; hu 7; w72 35; w71 141
19:22 w73 157
19:23 w75 699
19:26 g75 5/22 24
20:1 w75 300; w74 451; w73 669
20:6 w74 367
20:7 ka 127
20:10 g75 10/8 17
20:12 g71 8/22 10
20:14 g73 7/22 14
20:17 w74 246
20:19 w71 222
20:22 w73 474, 476
20:23 w75 291; g74 3/8 28
20:25 w73 607
21:3 w73 490
21:5 w72 274
21:9 w71 582
21:11 w73 504
21:17 w74 453
21:18 tp 43; w71 633
21:19 w71 582
21:23 w73 542
21:29 w74 616; hu 11
21:30 w74 616; hu 11
21:31 w74 616; hu 11
22:1 w74 533; w73 156; yb72 5/16; w71 387, 645
22:2 w74 420
22:3 w75 101; g75 11/22 13; w74 90; g73 4/22 14
22:4 w74 408
22:6 yb76 3/11; yb75 1/3; w74 81, 84, 268; yb74 4/30; g74 2/8 7; w73 552-4, 556-7; yb73 2/5; yb72 10/21; w71 341
22:7 w75 5; w71 766
22:11 w73 157
22:13 w74 589
22:15 w74 82; g74 4/22 15; w73 556; w71 592
22:26 w75 4; w71 767
22:27 w75 4; w71 767
23:1 w73 599
23:2 w73 599
23:3 w73 599
23:4 w75 567
23:5 w75 567
23:6 w73 599
23:7 w73 599
23:8 w73 599
23:13 yb75 3/10; w74 82; yb74 7/30; g74 4/22 15; w73 557; yb72 11/20; w71 592
23:14 yb75 3/10; w74 82; g74 4/22 15; w73 557; yb72 11/20; w71 592; bi8 1353
23:15 w72 116
23:16 w72 116
23:20 w74 453; yb74 3/4; w72 196
23:21 w74 167, 453; w72 196
23:22 g75 5/22 24; w73 461
23:23 w73 156, 461; g72 12/22 7
23:24 w74 272; w73 156, 461
23:25 w74 272; w73 156, 461
23:26 yb72 1/20; w71 150
23:29 w73 668
23:30 w73 668
23:31 w73 668
23:32 w74 452; w73 668
23:33 w73 668
23:34 w73 668
23:35 w73 668
24:3 w73 182, 541
24:4 w73 541
24:10 w72 275
24:16 w73 408
24:21 g73 3/22 15; w72 268
24:22 w72 268
24:23 yb76 7/27
24:25 w73 541
24:26 w73 541
24:27 w73 493; w71 312
24:29 g75 6/8 4; g74 5/22 27; w71 373; te 132
24:30 w74 589
24:31 w74 589
24:32 w74 589
24:33 w74 589
24:34 w74 589
25:8 w72 466; or 157
25:9 w72 466; or 157
25:10 w72 466; or 157
25:11 w75 486; w73 504; g73 9/8 17
25:12 w73 503
25:17 w74 61; w73 600
25:23 w71 350
25:27 w72 597
25:28 w75 647; g74 5/22 28; w73 186; w72 68
26:4 w72 127-8
26:5 w72 127-8
26:17 w71 373; te 134
26:18 g75 7/22 15
26:19 g75 7/22 15
27:2 g72 2/22 3
27:6 w72 740
27:9 w73 423
27:10 g75 7/22 3
27:11 w74 203, 344, 603; w73 197; yb72 12/18; w71 534; g71 9/22 28
27:15 g72 4/8 25
27:20 bi8 1353
27:23 yb75 2/19; w74 434; w73 39
28:1 w73 292
28:7 w72 196
28:9 g74 1/8 10
28:13 g74 11/8 28; yb73 10/23; w72 18, 335, 437; yb72 25
28:14 yb75 8/5; w74 211
28:20 yb76 4/9; w75 77; yb75 6/6; w74 530; ts 14; g74 3/8 27; w73 69; tp 118
28:22 w73 407
28:23 w73 542
28:26 w71 141
28:27 yb75 8/16; w74 499
29:1 w74 300; w72 40
29:15 w74 82; w73 557; w72 359
29:17 w73 556; tp 176; yb73 4/21; w72 270
29:18 w75 114; g75 1/8 6; g73 10/8 15
29:19 g74 4/22 15; w73 556
29:20 w74 104; w73 504
29:21 yb73 8/15; w72 270
29:25 w74 203; g73 11/8 7, 28; kj 78
30:6 g73 8/8 7
30:7 w75 232
30:8 yb76 4/20; w75 232, 571; w74 58
30:9 yb76 4/20; w75 232, 571; pm 211
30:11 w73 447
30:16 bi8 1353
31:1 w75 438
31:10 w75 16
31:11 w75 16
31:12 w75 16
31:13 g73 8/22 12
31:19 g73 8/22 12
31:29 w72 445
31:30 g74 5/22 6; w73 523
31:31 yb76 10/18

ECCLESIASTES

1:2 w73 639
1:4 w74 50
1:5 w71 349
1:6 w71 349
1:7 g72 1/22 17; g72 10/8 26; w71 349
1:11 ts 23
1:13 g72 9/8 27
1:14 g72 9/8 27
1:15 g72 9/8 27
1:18 g72 9/8 27
2:13 g72 9/8 27
2:14 g72 9/8 27
2:17 w73 490
2:18 w73 490
2:19 w73 490
2:21 w73 640
2:24 w74 167; g73 7/22 25; yb73 8/9; w72 206, 487
3:1 g75 12/22 11; w74 644; g72 11/22 11; w71 61, 263
3:4 w75 699; g75 7/22 13; g72 1/8 4
3:7 w73 542; g72 11/22 11
3:8 w74 438; g72 9/22 3; w71 263
3:10 ts 18
3:11 g75 10/22 4; ts 18
3:12 g73 7/22 26
3:13 yb73 1/14; g73 7/22 26; w72 206, 487
3:19 ts 49; g73 7/22 27; g72 8/8 27
3:20 g73 7/22 27
3:21 bi8 1353
3:22 w72 206; g72 9/22 16
4:1 w74 617; hu 13
4:2 w74 617; hu 13
4:4 w73 506
4:9 g72 2/22 5

g, Awake!; **ka**, God's Kingdom of a Thousand Years; **kj**, "The Nations Shall Know that I Am Jehovah"; **km**, Kingdom Ministry; **or**, Organization; **pm**, Paradise Restored—By Theocracy!; **po**, God's "Eternal Purpose"; **sg**, Theocratic School Guidebook; **sl**, Man's Salvation out of World Distress!; **te**, Listening to the Great Teacher; **tp**, True Peace and Security; **ts**, Is This Life All There Is?; **w**, Watchtower; **yb**, Yearbook. **Complete list on page 6.**

4:12 w72 36; g72 2/22 6
5:4 w73 607
5:5 w73 607
5:6 w73 607
5:7 w72 286, 543
5:8 w75 164; w72 267; w71 261
5:10 yb76 3/2
5:12 g74 2/22 9; g74 6/8 15
5:18 g74 8/8 4; g73 7/22 26; w72 206
6:2 g75 6/22 3
7:1 g75 12/22 28; ts 15; g74 12/8 27; w72 517; w71 387, 646
7:2 g75 7/22 15; ts 15; g74 12/8 27
7:3 g75 7/22 15; g74 12/8 27; g72 1/8 4
7:4 ts 15
7:5 w74 304
7:6 g72 1/8 4
7:7 w74 617; hu 13
7:8 w74 8; w73 370; g73 3/8 3; w72 68
7:9 w74 104; w73 370; w72 68
7:10 w73 643
7:12 w74 419; g74 9/22 10; yb73 6/25; w72 419; g72 9/8 27
7:16 w75 707; w74 575
7:29 w74 615; hu 10; g74 10/8 13; yb73 1/16; w72 230
8:9 w74 67; w73 165; g72 10/22 11
8:11 w74 293; yb73 2/6; w72 264
9:2 w73 639
9:3 w73 639
9:5 g74 12/8 26; w73 605, 639; g73 5/8 5; g72 6/8 5-6; g72 11/8 6
9:6 ts 70; g74 12/8 26; w73 605, 639
9:10 ts 93; w73 231; g72 6/8 6; g72 11/8 6; bi8 1353
9:11 w74 56; ts 12; g74 7/8 27; w73 288
9:12 w74 56
10:19 yb76 7/7
10:20 w72 268
11:6 yb76 1/5
11:7 g71 6/22 9
11:9 km 5/73 3; w71 593
11:10 km 5/73 3
12:1 w73 702; yb73 2/15; km 5/73 3
12:3 w72 412
12:4 w72 412, 414
12:6 w73 78
12:7 ts 47-8; g72 8/8 27
12:9 g72 2/8 28; sg 6; g71 11/8 27
12:10 w73 535; g72 2/8 28; sg 6; g71 11/8 27
12:11 w73 535; sg 6
12:12 g75 12/8 22; w73 207
12:13 w73 189, 640
12:14 w73 640

SONG OF SOLOMON

8:6 bi8 1353
8:8 w73 521
8:9 w73 521; w72 219
8:10 w73 522; w72 219

ISAIAH

1:4 tp 131
1:6 tp 131
1:13 g75 8/8 5
1:15 g72 10/8 18
1:16 w72 414
1:24 bi8 1354
1:25 pm 358; w71 239
1:26 pm 358; w71 239, 347
1:27 w71 239
2:2 w75 395; w74 40, 44, 572, 628; w73 381; ka 281; w72 607; pm 77; kj 384
2:3 w74 40, 44, 572, 628; w73 459; ka 281; w72 607; pm 77
2:4 w74 40, 44, 572; w73 38; ka 52, 281; pm 77; g71 12/22 24
2:10 sl 246
2:11 sl 246
2:12 sl 246
2:18 sl 246
2:19 sl 246
2:20 sl 246
2:21 sl 246
2:22 sl 246
3:1 bi8 1354
3:15 bi8 1352
3:16 w72 665
3:17 w72 665; bi8 1352
3:18 w72 665; bi8 1352
3:19 w72 665
3:20 w72 665
3:21 w72 665
3:22 w72 665
3:23 w72 665
4:4 bi8 1352
5:14 bi8 1353
5:28 kj 192
6:1 bi8 1352
6:3 yb72 3/29; w71 271
6:5 w74 363; ka 234; pm 111
6:6 ka 234
6:7 ka 234
6:8 yb76 4/18; ka 234; bi8 1352
6:9 w74 320
6:10 w74 320
6:11 bi8 1352
7:8 w71 672
7:14 bi8 1352
7:20 w73 140; bi8 1352
8:7 bi8 1352
8:9 w74 615; hu 11
8:10 w74 615; hu 11
8:14 w74 761; w72 443
8:19 g74 4/22 28; g71 5/22 27
9:1 w71 323
9:2 w71 323
9:6 sl 80-1, 361; w74 618; po 127; ts 167; hu 16; w73 103, 466; ka 133; tp 45; w72 177, 659; pm 272; g72 10/8 18; w71 198, 246, 275, 635; g71 9/8 28; g71 11/8 14
9:7 yb75 4/19; w74 618; po 127; hu 16; ka 54, 56; tp 45; w72 241; pm 272; g72 10/8 18; w71 198; g71 11/8 14
9:8 bi8 1352
9:17 bi8 1352
10:12 bi8 1352
10:16 bi8 1354
10:22 w72 443
10:23 bi8 1352
10:24 bi8 1352
10:33 sl 172; bi8 1354
10:34 sl 172
11:1 sl 173, 177; ka 140
11:2 sl 173, 175-6, 178; ka 140
11:3 sl 179; ka 140
11:4 sl 179-80; ka 140; yb72 11/25; w71 245
11:5 sl 179; ka 140, 142
11:6 sl 184-7; w74 345; ts 142; ka 142, 144-5; g73 10/22 26
11:7 sl 184-7; w74 345; ts 142; ka 142, 144-5; g73 10/22 26
11:8 sl 184-7; w74 345; ts 142; ka 142, 144-5
11:9 w75 89, 124; sl 184-7, 191-4, 196, 204; w74 181, 345; ts 142; g74 10/8 22; ka 142, 144-5; g73 4/22 21; w71 624; nc 28
11:10 sl 170-1, 197-200, 202-3
11:11 bi8 1352
12:1 yb73 3/30, 11/22; w72 81, 84, 173; pm 349
12:2 yb73 3/30; w72 84; pm 349
12:3 w71 656
12:4 w71 656
12:5 w71 656
13:10 pm 381
13:13 g75 8/22 28; w71 511
13:19 w75 136
13:20 w75 136, 294
14:9 bi8 1353
14:11 bi8 1353
14:12 yb74 8/19; w73 209
14:15 w73 209; bi8 1353
14:16 w73 209
14:19 sl 178
14:24 po 19
14:25 po 19
14:26 po 19
14:27 po 19
19:4 bi8 1354
21:6 bi8 1352
21:8 bi8 1352
21:11 w75 31
21:12 w75 31
21:16 bi8 1352
22:5 bi8 1352
22:12 bi8 1352
22:14 bi8 1352
22:15 bi8 1352
23:15 w74 303
23:16 w74 303
24:5 w73 306
24:6 w73 306
25:6 w74 292; ts 137; yb74 7/14; g74 10/8 22; dy 29; g73 6/22 13; w72 64, 582; g72 12/22 11
25:7 w74 292; w72 582; g72 12/22 11
25:8 w74 292, 603; ts 137; yb74 7/14; g74 10/8 17; w73 624; dy 29; w72 582; g72 12/22 11
26:7 w74 293
26:8 w74 293
26:9 yb76 11/25; w74 293; g73 4/22 20
26:10 w74 294; ka 137; tp 41; g73 4/8 19
26:20 g72 10/8 17
26:21 yb74 10/29; w73 300, 308; g72 10/8 17; w71 512
28:2 bi8 1352
28:7 w74 452
28:14 sl 336
28:15 sl 336; bi8 1353
28:16 w74 60; w71 77
28:17 sl 337; w71 77
28:18 sl 337; bi8 1353
28:19 sl 337
28:20 sl 337
28:21 sl 337
28:22 sl 337; bi8 1352
28:24 w75 517; w73 229
28:25 w73 229
28:26 w73 229
28:27 w73 229
28:28 w73 229
28:29 w75 517; w73 229
29:13 bi8 1352
29:16 w71 50
29:18 sl 150
29:19 sl 150
30:9 w74 35; g73 10/8 24
30:10 w74 35; g73 10/8 24
30:11 w74 35; g73 10/8 24
30:20 yb75 9/21; w74 339; bi8 1352
31:1 g72 10/22 25; kj 200
31:3 po 32; g72 10/22 25
31:4 w74 728
31:5 w74 728
32:1 w75 605; sl 362, 364; w74 292; ts 132; w73 427; tp 188; w72 459; w71 635; kj 405
32:2 sl 362; w74 292; ts 132; w73 427; tp 188; w72 459; w71 223; kj 405
32:15 w73 330
32:16 kj 405
32:17 fu 3, 29; w73 330; tp 23; g73 10/8 29; kj 405
32:18 w75 605; fu 3; g74 4/8 9; tp 23; g73 10/8 29; kj 405
33:15 g74 3/8 28
33:16 g74 3/8 28
33:22 sl 215

33:23 sl 215
33:24 sl 215; w74 134; g73 4/22 21
34:1 sl 216, 349
34:2 sl 216, 297, 349
34:3 sl 216, 297, 322, 349
34:4 sl 216-18, 297, 322, 349
34:5 sl 219, 231, 297, 322, 349
34:6 sl 219, 349
34:7 sl 219
34:8 sl 219-21, 228
34:9 sl 229
34:10 sl 229
34:11 sl 229, 231
34:12 sl 229
34:13 sl 229
34:14 sl 229
34:15 sl 229
34:16 sl 230
34:17 sl 230
35:1 w75 683; sl 138, 142; g75 3/8 6; yb74 12/8; g74 4/8 14; w73 211; tp 101; kj 31
35:2 sl 138, 141-2; g74 4/8 14; kj 31
35:3 sl 144, 145; w73 462
35:4 sl 144, 146, 148; w73 462, 469
35:5 sl 149-50; w73 212, 469
35:6 w75 683; sl 149-51; ts 136; g74 4/8 14; w73 212, 469
35:7 w75 683; sl 149, 151-2; w73 211
35:8 sl 155-6, 159; w73 469
35:9 sl 156-7, 163-4
35:10 sl 138, 163-6, 168; w73 211, 469; yb72 9/16; kj 31
37:16 po 29
37:19 bi8 1356
37:24 bi8 1352
38:10 w73 243; bi8 1353
38:14 bi8 1352
38:16 bi8 1352
38:18 ts 93; w73 243; bi8 1353
38:19 ts 93
40:8 w75 149
40:11 w73 39
40:22 g73 7/8 21; w72 4, 38
40:25 yb76 8/5
40:26 g75 6/22 19; g72 12/22 25
41:8 po 90; w72 731
41:9 w72 731
41:10 w73 555
41:14 w72 172
41:23 bi8 1356
41:27 w72 172
42:1 g71 12/22 27
42:2 g71 12/22 27
42:4 w73 103
42:6 w73 283
42:8 yb76 3/30; w75 231; g73 5/22 28; w72 250, 295; te 19
42:9 w71 467
43:1 sl 370; w72 172; kj 22, 172
43:2 sl 370; kj 22
43:3 sl 370; tp 43; w72 172; kj 22
43:4 tp 43
43:9 sl 104; g73 3/22 19
43:10 w75 45, 656; sl 104, 370; w73 427; ka 239-40; w72 188, 637, 731, 751; or 9, 132; yb72 11/5; w71 749; kj 22, 172, 307, 319
43:11 kj 22, 172, 307
43:12 yb76 6/19; yb75 150; w72 637, 751; or 132; kj 22, 172, 307
43:14 w72 172
43:15 w72 172
43:27 po 63
44:2 w72 172
44:8 w72 751; kj 319
44:9 bi8 1356
44:21 w72 172
44:24 w72 172
44:27 w71 315
44:28 sl 163; po 21; g74 7/8 28; w72 746; pm 32; kj 31
45:1 sl 163; po 21, 130; g74 7/8 28; pm 32; w71 315
45:2 w71 315
45:8 w74 293; ka 137
45:18 g75 6/22 19; g75 12/22 10; tp 38; g73 5/22 13
45:22 w72 587
46:8 po 21
46:9 po 21; g73 1/22 7; g73 3/22 19
46:10 po 21; g74 7/8 27; g73 1/22 7; g73 3/22 19; kj 361
46:11 po 21; g73 1/22 7; g73 3/22 19
49:8 sl 149; w72 375
49:9 sl 149; w72 375
49:14 bi8 1352
49:15 g72 2/8 3; w71 411
49:22 kj 31
49:23 kj 31
50:1 sl 157; w74 461
50:4 yb74 233
51:3 w72 182
52:1 w72 182; yb72 7/9; w71 446
52:3 sl 157; w72 81
52:5 w72 82
52:6 w72 82
52:7 w72 182; yb72 4/1, 7/29; w71 78-9, 286, 744
52:8 yb73 7/20; w72 182
52:9 w72 182
52:10 w72 182
52:11 sl 120, 155, 160; w73 336; kj 161, 176
52:12 sl 120, 155, 159
52:13 sl 31, 35, 37-9, 89; w74 601
52:14 sl 43
52:15 sl 43-4
53:1 sl 47; w72 174
53:2 sl 49-51
53:3 sl 52-5, 82; w74 601; ts 155; g73 9/8 28; w72 178
53:4 sl 66-8; w74 601; g73 9/8 28; w72 178
53:5 sl 66-9; g73 9/8 27; w72 178
53:6 sl 69; w72 178
53:7 sl 37, 69; po 146; w72 581
53:8 sl 37, 71-5
53:9 sl 71, 76-8; po 153
53:10 sl 78-81; w74 601; po 138; yb73 6/10; w72 174-5, 177, 242, 287; yb72 11/29; g72 2/8 7; w71 275
53:11 sl 35, 37, 81-3, 89; w72 175, 242
53:12 sl 84-6, 90; w74 346; po 146, 153; w73 231; g73 9/8 27; w72 174-5, 242; g72 2/8 8
54:1 w75 695; sl 92-4
54:5 w74 461; yb73 1/30
54:6 w74 461; w72 78-9
54:7 yb73 2/12; w72 78-9
54:8 yb73 2/12; w72 78-9, 82
54:11 yb73 2/26; w72 79
54:13 yb76 11/21; sl 94; w74 339; w73 533
54:17 yb76 3/16; yb75 65; w74 755
55:1 yb76 12/30; sl 95-9
55:2 yb76 12/30; sl 95, 99
55:3 sl 95, 102-3, 110
55:4 sl 95, 102, 104-6; w73 368
55:5 sl 107-8
55:6 sl 111; w74 461; w73 147, 432; g73 1/22 27; w72 183
55:7 w75 39; sl 111-12, 115; w74 461; ts 188; w73 147; g73 1/22 27; g73 8/22 8
55:8 sl 116, 129; w74 461; g73 1/22 27; kj 284
55:9 yb76 6/13; sl 116, 129; g73 1/22 27; kj 284
55:10 w75 700; sl 116-18, 121
55:11 w75 700; sl 116-18, 121; g75 12/22 10; g73 3/22 19
55:12 w75 700; sl 118, 120-1, 123, 128
55:13 w75 700; sl 118, 121-2, 125-6, 128; tp 101
56:6 w74 572
56:7 sl 203; w74 572; w72 183; pm 406
57:9 bi8 1353
57:15 w71 263
57:20 pm 74
57:21 tp 13
59:1 yb72 5/22
59:7 tp 13
59:8 tp 13
59:9 ka 325
59:10 ka 325
60:1 pm 157
60:2 w75 658; w74 560, 754; pm 157
60:3 pm 157
60:14 pm 157
60:17 yb74 4/18; w73 331
60:21 sl 178; pm 157
60:22 yb76 80; w75 86; sl 178; yb75 212; w74 188; pm 157; yb72 12/6; w71 88
61:1 po 145; g73 9/8 28; w72 660; w71 78; kj 66, 173, 190, 285, 311; g71 12/8 9
61:2 w72 368, 371, 660; w71 31, 78, 360; kj 66, 173, 190, 285, 311
61:3 pm 303; kj 66, 173
61:6 po 114
61:8 w74 153
62:2 ka 239
63:7 yb76 6/20
63:9 w73 101
63:14 w72 748
64:8 w71 566
65:11 g75 7/8 27; w74 135, 588; g74 6/22 13; yb73 11/20; w72 594
65:12 w74 135
65:13 w71 554
65:14 yb72 3/24; w71 554
65:16 sl 189-90
65:17 sl 189-90, 320, 356; gc 28; w74 330; ts 166; g74 4/8 13, 17; g74 10/8 17; w73 85, 360; yb73 2/13; g73 3/8 26; w72 231, 500; g72 11/8 7; w71 535
65:18 sl 189-90, 320, 356; g74 10/8 17; w72 231; w71 535
65:19 sl 189-90
65:20 g74 4/8 13; w73 82; w72 500
65:21 g74 4/8 13; w73 362; w72 500; g71 4/22 27
65:22 g74 3/22 26; g74 4/8 13; w73 82, 85;

g, Awake!; **ka**, God's Kingdom of a Thousand Years; **kj**, "The Nations Shall Know that I Am Jehovah"; **km**, Kingdom Ministry; **or**, Organization; **pm**, Paradise Restored—By Theocracy!; **po**, God's "Eternal Purpose"; **sg**, Theocratic School Guidebook; **sl**, Man's Salvation out of World Distress!; **te**, Listening to the Great Teacher; **tp**, True Peace and Security; **ts**, Is This Life All There Is?; **w**, Watchtower; **yb**, Yearbook. **Complete list on page 6.**

w72 500;
g72 11/8 7;
g71 4/22 27
65:23 sl 189-90;
g74 4/8 13
65:24 sl 189-90;
g74 4/8 13
65:25 sl 189-90,
322
66:1 po 128
66:6 w72 392;
kj 127
66:7 pm 171
66:8 w73 457;
pm 171
66:10 w73 457
66:12 w73 457
66:13 w73 457
66:14 w73 457
66:22 sl 320, 322
66:23 sl 279
66:24 sl 279;
ts 114; bi8 1355

JEREMIAH

1:1 w73 13;
kj 57, 229
1:2 kj 57, 229
1:3 kj 57
1:5 w74 509;
g73 12/22 28
2:2 g72 2/8 27
2:3 g72 2/8 27
2:11 bi8 1353
2:19 bi8 1352
2:21 yb76 12/27
2:34 w73 305
3:8 w74 461
3:12 w74 461;
w71 515
3:13 w74 461
3:14 ts 104;
kj 241
3:18 w72 442
3:22 w74 461
4:13 g74 2/22 14
4:22 sl 156
5:31 pm 309
6:10 w71 443
6:13 w74 36
6:14 w74 36;
w72 678
6:15 w74 36;
g74 3/22 14
7:4 kj 271
7:5 w74 83
7:6 w74 83
7:7 w74 83
7:31 w73 228;
bi8 1355
7:32 bi8 1355
8:7 g74 1/8 22;
w73 580; pm 219;
w71 59
8:9 w73 553
9:11 sl 152;
w73 149
9:23 yb76 4/1;
w75 571;
w74 532; tp 129
9:24 yb76 4/1;
w74 532; tp 129
9:25 w71 443
9:26 w71 443
10:2 w73 486
10:3 w73 486
10:10 w74 146;
w71 43
10:11 w74 146;
w71 43; bi8 1356
10:12 w74 146;
yb72 3/5, 3/19;
w71 43
10:22 sl 152
10:23 gc 14;
yb73 2/10;
g73 11/8 6;
g72 10/22 11
11:21 w73 13
13:20
g72 11/22 14
13:21
g72 11/22 14
13:22
g72 11/22 14
14:9 w71 654
14:22 pm 285
15:1 w72 435
16:20 w73 486
17:7 yb76 11/14
17:9
g74 8/22 18;
yb72 10/6;
w71 139, 142;
g71 11/8 4
17:10 w75 480;
w72 272
18:7 w75 138
18:8 w75 138;
w73 147
19:2 bi8 1355
19:4 kj 103
19:6 ts 115;
bi8 1355
19:7 ts 115
20:8 yb76 4/5
20:9 w71 575
22:16 tp 167
22:24 kj 295
22:25 kj 295
22:26 kj 295
22:27 kj 295
22:28 kj 295
22:29 kj 295
22:30 ka 62;
pm 119; kj 295
23:1 kj 295
23:2 kj 295
23:3 w74 282;
kj 295
23:4 w74 282;
kj 295
23:5 pm 230;
kj 295
23:6 kj 295
23:18 pm 213
23:19 pm 213
23:20 pm 213
23:21 tp 35;
pm 213
23:22 tp 35;
pm 213
23:29 w75 144
23:30 pm 212
23:31 pm 212
23:32 pm 212
25:3 w71 336;
kj 103, 229
25:4 w71 336
25:9 kj 103
25:10 kj 57
25:11 po 130;
g72 5/8 27;
kj 57, 130
25:12 kj 130
25:15 kj 316
25:16 kj 316
25:17 sl 221;
kj 316
25:18 kj 316
25:19 kj 316
25:20 kj 316
25:21 sl 221;
kj 316-17
25:22 kj 317
25:23 kj 317
25:24 kj 317
25:33 g72 6/8 8
25:34 w74 54
25:35 w74 54
26:17 kj 312
26:18 w72 743;
kj 312
26:19 w72 743
29:10 kj 130
31:9 kj 161
31:20 w71 412
31:31 po 159-60;
w73 47, 217;
w72 443, 678,
680, 685, 690;
g72 3/22 28;
w71 745;
bi8 1366; kj 118
31:32 w73 47,
217; w72 678,
680, 685, 690;
g72 3/22 28;
bi8 1366; kj 118,
241
31:33 w73 47,
217; w72 559,
678, 680, 685, 690;
g72 3/22 28;
w71 745;
bi8 1366
31:34 w72 678,
680, 685, 690;
g72 3/22 28;
bi8 1366
31:35 g71 6/22 12
31:40 ts 113
32:10 w73 288
32:11 w73 288
32:12 w73 288
32:13 w73 288
32:14 w73 288
32:17 g73 5/22 13
32:35 bi8 1355
37:5 kj 96
37:6 kj 96
37:7 kj 96
37:8 kj 96
37:9 kj 96
37:10 kj 96
37:11 kj 96
37:21 kj 108
38:6 yb73 10/3
39:3 kj 109
39:4 kj 109
39:5 kj 109
39:7 kj 137
39:16 kj 171
39:17 kj 171
39:18 w75 563
40:1 kj 125
40:2 kj 125
40:3 kj 125
44:21 g73 5/22 28
44:22 g73 5/22 28
44:23 g73 5/22 28
45:5 w75 563;
kj 171
46:10 bi8 1352
49:5 bi8 1352
49:26 w74 363
50:1 po 20
50:2 yb73 8/13;
w72 746
50:3 w72 746
50:25 bi8 1352
50:31 bi8 1352;
kj 128
50:32 kj 128
50:38 w71 315
50:43
g72 11/22 14
50:45 po 20
51:21
g72 10/22 25
51:30 w71 315-16
51:31 w71 315
51:32 w71 315
52:3 kj 266
52:4 kj 266
52:6 kj 109
52:7 kj 109
52:8 kj 109
52:11 kj 137
52:12 g72 3/8 27
52:24 w72 677;
kj 175, 198
52:25 w72 677;
kj 175, 198
52:26 w72 677;
kj 175, 198
52:27 kj 175, 198

LAMENTATIONS

1:1 kj 170
1:4 kj 170
1:6 kj 170
1:14 bi8 1353
1:15 bi8 1353;
kj 170
1:18 kj 170
2:1 bi8 1353
2:2 w72 660;
bi8 1353; kj 188
2:3 sl 295;
w72 660; kj 188
2:4 sl 295;
w72 660; kj 188
2:5 bi8 1353
2:7 bi8 1353
2:10 kj 170
2:18 bi8 1353
2:19 bi8 1353
2:20 bi8 1353;
kj 170
2:21 w72 587;
kj 170
3:7 kj 137
3:8 g74 1/8 10
3:20 bi8 1353
3:31 bi8 1353
3:32 ts 124
3:33 yb76 7/19;
w75 280; ts 124
3:36 bi8 1353
3:37 bi8 1353
3:40 w72 434
3:41 w72 434
3:42 w72 434
3:43 w75 148;
w72 435
3:44 w75 148;
w72 435
3:58 bi8 1353
4:4 kj 170
4:9 w72 587
4:10 w72 587;
kj 170
4:11 w72 660;
kj 188
4:16 kj 170
4:20 yb72 10/30;
w71 241; kj 220,
249
5:11 kj 170
5:12 w72 587;
kj 170
5:13 kj 170
5:14 kj 170

EZEKIEL

1:1 w72 102;
kj 37, 95, 210, 279
1:2 w72 102;
kj 37, 95, 210, 279
1:3 w72 102;
kj 37, 95, 210, 279
1:4 w72 102;
kj 38
1:5 w72 102;
kj 38, 196
1:6 w72 102;
kj 38, 196
1:7 w72 102;
kj 38, 196
1:8 w72 102;
kj 38, 72
1:9 w72 102;
kj 38
1:10 kj 39
1:11 kj 39
1:12 w72 103;
kj 41
1:13 w72 103;
kj 41
1:14 w72 103;
kj 41
1:15 w72 103;
kj 42
1:16 w72 103;
kj 42
1:17 w72 103;
kj 42
1:18 w72 103;
kj 42
1:19 w72 103;
kj 42
1:20 w72 103;
kj 42
1:21 kj 42
1:22 w72 104;
kj 45, 54
1:23 w72 104;
kj 45
1:24 w72 104;
kj 45
1:25 w72 152;
kj 46, 186
1:26 w72 152;
kj 46, 54, 143, 186
1:27 w72 152;
kj 46, 54, 143, 186
1:28 w72 152;
kj 46-7, 54-5, 143
2:1 w72 187;
kj 55
2:2 w72 187;
kj 55
2:3 w72 187,
199-200; kj 56,
67, 70
2:4 w72 187,
200; kj 56, 70
2:5 w72 187,
200; kj 56, 70
2:6 w72 200;
kj 71
2:7 w72 200;
kj 71
2:8 w72 200;
kj 71, 74
2:9 w72 200;
kj 71, 74, 113
2:10 w72 200,
253; kj 71, 74, 113
3:1 w72 253;
kj 75, 113

3:2 w72 253; kj 75, 113
3:3 w72 253; kj 75
3:4 w72 254; kj 77
3:5 w72 254; kj 77
3:6 w72 254; kj 77
3:7 w72 254; kj 77
3:8 w72 254; kj 77
3:9 w72 254; kj 77
3:10 w72 255; kj 80
3:11 w72 255; kj 80
3:12 w72 255; kj 81
3:13 w72 255; kj 81
3:14 w72 255, 278; kj 81
3:15 w72 255; kj 81
3:16 kj 86
3:17 yb73 11/16; w72 277, 728; kj 86, 181, 279
3:18 yb75 6/3; w72 277; kj 86, 181, 279
3:19 w72 277; kj 86, 181, 279
3:20 w72 277; kj 86, 181, 279
3:21 w72 277; kj 86, 181, 279
3:22 w72 279; kj 89
3:23 w72 279; kj 89
3:24 w72 280; kj 90
3:25 w72 280; kj 90
3:26 w72 280; kj 90
3:27 w72 280; kj 90
4:1 w72 310; kj 94
4:2 w72 310; kj 94
4:3 w72 310; kj 93-4
4:4 w72 310; kj 97, 142
4:5 w72 310; kj 97, 142
4:6 w72 310; kj 97, 100, 123, 142, 229, 251
4:7 w72 310; kj 100, 142, 229, 251
4:8 w72 310; kj 100
4:9 w72 325; kj 106
4:10 w72 325; kj 106
4:11 w72 325; kj 106
4:12 kj 107
4:13 kj 107, 109
4:14 kj 108
4:15 kj 108
4:16 w72 325; kj 108
4:17 w72 325; kj 108
4:27 w72 471
5:1 w72 325; g72 11/8 13; kj 107
5:2 w72 325-6; kj 107, 109
5:3 w72 325-6; kj 110
5:4 w72 325-6; kj 110
5:5 w72 325; kj 105
5:6 w72 325; kj 105
5:7 w72 325; kj 105
5:8 w72 325; kj 105
5:9 w72 325; kj 105
5:10 w72 325; kj 106
5:11 w72 325; kj 106
5:12 w72 325; kj 106, 110
5:13 kj 110
5:14 kj 111
5:15 kj 111
5:16 kj 111
5:17 kj 111
6:1 w72 356; kj 116
6:2 w72 356; kj 116
6:3 w72 356; kj 116
6:4 w72 356; kj 116
6:5 w72 356; kj 116
6:6 w72 356; kj 116
6:7 w72 356; kj 116-17
6:8 w72 357; kj 118
6:9 w72 357; kj 118
6:10 w72 357; kj 118
6:11 w72 358; kj 120
6:12 w72 358; kj 120
6:13 w72 358; kj 120
6:14 w72 358; kj 120, 122
7:1 kj 123
7:2 w72 391; kj 123
7:3 w72 391; kj 123
7:4 w72 391; kj 123
7:5 w72 392; kj 126
7:6 w72 392; kj 126
7:7 w72 392; kj 126
7:8 w72 392; kj 126
7:9 w72 392-3; kj 126
7:10 w72 393; kj 128
7:11 w72 393; kj 128
7:12 w72 393; kj 128
7:13 w72 393; kj 128
7:14 w72 394; kj 131
7:15 w72 394; kj 131
7:16 w72 394; kj 131
7:17 w72 394; kj 131
7:18 w72 394; kj 131
7:19 g74 1/22 8; w72 420; kj 132, 134
7:20 w72 420; kj 132
7:21 w72 420; kj 132
7:22 w72 420; kj 132, 135
7:23 w72 470; kj 137
7:24 w72 470; kj 137-8
7:25 w72 471; kj 137, 139
7:26 w72 471; kj 137, 139
7:27 kj 137, 139
8:1 w72 42; kj 142
8:2 w72 509; kj 143
8:3 yb73 1/21; w72 509, 659; kj 143, 164, 182, 185
8:4 w72 509, 659; kj 143-4, 164, 182, 185
8:5 w72 509; kj 145
8:6 w72 509; kj 145
8:7 w72 537; kj 147, 167
8:8 w72 537; kj 147, 167
8:9 w72 538; kj 147, 167
8:10 w72 42, 538; kj 147, 167
8:11 w72 42, 538; kj 147, 167, 195
8:12 w72 42, 538; kj 147
8:13 w72 572; kj 149
8:14 w72 572; kj 149, 151, 168
8:15 w72 585; kj 154, 168
8:16 w72 585; kj 154, 163, 168, 195
8:17 w72 585; bi8 1353; kj 154-5, 158-9, 165
8:18 w72 43, 587; kj 154, 165
9:1 yb73 3/31, 5/23; w72 43-4, 632; kj 162
9:2 yb73 8/7, 8/26; w72 44, 46, 632-3, 659-60; kj 163
9:3 ka 266; yb73 6/20; w72 48, 633, 659; kj 164, 182, 185
9:4 w75 395; w74 57; w73 428, 462; ka 266; tp 96; yb73 2/8, 2/28, 7/19, 9/9; w72 48, 287, 633, 637, 659-60, 693; w71 460; kj 164, 170, 173; g71 7/22 28
9:5 ka 266; w72 51, 633, 659-60, 693; kj 166, 174
9:6 ka 266; w72 51-2, 633, 659, 693; w71 460; kj 166-7, 170, 174
9:7 w72 52, 633; kj 167
9:8 w72 53, 634; w71 631; kj 168
9:9 w72 53, 634; kj 169
9:10 w72 53, 634; kj 169
9:11 yb73 2/22; w72 53, 638; kj 180, 186
10:1 w72 660; kj 184, 186
10:2 w72 48, 660; kj 184, 186, 192, 196
10:3 w72 660; kj 184-5, 196
10:4 w72 660; kj 185, 196
10:5 w72 660; kj 185, 196
10:6 w72 660; kj 187, 196
10:7 w72 660; kj 187, 196
10:8 w72 660; kj 187
10:9 kj 192
10:10 kj 192
10:11 kj 192
10:12 kj 192
10:13 kj 192
10:14 w72 102; kj 39, 193
10:15 kj 193
10:16 kj 193
10:17 kj 193
10:18 kj 193
10:19 kj 193
10:20 kj 193
10:21 kj 193
10:22 kj 193
11:1 w72 676; kj 194, 204
11:2 w72 676; kj 194, 204
11:3 w72 676; kj 194, 204
11:4 kj 195
11:5 w72 677
11:6 w72 677; kj 267
11:7 w72 677; kj 267
11:8 w72 677; kj 197, 267
11:9 w72 677; kj 197, 267
11:10 w72 677; kj 197, 267
11:11 w72 677-8; kj 197, 199, 267
11:12 w72 677-8; kj 197, 199, 201
11:13 w72 678; kj 201, 204
11:14 kj 203
11:15 w72 723; kj 203
11:16 w72 724; kj 203-4
11:17 w72 724; kj 205, 207
11:18 w72 725; kj 205, 207-8
11:19 w72 725; kj 205, 207-8
11:20 w72 725; kj 205, 207-8
11:21 w72 724; kj 205
11:22 kj 38, 210
11:23 kj 210
11:24 w72 725; kj 211
11:25 w72 725; kj 211-12
12:6 kj 93
12:11 kj 93
13:5 kj 214
14:7 w72 684
14:8 w72 684
16:4 g72 11/22 14
16:12 w74 319
17:1 kj 95
17:2 kj 95
17:3 kj 95
17:4 kj 95
17:5 kj 95
17:6 kj 95
17:7 kj 246
17:8 kj 246
17:9 kj 95, 246
17:10 kj 95, 246
17:11 kj 95
17:12 kj 95
17:13 kj 95, 228
17:14 kj 95, 228
17:15 w73 60; kj 95, 228, 246

g, Awake!; **ka**, God's Kingdom of a Thousand Years; **kj**, "The Nations Shall Know that I Am Jehovah"; **km**, Kingdom Ministry; **or**, Organization; **pm**, Paradise Restored—By Theocracy!; **po**, God's "Eternal Purpose"; **sg**, Theocratic School Guidebook; **sl**, Man's Salvation out of World Distress!; **te**, Listening to the Great Teacher; **tp**, True Peace and Security; **ts**, Is This Life All There Is?; **w**, Watchtower; **yb**, Yearbook. **Complete list on page 6.**

17:16 w73 60; kj 95, 228, 246
17:17 w73 60; kj 95, 228, 246
17:18 w73 60; kj 95, 228
17:19 kj 95, 228-9
17:20 kj 95, 229
17:21 kj 95
18:4 g74 1/8 19; w73 231, 442; g73 5/8 5; g73 6/8 6; g73 7/22 28; g72 11/8 6
18:20 w73 231, 442; g73 5/8 5; g73 6/8 6; g72 11/8 6
18:21 w73 442
18:23 w74 461; tp 43, 62
18:25 bi8 1353
18:27 w73 442
18:29 bi8 1353
18:30 w74 461; w73 442
18:31 w74 461
18:32 w74 461; tp 43, 62
20:1 kj 143, 214
20:2 kj 143
20:3 kj 143
20:4 kj 239
20:5 kj 239, 312
20:6 kj 10, 115, 239, 312
20:7 kj 10, 239
20:8 kj 10, 239
20:9 kj 10
20:10 g72 11/22 5; kj 10
20:11 g72 11/22 5
20:12 g72 11/22 5
20:15 kj 115
20:45 kj 215
20:46 kj 215
20:47 kj 215
20:48 kj 215
21:1 kj 215
21:2 w72 763; kj 215
21:3 w72 763; kj 215
21:4 w72 763; kj 215
21:5 w72 764; kj 215-16
21:6 w72 766; kj 218
21:7 w72 766; kj 218
21:8 kj 219
21:9 w72 765; bi8 1353; kj 219
21:10 w72 765; kj 219-20
21:11 w72 765; kj 221
21:12 w72 765; kj 221
21:13 w72 765; kj 221
21:14 w72 765; kj 222
21:15 w72 765; kj 222
21:16 w72 765; kj 223
21:17 w72 765; kj 223
21:18 kj 224, 266
21:19 w73 60; kj 224, 235, 266
21:20 w73 60; kj 224, 235, 266
21:21 w73 60; kj 224-5, 235, 266
21:22 w73 60; kj 225, 235, 266
21:23 kj 226, 228, 266
21:24 kj 228
21:25 sl 174; po 129, 173; w73 61; kj 229, 251, 346
21:26 sl 174; po 129; w73 61; kj 229-30, 346
21:27 sl 174; w74 236, 683; po 101, 129, 177; w73 61; ka 260-1; kj 214, 229, 232, 305, 346
21:28 w73 62; kj 236
21:29 w73 62; kj 236
21:30 w73 62; kj 236
21:31 w73 62; kj 236
21:32 w73 62; kj 236
22:3 kj 268
22:4 kj 268
22:5 kj 268
22:6 kj 268
22:7 kj 268
22:8 kj 268
22:9 kj 268
22:10 kj 268
22:11 kj 268
22:12 kj 268
22:16 kj 238
23:1 kj 238
23:2 w73 90; kj 238
23:3 w73 90; kj 238
23:4 w73 90; kj 238, 240-1
23:5 w73 90; kj 242
23:6 w73 90; kj 242
23:7 w73 90; kj 242
23:8 w73 90; kj 242
23:9 w73 90; kj 242
23:10 w73 90; kj 242
23:11 w73 91; kj 244
23:12 w73 91; kj 244
23:13 w73 91; kj 244
23:14 w73 91; kj 244
23:15 w73 91; kj 244
23:16 w73 91; kj 244
23:17 w73 91; kj 244
23:18 w73 91; kj 245
23:19 w73 91; kj 245
23:20 w73 91; kj 245-6
23:21 w73 91; kj 245
23:22 w73 91; kj 247, 261
23:23 w73 91; kj 247, 261
23:24 w73 92; kj 247, 261
23:25 w73 92; kj 247, 261
23:26 w73 92; kj 247, 261
23:27 w73 92; kj 247, 261
23:28 w73 92; kj 250
23:29 w73 92; kj 250
23:30 w73 92; kj 250
23:31 w73 92; kj 250
23:32 w73 92; kj 251
23:33 w73 92; kj 251
23:34 w73 92; kj 251
23:35 w73 92; kj 256
23:36 kj 257
23:37 w73 93; kj 257-8
23:38 w73 93; kj 257
23:39 w73 93; kj 257
23:40 w73 93; kj 257
23:41 w73 93; kj 257
23:42 w73 93; kj 257
23:43 w73 91; kj 260
23:44 w73 91; kj 260
23:45 w73 91; kj 260
23:46 w73 91; kj 262
23:47 w73 91; kj 262
23:48 w73 91; kj 262
23:49 w73 91; kj 262-3
24:1 w73 123; kj 265, 277
24:2 w73 123; kj 265, 277
24:3 w73 124; kj 266, 277
24:4 w73 124; kj 266, 277
24:5 kj 266, 277
24:6 w73 124; kj 267
24:7 w73 124; kj 267
24:8 w73 124; kj 267
24:9 w73 124; kj 269
24:10 w73 124; kj 269
24:11 w73 124; kj 269
24:12 w73 124; kj 269
24:13 w73 125; kj 270
24:14 w73 125; kj 270
24:15 w73 125; kj 271
24:16 w73 125; kj 271, 273
24:17 w73 125; kj 271
24:18 kj 273
24:19 kj 273
24:20 w73 125; kj 273
24:21 w73 125; kj 273
24:22 w73 125; kj 273
24:23 w73 125; kj 273
24:24 w73 125; kj 56, 273
24:25 w73 126; kj 276
24:26 w73 126; kj 276
24:27 w73 126; kj 276-7
25:3 w75 422
25:4 w75 422
25:5 w75 422
25:8 w75 422; kj 374
25:9 w75 422; kj 374
25:10 w75 422; kj 374
25:11 kj 374
25:15 w75 422
25:16 w75 422
28:1 kj 138
28:2 kj 138
28:7 kj 138
28:12 ts 82
28:13 ts 82
28:14 ts 82
28:15 ts 82
28:16 ts 82
28:17 ts 82
29:17 kj 34, 210
29:18 w75 714; kj 210
29:19 w75 714; kj 210
29:20 kj 210
29:21 kj 210
30:11 kj 138
31:15 bi8 1353
31:16 bi8 1353
31:17 bi8 1353
32:21 bi8 1353
32:27 bi8 1353
33:1 kj 280
33:2 kj 280
33:3 kj 280
33:4 kj 280
33:5 kj 280
33:6 w73 147; kj 280
33:7 w73 147; kj 281
33:8 w73 147; kj 281
33:9 w73 147; kj 281
33:10 w73 147; kj 281
33:11 w74 495; w73 147, 227; kj 281
33:12 kj 282
33:13 kj 282
33:14 w73 147; kj 282
33:15 w73 147; kj 282
33:16 w73 147; kj 282
33:17 w73 147; bi8 1353; kj 283
33:18 w73 147; kj 283
33:19 w73 147; kj 283
33:20 w73 147; bi8 1353; kj 284
33:21 w73 148; kj 218, 285
33:22 w73 148; kj 218, 287
33:23 w73 148; kj 288
33:24 w73 148; kj 288
33:25 w73 148; kj 288
33:26 w73 148; kj 288
33:27 w73 149; kj 289
33:28 w73 149; kj 289
33:29 w73 149; kj 289
33:30 w73 149; kj 291
33:31 w73 149; kj 291
33:32 w73 149; kj 291
33:33 w73 149-50; kj 291-2
34:1 kj 294
34:2 w73 165; kj 294, 296
34:3 w73 165; kj 296
34:4 w73 165; kj 296
34:5 w73 165; kj 296
34:6 w73 165; kj 296
34:7 w73 166; kj 297
34:8 w73 166; kj 297
34:9 w73 166; kj 297
34:10 w73 166; kj 297
34:11 w74 282; w73 167, 299; kj 299
34:12 w73 167; kj 299-300
34:13 w73 167; kj 299
34:14 w73 167; kj 299
34:15 w73 167; kj 301
34:16 w73 167; kj 301
34:17 w73 168; kj 303

34:18 w73 168; kj 303
34:19 w73 168; kj 303
34:20 w73 168; kj 303
34:21 w73 168; kj 303
34:22 w73 168; kj 303
34:23 po 125; w73 168, 295; pm 326; kj 304-6, 356, 364, 404
34:24 w73 168, 295, 427; pm 326; kj 304, 306, 356, 364, 404
34:25 w73 169; ka 145; kj 308
34:26 w73 169; pm 284; kj 308
34:27 w73 169; kj 308
34:28 w73 169; kj 308
34:29 w73 169; kj 309
34:30 w73 169; kj 309
34:31 w73 169; kj 311
35:9 kj 314
35:15 kj 76, 314
36:1 w73 220; kj 313
36:2 w73 220; kj 313
36:3 w73 220; kj 314
36:4 w73 220; kj 314
36:5 w73 220; kj 314
36:6 w73 220; kj 315
36:7 w73 220; kj 316
36:8 w73 220; kj 32, 316
36:9 w73 220; kj 32, 316
36:10 w73 220; kj 32, 316
36:11 w73 220-1; kj 32, 316, 332
36:12 w73 220; kj 316, 320
36:13 w73 221; kj 322
36:14 w73 221; kj 322
36:15 w73 221; kj 322
36:16 w73 222; kj 323
36:17 w73 222; kj 323
36:18 w73 222; kj 323
36:19 w73 222; kj 323
36:20 w73 222; kj 323
36:21 w73 222; kj 323
36:22 w73 223; kj 32, 325, 334
36:23 w73 223; w72 75; kj 32, 325, 407
36:24 w73 223; pm 349; kj 325
36:25 w73 223; pm 349; kj 325, 327
36:26 w73 223; kj 325, 327
36:27 w73 223; kj 325, 327
36:28 w73 223; kj 325, 327
36:29 w73 223; kj 327
36:30 w73 223; kj 327
36:31 w73 223; kj 327
36:32 w73 223; kj 327
36:33 sl 124; w73 221; kj 329
36:34 sl 124; w73 221; kj 329
36:35 sl 124; yb75 11/20; w74 667; w73 221; tp 101; kj 329, 331, 343, 355
36:36 sl 124; w73 221; kj 329
36:37 yb76 11/5; w73 220-1; kj 332
36:38 w73 220-1, 223; kj 332, 334
37:1 w73 250; kj 336
37:2 w73 250; kj 336
37:3 w73 250; kj 336
37:4 w73 250; kj 336
37:5 w73 250; kj 337
37:6 w73 250; kj 337-8
37:7 w73 250; kj 338
37:8 w73 250; kj 338
37:9 w73 250; kj 338
37:10 w73 250-1; kj 338, 341
37:11 w73 250; kj 339
37:12 w73 250; kj 339
37:13 w73 250; kj 339
37:14 w73 250; kj 339
37:15 w73 282; kj 344
37:16 w73 282; kj 344
37:17 w73 282; kj 344
37:18 w73 282; kj 344
37:19 w73 282; w72 442; kj 344
37:20 w73 282; kj 344
37:21 w73 282; w72 442; kj 345
37:22 w73 282; w72 442; kj 345, 356, 364
37:23 w73 282; kj 345, 356, 364
37:24 w73 283; kj 348, 356, 364, 404
37:25 w73 283, 295, 427; kj 348, 356, 364, 404
37:26 w73 283; kj 348
37:27 w73 283; kj 348
37:28 w73 283; kj 348
38:1 w73 293; kj 350
38:2 w73 293; kj 350, 394
38:3 w73 293; kj 350
38:4 w73 293, 295; ka 153; kj 350
38:5 w73 293; kj 350
38:6 sl 257; w73 293-4; kj 350, 354
38:7 w73 294; kj 355
38:8 sl 257-8; w73 294, 347; ka 153; w72 75; kj 34, 356
38:9 sl 258; w73 294; kj 356
38:10 w73 295; kj 358
38:11 w75 303; sl 258, 262; w73 295, 347; kj 358, 382
38:12 sl 259; w73 295-6; kj 358-9
38:13 sl 259; kj 359
38:14 kj 360, 382
38:15 sl 257; w74 171; po 23; kj 360
38:16 sl 257; w74 171; po 23; w73 295; w72 75, 133; kj 34, 360
38:17 kj 362
38:18 sl 262; w73 296; kj 365
38:19 sl 262; g74 5/8 19; w73 296; kj 365
38:20 sl 262; g74 5/8 19; w73 296; kj 365
38:21 w74 171; w73 296; kj 366
38:22 sl 265; w74 171; w73 296; kj 366
38:23 w73 295-6; kj 366
39:1 w73 344; kj 369
39:2 sl 257; w73 344; kj 369
39:3 w73 344; kj 369
39:4 w73 344; kj 369
39:5 w73 344; kj 370
39:6 sl 280; w73 344; kj 33, 370, 395
39:7 w73 344; w72 75; kj 33-4, 370-1, 407
39:8 w73 345; kj 372
39:9 w73 345; kj 372
39:10 w73 345; kj 372
39:11 sl 277; w73 345; kj 373
39:12 sl 277; w73 345; kj 373
39:13 sl 277; w73 345; kj 373
39:14 sl 277; w73 346; kj 375
39:15 sl 277; w73 346; kj 375
39:16 sl 277; w73 346; kj 375
39:17 sl 266, 276-7; w73 346; kj 376
39:18 sl 266, 277; w73 346; kj 376
39:19 sl 266, 277; w73 346; kj 376
39:20 sl 266, 276-7; w73 346; kj 376
39:21 w73 346; kj 378
39:22 w73 346; kj 378
39:23 w73 346; kj 378
39:24 w73 346; kj 378
39:25 w73 347; kj 380
39:26 w73 347; kj 380
39:27 w73 347; kj 380
39:28 w73 347; kj 381
39:29 w73 347; kj 381
40:1 kj 210, 383
40:2 w73 381; kj 383
40:3 w73 381; kj 383-4
40:4 kj 383
40:6 kj 384
41:20 bi8 1356
43:1 kj 386
43:2 kj 386
43:3 w73 351; bi8 1353; kj 210, 386
43:4 kj 386
43:5 kj 386
43:6 kj 386
43:7 kj 386
43:13 w73 425
44:1 kj 389
44:2 kj 389
44:3 kj 389
44:15 w73 140
44:20 w73 140
46:22 bi8 1356
47:1 w73 381; kj 387
47:2 kj 389
47:3 w73 382; kj 389
47:4 w73 382-3; kj 390-1
47:5 w73 383; kj 392
47:6 w73 413; kj 392
47:7 w73 413; pm 384; kj 392
47:8 w73 413; pm 384; kj 392
47:9 w73 413; pm 384; kj 392
47:10 w73 413; pm 384; kj 393
47:11 w73 414; kj 396
47:12 w73 414; pm 384; kj 396, 398
47:13 kj 400
47:14 kj 400
47:15 w73 425; kj 400
47:16 w73 425; kj 400
47:17 w73 425; kj 400
47:18 w73 425; kj 400, 402
47:19 w73 425; kj 400
47:20 w73 425; kj 400
47:21 kj 400
47:22 kj 400
47:23 kj 400
48:1 kj 400
48:2 kj 400
48:3 kj 400
48:4 kj 400
48:5 kj 400
48:6 kj 400
48:7 kj 400
48:8 w73 425; kj 400
48:9 w73 425; kj 401
48:10 w73 425; kj 401
48:11 w73 425; kj 401
48:12 w73 425; kj 401
48:13 w73 425; kj 400
48:14 w73 425; kj 400
48:15 w73 426; kj 401, 403

g, Awake!; **ka,** God's Kingdom of a Thousand Years; **kj,** "The Nations Shall Know that I Am Jehovah"; **km,** Kingdom Ministry; **or,** Organization; **pm,** Paradise Restored—By Theocracy!; **po,** God's "Eternal Purpose"; **sg,** Theocratic School Guidebook; **sl,** Man's Salvation out of World Distress!; **te,** Listening to the Great Teacher; **tp,** True Peace and Security; **ts,** Is This Life All There Is?; **w,** Watchtower; **yb,** Yearbook. **Complete list on page 6.**

48:16 w73 426; kj 401
48:17 w73 426; kj 401
48:18 w73 426; kj 401
48:19 w73 426; kj 401
48:20 kj 402
48:21 kj 402
48:22 kj 402
48:23 kj 400
48:24 kj 400
48:25 kj 400
48:26 kj 400
48:27 kj 400
48:28 kj 400
48:29 kj 400
48:30 kj 402
48:31 kj 402
48:32 kj 402
48:33 kj 402
48:34 kj 402
48:35 w73 428; kj 34, 406

DANIEL

1:2 bi8 1353
1:4 w75 101
1:8 w72 141
2:1 pm 375
2:20 kj 92
2:21 kj 92
2:22 kj 92
2:31 w71 620; nc 19
2:32 w71 620; nc 19
2:33 w71 620; nc 19
2:34 sl 312-14, 316; pm 375; yb72 10/8; w71 620; nc 19
2:35 sl 312-14, 318, 320; pm 224, 375; w71 620, 624; nc 19, 28
2:37 sl 311; w71 620; nc 19
2:38 sl 311; w71 620; nc 19
2:39 sl 311; w71 620; nc 19
2:40 sl 311; g72 6/8 16; w71 620; nc 19
2:41 sl 311; w71 620; nc 19
2:42 sl 311; w71 620; nc 19
2:43 sl 311; w71 620; nc 19
2:44 w75 621; sl 312; og 24; ts 133; g74 2/22 22; w73 389; g73 4/8 19; g73 4/22 18; g73 10/8 23, 25; w72 582, 657; pm 224, 376-7; yb72 4/15; g72 10/8 19; w71 4, 99, 282, 620; te 161; nc 20; g71 10/8 23
2:45 w75 490; sl 312, 318; pm 224, 376-7; w71 620; nc 20
2:47 bi8 1356
3:15 w74 170
3:17 w74 169
3:18 w74 169
3:29 w74 170
4:3 tp 74
4:12 tp 75
4:13 ts 152
4:14 ts 152
4:15 ts 152
4:16 po 176; ts 152; w73 645; ka 12, 186, 260; tp 74-5; g73 10/8 18; w72 655; kj 57
4:17 w74 164; ts 152-3; tp 74
4:20 ts 153
4:21 ts 153
4:22 ts 153
4:23 w74 164; po 176; ts 153; ka 12, 186, 260; g73 10/8 18; w72 655; kj 57
4:24 ts 153
4:25 po 176; ts 153; ka 12, 186, 260; w72 231, 655
4:26 w74 164; ts 153; w72 231
4:29 w73 644; ka 10
4:30 w73 644; ka 10
4:31 w73 644; ka 10
4:32 po 176; w73 644; ka 10, 12, 186, 260
4:33 po 176
4:34 ts 157; w73 646; ka 11-12
4:35 ts 157; w73 646; ka 11-12
4:36 po 176; ts 157; ka 11
4:37 ts 157; ka 11
5:16 w71 316
5:31 ts 158; w72 349-50
6:1 w72 350
6:28 w72 350-1
7:7 g72 6/8 16
7:9 po 32; w72 154; kj 50
7:10 po 32; w72 154; kj 50
7:12 kj 234
7:13 w74 748; po 177; ts 154; ka 258, 327; g73 9/8 27; w72 187, 580; g72 2/8 6; kj 55, 234
7:14 yb76 11/26; w75 622; og 25; w74 748; po 177; ts 154; ka 258, 327; g73 9/8 27; kj 234
7:17 g75 10/8 14; w73 676
7:18 ka 73
7:22 ka 73
7:25 w74 236
7:26 w75 622; og 25
7:27 w75 622; og 25; ka 73; w72 580
8:1 w71 712
8:2 w71 714
8:3 w71 714
8:4 w71 714
8:5 g73 1/22 8; w71 714
8:6 w71 714
8:7 w71 714
8:8 w71 714
8:9 yb75 247; w71 715
8:10 yb72 10/25; w71 715, 720
8:11 yb72 9/5; w71 714-15, 720
8:12 yb72 11/7; w71 715, 720, 722
8:13 yb72 11/14; w71 723-4
8:14 yb75 247; yb72 11/27, 12/14; w71 711, 724
8:15 w71 715
8:16 w71 715
8:17 w71 715, 724; kj 55
8:18 w71 715
8:19 w71 715
8:20 w71 715
8:21 g73 1/22 8; yb72 6/13; w71 715
8:22 yb72 6/13; w71 715
8:23 yb72 8/2, 8/22; w71 716
8:24 yb72 10/25; w71 714, 716, 720
8:25 g74 2/22 22; yb72 8/2, 11/22; w71 716, 720, 724
8:26 yb72 8/2, 12/19; w71 716, 727
9:1 w72 349-51; pm 132
9:2 pm 132; g72 5/8 27; bi8 1357; kj 314
9:3 bi8 1353
9:4 bi8 1353
9:7 bi8 1353
9:9 bi8 1353
9:15 bi8 1353
9:16 bi8 1353
9:17 bi8 1353
9:19 w71 654; bi8 1353
9:24 po 131; ka 95; g73 9/8 27; g71 12/8 7
9:25 po 131, 144; ka 95; g73 8/22 29; g73 9/8 27-8; w72 241; g71 12/8 7-9
9:26 sl 74; po 131, 145; w73 758; ka 299-300; g73 9/8 27-8; w72 241; g71 12/8 7
9:27 sl 74; g75 12/22 28; po 131, 145, 162-3; w73 767; ka 95, 299-300; g73 9/8 27-8
10:1 w72 350
10:13 w72 154
10:21 po 137
11:3 w71 715
11:4 w71 715
11:8 bi8 1356
11:31 g73 1/22 8; w71 723
11:35 po 173
11:36 bi8 1357; g71 7/8 9
11:37 w74 198; g71 7/8 9
11:38 w74 198; w72 741; g71 7/8 9
11:39 g71 7/8 9
11:40 po 173; g74 2/22 22; g71 7/8 9
11:41 g74 2/22 22; g71 7/8 9
11:42 g74 2/22 22; g71 7/8 9
11:43 g74 2/22 22; g71 7/8 9
11:44 w74 334
11:45 w74 334; g71 7/8 9
12:1 sl 252, 318, 355; w74 191; po 137, 185; yb72 4/13; w71 269
12:4 w75 750; sl 41, 316; po 173

HOSEA

1:4 g73 4/8 28
1:11 w72 442
2:18 w75 89; w74 345; g74 4/8 14; w73 415; ka 145
2:19 w72 549
4:1 w74 247, 433
4:2 w74 247, 434; tp 96
4:7 bi8 1353
4:11 w74 452
5:13 kj 242
5:15 w72 438
6:1 w74 462
6:4 w72 438
7:14 w72 438
7:15 w72 438
7:16 w72 438-9
8:7 w72 393; kj 129
9:8 w74 732
9:10 w73 589; ka 104; w72 684, 693, 752
12:1 kj 242
12:3 w73 496
13:14 bi8 1353
14:4 w74 462
14:8 bi8 1360

JOEL

2:12 g74 12/8 27; w72 439
2:13 g74 12/8 27; w72 439
2:28 ka 106; yb72 5/4, 7/18; w71 32, 96, 683, 685, 745
2:29 ka 106; w71 683, 745
2:31 w75 753; w71 32
2:32 sl 111; w74 729; w73 527-8; w72 695; kj 333
3:9 kj 33
3:10 kj 33
3:17 kj 33

AMOS

2:8 w74 459
3:1 po 119
3:2 w74 687; po 119
3:7 w74 163; w71 466
4:12 yb72 8/6, 10/1; w71 618; nc 16
4:13 w71 618; nc 16
5:15 w74 438
5:16 bi8 1353
7:7 bi8 1353
7:8 bi8 1353
9:1 bi8 1353
9:2 bi8 1353
9:5 bi8 1352
9:12 w71 655

OBADIAH

3 sl 219
4 sl 219
8 sl 219
9 sl 219
11 sl 221
12 sl 221
13 sl 221
14 sl 221
15 sl 221
16 sl 221
17 sl 232
18 sl 230, 232
19 sl 219, 232
20 sl 232
21 sl 219, 232

JONAH

1:1 w75 710
1:3 yb73 8/16; w72 213
1:9 w75 711
1:12 w75 711
2:2 bi8 1353
2:7 w75 711
2:9 w75 711
3:10 kj 77
4:11 w73 228

MICAH

1:1 yb73 7/18; w72 742

1:2 w72 712; bi8 1353
1:3 sl 298; w74 255
1:4 sl 298
2:7 yb76 6/28; w75 280
2:12 yb72 7/21
3:8 w71 575
3:9 w72 744, 749
3:10 w72 744, 749
3:11 w72 744; kj 133
3:12 yb73 8/2, 11/12; w72 744, 749; kj 133, 312
4:1 yb73 8/24, 9/7, 12/6; w72 746, 750
4:2 yb73 9/30, 12/27; w72 751
4:3 tp 103; yb73 12/15; w72 752; g72 10/8 19
4:4 tp 7, 103; yb73 12/21; w72 752; bi8 1354, 1357; g71 4/22 27
4:5 yb75 9/24; w74 378; w73 31, 632; yb73 4, 260, 10/21; w72 741, 754; bi8 1354
4:7 bi8 1354
4:9 g72 11/22 14
4:10 g72 11/22 14
4:13 pm 223; bi8 1354
5:2 w74 527; po 123; g73 3/8 28; g73 8/22 29; w72 241, 704, 743
6:8 w73 490; yb73 2/7; g72 3/22 4
7:7 yb76 1/31; w73 474; w71 263
7:18 w73 133
7:19 w73 133

NAHUM

1:2 w73 228
1:3 w73 228
1:9 sl 326, 348
2:4 kj 192
3:1 g72 6/22 28

HABAKKUK

1:8 g74 2/22 14
1:12 bi8 1353
1:13 w73 230, 458; w71 270
2:2 g72 2/8 27
2:3 yb76 1/30; w75 284; yb75 10/23; w74 57; w73 195; yb72 10/15
2:5 bi8 1353
2:14 w73 428; bi8 1354, 1357; kj 406
2:20 w73 746; w72 712
3:1 yb74 7/12; w73 746
3:2 yb74 7/19, 7/29, 8/8; w73 750-1; w71 631
3:3 yb74 8/26, 9/6; w73 751
3:4 yb74 9/6; w73 751, 753
3:5 yb74 9/21; w73 751, 753
3:6 yb74 9/26; w73 753
3:7 yb74 10/28; w73 753
3:8 w73 755
3:9 w73 755
3:10 w73 755
3:11 yb74 12/1; w73 755
3:12 yb74 11/21; w73 756
3:13 po 99; yb74 6/28, 11/21, 11/28; w73 747, 756
3:14 yb74 12/6; w73 747, 757
3:15 w73 747, 757
3:16 yb74 12/12, 12/20; w73 747, 757-8
3:17 w74 25, 40; yb74 12/26; w73 758
3:18 yb76 5/16; w74 25, 40; yb74 12/26; w73 758-9
3:19 yb74 12/31; w73 746, 760; bi8 1352-3

ZEPHANIAH

1:17 ka 325
2:2 yb75 1/1; w74 49; ts 187; w71 357
2:3 yb75 1/1; g75 12/22 11-12; w74 49; ts 187; w72 765; w71 357
2:11 bi8 1356
2:12 bi8 1353
2:13 w75 137; g72 6/22 28
2:14 w75 137; g72 6/22 28
3:8 sl 295; w74 42; w73 528
3:9 sl 295; w74 42; yb74 7/27; w73 528; w72 248
3:12 w74 729; w73 529; w71 446
3:13 w73 529
3:16 sl 370
3:17 sl 370

HAGGAI

1:1 pm 25, 36, 40, 176
1:2 pm 26, 30
1:3 pm 33
1:4 pm 33
1:5 pm 33
1:6 pm 33
1:7 pm 37
1:8 pm 37
1:9 pm 37
1:10 pm 37, 285
1:11 pm 37, 285
1:12 pm 40
1:13 pm 41
1:14 pm 42, 52
1:15 pm 42, 52
2:1 pm 54
2:2 pm 54
2:3 pm 54
2:4 pm 56
2:5 pm 56
2:6 pm 57-8, 60-2, 65-6, 70, 74-5
2:7 w75 394; sl 203; w74 572; w73 402; pm 57, 61-2, 66, 75-6, 80, 174; w71 285
2:8 pm 61, 83
2:9 w75 396; pm 61, 84-5, 90
2:10 pm 107
2:11 pm 107
2:12 w75 427; pm 107
2:13 w75 427; pm 108, 189
2:14 w75 427; pm 110, 189
2:15 pm 113
2:16 pm 113, 285
2:17 pm 113, 285
2:18 pm 106, 113
2:19 pm 113
2:20 pm 116
2:21 w75 454; pm 116
2:22 pm 116-17
2:23 w75 454; sl 321; pm 116, 118, 270

ZECHARIAH

1:1 pm 93, 95
1:2 pm 95
1:3 w72 430; pm 95, 100
1:4 pm 97
1:5 pm 97
1:6 pm 97
1:7 pm 127
1:8 pm 127
1:9 pm 127
1:10 pm 128
1:11 pm 128
1:12 pm 130, 132; g72 5/8 27
1:13 pm 133
1:14 pm 133
1:15 pm 133
1:16 pm 134, 141
1:17 pm 135, 137, 141
1:18 pm 141
1:19 pm 141
1:20 pm 143
1:21 pm 143
2:1 pm 154
2:2 pm 154
2:3 pm 155
2:4 pm 155, 157
2:5 pm 155, 157, 161
2:6 pm 162
2:7 pm 164
2:8 pm 164, 391; w71 111
2:9 pm 164, 168
2:10 w72 752; pm 170
2:11 ka 279; w72 721, 752; pm 170-1, 173
2:12 pm 170; bi8 1353
2:13 pm 170, 175
3:1 pm 177
3:2 pm 177
3:3 pm 179
3:4 pm 179, 181
3:5 pm 184
3:6 pm 184
3:7 pm 184
3:8 pm 186-7, 230
3:9 pm 186, 188-9, 198
3:10 w72 753; pm 191
4:1 pm 193
4:2 pm 193
4:3 pm 193
4:4 pm 194
4:5 pm 194
4:6 w73 402; pm 194-5, 203-4, 346
4:7 pm 194, 198, 346
4:8 pm 202, 346
4:9 pm 202, 346
4:10 pm 202, 346
4:11 pm 204
4:12 pm 204
4:13 pm 204
4:14 pm 204, 223
5:1 pm 208
5:2 pm 208
5:3 pm 209
5:4 pm 209
5:5 pm 217
5:6 pm 217
5:7 pm 218
5:8 pm 218
5:9 pm 219
5:10 pm 219
5:11 pm 220
6:1 pm 222
6:2 pm 222
6:3 pm 222
6:4 pm 223
6:5 pm 223, 225
6:6 pm 226
6:7 pm 226
6:8 pm 227; bi8 1353
6:9 pm 229
6:10 pm 229
6:11 pm 229
6:12 pm 230
6:13 pm 230-1
6:14 pm 230-1
6:15 pm 230, 232-3
7:1 pm 235
7:2 pm 235
7:3 pm 235
7:4 pm 237
7:5 pm 237; g72 5/8 27
7:6 pm 237
7:7 pm 237
7:8 pm 238
7:9 pm 238
7:10 pm 238
7:11 pm 238
7:12 pm 238
7:13 pm 238
7:14 pm 238
8:1 pm 240
8:2 pm 240
8:3 pm 241
8:4 pm 242
8:5 pm 242
8:6 pm 244
8:7 pm 245
8:8 pm 245
8:9 pm 246
8:10 pm 246, 285
8:11 pm 246, 285
8:12 pm 246, 285
8:13 pm 246
8:14 pm 249
8:15 pm 249
8:16 pm 251
8:17 pm 251
8:18 pm 252
8:19 pm 239, 252
8:20 w75 537; w74 628; ka 280; pm 253, 261, 365, 373
8:21 w75 537; w74 628; ka 280; pm 253, 261, 365, 373
8:22 w75 537; w74 628; ka 280; yb73 12/2; w72 721; pm 253, 261, 365, 373
8:23 w75 537-8; w74 572, 628; w73 459; ka 280, 282; pm 255, 257-8, 261, 365, 373
9:1 pm 261, 269
9:2 pm 261-2
9:3 pm 261-2
9:4 pm 261-2; bi8 1353
9:5 pm 261, 264
9:6 pm 261, 264
9:7 pm 261, 264, 266
9:8 pm 268
9:9 w75 620; og 21; w73 654-5; g73 2/8 28; g73 3/8 4;

g, Awake!; **ka**, God's Kingdom of a Thousand Years; **kj**, "The Nations Shall Know that I Am Jehovah"; **km**, Kingdom Ministry; **or**, Organization; **pm**, Paradise Restored—By Theocracy!; **po**, God's "Eternal Purpose"; **sg**, Theocratic School Guidebook; **sl**, Man's Salvation out of World Distress!; **te**, Listening to the Great Teacher; **tp**, True Peace and Security; **ts**, Is This Life All There Is?; **w**, Watchtower; **yb**, Yearbook. **Complete list on page 6.**

g73 9/8 27; pm 270, 272, 274
9:10 pm 270, 274
9:11 pm 275-6
9:12 w73 30; yb73 10/19, 12/1; w72 630; pm 275, 277-8; dn 27
9:13 pm 279
9:14 pm 279
9:15 pm 279
9:16 pm 281, 306
9:17 pm 281
10:1 pm 283, 285, 398
10:2 g75 1/22 5; pm 283, 286
10:3 pm 287, 289, 295, 303
10:4 pm 287, 289, 295, 303
10:5 pm 287, 290, 295, 303
10:6 pm 287, 292, 295, 303
10:7 pm 287, 292, 295, 303
10:8 pm 295-6, 303
10:9 w72 751; pm 295-6, 303
10:10 pm 295-6, 303
10:11 pm 295-6, 303
10:12 yb73 9/22; w72 751; pm 295-6, 301, 303
11:1 pm 303
11:2 pm 303
11:3 pm 303
11:4 w75 553; pm 305, 312
11:5 w75 553; pm 305, 308
11:6 pm 309, 314
11:7 w75 553; pm 310, 313
11:8 w75 553; pm 310, 312, 317
11:9 pm 310, 313
11:10 pm 310, 312-13; bi8 1353
11:11 pm 310, 313, 318
11:12 sl 54; pm 319, 321-2
11:13 sl 54; pm 319, 322, 324
11:14 pm 319
11:15 w75 555; pm 327
11:16 w75 555; pm 327
11:17 w75 555; pm 327, 356
12:1 pm 329, 331, 345
12:2 pm 329, 331, 333; kj 326
12:3 pm 329; kj 326
12:4 pm 329; kj 326
12:5 pm 329
12:6 pm 329
12:7 pm 336
12:8 pm 336
12:9 pm 336
12:10 g73 9/8 27-8; pm 339-41, 345, 348
12:11 pm 339, 341-2, 345
12:12 pm 339, 341, 343, 345
12:13 pm 341, 343, 345
12:14 pm 341, 343, 345
13:1 pm 345, 347-8
13:2 pm 351-2
13:3 pm 351, 353
13:4 pm 354
13:5 pm 354
13:6 pm 354
13:7 w75 78; ka 351-3; w72 528; pm 356-8
13:8 pm 356, 359, 361
13:9 pm 356, 359, 364
14:1 pm 365, 368, 370-1, 386
14:2 pm 365, 368, 370-1, 386
14:3 pm 94, 365, 368, 371, 375, 380, 392
14:4 pm 365, 371, 375, 379
14:5 pm 375, 378-9; bi8 1353
14:6 pm 381
14:7 pm 382
14:8 pm 383, 385, 406
14:9 w75 623; og 28; pm 383, 387
14:10 pm 383, 386
14:11 pm 383, 386
14:12 w75 637; pm 390-2, 399
14:13 w75 638; w74 244; w73 757; pm 390, 392, 399
14:14 w75 638; pm 390-1, 394, 399
14:15 w75 638; pm 390, 392, 399
14:16 pm 398, 406
14:17 yb73 12/14; w72 722; pm 398-9, 401
14:18 w72 722; pm 398-9, 401
14:19 pm 398-9, 401
14:20 w74 52-3; pm 398, 403
14:21 w74 52-3; pm 398, 403, 406

MALACHI

1:2 po 94
1:3 po 94
1:8 w72 703
1:12 bi8 1353
1:14 yb72 7/29; bi8 1353
2:9 ts 97
3:1 yb75 88; po 143; ka 234; w72 79; pm 360; w71 711; bi8 1354; kj 183
3:2 yb75 88; w73 336; w72 79; pm 360; yb 72 6/16; kj 183
3:3 yb75 88; w73 336; w72 180; pm 360; kj 183
3:4 pm 360; kj 183
3:5 w73 342; pm 361; kj 183
3:6 pm 361; yb72 3/18; g72 10/8 21
3:7 ts 52; w73 440; w72 431; pm 361
3:9 bi8 1353
3:17 w74 281
3:18 w74 178, 758
4:1 sl 279; w72 363, 661
4:2 sl 279; w74 755
4:3 sl 279
4:5 w74 298; ts 57; w71 239
4:6 w74 298; w71 239

MATTHEW

1:1 w74 105; po 142; w71 302
1:3 w72 241
1:6 w74 105; w72 241
1:12 ka 62; kj 230
1:16 w74 105; w72 241
1:18 w72 621; dn 11
1:20 po 138; bi8 1358
1:21 po 138; w71 58
1:25 w72 621; dn 11
2:1 w72 241
2:5 g73 3/8 28; w72 241
2:6 g73 3/8 28; w72 241, 703-4
2:11 w75 739; g73 12/22 5
2:20 bi8 1351
3:1 w72 681
3:2 w72 681
3:4 w75 464; w72 666
3:8 w74 469
3:13 po 144; w73 274; ka 65; w72 623, 681, 686, 715; dn 16; kj 62, 305
3:14 w73 274; w72 681, 686, 715; kj 62, 305
3:15 yb74 5/18; w73 274; yb73 6/6; w72 601, 681, 686, 715; kj 62, 305
3:16 w74 222; po 144; yb74 3/30; ka 65, 101; w72 601, 623, 681, 687, 715; dn 16; kj 62, 305; g71 12/8 9
3:17 w74 222; w73 168; ka 65, 101; w72 681, 687, 715; kj 62, 305; g71 12/8 9
4:1 po 146; g74 10/22 7; g73 12/8 27
4:2 w71 538
4:3 g74 10/22 7; w71 39
4:4 yb76 7/30; yb74 3/2; g74 12/8 21; w73 209; w72 306; or 55; w71 61; g71 12/8 27
4:5 sl 20; g74 10/22 7
4:6 g74 10/22 7; w71 39
4:7 yb75 6/13; w74 722; w73 209; w71 39
4:8 w75 619; og 21; w74 70; g74 10/22 7; w72 624; dn 16
4:9 w75 619; og 21; w74 70; g74 10/22 7; w72 624; dn 16; w71 39; te 53
4:10 yb76 12/3; w75 619, 716; fu 18; og 21; w74 70, 396; w73 209; w72 627; dn 22; w71 116; kj 398; te 139
4:11 w75 717; po 146; w72 627; dn 22
4:12 w75 619; og 20; w72 681
4:13 w72 681
4:14 w72 681
4:15 w72 681; w71 323
4:16 w72 681; w71 323
4:17 w75 619, 751; og 20; ts 128, 155; yb74 6/1; w73 651; w72 231, 681; w71 78
4:19 yb74 2/14; w73 270; kj 394
4:20 yb76 5/8
4:23 g75 6/22 8; yb72 2/12; w71 78
4:24 g73 5/22 15; g71 8/8 21
5:2 yb74 1/26
5:3 w75 645; yb74 3/7; w73 106, 436, 491; kj 310; g71 6/8 27-8
5:4 g74 12/8 28; g71 6/22 27-8
5:5 w74 377, 662; tp 38; g71 7/8 27
5:6 w73 107; g71 7/22 27
5:7 yb75 9/4; w74 494, 500, 505; w72 549, 554; w71 412; g71 8/8 27
5:8 g71 8/22 27-8
5:9 g72 4/22 21; w71 372; te 131; g71 9/8 27-8
5:10 w71 492; g71 9/22 27-8
5:11 w74 219; g72 12/22 6; w71 492; g71 10/22 27
5:12 g72 12/22 6; w71 492; g71 10/22 27
5:13 w75 646; g74 8/8 16; g71 3/8 26
5:14 w74 477
5:16 yb76 10/19, 12/17; w75 371
5:17 w72 686; g72 11/22 6
5:18 w71 480
5:19 w73 436
5:21 w75 646; g72 11/22 7
5:22 ts 111; yb74 8/27; bi8 1355
5:23 yb76 3/23; yb74 5/31; g74 11/8 27; w73 333; g72 11/22 7
5:24 yb76 3/23; g74 11/8 27; w73 333; g72 11/22 7
5:27 w75 646; w73 80; g72 11/22 7
5:28 w73 32, 80, 539; g73 11/22 27; w72 32; yb72 3/20; w71 142
5:29 ts 112; w73 80, 254; bi8 1355
5:30 ts 112; w73 80; bi8 1355
5:31 w74 671
5:32 g75 9/22 28; w74 511, 671, 703; tp 150; w72 31, 766
5:33 w75 646; w72 30; g72 11/22 7
5:34 g75 7/22 27; w72 30; pm 366
5:35 g75 7/22 27; w74 686; pm 366; w71 745
5:36 g75 7/22 27
5:37 w75 383; g75 7/22 27;

w73 63; w72 30; yb72 5/15; te 71
5:38 w75 646; g72 11/22 7
5:39 w75 648; g75 9/8 27; g74 3/8 4; w71 373; te 133
5:44 yb76 7/3; w75 524; g75 12/8 29; w74 147; tp 122; g71 1/22 6
5:45 w75 524; yb75 4/9; w74 120, 147, 177, 190, 465, 467; tp 122; yb73 9/21; w72 592; g72 2/8 9; g71 3/22 28
5:46 w74 465
5:47 w74 465
5:48 yb75 3/30, 7/4; w74 150, 155, 465; w71 565-6
6:1 g73 4/8 28; g73 8/8 28
6:2 w71 414
6:3 w71 414
6:4 w71 414
6:7 ts 67; w72 335; g72 11/22 27
6:8 ts 67; g72 11/22 27
6:9 w75 261; g75 12/22 14; w74 220, 235, 313, 448; g74 6/8 7; g73 4/22 19; w72 170; g72 11/8 6; g72 11/22 27; w71 647
6:10 g75 12/22 11; w74 235, 291, 625, 645; g74 6/8 7; w73 361, 389, 645, 689; g73 4/22 19; w72 170; g72 6/8 8; g72 11/22 27; w71 67-8, 131, 281; te 159
6:11 g74 6/8 7; g72 11/22 27
6:12 w74 497; g74 6/8 7; g72 11/22 27
6:13 g74 6/8 7; yb73 3/20; w72 329; yb72 3/6; g72 11/22 27
6:14 w75 675
6:15 yb76 11/16
6:16 g74 12/8 27; w71 536
6:17 g74 12/8 27; w71 536
6:18 g74 12/8 27; w71 536
6:19 w75 561; w73 408
6:20 yb76 3/27; w75 561; w73 158, 408; g72 5/8 4
6:21 w73 158, 408; yb72 12/23
6:22 yb76 6/11; w75 573; w73 407
6:23 yb76 6/11; w75 573
6:24 yb76 6/26; w75 232, 569; g73 5/22 27; w72 299
6:25 yb76 3/1; g75 9/8 28; w73 408; w71 573
6:26 w75 572; w73 408
6:28 g74 1/22 9; w71 554
6:29 g74 1/22 9; w71 554
6:31 yb76 9/13; g74 8/8 5; w72 196
6:32 yb76 3/1; w74 113; g74 8/8 5; w73 437; w72 196
6:33 sl 328; fu 26; w74 113, 250, 534; yb74 7/20; g74 8/8 5; w73 317, 437, 489, 591; yb73 1/27, 3/8; g73 6/22 13; w72 135, 196, 657; g72 5/8 4; g72 10/22 16; w71 767
6:34 w74 113; g74 8/22 19; w72 196
7:1 w75 92; g74 3/8 4; g74 11/22 27; w73 335
7:2 w73 335
7:5 g74 11/22 27
7:7 g74 6/8 5; yb73 6/26; w72 155; g71 1/22 6; g71 6/8 28
7:8 yb73 6/26; w72 155; g71 1/22 6
7:11 g75 9/22 3; w72 155
7:12 yb76 5/15; yb74 1/23; g73 3/22 7
7:13 w74 362; yb74 8/11; g74 1/22 18; w73 437; tp 28; g73 4/8 17
7:14 yb74 8/11; g74 1/22 18; w73 437; tp 28; g73 4/8 17
7:21 w73 102; g73 1/8 27
7:22 g75 6/22 8; w74 327, 447; g74 4/22 27; g74 10/22 10; w73 102; g73 1/8 27
7:23 yb76 10/5; w75 118; w74 327; w73 102; g73 1/8 27; g72 4/22 25
7:24 w71 638
7:26 w71 638
8:2 w72 581
8:3 w72 581
8:15 w75 717
8:16 sl 66
8:17 sl 66
8:20 w72 581; g72 10/8 30; kj 55
8:22 w74 95; w73 209
8:29 w74 383; bi8 1360
9:1 w75 669
9:10 w74 493
9:11 w74 140, 493
9:12 w74 493
9:13 w74 493; w72 551; w71 414
9:15 w71 538
9:16 w71 424
9:17 w75 200, 591; tp 41; w71 424
9:18 w72 448
9:25 w72 448
9:30 g71 12/22 27
9:35 w74 281; yb74 2/6; w73 270
9:36 w74 60, 281; g74 10/8 24; w71 412
10:5 w74 464, 691; w71 159
10:6 w74 464, 691; w71 159
10:7 or 8; w71 78
10:8 w74 447; w73 397; tp 32; g73 8/8 5; g72 12/22 4
10:14 w73 271
10:15 g75 10/22 13; ts 184
10:16 yb73 5/6; yb72 7/10
10:18 w74 414
10:19 w74 414
10:20 w74 414
10:22 w73 657
10:23 g72 12/8 23
10:27 or 114
10:28 w75 53, 286; g75 8/8 28; g75 10/22 11; ts 111-12; w73 208, 238; g73 7/22 28; bi8 1355
10:33 w74 370
10:34 g73 1/22 15; g72 12/22 6
10:35 g73 1/22 15; g72 12/22 6
10:36 g73 1/22 15; g72 12/22 6; w71 203, 533
10:37 tp 141; w71 203
10:38 bi8 1360
10:42 w75 714; w74 20, 78, 627; w73 264
11:11 g74 8/22 28; g73 5/8 7
11:12 ts 106; w72 90
11:16 w74 416
11:17 w74 416
11:18 w74 416
11:19 w74 140, 464; w73 29; or 114
11:20 ka 127
11:21 ka 127
11:22 w73 367; ka 127
11:23 ka 127; bi8 1361
11:24 ts 184; w73 367; ka 127
11:25 w74 180; yb73 1/5
11:27 w73 259; w71 265
11:28 g74 4/8 9; g72 11/22 4; w71 260
11:29 yb76 2/21; w74 103, 603; yb74 8/25; g74 4/8 9; w73 277; or 107; g72 11/22 4; w71 31, 260
11:30 w73 277; or 107, 184; g72 11/22 4; w71 260
12:7 w72 551; w71 414
12:12 g72 11/22 6
12:15 g71 12/22 27
12:16 g71 12/22 27
12:17 g71 12/22 27
12:18 g71 12/22 27
12:19 g71 12/22 27
12:21 w73 103
12:31 w75 39; g75 11/22 28; w74 76; ts 182
12:32 w75 39, 460; w74 76; ts 182
12:38 w74 748
12:39 w75 710; w74 748
12:40 w73 766-7; w72 580
12:41 g75 10/22 13; ts 184; ka 128
12:42 g75 10/22 13; ts 184; ka 54, 128; w72 106
12:43 ts 86
12:44 ts 86
12:45 ts 86
12:50 w71 75, 421; te 82
13:3 w73 684
13:4 w73 684
13:5 w73 684
13:6 w73 684
13:7 w73 684
13:8 w73 684
13:11 ts 152
13:13 w75 593
13:14 w75 593
13:15 w75 593; tp 43
13:16 yb72 8/13
13:17 yb72 8/13
13:18 w73 684; or 108
13:19 w73 684; or 108
13:20 or 108; g72 3/22 27
13:21 or 108
13:22 yb76 8/30; w75 570; w74 420; or 108; g72 3/22 27
13:23 w72 91; or 108; g72 3/22 27; km 2/72 3
13:24 yb76 10/1; sl 207-8; w74 480; ka 183
13:25 yb76 10/1; sl 207-8; w74 480; ka 183; g73 1/8 19
13:26 sl 207-8
13:27 sl 207-8
13:28 sl 207-8
13:29 sl 207-8
13:30 w75 594, 599; sl 207-8; yb75 33; w74 561; yb72 4/11; w71 174
13:31 yb76 10/16; w75 592-3, 595; sl 206-9; km 11/75 4
13:32 yb76 10/16, 12/14; w75 595; sl 206-9
13:33 yb76 7/23, 10/31; w75 597; sl 209, 211
13:34 w75 589; g73 6/8 7
13:35 w75 589
13:36 sl 207-8; w73 272
13:37 yb76 12/6; sl 207-8; pm 101, 362
13:38 w75 594, 599; sl 207-8; pm 101, 362
13:39 yb76 9/17; w75 594; sl 207-8; po 172; pm 101, 104, 362
13:40 sl 207-8; pm 362
13:41 sl 207-8; pm 362

13:42 sl 207-8; pm 362
13:43 sl 207-8; w74 561; pm 362
13:44 w75 594
13:45 yb76 10/3; w75 21, 594
13:46 yb76 10/3; w75 21, 594
13:47 yb76 9/26; w75 593-4
13:48 w75 593-4
13:49 w75 593-4
13:57 sl 52; w73 13
14:14 g75 6/22 7; w72 581; w71 412
14:20 g72 10/22 14
14:21 g72 10/22 14
14:24 te 62
14:25 te 62
15:18 w73 535
15:19 w73 535; g73 11/22 27
15:20 w73 535
15:24 w74 691
15:32 w71 412
15:37 g72 10/22 14
16:1 w74 748
16:4 w74 296, 748
16:6 sl 210
16:12 sl 210
16:16 sl 175
16:18 w74 600; po 158; w73 243; w72 717; bi8 1361
16:20 g71 12/22 27
16:21 yb72 2/27, 5/13; w71 109, 685
16:22 w74 296; w71 109; g71 5/22 9
16:23 w74 296; yb72 1/24; w71 110; g71 5/22 9
16:24 fu 31; w74 343, 600; w73 636; tp 183; yb73 12/4, 12/16; w72 697-8; or 17; bi8 1361
16:25 w74 600
16:26 w73 329
16:27 w74 297
16:28 w74 297
17:1 kj 305
17:2 kj 305
17:3 kj 305
17:4 kj 305
17:5 w73 168; kj 305
17:11 w71 239
17:12 g75 4/8 28; ts 57; w71 239
17:13 ts 57; w71 239
17:18 w73 700
17:21 w71 537
18:1 w75 723
18:2 w75 723
18:3 w75 723; w74 180; w71 367, 607
18:4 yb76 8/1; w75 723
18:5 w75 723
18:6 w75 723
18:8 ts 112
18:9 ts 112; bi8 1355
18:10 w74 220
18:11 w75 414
18:14 km 12/75 7
18:15 yb73 6/14; w72 465-6, 543; or 156
18:16 w72 465-6; or 156
18:17 yb75 4/15; w74 140, 463, 544; w73 703; w72 465-7; or 156; w71 746
18:20 yb73 4/10, 7/22; w72 407, 756
18:22 w74 154; w71 103
18:33 w72 551
18:34 te 65
18:35 w73 100; w71 103; te 65
19:4 w75 151; pm 8; te 15
19:5 w75 151; g74 12/8 15; w72 32
19:6 w75 151; w72 32
19:8 w73 155
19:9 w74 485, 511, 671, 703; w73 351; tp 150; w72 31, 766
19:10 w75 152; g72 12/8 6
19:11 g72 12/8 6
19:12 w75 158; yb73 2/19; g72 12/8 6
19:13 w75 435; w74 368
19:14 yb76 3/4; w75 435; w74 368; w73 29
19:20 w74 151; w71 567
19:21 w75 566; yb75 4/10; w74 420; w71 567
19:22 w74 420; w71 568
19:28 w73 427; g73 10/8 27; kj 405
20:4 w73 473
20:13 w73 473
20:14 w73 473
20:15 w73 473
20:23 g73 3/8 28
20:24 w75 725
20:25 w75 725
20:26 w75 725; w73 469; w72 581; w71 456
20:27 w75 725; w73 469; w72 581
20:28 yb76 6/1; w75 716, 721, 725; w74 200; ts 138; w73 239, 243, 465; g73 6/8 8; g73 7/22 3; w72 237, 687; or 108; g72 10/22 14; w71 456
20:34 w71 412
21:1 g73 2/8 28; pm 271
21:2 g73 2/8 28
21:3 g73 2/8 28
21:4 g73 2/8 28
21:5 g73 2/8 28; pm 271
21:11 po 143
21:12 g74 3/8 27
21:13 g74 3/8 27
21:16 yb74 11/20
21:31 ts 103; w73 367
21:32 w74 140; ts 103; w73 367
21:34 yb74 8/24
21:42 pm 188
21:43 w74 127, 685; w73 686; w71 184; kj 309, 330, 343
22:1 w74 636, 686, 690; ka 171
22:2 yb75 5/21, 6/12; w74 686, 690
22:3 yb75 5/29, 6/26, 8/15, 8/24; w74 686
22:4 yb75 7/18; w74 692
22:5 yb75 7/18; w74 692
22:6 w74 692
22:7 w74 693
22:8 w74 693-4
22:9 yb75 7/28; w74 693
22:10 w74 693, 697
22:11 yb75 11/4; w74 696-7
22:12 yb75 11/8, 11/22; w74 696
22:13 yb75 11/22, 12/16; w74 698
22:14 w75 108, 286; yb75 12/11; w74 636, 698
22:17 w74 140; w72 640
22:18 w74 140
22:19 w74 140
22:20 w74 140
22:21 yb76 11/9; w74 140; w73 63, 316, 741; tp 136; w72 640
22:32 g73 6/8 8
22:37 w74 538; yb74 3/11; w73 178; w72 563; or 183; g72 12/22 7; w71 146
22:38 w74 538; w72 563; or 183
22:39 w74 409; yb73 9/28; w72 563, 596; or 183; w71 305
22:40 w72 563
22:46 w75 554-5; pm 317
23:5 w73 192
23:7 w75 726
23:8 w75 726; w73 168; w71 331; kj 304
23:9 w73 168; kj 304
23:10 w73 168; w72 729; or 8; kj 304
23:11 w75 726; w73 168; kj 304
23:15 ts 112; bi8 1355
23:23 w73 504; w71 414
23:33 ts 112, 116; g73 3/8 28; bi8 1355
23:38 w74 399; kj 135, 146
23:39 w74 399
24:1 w74 681; pm 318
24:2 w74 429, 681; kj 210
24:3 w75 272, 621, 633, 686, 749; sl 19, 29; ml 26; og 24; w74 50, 244, 399, 717; po 172; g74 3/8 8; ka 167, 205-6; g73 7/22 5; bi8 1364; kj 210
24:4 ka 296, 320
24:5 w75 273; w74 682; ka 296, 320
24:6 w75 274, 388; ka 296; tp 79; w71 406; te 178
24:7 w75 274, 388; g75 10/8 13; w74 72, 195, 243, 682; g74 3/8 8; g74 5/8 18; ka 297; tp 14; g73 6/22 12; w72 339; g72 4/22 21; g72 7/22 12; g72 10/8 15-16; w71 69, 406; te 178; g71 10/8 16
24:8 g75 10/8 13; w74 682; ka 297; tp 84; g71 3/8 4; g71 10/8 16
24:9 w74 202, 682; po 178; yb74 12/24; w73 398, 657, 749; ka 298, 306; g73 3/8 25; w72 143, 340
24:10 ka 298
24:11 w74 100, 244; ka 298; tp 85
24:12 w75 37, 635; g75 11/22 15; w74 99, 244, 444, 682, 718; w73 691; ka 298; tp 19, 85; g73 3/22 5; g73 4/22 13; w72 340; g72 10/8 16; g72 12/22 6; w71 406; te 178; g71 5/8 6
24:13 yb75 11/11; w74 55; w73 40, 681; ka 298
24:14 yb76 7/24; sl 328, 343, 371; w74 4, 37, 183, 332, 334, 558, 682; po 174; w73 40, 658, 681; ka 227, 288, 298; tp 87; g73 4/8 17; g73 7/22 6; w72 656, 728; or 4; pm 140; yb72 4/7, 12/3; g72 10/8 16; w71 69, 302, 308, 401, 466; kj 62, 181, 301, 317
24:15 w75 741; sl 20; ml 21-2; w74 683, 717; ka 299; g73 1/22 8; w71 31, 718, 723; kj 257, 351
24:16 w75 741; ml 21; w74 683, 717; ka 299; kj 351
24:17 w75 340; ka 299; kj 351
24:18 w75 340; ka 299; kj 351
24:19 w75 158; ka 299; w72 108; kj 351
24:20 ka 299; kj 351
24:21 yb76 2/15; w75 272; sl 252, 316, 355; ml 25; w74 172, 400, 683; po 174, 181; w73 293; ka 299, 305, 316; g73 4/22 18; w72 629, 637, 657, 660; dn 25; g72 10/8 15; kj 112, 146, 161, 257, 269, 281, 351, 359
24:22 sl 252, 355; ml 25; w74 172, 683, 749; po 181; ka 299; w72 629, 657; dn 25; kj 146, 257, 269, 281, 351
24:23 w75 275; w74 750; ka 320
24:24 w75 275; w74 750; ka 320, 322; w72 88; pm 351
24:25 w74 750; ka 320
24:26 w74 750; ka 320
24:27 w75 275; w74 750; ka 320; bi8 1364
24:28 yb76 3/31; w74 750; ka 320
24:29 yb76 4/28; w75 276; w74 750; ka 323-4, 326
24:30 w75 272,

742; w74 698, 748, 751; ka 323, 327; g73 7/22 6
24:31 sl 201; w74 698, 751; ka 323, 328
24:34 w75 277; sl 357; gc 22; ml 25; g75 7/8 29; g74 4/8 18; tp 88; g73 4/22 19; g73 10/8 19; w72 583; g71 10/8 16
24:36 yb76 1/1, 1/22, 10/12; w75 9, 277, 768; sl 292; w74 56, 379
24:37 w75 10; sl 292; ka 332; w72 651; pm 11; w71 168; bi8 1364; te 127; g71 4/22 23
24:38 w75 10; sl 292; w72 651; w71 168; te 127
24:39 w75 10; sl 292; w72 651; w71 168; bi8 1364; te 127
24:40 w75 11; ka 335
24:41 w75 11; ka 335
24:42 w75 11; ka 336
24:43 w75 11
24:44 w75 11
24:45 w75 45, 77; ka 338, 341, 345; w72 458, 636, 731, 755; or 9; yb72 2/22, 8/31; w71 81, 462, 750, 756
24:46 w75 77; ka 347; w72 458, 731, 755; w71 462, 750, 756
24:47 w75 77; w72 458, 731; or 10; w71 462, 750, 756
24:48 w75 110; yb75 88; ka 358-9; pm 363
24:49 w75 110; yb75 88; ka 358-9; pm 363
24:50 w75 110; ka 358; pm 363
24:51 w75 110; ka 358, 361-2; pm 363
25:1 w75 593; w74 431, 478; ka 170
25:2 w75 593; w74 431, 478; ka 170
25:3 w74 478; ka 170, 176
25:4 ka 170, 176
25:5 w74 479, 506; ka 182
25:6 ka 191
25:7 w74 508; ka 191, 193
25:8 ka 194
25:9 ka 194, 200
25:10 w74 508; ka 200
25:11 w74 508; ka 202
25:12 w74 508; ka 202
25:13 w74 509; ka 204
25:14 w74 541; ka 213, 216
25:15 w74 541; ka 218, 247
25:16 w74 556; ka 220
25:17 w74 556; ka 220
25:18 w74 589; ka 247
25:19 ka 229
25:20 ka 241
25:21 w74 559; ka 241, 247; w72 731
25:22 ka 241
25:23 w74 559; ka 241, 247; w72 731
25:24 ka 248
25:25 ka 248
25:26 w75 111; w74 590; ka 248
25:27 w74 590; ka 248
25:28 w74 591; ka 253
25:29 w74 591; ka 253-4
25:30 w74 591; ka 253
25:31 sl 313; ml 26; w74 287, 626; w73 200; ka 258, 265; g73 7/22 5; w72 200; w71 238
25:32 sl 313; w74 287, 626; w73 200; ka 258, 265, 269; g73 7/22 5; w72 200
25:33 w74 287, 626; ka 258, 265, 269; g73 7/22 5
25:34 sl 359; w74 287, 626; yb74 6/12; g74 8/22 28; w73 495, 678; ka 270, 272, 291-2; g73 7/22 6; w71 559
25:35 w74 627; ka 270
25:36 w74 20, 627; ka 270
25:37 w74 627; ka 274
25:38 w74 627; ka 274
25:39 w74 627; ka 274
25:40 w74 250, 287, 627; po 184; ka 274-5; yb72 7/22; w71 421
25:41 sl 272; w74 381, 652; w73 238; ka 284
25:42 ka 284
25:43 ka 284
25:44 w75 717; w74 651; ka 286; w71 457
25:45 w74 250, 651; ka 287; w71 457
25:46 sl 274; yb75 4/25; w74 123, 377, 652; po 184; ts 181; ka 290-1
26:11 w75 70; w72 579
26:13 w74 574
26:14 sl 54; pm 321
26:15 sl 54; pm 321
26:16 sl 54; pm 321
26:17 pm 321
26:20 w73 175
26:26 w73 198; w72 166; g72 3/22 27
26:27 po 160; w73 198; w72 166
26:28 po 160; w73 198; w72 166; g72 3/22 27
26:29 w73 198
26:30 w73 198
26:31 ka 351; w72 528; pm 356
26:32 ka 351-2; pm 356
26:38 w72 527
26:39 w72 687; yb72 9/8; w71 273
26:40 w72 527, 687; w71 273
26:41 w72 527, 532, 687
26:42 w72 687; w71 273
26:43 w72 687; w71 273
26:44 w72 687; w71 273
26:45 w72 527
26:47 w71 685
26:52 g72 11/8 27
26:54 pm 357
26:56 ka 351; pm 357
26:57 w71 685
26:65 w71 273
26:74 yb73 11/27; w72 697
27:1 w71 685
27:3 pm 323; w71 685
27:4 pm 323
27:5 pm 323
27:6 pm 323
27:7 pm 323
27:8 pm 323
27:9 pm 323-4
27:10 pm 323-4
27:18 w75 8
27:20 w71 685
27:26 w71 110
27:29 g71 8/8 9
27:34 w71 249
27:41 ka 85; w71 685
27:46 w72 256
27:50 w72 714
27:51 w72 714
27:52 w75 639-40
27:53 w75 639-40
27:55 w75 717; w71 457
27:64 sl 77
28:1 w73 767; bi8 1362
28:10 w73 269
28:12 w71 685
28:16 w73 269; kj 176
28:17 kj 176
28:18 w74 179; w73 246, 263, 530; kj 176
28:19 yb76 11/20; w74 76, 422; yb74 1/10, 4/14; g74 3/22 27; w73 6, 269, 274, 530; yb73 3/10; w72 447, 691, 696, 701; or 4; w71 119; kj 62, 176, 179, 301, 307
28:20 yb76 11/20; w75 46; g74 3/22 27; w73 530; w72 447, 691, 696, 701; or 4; w71 119; kj 62, 176, 179, 301, 307; sg 49

MARK

1:4 w72 686
1:8 w74 363
1:11 w73 274
1:13 po 146; w72 627; dn 22
1:14 w71 31
1:24 bi8 1360
1:29 w75 669
1:31 w71 456
1:44 g71 12/22 27
1:45 yb74 6/2
2:1 w75 670
2:5 w73 412
2:10 w73 412
2:12 w73 412
2:15 w74 140
2:20 g74 12/8 27
2:27 w75 707; g74 4/8 11
2:28 g74 4/8 11; w73 11
3:5 w72 561
3:14 po 158
3:16 yb72 5/1
3:17 yb72 5/1; w71 435
3:21 g73 3/8 27
4:30 sl 206-9
4:31 sl 206-9
4:32 sl 206-9
5:7 bi8 1360
5:19 g71 12/22 28
5:30 sl 67
5:35 w72 448
5:40 w72 112
5:41 w72 112, 448
5:42 w75 262; w72 112, 448
6:2 g73 3/8 27;
6:3 w75 296; g73 3/8 27; g71 12/22 6
6:4 sl 52
6:12 w75 751
6:34 g74 10/8 24; w71 412
6:44 w73 15
6:52 g72 12/22 27
6:53 g72 12/22 27
7:8 w73 504
7:9 w73 504
7:21 w73 74
7:22 w73 74
7:23 w73 74
7:36 g71 12/22 27
8:11 w74 748
8:12 w74 748
8:15 sl 210
8:29 sl 175
8:34 yb75 8/28; w72 601
8:35 w73 231; g73 6/8 5
9:7 te 26
9:29 w71 537
9:33 w75 723
9:34 yb76 9/20; w75 723
9:35 w75 723; w74 401
9:38 w73 507
9:39 w73 507
9:40 w73 507; ka 278
9:41 w74 627; w73 507; ka 278
9:42 w73 507; w72 223
9:43 ts 112; bi8 1355
9:44 ts 112
9:45 ts 112; bi8 1355
9:46 ts 112
9:47 sl 275; ts 112; bi8 1355
9:48 sl 275; ts 112, 114
9:49 w71 670
9:50 w71 670
10:13 w74 368
10:14 w74 368
10:15 w74 368;

yb73 6/22;
w72 112
10:16 w74 368;
g72 11/8 10
10:17 w75 476
10:18 w75 476,
542; w71 325
10:27 w73 81
10:29 w73 403;
yb72 9/26
10:30 w74 214;
w73 403;
yb72 9/26
10:39 w72 517
10:42 w72 154
10:43 w72 154
10:44 w71 200;
te 106
10:45 fu 19;
w73 465
11:9 w75 620;
og 21
11:10 w75 620;
og 21
11:13 w72 95
11:14 w72 95
11:17 pm 406
11:19 bi8 1362
11:20 w72 96
11:21 w72 96
11:22 w72 96
11:24 w72 96
12:17 w74 63;
w72 267;
g72 12/8 19;
w71 765
12:29 g72 2/8 4;
g72 11/22 8;
g72 12/22 4
12:30 w72 596;
or 132; g72 2/8 4;
g72 11/22 8;
g72 12/22 4;
w71 146
12:31 w74 676;
g72 12/22 4
13:1 pm 318
13:2 kj 210
13:3 w74 399;
kj 210
13:4 w74 399
13:8 w74 72;
g74 5/8 18;
ka 297; w72 339
13:9 ka 298;
w71 541
13:10 sl 343;
yb74 10/10;
ka 298; kj 91
13:11 w73 406;
ka 298; kj 91
13:12 ka 298;
kj 91
13:13 yb76 2/25;
ka 298; kj 91
13:14 yb76 3/13;
ka 300, 302;
g72 12/22 28;
kj 351
13:15 ka 300;
g72 12/22 28;
kj 351
13:16 ka 300;
g72 12/22 28;
kj 351
13:17 ka 300;
g72 12/22 28;
kj 351
13:18 ka 300;
g72 12/22 28;
kj 351
13:19 sl 355;
w74 683; po 181;
ka 300, 305;
w72 629; dn 25;
g72 12/22 28;
kj 161, 351
13:20 sl 355;
w74 683; po 181;
ka 300, 318;
w72 629; dn 25;
g72 12/22 28;
kj 351
13:22 ka 322
13:32 w75 356;
w74 163;
g73 3/8 28
13:33 g71 11/22 4
13:35 bi8 1362
14:10 pm 321
14:11 pm 321
14:17 w73 175
14:21 w73 325
14:22 w73 198
14:23 w73 198
14:24 w73 198
14:25 w73 198
14:26 w73 198
14:27 pm 356
14:28 pm 356
14:49 pm 357
14:50 pm 357
15:23 yb74 5/8;
w73 183, 337;
w71 249
15:33 pm 341
15:41 w75 717;
w71 457
16:1 w73 766
16:2 w73 766
16:5 w73 766
16:6 w73 766
16:9 g73 8/8 6-7
16:10 g73 8/8 6-7
16:11 g73 8/8 6-7
16:12 g73 8/8 6-7
16:13 g73 8/8 6-7
16:14 g73 8/8 6-7
16:15 g73 8/8 6-7
16:16 g73 8/8 6-7
16:17 g73 8/8 5-7
16:18 g73 8/8 5-7
16:19 g73 8/8 6-7
16:20 g73 8/8 6-7

LUKE

1:3 yb76 1/20;
po 135;
g72 2/8 28;
sg 44
1:6 w74 535
1:15
g73 12/22 28
1:17 ts 57; sg 43
1:19 g73 5/22 14
1:25 w75 295
1:28 w75 295;
g71 8/8 9
1:29 g72 2/8 27
1:31 w74 69;
w73 711; w72 621;
dn 11; w71 302
1:32 sl 315;
po 135; w73 711;
w71 4, 242, 302
1:33 sl 315;
po 135; w73 711;
g72 10/22 14;
w71 4, 242, 302
1:34 w75 295;
po 136
1:35 w75 431;
po 136; ts 128;
w71 272
1:36 po 136
1:37 po 136;
g71 12/22 6
1:38 w75 220;
po 136
1:41
g73 12/22 28;
w72 114
1:44 w72 114
2:1 po 139
2:4 po 139
2:6 po 139
2:7 w72 743
2:8 w72 370
2:9 w72 370
2:10 w72 370,
685; kj 311
2:11 po 140;
w72 370, 685;
w71 241-2;
kj 311
2:12 w72 370;
kj 311
2:13 w72 370;
kj 311
2:14 sl 333;
po 140; w71 237;
kj 311
2:15 g72 9/22 7
2:17 w72 112
2:21 po 142;
ka 62
2:22 ka 62
2:23 ka 62
2:24 w75 221;
ka 62
2:25 g73 9/8 28
2:30 w71 58
2:36 kj 345
2:37 kj 345
2:38 g73 9/8 28;
kj 345
2:47 w73 532
2:51 sg 75
3:1
g75 12/22 27;
w73 767;
g73 9/8 28
3:3 w73 274;
w72 686
3:4 w73 274
3:8 w74 469
3:13 g74 2/22 28
3:14 w72 766
3:15 g73 9/8 28
3:21 ka 95;
g73 9/8 28;
w72 241
3:22 ka 95;
g73 9/8 28;
w72 241
3:23 w75 220;
w74 105; ka 62,
95; g73 9/8 28;
w72 241
3:27 kj 230
3:31 w74 105;
w72 241
3:33 w72 241
3:38 ka 71
4:3 w71 39
4:5 w75 236;
kj 353
4:6 w75 236;
w72 624; dn 17;
w71 39; kj 353;
te 53
4:7 w75 236;
w72 624; dn 17;
w71 39; kj 353;
te 53
4:8 w75 236;
g74 12/8 21
4:9 w71 39
4:10 w71 39
4:11 w71 39
4:12 w71 39
4:14 sl 177
4:16 g73 9/8 28;
te 157
4:17 g73 9/8 28
4:18 w74 361;
po 145
4:19 w72 371
4:21 g73 9/8 28
4:24 sl 52
4:29 g72 11/8 11
4:34 bi8 1360
4:38 g75 12/8 25
4:43 g73 4/22 18
5:4 yb72 7/30
5:10 kj 394
5:12 w75 90
5:13 w75 90
5:20 g74 11/8 28
5:30 w74 140
6:12 yb73 1/29
6:13 po 158
6:18 sl 67
6:19 sl 67
6:20 g71 6/8 28
6:21
g71 6/22 27-8;
g71 7/22 27
6:27 w73 501
6:28 w73 501
6:31 w74 676;
w73 324; w72 69
6:32 w74 120
6:35 yb75 1/17;
w73 473
6:36 w74 147,
499; w72 551;
w71 411
6:38 w74 46;
g74 6/8 4;
g74 12/22 4, 6;
w73 292; tp 177;
w71 346; te 146
7:34 w74 140
8:1 g73 4/22 18
8:2 yb76 6/15
8:3 yb76 6/15;
w75 717; w71 457
8:11 w73 684
8:15 g72 3/22 27
8:28 bi8 1360
8:31 w74 383
8:37 w73 287
8:46 sl 67
8:49 w72 448
8:54 w72 448
8:55 w72 448
9:20 sl 175
9:23 w73 337;
w72 518
9:24 w73 337
9:25 g74 9/22 11
9:29 w74 297
9:30 w74 297
9:31 w74 297
9:32 w74 297
9:33 w74 297
9:34 w74 297
9:35 w74 297-8
9:36 w74 297
9:42 w73 700
9:48 w75 724
9:62 w74 203
10:6 w73 271
10:7 w75 360;
w73 271
10:15 w74 78;
bi8 1361
10:19 w74 762
10:20 yb74 3/21
10:21 w71 606
10:22 w74 527;
g71 8/22 28
10:23 w75 305
10:24 w75 305
10:27 or 131;
te 38
10:29 te 38
10:33 w75 103;
w71 413
10:36 te 38
10:37 w71 413;
g71 8/8 27
10:40 w75 717
10:42 yb76 4/21;
w75 436; w73 271
11:1
g72 11/22 27
11:2 yb76 5/27;
g72 11/22 27
11:3 g74 6/8 7;
g72 11/22 27
11:4
g72 11/22 27
11:9 w74 361
11:10 w74 361
11:13 w74 115;
w73 405; w72 329;
g72 11/22 27;
kj 381
11:25 g75 2/22 28
11:27 w74 260;
g72 5/22 15
11:28 w74 260;
g72 5/22 15
11:31 fu 23; ts 184
11:32 ts 184
11:41 w71 413
11:50 w75 581;
g74 7/8 28;
w71 704
11:51 g74 7/8 28;
w71 704
12:1 sl 210
12:4 yb76 11/1;
g73 3/8 26
12:5 yb76 11/1;
ts 112; bi8 1355
12:14 w73 190
12:15 g75 5/22 4;
g74 9/8 4;
w73 158; w72 260
12:20 yb76 4/12
12:21 te 92, 94
12:31 w74 191
12:32 w74 287;
w73 199, 537;
ka 271; g73 5/8 6;
g72 11/8 7;
kj 177
12:36 bi8 1364
12:37 w75 716-17
12:42 w73 372;
yb73 3/16;
w72 731, 755;
or 9; w71 750
12:43 w72 755;
or 9; w71 750

12:44 or 9; w71 750
12:45 w75 110; ka 358
12:46 w75 110; ka 358, 361
12:48 w72 202
13:1 w75 8; w71 340
13:3 w75 751
13:12 g74 2/22 5
13:16 g74 2/22 5
13:17 w75 590
13:18 w75 590
13:19 w75 590
13:20 w75 590; sl 209
13:21 w75 590; sl 209
13:23 w73 464
13:24 w73 464; yb73 1/24
14:8 w71 199; te 104
14:16 w72 215
14:17 w72 215
14:18 yb73 4/27; w72 215
14:19 w72 215
14:23 w74 695
14:24 w74 695
14:26 w75 351, 381
14:28 yb76 9/6; yb74 12/28
14:33 w74 605; yb74 10/19; w73 278
14:34 g75 8/8 19
15:10 w72 201, 431
15:11 w72 432
15:12 w72 432
15:13 w74 81; w72 432
15:14 w72 432
15:15 w72 432
15:16 w72 432
15:17 w72 432
15:18 w74 81; w72 432
15:19 w72 432
15:20 yb75 3/13; w74 462; w72 432
15:21 w72 432
15:22 w72 432
15:23 w72 432
15:24 w72 432
15:25 w72 432, 568
15:26 w72 432
15:27 w72 432
15:28 w72 432
15:29 w72 432
15:30 w72 432
15:31 w72 432
15:32 w72 432
16:9 yb76 1/29, 11/23; w73 63-4
16:10 w75 201; yb75 6/1; w74 205, 530; w73 332; g72 4/8 28
16:11 w74 205
16:12 w74 205
16:13 w74 205
16:14 ts 102
16:16 w73 200
16:17 w71 480
16:18 ts 104
16:19 ts 99; g73 6/8 7
16:20 ts 99
16:21 ts 99
16:22 ts 99; w73 236; bi8 1361
16:23 ts 99; w73 236; g73 7/22 28; bi8 1361
16:24 ts 99; w73 236
16:25 ts 99
16:26 ts 99
16:27 ts 99
16:28 ts 99
16:29 ts 99
16:30 ts 99
16:31 ts 99
17:2 w74 78
17:4 w75 751
17:7 w74 372
17:8 w75 716; w74 372; w71 456
17:9 w74 372
17:10 yb75 8/19; w74 372, 532; w73 277
17:12 w73 366
17:14 w73 366
17:15 w73 366
17:21 w74 50
17:24 w74 750; ka 321
17:26 w75 748; ka 333; w72 652
17:27 w75 748; ka 334; w72 652
17:32 w73 58
17:33 w74 373
17:37 w75 11; w74 750; ka 322, 336
18:1 w72 329
18:7 tp 43
18:8 tp 43; yb73 3/3; w72 522
18:11 g72 11/22 28
18:12 g72 11/22 28; w71 536
18:13 g72 11/22 28
18:24 g71 11/22 27-8
19:1 w74 139
19:2 w74 139
19:9 w73 271
19:10 w73 271
19:11 w73 710
19:12 w74 61; w73 633, 710; ka 215, 229
19:13 w74 61, 542; yb74 6/20, 6/27; w73 713
19:14 yb74 9/18; w73 716
19:15 w73 717; ka 229
19:16 yb74 7/6; w73 717
19:17 yb74 7/18; w73 719
19:18 w73 719
19:19 w73 719
19:20 w73 720
19:21 w73 720
19:22 yb74 7/25, 7/31; w73 720
19:23 w73 720
19:24 w73 720
19:25 w73 720
19:26 w73 720
19:27 w74 541; w73 709, 720
19:40 w73 654
19:41 w74 425; kj 273
19:42 w74 425; kj 273
19:43 w74 425, 428, 681; kj 273
19:44 w75 139; w74 425, 428, 681; kj 273
20:20 te 136
20:22 g74 2/22 27
20:23 g74 2/22 27
20:24 g74 2/22 27
20:25 g74 2/22 27; te 136
20:33 g72 5/22 27
20:34 ts 178
20:35 ts 178
20:37 ts 174; w73 241, 249, 499
20:38 ts 174; w73 241, 249, 499
21:2 w75 19
21:3 yb76 8/9; w75 19; w74 574
21:4 yb76 8/9; w75 19
21:5 pm 318
21:6 w75 139; kj 210
21:9 w71 406
21:10 w75 684; w74 4; w71 69, 406
21:11 w74 4, 40, 72, 131, 195, 243, 318; g74 5/8 18; w72 339; g72 10/8 16; w71 69, 406; g71 3/8 4
21:12 yb76 9/19; w75 22; yb74 7/2; g72 7/8 20; w71 486, 491
21:13 yb76 9/19; w75 22
21:17 yb76 89; w71 486, 491
21:19 w73 40, 81; or 186
21:20 w75 138, 340; w74 426; ka 167, 300, 302; tp 92; w72 372; g72 10/8 20; g72 12/22 28; kj 232, 273, 352, 359; te 33; g71 12/8 5
21:21 w75 138, 340; w74 426; tp 92; w72 372; g72 10/8 20; g72 12/22 28; kj 232, 273, 352; te 33; g71 12/8 5
21:22 ka 300; w72 372; g72 10/8 20; g72 12/22 28; kj 232, 273, 352; g71 12/8 5
21:23 g74 11/8 11; ka 300, 303; g72 12/22 28; kj 232, 273, 352; g71 12/8 5
21:24 w75 621; sl 22, 41, 175, 243; og 25; w74 163; po 174; ts 159; w73 645; ka 12, 186, 260, 300, 303-4; g73 10/8 17; w72 351, 655, 748; w71 619, 621; kj 57, 176, 232, 273, 346, 352; nc 18, 21; g71 12/8 5
21:25 sl 283; w74 492, 656; g74 1/22 8; w73 618; dy 17
21:26 w75 635; sl 283; w74 656; g74 1/22 8; w73 618; dy 17; w72 339; w71 69
21:27 w74 163; tp 79
21:28 yb76 10/6, 12/5; sl 25; yb73 8/3; w71 406
21:29 tp 81
21:30 tp 81
21:31 yb76 5/2; w75 633, 635; tp 79, 81; w72 340; g72 10/8 15; w71 69
21:32 g75 10/8 13; tp 81; w72 3, 372; g72 10/8 15; w71 69; g71 10/8 26
21:33 w71 480
21:34 yb76 1/15; w75 281; yb75 12/5; w74 56, 59, 456; yb74 2/17; w73 57, 287; g73 6/22 13; w72 675; g72 10/8 21; g71 11/22 4
21:35 yb76 1/15; yb75 12/5; w74 56, 59, 456; yb74 2/17; w73 57; g73 6/22 13; w72 675; g72 10/8 21
21:36 w74 56, 59, 164; w73 57; w72 675; g72 10/8 21; g71 11/22 4
22:3 w75 654; pm 321; g72 6/8 27
22:4 pm 321
22:5 pm 321
22:6 pm 321
22:19 w73 198; g73 9/8 5; km 3/73 3; g72 3/22 28
22:20 w74 221; po 160; w73 198; w72 443, 678, 680, 686; g72 3/22 28; w71 745
22:24 w75 348, 727
22:25 w75 668, 727
22:26 yb76 8/20; w75 727; w72 703; w71 456
22:27 w75 727; w73 333; w71 456
22:28 w74 690
22:29 w74 690; w73 427; kj 405
22:30 w74 690; po 161; w73 427; kj 405
22:31 w75 654; yb74 253; w71 488
22:36 sl 87
22:37 sl 87; po 153; w72 174
22:38 tp 134
22:44 w71 274
22:45 g74 12/8 28
22:53 w75 653
22:66 w71 691
23:12 w75 8; w71 340
23:14 g73 9/8 16
23:17 w75 414
23:32 g72 11/8 27
23:34 w74 505
23:39 g74 4/8 14; bi8 1360
23:42 w75 623; og 28; g74 4/8 14; pm 12; w71 708; kj 392
23:43 w75 623; sl 90; og 28; w74 6, 362, 661; po 153; g74 4/8 14; ka 35; g73 6/8 6; pm 12, 395; yb72 9/25; w71 255-6, 617; kj 392; te 180; nc 13
23:44 pm 341
23:46 ts 52
23:56 w73 766

g, Awake!; **ka**, God's Kingdom of a Thousand Years; **kj**, "The Nations Shall Know that I Am Jehovah"; **km**, Kingdom Ministry; **or**, Organization; **pm**, Paradise Restored—By Theocracy!; **po**, God's "Eternal Purpose"; **sg**, Theocratic School Guidebook; **sl**, Man's Salvation out of World Distress!; **te**, Listening to the Great Teacher; **tp**, True Peace and Security; **ts**, Is This Life All There Is?; **w**, Watchtower; **yb**, Yearbook. **Complete list on page 6.**

24:15 ts 170
24:16 ts 170; w73 248
24:25 po 151
24:26 po 151
24:27 po 151
24:44 po 151
24:45 po 151
24:46 po 151
24:50 g72 9/22 6
24:51 g72 9/22 6

JOHN

1:1 w75 63, 173-6, 702-4; w74 307; w73 262, 524; ka 20; w72 486; g72 3/22 6-7; g72 5/22 27-8; bi8 1362-3
1:2 w74 307; w73 262, 524; w72 486; bi8 1363
1:3 w75 306; w74 307; w73 524; w72 486
1:4 w75 757
1:5 w75 757
1:8 ts 107
1:9 w73 442
1:10 sl 52
1:11 sl 52
1:12 w73 465
1:13 w73 465, 488
1:14 yb75 3/31; w74 298, 307; w73 263; g73 3/8 28; w72 106
1:16 w73 466
1:17 w73 466; g72 11/22 7
1:18 w74 209, 307, 527; w73 163, 259; w72 106; bi8 1363
1:21 ts 57
1:29 po 144; kj 283, 390
1:31 w72 715
1:32 ka 65; w72 715
1:33 ka 65; w72 715
1:34 po 144; ka 65; w72 715
1:36 kj 283, 390
1:41 w74 88; or 111
1:46 sl 50
2:3 w74 362; w71 439
2:4 w74 362; w71 439; bi8 1360
2:5 w75 717; w71 439
2:9 w75 717
2:14 w73 7
2:15 w73 7
2:16 w73 7; yb72 2/1
2:17 yb76 7/18; w73 7
2:19 w73 350
2:25 g74 4/8 12
3:13 g73 5/8 7; g72 8/8 28
3:16 yb76 4/14; fu 19; g75 1/22 22; w74 254; w73 133, 252, 465; tp 121, 167; g72 2/8 4; g72 10/22 14
3:17 w73 442, 651
3:19 w74 522; w73 7
3:20 w75 653; w74 522; w73 7
3:21 w73 7
3:25 w73 274
3:26 w73 274
3:30 w73 8, 274
3:36 w73 465; tp 123; w71 478; te 190
4:1 g74 3/22 27; w73 274
4:14 w73 380
4:19 bi8 1363
4:21 g73 8/8 27
4:22 w75 104; g73 8/8 27; w71 31
4:23 fu 8; w74 396; g73 8/8 27; w72 101, 751; g72 11/8 6; g72 12/22 7
4:24 yb76 9/11; fu 8, 10; w74 247; g73 1/8 27; g73 8/8 27; w72 101, 445, 751; bi8 1363
4:34 w73 327; w72 303
4:35 yb76 257; w74 541
4:36 yb76 257; w74 541
4:37 w74 541; w73 714
4:38 w74 541; w73 714
4:41 yb74 2/24
4:43 sl 52
4:44 sl 52
5:17 yb73 2/24; w72 486
5:18 w74 526
5:20 g72 2/8 4
5:24 w74 95
5:26 w73 240
5:27 w73 240
5:28 sl 363; g74 6/8 28; w73 240; tp 106; kj 390; g71 12/8 28
5:29 ts 183; yb74 11/6; w73 240; tp 106; kj 390; g71 12/8 28
5:30 yb76 8/17; w74 279
5:39 w74 180
5:42 w74 180
5:44 w71 323
5:46 po 148; g73 3/22 16
6:12 km 11/74 3
6:14 kj 233
6:15 g73 9/8 16; kj 233
6:27 yb73 8/30; g73 7/22 26
6:28 w72 694
6:29 w72 694; or 16
6:41 g73 3/8 27
6:42 g73 3/8 27
6:44 w75 309
6:48 po 149
6:49 po 149
6:50 po 149
6:51 w74 377; po 149; w73 199; g73 7/22 4; g72 9/22 7
6:57 w74 527
6:58 w74 377
6:63 w74 211
6:66 w73 404
6:67 w73 404
6:68 yb76 7/31; w73 404
6:69 yb76 7/31; w73 404
6:70 bi8 1363
7:1 w73 650
7:2 w73 650
7:3 w73 650; g71 12/22 27
7:4 w73 650; g71 12/22 27
7:5 w73 650
7:6 w73 650
7:7 yb74 7/24; w73 650
7:16 sg 50
7:24 w73 473
7:39 ka 102
7:41 sl 50
7:47 w75 707
7:48 w75 707
7:52 sl 50; w73 536; w71 323
8:28 w73 389
8:29 yb76 2/16; w73 389; yb73 6/23
8:31 w74 247
8:32 w74 247; w73 142, 701; yb73 3/12; g72 12/22 5
8:41 g71 12/22 7
8:42 g73 5/22 28
8:43 g73 5/22 28
8:44 w74 58, 146, 326; ts 81; g74 10/22 7; g73 5/22 28; g73 12/8 27-8; w72 232, 427; te 74
8:46 w73 650; w72 621; dn 11
8:48 w75 104; g71 12/22 7
8:51 yb75 2/28; w74 376
8:58 w74 527
9:1 g73 6/22 28
9:2 g75 4/8 28; ts 59; g73 6/22 28
9:3 g75 4/8 28; ts 59; g73 6/22 28
9:6 g73 6/22 28
9:7 g73 6/22 28
9:24 bi8 1363
9:25 bi8 1363
9:33 g73 3/8 28
10:3 w75 432, 693
10:4 w75 432; or 57
10:7 g72 3/22 27
10:9 kj 297
10:10 yb74 3/14; w73 329, 380; ka 134; kj 297
10:11 kj 297
10:14 w73 39; or 55; kj 177, 305
10:15 kj 177, 305
10:16 w74 287, 626; w73 169, 200, 732; ka 271; w72 174, 637; pm 79, 174; kj 174, 177, 307, 311, 319, 347
10:25 w73 700
10:27 w75 693; w73 39
10:29 w74 525
10:31 w74 525
10:32 w74 525-6
10:33 w74 525-6; w71 273; bi8 1363
10:34 w74 526; bi8 1356
10:35 w74 526; bi8 1356
10:36 w74 526
10:37 w74 526
10:38 w74 526
11:24 w73 243
11:25 w73 241
11:26 w74 377
11:39 tp 108
11:47 po 150
12:2 w75 717; w71 456
12:6 w71 507; bi8 1363
12:8 w75 70
12:20 w72 747
12:21 w72 747
12:23 w72 176
12:24 w72 176-7
12:25 w73 231; tp 165; yb73 8/20; w72 176-7
12:26 w72 176-7
12:27 w72 176
12:28 w72 176
12:31 w74 222; w73 491; tp 125; g73 7/22 5; w72 630, 653; w71 272; kj 353
12:37 po 150; w72 174
12:38 w72 174
12:49 w74 307
12:50 w74 307
13:5 te 29
13:14 w74 310; te 29
13:15 w74 310; w73 28
13:17 w72 668
13:19 g71 12/8 5
13:27 w75 654
13:31 kj 55
13:34 yb76 8/4, 10/17; w75 521; w74 603; tp 168; or 183; g72 2/8 4; g72 4/22 21; w71 191
13:35 yb76 238; w75 521; fu 27; g74 1/22 19; yb73 4/16; or 183; yb72 6/9; g72 2/8 4; w71 463
14:2 w73 63
14:6 ml 17; g75 1/22 28; yb74 1/14; g74 1/8 10; w73 176, 263, 388; w72 106; g72 11/22 28; g71 1/22 7
14:8 w73 388
14:9 yb76 1/10; w75 117; yb75 6/9; w74 149, 527; w73 259, 263, 388; g71 8/22 28
14:10 w74 307
14:12 w74 300
14:14 g75 1/22 28; g72 11/22 28
14:16 w74 380, 423; w72 730; g71 3/22 27
14:17 w74 423; w72 730; g71 3/22 27-8
14:19 g73 7/22 5
14:26 w75 145; w74 116, 414; w73 526; w72 730
14:28 w73 132; g73 3/8 28; w72 734; g72 5/22 28
14:30 w74 70; g74 10/22 8; tp 125; yb73 3/28; g73 11/8 6; g73 12/8 28; w72 653; w71 272; kj 353
15:2 or 109
15:5 g72 3/22 27
15:8 yb73 1/12; or 109
15:12 w72 581
15:13 w74 603; yb74 1/27; w73 458; w72 581, 740; g72 2/8 4
15:14 w74 310; w73 460
15:15 yb75 1/28; w74 310, 372
15:16 w75 733
15:18 w73 649
15:19 g75 12/8 3; w73 649, 658; tp 128; w72 198, 593; g72 12/8 20; kj 62
15:20 w74 522; w73 501; tp 128; g73 3/8 25; w72 142; yb72 1/5; w71 485
15:25 w73 652

15:26 w72 730
16:2 w75 654; w74 179
16:7 w74 423
16:8 w74 423
16:11 w72 653; kj 353
16:12 ts 179; w72 501
16:13 w74 423; w72 730; yb72 2/13; w71 461
16:23 g74 1/8 9-10; g72 11/8 6
16:27 g72 2/8 4
16:33 w75 83; w74 220; yb74 9/19; w73 491, 630, 649, 655, 659; g73 3/8 26
17:3 yb76 4/23; w75 117; ml 18; g75 1/8 28; w74 178; w73 329; w72 105; g72 11/8 6; w71 265, 477; te 188
17:6 w74 525; g74 1/22 19; w73 259, 543
17:7 w74 525
17:8 w74 525
17:9 w74 525
17:10 w74 525
17:11 w74 525; w73 259; tp 120
17:14 w75 426; g75 12/22 16; w74 215; w73 278; ka 282; tp 120, 128; w72 589; g72 10/8 18
17:15 tp 120
17:16 ml 26; w73 28, 200, 265; ka 282; w72 593, 639; yb72 10/4
17:17 w73 388; yb72 4/19; w71 560
17:19 w71 560
17:20 w73 272; kj 346
17:21 w73 272; kj 346
17:22 kj 346
17:25 g73 5/22 14
17:26 yb74 1/20; w73 259, 543
18:8 pm 357
18:9 pm 357
18:31 w73 652
18:36 w74 70; g74 11/22 6; ka 67; tp 126; w72 197, 589; g72 10/8 18; w71 532; kj 61, 153
18:37 g72 12/22 7
18:38 w75 7-8
19:1 w71 110
19:2 w75 8
19:3 w75 8
19:4 w75 7
19:6 w75 7
19:7 w71 273
19:11 w72 267
19:12 g73 9/8 16; w72 655
19:13 w72 655
19:14 w72 655
19:15 w75 620; og 22; w72 655
19:16 w75 620; og 22
19:17 g74 9/22 27
19:19 g74 9/22 27
19:25 w75 222; g74 9/22 27
19:26 g74 9/22 27
19:29 w71 249
19:30 w72 687; w71 249
19:31 w73 768
19:34 pm 340
19:37 pm 340
20:1 w73 766
20:14 ts 170; w73 248
20:17 ka 276; g73 2/22 28; g72 3/22 6
20:19 g73 7/22 4; g72 11/22 6
20:23 g74 11/8 28
20:26 w75 479; w73 248, 333; g72 11/22 6
20:27 w73 333; g73 7/22 4
20:28 w74 730; g72 3/22 6
20:31 yb76 7/16; w74 730; w73 102; g73 3/8 28
21:15 or 55
21:16 or 55
21:17 or 55
21:18 w71 768
21:19 w71 768
21:25 w73 326

ACTS

1:3 g72 9/22 5
1:4 ka 105; w72 730
1:5 ka 105; w72 730
1:6 w74 50; w71 4, 240-1; kj 233
1:7 kj 92, 233
1:8 w74 363; w72 691, 730; or 4, 7; w71 31, 159-60; g71 12/22 28
1:9 g72 9/22 5
1:10 g72 9/22 5
1:11 g73 7/22 4; g72 9/22 5
1:12 g72 9/22 5
1:18 pm 323
1:19 pm 323
1:20 w71 690
1:23 w71 319
1:26 w71 319
2:1 w75 106; w73 531
2:2 w75 106; w73 531
2:3 w73 531
2:4 g74 12/22 27; w73 526, 531; g73 8/8 5; yb72 7/25
2:6 w73 526
2:7 w73 526-7
2:8 w73 526-7
2:9 g73 8/8 5
2:10 g73 8/8 5; w72 671
2:11 g74 12/22 27-8; w73 526-7; g73 8/8 5; or 9
2:14 ka 106
2:15 ka 106
2:16 po 159; ka 106
2:17 w74 363; ka 106; yb72 4/8; w71 32, 331, 685
2:18 ka 106; w71 331
2:19 ka 106
2:20 ka 106
2:21 w74 729; ka 106; w72 695; yb72 4/8; w71 331; kj 333
2:22 po 150
2:23 w74 598
2:25 w73 527; w72 526; g72 11/8 6
2:26 g72 11/8 6
2:27 w73 238; g73 7/22 28; g72 11/8 6; w71 256; bi8 1361
2:28 w73 238
2:29 w73 238
2:30 w73 238
2:31 w73 238; g73 7/22 28; bi8 1361
2:32 po 159; w73 238
2:33 po 159
2:34 w74 236; w72 689, 696; pm 153
2:35 w74 236; w72 689
2:36 w74 236; ka 106; w72 655, 689, 696; kj 345
2:37 w72 689
2:38 w75 751; yb74 8/3; w73 275; tp 186; yb73 6/16; w72 689
2:39 w72 689
2:40 w72 689
2:41 w73 527, 531; w72 690
3:6 w73 103; w71 235
3:13 w72 690
3:14 w72 690
3:15 w73 263; w72 690
3:17 w71 235
3:18 or 15; w71 235, 238
3:19 w74 602; w73 636; w72 118, 690; or 15; yb72 5/27, 7/6; w71 236-7, 243
3:20 w72 690; w71 238
3:21 yb72 2/25, 8/27; w71 234, 239, 244, 287
3:22 w72 685; pm 316; w71 242
3:23 w72 685; pm 316; w71 242
3:24 w71 243
3:25 w74 690; po 162, 181; w71 243
3:26 w74 690; po 162; w72 690; yb72 9/28; w71 243
4:1 w72 690
4:2 w72 690
4:5 w71 685
4:7 w73 103
4:8 w71 685
4:12 w73 102; w72 700
4:13 yb76 11/6; w73 548
4:19 tp 137; w72 644
4:20 w73 473, 529; tp 137; w72 644
4:23 w75 615; og 12; yb72 5/13; w71 685
4:24 yb76 4/2; w75 615; og 12; or 8
4:25 w75 615; og 12
4:26 w75 615; og 12
4:27 w75 615; og 12
4:28 w75 615; og 12
4:29 yb76 4/2; w75 615; og 12; w73 529
5:3 g72 6/8 27
5:6 w75 728
5:8 te 73
5:10 w75 728
5:11 w71 746
5:29 w73 142, 473, 741; tp 137; w72 589, 644, 680, 736; or 8; g72 12/8 20; kj 326
5:30 g74 9/22 28; w72 680; bi8 1360-1
5:31 w72 680
5:32 w72 680, 730; w71 462
5:37 w74 139
5:38 w71 683
5:39 w71 683
5:41 yb72 5/6; w71 116
5:42 or 56; w71 751
6:1 w75 719; w72 704; w71 458
6:2 w75 719; w72 704; w71 320, 458
6:3 w75 719; w73 469; w72 704; w71 458
6:4 w75 719; w72 704; w71 458
6:5 w72 704
6:6 w72 704; w71 320
6:7 g75 3/22 19; w72 679
7:7 w75 736
7:8 w71 443
7:10 w72 703
7:16 w75 735-6
7:19 w72 114
7:20 w72 114
7:25 po 107
7:35 po 108
7:37 w72 685
7:38 w72 685
7:51 yb72 10/19; w71 443
7:54 w71 443
7:59 g72 8/22 28
7:60 w74 505; g72 8/22 28
8:1 w72 457, 691
8:2 w72 691
8:3 w72 691
8:4 w72 691
8:5 w72 691
8:6 w72 691
8:7 w72 691
8:8 w72 691
8:9 w72 691
8:10 w72 691
8:11 w72 691
8:12 w72 691
8:13 w72 691
8:14 w72 704; or 64
8:18 g74 12/22 27
8:20 kj 134
8:29 w74 421
8:33 sl 71-3
8:35 sl 37; w72 691
8:36 w72 691
8:37 w72 691
8:38 w72 691, 747
8:39 w72 691
8:40 yb75 5/8
9:2 w75 698
9:3 g73 7/22 4
9:7 w72 159-60
9:15 w75 733
9:20 w73 285
9:22 w73 285
9:30 g72 1/8 27
9:31 yb72 7/19; w71 10
9:36 g72 1/8 27; w71 414; g71 8/8 27
9:38 g72 1/8 27

9:39 w71 414
9:42 g72 1/8 27
9:43 g72 1/8 27
10:2 g71 8/8 27
10:6 g72 1/8 27
10:9 g72 1/8 27
10:14 kj 108
10:23 g72 1/8 27
10:24 or 111
10:27 w74 463
10:28 w74 463
10:30 w71 537
10:34 w73 518, 537, 735
10:35 w74 494; w73 518, 537, 735
10:37 w72 692
10:38 yb76 5/12; w72 692
10:39 g74 9/22 28; w72 692; bi8 1360
10:40 w73 351; w72 692
10:41 w72 692
10:42 w72 692
10:43 w72 692
10:44 po 166; w73 480; w72 692
10:45 po 166; w72 692
10:46 w72 692
10:47 w73 480; w72 692
10:48 w73 276; w72 692
11:2 w74 463
11:3 w74 463
11:8 kj 108
11:18 w74 378; w72 691; or 15
11:29 w75 717; tp 32
11:30 w71 686
12:2 w71 320
12:10 g72 9/22 7
12:25 w75 717
13:2 w75 716
13:5 w71 457
13:6 w74 325
13:7 w74 325
13:8 w74 325
13:9 w74 325
13:10 w74 325
13:14 g72 11/22 6
13:15 g72 11/22 6
13:16 g72 11/22 6
13:20 w74 507; po 121; ka 207-10
13:21 po 123
13:29 g74 9/22 28; bi8 1360
13:34 g73 7/22 4
13:42 g72 11/22 6
13:43 g72 11/22 6
13:44 g72 11/22 6
13:47 w75 733; w73 531
14:16 tp 64
14:17 yb76 4/3; w74 190, 371; tp 64; g72 10/22 7
14:23 yb76 11/24; yb75 164; w72 19; or 59; yb72 26, 8/5; w71 689
15:1 w72 704
15:2 w72 704; w71 686
15:3 or 16
15:4 w71 686
15:6 w71 686
15:13 yb72 11/8
15:14 or 12; g72 1/8 27; w71 655
15:17 w71 655
15:20 w74 352; g74 5/22 20; w72 531; yb72 9/6; g72 7/8 27; w71 118-19
15:21 g73 3/22 16
15:22 w72 703-4; w71 687, 759
15:23 w72 704; yb72 5/17; w71 687
15:25 w72 704
15:26 w72 704
15:27 w72 704
15:28 tp 164; g73 5/8 27; or 64
15:29 w74 351; g74 5/22 20; tp 164; g73 5/8 27; w72 531, 544, 564; g72 7/8 27
15:30 w72 704
15:32 w72 704
15:37 w75 344
15:38 w75 344
15:39 w75 344
16:2 w72 14; yb72 17
16:4 w71 687
16:5 or 64
16:7 w74 421
16:11 g72 11/22 6
16:12 g72 11/22 6
16:13 g72 11/22 6
16:15 w71 346; te 145
16:16 g74 4/22 28
16:29 w72 692
16:30 w72 692
16:31 g75 11/8 27; w72 692, 695-6; g72 11/8 6
16:32 w72 692, 696
16:33 w72 692, 696
16:34 w72 692
17:1 g72 11/22 6
17:2 yb74 5/1; w73 209; g72 11/22 6
17:3 w73 209; g72 11/22 6
17:16 w73 429
17:17 yb75 8/29; w73 430
17:18 w73 430; g72 11/22 17
17:19 w73 430
17:20 w73 430
17:21 w73 430; g72 11/22 17
17:22 w73 430
17:23 w73 429-30
17:24 w74 491; w73 431; w72 751; g72 11/22 18; kj 274
17:25 w74 120; w73 431; w72 592; g72 11/22 18; w71 345
17:26 w75 617; og 16; w74 220; po 47; yb74 1/17; w73 431, 517, 735; g72 11/22 18
17:27 w75 617; og 16; g75 5/8 4; w74 220, 368; w73 176, 431, 433, 735; g72 11/22 18; w71 429
17:28 w74 190; w73 433
17:29 w73 433
17:30 w75 751; w73 433, 441, 636; g73 1/22 27; w72 119, 695; or 14
17:31 g75 10/8 26; w74 278; ts 168; w73 248, 262, 433, 583, 740; ka 31; w72 119, 695; or 14; g72 11/22 18
17:32 w73 433; w71 324
17:33 w72 696; g72 11/22 8, 18
17:34 g72 11/22 8, 18
18:4 g72 11/22 6
18:12 w74 80
18:22 g72 1/8 27
18:23 g72 6/22 5
18:25 w73 275
19:1 w73 275; w72 696; g72 6/22 5
19:2 w73 275; w72 696
19:3 w73 275; w72 696
19:4 yb74 6/29; w73 274-5; w72 696
19:5 w73 275; w72 696
19:6 w73 275; w72 696; w71 751
19:7 w73 275; w72 696
19:9 w73 114
19:19 yb76 6/18; g74 2/22 6
19:22 w75 728; w71 457
20:7 g72 11/22 6
20:10 ts 42
20:17 yb73 3/4; w72 703; or 61; w71 687, 690, 695
20:19 w75 724
20:20 w73 373; or 56
20:21 or 16
20:24 w75 733
20:26 km 2/73 3
20:28 w75 370, 470, 733; w74 121, 367, 599; w73 39, 277, 374; yb73 4/1, 12/5; w72 19, 604, 703; or 8, 17, 53, 62; yb72 27; w71 690, 695, 751; bi8 1363-4
20:29 w75 470, 729; yb73 9/10; g73 1/8 19; w71 80, 628
20:30 w75 167, 729; w71 80, 628
20:34 yb76 8/12; w75 360; tp 32
20:35 yb76 10/2; g75 2/22 3; g74 12/22 3; w73 158, 292, 318, 328; g73 11/22 26; w72 408; g72 12/22 3; w71 345; te 143
20:37 w75 724
21:8 w74 336; g72 1/8 27
21:13 w74 169
21:15 or 61
21:16 g72 1/8 27
21:17 w72 704
21:18 w72 704; or 61; w71 687
21:25 g74 5/22 20; w72 64
21:30 w75 367
22:5 w71 691
22:9 w72 159-60
22:22 w73 214
23:1 w72 562, 657
23:5 w72 268
23:16 w74 537
23:23 g72 1/8 27
23:33 g72 1/8 27
24:15 yb76 10/4; sl 28; w74 279, 608; ts 181; g74 6/8 28; w73 244, 638; g73 4/22 20; w72 688; kj 390
24:16 w72 599
25:1 g72 1/8 27
25:4 g72 1/8 27
25:6 g72 1/8 27
25:13 g72 1/8 27
26:7 w73 282
26:14 g71 1/8 28
26:20 yb75 9/3; w74 469; w72 439
26:27 sl 222
26:28 sl 222; w71 541
27:6 g71 4/8 27
27:9 g71 4/8 27
27:11 w72 703
27:12 g71 4/8 27
27:17 g71 4/8 27
27:18 g71 4/8 27
27:19 g71 4/8 27
28:3 g73 8/8 5
28:5 g73 8/8 5
28:6 bi8 1363
28:8 g75 12/8 25

ROMANS

1:12 w74 203; yb73 10/13
1:18 ts 188; tp 42
1:19 tp 42; pm 147
1:20 yb76 1/12; yb75 1/22, 6/17; w74 147, 376, 643; g74 3/22 26; w73 163, 554; tp 42; g73 7/22 3; w72 35, 388; pm 147
1:21 w74 563
1:22 w72 586
1:23 w72 586; kj 157
1:25 g72 12/22 7
1:26 w75 364; w74 483; tp 153; w72 596, 667, 734, 768
1:27 w75 364; w74 483; tp 149; w72 667, 768
1:28 w74 487; g74 5/8 5; w73 183
1:29 w74 247
1:31 w72 551; w71 309
1:32 w72 768; w71 309
2:4 yb76 10/29; sl 301; w74 495
2:6 yb73 5/18; w72 588
2:14 yb76 5/11; w75 210; w73 37, 140, 164; tp 64; g73 5/8 27; w72 588
2:15 yb76 2/19; w75 114, 210; w73 37, 164; yb73 9/1; g73 5/8 27; w72 588
2:20 w74 179
2:21 w73 260; w71 332
2:22 w73 260
2:23 w73 260
2:24 w73 260
2:28 w74 14, 127; pm 255; w71 430
2:29 w74 14, 127; w72 199; pm 255; w71 430, 442, 444; kj 68
3:9 w72 588
3:19 ka 129; w72 588; g72 11/22 6
3:20 g72 7/22 27
3:23 w74 280; w73 199; tp 182; w71 272; g71 10/8 20; g71 12/8 28
3:24 w73 199, 262; w71 272
3:25 w72 175; w71 272
3:26 w73 262; w72 175; w71 272
3:27 w72 757
4:9 po 163; w71 272
4:10 po 163
4:11 po 163
4:12 po 163
4:16 w73 252
4:17 w75 82; w73 252; kj 335
4:25 ka 110

5:1 w74 252; ka 110; yb73 11/14; g73 5/8 6
5:3 or 182
5:4 or 182
5:6 w73 580
5:7 w74 190; w73 473; w72 550
5:8 yb76 4/16; w75 347; yb75 3/27; w74 154, 190, 254, 371; tp 167; g72 2/8 4
5:9 w74 252; w73 465; yb73 11/14; g73 5/8 6
5:11 w73 309
5:12 ml 15; w74 190, 598; ts 35; g74 10/8 13; w73 412, 464; tp 52; g73 6/8 8; g73 6/22 28-9; g73 10/8 26; w72 621; dn 11; g72 6/8 7; kj 394; g71 12/8 27
5:13 w73 464
5:14 w73 464
5:15 w74 599; w73 465; w71 429
5:16 w74 599; w71 429
5:17 w74 599; w71 274, 429
5:18 w75 430; w71 274
5:19 sl 82
5:21 w74 370
6:3 w74 252; w72 518
6:4 w72 518, 718
6:5 w74 255; w73 200, 740; w72 518, 718
6:6 w73 337; w72 518
6:7 w75 55; g75 10/22 7; w74 607; w73 311; w72 518
6:11 ts 104
6:13 w72 683
6:14 yb73 4/14; w72 672; g72 11/22 6-7
6:16 yb75 1/13; w74 370; g73 5/22 27
6:17 w74 184
6:19 w74 603; w73 339
6:23 w74 607; ts 35; w73 133, 329; g73 6/8 6; g71 12/8 28
7:4 ts 105; g72 11/22 7
7:5 w72 287; g72 11/22 7
7:6 g72 11/22 7
7:7 w73 464; w72 287; g72 11/22 7
7:8 w72 287-8; g72 11/22 7
7:9 g72 11/22 7
7:10 g72 11/22 7
7:11 g72 11/22 7
7:12 g72 11/22 7
7:14 w74 369
7:20 g75 5/22 28
7:21 w73 511
7:22 w73 511; g73 10/8 26; w71 433
7:23 w74 369; w73 511; g73 10/8 26; w71 433
7:24 w73 511
7:25 w74 252
8:1 w74 252; w73 199; w72 608
8:2 w74 252; w72 608
8:4 w74 312
8:5 w74 209
8:9 w75 106; g75 5/22 28; w74 421
8:11 w74 312; w73 351
8:15 w75 106; w74 448
8:16 w75 106; w73 730; g73 5/8 6; w72 636
8:17 w73 730; w72 636
8:19 yb72 1/9; w71 431
8:20 w75 584; w74 319; w73 606, 638-9; g73 10/8 27; w71 431
8:21 g75 3/22 5; w74 319, 348, 448; g74 10/8 22; w73 606, 638-9; g73 10/8 27; w71 431
8:22 w71 431
8:23 w73 466; w71 431
8:26 w75 121
8:28 w74 106, 191; ka 74
8:29 w75 431-2; w74 106, 254; ka 74, 115
8:30 w74 106; ka 74; w71 329
8:31 w71 566
8:32 w75 702; w74 371; w73 252
8:33 w74 96; ka 146; w72 608; w71 566
8:34 w71 566
8:38 w74 203, 539
8:39 w74 203, 539
9:1 yb76 2/26; w73 286; w72 562
9:2 w74 523
9:3 w74 523
9:5 g72 3/22 7; bi8 1364
9:6 w74 127; w71 430
9:7 w74 127; w71 430
9:8 w74 127; w72 172; w71 430
9:10 po 94; g74 2/8 16
9:11 po 94; ts 58; g74 2/8 16; w73 727
9:12 po 94; ts 58; g74 2/8 16; w73 497, 727
9:13 po 94; ts 58
9:16 w75 107; kj 360
9:22 w74 155
9:23 w74 155
9:27 w74 695; w72 173
9:28 w72 173
9:29 w72 173
9:30 w74 17
9:31 w74 17; w72 443
9:32 w74 17; w72 443; w71 430
9:33 w74 17; w72 443
10:2 w74 179; w73 437; g73 5/22 27; g73 11/8 28; g72 7/22 28
10:3 w73 437; g73 5/22 27; g73 11/8 28; g72 7/22 28
10:4 w73 437; g72 11/22 7
10:5 w72 694
10:6 w72 694-5
10:7 w72 694-5
10:8 w74 17; w73 416; yb73 9/4; w72 601, 694-5
10:9 w74 17, 19; w73 416; yb73 9/23, 11/24; w72 601, 694-6
10:10 w74 17, 19; w73 416, 479; tp 184; yb73 8/25; w72 601, 635, 694, 696; yb72 4/25; kj 333
10:11 kj 333
10:12 g74 10/8 19; kj 333
10:13 sl 111; tp 184; w72 695; kj 333
10:14 kj 333
10:15 w71 79
10:16 sl 48
10:17 sl 48
11:5 w74 695; w72 173
11:13 w75 733; sl 200; w71 320
11:15 w74 128
11:17 yb75 9/20
11:25 w74 127; w72 173
11:26 w74 126; w73 730; w72 173
11:33 w73 463, 489
12:1 tp 163; w71 670
12:2 yb76 7/22; w75 297, 725; yb75 9/10; w74 111, 261, 264-5; g74 9/8 6; w73 327; tp 111; g73 4/22 24; w72 453, 474; w71 138, 266, 585
12:3 yb76 8/18; w75 468, 725; g75 7/22 14; w73 334, 472-3; g73 3/8 3; w72 756
12:4 w73 373; kj 58
12:5 w73 373; kj 58
12:6 w73 372-3
12:7 w73 372-3
12:8 yb76 4/11; w73 372-3; or 65
12:9 yb76 11/27; yb75 3/23; w74 153; w72 286, 439
12:10 yb76 5/18; w75 725; w73 142; w72 757; g72 2/8 3
12:11 w73 328
12:12 yb76 1/23; yb73 10/9
12:13 w74 440; w73 372, 472
12:15 g75 7/22 15
12:16 w75 297, 725; w74 103-4, 532; w73 473
12:17 g75 6/8 4; g75 12/8 29; g74 3/8 3; g72 3/8 11; w71 580
12:18 yb76 2/1; g75 12/8 29; w73 128, 334; g73 5/8 23; g72 3/8 11; g71 12/22 24
12:19 yb76 2/1; g74 3/8 4; g74 5/22 28; w72 196, 640, 660; g72 3/8 11; w71 580
12:20 w75 676; w74 122; g72 3/8 11
12:21 tp 171; g72 3/8 11; w71 580
13:1 sl 297; yb75 238; ml 27; w74 62, 108; w73 63, 142; tp 135-6; yb73 7/5; w72 267, 501-2, 644, 657
13:2 tp 135; yb73 4/3; w72 267-8, 657
13:4 yb76 7/10; w75 719; g75 11/22 27-8; w72 268, 480
13:5 yb76 3/20; w75 75, 215; g74 2/22 28; tp 138; w72 589, 640
13:6 g74 2/22 28; tp 136; w72 267, 640, 657
13:7 g74 2/22 28; w73 316; tp 136; w72 267, 640, 657
13:8 w73 287; tp 28; yb72 4/5; g72 11/22 8; w71 127, 526, 766
13:9 w73 452; tp 28; w72 563; g72 11/22 8
13:10 tp 28; w72 563; g72 11/22 8, 18
13:11 yb76 5/5; g71 11/22 3
13:12 yb76 5/5
13:13 w74 13; w73 575
13:14 yb76 12/22; w74 13; w73 568
14:1 w72 757
14:3 w72 599
14:4 w74 437; yb73 9/6; w72 591, 757
14:5 w73 542; w72 564; g72 11/22 7
14:7 w73 277
14:8 g74 9/8 27; w73 277
14:9 w72 177
14:10 w73 320; g73 9/8 7; w72 591, 599
14:12 w73 542; w72 591
14:13 w72 757
14:14 w72 564; w71 314
14:15 w72 564
14:17 w73 187, 459
14:19 yb74 5/11; w73 139, 320, 332; w71 311
14:21 w75 300; w72 565; w71 314
14:22 w73 139
14:23 w72 564
15:1 w73 320, 333; yb73 10/17; w72 757
15:2 w73 31, 333; w72 666
15:3 w73 139, 333, 736
15:4 g74 10/8 21; w72 503, 635
15:5 yb73 3/27; w72 303

15:7 yb73 9/16
15:8 w75 721; w73 261
15:12 sl 171, 197
15:13 w72 619-20; dn 7-8
15:25 w75 718
15:26 yb76 6/24
15:27 w75 718
15:33 g72 10/8 17
16:4 w72 457
16:18 w73 568
16:20 w75 618, 622; og 19, 27; w74 106; yb73 6/15; w72 620, 623, 631; dn 8, 15, 29
16:25 po 156
16:26 po 156
16:27 w73 163

1 CORINTHIANS

1:10 yb76 9/14, 11/7; w75 732; w74 107; w71 301
1:11 w72 298; w71 301
1:12 w75 727; w71 301
1:13 w71 301
1:18 w75 429
1:19 w74 339
1:20 w74 339; g72 9/8 28
1:21 w74 339
1:23 w75 429; g72 9/8 28
1:24 w75 512; w72 106
1:25 g72 9/8 28
1:26 yb76 5/31; w73 535
1:27 w73 535; kj 358
1:28 kj 358
1:29 kj 358
1:30 w73 535; w72 106
2:1 w74 211; w73 374, 472
2:3 w75 199; w74 415
2:4 w73 374, 472
2:5 w74 211; w73 160, 374
2:10 w73 186, 402
2:11 w73 186
2:13 w74 211
2:14 w74 212; w73 463; w72 128, 306; w71 543
2:15 w74 212; w73 463; w72 306; w71 543
2:16 yb75 3/8; w74 209; w71 544
3:1 yb75 1/7, 8/26; w74 109, 209; w71 662
3:2 yb75 8/26; w74 109; w71 662
3:3 w74 109; w72 757
3:4 w74 109; yb72 1/11
3:5 yb76 8/31; w75 722
3:6 yb76 1/21; w73 273
3:7 yb73 4/20; w72 756
3:9 yb76 3/21; w75 708; yb73 11/29; w72 719
3:10 or 123
3:11 or 123
3:12 or 123
3:13 or 123
3:14 or 123
3:15 or 123
3:16 w74 491; w72 719
3:17 w74 491; w73 440; w72 719
3:21 w75 727; w72 756; w71 351
3:22 w75 727; w71 351
3:23 w75 174, 727; w71 351
4:2 yb75 6/19; w74 531
4:4 w73 310; w72 590
4:5 w72 590
4:6 w71 266
4:7 w74 299; w73 372
4:9 yb75 4/3, 4/17; w74 215-16, 318
4:10 w74 216, 219
4:11 w74 216, 219
4:12 w74 216, 219; w73 501
4:13 w74 216, 219
4:15 w72 512
4:21 w74 82; or 57
5:1 w75 75; w72 735
5:2 g71 6/22 27
5:3 w74 422
5:4 yb75 12/3; w74 422
5:5 yb75 12/3; w74 422, 467, 472
5:6 w75 428; sl 210; w74 466; w73 336
5:7 w75 604; sl 210
5:8 yb76 4/15; w75 604; sl 210
5:9 w74 223; tp 121; w72 592
5:10 w74 223; g74 3/8 28; tp 121; w72 592, 599
5:11 yb75 1/19, 6/30; w74 460, 464, 468; w72 196
5:12 w73 191
5:13 w75 94; w74 217, 460; w73 191
6:1 w73 703
6:2 w73 703
6:3 w73 703
6:4 w73 703
6:5 w73 703
6:6 w73 703
6:7 w73 703
6:9 w74 484, 494; g74 3/8 28; w73 356; w72 295
6:10 w74 205, 484, 494; yb74 2/4; g74 3/8 28; w73 356; w72 593
6:11 w74 486, 494; g73 8/22 6; w72 298
6:12 w73 145; w71 671
6:13 w73 145; w71 671
6:18 g75 5/8 6; g74 1/22 27-8; g74 2/8 9; w72 196; g71 1/8 4
6:19 yb74 11/9; w73 137, 277; tp 183; or 17
6:20 yb74 1/18, 11/9; w73 137, 277; tp 183; or 17
7:1 w73 31, 74, 595
7:2 w73 596; g72 12/8 5
7:3 g74 4/22 6; w73 352
7:4 w73 352; w72 736
7:5 w74 671; g74 4/22 6; w73 352; w71 538; g71 5/22 9
7:9 w74 703; w73 568, 596
7:10 w75 287; w74 511; w72 382
7:11 w75 287; w74 511; w72 382
7:12 w75 146; g71 11/8 28
7:13 w75 287; tp 177
7:14 w73 575, 671; tp 177; w72 361-2; w71 63
7:15 w75 575-6; w72 364, 383
7:16 w75 576; tp 177; or 186; yb72 2/14; w71 201
7:23 w74 158; tp 182
7:25 w75 146; g71 11/8 28
7:28 w75 152; g72 12/8 6
7:29 w75 351-2
7:31 w75 91, 352; w74 50; w73 138; w71 251, 352
7:32 w74 379
7:35 w74 379, 703; w72 107
7:36 w74 703; g72 12/8 4, 7
7:37 w74 703
7:38 w74 379, 703; g72 12/8 6
7:39 g75 9/22 28; yb74 4/2; w73 73, 153, 319, 477, 735; w72 365
7:40 yb76 4/27; w75 146; g71 11/8 28
8:1 w75 370; w74 180; g74 8/22 19; w73 291
8:2 w74 180
8:4 yb76 8/23; w75 218; g72 8/22 7
8:5 g72 3/22 6; w71 101; bi8 1356
8:6 bi8 1356
8:7 w75 218; yb73 9/20; w72 563; g72 8/22 7
8:8 g72 8/22 7
8:9 w72 564; g72 8/22 7
8:10 w72 564; g72 8/22 7
8:11 w72 564; g72 8/22 7
8:12 w73 139; w72 564; g72 8/22 7
8:13 yb76 9/25; w75 219; w73 139; g72 8/22 7
9:1 g72 5/22 27
9:2 g72 5/22 27
9:5 g72 5/8 12
9:11 w73 160
9:12 w73 160
9:16 km 2/74 7; or 5
9:22 km 12/75 8; yb72 4/12
9:27 yb76 9/5; w74 59; w73 285, 511; g73 5/8 6
10:6 w74 63; w72 685; pm 44; kj 237
10:7 w74 63; kj 237
10:8 w74 63; w73 588; w72 684; kj 237
10:9 w74 63; kj 237
10:10 w74 63; kj 237
10:11 w75 145, 428; ka 296; w72 503, 635, 685; pm 44; kj 237; g71 11/8 28
10:12 yb76 2/23; w74 112, 181; ka 40; w72 436, 531; kj 237; g71 11/8 28
10:13 w74 63, 203; yb74 3/25; w73 41; yb73 7/10, 10/10; w72 123, 138, 529; yb72 3/22; w71 114, 116
10:14 w74 395; w72 295, 530; g72 11/8 28
10:19 w74 145
10:20 w74 145, 396; g74 1/22 18; w73 181, 486, 606; g73 5/22 28; w72 754; w71 510-11
10:21 w73 181, 700
10:22 w73 181, 700
10:23 w75 268; w73 145
10:24 w73 144; g72 11/22 18; g72 12/22 4
10:25 g72 8/22 7
10:26 g72 8/22 7
10:27 g72 8/22 7
10:28 g72 8/22 7
10:29 g72 8/22 7
10:31 yb76 5/19; w75 300; yb75 1/26; w74 84; km 7/74 3; yb73 6/3; w72 179, 400, 591; w71 311
10:32 w73 736; w72 757
10:33 w73 736
11:1 w74 149; yb74 2/16; w73 99; w72 757
11:3 w75 434, 464; tp 139; yb73 1/26; g73 2/22 28; w72 266, 270, 730, 736; yb72 4/3; g72 2/22 7; bi8 1360
11:4 w72 446
11:5 w73 255; w72 446
11:6 w72 446
11:7 w72 445; g71 10/8 19
11:10 w72 447
11:12 g72 5/22 10
11:14 w73 140; w72 667; g72 5/8 16
11:15 w73 140; w72 667; g72 5/8 16
11:16 w72 457
11:23 w74 200; w73 198
11:24 w74 200; w73 198; km 3/73 3; te 169
11:25 w74 200; w73 198; w71 745; te 169
11:26 w73 198
12:1 g74 4/22 27
12:2 w72 693, 697
12:3 w72 697
12:4 w73 109, 373; w72 703; w71 502
12:5 w73 109, 373; w72 703; w71 458, 502
12:6 yb74 5/19; w73 109, 373; w71 502
12:7 w73 373; w71 502
12:8 w71 502
12:9 w71 502
12:10 g74 12/22 27; w71 502
12:11 w73 110

12:12 kj 58
12:13 kj 58
12:18 w74 137
12:20 g74 12/8 20
12:21 w74 316
12:23 g74 2/8 15
12:24 yb76 12/28; g74 2/8 15
12:25 yb76 12/28
12:26 yb72 6/26
12:28 yb76 2/2; w72 703
12:29 w74 447; g74 12/22 27
12:30 g74 12/22 27
12:31 g74 12/22 27
13:1 w73 524; g71 2/22 8
13:2 g73 4/8 28
13:3 g73 4/8 28; w72 415; g72 7/22 27
13:4 yb75 3/22; w74 439-40; g74 4/22 8; w73 292; w72 131
13:5 yb75 9/2, 11/3; w74 440-1; g74 4/22 8; w73 292; w72 131, 287, 739
13:6 yb75 6/25; w74 441; w73 292; w72 131
13:7 yb75 4/26, 5/10; w74 104, 441-2; w73 292; w72 131
13:8 yb76 8/28; w75 95; w74 442, 447; g74 12/22 27; w73 292; ka 391; w72 131; g72 11/8 7; w71 501
13:9 g72 11/8 7
13:10 w75 95; g72 11/8 7; w71 565
13:11 yb76 1/19; g72 11/8 7
13:13 w73 390, 691; g72 11/22 4
14:2 w72 160
14:9 w75 732; sg 56
14:18 w71 503
14:19 sg 56
14:20 yb75 2/27; w74 112; w71 565, 605-6
14:28 g73 8/8 5
14:33 w73 393; tp 45
14:34 w73 255
14:35 w73 255
15:5 w71 320
15:6 w73 269; g72 11/22 18
15:7 w75 222; w74 19
15:10 g75 6/22 4
15:13 ts 169; w73 248
15:14 ts 169; w73 248
15:15 ts 169; w73 248
15:18 sl 29
15:19 sl 29; g73 6/8 8
15:20 po 153; w73 239; g73 5/8 5
15:21 w73 239
15:22 w73 239, 465, 639
15:23 po 153; w73 246; bi8 1364
15:24 og 29; w74 96, 346, 604; ts 131; w72 463
15:25 w74 346, 604; ka 160; w72 463; pm 378
15:26 w74 346, 604; ts 119, 125; w73 604, 606; ka 160; w72 463; pm 378
15:27 w74 346, 604; w72 463; pm 378
15:28 yb76 12/7; w75 492; og 29; w74 346, 604; po 190; ka 154; g73 2/22 28; w72 463; pm 378
15:31 w72 519
15:32 w75 172; w74 216; ts 13; w73 70, 423; g73 6/8 8; g72 11/22 18
15:33 w74 93, 112, 153, 271, 564; yb74 3/20; w73 70, 144, 177, 423; yb73 5/10; w72 196, 304, 592; w71 606; g71 5/8 27-8
15:34 w73 70; g71 11/22 4
15:35 yb76 4/17
15:39 po 42; w72 32
15:40 w73 726
15:42 w72 687, 717-18
15:43 po 154; w72 687, 717-18
15:44 po 39, 154; w73 243; w72 687, 717-18
15:45 sl 80, 365; po 154; ts 38; w73 230; w72 659, 687, 717; w71 275
15:46 w72 717
15:47 w72 717
15:48 w72 717
15:49 ts 170; w72 717
15:50 g74 8/22 27-8; g73 7/22 4; w72 717
15:51 w74 256; ka 244; w72 717
15:52 w74 256; ka 244; w72 717
15:53 w72 622, 717; dn 13
15:54 w72 622, 717; dn 13
15:58 yb76 7/4; w74 57, 534; w73 405
16:13 w74 111
16:17 bi8 1364

2 CORINTHIANS

1:3 w74 497; w72 549
1:4 w73 185
1:8 w74 216
1:9 w74 216, 702
1:10 w74 216
1:11 w74 702; w72 603
1:12 yb76 12/13; yb73 12/8; w72 556, 565
1:19 tp 65
1:20 w75 455; w74 17; w73 261, 543; tp 65
1:21 w74 252
1:22 w75 105; w74 252
1:24 or 54
2:6 yb73 10/15
2:7 w74 466; g74 11/8 28
2:11 yb75 4/27; w74 466-7; w73 485; yb72 5/29; w71 116; g71 5/22 10
2:14 tp 96
2:15 tp 96
2:16 tp 96
2:17 tp 96
3:1 yb76 87
3:2 yb76 87; w74 125
3:3 yb76 87; w74 125
3:5 w74 367; w73 532; yb72 6/14; w71 332
3:6 w71 457, 692
3:16 w73 437
4:2 yb76 2/12; w73 471; yb73 7/29, 8/11; w72 566, 598
4:3 w75 658
4:4 w75 658; yb75 3/3; w74 561, 755; g74 10/22 8-9; w73 344; g73 4/22 19; w72 600, 629, 653, 754; dn 26; g72 11/22 19; g71 5/22 5
4:6 yb76 7/9
4:8 w75 518
4:9 w75 518
4:13 w75 304; w74 184
4:14 ka 403
4:15 w71 351
4:16 w74 380; w72 556
4:17 w74 380
4:18 w74 380
5:1 g73 5/8 6; w72 412
5:2 w72 412
5:5 w74 252
5:10 w72 589
5:14 w75 153; w74 200, 371; w73 277
5:15 w74 372; w73 277
5:17 w73 732; w72 608
5:18 w72 376
5:19 w72 376
5:20 w74 107, 147, 604; w73 401; ka 78, 278; w72 376; yb72 7/15; w71 622; kj 359; nc 24
5:21 sl 82
6:1 yb76 6/4; w74 496; yb73 1/7, 5/31; w72 297, 308, 375; kj 285
6:2 w72 375; kj 285
6:3 yb76 4/30; w72 570; g72 5/8 16; w71 765
6:4 yb76 4/30, 8/6; w75 721; w72 283, 285; g72 5/8 16; w71 692
6:5 w75 721; w72 283; w71 538
6:7 w73 159
6:9 yb76 10/24
6:10 yb76 10/24; w75 574; w73 158; w72 285
6:14 g74 1/22 18; w73 73, 319; yb73 6/12; w72 305; kj 161
6:15 w73 73; kj 161
6:16 g74 1/22 18; w72 719; kj 161, 275
6:17 sl 160; g74 1/22 18; w73 73, 336, 575; or 12; w71 639; kj 161
6:18 kj 161
7:1 yb74 7/8; w73 339, 409, 411, 543, 567; tp 163; yb73 4/15; w72 196, 414, 595; or 154; kj 161
7:2 w73 160
7:6 bi8 1364
7:7 bi8 1364
7:10 tp 181; w72 438, 636
7:11 w72 636
8:4 w75 718
8:9 g75 4/8 12
8:12 g74 1/8 28
8:18 w75 765; w71 766
8:19 w71 766
8:20 w75 718; w71 766
8:21 yb75 11/24; w74 151; w71 764, 766
8:23 yb76 10/8
9:1 w75 718
9:6 w73 292
9:7 yb76 7/28; g74 1/8 28; g74 12/22 4; w73 292, 372; tp 32; km 10/73 8
9:11 w75 718
9:12 w75 718
9:13 w75 718
10:1 w73 473
10:3 w73 159
10:4 w73 159
10:5 w73 159-60
10:10 bi8 1364
10:12 w74 270, 562
11:3 w73 160; w72 178, 191
11:4 w72 191
11:13 w73 160; w72 191
11:14 w74 327; g74 10/22 8; w73 160; w72 191
11:15 w74 327; w72 191
11:23 w75 721; w71 692
11:25 w75 721
11:26 w75 721
11:27 w75 721; w71 538
11:29 w74 153
12:1 sl 131, 133
12:2 sl 131
12:3 sl 131
12:4 sl 131, 134; pm 286, 396; kj 309
12:5 sl 131
12:11 w73 160
12:15 w73 286
12:16 w73 160
12:21 w73 575
13:5 yb73 2/14; w72 302
13:10 w73 504; or 57
13:11 yb75 3; w73 331, 335
13:14 yb75 3; w74 422

GALATIANS

1:4 w75 750; tp 186
1:6 w74 329
1:7 w74 329; g73 2/22 27
1:8 w74 329; g73 2/22 27
1:11 w74 329
1:12 w74 329
1:14 g73 11/8 27
1:16 w73 570

g, Awake!; **ka,** God's Kingdom of a Thousand Years; **kj,** "The Nations Shall Know that I Am Jehovah"; **km,** Kingdom Ministry; **or,** Organization; **pm,** Paradise Restored—By Theocracy!; **po,** God's "Eternal Purpose"; **sg,** Theocratic School Guidebook; **sl,** Man's Salvation out of World Distress!; **te,** Listening to the Great Teacher; **tp,** True Peace and Security; **ts,** Is This Life All There Is?; **w,** Watchtower; **yb,** Yearbook. **Complete list on page 6.**

2:2 or 63
2:7 w72 670
2:8 w72 670
2:9 w72 670; or 63; w71 687
2:11 w75 345; w73 285
2:12 w75 345; w73 285, 319
2:14 w75 345
2:20 w72 520
3:7 po 85, 163
3:8 w74 330; po 85, 163, 187
3:9 w74 330
3:11 w73 437
3:13 po 159; g74 9/22 28; w72 691; w71 274; bi8 1360-1
3:16 sl 224; w74 330; po 187; g73 8/22 29; g72 10/22 14
3:17 po 106, 112
3:19 w73 44, 581; w72 682
3:20 w72 682
3:23 g72 11/22 6
3:24 w74 17; w73 581; tp 65; w72 127; g72 11/22 7
3:25 w72 127; g72 11/22 7
3:26 po 163; w73 527
3:27 po 163
3:28 po 163; g74 10/8 19; w73 527; w71 570
3:29 sl 224; po 163, 187; w72 172
4:2 w73 581
4:3 w71 415
4:4 w74 621; hu 24; w73 580-1; ka 61; w72 685; g72 11/22 6
4:6 w75 106
4:7 w75 106
4:8 w73 486; bi8 1357
4:9 sl 351; g72 11/22 7
4:10 g72 11/22 7
4:11 g72 11/22 7
4:15 w74 575; w73 254
4:22 sl 94
4:23 sl 94
4:24 sl 94
4:25 sl 94
4:26 sl 94; ts 127; w73 141
4:27 sl 94
5:1 sl 94; yb74 4/20; w73 141
5:9 w73 338; w72 263
5:12 w73 286
5:13 yb76 8/25; w74 10; g72 11/22 8
5:14 yb76 8/25; g72 11/22 8
5:15 yb76 8/25; w75 347
5:16 w74 209, 415; w73 408, 511
5:18 w72 563
5:19 yb74 4/23, 5/6; w73 74, 574-5, 593; w72 196; g71 5/22 4
5:20 w74 110; yb74 4/23; w73 339; tp 161; w72 196; w71 248; g71 5/22 4
5:21 w74 110, 168; w73 505
5:22 yb76 12/25; w73 691; w71 664; kj 327, 331, 343, 381, 405
5:23 yb76 12/25; w73 142; yb72 8/9; w71 664; kj 327, 331, 343, 381, 405
5:24 w73 337
5:26 g75 6/22 27; w73 506; g73 3/22 13; g72 11/22 10
6:1 yb76 7/20; w75 268, 371, 530, 766; w74 104; w73 145, 503; yb73 9/18; w72 465-6, 604, 740; or 160, 166-7; sg 72
6:2 w72 757; or 183
6:3 w74 562, 575
6:4 w74 562, 575
6:5 w75 765; w74 183; w73 542
6:7 w74 212; g74 8/8 3; w73 76, 144, 680; yb73 3/14; g73 6/22 29; w72 392, 597; g72 12/22 17; g71 10/8 20
6:8 yb74 1/6; w73 76; yb73 3/14; g73 6/22 29
6:9 yb76 12/26; w74 446; w73 334, 502; w72 702
6:10 yb76 9/3, 12/26; w75 87, 310, 676; km 3/75 3; w74 122; w73 334; or 111
6:15 po 160; w72 199
6:16 w74 126; po 160; yb74 6/19; w73 748; w72 173; or 9; kj 332, 352

EPHESIANS

1:1 g75 1/22 28
1:4 w74 287; g74 7/8 28; w71 704
1:5 w74 287
1:8 po 157
1:9 sl 330, 333, 365; yb75 3/24, 11/21, 12/10; g75 4/8 14; w74 601, 616-17, 622; po 157; ts 131; hu 12, 14, 24; tp 59
1:10 w75 286; sl 330, 333, 365; yb75 3/24, 11/21, 12/10; g75 4/8 14; w74 601, 616-17, 621-2, 636; po 157; ts 131; hu 12, 14, 23-4; w73 583; tp 59; w72 171
1:11 sl 330; w74 616-17, 622; po 157; ts 131; hu 12, 14, 24; g74 7/8 28
1:12 sl 330; po 157; ts 131
1:13 sl 330; w74 252; w73 730; w72 636
1:14 sl 330; w74 252; w73 495; w72 636
1:15 w74 16
1:18 sg 73
1:21 w73 103
1:22 yb75 4/30; w72 729; w71 747
1:23 yb75 4/30; w74 619; hu 18
2:1 ts 104; w73 209; ka 36, 39; w72 607; g71 3/8 28
2:2 w74 735; g74 10/22 9; w73 136, 177; yb73 1/8; w72 262, 630; dn 27; w71 630
2:4 w72 549
2:5 ts 104; w73 464; ka 36, 39; w72 607
2:6 sl 132; yb75 7/15; w74 621; hu 23; ka 36, 39
2:8 g75 11/8 28
2:12 w72 691, 693
2:14 w74 619; po 165; hu 19; g72 11/22 7; g71 9/8 28
2:15 w74 619; hu 19; g72 11/22 7; g71 9/8 28
2:16 w74 619; hu 19; g72 11/22 7
2:17 g72 11/22 7; g71 9/8 28
2:18 g72 11/22 7
2:20 po 158; w72 719
2:21 w73 440; w72 719
2:22 w72 719; kj 275
3:5 w74 127; po 168
3:6 w74 127; po 168
3:7 w75 721
3:9 po 9, 167; w71 319, 569
3:10 po 9, 167; w71 319, 569
3:11 po 9, 11-12, 167
3:12 g74 6/8 5; w73 211
3:20 w74 315
3:21 w71 318
4:3 yb76 12/9; w75 758; w73 281; w72 731
4:4 w72 731
4:5 w74 16; g74 1/22 19; w72 731
4:6 w72 731; w71 318
4:7 w71 750
4:8 w75 667, 727; sl 85; w74 620; yb74 8/21; hu 21; w73 402; or 53, 55; yb72 11/1; w71 748
4:9 sl 85
4:10 sl 85; w74 620; hu 21
4:11 w75 726-7; sl 85; yb75 5/1; w74 111, 336, 620; hu 21; yb73 5/7; or 53, 55; w71 333, 748, 750, 752
4:12 w75 667, 727; sl 85; yb75 5/1; w74 111, 620; hu 21; or 53; w71 748
4:13 w75 667, 727; w74 111, 620; hu 21; w71 662-3
4:14 w75 668; w74 110-11; w71 662
4:15 w75 668; w74 111; pm 252
4:16 w75 668; w72 755
4:17 w74 562
4:18 w74 562-3
4:19 w74 562; w73 575; w72 93, 588; g72 12/8 7
4:20 kj 381
4:21 kj 381
4:22 w74 111, 312; w71 444, 763; kj 381
4:23 w75 119; yb75 2/8; w74 111, 210, 312; g74 12/8 21; w73 460; or 123; yb72 8/8; w71 138, 444, 543, 763; kj 381
4:24 w74 111, 210, 312; g74 12/8 21; w73 460; or 123; w71 444, 763; kj 381
4:25 yb75 5/24; w74 58, 313-14; w73 317, 597; pm 252; yb72 3/10; w71 306
4:26 w75 648; w74 314; w72 196
4:27 w75 648; w74 314
4:28 w74 314; g74 3/8 28; w73 317; g73 1/22 28; g73 8/22 7; w72 599; pm 211; yb72 3/10; w71 306, 533
4:29 yb75 7/24; w74 314, 435; yb72 8/30; w71 306; sg 56
4:30 w74 422; w72 756
4:31 w74 314; w71 164, 307
4:32 yb76 5/17; w75 675; g75 1/22 24; w74 154, 435; g74 5/22 5; w73 100, 335; tp 171
5:1 w75 285; yb75 1/5, 3/20; w74 144, 146, 154, 270; w73 99-100; g73 4/22 25
5:2 yb76 4/19; yb75 1/5; w74 146, 154
5:3 g74 2/8 9; g74 4/22 13; g73 5/8 4; g73 11/22 28; w71 305
5:4 g73 5/8 4; w71 305; sg 56
5:5 g74 1/22 27; w71 305
5:8 w74 572
5:11 w73 593
5:12 w73 593
5:13 w74 572
5:15 yb76 8/15; or 110
5:16 yb76 8/15; w73 502; w72 247; or 110; g72 12/22 6; w71 671
5:17 or 110; w71 671
5:22 w75 485; g74 4/22 7; yb72 3/25

5:23 w74 686; g74 4/22 7, 9; g74 5/22 5; yb72 4/24; g72 5/22 13
5:24 w74 317
5:25 w75 153; yb75 6/18; w74 317, 686; tp 140; g72 5/22 14
5:26 w74 317
5:27 w74 317
5:28 w75 153; g74 4/22 10; w73 154
5:29 w75 153; g74 4/22 10
5:32 w74 686
5:33 w74 91; g74 4/22 8, 10; w73 154; tp 140; w72 36, 271; yb72 7/3; g72 1/22 12; g72 9/22 27
6:1 yb75 4/21; g75 10/22 27; w73 318, 671; w72 164; g72 9/22 27; te 32, 138
6:2 yb75 4/21; g75 10/22 27; w74 265; w72 164; g72 1/22 12; g72 9/22 27; te 32
6:3 yb75 4/21; g75 10/22 27; w74 265; w72 164; g72 9/22 27
6:4 yb76 11/8; w75 156; yb75 2/23; w74 82; yb74 11/19; g74 2/8 8; w73 154, 561; tp 176; yb73 8/29; w72 114, 164, 260, 634; g72 9/22 27; w71 205
6:5 w72 598
6:6 w74 536
6:10 or 185
6:11 g74 10/22 10; w72 653
6:12 yb76 10/26; w75 655; w74 560, 735; g74 2/22 4; w73 512; yb73 12/9; g73 5/22 14; w72 653; w71 479, 511
6:18 g75 1/22 27; yb73 4/26; w72 329

PHILIPPIANS

1:1 yb76 10/27; w74 408; w73 469; w72 19, 21, 692; or 61; yb72 27, 30, 9/22; w71 690
1:7 yb75 172
1:9 g72 2/8 4; w71 266
1:10 w73 127-8; yb73 2/9; w71 266
1:21 w73 470; w72 519
1:23 bi8 1364-5
1:26 bi8 1364
1:27 w74 540
2:2 w74 316; w72 757
2:3 yb76 8/3; w74 299, 316, 413; g74 6/8 4; g73 7/8 4; w72 757
2:4 w74 202, 282, 316; g74 6/8 4
2:5 w74 409, 601; yb73 5/9; w72 177, 757
2:6 w74 601; w72 177; w71 355-6
2:7 w74 601; w72 177, 581
2:8 w74 409, 601; w72 177
2:9 w73 103; w72 177; pm 153; w71 649
2:10 w75 120, 492; sl 203; w73 103, 312; g73 2/22 28; w72 177, 756; w71 649
2:11 sl 203; w73 312, 530; g73 2/22 28; w72 177; yb72 9/14; w71 649
2:12 w74 532; bi8 1364
2:13 yb75 7/8
2:15 yb76 12/2; w75 757
2:16 w75 757; w73 535
2:20 w73 157
2:21 w73 157
2:22 w73 157
2:25 w72 553
2:27 w74 137
2:29 w72 553
2:30 w72 553
3:7 yb76 9/7; w73 158, 470
3:8 w73 158, 286
3:10 w73 740
3:11 w73 740
3:12 w74 659
3:13 w74 659; w73 500
3:14 yb75 11/6; w74 659; w73 500; w71 329
3:17 w73 319
3:19 w73 568
3:20 w72 183
4:1 w75 343
4:2 w75 343
4:3 w75 344
4:4 w74 576
4:5 w72 593
4:6 yb76 5/6; yb75 11/13; g74 8/22 19; w73 337, 512; w72 336, 543; g72 11/22 4
4:7 g74 8/22 19; w73 331, 337, 512; g72 12/22 6
4:8 w73 329, 479, 512, 540, 595; g72 11/22 4
4:9 w73 329
4:11 w75 124; w73 573; g72 3/8 4; g72 11/22 4
4:12 g72 3/8 4
4:13 w74 344, 522, 534; w73 375; km 4/72 3
4:22 yb73 10/16; w72 592

COLOSSIANS

1:4 w73 685, 691
1:5 yb74 6/26; w73 683, 688, 691, 718
1:6 yb74 6/26; w73 582, 683, 688, 718; ka 298
1:7 w73 691
1:8 w73 685, 691
1:13 yb74 3/17; w73 458, 686; w71 428, 431
1:14 w73 458
1:15 w73 132, 262; g73 3/8 28
1:16 w73 263
1:17 w72 486
1:18 w74 432; g73 5/8 7; w72 729
1:19 w73 263
1:22 w73 470
1:23 w75 721; w74 61; yb74 6/18, 7/1; w73 582, 683, 688, 718; ka 227, 298; yb72 11/19; g72 4/22 21; g72 11/22 8
1:25 w75 721; po 167; w73 692; w71 457
1:26 po 167; w73 692
1:27 po 167; w73 692
2:2 w73 263
2:3 yb76 3/6; w75 305; w74 180; w73 263; yb73 1/22; w72 105-6
2:6 w73 692
2:7 w73 692
2:8 yb75 5/6; w74 181; w71 415
2:9 w73 263
2:10 w73 263
2:13 w74 95; ts 104; ka 37; w72 607; g72 11/22 7
2:14 po 159; g74 1/8 28; g72 11/22 7
2:16 g74 4/8 11; w73 263; g72 11/22 7; g71 10/8 27
2:17 w74 176; g74 1/8 28; g74 4/8 11; w73 263, 415; w72 127; g72 11/22 7; g71 10/8 27
2:18 w74 213
2:19 w72 756
2:20 g73 8/8 28; w71 415
2:21 g73 8/8 28; g72 7/8 8
2:22 g73 8/8 28; g72 7/8 8
2:23 w75 12; w74 213; g73 8/8 28
3:2 w73 145
3:3 w72 520
3:5 w74 242; yb74 7/10; w73 75, 337, 567; tp 152; g73 11/22 27-8; w72 93, 530, 593; g72 12/8 7
3:6 w74 242; w73 75, 567
3:7 w74 242
3:8 w74 242
3:9 w74 148; g74 8/8 5; w71 586
3:10 yb75 2/5; w74 148; g74 8/8 5; g74 9/8 6; or 123
3:12 w74 411; g74 8/8 5; w73 371
3:13 yb76 9/30; yb74 4/5; g74 8/8 5; w73 334, 371
3:14 ml 28; w73 371, 458; yb72 5/18; w71 305
3:15 w73 334; w72 731
3:16 w75 30; yb73 3/25; w72 405
3:17 w74 76
3:18 w74 118; tp 141; yb73 10/29
3:19 yb76 9/1; w74 155; yb72 6/5
3:20 w73 671; tp 141; w72 733
3:21 yb72 9/12; w71 370
3:22 w72 269, 598
3:23 yb76 7/17; w74 84, 374; g73 7/22 26; w72 269; yb72 1/30
3:24 yb76 7/17; w75 716; w74 374; g73 7/22 26; yb72 1/30
4:2 yb76 12/20; g74 1/8 11
4:5 w73 502
4:6 yb72 12/22; w71 207
4:11 w74 203
4:17 w75 733

1 THESSALONIANS

1:9 w72 122, 693
2:3 w73 575
2:7 yb76 1/6
2:8 yb76 3/18, 11/17; w75 177; yb75 5/31; w74 338
2:9 yb76 4/4; w75 177; g74 1/8 28
2:10 w73 473
2:11 yb76 10/13
2:13 yb76 8/13; w73 150; kj 292
2:15 g73 5/22 27
2:16 po 173; g73 5/22 27
2:18 sl 355
2:19 yb76 6/22; w75 183; bi8 1364
2:20 yb76 6/22; w75 183
3:3 yb72 2/16
3:4 yb72 2/16
3:13 bi8 1364
4:1 yb76 2/14; w75 184
4:3 g75 5/8 8; g74 4/22 13; tp 148; w71 119
4:6 tp 148; g71 1/8 4
4:7 w74 160, 340; w73 339, 567
4:8 w74 340
4:9 yb76 3/22; w75 339; g72 2/8 3
4:11 g74 9/22 11; g73 7/22 26; g73 8/8 3; w72 206, 594

4:12 g74 9/22 11; yb73 12/7; g73 7/22 26; w72 594, 597
4:13 g75 5/8 23; w74 255; g74 12/8 28; w73 252, 452, 494, 606, 640; g73 5/8 5; g71 12/8 28
4:14 w74 255, 558; g74 12/8 28; w73 252, 640; ka 243
4:15 w74 255, 558; ka 243; bi8 1364
4:16 w74 255, 558; ka 243; w71 269; bi8 1365
4:17 w75 89; w74 255, 558; ka 243; bi8 1365
4:18 w74 255; g74 12/8 28
5:1 g72 10/8 14
5:2 w74 552; g74 4/8 7; ka 365; tp 72, 89; g72 10/8 14
5:3 w75 375, 682; g75 11/8 7; w74 40, 244, 552; g74 4/8 7; ka 365; tp 89; g72 10/8 14, 22; g72 11/22 14
5:4 w74 432; tp 72
5:5 w74 432, 572
5:6 w74 432; w73 362; g71 11/22 4
5:8 w74 644; g72 11/22 4
5:11 w73 467
5:12 yb76 6/5; g72 1/22 12
5:13 g72 1/22 12
5:14 yb76 3/26; w75 530-1; g75 4/22 20
5:15 g74 3/8 4
5:17 yb76 5/30; w74 211; g74 1/8 11; w72 332, 404
5:18 yb76 5/30; g74 6/8 6; yb73 8/4; w72 332
5:23 bi8 1364

2 THESSALONIANS

1:1 w73 319
1:3 yb74 2/23; w73 459
1:4 w73 459
1:5 w73 459
1:6 w74 170; g73 7/22 6
1:7 w74 170; g73 7/22 6
1:8 w74 170, 433; ts 164; g73 7/22 6
1:9 yb75 5/12; w74 123, 128; ts 164
1:12 g72 3/22 7
2:1 bi8 1364
2:3 w75 167, 202, 269; sl 213; po 170; ka 369-70; w72 469; kj 79
2:4 w75 203, 269; sl 213; po 170; ka 379, 396; kj 79
2:5 sl 213; ka 379; kj 79
2:6 w75 252; sl 213; ka 384; kj 79
2:7 w75 252; sl 213; po 170; ka 182, 385, 387; kj 79
2:8 w75 252, 271; sl 213; ka 388; bi8 1364; kj 79
2:9 w75 254; sl 213; w74 327, 758; po 170; ka 389; bi8 1364; kj 79
2:10 w75 254, 271; sl 213; w74 327, 758; ka 389, 392; kj 79
2:11 w75 271; sl 213; ka 392; w71 177; kj 79
2:12 w75 271; sl 213; ka 392; kj 79
3:6 w73 318-19; or 172
3:10 yb75 5/5; g73 7/22 26; g73 9/8 10; w72 583
3:11 w73 318; g73 7/22 26; g73 8/8 3
3:12 g73 7/22 26
3:14 w75 93; w73 318; or 171-2
3:15 w73 318; or 171

1 TIMOTHY

1:3 w73 208
1:4 w73 542
1:5 yb76 6/9; w75 529; w73 542; w72 598-9
1:6 w73 542
1:7 w73 542
1:8 yb76 8/24
1:9 yb76 5/26, 8/24; w75 309; yb73 6/4
1:10 yb76 8/24
1:11 yb76 8/24; w73 488; w71 345; kj 399; g71 6/8 27
1:12 w74 367
1:13 yb74 11/4; w73 268, 309; w72 562
1:17 w74 376
1:19 yb73 9/14; w72 598
2:1 w74 121
2:3 w73 106; or 14
2:4 yb75 2/16; w74 121, 179; yb74 2/11; w73 106; w72 389; or 14
2:5 w74 70, 200, 370, 599; po 188; w73 199, 244, 382, 465; w72 236, 678, 687; or 14; g72 9/22 7; kj 390
2:6 w74 70, 121, 200, 370, 599; po 188; w73 199, 244, 382, 465; w72 175, 236, 678, 687; or 14; g72 9/22 7; kj 390
2:7 w71 332
2:8 yb76 8/16; w75 409
2:9 yb76 7/5; w74 85; w73 472; w72 222, 667-8, 672; g72 5/8 16
2:10 w74 85; w72 668, 672
2:11 w73 255
2:12 w73 255; w72 271, 447
2:14 w72 178
3:1 yb76 9/21; km 12/75 6; w73 469, 475, 569; w72 10, 21; or 59, 61; yb72 12, 30, 10/28; w71 691, 695, 698; sg 191
3:2 yb76 2/17, 3/24, 3/29, 4/24, 10/21; w75 467-8; km 5/75 4; w74 530; w73 205, 470, 472; yb73 1/11, 1/19, 1/25; g73 3/22 4; w72 10-11; or 59; yb72 12-14, 12/5; w71 752
3:3 w73 470, 473; yb73 5/22, 6/19; w72 13, 581; or 59; yb72 15-16
3:4 km 7/75 3; w74 89; w73 471; yb73 7/23; w72 13, 126, 703; or 59; yb72 16-17
3:5 yb76 3/10; w75 469; w74 89; w73 471; w72 703; or 59
3:6 ts 82; g74 10/22 20; w73 471, 475; yb73 2/4; w72 14; or 59; yb72 18; g71 5/22 10
3:7 w73 473; yb73 8/6; w72 14, 597; or 59; yb72 18-19; g71 5/22 10
3:8 yb76 7/26; w75 720; g74 3/8 27; w73 470-1; w72 21; or 60; yb72 29, 12/12; w71 692
3:9 yb76 7/26; w73 471; w72 21, 598; or 60; yb72 29
3:10 w75 720; w73 470-1, 475; yb73 12/17; w72 21, 126, 597; or 60; yb72 29, 12/12; w71 692
3:11 g73 3/22 4
3:12 w73 470-1; w72 21; or 60; yb72 29, 11/13; w71 692
3:13 yb76 8/11; w75 720; w72 21; or 60; yb72 29; w71 692
3:15 or 12; w71 319
3:16 yb76 7/15; w75 119, 286; g72 3/22 7; g72 6/22 6
4:1 yb76 2/29; g73 2/22 27; w71 628; kj 160
4:2 yb76 2/29; w75 212; w73 357; yb73 11/7; w72 565; w71 628
4:3 w75 301; g75 5/8 28
4:4 w75 301
4:5 w75 542
4:6 or 55
4:7 w75 502
4:8 yb76 9/4, 9/22, 12/10; w75 119; g75 12/8 29; ts 125; yb74 11/24; w73 52, 55; g73 5/22 24; w71 352; g71 9/22 6
4:10 w74 529, 746
4:12 yb73 7/8
4:13 w73 204; sg 29
4:14 w74 408; w72 458; or 63; w71 691, 695
4:15 yb75 10/25; w74 114; yb74 4/10; sg 188; km 7/71 3
5:1 km 11/74 3; g72 5/22 14
5:2 w73 540; g72 5/22 14
5:3 g75 10/22 28
5:4 g75 10/22 28; g73 9/22 19
5:8 g75 10/22 28; w74 122; w73 703; g73 6/22 9; km 9/73 8
5:17 yb76 4/29; w75 471; g74 1/8 28; yb73 2/23; w72 458, 553; yb72 6/27; w71 687, 752
5:18 g74 1/8 28
5:20 w73 319; yb73 8/27; w72 16; or 168; yb72 21
5:22 yb76 8/10, 12/8; w75 93, 732; w72 14, 19, 126; yb72 17, 26
5:24 w74 212; w73 539
5:25 w74 212
6:1 w73 260
6:5 w71 767
6:6 yb76 2/5, 8/14; w75 119, 121, 123; g74 3/8 28; g73 9/8 11
6:7 g73 9/8 11
6:8 w75 123; g74 3/8 28; g73 9/8 11; g72 5/8 4
6:9 w75 569
6:10 w75 4, 569; w74 113; g74 8/22 19; kj 133
6:11 yb76 6/17, 12/12; w75 185, 756
6:12 yb76 6/17; yb75 12/29
6:13 sl 254
6:14 yb76 260, 6/17; w75 756; sl 254; w73 470
6:15 sl 254; g71 6/8 27
6:16 sl 254; w74 255; g73 7/22 4
6:17 yb76 2/18; w75 572; w74 249; g74 9/22 11
6:18 w75 572; w74 249; g74 9/22 11; w73 463
6:19 w75 572; w74 249; g74 9/22 11; w73 76, 329, 463
6:20 yb75 4/22

2 TIMOTHY

1:5 yb76 8/27; w72 114
1:6 w74 658
1:7 w75 373; w74 522
1:8 w74 219, 658
1:9 w74 658; g73 5/8 6; w71 703

1:10 g73 5/8 6
1:13 yb74 4/26; w73 528; sg 6
1:16 w72 555
1:18 w75 718; w72 555
2:2 w73 208, 462, 506
2:3 w74 680; g73 8/8 22
2:4 w74 680
2:8 w74 362
2:11 w73 728
2:12 g74 8/22 27; w73 728
2:15 yb74 6/5; w73 207-8
2:16 w73 206
2:19 w75 189; w73 594
2:22 w73 540; yb72 7/26
2:24 g75 11/22 12; yb73 1/10; sg 72
2:25 yb76 9/10; yb73 1/10; sg 72
2:26 yb76 9/10; w75 372; g71 5/22 9
3:1 yb76 10/20; w74 165; g74 3/8 16; g74 9/8 5; g73 7/22 5; w72 583; w71 588; kj 125; g71 10/8 16
3:2 yb76 9/15, 10/20; w73 553, 568; w72 583
3:3 g74 3/8 16; w72 583
3:4 yb76 9/15; g74 9/8 5; g73 4/22 13; w72 583, 754; g72 1/22 26
3:5 g74 9/8 5; w73 136; tp 18; g73 2/8 23; w72 3, 191, 583, 636; kj 125, 175
3:6 w72 191
3:7 w72 191
3:8 kj 13
3:10 w74 659
3:12 w74 216, 442; tp 128; g73 3/8 25
3:13 g73 10/8 22
3:14 w73 113; w72 114, 506
3:15 yb75 6/22; yb74 9/2; yb73 8/8; w72 114
3:16 yb76 1/3, 5/23; w75 141; gc 4; w73 505; g72 2/8 27; g72 12/22 28; w71 228; sg 15
3:17 w73 505; g72 12/22 28
4:1 ka 113, 119, 134, 143; w71 701
4:2 yb76 8/19; w73 472; w72 499; w71 120, 701; sg 49
4:5 yb76 2/3, 2/27; w75 368, 733; w73 370, 472; w71 753
4:6 bi8 1364
4:8 ka 242
4:11 w71 457
4:13 w74 553; km 11/74 3

TITUS

1:2 w74 645; w72 742
1:5 yb76 6/7, 12/15; w73 469; w72 9, 19; or 59; yb72 10, 26, 8/21; w71 689, 695
1:6 w73 470-1; w72 126, 597; or 59
1:7 w75 725; yb75 7/14; w74 531; g74 3/8 27; w73 470, 473; w72 9, 581; or 59; yb72 10, 8/21; w71 689
1:8 w73 472-3, 569; or 59
1:9 w75 730; yb75 7/14; w74 435, 531; w73 160, 472; yb73 1/31, 6/7; w72 12, 15-16, 703; or 59; yb72 15, 20-1, 11/21; w71 752
1:13 w72 565
1:16 w74 36; g73 10/8 23
2:1 yb76 4
2:2 yb76 4; w73 178; w71 286
2:3 yb76 4; w73 569
2:4 yb76 4; w73 569
2:5 yb76 4; w73 178
2:6 yb76 4
2:7 yb76 4; w73 319; or 57
2:8 yb76 4; w73 319
2:9 yb76 4; w73 142; w72 269
2:10 yb76 4-5, 32, 259, 11/12; w75 672; g74 3/8 28; w73 142; yb73 3/7; w72 269; or 132; w71 223
2:13 yb76 6/29; g72 3/22 7; bi8 1365
2:14 yb76 6/29; w75 311; or 57
3:1 w75 317; tp 135; yb73 2/21; w72 266; or 57
3:2 w73 473; tp 135; g73 1/22 4; km 3/72 4
3:4 sl 89; or 14
3:5 sl 89; g75 11/8 28; w72 607; or 14
3:6 sl 89; or 14
3:7 or 14
3:8 or 57
3:13 w75 318
3:14 w75 318

PHILEMON

8 w75 676
9 w75 676
13 w75 718, 728; w71 457

HEBREWS

1:1 yb76 1/9
1:3 g73 7/22 4; pm 153
1:4 w73 215
1:5 w73 215
1:6 w73 215
1:8 w71 635
1:9 w71 131, 635
1:10 w71 479-80
1:11 w71 479-80
1:13 pm 153
1:14 w74 64; w72 201; g72 6/8 28
2:1 yb74 5/5; w73 44, 206, 310
2:2 w73 44, 206
2:3 w73 44, 206
2:4 g75 5/22 28; w73 206; w71 501
2:5 sl 50; w74 662
2:6 sl 50
2:7 sl 50
2:8 sl 50; w74 662
2:9 sl 50; w74 662; po 188; w73 199, 382, 465; w72 687-8, 695; kj 390
2:10 w73 104; yb73 10/18; w72 178, 688, 695-6
2:11 w71 275
2:12 or 92; w71 746
2:13 w74 730
2:14 w75 53; w74 347; ts 174; w73 309, 605; ka 285; w72 622; dn 13
2:15 w75 53; g75 10/22 12; w74 200, 347; w73 604-5; w72 623; dn 14
2:16 w73 605; w71 608
2:17 w72 178, 549
2:18 w72 178
3:1 w73 199; tp 67; w72 718; kj 403
3:3 w73 216
3:4 gc 8; g74 10/8 8; w73 216, 554; g73 5/22 8; yb72 1/25; w71 43
3:5 w73 216
3:6 w73 216
3:12 w75 375; w71 149
3:14 yb76 3/12
4:4 g72 11/22 8
4:9 g74 10/8 22; g72 11/22 8
4:10 g72 11/22 8
4:11 g72 11/22 8
4:12 yb76 5/9; g75 1/22 6; w74 445; w73 160, 186, 207, 212; tp 143; g73 1/22 26; g73 8/22 6, 8; yb72 9/17; w71 148
4:13 w73 555; tp 143; w71 357
4:14 w73 216
4:15 ts 140; tp 66; w71 570
4:16 w74 137; ts 140; w73 211; w72 549
5:1 w74 157
5:2 w74 157
5:3 w74 157
5:4 w74 158; w72 716
5:5 w74 158; w73 216; ka 88; yb73 9/5; w72 716
5:6 w74 158; w73 216; ka 88; w72 716
5:7 w73 132; yb72 12/16; w71 274
5:8 w73 132; w72 175, 695
5:9 w72 175, 688, 695
5:10 po 155; w72 175, 688
5:11 w73 43
5:12 w74 110; w71 662
5:13 w74 110; w73 43; w71 662
5:14 w74 110-11; w71 565
6:1 yb75 2/13, 2/20; w74 109-10; g72 7/22 27; w71 662
6:6 bi8 1360
6:8 g75 10/22 7
6:10 yb76 6/16; w75 713, 719; w74 373; w73 261, 375, 408
6:11 yb76 10/10; g73 7/22 26
6:12 g73 7/22 26
6:17 w71 713; kj 316
6:18 yb76 1/18; yb73 7/4; w72 714, 742; g72 12/22 6; kj 316
6:19 w75 506; w74 644; w73 312; ka 100, 112; w72 526, 714; yb72 5/26; g72 11/22 4
6:20 ts 130; yb74 12/13; w73 104, 312; ka 100, 112; w72 526, 714; yb72 5/26
7:1 w74 159; pm 200
7:3 w74 159; ka 90
7:15 w74 159
7:16 w74 159
7:17 w74 159
7:22 w74 159; bi8 1366
7:23 w73 216
7:24 g74 1/22 18; w73 216; pm 405
7:25 w74 159, 200; g74 1/22 18; w73 216, 311; pm 405
7:26 w74 157-8; w73 311; w72 621, 686; dn 11; yb72 11/18; w71 272, 284
7:27 w74 158
8:1 w74 220; ka 92; pm 153
8:2 w74 220; w73 380; ka 92; kj 386
8:3 w74 158
8:5 w74 174
8:6 po 160; w72 685; bi8 1366
8:7 w73 217; w72 685
8:8 w73 47, 217; w72 685; bi8 1366
8:9 w73 47, 217; w72 685; bi8 1366
8:10 w73 47, 217, 415; w72 685; bi8 1366
8:11 w73 47, 217; w72 685
8:12 w73 47,

g, Awake!; **ka**, God's Kingdom of a Thousand Years; **kj**, "The Nations Shall Know that I Am Jehovah"; **km**, Kingdom Ministry; **or**, Organization; **pm**, Paradise Restored—By Theocracy!; **po**, God's "Eternal Purpose"; **sg**, Theocratic School Guidebook; **sl**, Man's Salvation out of World Distress!; **te**, Listening to the Great Teacher; **tp**, True Peace and Security; **ts**, Is This Life All There Is?; **w**, Watchtower; **yb**, Yearbook. **Complete list on page 6.**

217; w72 685, 690
8:13 po 157, 160; w73 217; w72 685, 690
9:1 ka 101
9:2 ka 101; w72 711
9:3 ka 101; w72 711
9:4 w72 711, 717; bi8 1366
9:5 w72 711, 717
9:6 w72 711
9:7 w74 175; w72 711
9:8 w72 711
9:9 w72 711; w71 536
9:10 w72 711
9:11 w72 713; g72 3/22 28; w71 498
9:12 w73 465; w72 713; g72 3/22 28
9:13 w74 176; w71 536
9:14 w74 176; w72 689, 700; g72 7/22 28
9:15 po 160; bi8 1366
9:16 bi8 1365-6
9:17 bi8 1366
9:18 w72 683; g72 3/22 28
9:19 w72 683; g72 3/22 28
9:20 w72 683; g72 3/22 28; bi8 1366
9:22 w72 700; g72 3/22 28
9:23 w73 381; w72 713; w71 498; kj 386
9:24 w74 158, 331; w73 351, 381; ka 100, 103; w72 713, 751; w71 498, 713; kj 274, 386
9:25 kj 274
9:26 w74 681; ka 295; yb73 9/26; kj 274
9:27 g72 3/22 28
9:28 w72 175; g72 3/22 28
10:1 sl 65; w74 176; g74 1/8 28; g74 10/8 21; w72 127, 700, 715; g71 10/8 27
10:2 w72 700
10:4 ka 96; w72 715
10:5 w74 158; w73 274; ka 96; w72 623, 686, 715; dn 16; w71 273; kj 177
10:6 w73 274; ka 96; w72 686, 715; kj 177
10:7 ka 96; w72 606, 686, 699, 715; kj 177
10:8 w74 221; ka 96; w72 606, 686, 699, 715; kj 177
10:9 yb76 1/24; w73 327; ka 96; w72 606, 686, 699, 715; kj 177
10:10 w74 221; ka 96; w72 606, 686, 715; kj 177
10:12 sl 42; w74 331; po 155; w73 309; w72 628; pm 153; dn 23; w71 239; kj 233
10:13 sl 42; w74 331; po 155; w72 628; dn 23; w71 239; kj 233
10:16 w73 47
10:17 w73 47
10:19 yb72 7/16; w71 713
10:20 w75 479; w74 222; w72 606; yb72 7/16; w71 713
10:21 yb72 7/16; w71 713
10:22 w74 136; w72 414, 598
10:23 km 7/75 1; w73 48; yb73 1/13; w72 696; yb72 6/4; w71 400
10:24 w75 317; w73 48, 253; w72 404; yb72 6/4; w71 400, 529
10:25 w75 317; yb74 9/20; w73 48, 253; w72 404; w71 400, 529
10:26 w74 370, 382; ts 181
10:27 w74 370, 382; ts 181
10:30 g74 3/8 4
10:32 w73 43
10:33 w73 43
10:34 w73 43
10:35 w73 43; w72 304
10:36 yb74 2/28; w73 43; tp 189; or 182
10:38 w74 203, 539; g73 4/8 27
10:39 w74 203, 249; w73 467
11:1 yb75 1/2; w74 16, 397; w71 304
11:4 yb74 3/16; w73 236, 435; w72 651
11:5 po 69-70; yb73 12/3; w72 651; w71 617; nc 12
11:6 yb76 1/26; w75 77; w74 136, 339; yb73 11/3; w72 244, 598; w71 93
11:7 sl 292; w74 23; tp 94
11:8 w74 23, 309
11:10 w73 495; w71 569
11:11 w73 247; w71 704
11:12 w73 247
11:13 w73 477, 495
11:16 w75 282; w73 495; w71 569
11:17 w74 309; w73 242
11:18 w73 242
11:19 w73 242
11:20 w73 447
11:21 w73 447
11:24 yb76 5/29
11:25 yb76 5/29
11:26 po 108; yb74 12/19; w73 158, 495, 500; w71 573
11:27 w75 234; w73 452, 632
11:30 w74 24
11:31 w74 24
11:33 w74 278; g71 10/22 28
11:34 g71 10/22 28
11:35 w75 54; w74 280; ts 175; w73 242; kj 335
11:38 w74 535
11:39 w73 200
11:40 w73 200, 242-3
12:1 w75 91, 111, 428, 494; g75 12/22 19; w74 199; w73 47; w72 701-2; w71 337
12:2 w75 91, 494; w74 199, 559; w73 47, 328; w72 701-2; pm 153
12:3 w74 199; w73 47, 279, 501; w72 702
12:5 w73 557; yb73 10/5; w72 17, 604; yb72 23
12:6 yb74 8/12; w73 557; w72 17, 266, 604, 740; yb72 23
12:7 sl 145; w74 82; w73 347; w72 17, 266; yb72 23
12:8 sl 145
12:9 sl 145; w74 82; w72 498, 604; g72 1/22 12
12:10 sl 145; w74 82; w73 557
12:11 sl 145; w73 557; w72 266; w71 660
12:12 sl 144-5; yb74 2/22
12:13 sl 144
12:14 w73 336
12:15 w74 212; w73 336
12:16 sl 224; w74 212; yb74 6/30, 8/29; w73 48, 336, 497
12:17 sl 224; w74 212; w73 48; w72 438
12:18 w73 217; pm 64
12:19 pm 64
12:20 pm 64
12:21 pm 64
12:22 w75 362; sl 190; w73 217; w72 752; pm 64, 67, 377; kj 234
12:23 w75 362; pm 64, 67; kj 403
12:24 w75 362; po 160; pm 64
12:25 yb73 4/19; pm 65
12:26 w75 363; sl 354; pm 65, 67, 70, 73
12:27 w75 363, 542; sl 354; pm 65, 67
12:28 sl 354; w73 218; pm 65, 67
12:29 sl 354; pm 65, 159
13:2 w75 359
13:4 w72 219, 454, 736; w73 155, 352, 539; tp 146, 149; g72 2/8 20
13:5 w74 202; km 2/74 6; w73 408; yb73 5/25; g72 5/8 4; g71 12/22 24
13:6 w73 408
13:7 w73 139; yb73 3/13; w72 404, 506, 703
13:8 w74 661
13:10 w74 252; ka 97, 109; yb73 8/1; w72 715; kj 386
13:11 sl 65; po 155; w72 715; kj 386
13:12 sl 65; po 155; w72 715; kj 386
13:13 sl 65
13:14 sl 65
13:15 w75 20; w73 260, 405; w72 700
13:16 g74 12/22 5
13:17 yb76 11/22; w75 529; w74 91; w73 142, 335; tp 142; yb73 5/13; w72 204, 464, 703-4, 755, 757; g72 1/22 12
13:18 g74 3/8 28; g74 12/8 4; w73 358; yb73 6/24; w72 603; w71 127
13:19 w72 603
13:20 w73 168, 351; kj 306, 386
13:24 w72 703

JAMES

1:2 w74 203; or 182; yb72 8/12; w71 115
1:3 w75 332; w74 203; or 182; yb72 8/12; w71 115
1:4 w74 203; or 182
1:5 yb76 2/20; w74 138, 154, 203, 318, 368, 415; w73 512; yb73 3/9
1:12 w73 81
1:13 w73 364; w72 649
1:14 yb74 2/12, 6/10; w73 364; tp 50; w72 649; w71 141
1:15 w73 364; tp 50; w72 649
1:17 w75 657; yb73 6/13; g72 2/8 9; sg 5
1:18 g74 8/22 27; w73 466
1:19 yb75 3/17; w74 104; g74 11/22 23; w73 504
1:20 g74 9/8 11
1:21 w71 31
1:22 w74 568
1:25 w73 463
1:26 w75 754; w72 68
1:27 yb76 10/9; w75 720, 754; sl 253, 327; w74 83; g74 1/22 19; w72 679; g72 12/22 4; kj 202
2:1 w74 104; w71 448
2:4 w74 104
2:5 kj 358
2:8 w72 553; w71 586
2:9 w74 104; w73 473; w72 553; w71 448
2:13 w74 497-9; w72 551-2, 554-5
2:14 yb75 4/6; w74 20, 25; yb74 254
2:15 w74 20, 570
2:16 w74 20, 570
2:17 w74 20; yb74 254
2:18 yb75 1/23; w74 20
2:19 w75 237; yb75 6/2; w74 21; w73 56
2:20 yb75 7/1; w74 22; w73 56
2:21 w74 22
2:22 w74 22
2:23 yb75 4/12; w74 22, 310

2:24 w74 22; w72 488
2:25 yb75 9/8; w74 24
2:26 yb75 1/30; w74 25; ts 49; yb74 255; g72 8/8 27
3:1 w73 503; w72 202; w71 333
3:2 w73 598; g73 2/8 3; w72 643
3:6 ts 112; bi8 1355
3:7 g72 7/8 4
3:13 yb76 9/27; w75 726; w73 541; w72 5, 203, 757; yb72 4
3:14 w72 203
3:17 yb76 12/21; w75 707; w73 332, 473, 541; yb73 2/18; w72 6-7, 592; yb72 5-7; w71 287
3:18 w73 332; w72 13, 757; yb72 16
4:1 w73 506; g72 10/8 17
4:2 w73 506; g72 10/8 17; w71 447
4:3 g74 1/8 9; w72 439; g72 10/8 17
4:4 yb76 9/18; w73 73, 424; tp 128; w72 589, 655; yb72 10/3; kj 258
4:5 w73 505
4:8 yb74 1/24; w73 439
4:9 g71 6/22 27
4:11 w75 94
4:12 w75 94
4:13 w73 470
4:14 w74 55, 701; w73 362
4:15 w74 701; yb73 7/12; w72 333
4:17 yb76 9/29
5:1 w71 447
5:6 w71 447, 539
5:7 w73 439; g73 3/8 3; bi8 1364
5:8 w73 439; g73 3/8 3; yb72 1/27; bi8 1364
5:9 w75 87
5:11 w73 105; w72 648
5:13 w74 138
5:14 w75 255; w74 138; g74 11/8 28; w73 512; or 162; w71 687
5:15 w75 255-6; w74 138; g74 11/8 28; w73 512; or 162
5:16 yb76 3/7, 6/6; w74 138; g74 11/8 28; w72 437, 603; or 162
5:19 w72 466; or 160
5:20 ts 42; w73 372; w72 466; or 160

1 PETER

1:1 g74 7/8 28
1:2 g74 7/8 28
1:3 w74 288; g74 8/22 27; yb73 10/31; w72 234
1:4 w74 288; g74 8/22 27; w73 495; w72 234
1:5 yb74 4; w73 362; w72 234
1:6 w75 22; w74 220; yb72 6/24
1:7 w75 22; w74 220; w73 362; yb72 6/24
1:8 yb72 257
1:9 yb72 257
1:11 w71 238
1:12 po 168
1:13 yb74 5; w73 362
1:15 w74 147; w72 583
1:16 w74 147; w73 99; w72 583; or 154
1:17 w75 59; w72 251
1:18 g73 11/8 27
1:19 w75 756
1:22 yb76 9/9; w75 338, 527; w74 368; g73 4/22 23
1:23 w74 222; w73 732
1:25 g75 10/8 9
2:1 yb76 5/22; w75 59; g73 4/22 23
2:2 yb76 5/22; km 7/74 3
2:4 w73 198; pm 188; kj 275
2:5 yb73 10/22; w72 718; pm 188; kj 275, 403
2:6 pm 188; kj 275
2:7 w74 600; pm 188
2:8 w74 600, 761; w72 443; pm 188
2:9 w74 600, 690; w73 62, 198, 394; ka 108; g73 5/8 6; w72 173, 718; pm 188; kj 403
2:10 w74 600
2:11 sl 308; w73 658
2:12 yb76 12/4
2:17 yb76 9/16; w74 46; yb73 7/24; w72 268
2:18 w75 708; w72 598
2:19 yb76 2/6; w72 598, 657
2:20 w72 598, 657
2:21 sl 69; yb74 11/27; w73 21; kj 62, 177, 283
2:22 sl 69; w73 274, 316; w72 235
2:23 sl 69; w74 410; g74 4/22 9; g74 5/22 28
2:24 w75 431; sl 69-70, 83; g74 9/22 28; w72 235; w71 274; bi8 1360
2:25 sl 70, 83; w74 463; kj 300
3:1 w75 154; g74 4/22 9; w73 475; tp 177; w72 446
3:2 w73 475; tp 177; w72 446
3:3 yb76 8/29; yb75 1/20; w74 118; w72 446, 667-8
3:4 yb76 8/29; w75 154; yb75 1/20; w74 118; w72 36, 446, 556, 668; yb72 9/19; w71 208
3:5 w74 310; w72 446
3:6 w72 446
3:7 w75 153, 408; yb75 6/16; w74 91, 155, 212; g74 4/22 11; w72 576; g72 5/22 14
3:8 w74 282, 317
3:9 g75 6/8 4; g74 5/22 27
3:10 w73 331
3:11 w73 331; g72 10/8 23
3:12 yb76 4/8; w75 293
3:14 w74 220; sg 94
3:15 w72 696; yb72 1/23; sg 94
3:16 w72 588
3:18 po 154; w73 248, 712; yb73 10/24; w72 235, 622, 687, 717; dn 13; g72 9/22 7; w71 607
3:19 po 78, 154; ts 85; g73 5/22 14; w72 428, 651; w71 607
3:20 yb75 11/15; po 78; ts 85; w73 309; g73 5/22 14; yb73 12/22; w72 651, 699; w71 607
3:21 w74 603; yb74 6/8; w73 31, 276, 309; tp 185; yb73 12/29; w72 120-1, 686, 699, 701; w71 671
3:22 yb76 8/2; w72 655, 701; pm 152
4:1 w72 519, 700
4:2 w73 277; w72 519, 700
4:3 w74 455; w73 277, 470, 575; w72 519, 700
4:4 w74 201, 455; w73 341, 501; g73 8/22 6
4:5 w74 201; w73 341
4:6 w73 208, 341; w72 519
4:7 yb76 7/1; w75 340-2; yb74 1/29; w73 341, 362, 368; yb73 8/17; w72 329, 404, 527, 532
4:8 yb76 12/18; w75 340-2, 529; yb74 10/1; w73 319, 371; w72 739; w71 574
4:9 w73 371-2
4:10 yb76 5/7; w74 532; yb74 10/18; w73 371-2; or 131
4:11 w73 110, 374
4:12 w71 493
4:13 w74 220; w73 362; w71 493
4:14 w74 220; g73 12/8 19; yb72 9/2; w71 493
4:15 w75 371; g73 12/8 19
4:16 w73 342; w71 493
4:17 w75 78; yb75 88; w74 335; w73 342; ka 138; w72 764; kj 217
4:18 w74 335; w73 342; ka 138; kj 217
4:19 w74 528; w73 342; w72 700
5:1 w72 15; or 53; yb72 19, 7/17; w71 688
5:2 yb76 3/28, 10/23; w74 367; w73 39, 469-71, 503; w72 15, 204, 581; or 53; yb72 19-20; w71 688
5:3 yb76 10/23; w75 730; w73 39, 374, 469, 503, 569; w72 15, 204, 581; or 54; yb72 19-20; w71 688
5:4 w74 367; w73 39
5:5 yb76 8/26; w75 299, 728; w74 265, 300, 317, 401, 407; w73 142
5:8 w75 369; w73 501; yb73 1/4; yb72 2/3
5:9 g74 10/22 9; or 7
5:10 w73 199, 279
5:13 w72 669

2 PETER

1:1 g72 3/22 7
1:4 sl 323; w74 222; w73 311, 740; ka 51; w72 622, 717; dn 13
1:5 w73 329
1:6 w73 329
1:7 w73 329
1:8 w73 329
1:10 w74 432; w73 730; w71 329
1:11 w74 432
1:14 g71 2/8 28
1:16 w74 298; bi8 1364
1:17 w74 298
1:18 w74 298
1:19 sl 284; w74 298
1:20 w75 144; sl 284
1:21 yb76 2/13; w75 144; sl 284; fu 5; g72 2/8 27; w71 228; kj 196; sg 15
2:1 w75 168; w74 14, 370, 598; w71 628
2:2 w74 14; w73 591, 597; w71 628

g, Awake!; **ka,** God's Kingdom of a Thousand Years; **kj,** "The Nations Shall Know that I Am Jehovah"; **km,** Kingdom Ministry; **or,** Organization; **pm,** Paradise Restored—By Theocracy!; **po,** God's "Eternal Purpose"; **sg,** Theocratic School Guidebook; **sl,** Man's Salvation out of World Distress!; **te,** Listening to the Great Teacher; **tp,** True Peace and Security; **ts,** Is This Life All There Is?; **w,** Watchtower; **yb,** Yearbook. **Complete list on page 6.**

2:3 yb76 8/7; w75 750; sl 303; w71 628
2:4 po 60, 78; ts 84; w73 485; yb73 11/10; g73 6/8 8; w72 427, 651; w71 607; bi8 1366
2:5 yb76 7/11; w75 747-9; sl 291; w73 485; g73 6/8 28; w72 651; kj 390
2:7 w73 575
2:8 w72 320
2:9 yb76 7/21, 9/28; w75 749; sl 351; w74 172
2:12 g72 7/8 5, 7
2:13 w75 755
2:14 w73 407
2:18 w73 575
3:1 sl 285
3:2 sl 285, 293; yb73 4/28
3:3 w75 280; sl 285; w72 678
3:4 sl 285; w72 678; bi8 1364
3:5 sl 290, 294; po 75; w72 308
3:6 w75 747; sl 290, 292, 294; w74 666
3:7 yb76 8/22; sl 293-4, 296-8, 311, 319; w74 95, 291, 666; po 187; g73 5/22 15; pm 71
3:8 sl 293, 299; w74 57; w73 196; kj 8
3:9 yb76 6/10, 11/11; w75 750-1; sl 299; yb75 5/30; w74 57, 154, 495; g74 4/8 17; w73 101, 197, 583; tp 57, 59; w72 246; or 15
3:10 sl 299, 303-7, 319, 351; g75 8/22 28; w74 666; po 187; w71 511, 635
3:11 yb76 260, 6/3, 12/1, 12/31; w75 694, 752, 757; sl 308-9, 357; w74 49; w73 361; w72 736
3:12 yb76 6/27, 12/1; w75 683, 752; sl 308-9, 311, 319, 351, 357; yb75 10/21; w74 49, 54, 666; po 187; w73 361, 543; g73 5/22 15; w72 661, 702, 736; bi8 1364
3:13 w75 261, 745, 752; sl 308, 320, 356; g75 11/22 16; w74 49, 666; po 187; g74 8/8 11; w73 85, 197, 245, 360, 382, 428; w72 4, 234, 500, 661; g72 11/8 7; w71 131; kj 373, 390; g71 4/22 23
3:14 yb76 260-1, 6/25, 6/30; w75 754, 758; sl 327, 330; w73 197, 339
3:15 yb76 2/7; w75 345, 754; sl 327-8; w74 484, 495, 573; w72 247; g71 2/8 28; g71 11/8 28
3:16 sl 327; w74 484; w73 206; g71 2/8 28

1 JOHN

1:3 yb75 4
1:4 yb75 4
1:5 w74 560; w71 436
1:6 yb75 5/27; w74 561, 565; w71 436
1:7 w75 460; yb75 4/29; w74 564; g74 3/22 28; w73 275; w72 607; w71 237; kj 388
1:8 w73 511; w72 436; w71 436
1:10 w71 436
2:1 w73 466; ka 113
2:2 w75 694; w74 223, 371; w73 244, 382; ka 113; w72 175, 608; kj 390
2:3 sl 195; yb75 5/18; w74 434, 566
2:4 yb76 6/21; sl 195; w74 434; yb72 7/11; w71 436
2:6 w74 568; w71 436
2:7 w71 191
2:8 w71 191
2:9 w74 569
2:10 w74 569
2:11 w74 569
2:15 yb76 4/13; w74 55; w73 457; tp 122; g73 8/22 14
2:16 yb76 6/8; w73 457, 569; tp 122
2:17 yb76 2/28, 4/13; w75 91; w74 50; w73 457; tp 122; g73 4/22 19; g73 5/22 15
2:18 w75 253
2:19 w71 265
2:20 w74 252
2:25 w74 376
2:28 w71 438; bi8 1364
3:2 w74 376; w73 466; g71 8/22 28
3:4 w74 495
3:5 w74 495
3:6 w74 495; w73 466; w71 265
3:7 w74 495
3:8 w75 176; w74 180, 495; w73 466; tp 126; w71 276
3:10 w73 467
3:11 w73 467; w72 650; w71 74, 463; te 80
3:12 w73 300; w72 650; w71 74; te 80
3:15 w74 442, 676; g74 7/22 27; w72 707; w71 142
3:17 w75 531
3:18 yb76 12/24; w75 531; w74 367; w73 331; w72 739
3:19 w73 211; w71 445
3:20 w73 211; w71 445
3:21 w73 211; w72 598; g72 7/22 28
3:22 yb76 5/20; w75 121; g74 1/8 10; g72 7/22 28
4:1 pm 352; g72 11/8 8
4:8 w75 522; sl 195; fu 28; w74 146; w73 133; tp 166; w72 650; w71 75, 265, 437
4:9 w71 437
4:10 w75 522; w71 437
4:11 w75 526; w74 154; w71 438
4:16 sl 195; w74 154; w73 227; w72 650; w71 437-8
4:17 yb76 7/29; w74 212; w71 438
4:18 yb76 9/8; w74 116; yb74 11/5; w73 210-11
4:19 yb76 9/2; w75 522; w73 452, 458; w72 304
4:20 yb76 9/24; w75 526; w73 333; w71 438
4:21 w75 526; w73 333
5:1 g74 8/22 27-8
5:3 sl 195; w73 253, 452; yb73 4/25; w72 304; g72 11/22 18
5:4 yb74 253; w73 659; g73 8/22 16
5:5 yb74 253; w73 659
5:7 w75 190; bi8 1366
5:8 w75 190; bi8 1366
5:11 w73 382; kj 388
5:12 w73 382; kj 388
5:13 w73 102
5:14 yb76 2/24; w75 402; g74 1/8 9; yb73 2/11; w72 389
5:16 w74 138; w71 383, 437
5:17 w71 437
5:19 yb76 5/3; w74 147; w73 344; tp 125; w72 639; w71 511; kj 394
5:20 g72 3/22 7
5:21 yb76 6/23; w74 62, 396; w72 295

2 JOHN

7 w74 465, 468-9
9 w74 465, 468-9; km 11/74 4; or 172
10 yb75 5/26; w74 465, 468-9; km 11/74 4; or 172
11 w74 465, 468-9; km 11/74 4; or 172

3 JOHN

8 w73 597

JUDE

3 yb76 3/5
4 w74 594-8; w73 575; w72 191
6 w74 640; po 77; ts 84; w73 181, 485; yb73 4/23; g73 5/22 14; g73 6/8 28; w72 427, 651; g72 7/8 6; w71 607
7 w74 485; ts 122; w73 181, 575; w72 736, 767; g72 7/8 6
8 w73 575
9 po 155
10 g72 7/8 5
12 yb75 58
14 w74 664; w72 651
15 w74 664; w72 651
19 w73 575
20 yb75 10/29; w74 378
21 yb75 10/26, 10/29; w74 378; or 160
22 w75 755; w72 466; or 160
23 yb76 10/30; w75 755; w72 466; or 160

REVELATION

1:1 w73 62; ka 324; g72 2/8 27
1:3 w73 205; ka 16
1:5 w72 607
1:6 ka 108
1:7 w74 751; g73 7/22 3; pm 341
1:10 w74 356
1:11 g72 2/8 27; w71 228; sg 15
1:17 w73 239, 243
1:18 yb74 6/6; w73 239, 243; km 3/73 4; bi8 1361
1:20 w71 751
2:1 yb72 11/15; w71 751
2:7 sl 90, 132
2:10 w73 243; w72 415
2:11 ka 41
2:14 w73 586
2:23 w75 480
2:27 ka 21
3:10 yb73 4/29; w72 528
3:12 ka 150; g73 2/22 28
3:14 w75 175, 701; w73 132, 262; g73 3/8 28
4:1 w73 62
4:6 kj 40
4:7 kj 40
4:8 w71 271; kj 40
4:9 kj 40
4:11 w74 593; w73 327
5:9 w74 121; po 183; g74 8/22 27; w73 518, 537; pm 151
5:10 w74 252, 288, 735; po 183; g74 8/22 27; ka 108; pm 151
5:11 w72 154; kj 50
5:12 w72 154; kj 50
6:1 ka 164
6:2 w75 768; w74 332, 355, 398; ts 160; ka 164; g73 6/22 12
6:3 w74 355; ka 164; g72 10/8 15
6:4 w75 684; w74 355; ts 161;

ka 164;
g73 6/22 11;
g72 10/8 15
6:5 w74 15,
195, 243, 355;
ts 161;
g73 6/22 11, 12;
g72 10/8 15
6:6 w75 3;
w74 15, 195,
243, 355; ts 161;
g73 6/22 11, 12;
g72 10/8 15
6:7 w74 355;
ts 161;
g73 6/22 11;
g72 10/8 15
6:8 w74 355;
ts 161; tp 14;
g73 6/22 11;
g72 10/8 15-16;
bi8 1361;
g71 3/8 4
6:9 g73 6/8 7
6:10 yb76 6/12;
w75 622; og 27
6:11 w75 622;
og 27
6:12 g74 5/8 19
6:14 w74 356
6:15 sl 246
6:16 sl 246;
g73 11/8 7
6:17 sl 246;
w74 356;
g73 11/8 7
7:1 w74 192;
w73 730; pm 146
7:2 w74 61,
192; w73 730
7:3 w74 61,
192; w73 730;
w72 636
7:4 w74 127;
w73 537, 730;
g73 5/8 6
7:7 kj 382
7:9 sl 107,
110, 201-2,
269, 328;
yb75 156;
w74 172, 623,
572; po 182;
hu 27; w73 107,
200, 382, 518,
537; ka 27, 29,
266, 268-9, 271;
yb73 12/20;
w72 376, 608,
638, 701, 721-2;
pm 78, 406;
kj 311, 347
7:10 w74 623;
po 182; hu 27;
w73 107, 113;
yb73 12/20;
w72 239, 376,
701, 721-2;
pm 78; w71 285
7:11 w73 113;
w72 701, 721-2
7:12 w73 113;
w72 701, 721-2
7:13 w73 64;
w72 701, 721-2
7:14 yb76 3/3;
w75 278, 396;
sl 168, 269, 316;
w74 172, 192,
724; po 182;
yb74 12/11;
w73 64; ka 275,
319; yb73 5/12;
w72 239, 377,
608, 701, 721-2;
kj 283
7:15 sl 203,
306; w74 724;
po 182; w73 64;
ka 53, 275;
w72 607, 721-2,
753; pm 80
7:16 sl 168;
yb74 3/24;
w73 107;
w72 255, 721-2;
kj 179
7:17 sl 168;
ts 165; w73 107;
w72 721-2;
kj 179, 181
8:4 w71 285
8:7 yb75 135
8:8 yb75 136
8:9 yb75 136
8:10 yb75 136
8:11 yb75 136
8:12 yb75 137
9:1 yb75 137
9:3 yb75 137
9:7 pm 294
9:8 pm 294
9:9 pm 294
9:10 pm 294
9:11 pm 294
9:15 yb75 138
9:16 yb75 138;
pm 295
9:17 yb75 138;
pm 295
9:18 yb75 138;
pm 295
9:19 pm 295
9:20 w75 755
9:21 w75 755;
w73 181, 339
10:8 w72 253;
kj 76
10:9 w72 253;
kj 76
10:10 w72 253;
kj 76
10:11 kj 76
11:2 pm 45-6
11:3 yb75 104;
w73 398;
pm 45-6, 205
11:4 pm 205
11:7 yb75 104;
w73 251; pm 46,
169; kj 342
11:8 w73 251;
pm 46, 169; kj 342
11:9 w73 251;
pm 47, 169; kj 342
11:10 yb75 109;
w73 229, 251;
pm 47, 169; kj 342
11:11 yb75 124;
w73 251, 398;
ka 356; w72 278,
750; pm 47;
kj 82, 342
11:12 yb75 124;
w73 251; ka 356;
pm 52; kj 53,
82, 342
11:13 kj 82
11:14 kj 82
11:15 yb76 10/28;
w75 661;
yb75 138; ml 26;
w74 237, 376;
ts 160; w73 645;
tp 70; yb73 10/20;
w72 351, 656,
709; pm 369
11:16 w75 662;
w72 709
11:17 yb76 10/7;
w75 362, 662;
w74 237; w72 709
11:18 yb76 10/7;
w75 362, 662;
g75 12/22 11;
w74 237;
g74 10/8 24;
w73 164; tp 101;
w72 661, 709;
pm 73, 370;
w71 561, 626;
kj 394;
g71 4/22 24-5
11:19 w74 221;
yb73 6/2;
w72 606, 709-10
12:1 kj 353
12:2 kj 353
12:3 ts 83;
w72 352, 427;
kj 353
12:4 ts 83;
w72 352, 427;
kj 353
12:5 sl 348;
w74 331; po 177;
w73 294, 617;
ka 21, 236; dy 15;
w72 352; pm 71;
kj 306, 353
12:7 w74 332;
po 155; w73 294,
617; dy 15;
g73 5/22 14;
w71 269; kj 353
12:8 w74 332;
kj 353
12:9 w75 655;
ml 19; w74 6,
332; ts 83;
g74 10/22 8;
w73 294, 617;
tp 125; dy 15;
g73 4/22 19;
g73 5/22 14;
g73 12/8 28;
kj 353
12:10 w74 6, 192,
332; kj 354
12:11 w74 332;
kj 354
12:12 yb76 6/14;
w75 362, 655;
ml 19; w74 6,
332; ts 163;
w73 294, 344,
617; yb73 12/10;
dy 15;
g73 4/22 14;
g73 6/22 12;
g73 7/22 5;
g73 12/8 28;
w72 628; dn 24;
kj 354
12:13 w73 619;
ka 29; dy 18;
kj 354
12:14 pm 379;
kj 354
12:15 kj 354
12:16 kj 354
12:17 sl 256;
w74 723; po 178;
w73 145, 619,
623; ka 29, 239;
dy 18, 26; pm 290,
380; kj 354
13:1 yb76 2/4;
w75 228, 235,
743; sl 250, 266;
w73 676; ka 22-3,
33; kj 363
13:2 w75 228;
sl 250;
g74 10/22 8;
w73 676; ka 22;
kj 363
13:4 w75 228
13:6 w74 170
13:7 w74 170
13:8 w75 228
13:11 sl 251,
266; ka 24
13:12 sl 251, 266;
ka 24
13:13 sl 251,
266; ka 24
13:14 sl 251;
ka 24; w71 723;
kj 256, 258
13:15 w75 743;
sl 251; ka 24, 33;
w71 723; kj 256,
258
13:16 ka 33
14:1 w74 127;
ts 130;
g74 8/22 27;
w73 199, 537;
g73 5/8 6;
w72 79, 181,
580; g71 7/8 28
14:3 g74 8/22 27;
w73 62, 401, 537;
w72 580
14:4 w74 108,
127, 431; ts 130;
g74 8/22 27;
w73 62; ka 73,
106, 173, 177
14:5 w74 108;
w73 741; w72 581
14:6 w74 761;
w73 405; w72 200;
w71 753; te 101
14:7 w74 761;
w73 405;
w72 200; te 101
14:9 ts 121;
kj 256, 258
14:10 ts 121;
kj 256, 258
14:11 ts 121;
kj 256, 258
14:12 ts 122;
or 186
14:13 w74 256,
559; ka 244
14:18 sl 348;
ka 21
14:19 sl 348;
ka 21
14:20 sl 348;
ka 21
15:1 w71 630
15:2 sl 282;
yb74 11/14;
w73 623, 660;
dy 26
15:3 sl 282;
w73 623; dy 26;
w71 658
15:4 sl 282;
km 6/75 3;
w71 515, 658
16:2 kj 258
16:8 w74 756
16:9 w74 756
16:12 w74 230;
kj 362
16:13 sl 256,
266; w73 294,
619; dy 19
16:14 w75 753;
sl 256, 263, 273;
w74 233;
g74 11/8 7;
w73 294, 297,
619, 745; ka 21;
dy 19; pm 94;
kj 113, 235, 298,
362, 366, 371
16:15 kj 113,
235, 298
16:16 yb76 11/2;
sl 256, 263, 273;
w74 77, 230, 318;
g74 11/8 7;
w73 294, 297,
619, 745; ka 21;
dy 19; w72 587,
753; pm 94;
g72 10/8 22;
kj 113, 235, 298,
362-3, 366, 371
16:17 w71 630
16:18 g74 5/8 19
17:1 sl 340;
w74 552;
w73 676;
g72 10/8 18;
kj 254
17:2 w75 692;
sl 340; w73 676;
kj 254
17:3 w75 743;
sl 341; w73 676;
ka 197, 394;
w71 718; kj 254,
256
17:4 sl 341;
ka 310; kj 254,
256
17:5 w75 691-2;
sl 235, 341;
w73 306, 676;
ka 197, 310;
tp 26; kj 254-6
17:6 sl 341;
w74 718;
w73 306, 308;
kj 254, 256
17:7 w74 552;
w71 718, 723-4;
kj 256

g, Awake!; **ka**, God's Kingdom of a Thousand Years; **kj**, "The Nations Shall Know that I Am Jehovah"; **km**, Kingdom Ministry; **or**, Organization; **pm**, Paradise Restored—By Theocracy!; **po**, God's "Eternal Purpose"; **sg**, Theocratic School Guidebook; **sl**, Man's Salvation out of World Distress!; **te**, Listening to the Great Teacher; **tp**, True Peace and Security; **ts**, Is This Life All There Is?; **w**, Watchtower; **yb**, Yearbook. **Complete list on page 6.**

17:8 sl 237; yb75 203; w74 552; ka 316; w71 718, 723-4
17:9 sl 235; w74 381, 718; ka 309
17:10 sl 235; g75 10/8 14; w74 381, 606, 718; ka 309, 315
17:11 sl 237; g75 10/8 14; w74 718; ka 309, 311, 315-16, 394; w71 718
17:12 w75 743; sl 239, 244, 253, 318; w74 552; ka 316-17; yb72 7/15; w71 622; kj 364; nc 23
17:13 sl 239, 244, 253, 267, 318, 346; w74 552; ka 317; yb72 7/15; w71 622; kj 364; nc 23
17:14 sl 253, 267, 318, 346; w74 552; g74 4/8 19; ka 317; yb72 7/15; w71 622; kj 364; nc 23
17:15 sl 239; w74 719; ka 311; tp 26; kj 254
17:16 sl 239-40, 245, 339; w74 53, 552, 719; g74 4/8 19; w73 676; ka 311; g73 4/8 18; g73 12/8 19; g72 4/22 25; g72 10/8 22; kj 254-5
17:17 sl 242, 244; w74 53, 719; g74 4/8 19; w73 676; ka 311; g72 4/22 25; g72 10/8 22; kj 254
17:18 w75 682; sl 234, 239, 341; w74 718; w73 676; ka 311; tp 26; g72 10/8 18, 22; kj 254
18:2 w72 587, 589
18:4 yb76 7/14; w75 85, 128, 694, 744, 754; sl 249; yb74 2/7; ka 197, 312; tp 35; or 12; g72 10/8 22; w71 533; kj 176, 254-5
18:5 w75 128; sl 249; tp 35; w72 661; kj 254-5
18:6 sl 249; w72 661; kj 254-5
18:7 sl 234, 238, 249; w73 165, 676; g73 12/8 20; w72 661, 724; kj 254-5
18:8 sl 247, 249; w73 676; tp 35; g73 4/8 18; g73 12/8 20; w72 587, 661; kj 191, 254-5
18:9 sl 270; w72 661; kj 191
18:10 w72 661; kj 191
18:11 sl 270
18:15 sl 270
18:17 sl 270
18:18 sl 270
18:19 sl 270; g72 10/8 22
18:20 sl 341; w74 719; kj 191
18:21 sl 248, 342; g72 10/8 22; kj 207
18:22 sl 342; kj 207
18:23 sl 342; w73 181; kj 207
18:24 sl 342; tp 26; kj 207
19:1 sl 248, 280; kj 207
19:2 sl 248, 343; kj 207
19:3 sl 248, 280; kj 207
19:4 sl 248
19:5 sl 248, 280
19:6 sl 248
19:7 w73 199, 694; ka 172; w71 275
19:8 w73 199
19:9 w74 431, 698, 700; w73 199; ka 172
19:10 w74 297, 414; w71 95, 286
19:11 sl 264; w74 238; ka 20; w72 765
19:12 sl 264
19:13 sl 264; w74 307; ka 20
19:14 sl 264
19:15 w75 620; sl 264-5, 348; og 23; g74 2/22 22; w73 621; ka 21; dy 23
19:16 sl 264; w74 238, 398; w73 621; ka 21; dy 23
19:17 sl 266, 275; w73 346; ka 22, 27; kj 376
19:18 sl 266, 275; ka 22, 27; kj 376
19:19 sl 269-70; w74 238; w73 622, 677; ka 22-3, 25, 27, 33; dy 24; g73 4/8 19; w72 661; kj 376
19:20 sl 269-70, 272, 274-5; w74 238, 381; ts 118; w73 677; ka 23, 25-7, 33, 157; g73 4/8 19; w72 661; bi8 1356; kj 376
19:21 sl 269-70, 274, 281; w74 238; w73 677; ka 22, 25, 27; g73 4/8 19; w72 661; kj 376
20:1 w74 6; po 186; w73 345; ka 29; w72 657; kj 371, 395
20:2 w74 6; po 186; w73 345; ka 18, 29; w72 657; kj 371, 395
20:3 w75 656, 683; w74 6, 347; po 186; w73 345; ka 18, 29, 43; w72 657; kj 371, 395
20:4 w73 728, 740-1; ka 18, 30-1, 33-4, 39, 80; g73 6/8 7; kj 391, 395
20:5 w74 7, 95, 346, 608; w73 728; ka 18, 34, 36, 39, 159; kj 391, 395
20:6 w75 689; g75 10/22 9; w74 106, 157; ts 183; g74 8/22 27; w73 199, 728-9, 740-1; ka 18, 30, 36, 39, 41; g73 5/8 7; w72 178, 718; kj 391, 395
20:7 w74 346; po 191; ka 18, 149; tp 57; kj 349
20:8 w74 346; po 191; ts 185; ka 149, 151, 153; tp 57; w72 273; kj 349
20:9 w74 346, 382; po 191; ka 149, 155; tp 57; w72 273
20:10 sl 272; w74 346, 381, 383, 652; po 191; ts 117; ka 149, 156, 285; tp 57; bi8 1356
20:11 w74 95, 291; po 187; w73 240, 364; ka 130; w72 231; pm 67, 69
20:12 sl 364; w74 95, 292, 382; yb74 5/21; w73 240, 244, 364; ka 130; g72 4/22 26
20:13 g75 11/22 28; w74 6, 95, 292; ts 119; w73 240, 244; ka 35, 130, 160; bi8 1361; kj 391
20:14 sl 269; w74 346, 381-2, 652; ts 118; w73 241, 246, 414, 606; ka 26, 147, 157, 160; g73 7/22 28; pm 386; w71 628; bi8 1356, 1361; kj 391, 396
20:15 w74 7, 345, 382; ts 118, 185; w73 241, 246, 414; ka 36, 138, 157; bi8 1356; kj 396
21:1 sl 324, 356; w74 95, 599; w73 85; yb73 5/5; w72 231, 500, 720; pm 68; g72 10/22 16; w71 511, 635; kj 388, 395, 403
21:2 sl 324, 359; w74 599; ts 143; w73 199; w72 720; pm 68, 150-1; w71 320, 569; kj 388, 395, 397, 403
21:3 w75 746; sl 324; ts 143; g74 4/8 15; w73 428; ka 160; g73 4/22 21; kj 395, 398
21:4 w75 746; sl 324; ml 30; w74 134; ts 119, 143; g74 4/8 15; ka 160; tp 105-6; g73 4/22 21; g73 5/8 6; g72 10/8 19; g72 11/22 16; kj 395, 398; te 182
21:5 w75 746; g74 4/8 15; w72 231; kj 395
21:7 w74 382
21:8 yb76 8/8; w75 52; w74 247, 382-3, 523; ts 119; g74 7/22 27; w73 136, 342, 555, 597; ka 158; w71 248; bi8 1356
21:9 w75 691; sl 324, 359; w74 599; w72 79; pm 151; w71 275
21:10 sl 324, 359; pm 150
21:12 pm 150; kj 402
21:13 kj 402
21:14 yb72 10/29; w71 320, 569; kj 402
21:21 w73 414; kj 397, 402
21:22 w75 492; w72 720; kj 388
21:23 w72 720
21:24 w72 720; pm 150
22:1 g75 10/8 27; w74 608; w73 414; pm 384; kj 388, 397, 403
22:2 w74 608; w73 414; pm 384; kj 388, 397, 403
22:3 pm 386
22:4 w72 720
22:9 w74 396; w72 201
22:15 g74 5/8 4; w73 343
22:16 sl 199
22:17 yb75 5/2; w74 660; w73 380; yb73 5/4; or 110; pm 151
22:18 g73 8/8 7
22:19 pm 213
22:20 w74 308; g72 8/22 28

ADDITIONAL REFERENCES

ADDITIONAL REFERENCES

ADDITIONAL REFERENCES

ADDITIONAL REFERENCES

ADDITIONAL REFERENCES

ADDITIONAL REFERENCES

ADDITIONAL REFERENCES